Praise for
Competent Christian Counseling

"The whole field of Christian counseling is an incredible tool in God's hands, bringing healing to children, adults, marriages, and families, and bringing many into a close relationship with Christ. *Competent Christian Counseling* does a wonderful job of helping Christian counselors employ the right methods and motives. I highly recommend this book."

—PAUL MEIER, M.D., cofounder, Meier New Life Clinics

"Christian counseling is facing both dusk and dawn. The era of professionalism with a biblical overlay is over. The season of biblically defined competence is at hand. It's a good time! *Competent Christian Counseling* effectively announces dawn."

—DR. LARRY CRABB, New Way Ministries

"It is a new era in Christian counseling, and this text will prove to be the compass directing the next generation of counselors toward higher and higher levels of competency. Counselors-in-training, those who teach them, and experienced parishioners—all of us are sure to benefit from the collective wisdom this volume provides. Our profession will be better for it, and the care of souls will benefit because of it."

—LES PARROTT, PH.D., Seattle Pacific University

"There is no endeavor in the world that deserves our best efforts more than the calling to help human beings experience spiritual transformation. That's why I'm so grateful for a state-of-the-art resource that reflects the wisdom of devoted practitioners."

—JOHN ORTBERG, PASTOR, Willow Creek Community Church

"Difficult times lead people to ask Christian therapists and pastors hard questions about life. Often these questions transcended the level of training of the caregiver. The goal of this book is to better prepare Christian caregivers for these challenges. This book is an excellent resource for reviewing the current base of knowledge in Christian counseling in a practical, inclusive fashion, while identifying research needs for the future."

—DR. MICHAEL LYLES, Lyles and Crawford

"A must-read for all counselors, lay persons, and professionals. Drs. Clinton and Ohlschlager have not only selected the most competent contributors but also make a substantial contribution themselves to this outstanding resource. *Competent Christian Counseling* is professional, with contributions from some of our country's leading specialists; biblically sound, with careful and reflective theological thought; and practical."

—ARCHIBALD D. HART, PH.D., FPPR
Graduate School of Psychology, Fuller Theological Seminary

"Although I am not a trained counselor, I have spent forty years in the care of souls, and I have read the basic works on Christian counseling throughout those years. I am excited to know that *Competent Christian Counseling* will help me as I continue to practice compassionate soul care. Dr. Tim Clinton and Dr. George Ohlschlager are giving us exactly what we need!"

—DR. JERRY VINES, pastor
First Baptist Church, Jacksonville, Florida

AMERICAN ASSOCIATION OF CHRISTIAN COUNSELORS

DR. TIMOTHY CLINTON

— AND —

DR. GEORGE OHLSCHLAGER

EXECUTIVE EDITORS

COMPETENT

CHRISTIAN

COUNSELING

VOLUME ONE

FOUNDATIONS & PRACTICE OF
COMPASSIONATE SOUL CARE

WATERBROOK
PRESS

COMPETENT CHRISTIAN COUNSELING, VOLUME ONE
PUBLISHED BY WATERBROOK PRESS
2375 Telstar Drive, Suite 160
Colorado Springs, Colorado 80920
A division of Random House, Inc.

All Scripture quotations, unless otherwise indicated, are taken from the *Holy Bible, New International Version®*. NIV®. Copyright © 1973, 1978, 1984 by International Bible Society. Used by permission of Zondervan Publishing House. All rights reserved. Scripture quotations marked (NASB) are taken from the *New American Standard Bible®* (NASB). © Copyright The Lockman Foundation 1960, 1962, 1963, 1968, 1971, 1972, 1973, 1975, 1977. Used by permission. (www.Lockman.org). Scripture quotations marked (TLB) are taken from *The Living Bible* copyright © 1971. Used by permission of Tyndale House Publishers, Inc., Wheaton, Illinois 60189. All rights reserved. Scripture quotations marked (NLT) are taken from the *Holy Bible, New Living Translation,* copyright © 1996. Used by permission of Tyndale House Publishers, Inc., Wheaton, Illinois 60189. All rights reserved. Scripture quotations marked (NKJV) are taken from the *New King James Version*. Copyright © 1982 by Thomas Nelson, Inc. Used by permission. All rights reserved. Scripture quotations marked (KJV) are taken from the *King James Version*.

Clients' names and identifying details have been changed to protect confidentiality.

Permissions statements for quoted material have been incorporated into the references section of this publication.

ISBN 1-57856-517-0

Printed in the United States of America
2005

10 9 8 7 6 5 4

To Ron Hawkins and Gary Collins,
my teachers, mentors, colleagues, and friends:
for believing in and caring for me, and for giving me deep love,
wise direction, and strong encouragement.

And to the citizens and, especially, the church of New York City
and the many courageous heroes who have emerged from out of the ashes:
Although this manuscript was completed before the events of September 11, 2001,
the AACC and I have been honored to serve the church of New York City, to walk
the sacred space and assist the heroes at Ground Zero, and to witness, in the midst
of terror and murder like we've never seen before, how God miraculously
brings life out of chaos and loves to shine out over all things.

—Tim Clinton

———————

To Lorraine, Noelle, Justin, and Rea,
my beloved ones:
This is for your better future.

And to the memory of
my father
WALTER WILLIAM OHLSCHLAGER (1917–1988)
who, in the face of divorce, disillusionment, and shattered dreams,
maintained his commitment to love and care for his broken family.

my brother
EDWARD JOHN OHLSCHLAGER (1953–2001)
for his love of life and dedication to the best things our father taught us.
His sudden heart attack and shocking death still deeply pains my family.

my friend and Christian counseling colleague
DAVID O. GATEWOOD (1943–2001)
who maintained his love for God and his delight in knowing Christ in the face
of terrible pain and an untimely death due to cancer and, through the Holy Spirit,
was filled with hope and wondrous visions of his heavenly home.

Though unknown to the larger world, these men are three of my enduring heroes.

—George Ohlschlager

CONTENTS

ACKNOWLEDGMENTS

No project of this scope is the product of just two people. We are honored to have many of our friends, colleagues, and collaborators in Christian counseling join us in this collective effort. Thank you all for your fine and timely work! Thanks also to our dear friends and colleagues Arch Hart, Diane Langberg, Ron Hawkins, and Ed Hindson for reading, analyzing, and commenting on many chapters. This book is far better because of your contributions to it.

We extend special thanks to Dan Rich, Dan Benson, and the staff at Water-Brook Press for your dedication and skill in bringing this book to completion. It has been a singular delight to work with you in your new publishing venture. Thanks also to Heidi Brizendine for her excellent assistance in keeping this project organized and moving forward with so many people involved in the production, and to Sealy Yates, agent and friend, who believed in the work from the start.

A very special thanks also goes to our long-suffering wives, Julie and Lorraine, and to our children—Megan and Zachary, and Noelle, Justin, and Rea—all of whom lived with mostly absent husband-fathers over the last six months of completing this book.

We both have enjoyed immensely the mutual stimulation and collaborative effort to complete this work, something we've been chipping away at together for nearly three years. As "iron sharpens iron" (Proverbs 27:17), the many (and usually late-night) "soul sessions" during which we have considered, debated, created, sharpened, expanded, argued, contracted, and reshaped our thinking and the presentation of this subject matter has made this a better book and has made both of us better men for the effort.

Though it sounds almost like a cliché because we've read it so often in the prefaces of many books, it is true that whatever is missing or deficient about this work is truly our responsibility. This book has only been improved by the efforts of those who have assisted us.

COMPETENT CHRISTIAN COUNSELING

The past fifty years of modern Christian counseling can be marked by the publication of some of its most defining books. Seward Hiltner published his classic *Pastoral Counseling* in 1949, while Wayne Oates published *An Introduction to Pastoral Counseling* ten years later. Jay Adams published his groundbreaking *Competent to Counsel* in 1970, and Larry Crabb published *Basic Principles of Biblical Counseling* in 1975. The original and revised editions of Gary Collins's "big yellow book," *Christian Counseling,* were published in 1980 and 1988. Jones and Butman's 1991 volume, *Modern Psychotherapies,* while it did not advance a model of its own, was a much needed Christian appraisal of the major psychotherapeutic systems.

MISSION

We believe the time is right—overdue, in fact—for a new and comprehensive work to serve as a resource and to guide today's Christian counselor.

Our mission is to draw truth and wisdom from God's Word, synthesizing the very best contributions from science, the arts and literature, and ministry to help construct a potent, contemporary perspective of Christian counseling—one that helps professional clinicians, pastors and pastoral counselors, and dedicated lay helpers to counsel effectively in their helping ministries. We outline some of the best practical skills and goal-directed action in the work of counseling, applied in both church and clinical settings.

Our hope is that this work will be regarded as a key work for the practice and process of Christian counseling in the twenty-first century. Our desire is that *Competent Christian Counseling* will become a primary reference, a resource guide, and a skills-based training tool for Christian counselors and pastors in the United States and worldwide—much as are the seminal Christian counseling works previously noted and as Egan's *The Skilled Helper* or Kottler and Brown's *Therapeutic Counseling* are for the general counseling professions.

DESIGN AND FORMAT

Competent Christian Counseling is both descriptive and prescriptive, focusing the universal process and explicating the "common factors" of helping that transcend the myriad theoretical schools of counseling.

This work of Christian counseling melds together (1) the foundations and teachings of Scripture, salted with the writings of the giants of church history on spiritual formation and pastoral care, and (2) some of the very latest research, theory, and practice in Christian counseling, in the broader fields of counseling and psychotherapy, and in the bio-psycho-social sciences, to produce (3) a Spirit-directed, twenty-first-century meta-understanding of Christian counseling that is counselor-friendly, effective in facilitating client change, and geared to helping people mature in the ways and wisdom of Jesus Christ.

Most important, we hope to offer God-honoring direction to practicing pastors and clinical colleagues, to students in training, and to our dynamic and emerging profession as it takes its place in the twenty-first century. Many see Christian counseling as a healthy and growing adolescent—full of energy and disorganized, but vibrant and directed toward a wonderful life. Almost daily, new developments are adding life, credibility, and challenge to our ministry. *Competent Christian Counseling* chronicles some of this life to date and challenges this ministry-profession to grow into adulthood.

Competent Christian Counseling is presented primarily from a practitioner's point of view. As hybrid writer-editors, we present what we hope is a reader-friendly resource. Each volume stands on its own: Volume one is an introduction in which we outline the foundations, core relationship issues, generic processes, major modalities, and future of Christian counseling. Volume two describes more advanced practice and addresses key clinical applications, controversial issues and tough cases. Volume three addresses legal and ethical dilemmas, includes many practice forms, and outlines a skills-based counselor training program.

These volumes progress according to the logic of the counseling process and the major applications and issues of the field. Theory is noted and issues are defined, but practice and process are emphasized as the third volume attempts to pull together the discipline to make it useful for helper and client alike.

We personally wrote or contributed to about half of the chapters, and many other leading counselors, pastors, and educators in our field contributed whole or partial chapters in their areas of expertise. We then connected and edited all of them so that the entire book flows logically and clearly with the voice of a teacher-practitioner. The first name noted in each chapter's byline denotes the primary writer of that chapter; the second and third names, if applicable, indicate secondary writers.

Each chapter outlines the knowledge requirements for practice, highlights some of the latest data, and details the process of a practical helping model. Sidebars emphasize key ideas, applicable quotes, and other nuggets of information that will help make the book useful. Some chapters also include relevant case studies and counseling interactions that provide practical application of the chapter's content. Case references are largely composite in nature—combining numerous cases and not representing any one client—and all names are changed to protect every client's right to confidentiality.

Our audience is the worldwide field of Christian counseling and pastoral care—the entire church that is dedicated to helping others—including licensed clinical professionals, pastors and church staff, parachurch counselors, students-in-training, lay helpers, and all those interested in counseling and helping ministry. In this preface we have assumed some knowledge and experience in Christian counseling practice. From here on, however, we limit our assumptions and endeavor to clearly explain as much as possible about our language and constructs.

OUR ORIENTATION

We are, first and foremost, practicing clinicians, consultants, and teachers who invest a significant amount of time and energy in Christian counseling ministry. As counselor-consultants we are daily challenged by clients to show that what we promote in our practices is also what we live out passionately in our personal and professional lives. From the client's perspective, it's not worth the trouble to change unless someone—the counselor—is modeling the fruits of a healthy life. Our faith, emotional health, social relations, and marriage and family life must all demonstrate integrity and growth—not perfection or perfectionistic striving, but a humble awareness that we are on the right highway toward the fullness of God's kingdom.

Since Christ is the One who holds us and our counseling ministries together, a central goal of this book is to facilitate a pragmatic understanding of truth and a call to unity in Christ himself. We invite all those who name the name of Jesus to join us in a Christ-centered inclusivism that recognizes the diversity of Christian counseling approaches as they are expressed in the broad range of practice distinctives.

We believe that far too much energy has been expended in parsing and asserting our differences in Christian counseling and in the church. In his high-priestly prayer (John 17), Jesus prayed that we would be one as he and the Father are one. Likewise, the unity of God's people is supported by the unity of God's truth revealed in Jesus Christ. This orientation toward unity and conformity in Christ, and the seamless unification of God's truth, sees and appreciates that the proverbial glass is half-full instead of half-empty.

LIFE-CHANGING PRACTICE

Our central focus in this book is practice. We are committed to moving beyond theoretical musing and the construction of academic models to a pragmatic understanding of how God comes alive and how people actually live in and grow by the helping endeavor. Psychology and theology are not devalued in this book; rather, they are balanced with an appropriate concern for the place of Christian spirituality and the presence of God in the process of counseling.

Hence, our perspective on Christian counseling places heavy emphasis on the so-called common factors that have been explicated in the research over the past two decades and revealed in the historical writings of the church on pastoral care. These are the core conditions for constructive change that cut across all counseling theories. In this model, counselor character is emphasized over knowledge, although we encourage learning all one can about the helping process in addition to developing exemplary character. Acquiring universal helping skills is emphasized over gaining deep understanding of counseling theories, although we address many important theoretical issues that are present across much of the counseling enterprise. Relationship and ethical factors are emphasized over technique, although we examine proven ways to build the helping relationship and the best techniques to apply in the helping context.

Overall, we emphasize the counselor's knowledge of and reliance upon God. We advocate yielding to God to guide and direct the helping endeavor in ways that cannot be understood with human knowledge, insight, or reasoning alone. This emphasis has significant theological and practice implications that we will address throughout the book. First is the role of the Bible in both the assessment and treatment of persons and its use in defining the goals and procedures for change. Second is the role and action of the triune God of all creation. How does Jesus Christ, for example, mediate our relationship with the Father and enable us to live more intimately with him? How does the role and action of the Holy Spirit operate in the counseling experience, and how does he guide and gift the helper to assist others to mature in Christ?

In volume one we outline a generic, or universal, counseling process that is becoming the accepted standard of practice around the world—a model of brief intervention that averages two to eight sessions per case. These developmental, case-managed steps involve counseling intake, data gathering and assessment, clinical diagnosis, goal setting and treatment planning, treatment and goal acquisition, and strategies for helping clients overcome their fear and resistance to counseling-based change. We outline effective skills and techniques across the wide range of applied practice modalities, then we consider the future of Christian counseling.

In volume two we will consider more advanced practice by reviewing clinical applications and controversial issues in our field. We address only the clinical applications of Christian counseling that are most common at present. We then present a model treatment planner to enable you to achieve excellence in your helping work. Our goal in the first two volumes is to be as comprehensive as possible but not exhaustive. Every chapter represents Christian counseling on the cutting edge, bringing together some of the best and latest research, theory, and practice so that you will be well versed on each topic.

We intend to follow these two volumes with a practical training resource, which will outline legal and ethical dilemmas, will include practice forms, and will contain skills-based exercises for learning clinical assessment and treatment. It will be designed to be used by students, interns in training, and clinical practice groups who will systematically review and upgrade their skills and training efforts within agencies and clinics.

THE BEST IS YET TO COME

Is God calling you to Christian counseling ministry? Have you already been called? You probably have been if you're reading this book. If so, we welcome you to a dedicated and dynamic family of Christian counselors all over the world! Even if you are not involved in Christian counseling, we believe these volumes will help give you a clear understanding of our field.

Are you called to remain in Christian counseling in spite of the pressures and fatigue you may experience after years—and even decades—of counseling ministry? We invite you to read on and be refreshed again, for the best is yet to come.

—TIM CLINTON and GEORGE OHLSCHLAGER

Forest, Virginia

SMORGASBORD SPIRITUALITY VERSUS THE ROAD LESS TRAVELED

GEORGE OHLSCHLAGER AND TIM CLINTON

Spirituality—whether it means getting in touch with angels, spirits, and higher powers or using crystals, meditation, or manuals on "experiencing God"—is a stylish pursuit these days (Gallup & Jones, 2000; Humphrey, 2001). The good news is that people are searching for something beyond themselves. The bad news is that our modern, market-based culture offers a smorgasbord of spirituality: The consumer is king (or queen), anything and everything is available for consumption, and "spiritualities" of all kinds can be tailored to fit individual preferences and needs.

This consumerist mentality allows a comfortable ride to nirvana and avoids the discomforts of sacrifice, suffering, and struggle, which have been the foundation of spirituality for nearly all of human history. The following definition of spirituality was published in the quarterly magazine of a major national behavioral health care provider and was written by a "trained pastoral counselor" with an earned MA degree:

> Spirituality is that quality of coming home to one's self, knowing that person [you are] for the first time and recognizing one's true feelings. It is that process of feeling at ease within self, feeling connected with inner feelings, and from that safe place of connection, that inner core, acknowledging, "I am okay." That is spirituality! (Berns, 2000, p. 12)

THE ROAD LESS TRAVELED

Thankfully, Jesus offers an alternative route. He is the One who offers to take our burdens onto himself, to carry our yokes so that we may find rest, love, hope, and even new life (see Matthew 11:28-30). He calls us to a higher road that, sadly, few choose to travel (see Matthew 7:13-14). Those who do, however, travel a wondrous road. God cares for each and every person on Earth, and nothing can compare to the promises we have in God's love.

Consider the experience of one couple in counseling as they encountered the power of the living God. Referred by their pastor, they came in together for their first session. They were attractive, middle-aged, physically fit, educated, and active in a variety of church and community activities. Both were accomplished professionals—he a college history teacher, and she an elementary school principal—and were quite comfortable financially. They had recently seen their last child leave for college, and now they were coming home each night only to each other.

He smiled quickly and easily, but guilt kept him from maintaining eye contact. Still, he maintained his casual persona, his easygoing style. It was clear he was ready to engage in counseling and wanted to be put at ease.

She was elegant, quiet, observant, and overly controlled, from her coifed hair to her tailored, color-matched, accessorized suit and pumps. She projected a closed-mouth smile that did not hide the enormous pain in her striking blue eyes.

I (George) knew I was on trial with both of them. They wanted to know if I could be trusted, if I could help them see their way through the chaos of his infidelity.

Neither wanted a divorce—or so they both said—but neither of them was able to say that the marriage would survive, let alone thrive and be a source of joy again. A black hole broiled at the core of their relationship, and it was pulling them both toward oblivion. They wanted my help to accomplish what was arguably impossible: to plug up the vacuous hole in their marriage and help them create a new center that would be stable, attractive, trustworthy, and full of love and hope and goodness.

His motivation to save the marriage was apparent, but it seemed superficial, glib, presumptuous. Nonetheless, he was hopeful, curious, full of guilt, and altogether confused about his long history of adultery. She was neither hopeful nor motivated. She seemed, at best, to be only half there, acting as if her mind was in another world. I knew that I had to direct my initial work toward her to help restore some hope.

As their story unfolded during that first session, I responded with a somewhat paradoxical move that is uncharacteristic at such an early stage in counseling. I spoke openly about my fears for them, disclosing my sense of inadequacy in the face of the enormity of their problem. He looked deflated by those disclosures, and I chose to live with that. I did not think his discouragement would dissuade him— and it did not.

This uncharacteristic (though accurate) display of doubt seemed to connect with her, however. It seemed to resonate with her own doubt. Perhaps she realized that I wasn't assuming success in this venture or taking her husband's transgressions lightly.

They told me that they had recently celebrated their silver anniversary by taking a world cruise. Shortly after their return home, the news came out that he—a Bible teacher, deacon, and head of the education committee at church—had been involved in a series of affairs for over twenty years. He reported the affairs in a mechanical, almost scripted way, constantly checking for her reactions.

She had never known about or even suspected his unfaithfulness. She told me how she had literally vomited and "nearly went crazy" upon hearing this news. It had poisoned her view of her entire marriage and had corrupted her memory of her entire adult life. Underneath her cool and classy exterior, she was devastated. She was genuinely heartbroken, and her mind screamed in pain and rage.

The waters here are really deep, I thought. I silently cried out, *God, help me. I can't do this alone.*

POLARIZATION

When they returned for a second session, the mood was disjointed, tense, and polarized. He had become convinced of—even cocky about—the certainty of their reconciliation. His hopefulness was encouraging, but he was too confident of success. With his reborn confidence, he had already shifted the problem from his adultery to her doubt and lack of confidence in the marriage.

Indeed, she was not sure of anything, either in their marriage or in any other area of her previously well-ordered life. Accustomed to being in control of her life, she now found that her world was turned upside down. Her husband's confidence galled and offended her, causing her to turn even farther away.

Over the next few weeks she sank into a deep depression that began to affect her health and work. She went to her physician and started a regimen of anti-depressant medication, but she missed increasing amounts of work and withdrew socially. After much coaxing, she finally began to talk about what her behavior was already communicating: her declining will to live.

He vacillated between concern for her and anger toward her. He wasn't really sure why she was behaving or responding the way she was. He was clueless, not understanding the horror of his betrayal and the depth of its impact on his wife. Both were tremendously stuck, and neither connected with what I was trying to do to help them get unstuck. They were drifting farther and farther away from each other and from God.

I was stuck as well and felt as if I was spitting into a storm. I was losing hope, but this time I fought against showing them my feelings. I addressed their case in weekly case consultation with my clinical colleagues, but this was only slightly helpful; I was already doing most of what they suggested. I was getting desperate, and I called out to God with fervor, "O God in heaven, *please* help."

MIRACLE IN A MUSEUM

Everything changed in a day—in minutes, really. He invited her to go to the city with him for a long weekend of shopping, museums, and the theater, something they hadn't done together in years. She reluctantly agreed to go, but it was clear that her heart wasn't in it. I encouraged them to "go and let go," to deliberately put their past behind them for three days and enjoy a weekend of renewal and refreshment. However, I had nagging doubts that they would be able to do it. O me of little faith.

They were at an art museum, and he was standing quizzically in front of a statue by the nineteenth-century French sculptor Rodin. Two naked figures were joined in this display: a man hunched over with his face full of agony and a beautiful woman lying supine across his back, exotic, erotic, luxuriant. She was exerting a weight on him, not of joy and pleasure, as one might expect, but of horrific suffering.

Suddenly the husband was convicted by the Holy Spirit as he contemplated this statue—the truth hit him "like a bolt of lightning," he said. He saw the full weight of his infidelity, the mad mixture of sinful secret pleasure and moral guilt, his woundedness from the divorce of his own parents, and his addiction to pornography and illicit sex that had haunted him his entire adult life.

In the suffering etched in that face of stone, he also saw the suffering he had inflicted on his wife and his marriage. He finally understood the full impact of what he had done. For the first time in his life he really felt it and was overwhelmed by its depth. He sat down on the floor of the museum and, with his face in his hands, wept uncontrollably.

His wife, who had been wandering elsewhere, returned and was surprised to find him in that state. When he regained some semblance of control, he haltingly and tearfully told her what had happened. He could not even look her in the face. The magnitude of his sin and the enormity of the suffering he had caused leveled him. Stricken by his demeanor, she looked quizzically and critically at the statue for a long time.

Then, Aha! She saw it too. In the gorgeous woman lying lustfully on the back of the man, all of the temptation and seduction and lies became clear. She was, as she later explained, both horrified and enlightened. She was also filled with a compassion for her husband that surprised them both and that overwhelmed her and melted a place in her frozen heart. She reached out to touch him tenderly. Later they confided to me that this moment in the museum was the first time she had touched him in months.

They both described the remarkable journey home. Brokenhearted, he repented with a contrition that only God can produce. He didn't demand that she forgive him, as he had done for weeks. He didn't even ask for forgiveness—he was convinced that his transgressions and lies were unforgivable. But she forgave him anyway, something she had not been able to do since the first revelation of his betrayal. She forgave him with an absolution that only God can create.

Theirs is a story at which a counselor can only sit back and marvel, thankful to have been given the honor of witnessing and participating in such a miraculous transformation. The entire interpersonal equation between this husband and wife had been transformed that day by the grace and greatness of our amazing God. This glib man yielded to God the weight of sin and pain that had crushed his soul for years and had nearly destroyed his marriage. This broken woman poured out a forgiveness that her frozen heart had yearned to give before it was forever turned to stone.

THE PROMISE OF CHRISTIAN COUNSELING

Nearly everyone who has heard this story agrees with me that God performed a miracle that day. He created a whole new marriage in a way that only he could script. He truly took what was damaged—ashen, dirty, stained beyond cleansing—and created something altogether new. In a few days' time this dead marriage and the two broken people living it were transformed into something alive and beautiful.

Everything in their counseling also changed after that day. Marital therapy and individual counseling became easy, fun, and successful beyond my best expectations. The truth, which was at first painful and horrifying and later deeply educative and enlightening, was setting them and their marriage free. Months later, I stood with their pastor as they renewed their vows in a delightful remarriage ceremony.

They are now living a vibrant life together that neither had thought possible, and they believe that God takes pleasure in them and in their marriage. They revel in that knowledge and in the delight of telling others the story of God's miraculous rescue. They are model citizens of both church and community and are deeply involved in ministry to other couples in distress.

Such is the promise of Christian counseling: the hope and the power of Christ. Such is the difference between the true spirituality found only through an encounter with the living God and the faddish, and often self-obsessed, New Age spirituality that attracts many "seekers" today. Such is also the difference, dare we say, between Christian counselors who actively invite God to be the heart of the helping endeavor and counselors who confess Christ but have no conscious commitment to incorporate that faith and the divine object of that faith into therapy.

We wish we could report that every marital intervention turns out so well. You know it doesn't. Furthermore, we don't know if this couple's marriage would have survived without God's miraculous intervention. Perhaps it would have. They might have stayed together, but probably in a duty-bound, conventional way in which they would have been useful to each other but never really pleased or honored each other again. Without God's intervention, their marriage likely would have been like so many others that have lost all true joy and spontaneity.

Exalting Christ in Christian Counseling

Overcoming the pain, bleakness, bills, boredom, and the brokenness of life seems to be a deep yearning, hard-wired into the soul of every person (a theme we will develop further in chapter 1). The world is full of modern gurus, including some who claim to be Christ himself, who promise to help anyone willing to pay for such an escape from life. Myriad promises and elaborate plans exist to help people find nirvana, strike it rich, reach some superconsciousness, change the world, or attain true inner peace.

Then there is the call of Christ. Jesus' timeless message still trumpets its hallowed, outrageous offense: "I bid you to come and die." But in that dying, something else is reborn: new life in the present and the seed of eternal life to come. This is true spirituality, not the false, man-made, human-centered, creature-glorifying variety. This is what everyone is seeking even if they don't know it yet—even if they come to it fighting, screaming, and complaining.

The simple, unvarnished truth is that God makes something happen in us that we cannot do by ourselves—nor can any other human being do it for us. Titus put it so clearly: "He saved us, not because of righteous things we had done, but because of his mercy. He saved us through the washing of rebirth and renewal by the Holy Spirit, whom he poured out on us generously through Jesus Christ our Savior" (3:5-6). Only Jesus, the God-man, living in us through his Holy Spirit, can make this life happen. This exclusivity, this one and only way, is heresy to a world that bows to the gods of hypertolerance and to an A-to-Z spiritual inclusivity. But it is true.

The couple whose story we've shared learned the secret of true spirituality, a spirituality forged in the crucible of lifesaving, marriage-saving redemption and forged in a manner and at a time that God chose for reasons that he alone knows. This spirituality is freely available to us from God simply for the asking. He is a great God—the great "hound of heaven," as Francis Thompson wrote—who loves us and pursues us until we exhaust our attempts to flee from him and yield to his glorious way.

God in Christ is the Great Physician, the only One who is able to apply healing salve to our aching souls. God in Christ is the Great Redeemer, seeking and saving the lost, redeeming our darkened and desperate lives from great travail. God in Christ is the Great Reconciler who forges new bonds and creates renewed relationships out of broken shards that otherwise would only cut and wound. God in Christ sends his Holy Spirit to us to shape in us the very same Spirit of the One who sent him.

Though it is a road less traveled; nonetheless, this is true spirituality. And though this is a book about Christian counseling—one that you will learn and grow from, wherever you are in your ministry or practice—we hope it is something more. We hope this book will exalt the living God and move you to invite the life and love of Jesus Christ to permeate every facet of your life and ministry.

PART I

INTRODUCTION TO CHRISTIAN COUNSELING

CHAPTER 1

CHRISTIAN COUNSELING AND COMPASSIONATE SOUL CARE

The Case for Twenty-First-Century Practice

TIM CLINTON AND GEORGE OHLSCHLAGER

There are five gospels of Jesus Christ—Matthew, Mark, Luke, John, and you, the Christian. Many people will never read the first four.

—GIPSY SMITH, AMERICAN EVANGELIST

W hat's happening to us?

The 24/7 pace and the pain of our day have taken over. The cry for relief is deafening; the need to simply slow down and live a simpler life is compelling. More than 50% of all adults in the United States now claim to be stressed out, too busy to make sense of their time-starved, cluttered, and unstable worlds (Barna & Hatch, 2001). Trapped in the difficult paradox of chasing excitement and pleasure, most people feel too fatigued and overworked to simplify, reflect, and satisfy deeper longings for meaning and renewal.

Faced with an uncertain future, many people believe they are falling farther behind and will never get the chance to stop and smell the roses. *It's too late*, they think. *I'm in too deep.* As a result, it is easy to conclude that significant numbers of individuals in today's world are overwhelmed and confused by lives that have turned out far differently than they were supposed to.

Crowded and pained lives lead to fatigue, even the mysterious "hurry disease" of CFS (chronic fatigue syndrome). We are even too tired and overwhelmed to exercise, eat right, sleep more, read a good book, be a coach, or teach a class. More forces than ever are tearing at our relationships and competing for our time, energy, and affection. Before long, tension builds, tempers flare, stomachs turn, ulcers bleed, and poor choices are made. Worse yet, hurt people *hurt* people (Wilson, 1993). Brokenness is everywhere.

Yet we go plodding onward, desperately hoping for a better day. Consumed in our quest for a better life, we do more, demand more, and stuff more into our thoughts and emotions, but not much changes. Like Solomon in his pursuits, we see the handwriting on the wall, which plainly reads, "All is vanity and vexation of spirit" (Ecclesiastes 1:14, KJV).

Maybe you know what we're talking about. No doubt you, like Job, have lived in triumph as well as travail. But have you pondered his lament? "Man who is born of woman is of few days and full of trouble. He comes forth like a flower and fades away" (Job 14:1-2, NKJV). Maybe you are living now in the bloom of life, and everything around you seems to be flowering with color, happiness, and success. If so, may God bless you so that you will enjoy it for however long it lasts (Ecclesiastes 3:11-12).

Or perhaps you or someone you love is heavy-hearted, tasting right now the bitter cup of pain and travail, suffering in despair, overwhelmed by the "dark night of the soul" (John of the Cross, trans. 1987). You know as well as we do that good times will not last, for triumph and travail move through our lives with the regularity of the seasons (Ecclesiastes 3:1-8).

People the world over are consumed by and sated with the dead promises of pleasure, wealth, power, comfort, and fame. They are empty but expectant as they search frantically for purpose, meaning, and value. In their hopeful quest, most end up echoing the words of Solomon: "That which is crooked cannot be made straight: and that which is wanting cannot be numbered" (Ecclesiastes 1:15, KJV). As a result, we believe a yearning for God—a sacred discontent—is gripping humanity and motivating a search for something more in life. And considering that more than six billion people now inhabit the planet, this search must be unprecedented in the history of mankind.

This global search is fomented by a world saturated with poverty, starvation, divorce, violence, father absence, rampant sexual abuse, fear, depression, religious oppression, war, drug abuse, abuse within the family, suicide, and despair. People everywhere—in countries rich and poor, from the First World to the Third World—are hurting, lonely, afraid, and confused. Many are also angry about life and what people, governments, armies, corporations, and even the church are doing (and not doing) to them. And why shouldn't they be?

Why shouldn't our children be, at some level, angry, frightened, and confused about the worldwide legacy of pain, death, indifference, injustice, and suffering they are inheriting? The twenty-first century is the time to find a way to overcome our personal and mass denial of these problems. We must pull our collective heads out of the sand and take an honest look at life. For as the ancient medical adage so truthfully states, "You can't treat what you can't see."

Yet many of these searching people also feel powerless, helpless, and hopeless (Allender, 1999, pp. 69-90; Langberg, 1999). Far too many seekers abandon their quest before they complete it, with degradation and despair an all too common result. Instead of confronting problems, people, and systems, they escape into private, secret, and desperate worlds of designer drugs, pornography, sexual addiction, gambling, shopping and mindless consumerism, idolized sports, rampant violence, and even suicide. Consider the story of one of our teenage clients from years ago.

ONE DESPERATE SEEKER

Sally was a bright, articulate, and severely depressed sixteen-year-old American high-school student brought in for counseling by her mother. It was immediately clear that she wanted nothing to do with being helped. She was angry with her divorcing parents—who were confessing Christians—and with her life situation. She was desperately searching, mostly hopeless, and borderline suicidal. During our time together in counseling, I was given a paper Sally had written for a class at her Christian high school. It was about Christ and the search for truth that we claim is found in him. Following is a portion of Sally's paper.

"WHO DO YOU SAY THAT I AM?"

I say Jesus Christ was a man sent from God in a last-ditch attempt to save the troubled human race. He performed miracles, preached to the masses about the promised kingdom of heaven, and died on the cross for our sins. Unfortunately, I don't believe he succeeded.

We and our fellow human beings are even more disgusting and self-destructive now than we were back then. We spend more money on nuclear weapons to destroy people than we do to feed people to save their lives. If we spent just one half of 1% of our military funding on food for the poor, every citizen of this country would have three well-balanced meals a day.

Don't get me wrong, I give credit to Jesus. He tried to send out a good message and did willingly go and die on a cross for us—a really amazing recognize them as the parallel tracks on which the Christian counseling train is speeding along. This dual focus is a theme we will return to repeatedly in this volume as we systematically present that which describes, inspires, instructs, and motivates competent Christian counseling.

The data regarding pastoral care and the helping professions is already extensive, and the material covered in this book is not intended to be exhaustive. We have, however, endeavored to write and bring together a comprehensive survey of our growing and dynamic field, highlighting the best data, knowledge, skill, and godly wisdom to honor God and to raise the standard of Christian counseling excellence in practice as well as ethics.

In this chapter, we will expand on the theme we introduced in the prologue and make the case for Christian counseling in the church and in the world. In the next two chapters, we will develop our treatise by defining Christian counseling more precisely, exploring and understanding it from a variety of perspectives, and then describing who we are and what we do as Christian counselors.

LIFE IN THE TWENTY-FIRST CENTURY: THE BEST AND WORST OF TIMES

In true Dickensian fashion, it appears to be simultaneously "the best of times [and] the worst of times" around the world. Hope and fear coexist in so many lives, inciting many contradictions. We in the industrialized West are the wealthiest people in history, yet the worry over the loss of our wealth if our economic system should fail is enormous. We are also the healthiest people in history, having nearly doubled our life expectancy in just one century, and yet we fear aging and the loss of our health like no generation before us. Technology dazzles us at every level, transforming the way we live with incredible speed. Yet millions of us wrestle with technology as if it were an amoral, metastasizing monster, one that will either fail us or overwhelm us with its destructive power.

In stark contrast, billions of Earth's citizens live on the precipice of starvation, disease, warring violence, and death, and they have no access whatsoever to our transforming technology. The worldwide gap between rich and poor, First World and Third World, is huge, and it grows larger every day. The optimists and pessimists of the world are both in their heyday. Optimists deny or minimize the worst, embracing and crowing only about the best of times. Pessimists see only doom and gloom, adopting a bunker mentality, loading up with guns and food, and waiting for the end. And there is plenty to fuel the selective perceptions of both extremes.

THE BEST AND WORST IN AMERICA

The contradictions inherent in American life are just as numerous and confusing. Barna and Hatch (2001) list the following troubling absurdities that abound in the United States:

- Divorce, homosexuality, and abortion are no longer moral issues to be decided on the basis of God's law, but on the basis of personal preference. We even call those who support abortion "pro-choice," as if God ceded to us the right to make such a determination.
- Pornography is generally protected as "free speech," but prayer at public schools and the posting of the Ten Commandments in courthouses is frequently outlawed.
- Widespread and public use of foul language is accepted as a right of personal expression; mass media broadcast such language without fear of reprisal.
- Lying and cheating are described as inappropriate behaviors, but most people believe that the problem is not lying or cheating but getting caught.
- Personal bankruptcy filings, based on the popular notion that people have no moral obligation to pay their debts, have increased every year for the last seven years.
- The prison population is larger than ever and continues to grow, due in part to a population that equates lawlessness with freedom and personal rights.
- Suicide among young people continues at alarmingly high rates and is fueled by the postmodern perspective that life has no real meaning.
- Racism, carefully masked, festers just below the surface of our society because many people believe they are better than others. In America it seems that the principle of equality is more theoretical than practical.
- Computer hackers have spawned an entire industry of software developers and law-enforcement specialists who focus on protecting people's computers from viruses and malicious hacking.
- The number of lawyers in the U.S. has nearly tripled since 1970. We have more lawyers than doctors, and the growth of the legal profession is eclipsing that of the medical profession. (pp. 82-83)

Furthermore, the biggest transfer of wealth in the history of the world is now taking place, and the annual GDP (gross domestic product, which is the entire wealth a nation produces) is nearing the unimaginable sum of ten trillion dollars ($10,000,000,000,000). In regard to material things, most American young people lack nothing and want for little. But a huge number of these same youth are suffering a crisis of meaning and purpose that we, as a nation, are currently failing to resolve. While emotional disorders account for about 10% of all adult suffering, the rate is 40% among America's youth and young adults. According to the Children's Defense Fund (1992), the following events happen in America every day:

- six teens commit suicide
- seven kids, ages ten to nineteen, are murdered

BOX 1.1—THE BEST AND WORST OF TIMES ACROSS PLANET EARTH

At the genesis of the third millennium since Christ, consider the following:

- It took thousands of years and hundreds of generations of human development for the world's population to reach three billion around 1950, and it took just fifty more years and two generations for the *next* three billion persons to be added. Projections estimate that by 2050 world population will increase another four billion, mushrooming to ten billion people worldwide in the lifetime of our children and grandchildren.
- The disparity of global wealth is also becoming extreme, and the gulf between rich and poor is constantly growing wider. For example, the combined assets of the world's three richest persons are greater than the combined gross national product (GNP) of twenty-six of the world's poorest countries.
- The combined assets of the world's 250 richest people are greater than the combined incomes of the poorest 2.5 billion people. Expressed symbolically, 250 ($R) > 2,500,000,000 ($P).
- The annual per capita income of Swiss citizens is $40,000; in Ethiopia it is $100. The United States average income is $29,340; the world average is $4,890.
- During the 1990s, sixty-one wars were fought around the globe, killing millions of people and forcing 300,000 children to become warriors.
- Polluting fuel emissions decreased 40% worldwide during the 1990s, yet 1.3 billion people do not have access to clean water. There are now 5 million deaths annually due to contaminated water and waterborne diseases.
- Access to clean water, in fact, may be as much a reason for future wars as access to oil because many parts of China, India, Africa, the Middle East, and the American West are running out of water.

- seven juveniles, ages seventeen and under, are arrested for murder
- eighty teens are raped
- five hundred teens begin using drugs
- one thousand teens begin using alcohol
- one thousand unwed teenage girls have a baby
- more than one thousand teenage girls get an abortion

- The United States consumes 1,100 cubic meters of water per citizen per year; Israel consumes just 100 cubic meters; Egypt, Jordan, and Lebanon, about 50; and Palestine in the Gaza Strip, just 20.
- While freedom, democracy, and economic opportunity have spread throughout the world since the collapse of the Soviet Union, these values have declined in most of Africa and the Islamic world.
- More than 100 million Americans now have access to the Internet, and Europe is rapidly approaching the same number. In Africa, only 1 million people have access; in the Middle East, only 900,000 have access.
- Modern banking technology now supports over 700,000 global wire transfers every day for about $2 billion total; $300 million (15%) of that is laundered money controlled by international crime syndicates.
- In 1975, 40% of the world's people lived in cities. In 2000, the figure reached 50%. By 2025, the figure is projected to be 60%.
- During the 1990s, nearly 400,000 square miles of the earth's surface was deforested—an area about the size of California and Texas combined.
- AIDS has infected 36 million worldwide, orphaned nearly 10 million children worldwide, and is laying waste the people, cultures, and political stability of many sub-Saharan African countries. Over 1 million children have been orphaned in Uganda alone, and that figure is expected to double by 2010.
- Children born today in Europe and most of North and South America can expect to live twice as long as those born in 1900. Children born today will, on average, live a full decade longer than those born in 1965.
- On the other hand, there are presently 200 million children in Third World countries who are starving or are seriously malnourished. (Revised and adapted from Barna & Hatch, 2001; Walch, 1999–2000; and various Internet sources.)

- more than twenty-seven hundred kids watch their parents separate or divorce
- more than four thousand teens contract a sexually transmitted disease
- more than one hundred thousand kids bring a gun or other weapon to school

The preceding statistics provide just a single day's snapshot of the trouble our children face: suicide, abuse, violence, pornography, abortion, drugs and alcohol, STDs, family breakdown, and the rampant moral and ethical confusion so prevalent in our culture and across the earth.

What is happening? How can things be so good and yet be so bad? Why are these contrasts so stark? Why is there so much suffering?

HURTING PEOPLE IN A BROKEN WORLD

Early in Genesis, we learn that the human race was made by and for God. Human beings lived in perfect harmony with God in the Garden of Eden, but brokenness and suffering entered the world because of the Fall (see Genesis 3). As Job 5:7 reminds us, "Man is born to trouble as surely as sparks fly upward." Our eyes are blinded to God's love because of pain and trouble. At best, we see through a glass darkly, and in our blindness, evil flourishes and our pain intensifies. We live in misery from the atrocities of this life and are easily overwhelmed, even defeated.

For some people in every nation, life is so painful and desperate that death, if not welcomed, is experienced as a sweet release. Proverbs 13:12 echoes the heart cry: "Hope deferred makes the heart sick," and this heartsickness is gripping more and more people every day. When hope is lost, when desires die, when dreams are shattered, we are broken. Some people give up and die in this brokenness, while others are desperately driven to search for new hope. The compelling forces that drive this search are (1) despair, or the cry of the suffering soul, and (2) discontent, or the drive either to idolatry or to an encounter with the living God. Let's look at both of these factors.

DESPAIR AND THE SUFFERING SOUL

Human suffering is universal; no one escapes it. It is ubiquitous. We can suffer in anything we do. Not only do we suffer because of our sins and deficits, but we sometimes suffer even when we do right and good. Suffering is pervasive. Wealth, comfort, and medication do not separate us from pain; they only temporarily numb it. Suffering includes the existential angst that everyone struggles with, the struggle to find meaning and purpose in living as well as the pain, grief, and sorrow that operate at a deeper level of intensity.

Furthermore, we experience suffering in our entire being. It can affect and damage body, soul, and spirit, twist our marriages, harm our family life, and hurt all our relationships. Counselors see some of the worst human suffering when counseling people who, for much of their childhood, were physically and sexually abused by those whom they loved and trusted. Listen to their heartwrenching, mind-twisting stories (Langberg, 1999):

> Does anybody know what it is like to be wanted only for your body parts? Your mind, your heart, your abilities, your interests are irrelevant. Even your body as a whole is unimportant. Only specific parts matter. That is who you are. [So I] hated and destroyed my body. The impulses to attack it are fierce. It is my enemy. If it weren't for my body, I would have been safe.... [I would] hit myself with sticks and punch myself. I let the ants bite me. I used to lie in the bathtub under the water [and] hold my breath, hoping I could do so until I died. (pp. 85-86)

> Feelings? Sure I have feelings—hate, rage, fear, and shame. They never go away. I never relax. I never feel safe. I can't bear up under them. I deaden my feelings with alcohol, pot, any substance I can find. That's the only way I know to keep my feelings under wraps. I don't remember the last time I cried. I am not sure I remember how. I am terrified that if I start, I will never stop. (pp. 99-100)

> He would turn me upside down on the bed and rape me. I would pick out a flower on the bedspread and concentrate on it. Eventually I would "go into" the flower. Then I could not feel what he was doing. (p. 114)

> My dad terrified me...but he was a wonderful man. Everybody loved him, and he was a great entertainer...but he would drink and come after me and my sisters. We would hide in closets and under the bed, but he would always find one of us. You could always hear him raping whoever he caught. Mother was either gone or just cooking dinner...but Mom and Dad loved each other, and he provided a good living for all "his girls." (pp. 112-113)

> I had two uncles who raped me. I feel so confused about myself. Why would men rape a boy? Does that mean I'm gay? Do I give off certain signals? I do feel odd around women. Yet I have been very promiscuous, as if somehow the more women I have sex with, the more likely it is that I can prove that I am really male. (p. 62)

I went to my pastor for advice and counseling. It was a vulnerable time in my life. I had certain feelings that something was not right, but I ignored these warning signals [as I never trusted] my own instincts. I decided to trust this man…but he was not trustworthy at all.… He abused me sexually and in other ways. (p. 120)

I concluded that God was untrustworthy, that he had also abandoned me, that he was unsafe and abusive. How was I to know anything different? It all fit together. I began to believe that my very creation was an accident of God's…I was unintentionally created, incorrectly made. This dark assumption accompanied me into my adult life and fashioned all my thinking. (pp. 129-130)

I live terrified of God, certain that if I cross him in any way, I will get beaten. Surely he does not love me or care for me, [and my] punishment will be eternal. (p. 130)

Suffering of this nature and intensity is horrific beyond words. Words, in fact, cannot contain or adequately describe the depth, the pain, the craziness, the evil of it. Like Jesus at the tomb of Lazarus, God knows the cry of our soul and weeps with us in our pain. The wrath that unregenerate perpetrators will face on Judgment Day for these kinds of crimes is unimaginable (see Matthew 18:6). Yet acknowledging these truths can so often paralyze a helper, who knows intuitively that little he or she says will be adequate to bring healing. That is normal, honest, and real. In many cases there truly are no words to match this suffering. Sometimes providing a faithful, caring presence is all one can do.

The point we wish to make here, however, is that this kind of suffering clearly demonstrates why nearly all people consider pain to be an enemy and why suffering is universally regarded as a revolting, diseaselike affliction that nobody wants and everyone is desperate to escape. Whether pain is deserved (1 Peter 4:15) or undeserved (1 Peter 2:21), whether we see it coming or it strikes like a thief in the night, nothing about it seems inherently good or noble or attractive. Jesus himself revealed his true humanity in his abhorrence of the pain and suffering he faced in his torture, crucifixion, and separation from his heavenly Father. Although he did yield—brokenhearted and exhausted—out of his higher love for us and his desire to please his heavenly Father, he desperately pleaded with God, "Take this cup from me" (Luke 22:42).

Yet suffering is also the "royal road" to experiencing the deeper things of God. Life is not a question of whether or not we suffer; that is a given for everyone born on planet Earth. The more crucial question is how we respond in the midst of suffering. The reality of heartache and hardship should not lead us to the false and twisted belief that God *causes* suffering. Since we cannot escape distress in this life, we are better off finding a way to live with it, finding meaning and redemption through it.

C. S. Lewis referred to pain as "God's megaphone." Paul Brand and Philip Yancey called it "the gift nobody wants." M. Scott Peck called pain and suffering "the road less traveled." A. W. Tozer (1977) said this about God's "night ministry":

> Slowly you will discover God's love in your suffering. Your heart will begin to approve the whole thing. You will learn…what all the schools in the world could not teach you—the healing action of faith without supporting pleasure. You will feel and understand the ministry of the night; its power to purify, to detach, to humble, to destroy the fear of death.… You will learn that pain can sometimes do what even joy cannot, such as exposing the vanity of earth's trifles and filling your heart with longing for the peace of heaven. (p. 122)

Truly helpful counselors are often those who have suffered themselves and yet have allowed God to transform and mature them through their hardships. Unfortunately, far too many sufferers allow pain to blind their eyes spiritually, to leach away their faith and courage, to bind up and freeze their hearts. But "wounded healers," as the late Henri Nouwen (1972) described them, show a winsome spirit, express joy, speak wisdom, and pour out love from their souls, which makes them wholly attractive to others, especially to people in pain.

This process is one of God's abiding miracles, one of the truly great paradoxical truths about life. The heart of this truth is beautifully expressed in 2 Corinthians 1:3-5:

> All praise to the God and Father of our Lord Jesus Christ. He is the source of every mercy and the God who comforts us. He comforts us in all our troubles so that we can comfort others. When others are troubled, we will be able to give them the same comfort God has given us. You can be sure that the more we suffer for Christ, the more God will shower us with his comfort through Christ. (NLT)

Christian counseling—and every form of soul-care ministry—starts with the God of all comfort. He pours out his comfort and care to us in our trouble and suffering as we search for meaning, purpose, and contentment. And as we are cured, redeemed, and made whole by his healing love and guidance, we are then able to offer that same help to others. On and on it goes, till we reach heaven, where wounds and pain will vanish forever.

DISCONTENT AND THE SEARCH FOR MEANING

While despair overwhelms some people, *discontent* best describes the struggle of others. A sacred discontent, an "existential struggle" for purpose and meaning, is part of the God-image that is hard-wired into the soul of every human (Allender, 1999). Augustine held that this discontent—this vague feeling of emptiness, this yearning for something more, this hole in the soul—compels us to search for connection, and we spend our lives trying to fill that emptiness with something that brings contentment. Pascal called it our "God-shaped vacuum." In our quest, we wander the earth and fill our lives with idols and lies. Either we die unfulfilled, or we experience connection with the Creator, who beckons us to come to him to find new life.

Viktor Frankl (1963), the famed Viennese psychiatrist and younger contemporary of Sigmund Freud, survived the Nazi death camp at Auschwitz. His deterministic training taught him that such a horrific experience should turn all people into groveling animals. Instead he encountered a few rare souls who rose above the hellish environment of mass death. These exceptional individuals comforted others, loved the loveless, and shared their meager rations. Frankl learned that one freedom could never be taken away from us: the freedom to choose our response—our attitude—no matter what the circumstances might be. He understood the divinely implanted trait that makes humanity unique from the animals: An individual can flourish even in the midst of great suffering.

Many people wonder if Frankl ever came to know Christ since his death-camp experience surely opened his eyes to the spiritual realm. It is only known, however, that in his later years he became something of a Jewish mystic. Experiences such as the one Frankl endured always seem to crash through our closed, godless, and mechanistic worldviews, opening the door to the spiritual, mystical, and heavenly realms. We have no doubt that these encounters are whispers (and sometimes shouts) from God about the invisible truths of life. Yet a choice must always be made. For those who search, God has no greater plan for his people than to bear witness to his truth (Matthew 28:19-20). Still, even among the twelve disciples—most of whom believed in Christ—Judas rejected Jesus and committed suicide.

SEARCHING FOR THE SACRED

Something seems to be happening. According to *Newsweek,* "Millions of Americans are embarking on a search for the sacred in their lives" (Kantrowitz, 1994, p. 53).

People are searching for God, however they name him. They're looking for something sacred beyond themselves to anchor life and to give it meaning in the midst of its suffering and chaos. Pollster George Gallup Jr. reported that 82% of Americans expressed a need for greater intimacy with God, an increase of 24% in just four years (Gallup & Jones, 2000).

During times of social upheaval, confusion, and moral decline, people often reach for something beyond themselves, and they have done so throughout history. In the Old Testament we see the recurring theme that God consistently allowed the Israelites, his chosen people, to experience the consequences of rebellion, whether by drought, moral and economic decline, or even conquest and enslavement by adversaries. If seen through the lens of God's interaction with humankind, history is surely a lesson on how forsaking God has not only adverse personal consequences but also corporate, systemic, and national consequences.

The positive outcome of Israel's corporate suffering was that it often brought about mass repentance, a renewed search for God's mercy, and national-religious-cultural recovery. Dallas Willard (1988) alluded to this dynamic when he claimed,

> Psychological, social, and political revolutions have not been able to transform the heart of darkness that lies deep in the breast of every human being. Amid a flood of self-fulfillment, there is an epidemic of depression, suicide, personal emptiness, and escapism.... So obviously the problem is a spiritual one. And so must be the cure. (p. viii)

SPIRITUALITY VERSUS RELIGION

During times of discontent, discernment is desperately needed as many seekers latch on to anything that promises hope or easy relief. G. K. Chesterton stated it well: "Once people stop believing in God, the problem is *not* that they will believe nothing; rather the problem is that they will believe anything" (Moreland, 1997, p. 34).

Clearly, many people no longer believe in religion. Religion and church life, for many seekers, is deemed to be too rigid, external, cognitive, organized, and, worst of all, sterile. In contrast to religion, the spirituality sought by so many seekers is experiential, intuitive, subjective, internal, interpersonal, emotive, dynamic, and, best of all, full of life. In this climate, the differences between religion—especially organized religion—and spirituality tend to be emphasized.

Mahrer (1996) artfully defined the difference this way: "Religion may be taken as referring to the beliefs, values, and practices of various established religions, [while] spirituality may be taken as referring to some kind of relationship between the person and a higher force, being, power, or God" (p. 435). Sperry and Giblin (1996) tell of one student's humorous distinction: "Spirituality is about going fishing and thinking about God and life, while religion is about going to church and thinking about fishing" (p. 517).

Religion and spirituality are, in fact, often seen as polar opposites in this post-modern conceptualization. Modern spirituality is person-centered, oriented toward immanence (inside you) rather than transcendence (outside and beyond you), and it may or may not have anything to do with God. Even if God is factored into the spiritual equation, it is a god that bears little resemblance to Yahweh of the Bible, the infinite-personal God of creation. The god of New Age spirituality is a pantheistic, universal, hypertolerant, and impersonal force that exists in all and is all that exists.

This lends itself to a freewheeling, anything-goes definition of spirituality that devolves into the subjective, self-focused psychospirituality that we introduced in the prologue. This modern marketplace approach to spirituality tends to deliver a tepid, feel-good pseudospirituality, and it usually denies the reality of evil, pain, sin, and shattered dreams. While we advocate a biblical spirituality that is centered in a relationship with the living God, we agree with Collins (1998) who asserted that for many seekers, rational thought is denied as more and more people look inside themselves to find fulfillment and enlightenment.

Search Patterns

The search for spiritual contentment is a road that quickly forks in two directions (Matthew 7:13-14). Many people, eager to quell the cry of their souls, choose the broad road or "highway to hell"—the path of darkness where evil festers and flourishes. The narrow road, on the other hand, is the path where God comes alive to those who truly seek him. He reveals his beloved son, Jesus Christ, and sends his Holy Spirit to transform the lives of all who invite him in.

People journeying on the wide highway are intensely engaged in the pursuit of short-term relief from suffering that inevitably leads to long-term sorrow. They become trapped in the many idolatries of denial: drugs, sex, money, powermongering, and whatever else numbs their pain. The few sufferers who flee into the arms of God can discover relief that lasts, purpose that remains, and direction that leads to a hope-filled future. Some people are trapped between these choices, wanting to find the right way but not sure where it is or in whom it is found.

The Highway to Hell

It is a vexing question why the highway to hell is the broader road. Yet as Proverbs 19:21 says, we have myriad plans to pursue happiness and satisfaction, but most schemes don't include God. Our natural bent is toward self-glorification and idolatry. Our unredeemed heart grabs and gloats, "*I want* to do it myself. *I want* the credit. *I want* people to be impressed with me."

Far too many people consider God boring, irrelevant, or demanding. They prefer to dabble in New Age, self-focused, feel-good spiritual pursuits rather than to pursue a path that calls for sacrifice or that deals with sin and our need for redemption. Dan Allender (1999) expresses this clearly in *The Healing Path:*

> When we demand that another person [or anything else] provide safety,
> certainty, fulfillment of our deepest desires—we turn from God to an idol
> for fulfillment of our needs. When we turn from God we inevitably
> demand from others the very things we miss in our relationship with
> God.... That demand is the genesis of lust and murder. (p. 53)

Many searchers go on—dare we say, *stumble along*—in blissful denial. Deniers take the easy road, embracing the latest fad, potion, gadget, guru, investment, partner, or plan that promises pie-in-the-sky satisfaction. The tragic irony is that for the short time the fix lasts, this wide and deceptive highway provides people the false sense that they have found it—whatever *it* is. The tragic truth, which these folks may or may not one day discover, is that our modern world will always offer the next new thing, the next quick fix. There will always be something more to be enamored with once our current attachments no longer satisfy.

Some of these people eventually wake up to find they have nothing of lasting value. Their lives of serial attachment to unsatisfying people, fads, and possessions will finally exhaust itself. This precipitates a crisis that branches into yet another choice between two divergent paths. Some people, shocked at what they discover, take the highway to hell that widens to superhighway status. They end up cynical, embittered, and despondent, forever complaining about life's injustices and evil. Some of these people will succumb to nihilistic rage, violence, murder, and suicide. All of us know people who have taken this path, including more and more young people!

THE NARROW WAY TO LIFE

Other people take the narrow path and find God as a result of their search. The difference this choice makes is profound, both in this life and in life eternal. God gives everyone a lifetime to choose denial and despair or him (Crabb, 1993). You have made and are living out a choice right now, whether you know it or not, or believe it or not.

Curtis and Eldridge (1997), in *The Sacred Romance,* describe our desire for connection as a longing "for intimacy because we were made in the image of perfect intimacy" (p. 73). They refer to the love and intimacy shared by God among the persons of the Trinity, the perfect intimate love between Father, Son, and Holy Spirit. This is the intimacy that humans long to participate in when they come to know God in a relational way. This is the deep, soul-filling contentment we desire and want to reproduce right here on Earth, in spite of our sins and limitations.

People everywhere need Christ. The question is and always will be, "Whom should I send as a messenger to my people? Who will go for us?" (Isaiah 6:8, NLT). We are designed to share in God's glory, reflecting, as Calvin put it, the "sense of deity written into every heart." But this rarely happens unless the messenger goes and tells the story. We hope the Christian counselor is willing to be that messenger and to say, "Lord, I'll go! Send me."

Counseling and the Quest for Spirituality

In addition to the reality of suffering and its effect on the human soul, the need for Christian counseling is evident when we consider the current directions in counseling and the behavioral sciences as a whole. Traditionally, mental health professionals have been either disinterested in religion and faith or downright hostile toward it (Collins, 1998; Richards & Bergin, 1997). Surely this is one of the reasons significant parts of the church remain so skeptical about psychotherapy. We remember how some of our classmates in graduate school were adamant about the gulf between faith and counseling. "I don't believe a Christian could ever be a professional counselor," one woman asserted in a class that was considering the role of religious and spiritual values in counseling. "Christians would push their 'toxic faith' positions on clients seeking help—especially their views about homosexuality and abortion" (Clinton, 1998, p. 30).

The "Faith Gap"
Many mental health professionals, including some of the field's leading lights, have characterized religious people, and especially Christians, as simpleminded, easily controlled, and thoroughly deluded (Ellis, 1971; Freud, 1927; Watson, 1924, 1983). Though no real empirical evidence exists to support these claims, faith has been viewed, from this naturalistic, antisupernatural mind-set, as something pathological. Christians are broad-brushed as manipulated masses who are intolerant, living in denial, and even dangerous to the commonweal due to their fanatical, fundamentalist beliefs.

In counseling, non-Christian therapists have tended to express values unknown or alien to many Christian clients (Bergin, 1983, 1991; Worthington, 1986). Many of these therapists simply have been uninterested in spiritual things, communicating directly or indirectly that spiritual issues are unimportant. Worse yet, some promote what many believers report to be unusual, non-Christian, and even anti-Christian New Age and pagan beliefs, challenging and even belittling a client's Christian values (Gross, 1978; Richards & Bergin, 1997).

Though the rise of interest in spirituality has blunted the sharp edges of these clashing worldviews, a significant faith gap still exists between Christian clients and the mental health professions. One survey showed that while 72% of the American population says that religious faith is among the most important factors in their life, only 33% of psychologists could say the same thing (Bergin & Jensen, 1990). A 1992 Gallup poll on mental health assistance indicated that over 60% of the respondents preferred a counselor with spiritual beliefs and values, and 80% wanted their own beliefs and values brought into the counseling process (Kelly, 1995).

THE MYTH OF VALUE-FREE COUNSELING

Values are best understood as personal beliefs about what is true, good, right, or virtuous. Without a moral compass and functional values in life—and in counseling—we would be aimless. Starting with Kuhn's seminal work in 1970 and permeating Bergin's work in the 1980s and 1990s, the myth of value-free counseling—even of so-called value-free, "objective" science—has been debunked.

Values and worldviews permeate counseling and psychotherapy, science, policy choices, and every other choice we make in life. This truth—one of the few good fruits to come out of postmodern thinking—sets us free to explore and debate our values. No longer can or should a counselor assert, in contravention to a client who complains about being set upon by unwanted counselor values, that he or she was doing value-free counseling. It simply doesn't exist. "No matter how or at what level the counselor is intervening, his or her values will have some kind of influence on the client" (Clinton, 1998, p. 31).

Informed consent, a key ethic in counseling, is as much about disclosure of values and beliefs as it is about theory and applied technique. Clients have the right to freely choose what values and beliefs they want influencing the counseling process. Conflict and unrealized goals are common outcomes when Christian clients work with counselors who do not share similar beliefs (Richards & Bergin, 1997).

SPIRITUALITY AND MENTAL HEALTH

As we have already discussed, spiritual pursuits of all kinds have become fashionable in this postmodern, post-Christian age. This is true in the helping professions as well. In fact, although the faith gap does exist, a strong argument could be made that spirituality is the "hot new thing" in the counseling world. A quarter-century ago, such a pursuit was absurd in the heady halls of the mental health professions.

Now one can hardly attend any conference in the mental health field without hearing about various people who are "getting in touch" with their spirituality. In fact, the theme for the 2001 annual conference of the American Counseling Association (2000) was "Counseling at Its Best: Celebrating the Human Spirit." Consider the number and variety of presentations in just *one track* at this conference that include the word *spirit* or one of its derivatives in the title:

- A Culture-Sensitive Model for Working with Spiritual Issues in Counseling
- African American Spirituality: A Living Journey Homeward
- All Paths Lead to God: Integration of Spiritual and Religious Identity in Multicultural Counseling
- Beyond Coping: Trauma, Grief, and Spiritual Growth
- Bringing Out the Best in the Human Spirit: Reality Therapy in Groups
- Celebrating the Holistic Spirit: Embracing Our Inner Voices
- Celebrating the Human Spirit: Culturally Competent Counseling at Its Best
- Combining Person-Centered and Feminist Therapy to Reach the Human Spirit
- Cultivating the Spirit of Mindfulness in Counseling and Psychotherapy
- Finding the Human Spirit: Counseling Children with Conduct Disorders
- Freedom of the Spirit: Spiritual Perspectives in Coming Out
- Helping Families Recover from Suicide: A Model for Spiritual Coping
- Integrating Spirituality, Humor, and Playfulness in Counseling
- Interventions in Psychospiritual Counseling
- Living in Two Cultures: Celebrating the Spirit of Native Americans
- Nurturing Women's Spirits: Phenomenological Studies of Leaderless Women's Groups
- Religious and Spirituality Issues with Gay and Lesbian Clients
- Spirituality and Jung: Resolving Dualities, Accepting Paradox, Creating Unity
- Spirituality in Adult Development: Implications for Counseling
- Spirituality in Counseling: Research and Implications for Counselors and Educators
- Spirituality in Supervision
- Tapping the Human Spirit to Enhance Cultural Awareness
- The Interplay of Sexual Identity and Spirituality
- The Native Spirit Reflected in Counseling Practice

- The Problem of Evil: The Underbelly of Spirituality
- The Therapeutic Power of Ritual in Celebrating the Human Spirit
- Using Your Spirit to Get a Faculty Position
- Women in Counseling: Nurturing Our Spirits

It should be obvious that the spiritual search we have described is also going on in the secular mental health disciplines, reflecting how widespread this is in the entire culture.

CHRISTIAN COUNSELING AND THE CHURCH

Thus far we have developed the case that Christian counseling is a response to the trends and dynamics in the larger social, cultural, and professional realms. Now we will focus on Christian counseling and the church. We agree with Collins (1993), who asserts that "counseling is not Christian when it ignores the church and when it is done in isolation from the community of believers...who come together for the purpose of worship, edification, transformation, and service" (p. 211).

Christ-centered soul care means recognizing that the *church,* more than the hospital or clinic, is the central place for healing, growth, and rich relationship. It means seeing people's pain as a soul wound as well as a psychological disorder at times. It means being invested in others—making a caring connection with someone—rather then merely engaging in skilled talking. It means concerning ourselves with who Christian counselors are. We value more the impact of the character and maturity of the counselor than what is done in terms of technique (Crabb, 1997).

Christian counseling is believing that the care and cure of souls is the work of God—a process of spiritual formation and discipleship—more than the work of psychotherapy. James 5:16 says to "confess your trespasses to one another, and pray for one another, that you may be healed. The effective, fervent prayer of a righteous man avails much" (NKJV). The Scriptures contain more than fifty "one another" passages that are essentially instructions for the care and counseling of believers.

As important as we believe—and passionately advocate—counseling and psychotherapy to be, they are secondary to, adjunctive to, and supportive of the gospel call and the discipling work of the church. "Good preaching proclaims the Word of God publicly; good counseling applies the Word of God privately. Both may be abused, but both also may be used by the Holy Spirit to change lives. Sometimes one is effective when the other is not" (Collins, 1998, p. 23). We see both as complementary gifts to the church.

The church must become more therapeutic in the sense of being a place that makes people feel accepted, wanted, and valued. These are often the necessary pre-conditions to ushering someone into a relationship with the living God. However, the church must never allow itself to be reduced to a mere therapeutic community or to let a purely therapeutic mission become the center of its purpose and call. While the call to care is vital in the church, there is no substitute for the primacy of Jesus Christ. Nothing must overshadow the meaning and power of his life, death, and resurrection.

Soul-care helpers are passionate about reflecting the life of Christ and assisting the sanctifying work of the Spirit to form true spiritual life in the souls of others. Soul-care helpers are quick to give and slow to crow. They know they are but the *agents* of healing, for only God can supply the medicine to cure ailing souls. Isaiah 61:1-2 reveals the heart of a counselor:

> The Spirit of the Sovereign LORD is upon me, because the LORD has
> appointed me to bring good news to the poor. He has sent me to comfort
> the brokenhearted and to announce that captives will be released and pris-
> oners will be freed. He has sent me to tell those who mourn that the time
> of the LORD's favor has come. (NLT)

ANSWERING GOD'S CALL TO CARE

Christian counseling is honorable work, a true calling to ministry in the church (burden bearing in Galatians 6:2; "the ministry of reconciliation" in 2 Corinthians 5:18). The ministers in Christian counseling are dedicated Christians who entreat and trust God to be the third person in the counseling endeavor. In his delightful book *If You Want to Walk on Water, You've Got to Get Out of the Boat*, John Ortberg (2001) declares that "a calling is something you discover, not something you choose" (p. 60). Noting that the root of *vocation* is the Latin word for "voice," Ortberg builds the case that the call to holy work is the result of careful and consistent listening to God.

Christian counseling must be holy work, and the call to do it takes place in that territory of the soul where "your deep gladness meets the world's deep need" (Ortberg, 2001, pp. 60-61). Many people become Christian counselors because they like helping people, and they believe that God has gifted and called them to a helping ministry. Over forty thousand of these helpers from all over the world are now members in the American Association of Christian Counselors (AACC), and they are joining at a rate of over a thousand per month.

Those who stay in the helping ministry are those who love doing it. (Yes, there is a downside to counseling, and you will discover it if you give your life away to others long enough.) Those who persevere in their call to counsel are those whose "deep gladness" is a wellspring that is constantly renewed for themselves and for those who come seeking help. Your giftedness must also be charged with a passion for ministry, a delight in seeing the light come on in clients' faces, a willingness to laugh and cry with clients, and a commitment to walk with your clients through some dark emotional valleys.

Christian counseling has become a compassionate force of twenty-first-century ministry-practice on behalf of the church, and it is comprised of committed soul-care helpers from a variety of backgrounds, affiliations, professions, and specialties. Soul-care ministry is centered in Christ and takes place not only in the church but also in hospitals, clinics, agencies, private practices, and homes, as well as via the Internet. It spans the entire continuum of care, from outpatient counseling to residential care, day treatment to full hospitalization. Soul-care ministry encourages the entire community of helpers, including pastors, chaplains and pastoral counselors, professional clinicians from all the mental health disciplines, and lay helpers of all kinds.

THE CASE-WISE WAY OF SANCTIFICATION

At least as critical to the rise of Christian counseling and the failures of the secular helping professions have been the problems and deficiencies of contemporary church ministry. Bruce Narramore argued that one reason so many believers have been willing to use Christian counselors is because the church "wasn't stemming the tide [by helping people overcome their troubled lives]. What was missing in the church was a practical application of our biblical knowledge to life" (see Stafford, 1993, p. 29).

Too many churches still live in denial. They will not admit that Christians need help. It is as if salvation solves every problem, and sanctification is an idea without practical import in church life. Henry Cloud asked, "In the church it is…unacceptable to have problems: that is called being sinful. In an AA group it is… unacceptable to be perfect: that is called denial. Which stance is more biblical?" (see Stafford, 1993, pp. 28-29).

Cloud further decried the deification of willpower in many conservative churches, as if Christians can somehow overcome sin and achieve spiritual maturity by merely choosing to do so. He considered this pull-yourself-up-by-the-bootstraps mentality to be essentially a denial of the gospel, a denial of our need for Christ in an ongoing work of redemptive sanctification because we are totally unable to accomplish it ourselves.

Larry Crabb believes that Christian counseling is a logical "response to a shallow sort of spirituality that developed out of fundamentalism in its [early twentieth-century] controversy with the modernists" (see Stafford, 1993, pp. 30-31). While conservatives rightly emphasized biblical integrity and moral absolutes, Crabb noted that "sanctification came to be seen as no more than chosen obedience" (pp. 30-31). Christian counseling emphasizes change from the inside out, a transforming life experience where God touches, heals, and reshapes the deepest recesses of heart and soul. "Simply telling people to try harder or pray more doesn't accomplish that" (pp. 30-31).

The excessive emphasis on personal morality and change in the conservative church is also deficient. Crabb is convinced that Christian growth and maturity—and the counseling and soul-care ministry that facilitates this—must be embedded in a community of believers and must be grounded in the church. Though he is opposed to a therapeutic mentality taking root in the church—the false but seductive idea that God exists primarily to help solve my problems, enhance my happiness, and fulfill my dreams—Crabb believes the church can and must become more caring and therapeutic in its ministry. That is, when believers are honest, accountable, receptive, and helpful to others in a small-group context, true sanctification can take place, and true ministry can come alive (Crabb, 1993, 1997).

CHRISTIAN COUNSELING AS MODERN DISCIPLESHIP

Another variant on relations between Christian counseling and the church revolves around the call to discipleship (Matthew 28:19-20). A common criticism of the evangelical church, which is related to the issues noted in the previous section, is that it is full of converts, but very few disciples (Barna, 2000). The priority of evangelism over disciple making has a long history among conservative Christians. While salvation and entry into church community is the crucial first step in the lifelong journey toward maturity in Christ, the growing-up process, which is equally important, is an area in which many churches fail or show considerable deficiencies.

Barna's research revealed that while many churches have discipling programs of various kinds, most are not really accomplishing the objective of discipleship. For example, fewer than half of the adults and teens attending conservative churches actually believed in moral absolutes. Only 20% of born-again believers were engaged in spiritual-growth programs with specific and measurable goals. Less than 10% embraced thirteen basic biblical beliefs or believed they were true. Barna (2000) concluded that a disjointed, "menu-oriented" approach to discipling was inadequate. "Churches feel they have fulfilled their obligations if they provide a broad menu of courses, events, and other experiences, but [this] approach leaves people confused and imbalanced" (pp. 251-252).

One way to correct this evangelism-discipleship imbalance is to recognize that Christian counseling often does double duty in the church. It helps resolve parishioners' trouble and suffering, and it assists them toward growth in intimacy, faith, and confidence in their relationship with God. In essence, Christian counseling should be seen, at least in part, as a person-focused, case-wise, and intensely formative process of discipleship.

Collins (1996a) assertively develops the thesis that church-based "people helping" is really an expression of the call to discipleship that God makes to every believer. Every soul-care helper must count the cost and be willing to sacrifice some level of personal comfort and preference in order to be fit for service, able to meet the needs of others and help them grow into a disciple of Christ's.

> The emphasis on discipleship is so central to the teachings of the New Testament and so basic to the Christian way of life that it cannot be ignored when a Christian enters a counseling or other helping relationship.... Helping that leaves out the spiritual dimension ultimately has something missing. It may stimulate good feelings and help people cope with stress, but it does nothing to prepare people for eternity or help them experience the abundant life here on earth—an abundance that only comes with commitment to Christ. (pp. 14-15)

THE GOAL OF CHRISTIAN COUNSELING

Christian counseling is not an end in itself but a ministerial and professional means of finding our true selves by finding new life in Christ. Each of us has a circle of friends, a circle of influence. So don't get lost in the myriad spirits of this age or in the vast forest of the helping professions—the human and social sciences—and miss the Tree of Life and the beauty of the Kingdom Grove.

Yes, this is a book about Christian counseling and its bright promise in the new century, but more than that, it is a book about Jesus Christ—about the living God, the Lord and Giver of Life, the One who gave us life abundantly. Our best hope is that, as you read this book, you will not only attain the wisdom to become a better helper, but you will encounter Jesus on a personal level and learn from him.

So then, may Jesus be exalted in everything we do, individually as counselors and corporately in the field of Christian counseling. He is the reason for our counseling, the goal of our work, and the way to achieve it. May he be seen in every chapter and heard on every page.

Whatever the reason for your interest in reading this book, we hope you will be "surprised by joy" as C. S. Lewis put it—delighted by what you learn and the One you come to know.

CHAPTER 2

COMPETENT CHRISTIAN COUNSELING

Definitions and Dynamics

TIM CLINTON AND GEORGE OHLSCHLAGER

There is a movement afoot to pool all the good ideas found in the many forms of counseling and psychotherapy in order to identify a set of converging themes: the principles, approaches, and methodologies that constitute the essence of helping.

—GERARD EGAN, *The Skilled Helper*

Counseling is difficult to define, for it has so many meanings, so many ways it can be understood. From a client's viewpoint, it is a relationship with a trained and caring counselor directed toward solving problems and reaching goals that he or she is having difficulty attaining. From a counselor's perspective, it is a multidimensional process that targets and works to change thoughts, feelings, behaviors, relationships, and environments by applying knowledge and skill to serve a client's best interest in personal growth and maturation. Broadly defined, counseling is a multidisciplinary profession with various standards of practice, ethics, training regimens, and identities.

Furthermore, the counseling professions are undergoing a paradigm shift as we enter the new millennium (Kuhn, 1970). Akin to the scientific transformation of medicine and the development of psychology and social work a century ago, the paradigm for understanding, practicing, and evaluating psychotherapy and counseling is being transformed as we move into the twenty-first century. (This transformation will be discussed in more detail in later chapters.)

Theory-based approaches to counseling, which challenged (and sometimes forced) the client to adhere to the preferred model of counseling, are giving way to a new practice paradigm. This new paradigm fits interventions to the individual, the problem, and the situation, and it accords greater respect to the competencies and limits of the counselor. Long-term psychotherapy is giving way to brief, empirically based treatments. Clients once viewed as needy, mostly passive recipients of expert help are beginning to be recognized as knowledgeable consumers and partners in counseling (Oliver, Hasz, & Richburg, 1997; Richards & Bergin, 1997).

Christian counseling and soul care is a healthy, vibrant part of this exciting transformation. A robust work of clinical, spiritual, and scientific development is taking place throughout our field (McMinn, 1996). Consequently, we need a simple yet potent model that shows the efficacy of Christian counseling across a wide range of applications. Still, as much as we need to have an effective model, we need even more to root ourselves in the redeeming power of Christ. The value of developing new practices will be undercut unless they are shaped by the Holy Spirit, built on the sure foundation of God's truth as revealed in the Scriptures, and salted with the writings of the great saints throughout church history. Christian counseling needs a broadly accepted, biblically based, Spirit-directed, and empirically validated model that invites Christ into the helping process to meet the deepest needs of individuals and families.

Counseling and the larger behavioral sciences represent a diverse population of many disciplines that use a wide variety of methods to care for people and help them change. If we add the classical pastoral care ministries of the church to our list, the following fields would be identified as members of a broad class of "helping professions":

- counseling (and psychotherapy)
- clinical and counseling psychology
- clinical social work
- psychiatry
- psychiatric nursing
- marriage and family therapy
- pastoral counseling
- pastoral care and visitation
- lay helping/counseling
- substance abuse counseling
- myriad other forms of specialized "niche" care

THE BREADTH AND THE ESSENCE

Beyond these more formal helping roles, Egan (1998) recognizes that helping is also done informally and indirectly by a number of other professions and groups, such as doctors, dentists, lawyers, business consultants, police officers, teachers, bartenders, hairdressers, and many other kinds of service workers. Most of these helpers claim and can demonstrate some level of success in helping people change. As Christians, however, we believe it is necessary not to consider change per se, but, more important, the direction and goal of that change.

McMinn (1998) goes deep into this additional step when he says,

> If God longs to be in relationship with us and if the deepest longings of the human soul point to God, then the goals of Christian counseling go much deeper than changing behavior. Even those who don't know God long for the things of God—peace, hope, love, and justice, to name a few. These longings are spiritual in nature and so it is inevitable that every counseling session that digs beneath the behavioral veneer of human experience has something to do with spirituality and religious experience. (p. 17)

This is the essence of Christian counseling that, we believe, is hidden in the person of Christ (see Colossians 1:26-27). At the heart of Christian counseling is the good news of Jesus Christ. This is a message of love and hope, of a God who cares for us so much that he sent his only beloved Son who, through his death, burial, and resurrection, made it possible for us to be reconciled with God. The power of this God-man who walked the earth two millennia ago makes change, redemption, and new life possible no matter how horrible the circumstances.

The competent Christian counselor, therefore, is a person who knows Jesus Christ intimately and is able to make him known to others. In Christ and by his power and wisdom, all of the best ideas, methods, and principles of helping converge. Jesus is the Alpha and Omega, the Lord of all truth (Johnson, 1997). Truth is revealed in him (special revelation) and in his creation (general revelation derived by empirical and reflective study). This essence is embodied truth, which is always revealed in the person of Christ who freely and supernaturally gives himself and his way to us when we earnestly seek him (Matthew 7:7-11).

In this chapter we will endeavor to consider this essence as well as the overall process by which it works. We do this to help Christian counselors be informed and guided by a cogent road map that will help those in need. Our desire is to honor Christ and help bring increasing maturity and unity to the church. We strive to be guides and catalysts, pointing the way and encouraging action so that the counseling ministry movement will be brought to a fuller maturity.

WHAT, THEN, IS CHRISTIAN COUNSELING?

In this chapter and the chapter that follows, we will address the questions that many people, both inside and outside the church, are asking: What is Christian counseling, who does it, and how is it different from other kinds of counseling?

We will answer these questions in a variety of ways throughout this book by exploring

- a brief history of the modern Christian counseling movement, including its long prehistory as pastoral care and spiritual formation in the church;
- structural, thematic, convergent, and other descriptions of the field by leading Christian counselors;
- the biblical and clinical grounds of Christian counseling, including the ten "control beliefs" or presuppositions upon which we base the development and practice of our Paracentric perspective on Christian counseling;
- a 3 x 3 x 3 pattern that outlines the core elements and process of competent Christian counseling by synthesizing the best data from these many definitions. This will outline a skeletal framework for Christian counseling and soul-care ministry-practice to which we will add tissue, sinew, and flesh throughout the rest of this book.

DEFINING CHRISTIAN COUNSELING: TWENTIETH-CENTURY FOUNDATIONS

This section reviews the twentieth-century historical and definitional threads that comprise the foundations of the model we present in this book.

DEFINITIONS AND DEVELOPMENT

Although modern Christian counseling has a short, post–World War II history of fifty-plus years, its prelude in the pastoral care and counseling ministry of the church is two thousand years old. This connection is vitally important because Christian counseling has been, in the form of pastoral care, a central and long-standing ministry of the church since its inception. It is not, as some critics contend, some sinister, secular interloper that has arisen in the twentieth century to confound and defeat the church (Bobgan & Bobgan, 1987; Hunt, 1987). In fact, so much of what is considered new and unusual—especially as it arises out of the psychosocial sciences—is, in fact, not new at all (see Ecclesiastes 1:9-11). Oden (1987), among others, has shown that the most sophisticated ideas and modern applications of counseling were clearly articulated in the pastoral care writings of the early church fathers and saints throughout history.

Consider, for example, the valuable and useful definition of counseling and soul care given by the great theologian-philosopher Thomas Aquinas (1225–1274) over seven hundred years ago:

Spiritual needs are relieved by spiritual acts in two ways, first by asking help from God, and in this respect we have prayer.... Secondly, by giving human assistance...by instructing...[or] by counseling, [which include]: *instruction* to the mind, *counsel* for practical action, *comfort* for sorrow, *reproof* and admonition for correction, *pardon* for sins, and *forbearance* for those who are weak. (Oden, 1987, pp. 51-52)

Contemplate the ministering prayer of Aelred, the abbot of Rievaulx in Yorkshire, England (1109–1167) and the insight he had nearly nine hundred years ago about the role of empathy in helping others:

Give me the power, dear Lord, to speak the truth straightforwardly, and yet acceptably, so that they all may be built up in faith, hope, and love.... Teach me therefore, sweet Lord, how to restrain the restless, comfort the discouraged, and support the weak. Teach me to suit myself to everyone according to his nature, character, and disposition, according to his power of understanding or lack of it, as time and place require. (Oden, 1987, p. 11)

Finally, consider the metaphorical wisdom of Martin Luther (1483–1546) on the balanced way that pastoral reproof should be conducted and how the confrontation of sin should take place:

For you have to inflict the wound in a way that you also know how to alleviate and heal it. You have to be severe in such a way as not to forget kindness. Thus God, too, puts lightning into the rain and breaks up gloomy clouds and a dark sky into fruitful showers. (Oden, 1987, p. 169)

As for the history of faith-based counseling, note some of the key dates and events in our development since 1949:

1949—Seward Hiltner published his classic treatise *Pastoral Counseling*.

1956—Christian Association of Psychological Studies (CAPS) was begun.

1959—Wayne Oates published *An Introduction to Pastoral Counseling*.

1960—Clyde Narramore published *The Psychology of Counseling*.

1965—Fuller Theological Seminary launched its PhD-level Graduate School of Psychology.

1968—Nouthetic counseling movement began with the establishment of the Christian Counseling and Education Foundation at Westminster Theological Seminary.

1969—Rosemead Graduate School of Psychology was established.

1970—Jay Adams published *Competent to Counsel.*

1972—*Journal of Psychology and Theology* was launched by Rosemead.

1974—Kenneth Hauck started Stephens Ministry.

1975—Larry Crabb published *Basic Principles of Biblical Counseling;* CAPS Bulletin was launched (now *Journal of Psychology and Christianity*).

1976—American Psychological Association (APoA) Division 36 was started for "psychologists interested in religious issues" (now "psychology of religion"); Minirth-Meier Clinic was launched.

1979—James Dobson launched Focus on the Family ministries.

1980—Gary Collins's "big yellow book," *Christian Counseling,* was published.

1988—First International Congress on Christian Counseling was held in Atlanta; New Life Treatment Centers were established.

1990—Rapha Hospital and Clinic system was established.

1991—Gary Collins and Tim Clinton assumed leadership of the American Association of Christian Counselors (AACC); in five years, membership mushroomed from seven hundred to nearly fifteen thousand.

1992—AACC launched its flagship magazine *Christian Counseling Today;* Second International Congress on Christian counseling was held.

1995—AACC introduced the provisional draft of its *Christian Counseling Code of Ethics.*

1996—Edward Shafranske edited the APA-published *Religion and the Practice of Clinical Psychology.*

1997—AACC launched *Marriage and Family: A Christian Journal;* P. Scott Richards and Allen Bergin published *A Spiritual Strategy for Counseling and Psychotherapy.*

1999—AACC World Conference attracted thirty-three hundred attendees, the largest single gathering of Christian counselors to date.

2001—AACC reached over forty thousand members in fifty states and nearly fifty countries and was divided into four major groups: mental health professionals, pastoral counselors, lay helpers, and students; AACC World Conference attracted nearly six thousand attendees.

STRUCTURAL DEVELOPMENT

The Christian counseling movement has advanced beyond a small guild of loosely affiliated practitioners and the largely academic exercise of theory building that integrates psychology and theology (McMinn, 1996; Worthington, 1994). Hundreds of thousands of professional and pastoral counselors—and millions more lay helpers—are now doing counseling ministry in every state and on every continent. As mentioned in the previous list, the American Association of Christian Counselors alone has over forty thousand members worldwide, making it one of the largest counseling associations in the world. Many other schools, organizations, institutes, journals, hospitals, clinics, and agencies now exist to develop and promote the idea and work of Christian counseling.

This field is also becoming more closely connected with the church as we recognize and respond to God's call to be the servant of the church and its people. We have entered an era of clinical practice and pastoral care that incorporates soul-care and spiritual-formation activities into the work of human, family, and societal change at all levels. Additionally, increasing numbers of people seeking therapy are now requesting faith-based counseling, which, we believe, is one reason why our profession is becoming a respected member of the panoply of twenty-first-century mental health disciplines (Clinton, 2001).

THEMATIC DEFINITIONS

Although they rarely capture the richness and complexity of any profession, thematic or formal definitions provide a helpful basis for understanding Christian counseling. Boundaries are clearly set and major themes, principles, and objectives are elucidated. In the following discussion, we will identify three primary classifications in the development of Christian counseling as an evangelical ministry movement, though each group has many subsets and variations.

1. *Integrationists.* Gary Collins (1988), one of Christian counseling's most influential worldwide ambassadors, has probably best defined the integrationist position, where biblical theology and the psychosocial sciences are integrated into a workable counseling model (see also Bouma-Prediger, 1990; Carlson, 1980; Carter and Mohline, 1976; Farnsworth, 1985; Johnson, 1997). Collins described the distinctive attributes and processes of Christian helping in his "big yellow book" titled *Christian Counseling:*

> Christian counselors use many techniques developed and used by non-believers, but Christian counseling has at least four distinctives:
>
> *Unique Assumptions.* No counselor is completely value-free or neutral in terms of assumptions.... Despite variations in theology, most counselors who call themselves Christian have (or should have) beliefs about the attributes of God, the nature of human beings, the authority of Scripture, the reality of sin, the forgiveness of God, and hope for the future....
>
> *Unique Goals.* Like our secular colleagues, the Christian seeks to help

counselees change behavior, attitudes, values, and/or perceptions.... But the Christian goes further. He or she seeks to stimulate spiritual growth in counselees; to encourage confession of sin and the experience of divine forgiveness; to model Christian standards, attitudes, values, and lifestyles; to present the gospel message, encouraging counselees to commit their lives to Jesus Christ; and to stimulate counselees to develop values and live lives that are based on biblical teaching....

Unique Methods. All counseling techniques...seek to arouse the belief that help is possible, correct erroneous beliefs about the world, develop competencies in social living, and help counselees accept themselves as persons of worth.... Christian and non-Christian counselors use many of the same helping methods.... But the Christian does not use counseling techniques that would be considered immoral or inconsistent with biblical teaching...[like encouragement to] engage in extramarital or premarital sexual intercourse.... Other techniques are distinctly Christian and would be used in Christian counseling with some frequency. Prayer in the counseling session, reading the Scriptures, gentle confrontation with Christian truths, or encouraging counselees to become involved with a local church are common examples.

Unique Counselor Characteristics. Research studies found that counseling techniques are most potent when used by helpers who are characterized by warmth, sensitivity, understanding, genuine concern, and a willingness to confront people in an attitude of love. Counseling textbooks stressed the importance of counselor qualities such as trustworthiness, good psychological health, honesty, patience, competence, and self-knowledge.... Surely Jesus Christ is the best model we have.... At times he listened to people carefully without giving much overt direction, but on other occasions he taught decisively. He encouraged and supported, but he also confronted and challenged. He accepted people who were sinful and needy, but he also demanded repentance, obedience, and action....

At the core of all true Christian helping...is the influence of the Holy Spirit. His presence and influence make Christian counseling truly unique. It is he who gives the most effective counselor characteristics: love, joy, peace.... He is the comforter or helper who teaches "all things," reminds us of Christ's sayings, convicts people of sin, and guides us into all truth.... This should be the goal of every believer—pastor or layperson, professional counselor or nonprofessional—to be used by the Holy Spirit to touch lives, to change them, and to bring others toward both spiritual and psychological maturity. (pp. 17-20, [italics added])

Furthermore, Collins asserted that Christian counseling has distinctive relationships with Jesus Christ, with the Holy Spirit, and with the church. In a more recent book on the biblical bases of Christian counseling, Collins (1993) distills a comprehensive definition of Christian counseling from an earlier work:

Attempts to define or describe Christian counseling tend to emphasize the person who does the helping, the techniques or skills that are used, and the goals that counseling seeks to reach. From this perspective the Christian counselor is

- a deeply committed, Spirit-guided (and Spirit-filled) servant of Jesus Christ
- who applies his or her God-given abilities, skills, training, knowledge, and insight
- to the task of helping others move to personal wholeness, interpersonal competence, mental stability, and spiritual maturity.

Christian counselors are committed believers, doing their best to help others, with the help of God. Such a definition includes believers who come from different theological perspectives, use different approaches to counseling, and have different levels of training and experience. (p. 21)

Believing integrationism to be the invalid importation of corrupting psychological theory into the church, some critics attacked it as false on its face (Bobgan & Bobgan, 1987; Bulkley, 1993; Hunt, 1987; Kilpatrick, 1983). But often such critics fail to discriminate between the gold and the junk in the psychosocial sciences when they assume all of psychology to be wholly secular and inherently corrupt, and they still criticize a Freudian-Jungian-atheistic straw man that most of psychology left behind long ago (Myers, 2001). We do agree, however, with the arguments that some integrationists have far too often borrowed uncritically from and have been far too enamored with psychology and the behavioral sciences and have not been enamored enough with the God of the Bible or with the church he is building (Powlison, 2001).

2. *Nouthetic counseling.* Jay Adams is the founder and one of the key leaders of the nouthetic counseling movement, one of many theoretical emphases that demonstrates both the vitality and the ferment in the Christian counseling field today (Adams, 1970, 1973, 1979). Although it is currently expanding in both range of practice and type of practitioner, most nouthetic counseling is anchored in Reformed theology and a more separatist community orientation. A great deal of nouthetic counseling is centered in the church and is practiced by the pastor and others under pastoral authority. Nouthetic counselors use the Bible almost always,

if not exclusively, as their resource. Adams (1979) provides insight into his beliefs about counseling when he says:

> The Christian's basis for counseling, and the basis for a Christian's counseling, is nothing other than the Scriptures of the Old and New Testament. The Bible is his counseling textbook.
>
> "Why?" you ask. "After all, the Christian doesn't use the Bible as his basis for...engineering, architecture, music—so why should he insist that the Scriptures are the basis for counseling?"
>
> The answer to that question is at once both simple and profound (because of its simplicity don't miss the profundity of its implications). The Bible is the basis for Christian counseling because it deals with the same issues that all counseling does. The Bible was given to help men come to saving faith in Christ and then to transform believers in His image (2 Timothy 3:15-17).... God assigns this life calling of transforming lives by the Word to the man of God, [and] the Holy Spirit strongly declares that the Bible fully equips him for this work....
>
> As future ministers of the Word, be just that—only that, and nothing else but that—ministers of the Word! Do not forsake the Fountain of living water for the cracked cisterns of modern counseling systems. (pp. xiii-xiv)

David Powlison (1997), perhaps this group's most thoughtful theorist and best advocate, defines some contemporary challenges for Christian counseling that must be addressed by all of us in the field. Calling Christian counselors who perceive life as being pervaded by God and lamenting counselors and ministers who leave God on the margins of their lives and practices, he endeavors to construct a vibrant and "systematic biblical counseling." (Nouthetic counselors have described themselves as "biblical counselors" for nearly a decade.) Powlison believes that the Bible is sufficient to "make us 'wise unto salvation,' [and useful for] a comprehensive description of transforming human life from all that ails us (2 Timothy 3:15-17)" (p. 3). Decrying the artificial split of spiritual and psychological concerns, he argues that

> [t]hose committed to systematic biblical counseling see that a practical biblical theology is not only possible, but necessary. We would affirm that "spiritual matters" include the details of practical human problems. Any contribution of extrabiblical sources is distinctly subordinate and secondary to the givens of a biblical model. Other sources may be informative and provocative: we may learn from and be challenged by our own experience,

popular fiction, history, the mass media, psychology.... But the "truth" of all these things must be judged by Scripture and reinterpreted according to the Spirit's wisdom. (p. 4)

At a time when the church was widely embracing psychology—and sometimes doing so without thought—movement called attention back to the Word of God and challenged counselors to think theologically. The primary criticisms of the nouthetic approach, however, are that it is narrowly conceived and too focused on a confrontational style of dealing with sin and behavioral change to the exclusion of tender soul care and sensitivity to life's grief. Nouthetic process tends to be weak on understanding the complexity of human motivation, and it struggles to develop an adequate theory of suffering and emotion.

3. *The community model.* Larry Crabb (1975, 1977, 1993, 1997, 2001), a preeminent leader in our field and a teacher, clinician, and writer, has also significantly influenced the development of Christian counseling. His view of Christian counseling evolved from an integrationist position to what he called "biblical counseling" to his current stance, which endorses and champions the community model. His practice and continuing search to understand God's Word have led him to believe that helping should be centered in the church and, specifically, that counseling should be connected to the body of believers in Christ.

Crabb's (1997) definition of Christian counseling bridges and incorporates some of the best elements of the integrationist and nouthetic approaches. His reflections on the state of the "talking cure" and its implications for counseling and ministry are, in our opinion, provocative and challenging. His thoughts are instructive as to where Christian counseling and soul-care ministry could, and perhaps should, go in the twenty-first century:

> Serious students of psychotherapy are suggesting that *rich* talking, not necessarily *trained* talking, is helpful.... A case can be made that training in specific theory and technique is less important in becoming a good helper than learning to be conscientious, nondefensive, and caring. Engage with patients, honor confidences, and let yourself actually care when they hurt....
>
> I conclude that we have made a terrible mistake. For most of the twentieth century, we have wrongly defined *soul wounds* as *psychological disorders* and delegated the treatment to trained specialists. The results for the church have been significant....
>
> 1. *We no longer see the church as a place for the substantial healing of personal wounds....* We regard relationships, the real business of the

church, as having little to do with profound soul care and, in so doing we have underestimated the power that God has placed in his family.

2. *The work of discipling has been wrongly defined as less than and different from the work of psychotherapy and counseling.* Maybe it isn't. Maybe discipleship, defined properly as curing the soul, is the reality, and psychotherapy is the imitation.

3. *Professional training is thought to be more important in developing the "skill" of helping than the sanctifying work of the Spirit.* If soul care involves pouring something good out of one person into another, if releasing what is good is more central to healing than requiring what is right or repairing what is wrong, then the helper must have something good to pour.… Only God can supply the medicine needed to heal someone's soul. (pp. 200-201)

More recently, Crabb (2001) developed an understanding of the human personality that draws from New Covenant theology, which he regards as perhaps the most neglected aspect of our theological foundation as counselors. Central to this teaching is the truth that, at conversion, every Christian has been given a new heart, which Crabb sees as an appetite for God and for his glory that supersedes all other desires. Spiritual direction, which Crabb defines broadly enough to encompass everything that is legitimately done in psychotherapy, delves deeply into the wounds of life and discovers that the battle between the flesh and the Spirit lies at the root of all nonorganically caused psychological disorders. In that sense, he regards spiritual issues as foundational to psychological struggles.

Central to Crabb's thinking is that suffering raises the core matter of our confidence and, therefore, our connection with God. Even Job's suffering, though worsened through the relational failure of his friends, fundamentally involved his relationship with and understanding of God. Crabb's strong emphasis on spiritual friends and community healing is seen by some as devaluing the role of pastoral and professional counseling. Crabb responds that he is merely calling those in the Christian counseling movement to build their thinking about internal dynamics on theological categories, after the manner of the Puritans.

Christian Counseling as a Convergent Development

At this point, it might be easy to conclude that Christian counseling is a fairly embryonic and disorganized enterprise. It is true that a creative ferment has always characterized our field and that many models of practice and soul care have been developed and offered (Collins, 1996). We choose to view this ferment as constructive, like an energized and dynamic adolescent pushing his way into adulthood and needing sure direction. In the quotation at the beginning of this chapter, Egan elucidates the essence of counseling as a convergent synthesis of the best themes, principles, approaches, and methods. Describing this process of counseling construction as a *convergence* best reflects the process that has shaped Christian counseling over this past decade.

In 1991, after a comprehensive review of counseling theory, Jones and Butman noted that no clear or preferred theory of Christian psychology or psychotherapy yet existed, and they called for believers to engage in theoretical integrationism, or "responsible eclecticism." Christian psychologist Everett Worthington attempted to direct Christian counseling development in this way by outlining a "blueprint for intra-disciplinary integration" that brings together psychology, theology, and spiritual development in the counseling process. Using a house-building metaphor, Worthington (1994, p. 81) constructed a four-part model for Christian counseling development:

1. *The foundation:* Jesus Christ, "the rock, the Son of God," the Holy One who "integrates faith and practice."
2. *The weight-bearing pillars:* the basic beliefs of "mere Christianity" and their use in answering fundamental questions about the place of Scripture and God's role in counseling, for example.
3. *The frame:* choosing the goals and methods of counseling and determining how the setting, the faith of the counselor, the expectations of the client, and the experience of both factor into these decisions.
4. *The covering:* the specific content that gives counseling its unique and individual character.

We also appreciate the recent work by Gary Moon and Mark McMinn. In revealing the work of his Institute for Clinical Theology, Moon (1997) proposed an orientation for both practice and training that combined personal piety, soul-care ministry, study and contemplation of devotional and spiritual classics, and spiritual formation in both counselor and client. Similarly, McMinn (1996) used a computer-related multitasking metaphor to argue that

> [t]he most effective Christian counselors are [multitasking experts] able to process several ideas simultaneously...[across] three essential categories... psychology, theology, and spirituality.

From a psychological perspective, effective counselors are able to participate fully in a treatment relationship while simultaneously stepping outside the relationship to view the problems of the client and the nature of the counseling relationship from a more objective vantage point. At the same time, as counselors empathize and reflect emotions from within the counseling relationship, they are also evaluating and assessing from outside the counseling relationship—noticing voice tone, nonverbal gestures, facial expressions, and styles of relating. This type of psychological multitasking requires excellent training, cultural sensitivity, and supervised experience to master. But there is more.

Effective Christian counselors also consider theological perspectives at the same time that they engage in the various psychological tasks of counseling. Historical and systematic theology, biblical understanding, and Christian tradition are all valued and considered essential components of counseling. These tasks require a basic working knowledge of the Bible, Christian history, and theological systems. But there is still more.

Multitasking for the Christian counselor also involves an understanding of the spiritual life of the client. How are the client's problems related to spiritual development? When is a problem simply a behavioral habit to eliminate or reshape, and when is a problem a reflection of deep inner yearnings for intimacy with God and others? How can a treatment relationship be crafted to foster humility and insight? When, if ever, should prayer or Scripture memory be used in counseling or prescribed to a client?... Training for spiritual sensitivity may begin in the classroom or by reading spiritual classics, but it must continue in the private lives of counselors. (pp. 269-270)

Bufford (1997), in his paper on consecrated counseling, noted that integration is used in many contexts with many different meanings. He then panned the use of integration as an organizing concept because it implies that our knowledge base is fragmented and needs to be put back together. He argues that integration is deficient terminology as it belies the unity of truth in a biblical Christian worldview (Carter & Narramore, 1979; Collins, 1977). Bufford cogently argues that Christian counseling is hard to define because there are two tracks to the field—spiritual counseling and mental health counseling—and the boundaries overlap. He asserts that Christian counseling is developing into a dynamic field encompassing ten themes or disciplinary issues:

1. pastoral counseling and psychology
2. Christian lay counseling

3. biblical counseling
4. professional psychotherapy and counseling for Christians
5. professional psychotherapy and counseling guided by Christian values
6. Christian marriage and family counseling and education
7. Christian antipsychology
8. missionary psychology
9. psychological measurement of Christian constructs
10. Christian recovery movement

Bufford (1997) goes on to define seven attributes of Christian counseling that, together, comprise the essential elements of consecrated counseling, which we believe holds much promise for future development:

1. pursuing excellence
2. working from a Christian worldview
3. incorporating Christian values
4. assuring the personal faith of the counselor
5. being confident of the personal calling of the counselor
6. recognizing and inviting into counseling the person and work of God
7. becoming skilled with spiritual interventions and resources

COMPETENT CHRISTIAN COUNSELING: TOWARD A PARACENTRIC CONVERGENCE

Moving from the previous half-century of developing thought and practice as well as from two thousand years of pastoral care ministry, we now propose thoughts on a twenty-first-century path for Christian counseling. We describe this as a *Paracentric* focus. In addition to introducing new language and a call for further development, our goal is to challenge all Christian counselors toward a more intentional development of a descriptive, prescriptive, and heuristic perspective that will help guide the practice, teaching, and research in our field for years to come.

Paracentric is a compound word that melds two crucial aspects of Christian counseling ministry. First is our yieldedness to the *Para*klete of God—the Holy Spirit—who is the invisible God present in counseling and who comes alive in wonder-working power by our invitation. *Paraklesis* and *parakaleo* are Greek New Testament words that mean "to come alongside someone to help," "to give aid," "to advocate for someone's best interest." These terms describe Spirit-directed and Christ-centered people committed to assisting others across the wide range of needs, from consolation to encouragement to confrontation.

We link this *Para* prefix with the idea of being centered—being single-mindedly focused on Christ and on our clients, clothed with integrity, and directed toward joy, maturity, and wholeness. A Paracentric focus represents a centered convergence in Christ as our exalted model and on the client as the clinical and ethical focus of our ministry. This focus should also reveal a wonderful divergent-convergent dynamic that captures and more accurately conveys the full arc of the helping process wherein

- the competent Christian counselor, yielded to an active, holy, and merciful God (1 Corinthians 1:18), meets the client at his or her point of need (diverging, becoming all things to all people [1 Corinthians 9:19,22]), and connects with the client to create a working alliance;
- This activity includes comforting the brokenhearted, supporting the weak, encouraging the discouraged, exhorting those who are motivated, entreating and guiding the misdirected, and warning the rebel and sinner. (The full scope of Spirit-led counselor behavior is described in 1 Thessalonians 5:14 and 2 Corinthians 1:3-7.)
- The counselor serves to refocus, facilitate, instruct, and reinforce goal-directed client action toward growing up into maturity (Ephesians 4:12-16) and living in more intimate relationship (John 17:9-13) with the divine object of our faith, Jesus Christ. This involves de-centering ourselves (Lamentations 3:20-24) and converging or centering on the Author and Finisher of our faith (Hebrews 12:2, RSV).

Christian counseling must be a biblical-clinical process that facilitates case-wise client sanctification. It is built on the sure foundations of Scripture, dependent on the inspired leading of the Holy Spirit, and selectively using the best of helping ministry resources and the bio-psycho-social sciences. Such counseling is not sterile or static. As we proceed, our purpose is not to present an elegant but ultimately useless model; rather, we wish to construct a dynamic framework, a living process that recursively grows and matures as it is used by the counselor and is influenced by God and the client (Worthington, 1994).

We have incorporated into this Paracentric focus many aspects of the twentieth-century definitions and developments of Christian counseling, attempting to synthesize the best of all the dedicated pioneers who have gone before us. We believe the title—*Competent Christian Counseling*—is the best short description of what a Paracentric focus is and does. *Webster's New World Dictionary* defines the three words that exemplify our model this way:

Competent: Answering all necessary requirements; suitable; fit; capable; well qualified and sufficient for the purpose.

Christian: A person professing belief in Jesus as the Christ; having the qualities demonstrated and taught by Jesus Christ, such as love, peace, kindness, faith, patience, and so forth.

Counseling: Opinion or advice, given upon request or otherwise, for directing the judgment or conduct of another; mutual exchange of ideas with advice and direction flowing from such exchange.

A Paracentric emphasis, then, is a convergence of the best knowledge and practice from the Scriptures and the clinical sciences as well as ancient and modern wisdom. It concentrates the relational encounter between at least three persons: God, the therapist as God's healing agent, and the client. Its goal is to skillfully assist the client by delivering timely knowledge, wisdom, guidance, and support. These resources are aimed at encouraging the client to grow in grace and maturity in Jesus Christ, to find joy in the midst of trouble, and to escape the snares of sin, shame, and despair. A Paracentric focus facilitates high levels of maturity, character, and relationship in clients. This focus is also characterized by

- the goal of delivering high levels of effective help that builds from the Scriptures and looks judiciously to other useful resources, in the power of the Holy Spirit, to facilitate maturity in Christ by means of well-qualified, dedicated, and caring Christians;
- its ministry as counseling, psychotherapy, consulting, discipling, helping, facilitating spiritual formation, mentoring, coaching, and peacemaking, done without prejudice or unjust discrimination, to all those who seek such help, both within and outside the church;
- the challenge to all Christian counselors, including pastors, chaplains, lay helpers, counselors, and clinical professionals, to attain a level of competence, even excellence, in responding to the call to be burden-bearers—counselors and helpers who can ably assist those who suffer and facilitate Christian growth.

TOWARD A CHRIST-CENTERED IDENTITY

This new helping paradigm needs an identity. We have already introduced the historic debate between nouthetic counselors and integrationists. Essentially, this divide has to do with epistemology—the nature of truth and our ability to know it. Nouthetic counselors argue, for example, that truth can only be known in the Christ revealed in the Scriptures and that any counseling models must begin and end within the textual truths of the Bible. Any extrabiblical inclusion of data in model presuppositions and process is inherently contaminated by the *noetic* effects of sin and must be avoided. Psychology may illustrate, but can never ultimately define or guide, the way we help others.

Integrationists, on the other hand, argue that "all truth is God's truth." God reveals his truth universally (general revelation in the world that is best known by scientific investigation) as well as by special revelation in Christ. Hence, integrationists borrow from extrabiblical resources believed to be consistent with scriptural truth and useful to the counseling encounter.

Although such debate is necessary, if we continue this dispute as it ensued in the twentieth century, we will reinforce a false, bipolar caricature of a field that is far more promising, complex, dynamic, rich, and diverse. While such disputes are indicative of a healthy and growing movement, future dialogue and interaction must become secondary to our common standing in Christ and our common mission in building up the body of Christ.

With the Paracentric emphasis, we want to encourage a more healthy dialogue that we hope will proceed with humility and compassion, respecting Christ's call that we be unified. Counselors, teachers, and writers from both perspectives are well represented in this book, and we are delighted that they have joined us in the higher mission of exalting Christ.

We further believe that the shrill criticism and rancorous debate among some Christian counselors and a few anticounseling critics is outdated, outmoded, and ill-suited to our mission: uplifting Christ as our model for counseling and for life itself. Hence, we put forth this new construction as a challenge to all. Hopefully, a new era in Christian counseling has begun.

The Paracentric Revelation

In introducing our Paracentric perspective, we want to emphasize that the process of developing any counseling direction is one of *unfolding revelation*. We propose to use these terms consciously and consistently, anchoring them deliberately in our language and interaction in order to

- *communicate* our dedication to Christ and Scripture, our yieldedness to the Holy Spirit and a more intimate relationship to the church and its helping ministry, and our commitment to providing a clearer description of Christian counseling as an emerging mental health discipline and ministry;
- *facilitate* a more refined and directed agenda for Christian counseling that moves us into the twenty-first century with a call to glorify Christ, to put our clients and parishioners before our reputations and careers, to respect the best findings of the human and social sciences, and to serve as a more united body of God's caring people;
- *operate* within the community of believers and our collegial counselors to continually learn, refine, simplify, amplify, and apply this perspective to the myriad issues we face as Christian counselors. Christian counseling must always be a work in progress, one that we hope will grow and

mature as you learn it, use it, and relate back to us what your experience with it can teach us.

CONTROL BELIEFS AND PRESUPPOSITIONS

All counselors operate from presuppositions that serve as *a priori* control beliefs. We have developed ten root values and baseline ministerial ethics that direct Christian counseling:

1. *Christ, our Lord of life and our model for counseling, is the embodiment of love and truth.* Proclaiming the lordship of Christ is a constant, Spirit-directed challenge to yield ourselves to God, to renounce our natural bent to the lordship of self or to the idolatry of our professional discipline. Our unity as Christian counselors is possible if Christ is lifted up above all things—if our doctrinal beliefs, our clinical disciplines and methods, and our favorite theories are consciously made secondary and are yielded to the King (John 12:32; 17:20-23). The Wonderful Counselor is the fount of life and our model for everything, the One we are called to imitate in all our helping endeavors (Colossians 1:19-22; Philippians 2:1-11). Everything about Christ—his behavior, questions, attitudes, parables, wisdom, emotions, prayer life, humility, teachings, death, and resurrection—is fit for study and for application as Christian counselors. This is true for our own development as helpers and as the way to direct clients in practice.

2. *The Bible is the sourcebook of revelation and relationship—the guidebook for treatment and renewal.* Christian counseling asserts a dedication to Christ, the God incarnate who was foretold in the Old Testament and revealed in the New Testament. The Bible is not only our source book, the ground of truth from which our helping proceeds, but it is also the guidebook from which we derive the principles for understanding, assessing, and treating others. Either by precept and direct instruction or by inference from the rich mine of narratives, poetry, proverbs, and parables, the Scriptures are also our primary source for any counseling methods, principles, and interventions that we can faithfully draw from the text (2 Timothy 3:16; 2 Peter 1:3). Any perspectives and resources needed for and used in counseling—whether they come from psychology, other sciences, classical and church history, good literature, or ancient wisdom—should be (theo)logical extensions of the Scriptures and evaluated in light of their truth-value according to the Bible.

3. *The church is the center of counseling and care activity.* Christian counseling must be Christ-centered and church-related since Christ lives in and dwells in his church (Colossians 1:18). Christian counseling as conceived in this book is a discipling, helping ministry of the church. It is Spirit-directed soul care that, while done both inside and outside the local body of Christ, must become more inti-

mately related to the church. Pastors are at the heart of the counseling and referral ministry, providing direct care to many and referring some to professional counselors or to lay helpers within the church. The combined helping network of pastor, professional clinician, and lay helper is like a three-legged stool that works most effectively when all three legs are functioning in relationship to each other.

4. *Science is synthesized within a larger construct of supernatural theism.* Christian counseling should be both empirical and extraempirical, synthesizing both scientific and supernatural interventions. It judiciously respects the findings of the clinical sciences and calls upon all Christian counselors to submit all our success claims to tests of empirical validity, and yet it subordinates and embeds all bio-psycho-social data within the revealed truth about God in the Bible. God's truth and his ways in helping ministry are never contradictory. We believe that Christian counseling can and must be empirically demonstrated and that tested verification will increase the power of our message to the world around us, especially to those who rely on and use the language of science. But let us be clear: We distinguish our Christian worldview, one that respects the correcting methodology of science, from the worldview of empiricism, which asserts that only those things that can be empirically proven truly exist. We reject both the fallacy that the material world is the only world that exists and that it allows no supernaturalism.

5. *Maturity in Christ is our ultimate goal; spiritual formation is our primary means.* The history of the church—especially from liturgical and contemplative traditions—is rich in the practices of soul care and spiritual formation. These rich practices, and the fruit they bear, are being revived in the Catholic renewal movement and are being discovered anew by evangelicals and by Christian counselors (Foster, 1998; Moon, 1997; Tan & Gregg, 1997). While the goals of many clients are shaped around better health, happiness, restored relationships, and greater well-being—goals that we can assist them in achieving—our *ultimate* goal is intimacy with our heavenly Father and maturity in Christ (Ephesians 4:20-24; Philippians 2:1-11). Hence, spiritual-formation activities are a primary means of availing ourselves of that precious grace God pours out to those who earnestly seek him. Explicit incorporation of spiritual-formation activities into counseling is central to the operation of competent Christian counseling.

6. *Christian counseling spans the bio-psycho-social-spiritual spectrum.* A paradigm shift is taking place in psychotherapy and in Christian counseling. The twentieth-century dedication to a mechanical objectivity and a preferred school of counseling (making clients fit the model) is giving way to a transtheoretical, eclectic practice that fits the treatment to the client. This is a systematic eclecticism that respects the common factors of change and uses assessments and methods that best help the

client across the entire biological, psychological, social-environmental, and spiritual-theological spectrum. This book reflects our bias toward a Spirit-directed and eclectic practice. The Holy Spirit, the Paraklete of God, is the third person present at all times in counseling. We consciously invite the Holy Spirit to join a process of spiritual formation that not only heals wounds, resolves problems, and reconciles broken relationships, but goes beyond this to facilitate intimacy with God, spiritual maturity, the development of the fruit of the Spirit, and dedicated service in church and community (1 Corinthians 1:18; 2:14; Galatians 5:19–6:5).

7. *Orthopraxy is as important as orthodoxy.* As committed evangelicals, we regard biblical orthodoxy and the creedal history of the church to be of great importance. However, right belief without living it out is a seductive fallacy and is all too prevalent in the modern church. As James put it, faith without works is dead (1:19-27; 2:14-26). We, therefore, seek to find in Christ the high call to ortho*praxy,* the active and holy living that reflects our belief in the way of Christ and that helps our clients and parishioners find the way that God has for them. In the language of Scripture, we can help people do all things through Christ (Philippians 4:13). In the language of counseling, insight is good, but it is not enough; there must be persistent action to bring about lasting change (Egan, 1998). Our clinical experience has taught us that, for many clients, action sometimes precedes insight and that working out one's weaker faith is essential to developing faith that is stronger and more mature.

8. *Counseling is a two-phased, sequential process: Brief therapy is mandatory for everyone, and long-term therapy is discretionary, chosen by some.* Solution-based brief therapy is showing promising results and is being well received in the Christian counseling community (Dillon, 1992; Kollar, 1997; Oliver, Hasz, & Richburg, 1997). Helping clients envision a hope-filled, healthy lifestyle, determine how to get there, and take action to achieve it is an essential skill for all Christian counselors. Brief therapy is not, however, a panacea for all problems (Kopta, Howard, Lowry, & Beutler, 1994). But in this age of therapeutic accountability, brief therapy has earned the right to be considered the therapy of choice, even the mandatory therapy for all clients at the beginning of counseling. However, there remains a necessary role for long-term therapy, which may be chosen by clients at the conclusion of brief interventions.

9. *Clients are valued over comfort, commodity, and compensation.* In the same way that Jesus asserted that the Sabbath was made for people and not people for the Sabbath (Mark 2:27), client concerns must supersede our commitments to counseling models, our own comfort zones, and our financial livelihoods. The people we serve must be first with us because they are first with God. This ethic supports the challenge of fitting our counseling models to people, rather than fitting people to counseling models, as was characteristic of twentieth-century therapy. It

also means that we give some service to those who are unable to pay (whether a portion or the full fee) because God has commanded us to serve, and he promises another kind of reward.

10. *Christian unity, counseling excellence, and ethical integrity take precedence over every personal theory, discipline, and preference.* Christian counseling honors the personhood, the personal identity, and the commitments of all Christian counselors. The worldwide community of Christian counselors is an extremely diverse, devoted, and dynamic group of people. Furthermore, we assert that, because of Christ, Christian counselors can avoid the fractious, divisive squabbles that tear at the unity of so many other helping disciplines. To do this, we must give heed to the call to remain united in Christ (Ephesians 4). This unity requires that our first allegiance always be to Christ, and it challenges us to pursue excellence in all our work and to maintain integrity in all our relationships, as befits anyone who would follow Jesus.

LIFTING UP CHRIST AND ANCHORING OUR ROOTS

Christian counseling must be dedicated to life in the body of Christ. If Christ draws all people to himself when he is lifted up (John 3:14-15; 12:32), let us deliberately and passionately lift up Christ in Christian counseling. Let us describe ourselves as Christian counselors and heartily identify with him and his way, his truth, and his life. Let us live in Christ and thirst after his Spirit so that within the body of Christ we may be reconciled to one another in the midst of our differences, and so that outside the body the world can know who we are without puzzlement, confusion, or revulsion. When Christ is honestly alive in something, he is attractive and powerful.

We believe the nature and process of Christian counseling is better and more accurately understood as *revelational.* That is, we are to be about the job of discerning, understanding, refining, and accurately communicating what God is revealing to us about counseling and the care of souls. At this stage of Christian counseling development, we believe the question we should ask is not "How are psychology and theology integrated?" but rather "How does God's special revelation in Christ relate to and direct his general revelation in nature?"

Put another way, we would ask this three-part question: (1) How does Christ, who is alive in every believing helper by the power of the Holy Spirit, (2) animate and direct the contemporary sciences (not only psychology and theology, but biology, sociology, and anthropology, to name a critical few), the ancient wisdoms of history, and the great works of art and literature, (3) to assist us in this time, place, and culture to build up God's people and his church to spiritual maturity, wholeness, health, and vital living?

We believe that this question, framed in this way, also sets us squarely in the

BOX 2.1—THE MANY EXPRESSIONS OF THE NEW TESTAMENT LANGUAGE OF CARE*

The Paracentric practice of compassionate helping is rooted in the many expressions of counseling and helping in the New Testament. Beginning with the most widely used term that grounds our focus—*parakaleo* and its various derivatives—the language of caring in the Bible is rich in meaning, broad in application, and full of the mercy and power of God.

1. *Parakaleo* literally means "to call to one's side" (or to call to one's aid). This word and its various forms convey a broader meaning of care and have much wider application than *noutheteo*. *Parakaleo* can mean anything across the spectrum of needful care from "comforting" and "consoling" to "encouraging" to "beseeching" and "exhorting." It occurs 109 times in the New Testament—10 times more frequently than *noutheteo*—and it can be translated as "summon," "beseech," "invite," "ask," "implore," "exhort," "console," "comfort," "encourage" (Philippians 2:1, 4:2; 1 Thessalonians 3:2, 4:10; Romans 12:8; 2 Corinthians 7:6, 12:18; 1 Timothy 1:3; Hebrews 13:19,22).

2. *Paramutheomai* means to "comfort," "soothe," "console," or "encourage" (1 Corinthians 14:3; Philippians 2:1; 1 Thessalonians 2:11-12), especially in connection with someone experiencing deep grief due to a death or tragic event. It is used, for example, in reference to those consoling Mary at the death of her brother, Lazarus (John 11:19-31).

3. *Noutheteo* comes from the root meaning "mind" (*nous*), that is, the seat of reflective consciousness, involving the faculties of perception, understanding, feeling, judging, and determining. Influence is placed upon overcoming the (resisting) mind by means of "admonition, advice, warning, reminding, teaching, and spurring on" in order to correct a person's behavior and redirect his ways. The word is found eleven times in the New Testament, ten times in the Pauline epistles (1 Thessalonians 5:12-13; Colossians 1:28, 3:16), and once in Acts 20:31 where Luke quotes Paul.

4. *Makrothumeo* literally means "long-tempered" and carries the idea of forbearing, enduring, suffering, and being patient. The concept of patience may be negative in the sense of resignation or desperate endurance, or it can be positive in the sense of persistence and long-suffering, as "an unswerving willingness to await events rather than trying to force them" (James 5:7; Hebrews 6:15).

5. *Antechomai* refers to holding or supporting someone or something fragile.

---

* We are pleased to acknowledge the assistance of Professor Ian Jones from Southwestern Baptist Theological Seminary in developing this material.

It conveys the idea of taking an interest in and paying careful attention to someone, and, hence, helping them (Matthew 6:24; Luke 16:13; Titus 1:9).

(*Note:* We could promote 1 Thessalonians 5:14 as the penultimate Christian counseling verse of the New Testament as it incorporates all five of these primary Greek words: "And we urge *[parakaleo]* you, brothers, warn *[noutheteo]* those who are idle, encourage *[paramutheomai]* the timid, help *[antechomai]* the weak, be patient *[makrothumeo]* with everyone.")

6. *Therapeuo,* which is the root word for the terms "therapy" and "therapeutic," means to "care for," "wait upon," "treat," "heal," and "restore." It is used for physical or medical healing as well as miraculous cures (Matthew 4:23-25; 8:7,16; 9:35; 10:8; Mark 1:34; 3:2,10; Luke 5:15; 6:7,19; 9:1,6). We are convinced that competent Christian counseling (an experience in *therapeuo*) is conducted by dedicated caregivers (*therapons,* who attend to the needy) who bring the life of Christ into the healing session.

7. *Iaomai* also refers to healing or curing; however, while it can imply moral or spiritual healing, it is usually used in a medical sense (Matthew 8:8; 13:15; Mark 5:29; Luke 5:17; 6:19; 17:15; John 4:47; Acts 9:34; 10:38).

8. *Katharizo* means "to cleanse" or "purify," in both a medical and a spiritual sense. In a medical context, the term usually refers to the healing of a leper (Matthew 8:2; 10:8; Mark 1:40-41; Luke 5:12). Moral and spiritual cleansing comes through the word and work of Christ (Ephesians 5:26).

9. *Hugiaino* means to be in good physical health or to possess a sound doctrine or teaching (Luke 5:31; 1 Timothy 1:10; 2 Timothy 4:3; Titus 1:9; 2:1).

10. *Sozo* is used seventy-three times in a theological sense in reference to "saving," "keeping from harm," "preserving," or "rescuing" people from sin, sickness, judgment, and death (Matthew 1:21; 14:30; 24:13; Mark 16:16; Luke 8:12; John 3:17; Romans 11:26; 1 Timothy 1:15; James 2:14). The word also refers to being made whole or freed from disease in a medical sense (Matthew 9:21-22; Mark 5:23,28; Luke 8:48; 17:19; Acts 4:9).

11. *Boule* comes from the root meaning "will." It can mean "counsel," "advice," "resolution," or "decision." It is often translated as "counsel" in Scripture. The word occurs more than a hundred times in the Septuagint, where it is used seventy-four times to translate the Hebrew word *etzah* (1 Corinthians 4:5). The verb *bouleuo* conveys the idea of taking counsel together or resolving an issue (Acts 5:35; 27:39; Luke 14:31; John 11:53; 12:10). Another form of the word is *sumbouleuo,* which is often used in the Septuagint to translate *yaatz.* It refers to the "giving of advice by one person to another" and is regularly employed in reference to the evil plots by the Jews against Jesus and the early church (Matthew 26:4; John 18:14; Acts 9:23).

realm of obligation to Christ to fulfill the Great Commission—to go out into all the earth and make disciples (Matthew 28:18-20). As stated in the previous chapter, we promote the view that one important way to see and understand Christian counseling—and its caring and case-wise Christian helpers—is as an integral part of the discipleship call of the church.

As we face a new paradigm for practice-ministry, we must grasp as our major concern the two interrelated revelations of the living God: Christ and his created order. The truth to be discovered in Christ facilitates unity in our field. This necessitates a serious and ongoing work of biblical exegesis, historical scholarship, and research into the bio-psycho-social sciences and the careful practice of the best and most biblically compatible findings.

Such work cannot be limited to only a few; the best minds and the most faithful hearts in this field must join together. So many of you, in numerous roles, forms, and varieties, are doing exactly that. When we must stretch and grow, let's pledge to not be combative and, instead, stand shoulder to shoulder in our common cause.

While we will always be challenged and will always engage in robust debate, let us concentrate our resources on the real enemy—the "[spiritual] rulers of the darkness of this age" (Ephesians 6:12, NKJV). Let us work toward spiritual renewal, Christian unity, God-honoring scholarship, and great fruitfulness in Christian counseling.

Covenantal Roots

Inherent to this Paracentric perspective is the truth of covenant relationship—the biblical doctrine that signifies the relationship between God and humanity. We believe that all of life is ultimately referenced back to God and that we—the church and humanity, individually and corporately, saved or unsaved—are in some form of relationship with God. From Adam through Abraham, Moses, and David to Christ himself in his death and resurrection, we all live in some form of covenant relationship with God.

A central purpose of Christian counseling, then, is the revelation, the encouragement, and the growth of that covenant relationship. Stated another way, Christian counseling facilitates that covenant by helping men and women become reconciled and related more intimately to God. *Covenantal discipleship* could be another name for the ministry of Christian counseling that is outlined in this book.

Farnsworth (1985), who has given us the language and challenge of covenantal counseling, recognizes that God is a covenant-maker and that humans are called to be covenant-keepers. Farnsworth asserts that this all-encompassing view of life has major implications for both individuals and covenant communities. Counseling in a covenantal perspective becomes a practice of *transformational soul care,* a process by which helpers facilitate the transformation of people and covenant communities by the power of the Holy Spirit so that they will be conformed to Christ's image (Romans 8:29).

Farnsworth asserts that Christian counseling without the body of Christ is deficient. He believes that a priority of the church should be the development of small-group ministries through which love, support, and encouragement can flow in a way that it cannot in any other setting. This covenantal connectedness is also the theme of one of Crabb's (1997) latest books. Connectedness in the body of Christ is the key to transformed living; connectedness invites and releases the Spirit of Christ to do his life-changing work.

Biblical counselors Hindson and Eyrich (1997) challenge us on another aspect of covenantal relationships: to build our counseling ministries on the eternal truths of God as revealed in the Scriptures. Asserting that our theological worldview shapes the values and practice of our counseling ministries, Hindson and Eyrich call us to develop a mature theology based on seven pillars of the faith, added to the previously mentioned pillar advocating the need for connectedness in the body of Christ:

1. the divine inspiration of the Bible, which allows us to confidently tell the truth—that we cling to by faith—to those who need to hear it
2. the existence of an infinite, personal God, who calls us to an allegiance that demands we forsake the "gods" we create for ourselves
3. the uniqueness of Jesus Christ, the only God-man of all history, the promised Messiah and Savior of humankind
4. salvation by grace alone, which enables us to see and communicate God's gracious life continuously offered to us, a life that is impossible to realize by our own efforts
5. the substitutionary atonement of Christ—we are sinners who deserve death, but Christ chose to die in our place so that we might live in him
6. personal spiritual regeneration, being born again in newness of life by the Holy Spirit
7. personal spiritual sanctification, the lifelong process of progressive maturity that is the fruit of God's forming in us the very life of Christ

CLINICAL AND EMPIRICAL ROOTS

The concept of a Paracentric focus is not new (Ecclesiastes 1:9-11); only the name is new. It is built on the foundation established by those who have gone before us. In keeping with our dedication to the centrality of Christ and to excellence and unity in practice and in order to honestly reveal our biases as Christian practitioners and teachers, we judiciously draw the best data from the following systems:

- *cognitive-behavioral therapy*—especially in its Christian form, where the "renewing of the mind" involves renouncing the "lies we believe" and embracing and living out biblical truth (Backus, 1985; Thurman, 1989);
- *contemporary and classical approaches* to biblical counseling and pastoral care—especially the application of biblical truth with the goals of spiritual maturity and ministry to others in the context of the church as a caring and dynamic community of believers;
- *historical, contemplative, and contemporary approaches* to comprehensive soul-care ministry, spiritual formation, and Christian discipleship and mentoring;
- *the applied integration of psychology and Christian theology,* focusing on systematic and technical eclecticism and applied intradisciplinary integration;
- *narrative therapy*—especially the use of stories and metaphors about biblical characters and truths as well as life accounts of the saints throughout the history of the church;
- *object-relations work and neoanalytic therapy*—especially defense mechanisms and transference/countertransference dynamics;
- *Frankl's logotherapy*—especially his use of paradox and the universal search for meaning, purpose, and value;
- *interpersonal and social systems therapy*—especially marriage and family-systems dynamics and the best contributions of developmental and social psychology;
- *ecological social work and task-centered practice* and *the person-in-environment* approach to intervention.

COMPETENT CHRISTIAN COUNSELING: GOALS, PROCESS, AND DYNAMICS

Clement of Alexandria said, "Now the modes of all help…are three.… The spiritual guide, accordingly, having received from God the power to be of service, benefits some by (1) disciplining them and bestowing attention…, (2) exhorting them…, [and] (3) training and teaching them."

Clement's ancient wisdom recognized the core principles of helping and distilled them into a threefold model for learning. We adopt his view that different clients require different approaches to be reached effectively. We also adopt his use of a three-factored model, a heuristic device that should be useful for counselor practice and training. In this paradigm, Christian counseling is a 3 x 3 x 3 endeavor. Here, we apply a multifaceted lens to outline various three-factor characteristics that shape the goals, process, and dynamics of helping.

CHRISTIAN COUNSELING AND THE CHURCH: A THREEFOLD PURPOSE

Christian counseling is increasingly being drawn into more and more intimate relationship with the worldwide Christian church. In fact, apart from Christ and his church, Christian counseling loses both its validity and its power. This does not mean that all Christian counseling is done within the four walls of the church, but that every aspect of it is somehow tied to the church. In recent years, the essential task of the church has been explicated according to a threefold purpose:

Up—to know and worship God

In—to love and serve one another

Out—to make disciples of all nations

THREE OBJECTIVES OF THE CHURCH AS A HEALING COMMUNITY

Remediation: The church as a spiritual hospital. Possibly the most difficult task facing the church is to commit itself to being a spiritual hospital and to organize to carry out this role. Many people coming into the contemporary church are serious casualties of a hostile world. They have severe and multiple wounds that demand tremendous time and energy to repair and heal. The church is called to save, *not shoot* its own wounded. The cost of this kind of service is high and demands a high level of sacrifice.

Prevention: The church as a spiritual school. Egan (1998) tells a wonderful story about the limits and frustrations of remedial helping. Two helpers were pulling drowning people out of a river, cleaning them up, and sending them on their way, but the number of people in danger of drowning never abated. Nearing exhaustion, the two helpers finally decided to move upstream to see if they could keep people from falling in. Moving upstream—stopping problems before they become overwhelming—is what prevention is all about. Education and discipleship should be seen as forms of primary prevention in the church.

Transformation: The church as a kingdom community. The King lives in and through his people. The kingdom is present and future, here now and heaven tomorrow. Nothing is impossible for the King and his kingdom community. Living in and serving through a kingdom community elevates helping to its highest power and bears powerful fruit.

THREE PHASES OF THE COUNSELING PROCESS

Like many life processes, counseling has a beginning, a middle, and an end. Egan (1998) has been a worldwide leader in educating and training helpers according to this three-phased process, which he describes as a natural problem-management process. We appreciate his process because it is universal and simple, and we have adapted it by integrating a decidedly Christian focus.

Phase One: Building trust to help explore and define the problem(s). The primary goal of phase one is to help clients tell their story—as clearly and accurately as possible—by building and using a trust relationship. Of crucial importance here is the role of the helping relationship in creating a climate of spiritual and social influence. Problem issues as well as resources for resolution are identified. Transition from phase one to phase two is accomplished when there is a mutually developed focus on which key client concerns call for initial action.

Phase Two: Developing a vision for transformed living. This phase—what Egan calls "developing a preferred scenario"—helps clients define and own what they want. We explore with clients the possibilities of "putting on" new life in Christ, and we encourage commitment to "put off" the old nature. However, we take care not to impose our personal values on the client since we must respect client receptivity and consent as well as avoid fostering client dependencies that hinder maturity. Goals are specified, and resources are employed to achieve them.

Phase Three: Taking action for change and living abundantly. In this final phase, goals are affirmed and various strategies for achieving goals are brainstormed and assessed. The right strategies are linked into a working plan, and clients are encouraged to go "do it." As people actually work their new plan, counselor and client evaluate and revise the plan of action to conform to new realities.

Important to Egan is the challenge not to become slavish in applying this model. He cautions helpers to beware of the following pitfalls in the use of any model: rigidity, overcontrol, virtuosity, and ineptness. In Christian counseling, we have a universal moral standard of truth that is embodied in the person of Christ and is revealed in the Scriptures. There are no rigid formulas, however, for applying God's truth, no one-right-answer equations for counseling. Staying flexible, applying principles of Christian living, and living by God's grace are crucial to the effectiveness of the competent Christian counselor.

Three Phases of Client Change

Howard, Leuger, Maling, and Martinovich (1993) have shown empirically that the recovery or change process in psychotherapy is a three-phased sequence, lending empirical support to our three-phase process:

1. A sense of subjective well-being is embraced, which includes hope and empowers action.
2. Symptom relief is effected, which reinforces hope and fuels further motivation for change.

3. Overall life functioning improves and is generalized to reinforce counseling gains for the long term.

THREE LEVELS OF GOALS

Immediate goals. Clients often come into counseling in crisis, demoralized and in pain, and often with a distorted, tunnel-vision view of the problem and its solution. Goals at this level are client-centered and short term: symptom reduction, pain control, crisis alleviation, and stabilization. Focusing the crisis, reinforcing strengths, and marshaling resources for change are usually the first, immediate goals defined by client and counselor alike.

Intermediate goals. As crisis issues abate in the present and stability develops once again, many clients quit counseling. For those who continue, attention begins to widen and includes consideration of the behavioral and belief patterns and the environmental conditions that trigger periodic crisis. Changing rooted patterns of dysfunctional beliefs, habitual behaviors, and recurring interpersonal styles is the work of long-term therapy.

Ultimate goals. For Christian counselors, the ultimate goal of helping is to bring clients to a saving knowledge of Jesus Christ, to assist clients to grow in maturity and in intimacy with Christ as an end in itself as well as a resource for future living, and to help clients learn to become dedicated servants to family, church, and community. The art of mature Christian counseling is learning how to assess, advocate, and assist the achievement of these objectives at each stage of counseling.

THREE PERSONS IN COUNSELING

Counseling is an intensely relational activity that involves a counselor and client and, if marriage, family, or group therapy is being done, many other people as well. Christian counseling, on the other hand, involves three persons at the very least: *the client, the counselor,* and *God,* who wants to be invited to participate in every session. The true power to change comes from the Holy Spirit's active involvement in the process as he encourages, consoles, challenges, convicts, and transforms the client into the likeness of Christ.

THREE ROLES IN THE COMMUNITY OF CARE

The organization of Christian counseling involves:
- pastors and ministry leaders
- professional counselors
- lay helpers

The core structure of competent Christian counseling revolves around pastors and is centered in the church. A pastor is often the first person parishioners turn to for help, and he or she must decide whether to provide help directly or refer the person to lay helpers or professional counselors. The pastor is like a generalist or family physician in the managed-care paradigm. He or she is the first contact who delivers remedial care or refers the patient on to a specialist, if needed. Professional counselors and lay helpers are adjunct resources that parishioners turn to on their own or on referral from their pastor or someone else.

THE THINKING-FEELING-ACTING PERSPECTIVE

The thinking-feeling-acting (TFA) perspective is a heuristic device that provides guidance to counselor and client in the face of complex and confusing client data. Though the human personality and social organization are more complex than the thinking-feeling-acting dimensions, the TFA paradigm is sufficient to organize and direct much counseling work.

1. Most people seek counseling help because they *feel bad,* and they can't shake it.
    a. The power of emotions to motivate and shape attitudes and behavior is profound. (Felt disturbance motivates change and action.)
    b. Our feelings reveal important issues about our relationship with God and with his people.
    c. Is feeling good the proper goal? The answer is yes and no. As an immediate goal, it can be proper since the alleviation of pain is often an essential motivator toward right action. As an ultimate goal, it is not sufficient since one is called to maturity whether suffering is alleviated or not.
2. Do good to feel good (right action brings peace in the long run).
    a. Your behavior reflects your beliefs and influences your emotions.
    b. "Be doers of the word, and not hearers only" (James 1:22, NKJV).
    c. Beware of behavioral religion (legalism, the leaven of the Pharisees).
3. Transformed thinking: Telling yourself the truth is the first step toward believing it and being transformed by it (Backus, 1985, 2000; Thurman, 1989, 1995; Vernick, 1999).
    a. As you think, so you are—our inner world shapes the outer presentation.
    b. Lies and unbelief are invariably at the root of wrong actions and bad feelings.
    c. Owning and renouncing our lies are central goals to spiritual maturity, to confessing the truth through faith in Christ, who is the way, the truth, and the life (John 14:6).

BECOMING A CHRISTIAN COUNSELOR

If you are feeling overwhelmed right now, that's normal. We've all felt this way, but rest assured that you're on the right track. The information *is* overwhelming; the challenge is daunting. However, when you come to believe that God is able—that he will shape and guide you and will walk with you through your growth and development as a Christian counselor—you will learn to relax. And you may as well relax, for learning is a lifelong journey, and the best helpers never stop growing.

The two of us have been learning, practicing, supervising, and teaching Christian counseling and related work for a combined total of forty-five years. We are still learning, and we sense that our best education is yet to come! Becoming a Christian counselor, a pastor or teacher, a helper of any kind, is an ongoing process. The fact that you are reading this book is evidence that you have already begun this fascinating journey. You will develop a style and become proficient in helping in a way that is uniquely your own, shaped and honed by your experience with God, your clients, and your colleagues (Ohlschlager & Clinton, 1997).

As you improve and develop a reputation for excellence and integrity in counseling, you will also discover a common bond with other helpers that crosses geography and disciplines, language and culture, and even time and history. You will begin to discern and learn, and you will be humbled and delighted at the way God uses thousands of people and centuries of history and wisdom to help shape you into the very best counselor you can be.

In the midst of the many perspectives on Christian counseling, we want to remind you of an old axiom that one hears in graduate training: *The most important counseling tool is you.* Understanding and rightly applying the "use of self" is a crucial counselor variable. The excellence of the counselor's life and the quality and intensity of the counselor-client relationship empower change in counseling.

Kottler and Brown (2000) envision the development of a personal style of counseling as a developmental life process moving through five stages:

1. *Entry.* The first step is the decision to pursue a counseling career or ministry and entering into formal and not-so-formal training to achieve it. This includes exposure to a wide range of theories and approaches, with the attendant exploration and confusion about them.
2. *Mentorhood.* Later in the training process, during practicums and intern training, you attach yourself to a particular school or to a supervising mentor with whom you identify and who you want to imitate. You study and learn in depth from your mentors, and you may continue to identify primarily with them for the rest of your career.

3. *Eclecticism.* Practice experience "helps to shatter the illusion that only one theory works" (p. 171). You become more flexible and experiment with new ideas and techniques as necessitated by client need and case problems.

4. *Experimentation.* Immersed in practice and the clinical-ethical dilemmas that are inherent in counseling work, you are constantly testing your preferred theoretical style, using and refining what works and incorporating new material to fill the gaps and deficiencies in your approach.

5. *Pragmatism.* "Not all counselors reach the stage of pragmatic flexibility; nor do they want to" (p. 171). Others develop a method of testing and incorporating new ideas and processes to increase positive client outcome. Three guiding questions shape the ethical pragmatist: (1) What is going on here? (2) What do we want to accomplish? and (3) How will this intervention get us there?

Making sense of the information in this book, shaping it into a useful treatment approach, and applying it effectively and consistently in the lives of hurting people is an intensely personal exercise. In your favor, clients are usually unwilling to explore the nuances and ramifications of any theoretical position beyond asking, "Will this work for me and mine?" On the other hand, they are almost always interested in you as a counselor. What you do, say, and believe surely affects the counseling outcome. So then, we would like to add a sixth level of development that characterizes the competent Christian counselor.

6. *Maturity.* As we stated earlier, maturity is the goal for both the client and the counselor. The mature counselor is shaped by the Holy Spirit and life experience to become more like Christ himself. As Croucher (1991) so artfully put it, "Spiritual formation is the dynamic process whereby the Word of God is applied by the Spirit of God to the heart and mind of the child of God so that she or he becomes more like the Son of God" (pp. 1-2).

CHAPTER 3

THE NEW CHRISTIAN COUNSELORS

Who We Are and What We Do to Help Others

GEORGE OHLSCHLAGER AND TIM CLINTON

The Christian counselors best prepared to help people are not only those who are highly trained in counseling theory and technique and in theology but also personally trained to reflect Christian character inside and outside the counseling office. This character cannot be credentialed with graduate degrees or learned in the classroom; it comes from years of faithful training in the spiritual disciplines—prayer, studying Scripture, solitude, fasting, corporate worship.

—MARK MCMINN,

Psychology, Theology, and Spirituality in Christian Counseling

Regardless of the discipline or setting Christian counselors work from, some basic roles and behaviors are common to nearly all counselors, and some are unique to Christian counselors (Collins, 1988; Egan, 1998; Kottler & Brown, 2000). We consider the following ten tasks to be the baseline role behaviors that competent Christian counselors should be able to perform.

1. *Intake and assessment* involves inviting clients into counseling, helping them relax and tell their stories, and using well-honed skills of observation, information gathering, and interpreting to accurately assess client problems and goals and determine what it will take to help clients achieve them.

2. *Case formulation and treatment planning* involves making judgments about why people behave as they do, whether these judgments are simple and

commonsensical, complex and psychological, derogatory or affirming. Moreover, most helpers have explanatory theories about the causes and influences of human behavior that guide their thinking about counseling. Every Christian helper needs a biblical-pragmatic understanding of people's problems in order to help define and direct God-honoring solutions.

3. *Individual counseling* consists of working in a unique, one-on-one-with-one framework that acknowledges and invites God's presence to help clients change in a direction that fulfills their goals as well as the higher interests of God. The dynamics of individual counseling are fairly similar whether one is a clinician, a pastor, or a lay helper. There is greater difference between the goals and dynamics of brief counseling versus long-term psychotherapy than there is in the role differences of individual counseling per se. We will outline these differences in detail later in this book.

4. *Marriage and family interventions* focus on understanding and intervening at critical junctures of marriage and family life in order to disrupt harmful relational patterns and replace them with new and more useful, caring, and life-promoting behaviors. Knowledge of the principles of family and social systems and skill with these processes are essential.

5. *Group counseling and discipling* involves being able to assemble clients into a working group with common goals and then to facilitate, guide, educate, and challenge them to achieve individual and group goals. This includes teaching them to do the same kinds of things for others.

6. *Spiritual direction and incorporation* refers to the ability to recognize and skillfully respond to the spiritual issues in people's lives, including their awareness; their level of maturity, knowledge, and truth; the value of that knowledge to them; blocks and frustrations; and their motivation for further growth. The competent Christian counselor is well-grounded in the knowledge and use of the Bible and is sensitive to the leading of the Holy Spirit. He or she is able to artfully introduce spiritual issues into the helping process and to motivate consideration and action by the client.

7. *Case evaluation and management* involves using one's abilities to evaluate case progress by simple single-case and pre- and post-test clinical designs and to constructively manage a client's case, assessing and acting on consultation and referral needs to fulfill client goals and expectations.

8. *Supervision and case consultation* involves the ability to participate in case presentation, analysis, and consultation in both individual and group collegial settings. Learning from good supervision and consultation is a key modality of professional growth in the early years of counseling practice.

9. *Networking and referral* consists of the knowledge and connection you have with your community—your church and your larger geographic community of service—on behalf of your client. Finding other resources for your client is a constant challenge, and the competent Christian counselor knows how to find help when he or she cannot provide it themselves.

10. *Research translation and technology application* refers to a counselor's ability to (1) understand and translate the best research findings into usable tools and programs for clients, and (2) use the tools of technology such as telephones, computers, e-mail and online resources, and specialized testing and evaluation equipment on behalf of clients.

ADVANCED ROLES AND BEHAVIORS

Experienced professional counselors and pastoral counseling specialists should also be competent in some or all of the following ten advanced roles and behaviors.

1. *Clinical practice with "hard cases"* refers to the expertise necessary to manage and assist goal acquisition in the more chaotic and severe cases, which go beyond the skill and competence of novice and most generalist practitioners. (Box 3.1 lists some of the common cases and hard cases with which Christian counselors work on a consistent basis.)

2. *Clinical research* is the ability to design and carry out competent research that evaluates the clinical efficacy and biblical integrity of counseling models and techniques and advances the knowledge base of Christian counseling by the empirical development of our field.

3. *Clinical training and education* calls forth the teacher of Christian counseling, both in an academic setting and in a variety of teaching and training modes, such as distance education, online and video-based learning, and training in church, hospital, agency, and clinic settings.

4. *Testing and evaluation* consists of high-level personality, mental, neurological, and organizational testing and assessment for ethical use by a variety of people and venues, including clients, churches, courts, and legislators as well as business, political, and academic organizations.

5. *Delivering supervision and consultation* is a necessary and consistent activity of the experienced professional, whether geared to client or clinician or organization. While all counselors need the facility to participate in and receive supervision and consultation, the expert must be able to deliver high-level, solution-focused supervision and consultation.

Box 3.1—Life Issues Addressed by Christian Counselors

The Soul Care Bible (Clinton, Hindson, & Ohlschlager, 2001), developed with nearly a hundred leaders in counseling and pastoral ministry, reveals biblical ways of living through myriad problem issues that Christian counselors face daily. Some of the more common issues include:

Abortion	Doubt	Perfectionism
Aging	Failure	Prayer
Anger	Faith	Pride
Anxiety	Fear	Relationships
Bitterness	Forgiveness	Self-Esteem
Boundaries	God's Promises	Singleness
Crisis Intervention	Grief and Loss	Spiritual Growth
Criticism	Healthy Living	Stress
Dating	Jealousy	Teen Sex
Death and Dying	Legalism	Temptation
Decision Making	Marital Conflicts	Trust
Depression	Obedience to God	Women's Issues
Discouragement	Parenting Issues	Worry

Some of the hard cases that are often best referred to and counseled by expert Christian helpers include:

ADD/Hyperactivity	Gender Identity	Satan Worship
Alcoholism	Problems	School Violence
Bipolar Affective	Homicidal Threats	Severe Depression
Disorders	Homosexuality	Sex Addictions
Child Conduct	Mental Illness	Sexual Abuse
Disorders	Obsessions and	Sexual Dysfunction
Complicated Crises	Compulsions	Spiritual Warfare
Debilitating Phobias	Panic Attacks	Spousal Abuse
Divorce	Post-traumatic Stress	Suicide Threats
Drug Abuse	Psychotic Behavior	Trauma Exposure
Eating Disorders	Recurring Trouble	Unresolved Grief
Gambling Addictions	and Conflicts	Violence and Assault

6. *Administration* combines the art of leadership with the science of management to shape and direct an organization of committed people toward achieving a specified goal. Knowledge and skill in planning, evaluating, budgeting, accounting, and managing human resources, as well as relating with boards, client groups, and community, are all brought to bear in administrative services.

7. *Program development and evaluation* is closely related to administration and entails taking the data of our field, translating it into workable programs, and evaluating its ability to advance human, church, clinic, and organizational goals.

8. *Case advocacy and courtroom and legislative testimony* is provided by Christian counseling leaders on behalf of their clients, for their organization, for Christian counseling, and for Christ and the church. They are also able to give expert testimony in church councils, in corporate boardrooms, and in the courts and legislatures of the various governments of the world.

9. *Mediation and arbitration* involves peacemaking, which we are convinced is a central role for the modern Christian counselor to adopt and become proficient in doing. We believe that conflict resolution skills will increasingly be seen as a nearly seamless extension of counseling expertise in the future.

10. *New practice expertise* in a niche skill reflects the cutting edge of Christian counseling and the helping professions and is an attractive part of the repertoire of the modern Christian counselor. Practice skills include such areas as forensics, sex therapy, life coaching, clinic consultation, and lay training.

CHRISTIAN COUNSELING PRACTICE VIGNETTES

Another way to give our field concrete, human personality is to describe what Christian counselors actually do. Showing the behavior and diversity of the people who identify themselves with our movement gives practical clarity to the abstract and academic definitions in the previous chapter.

Helping is multi- and interdisciplinary in nature and includes such techniques as sex therapy, forensic evaluation, and behavioral contracting (a universal technique). It is more like the multidisciplinary domain of orthopsychiatry than it is like the singular discipline of psychiatry. Christian counseling is conducted by adherents of all the mental health disciplines and all denominations of the church (Bufford, 1997). The following vignettes represent a composite portrait of the variety and diversity of Christian counseling and compassionate soul care.

Ann is a licensed professional counselor (LPC) who has been part of a Christian group practice in a mid-size Midwestern city for eight years. She sees twenty to twenty-five clients weekly consisting mostly of individuals, married couples, and two families, and she leads a group of adult women who were sexually abused as children. She has developed positive relationships with the pastors and staff from around twenty churches in her community who depend on her as a reliable referral resource for difficult and time-consuming cases. Last year she was invited to join the staff of one of the larger churches in the area as minister of counseling, but she decided that God wanted her to remain in her practice setting so she could be available to the larger geographic church she has served for years.

Bill is the senior pastor of a growing evangelical church in the intermountain West. He has two other staff members—a worship/music leader and an assistant pastor whose main work involves family, children, and youth ministry. Bill is a dynamic pastor, dedicated to his church and much loved by his congregation. He is a gifted helper and usually spends twenty-plus hours a week in pastoral care, counseling, and visitation. Over the past year, however, he has been giving close to thirty hours a week to these tasks. He is tired and sometimes feels overwhelmed by the demand and the severity of problems he is facing, and his time for prayer and sermon preparation has begun to suffer. Bill has started referring his toughest cases to professional Christian counselors and is exploring ways to develop a safe and dynamic lay-helping ministry that emphasizes small groups and home-based care.

Jeannie is a widowed single parent who leads a very active life and has two children, a young married daughter and a high-school-age son. She works full-time as a medical receptionist and is active in her local Mennonite church. She is well known for her caring heart and easy manner with hurting people, and she spends much time helping those who have lost spouses and other family members. Every Wednesday night she leads a grief sharing group at her church. She also participates in lay-helper training using the "Caring for People God's Way" program.

Bob is a consulting neuropsychologist who, with his private practice in clinical psychology, is connected to the neurology department of a big-city hospital. One time he was called in to consult with a couple whose twelve-year-old boy had suffered a brain injury in an auto accident. Though the prognosis was cautiously optimistic, the boy's rehabilitation was not going well, and the family was highly stressed. Toward the end of the initial family interview, the boy's mother asked if Bob was a Christian and if he would pray for the boy. Bob stopped, considered, then consented and prayed with the family, asking God to be in charge of the boy's healing and recovery. He wondered how marital and family dynamics affected the boy's rehab as he noticed that the mother prayed loudly and effusively for healing, while the father remained silent and withdrawn.

Steve is associate pastor for family life at a large Southern Baptist church in Texas, a position he has held since seminary graduation. Three-fourths of his time involves marital and family counseling and family-life education. A committed biblical counselor, Steve keeps an open Bible on his desk, refers to it frequently in sessions, and gives his parishioners homework shaped around biblical stories and injunctions. He is a serious student of the Scriptures and is admired for his ability to bring biblical truth and healing words to his parishioners' lives. After toying with the idea of doctoral-level clinical psychology training, Steven instead returned to his seminary alma mater to pursue a doctor of ministry (DMin) degree in pastoral care and counseling.

Kate is a licensed clinical social worker (LCSW) at a community mental health center in the rural Blue Ridge Mountains of southwestern Virginia. As the "designated Christian" on staff, she serves Christian clients and the church in the rural enclaves of the center's catchment region. Kate, who counsels with Christians who come in seeking Christian care, has become a trusted referral source to many area pastors and consults with them on issues of faith and mental health. She became well known in her role as a crisis and post-traumatic stress specialist during the aftermath of a tornado. Kate is not allowed to proselytize her non-Christian clients, and she has had to fight her clinical supervisor to maintain her right to openly display a cross and other images of Christ in her office.

Ken is a recovering drug addict who accepted Christ at age thirty-five and has been "clean and sober" for nearly ten years. He serves as a deacon in his church and is involved with the Promise Keepers ministry in his area. Ken leads two small recovery groups at his church, which draw members from numerous churches in his community, and he assists in lay-helper training by professional Christian counselors. Ken uses a Twelve Step model that has been reinterpreted biblically, and he finds it very helpful in his work with addicts. Though some people in his church question his capability for ministry and his use of a Twelve Step program, Ken is well-supported by his pastor and is highly trusted by the entire recovery community in his region.

Richard is a board-certified psychiatrist and family practitioner who became a Christian in his midthirties. After years of family practice, he returned to medical school and completed a psychiatric residency. He maintains an active psychiatric practice with a Christian clinic that provides "vertically integrated" care, delivering a full range of medical, psychiatric, and behavioral services. This one-stop health care resource has become attractive to many managed-care providers. He derides the profits-over-people orientation of managed care and resists its pressure to relegate him to a purely medications-only practice. He has adapted well in a clinical delivery system that balances cost and care. He deliberately spends extra time with most patients and often prays with them, addresses family concerns, and encourages them to embrace Christ and the spiritual challenges of healing.

Sara is a young clinical psychologist and assistant professor of psychology in an established doctor of psychology (PsyD) program on the West Coast that emphasizes the integration of psychology and theology in clinical practice. In addition to conducting integration research and clinical practice development, Sara is dedicated to research and practice in selecting mission candidates and improving their adjustment to the rigors of missionary life. She also maintains a limited clinical practice and supervises master's and doctoral students in the school's practice clinic. Currently she is collecting data and writing her first book on how Christian psychology can help improve missionary training and life effectiveness while reducing missionary burnout and missions bailout.

Eric is a specialized pastoral psychotherapist who has worked for many years in a community pastoral counseling center supported by client fees and subsidies from three large churches that cosponsor the center. Describing himself as a post-liberal who was CPE-trained (clinical pastoral education) in liberation theology and Jungian therapy, Eric now works from an explicitly Christian frame of reference. He has learned over the years that "Christ is the one who really makes the lasting difference" in people's lives. Due to the length of time and the excessive costs of doctoral studies and the complaints he now universally hears from professional colleagues about managed care, he gave up his plans to pursue his PhD and professional licensure. Instead, he is pursuing specialized training in mediation and coaching to enhance and expand his practice.

Ruth is a certified school counselor who has served ten years as the director of a multistaffed counseling center at a large public high school in the Midwest. Most of her time is spent in administration, supervision, and training activities with her staff, but she spends some time in counseling and mentoring relationships with a variety of students. She developed and supervises an award-winning peer helper program in the school and does both individual and group supervision and training with student helpers who serve in academic-tutoring and peer problem-solving roles. Two trends are currently challenging her: (1) an increase in difficult, even chaotic, multiproblem cases of some students that tax the abilities and resources of the center, and (2) the decreasing budget for school counseling at a time when the need for intervention services is greater than ever.

Distinctives and Similarities in Christian Counseling

You may be questioning how, in the midst of all this diversity of practice, Christian counseling is different from (or similar to) any other kind of counseling. In order to understand the uniqueness of Christian counseling, it is necessary to understand how, when, where, and why Christian counseling is different from secular counseling. These differences can be pulled together by distinguishing the differing presuppositions inherent to Christian and secular counseling endeavors.*

Goals: Maturity in Christ versus happiness and self-fulfillment. Maturity in Christ is a foreign, even offensive, concept to secular counseling, which targets human satisfaction as the primary, if not sole, goal of therapy. While happiness or contentment is a desired by-product of following Christ, sometimes Christian maturity follows a painful road that must be traveled for maturity to develop. The goal of self-fulfillment often corrupts to self-aggrandizement, an all-too-common selfishness that easily avoids the sometimes painful lessons of Christian growth.

Ground: God revealed in the Scripture versus human wisdom and imagination. We do not dispute the value and use of human wisdom and imagination. However, unless these powers are submitted to the lordship of Christ, the results are often vain and temporal and lead to either human debasement or pride and self-exaltation. All Christian counseling must be grounded in and evaluated against the revelation of God in the Old and New Testaments.

Process: Transformation versus adjustment. Christ transforms us from the inside out through the operation of the Holy Spirit in our lives and relationships. For highly mature believers, this inner life serves as an anchor of peace and wisdom in the face of external storms. An adjustment model inherently presumes the greater power of external forces and serves to help others adjust to them without reference to Christ. Transformation of the inner person empowers people to complete the work of sanctification in two dimensions: internal change and external adjustment.

Means: Working out our salvation versus pragmatism (whatever works). Closely related to the above propositions, the means by which we grow comes either from

---

* This section is adapted from unpublished lay-helper training materials that George Ohlschlager
  developed and used with Peter Mosgofian among churches in Eureka, California, during the 1990s.

God or from our own efforts divorced from God. No doubt human effort effects change, but change can be easily directed toward evil or ineffectual ends. We consider ourselves biblical pragmatists, evaluating the moral and spiritual quality of our goals and methods from the standpoint of biblical revelation, for there are many ways that seem right to all of us (Proverbs 14:12). Working out our salvation is a functional process for making life work well by applying biblical principles, but it always points to a deeper relationship with Christ.

Values: Absolute and eternal versus situational and temporal. In this postmodern, post-Christian age, it is easy to get caught up in the situational and relativistic values of some clients, which challenge our own values at times. Sometimes it is difficult to uphold and advocate God's standards. If honesty is the best policy, we need to be able to translate that into language and stories that persuade clients who present powerful justifications for lying in some instances.

CHRISTIAN COUNSELING AS COMMON TO ALL COUNSELING

Lest you believe that we only affirm the uniqueness and value of Christian counseling, we believe that Christian counseling also has much in common with other forms of counseling. In truth, much of Christian counseling—the process much more than the content—is very much like counseling in general.

Goal-oriented. Within the first few words of the definitions by Collins and Ellis in box 3.2, we can see that both forms are goal-directed. This may seem so obvious as to not bear pointing out. However, you know the importance of clear and mutually agreed-upon goals when a client comes to you complaining of the time and money wasted with a therapist who "went nowhere. We just seemed to go around in circles, talking about things all over the map, and I left more frustrated than when I began."

Greater maturity. The object of goal-directed counseling is to leave clients better off, or more mature, than when they began counseling. Though the conceptions of what "better off" means may be quite diverse, even radically different, in Christian and secular circles, there is indeed some overlap that creates a rich storehouse of knowledge to draw upon in counseling. Finally, this goal of maturity is one that, when advanced, allows the individual to live in the future with less distress and to live more effectively and deliberately.

Diversity. Another general similarity between Christian counseling and other counseling professions is the great diversity of practice in our field. Christian counselors represent the full spectrum of gender, counseling disciplines, education and licensure, applied fields of practice, and settings where practice happens. In this regard, Christian counseling has more in common with a problem-oriented, multidisciplinary specialty practice—something like a career counseling or forensic mental health practice—than with psychology, social work, or any other single-discipline profession. No wonder Christian counseling is so vibrant and alive and, at times, so noisy and controversial.

CHRISTIAN COUNSELING: UNITY IN DIVERSITY

Christian counseling is truly a diverse, multidisciplinary practice, founded upon our essential unity in the person of Christ. The many degrees and disciplines in the

---

BOX 3.2—COMPARING GOALS IN CHRISTIAN AND SECULAR COUNSELING

Two different definitions of counseling goals are advanced by Gary Collins and Albert Ellis (Collins, 1988; Ellis & Greiger, 1977). Notice the uniqueness and similarities when comparing their respective definitions of Christian and secular counseling.

> Jesus…had two goals for individuals: abundant life on earth and eternal life in heaven. The counselor who follows Jesus Christ has the same ulti-mate goals of showing people how to have abundant lives and of pointing individuals to the eternal life that is promised to believers. If we take the Great Commission seriously we will have a strong desire to see all of our counselees become disciples of Jesus Christ. If we take the words of Jesus seriously we are likely to reach the conclusion that a fully abundant life comes only to those who seek to live in accordance with his teachings. (Collins, p. 39)

> The main goals in treating psychotherapy clients are simple and concrete: to leave clients, at the end of the psychotherapeutic process, with a mini-mum of anxiety, guilt, depression (or self-blame), anger, and low frustra-tion tolerance (or blame of others and the world around them). Just as importantly, to give them a method of self-observation and self-assessment that will ensure that, for the rest of their lives, they will continue to make themselves minimally anxious and hostile. (Ellis & Greiger, p. 189)

following list that make up the Christian counseling family do not even include the myriad backgrounds of lay helpers in ministry everywhere.

Psychology
PsyD, clinical psychology
PhD, clinical psychology
PhD, counseling psychology
EdD, educational psychology
EdD, counseling psychology

Pastoral Counseling
MA, pastoral counseling
MDiv, pastoral counseling
ThM, pastoral counseling
DMin, pastoral counseling
PhD, pastoral counseling

Psychiatry/Medicine
MD, psychiatry
MD, family practice

Social Work
MSW, clinical social work
PhD/DSW, clinical social work

Professional Counseling
MA, counseling
MA, counseling psychology
MEd, counseling
PhD, counseling/counselor education
EdD, counseling/counselor education

Marriage and Family Therapy
MA, marriage and family therapy
MA, counseling
PhD, marriage and family therapy
PhD, counseling/counselor education
DMFT, marriage and family therapy

Professional Licensure and Certification Tracks

Nearly twenty-five thousand AACC members are either professional clinicians or pastoral counselors. Professional Christian counselors have attained the requisite training (and one of the degrees noted above) and are licensed—like a physician or lawyer—to practice independently by each of the fifty states in a mental health discipline, or they have earned national certification signifying expertise in a particular field or subdiscipline of practice, or both. Many pastoral counselors are ordained ministers and also have specialized training and certification in pastoral counseling or a related discipline. Some of the licenses and certification specialties currently available include:

Biofeedback
Career Counseling
Clinical Social Work
Criminal/Offender Treatment
Clinical/Counseling Psychology
Cognitive Therapy
Corporate/Organizational Consulting

Drug and Alcohol Counseling
Educational Psychology
Employee Assistance
Financial/Credit Counseling
Forensic Mental Health
Gerontology
Hospital/Prison/Military Chaplaincy

Marriage and Family Therapy
Mediation/Conflict Resolution
Medicine and Psychiatry
Mental Health Counseling
Neuropsychology
Pastoral Counselor
Pastoral Psychotherapist
Professional Counseling

Psychoanalysis
Psychometrics/Testing
Rehabilitation Counseling
School/Guidance Counseling
Sex Education/Therapy
Sex Offender Treatment
Supervision
Trauma Debriefing

THE AACC MEMBERSHIP SURVEY*

At the 1999 World Conference of the American Association of Christian Counselors (AACC), we distributed a survey that queried members' beliefs, counseling practices, values, and professional development needs. Although conference attendees may or may not be representative of AACC or of Christian counselors as a whole, a sampling of the results of this data yields the demographics on the following pages regarding Christian counselors and their practices.

A number of hypotheses—testable questions—are suggested from this limited data about the characteristics and accomplishments of Christian counselors. Unlike practitioners of broader counseling professions, most Christian counselors are conservative, Bible-believing evangelicals who are serious about explicitly incorporating their religious beliefs and practices (especially prayer and the use of Scripture) into their counseling practices.

Like the counseling professions in general, most Christian counselors are women (by a slight majority), identify with the counseling profession (though many disciplines are represented), and practice at the master's level (though doctoral-level achievement is well represented). Most are engaged in direct counseling practice; work in private practice, a clinic, or a church; and identify marriage and family therapy and individual psychotherapy as their primary activities. Seventy percent have six or more years of experience as counselors, and 90% believe that relationship is more important than technique.

On ethics, issues, and values, most Christian counselors take a conservative stance where biblical direction is clear (homosexual behavior, for example) but show more varied views on issues where the Bible is not as clear (as in media violence or the boundary lines of divorce). Most counselors practice with a high

---

* Survey results that do not total 100% are due to respondents failing to answer all the questions.

DEMOGRAPHICS		
Gender:	male	46%
	female	54%
Age:	20s	2%
	30s	22%
	40s	24%
	50s	26%
	60s and above	24%
Highest degree:	BA/BS	12%
	MA/MS/MEd	34%
	MDiv	12%
	MSW	10%
	PhD/EdD/PsyD	14%
	Other (MD, DMin, JD, ThM, MRE)	12%
Years of experience:	none	4%
	1–5	26%
	6–10	24%
	11–15	24%
	16–20	10%
	21–25	4%
	26–30	4%
	30 or more	4%
	10 years or less	54%
	more than 10 years	46%

ETHICAL DILEMMAS		
Ever had strong sexual feelings toward a client?	yes no	14% 86%
Ever acted out in sexual misconduct?	yes no	– 100%

ETHICAL DILEMMAS (continued)		
Ever been publicly sanctioned for sexual misconduct?	yes	2%
	no	98%
Have trouble maintaining confidentiality?	always	–
	often	–
	sometimes	8%
	rarely	34%
	never	40%
Have trouble with competence, ability to help?	always	–
	often	2%
	sometimes	6%
	rarely	32%
	never	40%
Have trouble finding good professional referrals?	always	–
	often	18%
	sometimes	24%
	rarely	22%
	never	4%
Have trouble finding good lay helpers?	always	2%
	often	38%
	sometimes	24%
	rarely	10%
	never	4%

COUNSELOR IDENTITY AND PRACTICE		
Primary practice discipline:	counseling	62%
	psychology	14%
	social work	8%
	marriage & family therapy	6%
	pastoral ministry	8%
	other	2%
Primary work activity:	counseling practice	78%
	teaching	10%
	pastoral ministry	8%
	supervision	2%
	administration	2%

COUNSELOR IDENTITY AND PRACTICE (continued)		
Primary practice setting:	private practice	40%
	clinic/agency	14%
	church	22%
	parachurch ministry	10%
	school	4%
	hospital	2%
	other	6%
Primary description of practice:	marriage/family therapy	26%
	generalist	20%
	brief therapy	16%
	long-term psychotherapy	22%
	pastoral care and counseling	16%
Theoretical orientation:	cognitive-behavioral	24%
	biblical-nouthetic	24%
	family systems	20%
	eclectic/integrationist	20%
	psychoanalytic/object relations	8%
	spiritual direction	8%
Counseling hours per week:	0–5	14%
	6–10	22%
	11–15	14%
	16–20	20%
	21–15	14%
	26–30	2%
	31 and more	10%
Advertise publicly as a Christian counselor:	yes	54%
	no	46%
Most referrals come from:	clients	52%
	pastors	20%
	physicians	18%
	schools	4%
	yellow pages	6%
Pray with clients in session:	always	24%
	often	34%
	sometimes	26%

COUNSELOR IDENTITY AND PRACTICE (continued)		
Pray with clients in session:	rarely	12%
	never	2%
Refer to Scripture in session:	always	16%
	often	54%
	sometimes	26%
	rarely	4%
	never	–
Relationship is more important than technique in Christian counseling:	always	48%
	often	42%
	sometimes	6%
	rarely	4%
	never	–
Encourage development of spiritual disciplines:	always	42%
	often	36%
	sometimes	16%
	rarely	2%
	never	–
Encourage particular denominational beliefs:	always	2%
	often	4%
	sometimes	14%
	rarely	26%
	never	54%

degree of awareness and adherence to ethical standards and struggle with many of the same ethical problems as their secular colleagues. Though denominationalism is waning as a basis for counselor identity, most helpers are supportive of Christian counseling as a distinctive identity, both individually and corporately, and are dedicated to improving their own skill and competence as helpers.

CORE CHRISTIAN COUNSELOR TYPOLOGIES

Christian counseling, as we show in many ways throughout this book, is not a monolithic enterprise. It is not a field with just one model of counseling, just one organization that represents it, or just one type of practitioner. In fact, at no point in its young history was Christian counseling ever simple (Collins, 1980). We cannot even divide it into a bipolar entity, reflecting the clash between biblical counselors and integrationists as noted in chapter 2. As with the fall of the Soviet Union and the collapse of the bipolar political world in 1989, we relegate to our twentieth-century history the false dichotomy of Christian counseling as a nouthetic-integrationist dispute. Christian counseling has now become far too rich, too complex, and too interesting and diverse for such simplistic categories.

Categorization is important, however, for identity, description, analysis, and purposeful professional development. We do recognize a variety of ways to categorize Christian counseling in a more refined sense and thereby describe an observed typology of Christian counselors.

As you will recall from chapter 2, we, as an organization, have distinguished three global types of Christian counselors in the establishment of the major divisions of the nearly forty-thousand-member AACC: pastors and pastoral counselors, professional clinicians, and lay helpers.

Presently, the division for pastoral counselors has more than ten thousand members, the division for mental health professionals has nearly fifteen thousand members, and the lay helpers division has over fifteen thousand members. Students make up most of the remaining membership (Clinton, 2001).

Based on our observation, one could further categorize the field according to the following trait-based typology of ten different kinds of Christian counselors. The following distinctives are not hard and fast, but they reflect overlapping categories of identity and role descriptions of counselors in the AACC. Though the first two types most closely adhere to descriptions of integrationists and biblical counselors, we are able to delineate significant numbers of each of these ten types among our worldwide membership. We also note what we all could learn from each type of helper.

1. *Professional clinicians* comprise mainly psychologists, psychiatrists, and other clinical professionals who are trained in and identify primarily with their mental health discipline. Professional clinicians are steeped in the processes and language of science, psychology, biology, psychiatry, behavior and social change, and psychopharmacology. They are oriented to integration, professionalism, and clinic and private practice. We could all learn from their extensive knowledge of behavioral, familial, and social change; their commitment to empirical evidence; and their understanding of how all realms of living—biological, psychological, social, and spiritual—operate and interrelate.

2. *Pastoral or biblical counselors* most often are pastors and seminary-trained counselors who use the Bible as their primary reference for all counseling and interventions. Trained primarily in theology and geared more to spiritual growth than to psychology, pastoral counselors are oriented to pastoral and church-based

practice but are increasingly involved in clinic practice and professional development. We could all learn from their dedication to Christ, their high view of the Scriptures, and the rich way they apply biblical truth to human problems and to the need for maturity in Christ.

3. *Recovery counselors* usually incorporate the Alcoholics Anonymous Twelve Step and addictions modality. The God of the Bible is the "higher power," and the helpers are "wounded healers." These professionals are very group-centered, church-based, and lay-intensive. Their practical dedication to gospel truth is instructive: We are all powerless to change in the ways we should, and sanctification as a willful pull-yourself-up-by-the-bootstraps effort is insufficient. These helpers know that God alone can empower us to accomplish what he calls us to do, and we must seek that power from him every day, or we delude ourselves.

4. *Lay or peer counselors* are recognized for their inherent empathy, listening ability, nonjudgmental ways, compassionate caring, and friendly helpfulness and receive specialized training to enhance these qualities. They are very lay-intensive. We could all learn from their natural friendliness and the ease with which they relate to people, and we should seek to imitate their interpersonal model, which evinces the best kinds of helping and human relations.

5. *Charismatic counselors* emphasize personal transformation and Holy Spirit power, which can include "signs and wonders" in counseling and Spirit gifts relevant to helping such as discernment, wisdom, words of knowledge, and prophecy. These counselors tend to stress inner healing, miraculous interventions, and the experiential presence of Christ. Their reliance on the Holy Spirit, their giftedness in spiritual discernment and wisdom, their facility with spiritual warfare, and their practiced belief in divine healing challenge us all.

6. *Liturgical counselors* are pastor- and church-oriented (even denomination-oriented) counselors whose help is linked with the liturgical process and calendar. Healing and maturity come partly through the faithful practice of the sacraments in the context of body life and community. We could all learn from their respect for the ebb and flow of life, the seasonal nature of human triumphs and troubles, and the power of liturgical celebration to give meaning to life.

While the next four types are also theoretical orientations that are likely to be used by many different types of counselors, they are substantial enough to be considered the primary identification of many Christian counselors ("I am a cognitive [or systems] therapist," for example).

7. *Cognitive/belief counselors* are oriented to individual and internal change. They work to identify and root out false beliefs, lies, curses, vows, and dysfunctional thinking and replace them with biblical and rational truth as well as the tools

to act and live out change accordingly. This orientation seems to be equally represented among both professional and pastoral counselors. We could all learn from their dedication to the axioms that truth is tangible and that ideas have consequences as well as from their understanding of how thoughts, feelings, and behavior interact together to influence the whole person.

8. *Family, systems, and relational counselors* emphasize family dynamics and interpersonal relationships as a primary healing force. They are social systems–oriented and network-focused. They are well represented in church and as professional counselors and therapists, and they are big on body life, community, and small groups. They have much to teach us about family values, understanding the power of systems and relational change, and adopting a balanced view of the individual living in the community.

9. *Social justice counselors* are primarily ecological social workers and systems-oriented therapists who have broad political and social justice concerns. They are concerned with client poverty, powerlessness, and marginalization, and they are sensitive to the corrupting influence of money, power, and secular culture. Social justice counselors are oriented to fixing the person and the social system together. We could all learn from their dedication to human rights, their understanding of the corporate and institutional structures of evil, and their conviction that personal change without peace or justice in the larger community is often fruitless.

10. *Eclectic counselors* meld together two or more of these types into one integrated role, rather than identifying completely with any one particular type or model of counseling. This, in fact, is the goal of becoming a truly competent Christian counselor—being able to fit the best perspective of change to the particular client need before you. As you mature and expand the range and power of your helping ability, you will likely see yourself becoming more Spirit-seeking, more prayerful, and more responsibly and pragmatically eclectic.

THE POWER OF OUR UNITY IN CHRIST

If all this deconstruction and discriminate analysis of Christian counseling is somewhat confusing, permit us to now return to our centering source—the person of Jesus Christ. He and his ways are the common threads woven throughout the work of all Christian counselors. At our invitation his living presence and divine influence are available in the counseling endeavor through the Holy Spirit. He is the invisible person who sits with us and our clients, charging our hearts with his hope, drawing out the truth, enlightening our eyes, and anchoring our walks with his promise. He is the source of life-changing soul care.

Christ's influence, which can be either subtle or overt, empowers constructive change in the lives of many people. Christ is the One who reveals himself and invites all to follow him. He is the One from whom we learn to change and grow on the path of sanctification, saved by the act of justification—the free gift of Christ's atoning sacrifice that is received by faith alone. He is the One who guides the way and constructs the path to transformation and maturity.

Furthermore, Christ is the One who holds the profession of Christian counseling together, like a sun that holds otherwise chaotic planets in a firm and stable gravitational grip. Christ is the head of the practice and the profession of Christian counseling, and he is able to gather all of us otherwise squabbling and unruly children into one united family fold. Christ will bring Christian counseling to maturity in this century, and his Spirit will bear much fruit for his kingdom in the new millennium.

Christian counseling rests on a bedrock of truth, which is expressed clearly in Christ and in a core of clear principles for preferred living. This truth is the high calling of Christ himself, and it must be pursued with all diligence in our helping endeavors. It is also a truth that should be applied flexibly according to client need and readiness, at the right time, for the best chance for positive response. We assert that the truth of Christ should be communicated in accord with the needs and limits of the people we serve. This is a central theme of *Competent Christian Counseling*.

The modern-day ministry of Christian counseling, which also has some very ancient roots, is maturing into a worldwide and essential ministry of the whole Christian church. We are dedicated in this book and by our vocations to nurture and foster this ministry. We are convinced that Christian counseling is here to stay and that it is not inherently evil, corrupted, or seductive in relation to the church. It is but one force among many that God has given the church for the building up of individual believers and faith communities in the way of Christ, and there remains much to learn before its ministry matures and fulfills its extraordinary promise.

BASIC ASSUMPTIONS

We have conceived the following essential counseling attributes as the core assumptions (the Fourteen A's) of Christian counseling excellence:

1. *Authority.* The revelation and place of God and the role of scriptural truth; the training, experience, and credentials of the therapist; and the therapist's orientation to counseling, including primary values and ethical commitments.

2. *Anthropology.* The view that men and women are creatures of God, both bearers of the God image and sinners who have turned away from God.

Humans are ultimately answerable to God and are the repositories of his saving and life-changing grace.

3. *Atmosphere.* The totality of skills and conditions that join counselor and client together and facilitate desired change.

4. *Advocacy.* The act of supporting and acting as an advocate for the client's best interests, whether that advocacy is directed to the church, to the world, to an HMO, or to the client's family and friends.

5. *Accountability.* The duty of adhering to a rigorous code of ethics in counseling and to be ethically connected to others who can support and monitor the work of counseling so that excellence is achieved and maintained.

6. *Attending.* A foundational relationship development skill that gives clients the counselor's undivided attention in a way that assures them that the helper cares and is committed to them.

7. *Assessment.* A formal process of interviewing, fact-finding, and goal defining at the initial stage of counseling and an ongoing clinical process throughout each successive stage.

8. *Alignment.* The process of understanding clients' preferred relationship styles and joining with them to mutually view their life and harmoniously define their future.

9. *Analysis.* The case formulation process that defines and links what is going on, what is blocking progress, and what to do to change things and move forward again.

10. *Agenda setting.* The logical extension of case analysis that sets forth a practical treatment plan with enough detail to direct client action.

11. *Action.* The process of working out the treatment plan in pursuit of counseling goals. Helping the client get started and maintain deliberate change-directed behavior.

12. *Application.* Back-end assessment and analysis of the fruits of change that consider how to generalize change to other areas of one's life and how to teach others to effect change.

13. *Adversity.* Acknowledging the truth that change is hard and often frightening. Counselors should encourage clients to see change as a normal part of life and to overcome the universal tendency to hide, avoid, and quit before things turn around.

14. *Accessibility.* The counselor's challenge to stay with clients and be available to them through the hard times of counseling—a necessary agreement in exchange for client accountability.

PART II

THE ROOT
FOUNDATIONS
OF CHRISTIAN
COUNSELING

CHAPTER 4

THEOLOGICAL ROOTS

Synthesizing and Systematizing a Biblical Theology of Helping

RON HAWKINS, EDWARD HINDSON, AND TIM CLINTON

We wake, if we ever wake at all, to a mystery.
—ANNIE DILLARD, *Teaching a Stone to Talk*

The scene was packed with emotion as the son pleaded, "Dad, why didn't you tell me?" Some weeks earlier, the father had been given a diagnosis of terminal cancer, but he hadn't wanted to tell anyone.

With tear-filled eyes, he turned to his son. "I didn't want you to define me by my cancer; I just wanted to remain 'Dad' and not become 'the cancer patient.'"

What defines you? What defines *your* counseling?

In this life, what you believe about God matters. And it matters in counseling. Known as the queen of the sciences, theology is the study of God that encompasses what we believe about God and his existence, his nature, his attributes, his influence, and his involvement in our lives.

Every counselor has a theology that defines and directly influences the counseling process, including a counselor's perceptions and actions. A comprehensive biblical theology—a theology of soul-care helping—is essential in order to establish the foundations of Christian counseling and to guide the practice of Christ-centered counseling (see Adams, 1970; Benner, 1988; Collins, 1993; Hindson & Eyrich, 1997; Powlison, 1997).

Following is a classic outline of the study of systematic theology as it is usually presented to first-year seminary students in the United States and Europe. This outline will provide a helpful point of reference as we develop our theology of soul-care helping.

Bibliology—the doctrine of Scripture
Theology Proper—the doctrine of God

Paterology—the doctrine of God the Father
Christology—the doctrine of God the Son
Pneumatology—the doctrine of God the Holy Spirit
Anthropology—the doctrine of human beings
Hamartiology—the doctrine of sin
Soteriology—the doctrine of salvation
Ecclesiology—the doctrine of the church
Angelology—the doctrine of angels
Eschatology—the doctrine of the future

THEOLOGY AND CHRISTIAN COUNSELING TODAY

Christian counseling is deficient in its theological roots and spiritual practices. There, we've said it. In this and the next chapter, we hope to facilitate some corrective action by filling this deficiency with a God-exalting theology and a program of spiritual formation geared specifically for Christian counselors.

Lamenting the current state of Christian counseling in this regard, Hart (2001) has challenged us:

> For some time now, experts have been telling us that the stock market is due for a major correction. Already we are beginning to see the economy "cool" with stocks jumping around like a cat on a hot tin roof. Well, I have the same fears about where we are headed in some of the things we do as Christian counselors, particularly our uncritical adoption of the secular psychological concepts. We have run ahead of our theological foundations in developing our understanding of a "Christian" approach to counseling— and we are due a major correction here as well! (p. 8)

McMinn (1996) recently called attention to the importance of theology in counseling:

> Effective Christian counselors also consider theological perspectives at the same time that they engage in the various psychological tasks of counseling. Historical and systematic theology, biblical understanding, and Christian tradition are all valued and considered essential components of counseling. (p. 270)

Effective counselors, in McMinn's view, are those given to *multitasking*, the ability to simultaneously and appropriately utilize—for the benefit of the client— the insights and skills gained from the study of theology, psychology, and spirituality (p. 269).

These concerns for building Christian counseling on a biblical-theological foundation are not new. In the 1970s Jay Adams stood Christian counseling on its head from his pastoral theology chair at Westminster Seminary. Convinced that counseling was a pastoral function being usurped by the secular psychological establishment, he insisted that

> contrary to what some may think, Christians have not suddenly burst upon the scene challenging psychiatrists and clinical and counseling psychologists; rather [the historical facts show that] the latter are the newcomers who moved in to supplant the church in its work of counseling. Historically speaking, therefore, competition is quite an accurate word to describe the situation. (1979, p. x)

Many were upset with Adams's provocative approach, confrontational style, and antipsychology pronouncements. However, his seminal and prophetic work has sensitized most Christian counselors to the need for greater thoughtfulness regarding the necessary and powerful influence of biblical and theological data by people in helping ministry. Christian counseling is listening, as these concerns are increasingly reflected in the various works of numerous leading authors in our field (Benner, 1988; Collins, 1993; Crabb, 1999; McMinn, 1996; Moon, 1997).

Strengthening counselor competency through multitasking, while necessary, is not easy. Theologians have seldom allied themselves with the challenges related to strengthening counselor competence. Additionally, counselors overwhelmed with meeting the needs of people have seldom had the time to call upon theologians for help. Both have too often lived like disconnected cultures, each with its own set of *shibboleths* and recommendations for resolving humanity's ills. Sometimes these two worlds have even expressed distrust and a general low regard for one another.

Multitasking is also demanding because there is so much to learn. Must we do so? The only correct answer is *yes!* In fact, consciously or without realizing it, every counselor already embraces a theology that impacts his life and practice. Bergin (1991), Worthington (1988), and others have clearly shown that we cannot divorce counseling from its moral, theological, and philosophical roots. This makes it a given that we are all doing theology whenever we practice counseling. The obvious questions, then, are: Are we doing theology well or poorly? Is the theology we are doing—that which inevitably informs our counseling—biblical theology or bad theology? We believe the choices are as black and white as the questions we state. There is a sharp divide between truth and untruth.

Counselor competence is greatly enhanced when we build from a solid theological foundation. It is hard work, but counselors can derive great personal and professional benefits from the study of theology. Not only do we strengthen our people-caring skills, but we also draw closer to the God who made us and gifted us for our helping ministries, for, at its core, theology is the study of God. Our hope is that Christian counselors will learn and impart to their clients a living and experiential theology that reveals the truth of the personhood of God and of his desire for relationship with us. The only other option is to merely learn *about* God by studying a sterile systematic theology. This might leave you full of knowledge, but it may also leave you intellectually proud and ultimately bereft of life.

Answering the following questions and reflecting upon the significance of the answers for counseling will provide the structure for this chapter. What is theology? What is at the heart of theology? With all the other challenges demanding our energy and time, why do counselors need to work at theological literacy? Where should counselors who wish to develop multitasking skills and to reinforce their theological understanding begin? How does a counselor apply theology? What principles guide counselors as they seek to arrange theological material in ways that advance counselor effectiveness? What areas of theology are particularly critical for enhancing counselor competence—and why are these areas of theological investigation so crucial to the counseling process?

THEOLOGY DEFINED

The dictionary defines theology as "the study of God, his attributes, and his relationship with man and the universe" (Landau, 1975, p. 763). Internationally renowned theologian Millard Erikson (1985) proposed that we understand theology as

> that discipline which strives to give a coherent statement of the doctrines of the Christian faith, based primarily on the Scriptures, placed in the context of culture in general, worded in a contemporary idiom, and related to the issues of life. (p. 21)

Grenz (1994) offered the following amplification of Erikson's definition:

> Theology is primarily the articulation of a specific religious belief system itself (doctrine). But it also includes reflection on the nature of believing, as well as declarations concerning the integration of commitment with personal and community life. The Christian theologian seeks to set forth a coherent presentation of the themes of the Christian faith. (p. 5)

Our theology informs and even shapes our worldview. Hence, it logically follows that our theology also informs and even shapes our counseling theory and practice.

According to Sire (1997), a worldview is "a set of presuppositions (or assumptions) which we hold (consciously or subconsciously) about the basic makeup of the world" (p. 17). Looking through the lens of a counselor, Collins (1993) reminds us that "Our worldview determines how we think about human nature, evaluate the causes of emotional problems, decide on treatment strategies, and evaluate counseling progress" (p. 13). The counselor's theology and worldview deal with, among other things, what we believe about God, humankind, and the created universe; about Jesus and salvation; about the Holy Spirit and his work in believers and in the world; about the church; and about the future completion of God's program.

Clearly, Christian counseling cannot be done effectively apart from theological covenants. This is a central reason why we stressed the nature and the importance of covenantal counseling in chapter 2.

THE NEED FOR THEOLOGY

Counselors and clients are constantly confronted with assertions regarding the truthfulness of opposing ideologies—what we believe and what we value. Multiple voices in our pluralistic society call out for a hearing, asking that the ideas they promote be received as the truth. This has caused many people to be confused and anxious. Others have adopted a relativistic mind-set—giving equal weight to all truth claims. Good theology helps filter out the theological and philosophical error that pervades so much of our world today.

Good theology provides the foundational authority of truth against which we can assess our beliefs and practices. It can assist the truth-finding functions of modern counseling, overcoming confusion and assisting with the management of anxiety. Biblical theology grounds the counselor and those we seek to help in the truth as revealed through the Holy Spirit. Counselors who are intentional in building a worldview grounded in biblical and theological truth are far less likely to assemble assumptions in conflicted bits and pieces. They are also less likely to borrow uncritically from a variety of psychological theories that are often at odds with one another and are at times opposed to the fundamental tenets of our faith.

POLEMICS, CATECHETICS, AND SUMMARIZATION

There are three important factors in theological reflection:

1. *Polemics* speaks to the need to clarify and distinguish biblical beliefs from proposed alternatives as well as to distinguish truth from error.
2. *Catechetics* deals with the imparting of instruction and training in skills that promote maturity in Christ (Ephesians 4:11-14).

3. *Summarization* involves the systematic arrangement of the major themes of Scripture that clarify God's nature and work.

These attempts to systematize the propositions of Scripture "seek to emancipate theology from any one cultural context in order to produce a statement of truth that is timeless and culture free" (Grenz, 1994, p. 7). This work requires a measure of humility as we seek to keep our personal and cultural biases from distorting our statements on "truth" and to keep ourselves committed to the Word.

As a redeemed people, we are often countercultural since we elevate the Word of the self-revealing God to a position superior to that of human opinion. As Christ-followers, we are under the authority of God's Word and are called to formulate our identities, ideas, actions, and commitments in submission to the Word. By virtue of our pivotal ministry in the covenant community, we are often required to transmit theological information to people in desperate need of truth-based thinking. In that position, we must attain to a higher level of theological sophistication than we have in the past. Far too many of us have witnessed the damaging effects of poor theology in counseling and the absence of a clear theological undergirding for many approaches to counseling.

While we, as counselors, may not analyze and debate at the level of the professional theologian, we dare not rest until we understand the significance of the great acts of God for human healing, the power in our traditions, the healing in our sacraments, the value of our covenants, the restorative power of our communities, and the content of our sacred documents. Above all, Christ, his global church, and its long and rich history are relevant to the care and curing of souls. Like teachers in the community of faith and because of our aspirations and giftings, we must be humbled by the reality that we are held to a higher level of accountability and will receive a weightier final judgment (1 Corinthians 4:1-2; James 3:1).

START WITH THE SELF-REVEALING GOD

Where do we begin this journey? Some like to begin with the assertion of God's existence, proceed to an amplification of his character and works, and then offer an examination of the implications of all this for our work. Others would prefer to begin with the Bible, the means of our knowledge of God. They ask how we can begin with God without first studying his revelation of himself in general and in the special revelation of the Scriptures.

Erikson (1985) offers another solution that may help bridge this gap. He proposes that we presuppose both the authority of the Bible and the existence of God as forming a foundational idea. We then proceed to develop the truths and ideas that flow from this core idea and evaluate the confirming evidence for their truthfulness.

> On this basis, God and His Self-revelation are both presupposed together, or we embrace the idea of the self-revealing God as a single presupposition. Our starting point would then be something like this: There exists one tri-une God, loving, all powerful, holy, all-knowing, who has revealed Himself in nature, history, and human personality, and in those acts and words which are now presented in the canonical scriptures of the Old and New Testaments. (p. 33)

This basic proposition can then be broadened into a theological system by identifying the support throughout Scripture for its various assumptive elements. We can examine ideas and proceed to their validation or invalidation based on the degree of support they receive in the Scriptures. Moving forward from God's special revelation in Christ, we can examine other sources in our quest for the knowledge of God and truth. God has also revealed himself in myriad ways (general revelation) in such areas as nature and science, world history, great art and literature, and human personality (Collins, 1993; Grenz, 1994; Morris, 1976). We may and should examine these for insights into the character of the self-revealing God, while bearing in mind that these sources will be clearly subordinate to the Bible.

BUILDING A HELPING THEOLOGY:
A WISDOM METHODOLOGY

In the book of Ecclesiastes, Solomon, the wisest man of his time, sought to answer the question of meaning or profit in life (1:1-3). Writing in the wisdom tradition, he taught that God made man upright, but that man through disobedience has fallen into sin and death (7:2,20). Hence, there is not a person on Earth who never sins (7:20), and we live in a broken world where there are so many things wrong that they can't be added up (1:15).

Ecclesiastes is of great importance because it describes in detail the deep hurts humans experience in the post-Edenic world (after the Fall of Adam) and offers wisdom's direction for the successful resolution of the pain (7:11,12). In ministering to these hurts, Solomon advocated a method—a way of doing theology—that flows from divine wisdom and can result in the restoration of meaning for humans who are immersed in vanity and suffering. Listen to the words of the biblical text:

"Vanity of vanities," says the Preacher, "All is vanity." And moreover, because the Preacher was wise, he still taught the people knowledge; yes, he pondered and sought out and set in order many proverbs. The Preacher sought to find acceptable words; and what was written was upright—words of truth. The words of the wise are like goads, and the words of scholars are like well-driven nails, given by one Shepherd. And further, my son, be admonished by these. Of making many books there is no end, and much study is wearisome to the flesh. Let us hear the conclusion of the whole matter: Fear God and keep His commandments, for this is man's all. For God will bring every work into judgment, including every secret thing, whether good or evil. (Ecclesiastes 12:8-14, NKJV)

SENSITIVE TO CONTEXT

We encourage Christian counselors to embrace a theological method that is in the wisdom tradition and is sensitive to context. In Ecclesiastes, Solomon spoke in the context of his day. He identified elements in that context that were damaging those he sought to help and proposed alternatives rooted in divine wisdom. It is this "wisdom from above" that Solomon believed would, when embraced, lead to heightened meaning and wellness.

Solomon spoke the truth, applicable at multiple levels—to the crisis in his culture (particularly within the covenant community) and within his own soul and spirit. The community he served was struggling with vanity (1:3). Vanity *(hebel)* reflects an inability to attach a sense of permanence, direction, or meaningfulness to life (Leupold, 1952; Von Rad, 1974). Modern counselors face a similar challenge of communicating empathically as we respond to the needs of the cultures, the communities, and the people we serve. This contextual application is a central feature of our theological method here.

CENTERED IN THE NEEDS OF PEOPLE

Solomon's work was carried out within and on behalf of people who constituted the covenant community. This wise preacher was focused on meeting their needs. The term *preacher* may be better understood as teacher, counselor, or elder—anyone who convenes a "people meeting" for the purpose of matching knowledge and wisdom to the needs of the people (Leupold, 1952, Wright, 1991). This wise helper was focused on the people and their social and cultural context and followed a theological method that resulted in the acceptance of his teaching. His words were honored, in part, because of their demonstrated efficacy in meeting human needs. Wisdom connected the teacher to the continuous service of the community as a whole and to its constituent parts represented by each person.

The apostle Paul also viewed this work as essential to the life and work of the believing community. In Paul's ecclesiology every member of the church is at some level a helper, able to speak intelligently about what God has done for him or her through the Word and the Spirit. Paul advocated that each member be invested in the growth of others in the body (Ephesians 4:1-16). He insisted that all believers be filled with goodness and care for one another, and he taught that this is a required ministry for all people in the community we call the church (Romans 15:14).

Covenantal community and the responsibility for attending to member maturity is at the heart of the New Testament assembly envisioned by the author of Hebrews (10:24-25). Members of the assembly come together for the purpose of encouraging one another and stirring up one another to love and good works. The theological method advanced by Solomon focused on suiting the words of Scripture to the needs of people in such a way that men, women, and children are put on the path to wellness, impressed with the relevance of God's Word for meeting the challenges of their daily lives.

ROOTED IN DIVINE WISDOM

As counselors, we should convene our sessions deeply aware of how dependent we are on divine wisdom. We all live in a fallen world, and those we serve are burdened with the task of finding meaning in life and are struggling with their bondage to sin.

Solomon understood the need for personal wisdom as the crucial prerequisite for guiding the covenant community (Ecclesiastes 12:9-10). It was his confession of personal inadequacy and his subsequent petition for divine enablement that resulted in his unusual anointing with wisdom (1 Kings 3:5-14). A similar confession and petition is required of all who would desire to obtain this type of wisdom—a wisdom that comes to us through Christ, the Scriptures, and the Spirit as a free gift from God (1 Corinthians 1:30; 1 Corinthians 12:1-11; 2 Timothy 3:15-16). James 1:5 reminds us, "If you need wisdom—if you want to know what God wants you to do—ask him, and he will gladly tell you" (NLT). Solomon's competence as a king required the gift of this wisdom received from Yahweh, Israel's shepherd. Every counselor today equally needs this divine gifting from the Holy Spirit—the church's *paraklete*—to assure our competence (Ecclesiastes 12:11; 2 Timothy 3:16).

Those who seek direction in life often ask, "What shall I do? Where can I find meaning?" What a privilege we have to offer wisdom from God that directs people into the way of value and meaning (Ecclesiastes 12:9-10). Wisdom enables Covey's (1997) "sharpening of the saw" that allows counselor and client to live life with a degree of connection and impact.

Grounded in the Authority of the Scriptures

Solomon also advanced the central place of the Scriptures in the theological method (Ecclesiastes 12:9-12). While many sources, such as professional journals, writings of church fathers, and programmed treatment manuals, promise to help people discover meaning or significance, Solomon counseled caution with these extrabiblical sources. The true answer to meaning and profit is found in the counsel of the words that have been given by Yahweh, our loving Creator. Any extrabiblical materials should be used judiciously, and only after the counselor is confident that such materials honor the goal of facilitating Christlikeness and are fully consistent with the truths of Scripture.

The words that are acceptable have come from God himself and are at the heart of wisdom's message. Counselors must be careful not to add anything to these instructions that dilutes or compromises their power to speak truth to broken people living in a broken world. The counsel given by the counselor is authoritative only to the extent that it is a faithful exposition of the truth received in the special revelation found in Scripture.

In the New Testament, the apostle Paul gave similar counsel to Timothy. Struggling with fear (2 Timothy 1:7), Timothy was told by his aged mentor to give great energy to the study of God's Word, correctly handling the word of truth (2:15). The Word had demonstrated its power to save and would now demonstrate that it had the power to make him wise for overcoming his fear. In fact, the Scriptures in their totality are given by divine inspiration and contain the doctrine, reproof, correction, and instruction required for bringing Timothy to full maturity in Christ (3:15-17). Second Peter 1:3 reminds us: "His divine power has given us everything we need for life and godliness through our knowledge of him who called us by his own glory and goodness."

Counselors must proceed with extreme caution as they grapple with truth. Assertions regarding "absolute truth" can be dangerous, and truth is sometimes used in the service of pride and in the reduction of theology to an academic exercise divorced from the practical needs of the community of faith. This so-called "truth" only serves division, argumentativeness, and a convenient theology that doesn't result in a heart broken and able to minister to the needs of the communities we serve. God's wisdom, the humility required for its reception, and a willingness to submit to the authority structures of the covenant community deliver Christian counselors from such aberrant misappropriations of truth.

Permeated with Passion, Compassion, and Practicality

Counseling requires a model for doing theology that is rich in *passion, compassion,* and *practicality.* Deeply invested in our work, we perspire over the inspired "givens" in the Scriptures (2 Timothy 2:15; Luke 4:4; Hebrews 4:12; John 5:39; 2 Timothy 3:15; Ecclesiastes 12:9-10). We ponder, seek out, and set in order the passages from God's Word that meet client needs. Counselors summarize and systematize the various parts of God's Word into a harmonious whole, focused on meeting the needs of the individual and his culture. It is this passion for applying truth in real-life ways that meets real needs.

Tillich (1951) embraced this challenge in his theological method and characterized his theology as an "answering theology." In his view, the helper moves back and forth between two poles. One pole is the Bible. This assures that the theological method is embedded in authority. The other pole is the context of our lives, which includes the cultures, traditions, and systems that impact or have impacted our attributions and interpretations. This assures that the theological method is wedded to relevance. Attention to these two poles assures that counselors are employing a theological method that allows them to speak with compassionate authority to real needs.

CHARACTERIZED BY FLEXIBILITY

The model Solomon proposed meets the need for flexibility in the application of theological truth. Theology, systematically expressed and artfully arranged to meet needs, comprises two clearly differentiated types of words to accomplish two very different purposes. There are words that secure and stabilize people like deeply embedded nails or tent stakes (Ecclesiastes 12:11). These are a delight to deliver and are frequently received with joy. There are also goading words of reproof and correction that are equally needed and yet are often more difficult to speak and more difficult to receive (Ecclesiastes 12:11; 2 Timothy 3:16).

Counselor competence demands that we deliver both nails and goads in language that is compassionate and is contemporary and sensitive to context (Anderson, 1995; Grenz & Olson, 1996; Horton, 1994). Attention to the contextualization of transcendent truth secures for it a degree of relevance that enhances one's ability to speak with clarity to the needs of hurting people in successive generations. Paul practiced this responsibility to be relevant and flexible in his evangelistic and discipling ministry. At Mars Hill his passion for relevance in the communication of the gospel dictated his choice of subject matter and demonstrated his flexibility and concern for contextualization (Acts 17:16-34).

The primacy of flexibility in context is seen in Paul's directives to the believing community in 1 Thessalonians 5:14 governing discipleship and counseling. Here, Paul advised action according to the situational and personality needs of the believing person. He counseled admonition for rule breakers, comfort for the timid, support for those troubled with life-dominating sins, and patience for all. A static or one-size-fits-all approach does not work for all people. What is needed is a compassionate theological method that is flexible and sensitive to context.

AUTHORITATIVE IN ITS DECLARATIONS

While there is a great deal of tenderness attached to the theological method advanced by Solomon, there is also power and authority in its declarations of what is true. In the demand for a heart focused on meeting the needs of people, we ultimately see the loving heart of God. However, the theological method built on the wisdom foundation also gives full weight to the toughness of God. Solomon closed his instruction on theological method with full attention to the God who gives commandments, establishes consequences, and ultimately judges all things—even the secret things of the heart.

According to a recent poll, 66% of Americans believe that "there is no such thing as absolute truth" (Barna, 1998, pp. 83-85). Postmodernists affirm that "there are no absolutes, truth is relative, reality is socially constructed and moral guidelines are only masks for oppressive power" (Veith, 1994, p. 72). While not diminishing any of what has been said to this point, counselor-theologians will utilize a theological method that is countercultural in its insistence upon submission to the self-revealing God who speaks authoritatively through the Scriptures.

A THEOLOGY FOR LIVING

According to Volf (2001), systematic theology should be "a transforming theology applied to real-life issues." This theology is not a rigid, sterile system of propositions to be learned in rote fashion. Rather it is an experiential and living theology, rational yet practical, and eminently useful for teaching and for life-changing learning.

We now turn our attention to some key doctrines and their application to counseling. This exercise—the doing of living theology—is a lifelong journey for all of us.

THEOLOGY PROPER: THE EXISTENCE AND CHARACTER OF THE INFINITE AND PERSONAL GOD

What do you know and believe about God? Laney (1999) believes that knowing God better "will help us deal with our doubts, prepare us to better cope with unexpected circumstances or tragedies in life, and provide increased wisdom for making life's decisions in a manner consistent with God's character and will" (p. 15). To accomplish these goals it is necessary to affirm the existence of the infinite, personal, creator God. This God creates *ex nihilo*—out of nothing—a testimony to his creative omnipotence (Genesis 1:1; 2:7). He is Almighty God and rules in his sovereignty over nations, time, and all of creation in a way that brings to pass without equivocation his predetermined purposes (Psalm 48:1-14; Ecclesiastes 3:11). All that he creates is good, exists for his glory, and bears the mark of his creativity (Psalm 19:1-4). God *is*.

Nowhere is his glory more fully evidenced than in the creation of humanity— male and female. Not the product of an impossible evolutionary spiral or the mere assemblage of the dust of the stars, male and female are special creatures who possess a unique dignity (Genesis 1–3; Psalms 8:1-9; 139:13-16). Created in the image of God and bestowed with a special assignment to rule over the earth (Genesis 1:26-28), humankind has the privilege of having a self-conscious connection to and relationship with the Creator (Genesis 3:8-9; Malachi 2:13-16). As a result, we celebrate with David the dignity that is inherent to humanity, the awesome nature of God's creative power, and the importance of the role he plays in new beginnings (Psalm 139:13-16).

Christian counselors also affirm with the writer of Hebrews that those who would come to God must believe that he is and that he rewards those who diligently seek him (11:6). We are humbled by faith wherever we encounter it, and we understand that it is an essential requirement for man's approach to God (Ephesians 2:8-9). Faith is awakened by hearing the Word of God, and that hearing is uniquely connected to the ministry of the Holy Spirit (Romans 10:17). According to Paul, saving faith is the gift of God (Ephesians 2:8-9). God is glorified when we witness the birth of faith in his saving grace and in his authoring of new beginnings. As counselors, we champion and celebrate these new beginnings.

Coming to God is the first step toward healing and toward a dynamic relationship with him. Counselors affirm and speak with encouragement and comfort of God's enthusiasm for connecting with all who seek him (Ephesians 1:1-6). More than that, we affirm that the God revealed in Scripture possesses a dominating passion for maintaining an intimate relationship with his creation (Genesis 3:8-20; Hosea 11:1-9). God so delights in the engagement of his creation that he pursues those distanced from him and invasively intrudes with his inflamed compassion in the effort to seek their return (Hosea 3:1-5).

This ardent motivation is rooted in God's nature as triune and flows from the essence of who God is within himself (John 17:20-26). What a privilege to share with others the essential need for unbroken unity and connectivity that is at the core of God's triune character! This driving passion provides the foundation for understanding God's extended efforts to communicate and connect with fallen men and women. He is a pursuer-God, no matter what our condition may be. This explains God's invasiveness and helps us understand why he searched for Adam, why he covered humanity in its shame, and why in the fullness of time the Son of Man came to seek and to save the lost (Genesis 3:8-9; Luke 19:10). Healing power resides in such a rich view of God's inexhaustible, investing love.

God's compassion, however, does not compromise his holy transcendence. We affirm that while man is on the earth, God is in heaven (Ecclesiastes 5:2). He is a holy and sovereign God, the commandment-giver, the Judge over all creation, the Issuer of consequence—altogether separate from his creation. He possesses all power and blends together the events of our lives in a way that is beautiful and is always done for his glory and our good (Ecclesiastes 3:11; Romans 8:28). He feels no obligation to provide us with an explanation for his action or perceived inaction, and he often leaves us to trust in his faithfulness, mercy, and lovingkindness, which are amply attested to in Scripture.

At times we are forced to suspend our limited reasoning powers and adopt a submissive reverence for his authority that knows its inception in trust and faith (Ecclesiastes 3:14). Like Joseph, we are sometimes able to see God's purpose in the difficult circumstances of our lives and say, "You intended to harm me, but God intended it for good to accomplish what is now being done, the saving of many lives" (Genesis 50:20). More often he moves in ways that are past our knowing. Equipped with the knowledge of God's character and unfailing love, we can affirm on the authority of the Word that he is, in all circumstances, too loving to be unkind and too wise to make a mistake. However, his utilization of men and women in his missioning, and his engagement of us in his purposes, is the cause of both our greatest joy and our greatest pain (2 Corinthians 1:3-7).

Our understanding of the character of God shapes our response to the needs of people as well as the message of hope and deliverance that we bear. We must work to possess a knowledge of God that expels ignorance and tears down lies that have been the source of untold misery. Godly counselors can help establish at the core of human personality an idea of the true God who has demonstrated the power to heal and transform the darkest of human minds for the restoration of body, spirit, and culture. Our greatest joy as counselors is derived from seeding the minds of people with an accurate knowledge of the character of God. Guiness (1977) challenges that

> sometimes when I listen to people who say they have lost their faith, it
> strikes me as less surprising than they suggest. If their view of God is what
> they say, then it is more surprising that they did not reject it much earlier.

Some people have a view of God so fundamentally false that it is a lie.
Their picture is not of God but an idol. (p. 92)

Some client caricatures of God are not just unattractive, they are so ugly as to be scary—ghoulish distortions that make God seem more like a monster than the loving Father that he is. Our theological competence as counselors determines our ability to articulate correctly the character of God to our clients and to establish the significance of his character in meeting people's deepest needs and expanding their hope for ultimate transformation.

ANTHROPOLOGY: THE DIGNITY AND FALLENNESS OF HUMANITY

Is humanity (male and female) created straight from the heart and hand of God, or are we the product of a billion years of evolutionary randomness? Is the nature of man innately good and able to achieve whatever the mind can imagine? Or do evil and the power of sin constantly thwart our attempts to do good and solve our deepest struggles?

The answers to these questions and others like them shape our mission and efforts in the therapeutic encounter (Allen, 1984; Custance, 1975; Hoekema, 1986). Answering questions like these with ideas formed independently of Scripture will lead to a tragic undertreatment of crucial issues at the core of human personality (Hart, 1992; Menninger, 1973; Mowrer, 1960). Scripture is emphatic in its description of the human condition. "We simply cannot come to a biblical understanding of man...if we do not come to grips with the awfulness of man in rebellion, separation and death. We are profoundly fallen" (Allen, 1984, p. 102). All have sinned, and in our union with Adam, we have fallen into the abyss of death, which opened as a consequence of his choice (Romans 3:23; 6:23).

We have previously spoken of male and female as image-bearers. Even in fallenness, humanity bears the mark of God's image. According to Allen (1984), "We are in danger of overstating the results of the Fall if we judge that man after the Fall is no longer a creature of dignity bearing the image of God" (p. 104). Hence, we live in a paradoxical state—carrying dual conditions within our single personage that emphasize both the dignity and fallenness of humanity. The redeemed, it should be noted, are twice special: (1) through God's invasive and gracious superintendence in our genesis, and (2) by God's bestowal of supernatural gifts through the Holy Spirit in our re-genesis or new birth (Psalm 139:13-16; 1 Corinthians 12:6-11). Thus, our specialness as humans resides not in what we may do but in who we are, because God who formed us placed his image and his gifts within us.

This is not to diminish the fact that we are equipped by God to do something significant. Humanity is an instrument in his divine hand; God bequeathed to the male and female a marvelous purpose: to multiply, replenish, subdue, have dominion! These words are part of a creation mandate given by the Creator to his beloved team (Genesis 1:26-28). Adam and Eve came to the challenge with their own distinctiveness, prepared by God for an impact requiring their unique contributions. Fulfilling divine mandates always requires a team effort—the parts working in concert, each part bearing its own weight, contributing its distinctive qualities for the accomplishment of the assigned mission (Ecclesiastes 4:9-12; 1 Corinthians 12:1-31). Autonomy and distinctiveness give birth to our significance, but also to reflection on self, position, rights, responsibilities, and freedom of choice.

The Christian counselor must be able to diagnose correctly the theological malady that is at the core of humanity's dilemma. Created upright and empowered with the imagination resident in the divine image at the core of human personality, male and female are free to dwell on what-ifs (Genesis 3:1-6; Ecclesiastes 6:9). However, in the service of autonomy, desire is free to wander, and because of our sinful bent, the tragic result is idolatry, rebellion, and disobedience to divine commandment. Unless we repent and turn, we will become destructive, abandon our postings, and vandalize the very *shalom* of God (Ecclesiastes 10:4). The friend of God becomes his enemy (Romans 5:8).

Vanity, sin unbridled, the parched quest for profit, and the vexing reality of a world encased in death, shatters *shalom*. The whole planet is engulfed in the intermixture of the times, washing antiphonally over its death and brokenness (Ecclesiastes 3:1-13). People seldom understand that the gift of pain is God's loving goad designed to break them loose from the groaning of this life and to pull them toward home (Ecclesiastes 1:13; 3:10; Hosea 2:14-15; Luke 15:17-18).

The Christian counselor has heard the curative prescription from God. The diagnosis offered regarding humanity's potential and fallenness is accurate; the prescription for treatment is a radical and God-provisioned one. Misdiagnosis will only serve to widen the chasm between Creator and created and will prolong the experience with sin and its devastating wages.

Christology: The Uniqueness of Jesus Christ

In the beginning was the Word, and the Word was with God, and the
Word was God…. All things were made by him; and without him was not
any thing made that was made…. The Word was made flesh…(and we
beheld his glory, the glory as of the only begotten of the Father,) full of
grace and truth. (John 1:1,3,14, KJV)

Jesus Christ is central to the resolution of humanity's fallenness (Romans 5:8; Hebrews 1; Erikson, 1991; Yancey, 1995). Eternally preexisting with the Father and Holy Spirit, Jesus Christ is God (Colossians 1:15-19). In Christ's incarnation we have heard from God, for Christ is the ultimate revelation of the self-revealing God. The birth of Jesus Christ bears witness to God's promises realized in our material, real-time universe as a testimony to his faithfulness and his miracle-working power. We know that the Incarnation took place outside of normal means: The Son conceived in the womb of the Virgin Mary was the direct result of the miraculous, life-giving work of the Holy Spirit (Luke 1:34-38).

The birth of Jesus Christ became the template, the firstfruit of the grand paradigm for what God will do again and again in his work of reclaiming those fallen in Adam (John 3:3-8). He will plant life where there was none and will, through the supernatural work of the Spirit, create new beginnings independent of human involvement. It can be sheer joy for the Christian counselor to reflect on and share the implications of the birth of Jesus Christ for new beginnings in the lives of clients.

Jesus is in mission because God refuses to give up or to give over his creation to Satan and his work as destroyer (1 John 3:8). God will work in anything—pain, suffering, beauty, even rebellion—to win the hearts of men and women. We dare not underestimate the cosmic proportions of the spiritual battle that is at the core of Adam's fall and Jesus' death (Ephesians 6:10-17). Jesus came to destroy the works of evil, to be God's Word to Satan as well as God's Word to the fallen sons and daughters of Adam. He is the second Adam; he is fully human and fully God (Romans 5:12-21).

In his humanity, Jesus Christ came as a fellow sojourner, one who would be tempted in all matters as a man and yet remain without sin (Isaiah 53; Luke 4:1-13; Hebrews 4:15). This second Adam gives birth to a new race. In the power of his resurrection, Christ leads a new exodus and brings a new Israel out of the Egypt of this world. He is the Passover Lamb, and his death is the death of the sinless Lamb of God who takes away the sin of the world (Hebrews 9:11-28; 1 John 2:1-2).

He died in our place, taking the wrath of God for our sins (Isaiah 53:1-7). We have redemption and the forgiveness of sin because of his death at Calvary (Ephesians 1:7). God is completely satisfied with the substitutionary blood atonement of his Son, just as he was with the Passover blood in Egypt (1 Corinthians 5:7). The blood of Jesus Christ is the covering on the mercy seat that separates the believing sinner from the condemnation of the law (1 John 2:2). In Christ, God was reconciling the world to himself, not counting men's sins against them but creating a new creation. The old has gone; the new has come (2 Corinthians 5:16-19)!

Faith in Christ's work results in the imputation of a new righteousness: Christ's righteousness becomes ours. As a result, we (in Christ) can now stand before God forgiven and cleansed (Romans 5:12-21). God has made Christ to be for us our righteousness, holiness, and redemption (1 Corinthians 1:30). When we confess our sins, he is faithful to continue the forgiveness first experienced in our conversion (1 John 1:9). Beyond that, he delights in his role as advocate—the atoning sacrifice—for the believing sinner (1 John 2:2).

The cumulative impact of what Jesus Christ does for the believing sinner results in the creation of a new person empowered to taste of life in a new and healthful manner. That person is in union with Jesus Christ.

Union with Christ is really the central issue in the message to be shared with clients. Pink (1971) began his work on union with these words: "The present writer has not the least doubt in his mind that the subject of spiritual union is the most important, the most profound, and yet the most blessed of any that is set forth in the sacred scriptures" (p. 7). This new relationship, rooted in grace, is the free gift of God for all who receive it (Ephesians 2:8-9). We cannot work our way to God, for he has worked his way to us. Grace is the basic theological tenet that is at the core of all Christian ministry, especially counseling (Hindson & Eyrich, 1997; Seamands, 1989).

In the ascension of Christ, Christian counselors find a witness to his ongoing investment in the lives of the redeemed. We can share with clients that Jesus Christ, from his position at the right hand of the Father, is unceasingly praying for his people (Romans 8:34; Hebrews 7:25). In fact,

> [i]n Christ, the eternal Christ, who suffered, rose, ascended, who is seated now at God's right hand supreme over all the forces of the universe: in Christ, in the heavenly sphere wherein He now abides, in the region of spiritual activities, all spiritual blessing is ours: in Christ God has blessed us. (MacArthur & Mack, 1994, p. 130)

Believing clients are encouraged by the knowledge that the One who was tempted in all things, even as they are, ascended to heaven and eternally intercedes for them. Additional encouragement comes from the reality that the ascended One is coming again as Judge and ultimate righter of all wrongs. Our futures are secured by his power; we who are in the second Adam will ultimately enter into the fullness of all God intended for the first Adam (Acts 1:11; 2 Thessalonians 1:4-10). The new heaven and the new earth are the inheritance of all who are in Christ.

What a message of hope to share with anxious, troubled, and fallen people who stream into our offices. In the first Adam we all are dead, but in Christ we are made alive. Hence, we must "argue that Jesus' teachings set the agenda...for He addressed those concerns that are most fundamental to human nature and the development of wholeness within persons" (Weyerhaeuser, 1988, p. 317). Therefore, a central element in our counseling is our witness to the significance of the words and work of Jesus Christ for the client's journey toward wholeness. In giving that witness, we expectantly work to see faith awakened, hope born, and God's love flooding the lives and relationships of persons once cold and dead.

PNEUMATOLOGY: THE POWER AND MINISTRY OF THE HOLY SPIRIT

When Jesus spoke to his disciples about his departure, they were deeply troubled. He comforted them by saying, "I will ask the Father, and He will give you another Helper, that He may be with you forever; that is the Spirit of truth, whom the world cannot receive, because it does not see Him or know Him, but you know Him because He abides with you and will be in you" (John 14:16-17, NASB).

MacArthur and Mack (1994) explain that

the word *helper* in verse 16 is the Greek word *parakletos*, meaning someone called to another's aid. It describes a spiritual attendant whose role is to offer assistance, succor, support, relief, advocacy, and guidance—a divine Counselor whose ministry to believers is to offer the very things that so many people vainly seek in therapy! (p. 134; see also chapter 2 of this book)

This is the same Holy Spirit who hovered above the waters in Genesis and brought order out of chaos (Genesis 1:2). In the Gospels, he entered the tomb where the body of the Lord Jesus lay in death, broke death's bondage, and brought Jesus back from the grip of death (Romans 1:4). He entered the womb of the Virgin Mary and, without human agency, quickened the egg in her womb, giving genesis to the God-man (Luke 1:26-38).

Our conceptualization of the resources available for empowering change in people's lives is dramatically impacted by our understanding of the Holy Spirit's power to transform (Carson, 1987; Pache, 1954; Williams, 1994). We enjoy and depend upon the presence of our empowered ally. While we may work with those who don't know God or are estranged from him, the Holy Spirit is always at work to win their hearts—convicting them of what is right and wrong and of a coming judgment (John 16:5-15). When we are working with members of the covenant community, he is the One who, from his position as indweller, empowers people for radical change. Humbled in a partnership with the divine, we must seek always to be in step with the Spirit—to not lag behind or rush ahead of him. When we work in harmony with the Spirit, we frequently witness the miracle of regeneration and subsequent transformation.

As we counsel, speaking to the hearts of broken men and women, we view all who are in Adam as prisoners of death (Ephesians 2:1-3). We believe that people come to life only through the quickening process of the new birth. The Holy Spirit alone can make one alive, implant faith in unbelieving hearts, enable the embrace of the gospel, call to the Savior, and seal us to God forever. In performing these acts, the Holy Spirit lays the foundation for the future, for the complete transformation of the people in whom we are seeking to encourage growth (2 Corinthians 3:16-18).

The Holy Spirit is just beginning his work when he invades us for the purpose of regenerating and indwelling. He comes also to equip us for ministry. He accomplishes this through the imparting of gifts as he determines (1 Corinthians 12:11). Ministering out of these gifts is a cause of great joy for Christ's disciples, creates impact for the church in mission, and brings glory to God in his church.

The indwelling and equipping are accompanied by empowerment for ministry, spiritual warfare, and fruit bearing. This work of the Spirit empowers the believer and provides opportunity to foster loving relationships in the community of faith. The work of the Spirit occurs against the adversarial demands of the world, the flesh, and the devil. The process that follows regeneration and brings defeat to these anti-God forces is the process of sanctification.

Sanctification follows regeneration and is the process by which the Holy Spirit progressively conforms the regenerated person into the likeness of Christ (Romans 8:29; 12:1-2). It is the process by which the Spirit produces personal holiness within our hearts and lives. A major agency in sanctification is the Word of God. Jesus said to the Father, "Sanctify them by the truth; your word is truth" (John 17:17).

Paul commanded the Colossian believers to make certain that "the word of Christ dwell[s] in you richly" (Colossians 3:16). When we allow the Word to dwell in us richly, Colossians 3 assures us, our lives will result in singing, thankfulness, and submission. In Paul's letter to the Ephesians, we see the same results from obedience to the command to be filled with the Spirit (Ephesians 5:18–6:9). The Word of God is the primary catalyst assuring that the Spirit of God is working to further the processes related to sanctification. Sadly, we, though regenerated, can limit the Spirit's work through the choices we make. One example is when we speak corrupting words, which grieves the Holy Spirit and hinders his sanctifying work in believers' lives (Ephesians 4:29-30).

The Holy Spirit, through regeneration and sanctification, produces spiritual and behavioral changes in people. How humbling to be allied with the One who has the power to produce such radical change in the lives of people! The Holy Spirit's work magnifies the influence of our efforts beyond the normal and puts us in step with the desires and purposes of God.

ECCLESIOLOGY: THE ROLE OF THE CHURCH

Transformation as a process is hindered or fostered within the structures and resources provided by community. Transformation is a family process. In regeneration, we are connected not only to Jesus but also to his body—our new family, the church (1 Corinthians 12:13). "Fundamentally, the church of Jesus Christ is neither a building nor an organization. Rather, it is a people, a special people, a people who see themselves as standing in relationship to the God who saves them and to each other as those who share in this salvation. Stated theologically, the church is a people in covenant" (Grenz, 1994, p. 605).

The church is also a separated community. The people of God are carved out from humanity, living as God's treasure. God's redemptive acts in history, which parallel and portend our own redemption and deliverance, fill us with hope and form the core of our new identity (Deuteronomy 6:20-25; 7:17-26).

This identity is further shaped within the context of intimate community (John 17:6-19). In the covenant community people are cared for, encouraged, exhorted, and supported for growth in spite of their failures (Hebrews 10:24-25). For many people, this is the first experience with grace-based relationships (Ephesians 4:17-32). Within a community committed to acceptance, education, and appropriate discipline and consequences for conduct unbecoming a disciple of Jesus Christ (often administered by God himself), people are brought to maturity.

The spiritual reparenting required is often best accomplished through cell groups that assemble for the purpose of Bible study, encouragement, exhortation, worship, and the practice of a series of spiritual disciplines within a circle of accountability (Foster, 1988; Willard, 1998). In keeping with our giftedness, no member of the believing community is excused from involvement with these groups or the means of personal spiritual growth they seek to establish (Ephesians 4:14-16).

The reparenting ministry that is at the heart of discipleship is the work of the entire church. Central to the life of the covenant community is a commitment to challenge and call forth holy change. This involves a call to repentance and an openheartedness that accompanies confession and repentance for wrongs committed (2 Corinthians 6:11–7:16).

Reparenting fallen sinners, who have inherited sin patterns from the Adamic connection and from sinful family systems, is difficult work. It requires a community focused on establishing in its members behaviors that imitate the standards established in the second Adam. It requires submission to and partnership with caring members of the body of Christ who speak lovingly but truthfully to sin issues while jealously guarding the flame ignited in salvation (Ephesians 4:20-32). These guardians of the flame are an open-hearted, transparent, and prayerful group who are dominated by a vision for the restoration and maturity of the one-time offender (Isaiah 42:3; Luke 17:4; Galatians 6:1).

As a result, various approaches must be employed with different members of the body. "The entire process of helping needs to be adapted to the status and needs of the client" (Egan, 1998, p. 62). The unruly need to be confronted and rebuked. They have made an idol of their own opinions. The timid (the "little of soul"), like Timothy, need to be comforted. It is inappropriate to begin by rebuking Timothys for timidity and fear; they first require words of encouragement. The weak require a commitment of God's family to support them through the myriad challenges related to overcoming a life-dominating sin. All of these kinds of people will require large doses of patience from fellow members of the body (1 Thessalonians 5:14).

Having heard God's marching orders given in the Great Commission (Matthew 28:19-20), we understand, perhaps better than many in the present-day church, that the army is hurting. "People today are much more wounded. They suffer from relationship wounds (consider the high percentage of marriages that end in divorce); emotional wounds (broken, dysfunctional families leave long trails); the wounds of abuse (sexual abuse alone has been perpetrated upon one quarter of all female baby boomers); the wounds of drug and alcohol addiction; and so much more" (Murren, 1991, p. 220). The church must awaken to the care of the family and to a renewed focus on discipleship that meets the needs of people where they really are and not where we would like them to be.

ESCHATOLOGY: A SECURED FUTURE

As Jesus taught in John 14:1-6, much of counseling is helping people see and live beyond their circumstances, which is a top-down perspective. Who doesn't wish for a better tomorrow? Frankl (1984) learned the stark reality of this truth in a Nazi concentration camp:

> The prisoner who had lost faith in the future—his future—was doomed.
> With his loss of belief in the future, he also lost his spiritual hold; he let
> himself decline and became subject to mental and physical decay. Usually
> this happened quite suddenly, in the form of a crisis, the symptoms of
> which were familiar to the experienced camp inmate. We all feared this
> moment—not for ourselves, which would have been pointless, but for our
> friends. Usually it began with the prisoner refusing one morning to get
> dressed and wash or to go out on the parade grounds. No entreaties, no
> blows, no threats had any effect. He just lay there, hardly moving. If this

crisis was brought about by an illness, he refused to be taken to the sickbay or to do anything to help himself. He simply gave up. There he remained, lying in his own excreta, and nothing bothered him anymore. (p. 83)

Grasping the idea of a certain future secured for us through the finished work of Jesus Christ removes the fear and anxiety, rooted in uncertainties, regarding our tomorrows. "All predicates of Christ not only say who he was and is, but imply statements as to who he will be and what is to be expected from him. They all say: 'He is our hope' (Colossians 1:27). Hope's statements of promise anticipate the future. In the promises, the hidden future already announces itself and exerts influence on the present through the hope it awakens" (Moltmann, 1993, p. 18). Hope allows the present to be filled with the *shalom* that God provides for those who are at rest in his sovereignty, promises, and faithfulness.

Hebrews 11 is commonly called the "faith hall of fame" chapter in the Bible. It contains the records of the lives and actions of people of faith. Each one was able, by faith, to reach into a yet unrealized future and live as if God's promises were present experience. "They did not receive the things promised; they only saw them and welcomed them from a distance" (Hebrews 11:13). This pulling of a promised future into the present transformed the way in which these people experienced the circumstances of their lives.

Paul referenced this transformation when he said, "Brothers, we do not want you to be ignorant about those who fall asleep, or to grieve like the rest of men, who have no hope" (1 Thessalonians 4:13). It is understood that believers who lose loved ones will experience grief, but they will not experience it like their unconverted peers. Hope promises a trumpet in the future and a returning Jesus who will unite all who are in him for a joyous experience of eternity in his presence. This future reality transforms the believer's experience of something as painful as death.

Jesus, because of the joy he clearly saw in his future, was able to endure the cross (Hebrews 12:1-2). Jesus understood the need of his disciples for a future. He promised them that where he was going, he would one day take them (John 14:1-4). He promised them a future. Jonathan understood David's need for a future and said to him, "You will be king over Israel.... Even my father Saul knows this" (1 Samuel 23:16-17). Paul told the Corinthians that when the earthly tent (body) they presently occupied collapsed, they had a building of permanence in heaven prepared for them by God (2 Corinthians 5:1-8).

Finding meaning in this life is not a luxury. We might say that meaning is a kind of spiritual oxygen that enables our souls to live. It involves a "going beyond"—a transcendence of whatever state we are in toward that which completes it. The meaning of present events in human life is largely a matter of what comes later. Thus, anything that "has no future" is meaningless in the human order. That is why we try to avoid it as much as possible. It stifles us. (Willard, 1998, p. 386)

The power of a secured future for healing and wholeness in the present is the heart of our message (1 Corinthians 15). Members of the family, the church of Jesus Christ, born and changed through the ministry of the Spirit, have a future—an eternal future. When we are able to help clients grasp that future, they gain a platform for assurance and stability that impacts every area of their intra- and interpersonal worlds.

INSTRUMENTS OF HEALING

What an awesome God we serve! As Christian counselors positioned for powerful healing ministries in the church and in the culture, we find ourselves cooperating with the Holy Spirit as he works in the lives of the unregenerate, convicting and convincing them of the truth. Challenged to see every person perfect in Christ, we become conduits through which the Spirit leads people from death to regeneration to maturity in Christ. We have the joyful opportunity to connect people to church communities where the power of healing relationships brings freedom from habitual, hurtful relational patterns.

In your counseling, don't neglect, stifle, or taint the work of God. Working in harmony with him, we have the privilege of engaging people in relationship with the Word of God and with the spiritual disciplines that will enrich their experience of God's *shalom*.

CHAPTER 5

ROOTS OF SPIRITUALITY

Spiritual Formation in Scripture, the Church, and Counseling

EDWARD HINDSON, GEORGE OHLSCHLAGER, AND TIM CLINTON

That there is a crying need for the recovery of the devotional life cannot be denied. If anything characterizes [life in the modern church], it is the absence of spiritual discipline.... Yet such disciplines form the core of the life of devotion. It is not an exaggeration to state that this is the lost dimension in modern Protestantism.

—DONALD BLOESCH, *The Crisis of Piety*

Tim: *The room at Duke University Medical Center was charged with high emotion. It was the night before what physicians call the "new birth," my father-in-law's near-experimental treatment of stem cell infusion (his own cells) to halt the advancing bone-marrow cancer that was killing him. A mixture of anticipation, anxiety, confusion, occasional nervous laughter, and hope were all present as we discussed and considered the next day. Finally we stopped and prayed, asking God for peace and an abiding sense of his presence in our midst.*

Immediately the Spirit of God came upon us all, filling the room and calming us, offering joy, hope, and relief. In that moment we all looked at one another in wonder—it was clear that everyone there knew the presence of God was upon us. The anxiety, confusion, and fear washed out of that room like dirt washed down a drain, and we praised God and gave him thanks for his wonderful love and care shown to us that night.

God cares for us (1 Peter 5:7) and longs to be in relationship with each one of his human creation. He longs to know us and to be known intimately by us. We are the beloved of God. We are God's loving workmanship, for if anyone be in Christ he is a new creation (2 Corinthians 5:17). "While God loves us just the way we are, he loves us too much to leave us that way. Because he loves us he wants to see us 'become like his Son' (Romans 8:29)" (Oliver, Hasz, & Richburg, 1997, p. 17).

Salvation is not the end but the beginning of spiritual life. Conversion is like getting the gift of a strength-building workout machine that we could not afford and had no way of earning. Sanctification comes by using that gift to build one-self up to spiritual maturity. It is like choosing to use that machine every day to grow into the strongest and best-shaped specimen we can be. Just as a workout machine is used to build up the body, the spiritual disciplines are used to build up the soul into spiritual maturity.

Spirituality, then, is a lifelong developmental process, dynamic and life-changing to the core. It is the realization that we were made to know God—not just to know *about* him—and we can't be fully satisfied until we do. There is a voice within the human soul that cries out for more than riches, comfort, power, and pleasure, more that just a limited temporal existence. Augustine, the theologian, called it the "restless heart." Blaise Pascal, the philosopher, called it the "God-shaped vacuum in the human soul."

The apostle Paul said, "The mind controlled by the Spirit is life and peace" (Romans 8:6; see Collins, 1998). That is the fruit we experience when God changes us from the inside out, making us ever more like Christ himself. Reflect on the "fire of love" that God created in the heart of Richard Rolle (1993), one of England's great spiritual leaders in the 1300s:

> I cannot tell you how surprised I was the first time I felt my heart begin to warm [during prayer]. It was real warmth too, not imaginary, and it felt as if it were actually on fire. I was astonished at the way the heat surged up and how this new sensation brought great and unexpected comfort. I had to keep feeling my breast to make sure there was no physical reason for it. But once I realized that it…was the gift of my Maker, I was absolutely delighted [by how] this spiritual flame fed into my soul. Before the infusion of this comfort, I had never thought that we exiles could possibly have known such warmth, so sweet was the devotion it kindled. It set my soul aglow as if a real fire were burning there.…
>
> But this eternal and overflowing love does not come when I am relax-ing, nor do I feel this spiritual ardor when I am tired out…nor…when I am absorbed with worldly interests or engrossed in never-ending argu-ments. At times like these I catch myself growing cold; cold until once again I put away all things external, and make a real effort to stand in my Savior's presence; only then do I abide in this inner warmth.…
>
> All love which is not God-directed is bad love and makes its possessors bad, too. And this is the reason why those who love worldly splendor with

an evil love catch fire of a different sort and separate themselves even further from the fire of divine love…. Indeed such people become like what they love, for they take their tone from the greed of their day and age…. [They are] blinded by a counterfeit "fire of love" which both devastates virtue and encourages vice in its growth….

As the Bible says, there is nothing worse than the love of money (1 Timothy 6:10), for it means that one's heart is everlastingly bothering about the love of the transitory and not giving itself a chance to acquire devotion. Love for God and love for the world cannot coexist in the same soul; the stronger drives out the weaker. (pp. 160-163)

In the New Testament, the encounter between God's Spirit and the human spirit is a fundamental aspect of the Christian experience (Galatians 5:17; Titus 3:5-6). It is "by the Spirit" that people encounter God and experience this life (Galatians 5:16-26). Living in the Spirit is an area of struggle for believers, but it is also where we meet God personally; it is where God comes alive. Encountering the living God always changes and transforms us, as God is big on making us anew. We will never be the same.

The term *spiritual* (in the Greek, *pneumatikos*) conveys the idea of belonging to the realm of the Spirit. *The Eerdman's Bible Dictionary* (1987) notes that terms such as *heart, spirit, soul,* and *mind* refer to differing aspects of human existence, life, and consciousness. The inner life of human beings embodies the nature and essence of the Spirit. In the New Testament, the term *spiritual* is almost exclusively a Pauline word. Outside of Paul's letters, it occurs only in 1 Peter 2:5. Paul uses the term three ways: (1) as an *adjective,* a spiritual something, as in "spiritual gifts"; (2) as a *masculine noun,* as in a "spiritual man"; and (3) as a *neutral noun,* as in "things of the Spirit" (see Brown, 1971).

Willard (1988) says that a spiritual life "consists in that range of activities in which people cooperatively interact with God—and with the spiritual order deriving from God's personality and action" (p. 18). John Calvin, the great theologian, referred to the Holy Spirit as the "inward teacher" *(interior magister)* who speaks to our hearts. Calvin (1960) wrote, "But we must bring a ready teachableness; we must listen hard and pay attention if we want to progress in the school of God. Most of all, we need patience until the Spirit makes plain what we seemed to have often read or heard in vain" (p. 88).

The New Testament emphasizes that the true Christian life is a life in the Spirit (Romans 8:5-6). We are challenged to "live by the Spirit" (Galatians 5:16); to "be filled with the Spirit" (Ephesians 5:18); to produce the "fruit of the Spirit"

(Galatians 5:22); to "keep in step with the Spirit" (Galatians 5:25); and to exercise the "gifts" of the Spirit (Romans 12:6; 1 Corinthians 12:1). Biblical Christianity is a spiritual journey with Jesus Christ led by the Holy Spirit.

Over a century ago the Scottish pastor Robert Candlish (1879) wrote, "For some, their life is not a walk with God, but a brief tumultuous rush of excitement, ending soon in vacancy, or something worse" (p. 105). Whenever we fail to develop spiritually, our inner life suffers. Instead of listening to God and walking with God, we lose almost all sense of God's presence in our lives; our hearts become deadened and God's voice is barely audible to our souls.

REDISCOVERING SPIRITUAL LIFE

Willard (1988) emphasized the importance of spiritual disciplines as the tools of grace. He separated them into two categories: (1) *disciplines of abstinence* (solitude, fasting, frugality, sacrifice, abstinence) and (2) *disciplines of engagement* (study, worship, prayer, service, fellowship) (p. 158). In his classic work *Celebration of Discipline,* Richard Foster emphasized spiritual disciplines as a means of spiritual growth into Christlikeness. Reflecting his Quaker background, Foster (1998) separated those disciplines into three categories: (1) *inward disciplines* (meditation, prayer, fasting), (2) *outward disciplines* (simplicity, solitude, service), and (3) *corporate disciplines* (confession, worship, celebration).

Tan and Gregg (1997) pointed out the importance of spiritual disciplines as "power connectors" to the presence and power of the Holy Spirit, who enables us to grow spiritually. Like Foster, they suggested three groups of spiritual disciplines but with a slightly different way of categorizing them: (1) *solitude,* drawing near to God in solitude, listening, prayer, study, and meditation; (2) *surrender,* yielding to God in repentance, submission, fasting, and worship; and (3) *service,* reaching out to others in fellowship, simplicity, service, and witness.

However we categorize the spiritual disciplines, they all refer to practices or activities that facilitate spiritual growth and maturity in Christ. Tan especially emphasizes the need for Christian counselors to live by these disciplines in their own personal lives and to apply them in their professional counseling sessions where proper ethical consent from the client has been given. Tan (1998) writes: "The disciplines enable us to access the presence and power of the Holy Spirit, whose ministry as the Divine Counselor or Helper is crucial in effective Christian counseling" (p. 20).

Christian psychologist Larry Crabb has also called for the church to take a more active role in shepherding God's people. He emphasizes that the core issues behind most emotional problems are, in fact, spiritual. Crabb (2001) argues for "a way that leads to a joy-filled encounter with Christ, to a life-arousing community with others, and to a powerful transformation of our interior worlds that makes us more like Jesus" (p. 198). However, he warns that too many Christian counselors bypass true spirituality in their haste to solve problems that make people uncomfortable, even when God may use that discomfort to draw them to himself: "Counselors who value technique above conviction and theory above character will not adequately shepherd their clients" (Crabb, 1998, p. 15).

Although we recognize that some Christian counselors will not agree that shepherding is a valid counseling role, we would encourage explicit incorporation of shepherding roles into competent Christian counseling since this is a central metaphor in Christ's description of his care and comfort for those he loved.

Similarly, Christian psychologist Mark McMinn (1996) writes, "Unlike competence in psychology and theology, understanding spirituality does not lend itself to credentials.… Spiritual training is experiential and often private. It is rarely found in the classroom or represented by graduate degrees, but it is found in private hours of prayer and devotional reflection" (p. 11).

McMinn goes on to point out that no matter how disciplined we become, we never can be fully spiritually competent. "Christian doctrine teaches that we are spiritually incompetent, in need of a Redeemer. The spiritual life directs us away from illusions of competence and causes us to confront our utter helplessness and dependence on our gracious God" (pp. 11-12).

The challenge of balancing Christian theology, psychology, and spirituality is what stretches the mind and heart of the Christian counselor. Without a biblical theology, McMinn suggests, we can easily drift into a world of narcissistic spiritualism that focuses on our search for God without recognizing his search for us. We can easily find ourselves asking, "What's in it for me?" instead of asking, "How can I find God?"

LOST GOD, LOST SOULS

Apologist Francis Schaeffer (1968) warned Christian thinkers to be careful not to say the same thing about life and reality that unbelievers are saying, only with Christian words and phrases. The Scriptures alone tell us the truth about God and ourselves. From the Bible we understand that we have been created in God's image. "That fact that man has fallen," wrote Schaeffer, "does not mean that he has ceased to bear God's image" (p. 88). We have become neither machine nor animal.

As we noted in the last chapter, the marks of our divinely created humanity are still with us: love, creativity, rationality, our wonder at beauty, the longing for significance, our fear of nonbeing, the desire for relationships, and the ability to understand eternity and infinity. Even if sin renders us unable to be perfect or to fully achieve satisfaction in these things, all of these invisible-yet-powerful traits of the God image remind us that we are personal beings. We are people with hearts and souls that long for God.

The greatest tragedy of postmodern society is its loss of transcendence. Without God, our lives tend to become a jumble of activities designed to deaden the pain of our hearts. Our inner being cries out for God, but we silence the cry with our busy pursuit of material gratification. Only at the end of the pursuit do we finally ask what is still missing.

According to Moore (1992), "The greatest malady of the twentieth century [was] its loss of soul. When the soul is neglected, we experience obsessions, addictions, violence, loss of meaning, and emotional pain" (p. xi). No one has made a better assessment of the last century. As our society has become more complex and technological, it has also become more superficial. The emptiness of our times is revealed in a spiritual vacuum that cries out to be filled by the divine. We are no longer a predominantly Christian society. The heart and soul of the Western world have been polluted by the secular pursuit of life without God.

Colson (1989) referred to our spiritual darkness as "the New Dark Ages." The barbarians of spiritual neglect are again threatening the soul of society, and we may not be able to withstand the assault. Without a solid spiritual foundation, society quickly turns to selfism, relativism, and materialism. But such indulgence always leaves us empty and wondering if there's anything more to life than what we've experienced. Ironically, excessive materialism almost always leads to mysticism. Society is never content without belief in some supernatural power.

REVIVING THE SOUL

"Most Christians have lost the life of their heart, and with it, their romance with God," wrote Curtis and Eldredge (1997, p. 10). No one escapes periods of living in a spiritual desert. None of us can avoid times where we are merely going through the motions religiously. "These people say they are mine. They honor me with their lips, but their hearts are far away" (Isaiah 29:13, NLT).

We normally start the journey well, excited about the discovery that God is truly on our side. But somewhere along the way we become bogged down by the mundane and overwrought by the cares of life. Consumed by the tyranny of the urgent, we lose sight of our ultimate destination. When that happens in our lives as believers, it robs us of the joy of the journey. In some cases we almost forget that we are on a spiritual journey.

God has many ways of calling us back to himself.

- *God is silent.* Sometimes God is silent, but he never intends that he not be heard. In every relationship, remember that you cannot *not* communicate. Silence always sends a message that God wants us to learn from. After Abraham and Sarah put reason above revelation in the matter of having a child, God apparently did not speak to them again for thirteen years (see Genesis 16:16; 17:1). Silence from God is often a challenge to build and grow one's faith in him. Faith and trust are not engaged when we are always in contact with someone; it must be exercised when our beloved is distant. It is then that we are challenged to trust that he or she will be faithful and return to us in love. So it is with God. Besides, when we haven't heard from God in a long time, we are more likely to listen when he does speak.

- *God whispers.* Sometimes God speaks to us in whispers. Elijah was in deep depression, hiding in a cave and fearing for his life, when he heard the voice of God's "gentle whisper" (1 Kings 19:12). Many times when God whispers to us, he wants us to slow down, quiet down, bow down. He desires that we be still and listen for him amid all the noise and clutter of our lives. A whispering God also challenges us as to our first love. If we love God above all else, we will pursue him and learn to separate his voice from all the other noise in our lives because love desires to be in touch with one's beloved.

- *God shouts.* Sometimes God shouts at us through our physical and emotional pain, our human failures, and our personal and financial crises. In our times of greatest need, we are more likely to hear his voice correcting us, consoling us, and reminding us that we are his. Sometimes he speaks loudly and repeatedly; sometimes he speaks through people and situations. While many of us would like to hear God speak loud and clear, it is rare that God does so. In fact, it seems that he does so most often when we are too thickheaded or dead-hearted to get it by other means. God's shouting is often an indication of our ignorance of him, of our lack of tuning in to his still, small voice, of our overattachment to the things of the world, or of our own spiritual immaturity.

Feeling alone and isolated during a difficult time will break us of self-sufficiency. It drives us to the only One who truly loves us. Jesus himself experienced feelings of being alone and isolated. His rejection, arrest, trial, and crucifixion would test the limits of his humanity. His disciples, too, would suffer isolation, persecution, and even death in his absence. But Jesus offered them the wonderful gift of his comfort. He promised to send the Holy Spirit as their counselor (*parakleton* [see

John 16:5-15]). He assured us that our own personal spiritual Counselor would keep our relationship with God vital and real every day.

Collins (1998) writes that "Life is a spiritual journey. It is part of the human condition to be restless, aware that something or someone greater than we exists" (p. 1). Collins observes that, in light of this restless search, there is a new spiritual awakening today unprecedented in modern times. "It is an unconventional and revolutionary movement," he suggests, "that is changing psychiatry, education, health care and thousands of churches" (p. 5).

Resurrecting Modern Soul Care

Christian soul care is a journey of healing, sustaining, reconciling, and guiding. It includes both the care and cure of the soul. As such, Christian soul care makes abundantly clear that the care of souls is a Christian activity that expresses the love of God to the needs of the human soul.

The term for "soul" in the Greek New Testament—*psyche,* which is translated from the Hebrew word *nephesh*—was used 101 times and referred to one's inner life, the self, the living personality. Furthermore, since the Hebrew and Middle Eastern mind emphasized the essential unity or wholeness of the person, the term is used interchangeably with "spirit" (*pneuma,* or *ruah* in Hebrew), "heart" (*kardia,* or *leb* in Hebrew), and "mind" (*nous* in the Greek). The biblical soul is the undifferentiated, immaterial life force that was created by God to be in relationship with him and, if redeemed, will live in eternity with him (Genesis 2:7; Deuteronomy 13:3; 1 Peter 1:22).

Beginning with Hume and the rise of modern science, and continuing through Kant and the rise of modern philosophy, the concept of the soul as an invisible religious reality began to fade. Logical positivism and the rise of modern American psychology effectively killed it. In James's (1890) treatise on *The Principles of Psychology,* where this newly forming discipline was conceived as a natural science, the soul concept was criticized for having no empirical access. Watson's (1924) behavioristic obsession with observable behavior and the rise of twentieth-century empiricism put the nails in the coffin of soul understanding and soul care, a situation that held fairly firm until the 1990s.

Johnson (1998) notes four major objections and four good reasons to acknowledge and study the soul. The objections are that (1) acknowledging the soul furthers the confusion around mind-brain study by introducing another term synonymous with mind or brain processes; (2) there is no verified evidence for the existence of the soul, an argument that merely reveals the limits of reductionistic naturalism; (3) soul creates another confusing dualism due to the question of whether there is some substance to the soul and, if there is, how it all works together; and (4) the concept of soul still carries with it that moral-religious baggage that scientists don't address and often don't like to deal with.

Johnson (1998) gives the following reasons for resurrecting the soul and considering its care. The idea of the soul

- is thoroughly biblical, and therefore, its existence is authoritatively established;
- is an excellent term (no other good term exists) for representing the entirety of the inner life—"emotions, desires, motives, the unconscious, memories, strategies, intentions, dispositions, thoughts, plans, and beliefs, as well as such processes as reasoning, perceiving, attending, organizing, choosing, communicating, obeying, believing, rejoicing, and so on" (p. 23);
- is heuristic, helping us make clearer sense of the conceptual dualism of body and soul. The soul understood this way helps us clarify and conceptualize other dualistic descriptors such as mind and brain, subjective and objective, inner dynamics and observed behavior, as well as the varied and complex ways that the two realities of body and soul interact and influence each other;
- implies—in its moral-religious connotation—that humans are always in some kind of orientation toward God.

Johnson goes on to assert some excellent reasons for reintroducing and referencing the soul in our modern discourse on counseling, including how it reasserts the lordship of Christ over psychology and over every arena of life:

> Turning away from the soul in modern Western thought was a discursive symptom of a more pervasive historical dynamic: the movement of Western culture away from Christ's Lordship.... The demise of the soul provides a powerful analogy of what has happened to the whole field of psychology. The soul in psychology was removed and poorer, secular substitutes have been put in its place as the focus of the discipline.... Through post-structural lenses, one can discern in this linguistic coercion a transfer of cultural power from the supernaturalists to the naturalists.... An anti-supernaturalistic dynamic has...been at work....
>
> The term *psychology* has a history that is rooted in the Christian tradition. Christians have engaged in the study (and treatment) of the soul for centuries...[the] soul is a useful term that could profitably be re-enlisted to inform a contemporary Christian psychology (and psychology in general). (p. 24)

THE EXPERIENTIAL SOUL: VISIONING GOD AND DISCERNING HIS VOICE

The soul is the living bridge between the material and the spiritual realms of living. It is the arena in which God is encountered and desired. Augustine called spirituality a "holy longing." Curtis and Eldredge (1997) call it a "sacred romance." They write,

> This longing is the most powerful part of any human personality. It fuels
> our search for meaning, for wholeness, for a sense of being truly alive.
> However we may describe this deep desire, it is the most important thing
> about us, our heart of hearts, the passion of our lives. And the voice that
> calls us in this place is none other than the voice of God. (p. 7)

Humanity was created by God for fellowship with him. We are never fully satisfied without him, and something deep within the human heart knows this to be true: In the depth of human agony and personal crisis, even the most irreligious will cry out, "Oh, God!" We know intuitively that he is there (see Romans 1:19-22). His voice is calling to us from every sunset, every waterfall, and every newborn baby.

But all too often his voice is silenced by the din of activity that causes us to focus on the creation rather than on the Creator. This worldly focus causes us to lose our otherworldly interests. This level of spiritual experience, which Lewis (1969) called the "self-forgetful place" and Groeschel (1983) called the "illiminative way," is often dismissed by Christians who have not known God with such intimacy or intensity. Haynes (1998) warns that

> Christian clinicians who do not yet relate to concepts that aid souls more
> advanced than ourselves should be careful not to speak categorically against
> [what] we or others may need to turn to in the future. It could also be
> unfortunate to [misunderstand or stifle these kinds of] spiritual interven-
> tions. (p. 51)

Yet in so much of modern-day living, when God speaks, we silence or distort his voice with outward activity. We go for counseling, join a small group, read a book, or get religious. Curtis and Eldredge (1997) express it, "The voice in our heart dares to speak to us…listen to me—there is something missing in all this.… You were made for something more [and] you know it" (p. 2). It is this "sacred romance"—to know and love God with all our hearts—that calls to us deep within. It is more than God engaging our intellects. It is his passionate appeal to capture our hearts.

The Journey of Faith

Faith is so important that it is mentioned more than three hundred times in the Bible (see Hindson, 1996, pp. 15-22). The first reference to believing God is found in the story of Abraham. Scripture says, "Abram believed the LORD, and he credited it to him as righteousness" (Genesis 15:6). This particular step of faith was so important that it was referred to three times in the New Testament (Romans 4:3,22; Galatians 3:6; James 2:23). Abraham's faith was such that he placed his total well-being, his entire future, and that of his whole clan in the care of an invisible God whom Abraham believed had his best interests at heart.

For Abraham it all began four thousand years ago in a burgeoning metropolis near the Persian Gulf. At the time, he was wealthy, successful, and prosperous. The last thing he needed was to abandon everything and follow God. But God asked Abraham to leave everything that was near and dear to him and go to a land he would show him. Abraham had no idea where it was. All he knew was that God promised to bless him and make him into a great nation.

Abraham said yes to God's call and stepped out in faith on a spiritual journey that would change the course of history. Abraham's God-led journey brought him to a new land that was full of unfriendly strangers, and he experienced a difficult famine, a disastrous trip to Egypt, and problems with relatives. Abraham's spiritual journey was also filled with personal challenges. He lied about his wife, embarrassed himself in front of strangers, and ran ahead of God's timing.

It wasn't until Abraham was ninety-nine years old that God finally clarified his calling in Abraham's life. "I will confirm my covenant between me and you," he explained (Genesis 17:2). God told Abraham he was making an everlasting covenant with him and his descendants through a son to be born to his wife, Sarah. Both Abraham and Sarah laughed at the idea of having a child in their old age, and when the baby was born they named him Isaac ("laughter"). They had laughed at God, but now they were laughing with God. He had kept his promise—the son of the covenant, the forefather of God's people, had been born.

The power of faith rests in the object of our faith, not in the faith itself. At the foundation of all love is a belief in the object that is loved. If you do not believe in a person, you cannot love him. The same is true in our relationship with God. Without faith, it is impossible to know him and love him. Faith is the starting point in our spiritual journey. We must begin with God—believing that he exists, believing that he cares, believing that his love is real.

The journey of faith is not a blind leap into the dark. It is much more than that. It begins with the assurance that God is really there. It moves ahead with great challenges, sometimes with moments of spiritual ecstasy and sometimes with long periods of spiritual drought. But ultimately the journey of faith is a spiritual pilgrimage that diminishes our confidence in earthly things and focuses our hopes on heaven. Every heartache, every disappointment with life, and every human mistake and failure points us to Someone beyond ourselves. Each struggle on the journey reminds us that we need God.

When God calls, we must respond in faith. The difficulty is that so many voices today compete for our spiritual affections. We must identify his voice and decide if we will follow it. We must believe that he is really God, that he is here after all, and that he cares about us individually and personally. Believing is the first step on the journey of faith, which will ignite your soul, stretch your mind, and quicken your heart. If you embark on the right path, you and others will see a winsome spirituality in the growth and development of your redeemed self. Collins (1998) and McDermott (1995) adapted Jonathan Edward's classic *A Treatise Concerning Religious Affections* to show that your life will

- be full of the Holy Spirit, demonstrating spiritual fruit and having a supernatural impact,
- show an attraction to God and his ways for its own sake,
- see and be attracted to the beauty of God's holiness,
- be characterized by a refined level of spiritual discernment, a knowledge of the holy,
- show deep-seated convictions that will empower faith and anchor belief in Christ,
- show a humility that is attractive and approachable,
- exhibit a change in nature and behavior, turning away from bad habits and embracing the good,
- show a Christlikeness that others will notice and be moved by,
- demonstrate an awesome awareness of God's ways and purposes in all of life,
- demonstrate an integrity that will be respected by believers and nonbelievers alike,
- show a hunger for God and a consistent desire to know him more deeply,
- become a model of Christian living and maturity that others will want to imitate.

RECONCILED AT THE CROSS

The primary symbol of the Christian faith is the cross of Jesus, which represents his substitutionary sacrifice (death) for our sins so that we could be reconciled to God (2 Corinthians 5:18). The first step toward reconciliation with God is to admit that our relationship with him has been damaged by our sin. Sin hasn't merely bruised our relationship; it has completely severed it. Worse, sin has placed us in an adversarial relationship with God that can cause us to spend a lifetime justifying ourselves instead of allowing him to repair the relationship.

The broken relationship between us and God is not merely a superficial rift. Were it not for God's grace, it would entail a hopeless standoff. But God took the initiative to correct the problem by sending his Son, Jesus, to take our sin upon himself so that it would no longer be an obstacle between us and God. Grace makes this provision possible, and faith accepts it as a free gift.

"God and sinners reconciled!" wrote Charles Wesley in the eighteenth century. That's the first step in bringing the soul to life, realizing that God is not the enemy. He is the lover of your soul. You were made for him, and without him, you are alone in the dungeon—in the darkness of your inner self. But as Wesley (1680) also wrote in his famous hymn, "And Can It Be":

> Long my imprisoned spirit lay,
>   Fast-bound by sin and nature's night.
> Thine eye diffused a quick'ning ray.
>   I woke, the dungeon flamed with light.
> My chains fells off, my heart was free,
>   I rose, went forth, and followed Thee.

Overcome by God's irresistible passion, faith wells up within our hearts, takes hold of his grace, and surrenders to his love. Light dispels the darkness, and our souls are ablaze with his presence. It is this "first love," as Jesus calls it (Revelation 2:4), that is God's continual desire for us. We first find it when we find him. But we lose it when we lose sight of him in the rituals and routines of the Christian life. And we will only discover it again when we rediscover him, when we grow in intimacy and maturity in Christ. As the title of a book by Arterburn and Felton (2000) states it, we need "more Jesus, less religion."

The picture of Jesus knocking on the door in Revelation 3:20 is often represented as Christ knocking on the door of the unbeliever's heart. But when we look carefully at the context (3:14-22), it becomes clear that he is actually knocking on the door of the church! The church of this passage was in danger of locking the Lord of life out. That's how we lose him: We fill our churches and our Christian lives with everything but Jesus until there's no room in our hearts.

True spirituality is centered in a personal relationship with Jesus Christ. Without him, robust theology deteriorates into human philosophy, intellectual arrogance, and hungry souls. Wilson (1998) described this desertlike condition well:

> Like many sincere evangelicals, my faith life had consisted largely of learn-
> ing denominationally approved definitions of terms *about* God rather than
> learning how to experience increasing intimacy *with* God. Yet all my correct
> theology left me hungering to know God more deeply. (p. 15)

Without personal intimacy with Christ, spirituality becomes little more than a narcissistic quest for a mystical experience. We believe this is characteristic of much of the interest in spirituality among nonbelieving baby boomers. But to really know Jesus is to know life as it was meant to be—a sacred romance with the Lover of your soul.

SPIRITUAL FORMATION IN CHRISTIAN COUNSELING

Now we turn to the practice of spiritual disciplines in Christian counseling. The spiritual disciplines are the "solid food...for the mature" (Hebrews 5:14) who have grown beyond the milk of the basic teaching of the faith. Like nothing else, these essential disciplines should first be alive in the life of the counselor, who then is able to give that life to clients and parishioners seeking help (see 2 Timothy 2:1-2).

A character in Lewis's (1969) *The Screwtape Letters* confesses late in life that he saw he had spent most of his life doing neither what he ought nor what he liked. Instead of coming to the end of our lives with this kind of regret, we can choose today to embrace Christ as never before and learn to live out his virtues in a mean-ingful way. Thomas (1998) says that spiritual formation is the reshaping of the inner man—that is, being formed spiritually from the inside out—transforming from a selfish and carnal existence to a holy and joyful one (see 1 John 3:3; Philip-pians 2:12-13).

Teaching and encouraging clients to learn and practice the spiritual disciplines follows Tan's proposal (1998, 1997) for explicit integration of biblical and spiritual practices into counseling. We agree with Tan (1998) that the spiritual disciplines "should have a central role in Christian counseling" (p. 8). In a Paracentric focus, the spiritual disciplines are consistent with a brief, solution-focused approach, yet we recognize that being transformed by the process of spiritual formation takes time and is a lifelong journey. Much of the work is done in the church—before and after time spent in counseling—or when long-term therapy is elected by the client. Counselors in long-term therapy are able to invest the time necessary to oversee the transformation that takes place as believers mature spiritually.

The incorporation of the spiritual disciplines in counseling is consistent with a proactive, strength-based approach to human change. This view asserts that often the best way to solve personal problems is not to attack the problem but to build positive and generalizing strengths—mature spiritual disciplines—into a person. A key principle of the emerging discipline of positive psychology, this strength-based approach recognizes the generalizing effect such work has on over-all client welfare. Consider, for example, the value of obtaining wisdom from God and how such wisdom prevents and pushes out the besetting problems of living.

> Cry out for insight and understanding. Search for them as you would for lost money or hidden treasure. Then you will understand what it means to fear the LORD, and you will gain knowledge of God. For the LORD grants wisdom! From his mouth come knowledge and understanding. He grants a treasure of good sense to the godly. He is their shield, protecting those who walk with integrity. He guards the paths of justice and protects those who are faithful to him.
>
> Then you will understand what is right, just, and fair, and you will know how to find the right course of action every time. For wisdom will enter your heart, and knowledge will fill you with joy. Wise planning will watch over you. Understanding will keep you safe.
>
> Wisdom will save you from evil people, from those whose speech is corrupt....
>
> Wisdom will save you from the immoral woman, from the flattery of the adulterous woman....
>
> Follow the steps of good men instead, and stay on the paths of the righteous. For only the upright will live in the land, and those who have integrity will remain in it. (Proverbs 2:3-21, NLT)

Competent Christian counselors should be familiar with an array of spiritual formation strategies that can be taught to clients as the means to spiritual maturity and intimacy with God. Moon (1997) refers to the inclusion of spiritual forma-tion in counseling as the practice of "clinical theology." Much of this activity hap-pens in the life of a client as a form of spiritual homework. However, counselors should stress that spiritual formation is not about time with God, as if there were some Twelve Step program to track as a formula for growth. It is about relation-ship, and like any relationship, time spent with another person is only one of the variables that make that relationship beloved or not.

From a broad clinical perspective, spiritual formation work can be seen as (1) a set-aside that one incorporates into one's daily routine as a new activity to learn and grow into, and (2) a stop-and-substitute activity—stopping the well-learned but bad thoughts and habits of the world and replacing them with the positive dis-ciplines of the life of Christ.

Spiritual formation work is the means by which we exchange our old dead life of sin for new life in Christ Jesus. We begin to feed our new nature in Christ and grow up into life abundant as a result, and we simultaneously starve our old nature, refusing to give place to the worry, doubt, fear, confusion, greed, anger, vengeance, and vanity that too often seethe within our souls.

Resources for the Disciplined Life

We will briefly review some key disciplines that are highly valuable for personal sanctification and change. While the literature is now vast on this subject, we rely here primarily on the broad-ranging work of these nine contemporary guides:[1]

1. Foster's contemporary classic *Celebration of Discipline* (1998) and selections from his Renovare program using *Devotional Classics* (Foster & Smith, 1993)
2. Tan and Gregg's treatise *Disciplines of the Holy Spirit* (1997)
3. Moon's *Homesick for Eden* (1997), the story of his transformation from practicing exclusively as a psychologist to becoming a spiritual director for some clients
4. Whitney's concise outline of *Spiritual Disciplines for the Christian Life* (1991)
5. Thomas's work titled *The Glorious Pursuit: Embracing the Virtues of Christ* (1998)
6. Ortberg's *The Life You've Always Wanted* (1997), an analysis of our missed appointment with God's way of living and how to find it and live it
7. McMinn's practice volume on *Psychology, Theology, and Spirituality in Christian Counseling* (1996)
8. Vine's narrative on living the *Spirit Life* (1998)
9. Arterburn and Felton's book *More Jesus, Less Religion* (2000), a polemic on the call to a living faith and the dangers of religious legalism

First, however, we will consider the importance of informed consent and the ethics of introducing and teaching the spiritual disciplines in counseling. We will then review six spiritual disciplines, outlining the first three—worship, prayer, and learning the Bible—more in depth, while briefly noting the final three.

Ethical and Legal Issues

When introducing and teaching the spiritual disciplines in counseling, the Christian counselor becomes more than a counselor. He or she becomes a soul-care artisan, a discipler, a mentor, a spiritual director, and a guide into the deeper way of Christ. He or she is an agent of God, a facilitator of the holy. These roles may be central or peripheral and adjunctive, but they are distinct from what the culture, even the church, often understands counseling to be.

Disclosure and consent become critical ethical tasks when practicing the explicit spiritual counseling that combines professional mental health practice with spiritual guidance. *Disclosure* requires that you provide adequate information to the client about how you do spiritual formation in the counseling process. Some counselors operate within a spiritual framework from the inception of counseling, while others introduce spiritual disciplines during or near the end of brief therapy in which clinical problem solving was the focus. *Consent* entails your client's permission—even an expression of his or her desire—to engage in the work disclosed.

We encourage you to use the disclosure and consent process as an assessment of how ready your client is to grow spiritually. Significant resistance or confusion about spiritual formation may require that you retreat from this approach or spend extra time in psychoeducation to better prepare the client for what you are planning. Spiritual formation can also be seen as part of the support system for maintaining the gains made in treatment over time. We believe that the more such work is stitched into the fabric of counseling, the less likely it is to be viewed as alien or merely appended to the process.

Nonetheless, challenge by the culture and its legal authorities should be anticipated. Some strict constructionists sitting on mental health licensure boards will likely raise questions as to whether spiritual direction is outside the scope of practice of the statutory definitions of psychology, social work, professional counseling, and marriage and family therapy. That is why Christian counseling must be defined—as we plan to do with the mental health practice credential of the newly developing American Board of Christian Counseling—as an adjunct, specialty practice that is appropriately attached to and derived from the core practice as it is legally defined.

McMinn (1996) notes that such practices are unlikely to be reimbursed by third-party vendors, which raises questions about counselors who are tempted to hide spiritual practices under the cover of psychological interventions in order to get paid. However, because managed care providers and other vendors are becoming increasingly results-oriented and sensitive to religious subscribers who demand Christian counselors, we have not found reimbursement to be a major problem for AACC membership who engage in explicit spiritual practices.

Each and every counseling environment provides a unique situation related to using the Word, prayer, and spiritual direction with clients. We should not give specific or inflexible directions in these situations. White (1987) notes that care must always be taken when introducing religious issues into counseling, for if some clients are "confronted too soon, some aspects of the client's faith might be undermined. Even when therapists sense the appropriate moment to deal with a religious issue, they must go gently, at the client's pace" (see Benner, 1987, p. 39). White directs counselors to uncover the issue "when it works naturally into the session but never imposing their own convictions" (p. 39).

Counselors have the responsibility of knowing what is and isn't legally allowed in their particular organizations and circumstances. Christian counselors must live and work with the tension of carefully avoiding "imposing" their own beliefs and value systems on their clients, while at the same time *never* compromising their personal convictions.

The First Discipline: Worshiping in the Spirit

Counselor and client together should come to God with a spirit of expectancy—expecting good things, for God does not give us stones when we ask for bread (Matthew 7:9-11). Worship is the highest human response to God's initiative of love. He beckons us; we worship him. It is *that* simple.

Philippians 3:3 calls us to worship God in the Spirit, which exalts the "splendor of his holiness" (Psalm 29:2). Tan and Gregg (1997) call worship "lovemaking with God" (p. 142). Foster (1998) describes it as "being invaded by the Shekinah of God" (p. 158), surrounded by and filled with his radiant glory that signifies his closeness, his intimate presence. True worship is singing, shouting, dancing, and delighting in his goodness and glory (Psalm 100:2; Colossians 3:16).

Spiritual formation, understood biblically, means to join daily with the Holy Spirit to worship, celebrate, commune, and live in his presence. We do this by inviting him and giving him a place in our lives. We make room for him by confessing our sins, renouncing our dark ways, and asking him to fill us up with himself. Paul died every day (1 Corinthians 15:31), and he wanted to be like Jesus in his death so that by the Holy Spirit he might be made alive in him and grow stronger in him day by day (Philippians 3:10-11).

The Spirit life is to be celebrated with joy and song and laughter and praise. Sing out loud, lift holy hands, shout at points of emphasis, and laugh with delight, knowing God is smiling and laughing with you. Foster (1998) warns against turning the spiritual disciplines into law, the way of death: "When the disciplines are turned into law, they are used to manipulate and control people" (p. 10). In contrast, combining worship and celebration sets us and others free to rejoice in the Lord, to worship in spirit and in truth, and to worship in a way that delights God.

Worship bears wonderful fruit in the lives of those who do it heartily. It is a powerful source of joy and of building up one's faith in and attraction to God. It is an activity that can quickly reap the kind of clinical fruit you want to see in your clients. It infuses hope, strengthens faith, identifies blocks in relationship with God, and even changes a pessimistic orientation to a more optimistic one as worship becomes a more desired and frequent discipline.

We promote worship as both an individual and a corporate activity to be done daily. Individually it can be done as spontaneous praise or added to prayer or personal devotional time, and corporately it can be done whenever there is a time of fellowship with other believers.

Be careful, however, to understand and respect the worship history and style of your client. Form of worship is truly a secondary consideration when worship is robust and joyful, but when it is alien or pro forma behavior, the form of worship can be too primary for some people. Encouraging it as a freewheeling love response can be disconcerting, and it may be resisted.

True worship can also diagnostically identify the blocks a person has in relationship with God. Worship does not happen if one is angry with God, afraid of him, or confused about his character and care. Assessing your clients' ability to enter worship can be a good indicator of issues to address with them at some point during counseling about healing their relationship with their Creator and Divine Lover.

The Second Discipline: Prayer and Interceding with the Spirit

"To be a Christian without prayer," said Martin Luther, "is no more possible than to be alive without breathing" (see Tan & Gregg, 1997, p. 66). We are invited to "approach the throne of grace with confidence, so that we may receive mercy and find grace to help us in our time of need" (Hebrews 4:16). We are called to "pray continually" (1 Thessalonians 5:17); to "pray for each another" (James 5:16); to never give up in prayer (Luke 18:1-8); to model the Lord's Prayer (Matthew 6:7-13); and to keep on asking, seeking, and knocking on heaven's door for every good thing of God (Matthew 7:7-11).

Prayer is a common, though not constant, activity that Christian counselors engage in with clients (Ball & Goodyear, 1993; Moon, Bailey, Kwasny, & Willis, 1993). It is likely the most varied and variable of all the spiritual disciplines in the many ways it is taught and practiced. This will be reflected in this book as we present prayer as a counselor character builder (chapter 8), a discipline to teach clients (herein), an intervention (chapter 10), and a specific and multivariate application (as will be seen throughout most of the following chapters).

Prayer has also been the most researched of the spiritual practices, although much research has yet to be done. Meditative prayer, contemplative prayer, and imaginal prayer have all shown some beneficial effect in counseling (Carlson,

Bacaseta, & Simatona, 1988; Driskill, 1989). Carlson et al. (1988) showed that prayer and meditation on Scripture helped reduce anxiety better than progressive relaxation training or no treatment. Propst (1980) showed that imagery in prayer, especially imagining Christ being close and going into a difficult situation with the client, helped reduce depressive symptoms.

McMinn (1996) frames the issue rightly by stating that whether we should pray with clients is the wrong question. "Instead we ought to ask, 'Which forms of prayer should we use with which clients under which circumstances?' " (p. 65). Prayer should be tailored as much as possible to each client's particular issues and history, including his or her own history of behavior and acceptance of prayer. Prayer always reinforces the reality that Christian counseling is an exercise involving the invisible-but-always-present person of the Holy Spirit. That awareness always changes things in counseling, and it is important that you are able to discern client strengths and weaknesses in this realm.

Make a practice of praying before sessions and silently during sessions. Ask the Holy Spirit to give you discernment, insight, and direction as you seek to help clients—and be open to communicating to your client words of wisdom you may receive from God during prayer. Stay flexible and make a practice of allowing each session to dictate whether you pray with the client. There are times when the client will ask you to pray; at other times you may ask the client if he or she would like to pray. Sometimes you may end the session with prayer, and at other times not. Rather than holding to an inflexible prayer policy, you need to tailor your practice to each client on a case-by-case, session-by-session basis in light of the issues and ethics that are most prominent.

How and when to fit prayer into the counseling session poses another challenge for Christian counselors. Because of limited research (McMinn, 1996), counselors are left to their individual discretion regarding this issue. When clients ask you to pray with them, you must assess whether you believe it is in their best interest. Most times it clearly is; at other times, such requests are made to deflect issues and detour the work at hand.

THE THIRD DISCIPLINE: BIBLE STUDY AND MEDITATION IN THE SPIRIT

When the devil tempted the famished Christ to turn stones into bread, Jesus answered that "Man does not live on bread alone, but on every word that comes from the mouth of God" (Matthew 4:4). Many evangelicals would argue that the first and foremost discipline—the one from which all others issue—is the study and application of the Holy Scriptures in our lives. If the oft-held notion that the

Bible is one of the least-read books by those who confess to be Christian is true, then it is certainly true among the ranks of those who come seeking help for serious problems in living.

We could even hypothesize an inverse relationship between problem suffering and the degree of investment in and knowledge of the Scriptures. We do not believe that immersion in Scripture causes an avoidance of tragedy and suffering; rather, the person steeped in God's Word is better prepared to manage the suffering of life without being overwhelmed by it (Psalm 119). The very process of developing a discipline of Bible reading and devotion has a consistent, life-changing effect in our witness. For it is true, as the psalmist asserted, that "Your statutes are my delight; they are my counselors" (Psalm 119:24).

Reading and hearing the Word. This simplest of tasks is often the least disciplined one in the lives of believers. Yet Jesus asserted that those who hear and obey the Word of God are blessed (Luke 11:28). We encourage developing the discipline of hearing the Word by daily reading the Scriptures aloud (let your ears hear the words of your mouth) or by listening to recordings of Scripture. When God's Word is heard as well as read, it takes deeper root in the mind and is easier to recall when it is needed throughout the day.

Studying the Word. So many good study Bibles are currently available that the biggest problem one may face is which one to use! We have an obvious bias toward *The Soul Care Bible* (2001). This, we believe, will become a preferred study resource for counselors and clients because we have embedded into the Scriptures more than a hundred of life's most common problem issues and what to do about them. We also encourage the method of inductive Bible study by anyone who is serious about studying and applying the principles of godly living (2 Timothy 2:15).

Memorizing the Word. It seems that memorizing Scripture is becoming a lost art in the modern world. But for counselors and pastors, it is a source of significant ministerial power and a natural extension to disciplined study and meditation on the Word. Psalm 119:11 speaks of hiding the Word in the heart and of the effect this practice has against sinful living. Counselors who report on client memorization and meditation often tell of how such discipline generalizes to better time management, greater peace and contentment, quicker recovery from past hurts, and better general mental and memory function.

Meditating on the Word. Meditating on the Word goes hand in hand with the disciplines of solitude and simplicity. When Moses commissioned Joshua to lead the Israelites, he instructed him to "Study this Book of the Law continually. Meditate on it day and night so you may be sure to obey all that is written in it. Only then will you succeed" (Joshua 1:8, NLT). Some of you have memorized and regularly

meditate on the "Jesus prayer" or the AA-based Serenity Prayer and know the blessings that you derive from such practice. Focus on God's promises and select a verse
to think deeply about, to repeat in your mind with different emphases, to pray to
God, to apply to an issue in your life. Imagine how you will live differently by obeying this verse. Sing and praise and give thanks for the verse's promise. Restate and
rewrite it in your own words; journal about it; love God because of it.

Be aware that introducing Scripture always risks triggering disputes about the
Bible's reliability, truthfulness, interpretation, and history. Some clients will want
to study and focus on the Bible as a way to deflect being confronted with their own
failings or contributions to relationship trouble. A well-meaning Christian counselor can be easily detoured by zealous clients who are dedicated to Bible study but
not necessarily to facing the core trouble in their lives.

Therefore, as with prayer, the better policy is not to push a rigid practice that
hauls out the Bible with every client. Take time to learn how clients approach the
Scriptures and track their entry into the Word as much as possible. As circumstances allow, incorporate into your discussions references to Scripture you have
memorized. Communicate biblical principles, injunctions, and stories as an organic
part of your verbal interaction with clients.

THE FOURTH DISCIPLINE: SOLITUDE AND LISTENING TO THE SPIRIT

Since God rarely shouts his message but most often whispers it, it is essential to
become disciplined in the art of solitude—learning to become still so we can hear
what God is whispering to us (Psalm 46:10). Far too often our confusion about
hearing and discerning the voice of God comes not because God mumbles or
doesn't speak clearly or chooses to hide among other voices, but because we haven't
turned down the volume of our daily lives to hear what God is saying. We tend to
demand that God raise his decibel level; he in turn calls us to slow down, be quiet,
and learn to hear his clear-but-soft voice.

THE FIFTH DISCIPLINE: CONFESSION AND REPENTANCE BY THE SPIRIT

The Christian counselor who becomes serious about spiritual formation in the
lives of receptive clients will also get serious about sin. Sin is not a welcome concept in much of the mental health field, but the competent Christian counselor
should be quite comfortable with it (that is, in dealing with sin, not in living in
it!). Yet confession of sin and repentance—turning away from sin and toward new
life in Christ—are central practices in spiritual living.

Christian counselors will, at times, engage clients in the confession of sin.

They will challenge sinful behavior, lament over sin and its consequences, guide repentance, and encourage remorse. They will also seek to understand and root out the many lies, deceptions, justifications, and deflections of sinful behavior and attitudes. Counselors will "get dirty" with the sins and lies of clients and must be able to "wash themselves" daily and protect themselves from the moral infection that sin will seek to lodge in their souls if they don't take proper protective precautions.

THE SIXTH DISCIPLINE: SIMPLICITY, COMMUNITY, AND SERVICE

Give and it shall be given to you. This is a central principle of body life in the church. The disciplines of simplicity, community, and service are more horizontal—more person-centered—than the God-centered disciplines of worship, prayer, and Bible study. Helping clients become other-focused will go far to break patterns of selfish living and self-absorbed obsessions with pain and suffering that seem to go hand in glove with many emotional disorders.

Simplicity helps people prioritize personal values, take power out of greediness and obsessions with money, and create time and space to spend with God and others. *Community* involves living more attached to and in fellowship with the body of believers of which God wants all Christians to be a part. *Service* is also community-centered, doing for others rather than demanding or assuming that others exist to serve us.

In its most basic forms, spirituality is knowing God intimately, becoming like Jesus Christ, and being filled with the Holy Spirit.

CHAPTER 6

BIOLOGICAL ROOTS

Psychiatric Medicine, the Brain, and Drug Treatments

MICHAEL R. LYLES

Medicine is not merely a science but an art. The character of the physician may act more powerfully upon the patient than the drugs employed.
—PHILIPPUS PARACELSUS, A.D. 1525

During the past few years, medical science has changed profoundly. With the announcement of the completed survey of the human genome, medicine, biology, genetics, the neurosciences—all of the human sciences, in fact—were transformed nearly overnight. The difference between twentieth-century medicine and twenty-first-century genome- and proteome-based medicine will be as great as, if not greater than, the difference between medieval and modern medicine. The Human Genome Project, the detailed mapping of the human genetic code, is having and will have as much impact on medicine and the human sciences worldwide as the Manhattan Project, the making of the first atomic bomb, had on physics and international relations in the 1940s.

As we continue our exploration of the foundations of Christian counseling, we now add biology to the critical concerns about human behavior and clinical treatment. Although the Human Genome Project may tempt some to accept the modern thesis that biology is destiny, I as a Christian affirm that biology, while critically important, is *not* destiny. Our ultimate identity, the Scriptures reveal, is in Christ. God can and does work through medicine and healthy living in mighty ways; however, they are just vehicles of treatment that can contribute to our growth and development as persons. They cannot save us, sanctify us, or usher us into the presence of God. That is the work of Christ alone.

The Real Mental Health Care System

Twenty percent of Americans will suffer from a significant mood or anxiety problem during the course of their lifetime (Kessler, McGonagle, & Zhao, 1994). Many more will suffer from psychosis, addiction, and other mental disorders that cause tremendous impairment in all aspects of their lives. Most of these individuals and their families do not understand why they experience these symptoms and they are very alarmed. They struggle in their quest to find answers and solutions that will lead to relief. This search usually involves turning to trusted family members and friends for direction and for appropriate avenues of getting help (Kleinman, 1980). Often they consult with psychiatrists and psychologists only after seeking help elsewhere. In fact, some secular studies estimate that only 20% of those with emotional problems consult a psychiatrist or psychologist first (Regier et al., 1993, p. 21). This number may be even lower in the Christian community, where concerned laypersons, pastors, and pastoral counselors serve as the point of first and most trusted counseling contact (Lyles, 1992).

The role and responsibilities of the Christian counselor in this situation revolve around five duties (Bell, Morris, & Holzer, 1976):

1. The counselor must help the client acknowledge that he has a problem earlier than the client would have realized on his own. As with many traditional medical illnesses, early acknowledgment of emotional struggles by the client often results in a better treatment prognosis. In order to accomplish this, the second duty must be embraced.

2. The counselor must help the client interpret his symptoms and form an explanatory model for why he is ill. This explanatory model may comprise spiritual, physical, and psychological components.

3. The counselor must provide client care at the level consistent with the counselor's gifts and talents. When the client needs a form of help or treatment beyond the counselor's capabilities, the counselor must be prepared to proceed with the fourth duty.

4. If necessary, the counselor should refer the client to someone else, such as a family physician or a psychiatric specialist. This requires that the counselor be familiar with community medical and mental health professionals who would be appropriate for the referral.

5. After referral, the counselor assumes a role of monitoring the care that the client is receiving from a specialist.

Given the many roles that Christian counselors play, it is imperative that we understand the variety of influences that can lead to emotional and behavioral problems. This chapter will focus on the biological variables that can significantly contribute to human behavior.

THE BRAIN: "FEARFULLY AND WONDERFULLY MADE"

Any understanding of the biology of behavior must begin with a consideration of the brain (Lewis & Oeth, 1995). As a physician, I continue to marvel more at the complexity of the brain than I do any other organ in the body. The ability to move begins in the motor area of the brain, and all of our major senses, such as sight and taste, are brain-mediated. The brain also controls basic body drives such as hunger, sleep, and respiration.

This complex electrical organ serves as the control center for other organs in the body. Organs such as the thyroid gland, adrenal glands, testes, and ovaries are directly controlled by the hypothalamus and pituitary areas of the brain. Thus an abnormality in the brain has the potential to translate into a number of physical symptoms in other parts of the body. I tell my patients that a fire in one small area of the brain can produce smoke all over one's body.

ANATOMY OF THE BRAIN

The brain is organized into topographical areas and anatomical lobes that are associated with different functions. The areas in the brain where a "fire" is most likely to produce emotional and behavioral "smoke" are the limbic system, prefrontal cortex, and temporal lobes. The *limbic system* comprises a number of components, including the basal ganglia, the cingulate system, the amygdala, and the hippocampus. It occupies the very center area of the brain at the top of the brainstem—analogous to where the seeds are in an apple. The limbic system is the "CD player of the brain" in that it adds the music (feelings) to the lyrics of our thoughts and behaviors. It has been implicated in a number of psychiatric disorders. The basal ganglia store patterns of learned behavior and our emotional reactions to them. This area of the brain also calibrates our cruising levels of alertness and anxiety. Abnormalities here can result in anxiety and panic disorders.

The cingulate system is involved in shifting attention and focus and in controlling pleasure drives. Aspects of the cingulate system have been implicated in obsessive-compulsive disorder (OCD) and in addiction. The amygdala seems to moderate the volume control on our feelings so that abnormalities here could result in anger and agitation problems as well as loss of control. The hippocampus has become famous in scientific circles due to discoveries showing that new brain cells seem to be generated here and then transported to other areas of the brain.

This is exciting news with great implication for research into new strategies for treating degenerative brain diseases such as Alzheimer's disease. Research has also revealed that disorders affecting the limbic system, such as depression, can hamper the hippocampal formation of new neurons over time. Thus I wonder whether we will someday find that patients with untreated chronic depression will develop brain damage due to the lack of the regenerative functions of the hippocampus.

The *prefrontal cortex* lies at the front of the brain just behind the forehead. It is the "CEO" of the brain, controlling the expression of emotions, impulses, thoughts, and behaviors. It is involved in concentration, critical thinking, and organization. Abnormalities here have been associated with schizophrenia, depression, and attention deficit (ADD) and attention deficit hyperactivity disorders (ADHD). The *temporal lobes* are located on the sides of the brain in the area above and behind the ears. Memory (including emotional memory), learning, language, and creativity have been associated with this area of the brain. Abnormalities in the temporal lobe have been associated with irritability and outbursts of anger.

BOX 6.1—THE MAN WITH AN UNCLEAN MIND

Paul was a thirty-year-old who had struggled for several years with intrusive thoughts of a blasphemous and vulgar nature. The thoughts would appear "out of nowhere" and cause him great concern. Early on, he found that washing his hands repeatedly or counting by three to three hundred would partially relieve the symptoms for a few hours. Paul experienced a "conversion to Christ" and experienced tremendous joy in his life, but the disturbing thoughts continued. He sought the advice of his pastor and several Christian friends. They defined his problem as spiritual oppression and referred him for "deliverance" work. He went to four deliverance services without relief. The minister at the fourth service, however, redefined his difficulties as a medical problem—obsessive-compulsive disorder—and referred him to me. With appropriate medical therapy, Paul was symptom-free in two months and has continued so for several years.

HOW IT ALL WORKS

Now let us put this background information together in a practical example. These systems do not work independently; they coordinate with each other, forming highly integrated networks. Let me give you an example: My wife goes to the mall and falls in love with a new leather furniture ensemble for our home. Her limbic system is on fire with emotional desire. Her basal ganglia remind her of how good this leather felt when she sat on her sister's new couch at Thanksgiving. Her temporal lobes remind her of seeing this furniture in a decorating book and how good it smelled in the showroom. Her cingulate system envisions us holding hands on the sofa.

About that time, I remind her that she also wants a new car, and that we cannot afford both. Hopefully her prefrontal cortex will kick in and she will agree with me. If she has untreated depression, ADD or ADHD, bipolar disorder, a frontal lobe tumor, multiple sclerosis with brain lesions, or traumatic brain injury to the frontal lobe, the prefrontal cortex won't kick in. Instead, her amygdala will become activated and I will be kicked out and in need of new neurons from my hippocampus to replace the ones lost in my head's collision with a frying pan.

One might ask how we know all of this information about anatomical functions. Animal models have been studied for decades, but human study has been made more practical with advances in technology. Initially, brain function was studied by looking at the effects of tumors, cysts, and epilepsy on different areas of the brain. In some cases, electrodes were placed in brain tissue to elucidate function. Now anatomical study is far easier with CT (computerized tomography) and MRI (magnetic resonance imaging) scans.

Functional studies have developed so rapidly that we can now take a picture of the brain's metabolic activity in real time. Brain scanning techniques—such as rCBF (regional cerebral blood flow), PET (positron emission tomography), SPECT (single photon emission computed tomography), and functional MRI—are rapidly advancing our understanding of brain function at a macroscopic level as detailed above. The real news, however, is occurring at a microscopic level, pertaining to how nerve fibers work in the brain, such as, for example, their physiology.

MICROSCOPIC CELL PHONES AND NERVE PHYSIOLOGY

If you cut through any of the areas of the brain noted above, you will see fibers similar to wires in an electrical cord crisscrossing everywhere. This is because the brain is an electrical organ: Its tissues comprise nerve fibers (neurons) that conduct electrical impulses. These nerve fibers are organized in functional highways that carry messages either from one area of the brain to another or from the brain to other areas of the body. The messages are handed off from one nerve to another like the baton hand-off in a relay race. The only difference is that the nerves cannot touch one another since they are electrically charged and would short out. In humans, short circuits are called *seizures* (see Stahl, 2000).

In fact, great care has been taken by the Creator to keep the nerves of this system from touching each other. There is fatty insulation along the shaft of the nerve fiber similar to the insulation on an extension cord. The nerves meet at the ends of the fiber but are held apart by synaptic clefts. These are anatomical gaps between the nerves that hold them close together without touching. This is an amazing feat when you consider that this nerve intersection looks like someone has uprooted two mature oak trees and intertwined their limbs. Because nerves cannot and do not touch each other, there is a need for a communication network that would allow the nerves to talk to one another in a wireless fashion across this synaptic cleft space. In other words, since they absolutely cannot touch each other in any shape or fashion, regular telephones won't work; the nerves need cell phones.

Neurotransmitters are the cell phones that the nerves use to talk to each other. They are protein substances that are usually made in the nerve ending and are kept in storage bubbles (called vesicles) until they are needed. There are approximately two hundred different neurotransmitters in the brain. Thus when a nerve sends a message to another nerve, the message is sent to the specific neurotransmitter that will convey that message.

This is possible because these neurotransmitters exist in highly specialized highways, which the nerve can turn to with different needs. For example, if you live in Atlanta and get hungry, you have several options available. If you want seafood, you can get on I-75 and drive to Florida. If you want barbecue, get on I-20 and go to Alabama. If you want peaches, get on I-85 and go to South Carolina (the real peach state). Likewise, the nerve has several choices relating to behavioral and emotional "hunger." If it is feeling stressed out and depressed, it can get on the *serotonin* highway and send messages to access this option. If it is confused and can't think straight, it can get on the *dopamine* highway and send messages to deliver more of this commodity. If it is tired and lacking motivation and energy, it can order up a helping of *norepinephrine*. If feeling fearful and anxious, *GABA* (gamma aminobutyric acid) is the neurotransmitter destination of choice. In other words, different neurotransmitters can be recruited depending on the neuronal system needs. Sending a message is clearly a very complicated enterprise for a nerve.

Once selected, the neurotransmitter is then released. It travels across the synaptic cleft and attaches to the receiving nerve on areas called receptors. Each neurotransmitter has a receptor that is specific for its shape and size. It's akin to a key fitting into a lock. Once the message has been passed on to the receptor, the neurotransmitter may be either recycled by re-uptake pumps, which vacuum it back into the sending nerve, or it may be destroyed by enzymes called MAO (monoamine oxidase) and COMT (catecholamine-O-methyl transferase) in the synaptic cleft. Re-uptake pumps and these enzymes serve to regulate the amount of neurotransmitter that would be hanging around the vicinity of the various receptors. This is necessary because receptors can take only so much stimulation. If overstimulated for an extended period of time, the receptors will become less sensitive to the neurotransmitter and turn themselves off (a process called down-regulation). If not stimulated enough, receptors change their density and sensitivity to become more responsive to whatever neurotransmitter is there.

The appropriated, stimulated receptor is usually connected via a linkage called G proteins to the "second messenger system." The second messenger system can be thought of as the computer chip that reads the message off the neurotransmitter. It is called the second messenger system (the neurotransmitter was the first messenger) because it takes this message and transmits it to the nerve's DNA (deoxyribonucleic acid) for final processing. The DNA then determines how, or whether, the cell will react to this message.

DNA and the Brain

A large amount of psychiatric research has been dedicated to understanding how the DNA participates in this communication process. We know that the message from the receptor is transcribed to the DNA by something called *transcription factor*. Transcription factor sits on DNA strands like a needle on a vinyl record. In response to the input from the receptor, it will travel up and down the DNA strand turning on and off different sequences of DNA. The resultant DNA pattern then sends an e-mail in the form of messenger RNA (ribonucleic acid) to the cell to make adjustments in response to the message.

To better understand this process, consider my son, who is a high-school football player. He used to be a quiet and studious child. Then something happened: In his mind, he became a jock. Unfortunately, his body strength didn't match his mental image, so he began lifting weights to build muscle mass. Weightlifting strained his muscles, leading the muscles to produce protein transmitters that told muscle receptors that he was breaking down muscle. The receptors conveyed this message to the DNA, which initially ignored it. The DNA thought that this would be a phase that would pass and not require adjustment. So after two weeks of lifting, my son looked the same. After two months, however, the DNA became convinced that he had lost his mind and determined that more muscle had to be made. Thus the e-mail went out, and he now looks like a linebacker.

In the brain, challenges in the environment can trigger the DNA to make adjustments. Chronic stress, for example, can cause serotonin levels to fall. Decreased serotonin levels cause receptors to trigger the transcription factor to turn on DNA to make serotonin. Under normal circumstances, the situation is rectified. When this process does not occur, we get disease states.

Disease States: When Normal Is Not at Home

An understanding of normal brain anatomy and physiology serves as the basis for understanding important theoretical aspects of how these systems can fail and cause disease states. Neurotransmitters can have faulty synthesis (ribosomes), sluggish release (storage bubbles), too rapid recycling (re-uptake pumps), or too much enzymatic destruction (MAO, COMT), resulting in low neurotransmitter volume to perform the cell phone functions. Receptors could be faulty in responding to neurotransmitters even in the face of normal neurotransmitter function, in essence forming bad antennae on the cell phone. This would then impair the transmission of the signal into the DNA. Then the DNA computer chips could malfunction due to faulty inherited genes and chromosomes, derailing the whole process even if everything else is functioning properly.

Depressive disorders appear to be related to dysfunction in serotonin, norepinephrine, or dopamine systems in the anterior frontal lobes. Anxiety disorders, such as panic disorder and OCD, seem related to problems in GABA, serotonin, or norepinephrine systems in the cingulate regions. Psychosis seems to be a dopamine-excess problem in certain areas of the limbic system. ADHD and ADD appear to be related to problems with dopamine and norepinephrine control in the frontal and cingulate areas. Bipolar disorder (manic-depressive psychosis) appears to be a second-messenger system problem involving several areas of the brain. Finally, some addictive disorders can be related to dopamine and serotonin problems in several areas of the limbic system, especially the anterior cingulate area.

Drug Therapy: The Usual Suspects

Most of the drug treatments for these disorders are theorized to focus on correcting the previously noted dysfunctions (Nemeroff & Schatzberg, 1999). While the mechanisms of action of many of these drugs are not fully known, some effects have been well characterized (DeBattista & Schatzberg, 2000). Antidepressants focus on increasing serotonin, norepinephrine, and dopamine volume by slowing down recycling pumps, decreasing enzyme activities between the nerves, or affecting receptor responsiveness. Antipsychotics work to decrease excess dopamine activity by blocking dopamine receptors, so that the excess dopamine cannot overstimulate them. Antianxiety drugs work by increasing either serotonin or GABA activity or by balancing norepinephrine activity. Mood stabilizers are believed to work by stabilizing nerve membranes and second-messenger systems. ADHD treatments focus on normalizing dopamine and norepinephrine systems in the frontal lobes and cingulate areas. We will now focus in on some of the more common medications used in pharmacotherapy.

ANTIDEPRESSANTS

Antidepressants are used to treat a variety of syndromes besides depression, including panic disorder, OCD, phobias, generalized anxiety disorder, pain syndromes, eating disorders, headaches, premenstrual dysphoric disorder, ADD, and sleep disturbances. Antidepressants are often categorized by their suspected mechanisms of action.

Several of the more popular antidepressants focus on increasing serotonin activity in the brain. These include Prozac (fluoxetine), Paxil (paroxetine), Zoloft (sertraline), Celexa (citalopram), Luvox (fluvoxamine), and Serzone (nefazodone). Drugs focusing on norepinephrine and serotonin include Effexor (venlafaxine), Remeron (mirtazapine), and many of the older drugs, such as Pamelor (nortriptyline), Tofranil (imipramine), Norpramine (desipramine), Anafranil (clomipramine), and Elavil (amitryptyline).

Wellbutrin (bupropion) focuses on increasing dopamine and norepinephrine activity. MAO inhibitors such as Nardil (phenelzine) and Parnate (tranylcypromine) are highly potent drugs with very high efficacy rates. But I call them the nuclear weapons of psychiatry because due to a number of dietary and medication restrictions that can prove fatal, they can kill the enemy (the disease) but also kill the patient if not used properly. Patients taking MAO inhibitors should wear a Medic Alert bracelet or have some type of identification that indicates they are on this medication in the event they become unconscious and require emergency medical care.

Potential side effects of antidepressants include nausea, dry mouth, constipation, sedation, nervousness, diarrhea, insomnia, sexual problems, headache, changes in blood pressure, and weight gain. The older medications can affect heart rhythm and aggravate prostate and glaucoma problems. All of these drugs differ in the degree to which they can cause any one of these side effects. The abrupt cessation of most of these drugs can cause a discontinuation syndrome characterized by dizziness, nausea, headache, anxiety, and depression. Therefore, they should be tapered down when discontinuation is indicated.

Furthermore, drug interactions are possible between these medications and other prescription and over-the-counter medications and herbal preparations (DeVane & Nemeroff, 1999; Wong, Smith, & Boon, 1998). Even caffeine can increase the anxiety and insomnia associated with some of these drugs. Side effects can be avoided or minimized by prescribing the antidepressant at the lowest effective dosage, as most of the side effects increase with higher dosages. Most of these drugs begin taking effect in two to six weeks.

BOX 6.2—THE WOMAN WHO IRONED SHEETS

Jean was a born-again Christian who had experienced depression since she was nineteen years old. It started after the birth of her first child. Her typical day consisted of "praying her way" out of bed to cook, clean, and iron her children's laundry and sheets. After twenty-five years of struggling with depression, she sought help and was diagnosed with major depressive disorder. She was placed on an antidepressant and was free of depression in six weeks. She joined a Bible study, started bowling, took piano lessons, and went out to lunch with her new friends once a week. She eventually became the pianist at her church. The children did suffer, however, as her twenty-year-old son was forced to do his own laundry.

MOOD STABILIZERS

Mood stabilizers are used in the treatment of bipolar disorder. These drugs include lithium carbonate and a variety of anticonvulsants, such as Depakote (a form of valproic acid), Tegretol (carbamazepine), Lamictal (lamotrigine), and the research drugs Topamax (topiramate) and Gabitril (tiagabine). Blood levels must be obtained on lithium and Depakote, which are the two most highly rated drugs for bipolar disorder. Lithium levels should fall between 0.7–1.2 mEq/l and Depakote between 75–100 mg/ml.

All of these drugs can cause serious side effects; therefore, close monitoring is necessary. Lithium can cause tremors, diarrhea, thirst, memory problems, weight gain, thyroid slowing, acne, and kidney problems. Depakote can cause drowsiness, upset stomach, diarrhea, tremors, hair thinning, and liver and pancreatic irritation. Supplemental selenium and zinc can help counter the hair thinning. Tegretol also must be monitored by blood level, preferably 4–12 mg/ml. It can interfere with the effectiveness of oral contraceptives. Tegretol blood levels can also decline over time related to changes in the liver. Lamictal is gaining support as a good treatment for patients who have more trouble with depression than mania. It can cause sedation, insomnia, dizziness, nausea, blurred vision, irritated esophagus, and severe skin rashes. In fact, a skin rash is a reason to immediately discontinue this medication.

Topamax is known for one significant side effect: decrease in appetite with resultant weight loss. Often patients will need to take an antidepressant with their mood stabilizer for brief periods of time during the depressed phase of this illness. However, if they take too much or stay on the antidepressant too long, they can become manic.

ANTIPSYCHOTICS

Drugs used in the treatment of psychosis include first-generation drugs, such as Haldol (haloperidol), Loxitane (loxapine), Stelazine (trifluoperazine), Navane (thiothixene), Mellaril (thioridazine), and Thorazine (chlorpromazine). These drugs work to block excessive dopamine activity in the brain. Their side effects can include muscle spasms, restlessness, rigid gait and facial expression, tremors, tight muscles, dry mouth, constipation, blurred vision, changes in blood pressure, changes in EKG (electrocardiogram), and weight gain. With long-term use of these drugs, patients can develop involuntary muscle movements called tardive dyskinesia. With poor hydration, patients can develop neuroleptic malignant syndrome, which can lead to death if not detected early and treated. Symptoms consist of fever, muscle rigidity, confusion, increased pulse, sweating, and muteness.

Newer-generation antipsychotics include Clozaril (clozapine), Risperdal (risperidone), Zyprexa (olanzapine), Seroquel (quetiapine), and Geodon (ziprasidone). These drugs work on serotonin systems in addition to dopamine systems. This added component has contributed to a better performance of these drugs in treating all the symptoms of psychosis in comparison to the first-generation drugs. Some of these drugs have also shown a degree of usefulness in treating mood disorders as well as psychosis. They have similar side effects to the first-generation drugs but have far fewer quantitative risks. Clozaril requires blood monitoring because of problems with lowered white blood cell counts. Cataracts and thyroid hormone changes have been reported in limited cases with Seroquel.

The major concerns with the second-generation drugs have been cost and weight gain. Some people have gained enough weight that blood-sugar control has become a problem, and other patients have experienced changes in their EKGs. Though rare, prolactin levels can go up, leading to the production of breast milk. However, these drugs have been dramatically helpful to many patients who did not respond to first-generation drugs, reducing the need for hospitalization and greatly improving quality of life.

ANTIANXIETY MEDICATIONS

Anxiety problems are addressed by several classes of drugs, including antidepressants, beta blockers, and anxiolytics. Beta blockers are cardiovascular drugs that block adrenaline (beta) receptors, thus preventing many of the physical symptoms of anxiety. Inderal (propranolol) is an example of these drugs. Side effects include fatigue, dizziness, and worsening of asthma. Often patients with cardiac disease cannot take these drugs. These medications are usually used in specific situations where anxiety may get triggered for short periods of time, such as during public speaking.

Anxiolytics are represented by benzodiazepines and BuSpar (buspirone). The benzodiazepines are potentially habit-forming (the first time we have said that) and therefore are reserved for short-term use. They include Xanax (alprazolam), Valium (diazepam), Librium (chlordiazepoxide), Tranxene (clorazepate), Ativan (lorazepam), and Klonopin (clonazepam). Sedation is the major side effect of using these drugs. Also, patients can develop tolerance with long-term usage, thus requiring progressively higher dosages over time. Many commonly used sleeping pills are similar to the benzodiazepines and include Halcion (triazolam), Ambien (zolpidem), Restoril (temazepam), and Sonata (zaleplon). These drugs should be used cautiously as they can cause next-day impairment with confusion, sedation, and difficulty operating machinery or vehicles safely.

BuSpar is a nonaddictive anxiolytic that is designed for long-term use. It reduces anxiety by increasing serotonin activity in a fashion different from most antidepressants. Unlike benzodiazepines, which start working immediately, BuSpar takes two weeks to start working. Potential side effects with this drug include lightheadedness, dizziness, dry mouth, nausea, and decreased appetite.

PSYCHOSTIMULANTS

Psychostimulants are used in the treatment of ADD and ADHD and occasionally in difficult cases of depression. Examples include Ritalin (methylphenidate), Concerta (sustained release methylphenidate), Dexedrine (dextroamphetamine), Adderall (four amphetamine salts), and Cylert (pemoline). They all work to increase dopamine and norepinephrine activity in the brain. In general they do have abuse potential and are designated as controlled substances by the U.S. Drug Enforcement Administration.

Potential side effects include insomnia, temper problems, decreased appetite, agitation, tics, and decreases in the rate of growth. Most of these drugs are short acting and can produce rebound when they are wearing off. (*Rebound* refers to the return of the symptoms of ADHD in a rapid fashion when the medication wears off.) Long-acting products such as Concerta seek to avoid this. Cylert has fallen into infrequent usage due to concerns about liver toxicity. (Liver function tests are recommended on a biweekly basis for patients taking this drug).

DRUG TREATMENT: SUMMARY CONCERNS

This brief survey demonstrates both the promise and the challenge of psychiatric medications. They have tremendous potential to help people with problems that can destroy their lives psychologically, medically, and spiritually. However, they must be used with care and at the discretion of someone who is skilled in their administration.

A Corvette is a wonderful car that can give you much joy if you know how to drive it properly. If you operate it improperly, it can kill you. In like fashion, the drugs we've discussed here can either help dramatically or cause more problems, depending on how they are used. I am not just referring to major issues, such as choice of drugs and dosing. Subtle issues can make a big difference as well. For example, Geodon works faster if taken with food. Ritalin often works better on an empty stomach. Luvox can produce more side effects if caffeine is not restricted. Several drugs are less effective if the patient smokes. Excellent results are not an accident, and there are many variables to be considered.

Furthermore, pharmacology is not the only treatment needed. Appropriate psychotherapy needs to accompany the medication even when medication yields a good result. The family of the woman "who ironed sheets" reacted quite negatively to the changes in her life and needed family therapy. The man "with the unclean mind" was encouraged by his Christian friends to stop his medication as an act of faith, and he later relapsed. Imagine his spiritual and psychological state at that point.

There is one other issue we should address: I am often asked if a Christian should be treated only by a Christian psychiatrist. First, there's the practical problem that there are not that many Christian psychiatrists. If therapy is the goal, the value system and worldview of the psychiatrist are very important. However, it is not critical to see a Christian when medication is the issue. In those circumstances, I vote for a skilled technician working in concert with a Christian therapist.

In fact, I would prefer a highly skilled agnostic to a less-skilled Christian physician in all areas of technical medicine. The patient can recruit many people to pray for the prescribing physician, who may be a psychiatrist, but in many situations, may be a family doctor or gynecologist. The key is finding out whether this physician has a good reputation as a diagnostician and psychopharmacologist. The diagnostic skills are crucial, since many medical illnesses (such as thyroid disease) and medications (such as corticosteroids) can mimic psychiatric disorders (Hutto, 1999). It is the responsibility of Christian therapists to find out what resources are available in their communities for this type of assistance.

BOX 6.3—THE PREGNANT LADY

Jane was in the third trimester of her first pregnancy and was very depressed with suicidal thoughts. She asked her obstetrician about taking an antidepressant, but the doctor was not comfortable giving a conclusive answer to her question. The patient contacted me and inquired about driving eight hours (while pregnant) for a consult because she wanted to see a Christian. I directed her to a secular psychiatrist I knew who practiced near her home and was an expert on pregnancy and depression. The patient already had a Christian therapist, but she needed a skilled medical specialist within a reasonable distance of her home. Her concern was really about trust and comfort level, not about technical expertise. A brief conversation allayed her fears.

BEYOND CHEMICAL IMBALANCES

Current research endeavors are moving beyond fine-tuning neurotransmitter imbalances. Research on the human genome is serving as a basis for developing diagnostic and treatment interventions based on DNA technology (Mundy, 2001). The relationship of the brain to the adrenal glands is promoting study of how adrenal gland hormones contribute to mood and anxiety disorders. Products are being researched that focus on other brain substances, such as substance P. Magnets are also under review as a treatment for depression in rTMS (repetitive transcranial magnetic stimulation). Finally, a surgically implanted pacemaker (the vagus nerve stimulator) has been developed for patients with intractable depression.[1] This device is implanted in the armpit, with a wire running underneath the skin into the neck where it is attached to the vagus nerve. The vagus nerve sends 80% of its fibers to the limbic system, thus affording researchers an opportunity to directly jump-start that area of the brain.

WHERE THE RUBBER MEETS THE ROAD

This chapter has given an overview of the biological components of behavior and the treatment alternatives that flow from this understanding. However, two major problems exist. First, patients are suspicious and fearful of the disorders and treatments that we have discussed. Health professionals are commonly questioned by patients about the potential of these treatments to cause side effects and long-term harm. These are legitimate questions that deserve an answer specific to each patient's situation. In fact, patients have a right to know at least the following about their treatment (Lyles, 1999):

- Patients should be told the diagnosis of the disorder or disease for which they are taking this medication.
- Patients should be informed as to why this particular treatment was selected.
- Interactions between this medication and other medications or medical problems should be detailed.
- Patients should have a general idea about how this treatment is supposed to help.
- Patients should have an estimate of how long the treatment will last.
- Patients should be forewarned if the treatment will be expensive.

It has been estimated that, at three months of treatment, only 50% of patients continue taking their medications. This statistic could reflect a failure to clearly address the patients' questions and therefore a lack of proper preparation for this kind of long-term treatment.

Patients seldom ask the most important question: What will happen if the disorder remains untreated? A body of literature is emerging that answers this question in regard to depression. Besides the obvious impairments in mood and relationships, untreated depression affects multiple areas of a person's life. It is one of the top three causes of disability and diminished work productivity. It can complicate treatment from diabetes and hypertension. It can dramatically worsen recovery from strokes and heart attacks to the point that untreated depression is considered a risk for cardiac mortality (Musselman, Evans, & Nemeroff, 1998; Penninx, Beekman, & Honig, 2001). Nursing-home patients with untreated depression have higher death rates. Suicide and substance abuse are overrepresented in patients with depression. Then there's the gnawing issue of whether untreated depression causes hippocampal brain damage (Vogel, 2000). The biological treatment of depression does carry risks; however, one must recognize that the failure to treat also carries risks.

BIOMEDICAL CONCERNS AND THE CHRISTIAN COUNSELOR

The first problem relates to the patient who may be suspicious and fearful of the disorders and the treatments. The second problem relates to the Christian counselor who is playing all the roles described earlier in this chapter. How do you decide whether the treatment plan for the problems your client is presenting requires a biological component? When should you consider referring for a medical evaluation, especially given the many medical conditions that can masquerade as emotional and behavioral problems?

Christian counselors should consider the following presentation as clinical clues for suspecting biological contribution:

- the presence of repetitive episodes of similar symptoms
- a family history of similar symptoms
- symptoms that are out of proportion to the situation
- symptoms that are out of character for the individual
- consistent changes in bodily functions such as sleep, appetite, gastrointestinal function, pleasure drives, and cognition
- an apparent lack of volitional control (such as crying spells in embarrassing situations)
- significant impairment in several areas of the person's life
- association between the onset of symptoms and changes in medical status or medications
- presence of suicidal ideation, delusions, or hallucinations
- persistence of the symptoms despite psychological and spiritual progress

Attention to these issues will guide the therapist in determining whether a medical evaluation is necessary.

CHAPTER 7

PSYCHOSOCIAL ROOTS

From Theoretical Schools to a Clinical Superscience

TIM CLINTON AND GEORGE OHLSCHLAGER

Empirical (quantitative) research on religious and spiritual issues in mental health and psychotherapy has mushroomed during the past decade, as documented by the review of Worthington et al. (1996).... When Worthington and his colleagues do the next ten-year review of the research...we hope a spiritual strategy for personality and psychotherapy will be solidly grounded in and supported by both quantitative and qualitative empirical research.

—RICHARDS AND BERGIN,

A Spiritual Strategy for Counseling and Psychotherapy

The chapters on theology and spirituality emphasized that humankind was made *by* God and *for* God. We were made in God's image to share in his glory and enjoy intimate fellowship with him. The chapter on biology discussed the powerful influence of nature, of our genetic heritage, and of the biomedical forces that shape life in this material world. We will now consider the influence of human behavior—the nurture side of our nature-nurture-spirit quest—and how we are shaped by the drives, desires, demands, and limits of the psychosocial forces of living.

Thoughts, feelings, and actions (the TFA approach we introduced in chapter 2 and will develop further in this chapter) are indeed the primary coins of the counseling realm. But we reassert our need to be as knowledgeable as possible in *all* the realms of life that we explore in this book. Therefore, we reject the black-and-white view that incorporating any psychosocial data unavoidably corrupts Christian counseling. In its extreme form, this view fails to understand or consider the modern field of psychology (Myers, 2001). It paints a caricature of the issues and presents a false dichotomy that forces an unnecessary choice—a choice that restricts understanding and appreciation of the fullness, complexity, and paradox of life.

However, we do agree that in recent years the role of psychology has been overrated and has held too much sway in some corners of the church in defining ultimate truth and the ways we can know it. This is especially true in the epistemological and teleological realms. While psychology as an organizing system of ultimate beliefs must be rejected as a false religion, it does not follow that all psychological data must be rejected as well (Vitz, 1977). We refuse to participate in this failure to discriminate "baby from bathwater," but we will readily throw out any "dirty water" that would pollute or attempt to supplant the truth of the gospel.

The ultimate *why* questions of life—those that reflect meaning, purpose, and value—are best answered by the theological and spiritual realms of living. Psychosocial (and biological, anthropological, cultural, political, and economic) data can assist us in identifying and understanding clinical issues and behavior and interaction patterns and can deliver specific treatment considerations. Bio-psycho-social data has significant value in helping us answer the *what, when, where,* and *how* questions about life. Our burgeoning knowledge base illuminates and guides the pursuit of ultimate truth, but it cannot do so apart from the revelation of truth through God in Christ (see Powlison, 1997).

SCHOOLS OF THERAPY: THE TWENTIETH-CENTURY PARADIGM

"What is your orientation/theory/approach to practice?" For most of the twentieth century, the training and practice of psychotherapy was something largely done according to a preferred theory or school of thought. Counselors and psychotherapists were identified by the set of organizing principles that distinguished them as proponents of a certain psychological theory. Many counselors still associate themselves with a preferred school of thought that influences their practice: "I am a cognitive therapist" (or family, psychoanalytic, object-relations, Adlerian, Jungian, Klienian, behavioral, gestaltist, or eclectic therapist). Christian counselors may also add on one of several prominent types, calling themselves nouthetic counselors, integrationists, temperament counselors, or spirituotherapists.

Theory, in itself, has significant value both in the development of science in general and in the growth of psychotherapy in particular. Since every counselor has a theology of counseling (as we discussed in chapter 4), so every counselor has a theory of counseling—an organizing road-map-of-the-mind that provides explanation and meaning to human behavior as well as the social organization of modern life. Simply put, good counseling theory "assists the counselor in predicting, evaluating, and improving results" (Brammer, Shostrom, & Abrego, 1989, p. 6).

Krumboltz (1966) reminded us decades ago that the "way we think about problems determines to a large degree what we will do about them" (p. 4). Behind every theory, then, is a set of beliefs and values, a philosophical context that influences how you practice counseling (Gibson & Mitchell, 1995). Inherent to each theory is a unique perspective on personality, abnormality, health, the "good life," and how to conduct psychotherapy—theory and application that must be sifted through to grasp the beliefs and values of each element (Jones & Butman, 1991).

The Primary Schools of Counseling

By the 1950s, about a dozen major theories were identified and classified under four broad orientations, what we might call the superschools of therapy: (1) psychodynamic, (2) behavioral, (3) humanistic, and (4) existential. Today, most schools of thought combine humanistic and existential therapies and add family and systems approaches as a fourth major orientation. In fact, most courses and texts on counseling theory still follow this fundamental format or emphasis (Burke 1989; Corey, 2000; Corsini & Wedding, 1995; Parrott, 1997). For example, Christian psychologists Jones and Butman (1991) list the following twelve therapies and their many derivatives under the broader categories of dynamic, behavioral, humanistic, and family system psychologies:

1. classical psychoanalysis
2. contemporary psychodynamic psychotherapies
3. Jungian therapy
4. behavior therapy
5. rational-emotive therapy
6. cognitive-behavioral therapy
7. Adlerian and reality therapies
8. person-centered therapy
9. existential therapy
10. gestalt therapy
11. transactional analysis
12. family therapy

The Trouble with "Schoolism"

This "schoolism" approach has caused significant problems, both in the church and in the counseling professions. In parts of the church, certain brands of psychology and therapeutic mind-sets have been uncritically accepted without attention to their anti-Christian roots. Sadly, many practicing counselors have borrowed from theories, ideas, and strategies that are incompatible with their own Christian beliefs and values. This is surely a big cause of the debate about the role of psychology in the church.

Another problem associated with schoolism is that the preferred school or theory was traditionally counselor-chosen and directed, not scientifically established or client-driven. Therapists learned the pet theories of their graduate-school professors and mentors. If your teacher was a Freudian, a Skinnerian, or a Rogerian—representing the three major schools of twentieth-century therapy—you became a psychodynamic therapist (honoring Sigmund Freud) or a behavior therapist (honoring B. F. Skinner) or a client-centered therapist (honoring Carl Rogers). The counselor tended to approach every client in a similar manner, regardless of client uniqueness and need. Client variables were not the primary concern; practicing with pure adherence to one's favored school of therapy was what counted. Although experienced counselors began to diverge from the school-of-thought mold and look increasingly similar to one another in practice, an allegiance to the school or theory of choice was paramount (Fiedler, 1950).

This schoolist approach even shaped the standard of care in counseling and psychotherapy. If sued for malpractice, counselors could successfully defend against liability by showing that they had practiced according to the tenets of the theory they espoused, whether or not the client got better. If the client did not improve or got worse, the individual was generally just directed to find another therapist. This schoolist approach, theory-laden and nonscientific, was essentially how medicine was practiced in the nineteenth century.

The third major problem with schoolism is a pragmatic one: The approach didn't work with every person in every situation. Clinicians presented client cases that stubbornly refused to yield to a schoolist understanding and intervention. It did not matter if a counselor was identified as a Freudian, Jungian, behaviorist, gestaltist, cognitive therapist, family therapist, or any other school; a schoolist orientation was, by itself, an increasingly deficient model of human-social description and of therapy. The inherent weaknesses of the schoolist approach were coming to light and a crisis began to brew.

TRANSITIONS TOWARD A NEW PARADIGM

The crisis in psychotherapy has always been shaped around the question of efficacy: Does counseling really work and, if so, can it work consistently with many different people and needs? This question has elicited much recrimination and soul-searching in the field (Gross, 1978; Masson, 1988). The ferment in the helping professions has branched in two primary directions, and everyone who travels the highway of counseling development and learning is now facing a fork in the road.

TRAVELING THE GREAT DIVIDE

One fork leads down a more-of-the-same route—schoolism with hundreds of lanes of traffic. The schoolist orientation has mushroomed in the last quarter-century with a veritable explosion of many new and different therapy models, all seeking (and most claiming) to improve on the evidence of poor outcomes with a schoolist approach. It was recently estimated that literally hundreds of distinct therapy models are currently available to the modern Western consumer and counselor-trainee (Corsini & Wedding, 1995).

So the schoolist approach is alive and well as we begin the new century, but it has morphed into a hydra-headed beast. Counseling innovators have produced myriad models of counseling and clinical intervention, and it seems likely that more and more models will continue to be developed and promoted with great vigor. Modern schoolism is both highly fragmented and entrepreneurial. For example, a 2001 issue of the *Family Therapy Networker* (now the *Psychotherapy Networker*) contained articles and ads for fifty-one different therapy and change models, some of which the authors have trademarked (January/February 2001).

There seems to be a dedicated minority of business-savvy clinicians who are able (or at least willing) to concoct an elixir of techniques that promise a breakthrough in counseling results. The claims that are made for many of these systems are highfalutin and overly optimistic. Do these marketing phrases sound familiar?

- "EMDR, a specialized approach, accelerates the treatment of a wide variety of psychological complaints and self-esteem issues."
- "TFT is highly effective, powerful, and innovative psychotherapy."
- "Your workshop was the most outstanding, intense, and joyful learning experience I can remember."

We suspect that most of you have seen similar ads and that your responses range from intrigue to a sarcastic snort at the marketing mania of these myriad therapy schools. The best spin we can put on this proliferation of schools and models is that it demonstrates a quest for truth, since no single theory has the ultimate answer.

Fortunately, the other fork leads to a road less—but increasingly well—traveled. By the 1980s, schoolism was giving way to a whole new approach: The paradigm began to shift toward empirically refined therapy based on client need and driven to improve client outcomes however they were measured. During this time, counselors and researchers discovered some crucial truths that are still chang-ing our field. One of these truths was that the most helpful counselors—those who consistently produced the best clinical outcomes—looked more and more alike in practice, regardless of the theory or school they worked from. These pioneering practitioners and researchers described what we now call the "common factors" of effective psychotherapy. In addition, the evidence revealed again and again that no theory or model was dominant in positive client outcome.

This evidence gave rise to eclecticism (Norcross, 1986; Smith, 1982). *Eclectic* means "drawn from many sources," and drawing what seemed useful from various theories allowed for more openness and flexibility in counseling. Counselors who embraced this approach worked to become acquainted with many different theo-ries and practices and, most significantly, were free to match treatment to the needs of clients. Clients and patients were finally becoming more important than coun-selor knowledge and skill with a particular way of therapy. The educated, active, and well-informed consumer of counseling—to say nothing of the insurance ven-dors who were paying for it—demanded nothing less than what we all demand as consumers: good results from the work done.

Unfortunately, this early eclecticism was overwhelming in its knowledge de-mands. It also encouraged indiscriminant selection of bits and pieces from diverse sources, resulting in a hodgepodge of inconsistent concepts and interventions (Smith, 1982). This method was sometimes sarcastically referred to as "electric counseling," implying that the practitioners were trying out any and every method that "turned them on." Understandably, this kind of counselor can do more harm than good if he or she does not thoroughly understand the theories and techniques being drawn upon (Parrott, 1997, p. 390).

These problems, however, gave rise to a systematic eclecticism, which attempted to pull together more compatible approaches to therapy and develop a logical and developmental counseling theory (Egan, 1998; Norcross, 1986). This newer eclectic approach refused to engage in the grab-bag approach, rejecting any ill-defined, inconsistent, or random collection of philosophies, purposes, and techniques. This pursuit resulted in a rapid maturing of the entire field and remains a major engine of empirical and theoretical growth in the helping professions. Furthermore, according to survey data from clinical and counseling psychologists, the most widely used approach to counseling is an eclectic one (Norcross & Prochaska, 1982; Smith, 1982).

This brief history reveals why the primary aspects of counseling that we em-phasize in this book—the quality of the therapeutic relationship, the primary skills or common factors that cut across the various schools, and the emphasis on briefer and more focused interventions—started to come to the fore in the mental health professions. The revolution was now ablaze, and the paradigm shift started to take place in earnest.

TOWARD TWENTY-FIRST-CENTURY METATHEORY

The twenty-first-century paradigm shift is driven by a consumerist culture where client satisfaction is paramount and is grounded on robust scientific development that is transforming the entire enterprise. Pragmatic eclecticism and the relationship between common factors and positive outcomes in therapy have pushed the development of an overarching metatheory. This emphasis on theoretical integrationism—which parallels the integrationism and eclectic convergence going on in Christian counseling (see chapter 2)—involves constructing a theory of theories, one that seeks to incorporate all the best findings that have defined the very essence of counseling (Egan, 1998). In the past it became necessary to develop a metatheory to bridge and organize the enormous and complex data of human life and help-directed practice. The rise of metatheory as a preferred mode of counseling development has allowed counselors "to operate within [a] holistic framework by integrating moral concepts with physiological/sensorimotor issues [and] to reconstrue counseling and therapy as basically spiritual in nature" (Blakeney & Blakeney, 1992, p. 42). It also organizes data in heuristic ways, resulting in practice guidelines that help discriminate success or failure (McWhirter & McWhirter, 1991). We firmly believe the recent trend in Christian counseling, that of biopsycho-social-spiritual therapy, will prove to be just this kind of useful metatheory.

HEDGEHOGS AND FOXES OF MODERN PSYCHOTHERAPY

Another way to characterize and summarize the divide we face is to look at the hedgehogs and foxes. English historian Isaiah Berlin used these creatures as a metaphor to describe how the major thinkers of history have shaped world culture. Foxes know and understand the influence of many things, articulating the complexity of multiple factors in human and social change. Hedgehogs identify and advance one big idea, propagating a grand theory, the glorious goal toward which change should be directed.

Among New Testament writers, for example, Paul's theology and ministry—his Spirit-led instruction to many churches—reveal the complexity and variety of a fox. Conversely, we see classic hedgehog traits in James, who expounded on the relationship of faith and works, and Matthew, who wrote a gospel for the Jews.

Five hundred years ago, the artist-inventor-philosopher-visionary Leonardo da Vinci was a consummate fox. Martin Luther, on the other hand, was a single-minded hedgehog with his bold anthem of *sola fide*—salvation by faith alone. Influencing our modern political-economic era were hedgehogs Karl Marx and Adam Smith, the progenitors of communist and capitalist political and economic theory. Thomas Jefferson, in his wide-ranging work on politics, education, architecture, and statecraft, was a fox extraordinaire.

In a compelling analysis of modern psychotherapy, family therapist Bill Doherty (1998) asserted that the schoolist approach of twentieth-century psychotherapy reflected the work of our best-known hedgehogs. Freud and Jung developed psychoanalytic theory, Watson and Skinner developed behaviorism and instigated the rise of scientific psychology, Rogers and Perls gave impetus to humanistic and third-force therapy, while Haley, Bowen, Minuchin, Whitaker, and others shaped the contours of family and systems therapy. These seminal thinkers combined innovative brilliance with influential platforms to propagate their models.

As we have argued, however, there is an undeniable downside to these familiar schools that is increasingly experienced by modern practitioners. The single lens of the hedgehog ("My school is the best and only way to do it") is being shown to be a deficient model in view of the multiple influences and complexities of modern life. Doherty (1998) pinpointed the issue and explained why the current transformation is taking place in our field.

> Ours was a profession dominated by brilliant, single-minded innovators who were reluctant to recognize the value of knowledge outside their explanatory system. Although the twentieth century of psychotherapy belonged to the intensely focused hedgehogs who were masters of a circumscribed domain, the twenty-first century, I think, will belong to intellectually flexible, broad-ranging foxes. Fox therapists know that nothing in the landscape of therapy is as simple or as local as it once was. They know that human problems are about genes, the environment, the unconscious, behavior, cognitions, the family, the economy, social institutions, race, gender, social class, morality, spirituality, politics, the broader culture, history, and sometimes even the ecosphere. If the hedgehog's cry was "Eureka! I've found it!" the fox's mantra is "I think it's more complicated than that." (p. 50)

Foxes and Hedgehogs March On

Many hedgehog therapies will be and are being proven to be useful at particular times with a few clients who have certain problems. Current data indicates that no single theory or model adequately accounts for the complexity of human behavior (Goldfried, 1982; Ivey, 1994). Furthermore, no single theory is always helpful for individual clients with certain varieties of specific problems (Beutler & Clarkin, 1990; Seligman, 1994, 1995).

We might by now predict that the universal and superior claims of these systems, like all systems that have come before, will be analyzed and challenged. Some will be challenged on moral and spiritual grounds; some will be challenged, even disproved, when rigorous empirical research is brought to bear. We appreciate the work of Benner (1987), who invited forty-six clinicians and researchers to analyze fifty of the most prominent models of psychotherapy from a Christian perspective. This kind of work should help us sift and cull the very best material, rejecting that which is useless or harmful, from the myriad schools of counseling and psychology.

In spite of the proliferation of hundreds of counseling models today, Doherty is convinced that the future will not belong to the therapeutic hedgehogs. We agree with Doherty that the foxes will gain parity and likely will eventually dominate our field and its future development. They are already beginning to assert considerable influence through empirical study and meta-analysis of psychotherapy, especially in research labs and academic centers. This work is describing with greater precision those elements of productive change that are identifiable across all the hedgehog models.

The foxes of empirical analysis are transforming psychotherapy from a school-based, hedgehog loyalty to a scientific enterprise that is eclectic in nature, more effective in outcome, and more efficient regarding the use of time and resources. The research of the past decade has shown that counseling success is a complex equation of problem duration and intensity, counselor attitude and experience, counselor-client matching and the quality of the working alliance, client readiness and motivation, and many other factors (Brammer, Abrego, & Shostrum, 1998; Corey, 2000).

DOES COUNSELING WORK?

The question of effectiveness—"Can we consistently deliver the help we promise?"—is now common to consumers of counseling services, to managed care and insurance executives, to state mental health licensure board administrators, and to behavioral science researchers who work in a specialized arena called psychotherapy outcomes research. The short answer is a cautious yes. Eysenck (1984) challenged the profession early on when he claimed that psychotherapy had little or no demonstrably positive effect. The mass of recent outcomes research indicates that counseling does indeed help and that the best counseling—or, more to the point, the best counselors—help the most (*Consumer Reports,* 1995; Lipsey & Wilson, 1993; Seligman, 1998; Smith, Glass, & Miller, 1980).

Nevertheless, skeptics outside our ranks (Gross, 1978; Kaminer, 1992) and some critics inside (Szasz, 1978; Zilbergeld, 1983) remained unconvinced. Much has been written about bad counseling, inept and abusive counselors, overly politicized power plays, and coercive mental health systems that trample on the rights of vulnerable, chronically mentally ill people around the world.

Masson (1988) wrote a searing analysis claiming that psychotherapy is a multibillion-dollar venture that simply profits from people's misery. While some of these charges are sensationalist, apparently motivated to sell books, others are not. We hope that Christian counselors will be in the forefront of cutting-edge movements that point out and correct abuses of the field, protect and champion the rights of mental health patients worldwide, and work to improve the quality of service in everything we do.

It's true that much research shows that some people will improve with or without counseling. So while we are able to answer affirmatively on the question of counseling's efficacy, the response to a query about the *need* for counseling may bring us up short. If most people are going to get better anyway with the passage of time, some may choose to forgo counseling altogether and suffer a tolerable amount of loss during their trouble. With these thoughts in mind, let us examine the evidence and highlight factors that consistently correlate with the delivery of effective service.

It is now known that counseling surely does work, and the tools we use are continually being refined to constantly improve effectiveness. In reality, however, not all counselors are good helpers, and not all use the best and most efficient methods. As Egan (1998) says, "Although helping can and does work, there is plenty of evidence that ineffective helping also abounds. Helping is a powerful process that is all too easy to mismanage" (p. 12). Even worse, there are inept, poorly trained, unmotivated, and self-absorbed helpers both within and outside of Christian counseling who pose a serious problem (Ohlschlager & Mosgofian, 1992).

For example, using a long-term psychodynamic approach with a person complaining of depression or phobic fears will border on the unethical (see Klerman, 1990; Stone, 1990). Short-term cognitive-behavioral and possibly pharmacological interventions are clearly the current treatment of choice and the one almost exclusively demanded by managed care. Even if psychodynamic principles are applied to long-term therapy once symptom relief is attained, relief of symptoms will be demanded within a few sessions. However, a less-structured psychodynamic or existential approach may be indicated for someone struggling with depression due to such issues as personal loss, beliefs and values, and meaning in life, and the client may elect to continue counseling to address these deeper issues.

KEY STUDIES ON OUTCOME AND EFFECTIVENESS

In 1950 Fiedler published a landmark study analyzing the traits and relationships among psychoanalytic, nondirective, and Adlerian therapists. He found that experts in all three orientations were much more alike than different in their counseling styles, while inexperienced nonexperts were more different than alike (even those practicing within the same theory). With the first scientific evidence that may have initiated the current paradigm shift, Fiedler posited that the therapist's *style* of counseling and *way of relating* were more significant variables for success than one's *theory*.

In 1961 Frank wrote his now classic treatise *Persuasion and Healing*. He analyzed the common factors of healing and change across the multitude of therapeutic schools, even across cultures. He noted that healing takes place when a rationale for improvement is promoted and understood, when there is a ritual by which it proceeds, and, most important, when a healthy therapeutic relationship exists. Frank noted that the best healers were those who

- instilled hope in their clients,
- respected and strengthened the healing relationship,
- imparted special knowledge to the client,
- engaged clients in a collaborative process of mutual learning,
- were able to emotionally arouse the client to greater insight and increased motivation to change,
- facilitated constructive behavioral change in the client.

Consistent with Frank's analysis, Lambert (1986) reviewed the already vast literature in psychotherapy outcomes research. His meta-analysis distilled and attempted to quantify myriad variables into the following four factors that account for psychotherapeutic change:

1. Expectancy factors—or hope—accounted for 15% of change.
2. Counselor-directed relationship variables that existed across all theories—such as acceptance, empathy, warmth, and encouragement—accounted for 30% of change.
3. Client variables—such as faith, courage, coping skills, motivation for change, fortuitous events, and the quality and availability of support systems—accounted for 40% of change.
4. Therapy techniques—which many tend to believe is the most important aspect in healing—accounted for 15% of change.

In two separate studies and research reviews, Frank (1971) and Whiston and Sexton (1993) considered the factors that lead to psychotherapeutic change. Both studies concluded that the *relationship* between counselor and client accounted for a significant amount of the positive change experienced in counseling. Clients working in a context of respect, warmth, empathic understanding, and common values showed significant levels of improvement and progress.

RESEARCH FOUNDATIONS OF THE NEW PARADIGM

The effectiveness of psychotherapy across a variety of conditions and counselor-client variables is now well established. Lambert and Bergin (1994) and Lambert and Cattani-Thompson (1996) reviewed counseling effectiveness and drew the following conclusions based on research available at the time:

1. Generally, counseling works. Most counseling effects are positive, and clients report satisfaction at the end of treatment. The best results are shown by the "best helpers" working with the most active clients. The most important factor here is a strong therapeutic relationship and not necessarily the skill used in applying techniques or theories.

2. With at least half of all clients, counseling success is attained in five to ten sessions. Brief therapy needs to become more intentionally practiced by all counselors.

3. A sizable minority of clients (20–30%) need long-term therapy or more intensive and multiple treatments. Clients in this group tend to have entrenched personality disorders, have chronically poor relationships, are poorly motivated, and perhaps are even hostile toward counseling.

4. Some clients do, in fact, get worse during counseling. Since many counselors are insensitive to negative change, effective client monitoring is essential to the relationship and to any needed treatment adjustments.

5. For the majority of clients, improvement remains strong for one to two years after treatment. The chance of relapse can be reduced by (a) helping clients see that *they* did the work of change and that it is in their power to maintain it, and (b) preparing them to view future problems and setbacks as natural and temporal rather than a failure of the counseling process.

6. Results are influenced more by client variables than by either a counselor's attributes or counseling techniques. Poor outcomes are associated with low motivation, high defensiveness, failure to take responsibility, and the severity, persistence, and complexity of problems.

7. The quality and process of the counselor-client relationship is the next best predictor of counseling success. High levels of attending, listening, empathy, and respect are crucial to positive outcomes. Specifically, using checklists to gather written feedback from clients on a weekly basis helps to focus and move toward goals.
8. A growing body of evidence demonstrates that certain techniques are helpful across a spectrum of problems and symptoms. National psychiatric and psychological associations are developing step-by-step, research-supported treatment protocols that Lambert encourages helpers to use.

How Much Therapy Is Enough?

In general, current research supports the proposition that, in many cases, short-term or brief therapy is as effective as long-term psychotherapy (Garfield, 1994; Hampson & Beavers, 1996). As we will discuss in chapter 14, brief therapy has been found to be efficacious with a wide range of personal problems, including depression, anxiety, panic disorders, and relationship problems (DeJong & Berg, 1998; Hampson & Beavers, 1996). Research shows that people entering therapy expect it to last no more than ten sessions and that the majority of clients terminate before the tenth session anyway (De Shazer, 1991).

However, in an important article by Kopta, Howard, Lowry, and Beutler (1994), symptomatic recovery was tested according to the number of sessions necessary to reach a "clinically significant improvement"—providing an empirical measure of change from dysfunctional to functional modes. The Symptom Checklist-90-R was applied to three primary symptom groups: acute distress, chronic distress, and characterological problems. For each of these groups, the researchers studied the range and mean number of sessions it took to help clients reach "clinical improvement." A diverse range of therapists—including practitioners of psychodynamic, cognitive, behavioral, and eclectic approaches—were included in the study. This research found that the greatest degree of constructive change occurred in the first eight to ten sessions, supporting the belief that brief therapy is effective. Findings also indicated that constructive change continued across a wide range of issues beyond ten sessions, and improvement continued through fifty-two or more sessions (weekly therapy for one to two years).

The second finding supports the value of long-term psychotherapy, contradicting radical arguments from managed care that long-term therapy is both wasteful and ineffectual. While the rate of positive change began to flatten out after eight to ten sessions, a consistent though slower rate of improvement remained up to fifty-two sessions and beyond.

Data on the three symptom groupings was remarkable. Acute distress symptoms (anxiety, mild depression, compulsive behaviors) were most amenable to psychotherapeutic change. Client improvement rates were between 68% and 95% at fifty-two sessions, and the mean number of sessions to achieve a 50% change rate by clients (denoted as ED50) was five sessions for this group.

Chronic distress symptoms (stronger levels of anxiety and depression, phobias, obsessive thoughts and behaviors, cognitive disturbance, and interpersonal distress) showed 60% to 86% reduction of symptoms at fifty-two sessions, and the mean ED50 rate was fourteen sessions.

Characterological problems were, of course, the most resistant to change. These included personality disorders, hostility, frequent arguing, paranoia, psychosis, sleep troubles, chronic blaming, and never being close to others. The best recovery rate at fifty-two sessions was only 59%, and numerous symptoms failed to reach a 50% level of improvement. Discounting this subgroup of symptoms to avoid the skewed result, the mean ED50 rate was thirty-one sessions.

BOX 7.1—CORRELATION OF SESSIONS WITH SYMPTOM GROUPINGS (KOPTA ET AL., 1994)

- Acute (and milder) symptoms: 5 sessions average
- Chronic (moderate) symptoms: 14 sessions average
- Personality (severe) symptoms: 31 sessions average

While this data contradicts the notion that brief therapy is a panacea for *all* problems, it does support the notion that we develop a two-phased, sequential counseling model (which we presented in chapter 2): (1) brief therapy (one to twenty sessions) is recommended for all clients, and (2) long-term therapy is discretionary for clients who want and are able to obtain it.

RESEARCH ON CHRISTIAN COUNSELING

Up to the mid-1980s, research on Christian counseling was both sparse and weak. In 1986, Worthington, a Christian psychologist and professor, published a systematic review of the research on religious counseling to that date. He concluded that:

1. No support has been found that religious counseling has any more beneficial effects than does secular counseling in working with religious clients. In fact, little is known about what really makes religious counseling

distinct from secular counseling, although theory abounds.… The only good studies show secular and religious counseling to be equally effective with religious clients.

2. Most of the research had focused on pastors and pastoral counselors, who tended to report that they had not received good counseling training in seminary and did not consider themselves to be skilled counselors.

3. In general, the little research that did exist suggested that evangelical and conservative pastoral counselors were not as effective as helpers from a more liberal theological persuasion.

4. Almost all the research consisted of self-report surveys; no data was found in which the counseling process was actually observed and evaluated. Furthermore, no studies focused on professional therapists who identified themselves as Christians and sought to bring Christ into the counseling endeavor. (pp. 429-430)

The Faith Factor: The Missing Ingredient

We believe these results can be interpreted in one of two ways: Either Christian counseling does not work (or is no more effective than good secular counseling), or the validity of Christian counseling practice has not been adequately examined. In support of this latter hypothesis, a study by Larson, Sawyers, and McCullough (1998) revealed that out of 2,348 research articles in four prominent psychiatry journals only 2.5% studied one or more religious variables. In only three studies was religion the control variable.

Larson concluded that many mental health professionals saw Christianity or any religious commitment as outdated, anti-intellectual, even harmful to emotional health. Quite to the contrary, Larson, at the 1999 AACC World Conference, identified emerging research that showed religion to be both a positive and a negative health effect. He showed that religious commitment benefits 84% of the people in their mental and physical health. The ratio of benefits to harm was 30:1 in mental health and 20:1 in physical health. Noebel (1995) asserted, "Trying to separate the saved from the secular is like trying to [sever] the soul from the body—a deadly experiment. We must recognize that all worldviews have religious implications" (p. 18).

The Good News of Recent Research

The research on Christian counseling done since Worthington's review involves studies with better design, and they are much more hopeful, even if such studies remain limited in number.

Tisdale et al. (1997) reviewed a Christian inpatient program that used multimodal treatments for at least ten days with Christian patients, 95% of whom were diagnosed with major depression. At discharge, significant improvement was shown in the areas of personal adjustment, depression, overall psychiatric symptoms, and God-image. These gains remained largely intact at six- and twelve-month tests. Due to the applied practice setting, the researchers were unable to compare subjects to a control group or to delineate the relative contributions of the various therapeutic modes. Hence, this research model might be deemed quasi-experimental. Nevertheless, it is important in that it shows us how to go about empirically evaluating outcomes in applied settings of Christian counseling.

Johnson (1993), adopting a stricter comparative treatments standard of research in psychotherapy outcomes, found only five studies that compared religious and secular treatments with faith-oriented clients. In contrast to the often dramatic claims about the effectiveness of Christian counseling, it was shown to work better than secular counseling in only two of the studies, while the other three were equivocal.

Probst, Ostrom, Watkins, Dean, and Mashburn (1992) compared the use of religious versus nonreligious imagery in the treatment of depression and found religious imagery to have superior efficacy. Their study found that clients in pastoral counseling and in a cognitive-behavioral program with religious content showed significantly less post-treatment depression than clients in a cognitive therapy program with no religious content. (This is perhaps the best outcomes study done on Christian counseling to date.)

Recent research on people seeking to change homosexual behavior showed that religious motivation was a significant factor in controlling and assisting abstinence. A religious-based program for controlling homosexual behavior was reported by Schaeffer, Nottebaum, Smith, Dech, and Krawczyk (1999) in the *Journal of Psychology and Theology*. This study indicated that 61% of males and 71% of females remained chaste and avoided same-gender behavior one year after treatment. Furthermore, a remarkable 94% of those who relapsed said that they were still committed to their therapy objectives.

At a higher level of generality, and therefore more indirectly, a growing wealth of evidence supports the Christian counseling endeavor. Religious commitment and positive religious behavior (weekly church attendance, for example) have been shown to correlate positively with a variety of health and relationship variables. These include longer life, lower suicide rates, less depression, reduced alcohol and drug abuse, reduced criminal behavior, fewer divorces, higher levels of marital and sexual satisfaction, and reduced hospitalization and mental illness relapse (Gartner, 1996; Gartner, Larson, & Allen, 1991).

For nearly a decade, Harold Koenig (2000), professor, founder, and director of the Center for the Study of Religion, Spirituality, and Health at Duke University Medical School, has conducted research on the physical and mental health benefits of a robust faith. These groundbreaking studies show empirically that, when compared to nonbelievers or people of nominal faith, people who embrace a deep faith in Christ and are frequently involved with their faith communities

- cope better and experience less depression and anxiety in the face of problems,
- are more likely to grow psychologically and become stronger physically and mentally when faced with a personal health crisis,
- have greater overall indices of mental health and social support,
- show less abuse of alcohol, drugs, and cigarettes,
- show overall better mental and physical health, greater social support, and healthier lifestyles in general,
- have stronger immune systems that better fend off disease and protect against infections,
- have lower blood pressure and rates of hypertension,
- live longer and use fewer expensive health services,
- experience less depression and have greater quality of life when ill.

THE NEW PARADIGM: CONVERGENCE OF A TWENTY-FIRST-CENTURY SUPERSCIENCE

The new counseling paradigm of the twenty-first century, then, reveals the development of a clinical superscience that tracks the transformation of twentieth-century medicine as a scientific discipline and practice. The core principles arising from this empirical eclecticism of the late twentieth century are significant for helpers today. In the aggregate, the shifts in practice are so great as to warrant an assessment of a "paradigm shift" in the field (Kuhn, 1962). These shifts have to do with the assessment of human problems, the structure and process of therapy, and the methods used to bring about therapeutic change. Empirically supported treatments (ESTs) are now tied to nearly thirty different psychiatric disorders (as categorized by the *Diagnostic and Statistical Manual of Mental Disorders,* [DSM]), and the paradigm is well-established for ESTs to be developed across the entire panoply of psychiatric disorders during the first decade of the twenty-first century.

BASIC PRINCIPLES
Several principles have emerged that will continue to guide the practice and study of counseling in the years to come.

Life is complex, and human behavior is multidimensional. Doherty (1998) notes that "human behavior is the product of many weak forces.… We know that there are many contributing factors to human problems, but few singular, overwhelming causes that alone are sufficient to create and maintain them.… Most psychosocial problems arise from countless influences interacting simultaneously, most of them relatively weak when standing alone" (pp. 50-57).

Similar to the events-cascade scenario in which an array of small, simultaneous events leads to a newsworthy disaster, the future of problem analysis done by responsible helpers—Christian and non-Christian—will consider biological, psychological, spiritual, social, cultural, economic, and environmental factors. Though still appealing to those overwhelmed by the complexity of modern life and looking for simple answers, the hedgehog alternative of presenting one right answer, a single cause, or a magic bullet will recede in its influence.

Brief therapy is becoming the norm. Numerous forces are converging to indicate that counseling is and will be further hewn into brief (or at least brie*fer*) interventions consuming less time and money. The outcomes research that showed that most improvement comes within the first ten counseling sessions also revealed that the move toward brief therapy is already underway.

We must admit that managed care has only hastened the shift toward brief therapy; however, it did not initiate the shift. Even so, the relentless cost-cutting objectives of managed care have institutionalized denial of treatment and the authorization of a predetermined number of sessions. While many consumers are rightfully screaming about managed-care abuses and are beginning to fight back in courts and legislatures, many others agree with the objective of brief, limited therapy.

The new therapy is outcomes-driven and grounded in service accountability. The methods of this brief therapy paradigm are goal-directed or solution-oriented. They are driven by the demands for results or outcomes accountability, which has generated a consumer pragmatism on the field. The new catch phrase is "use it if it works." More and more counselors are learning and applying an eclectic mix of therapy models and techniques.

The TFA System: Thinking/Feeling/Acting

As we said in chapter 2, some people have suggested that focusing on how people think, feel, and act is essential for increasing counseling effectiveness (Corey, 1986; Ellis, 1982a; L'Abate, 1981). This belief led Hutchins (1984) and Hutchins and Cole (1992) to espouse a model called the TFA System. This model is designed as a means for "examining theories, techniques, behavioral problems, and interactional patterns that exist between people" (1984, p. 573). Hutchins (1984) offered the following definitions of thinking, feeling, and acting orientations:

> *Thinking orientation.* People who have a thinking orientation are characterized by intellectual, cognitively motivated behavior. They tend to behave in logical, rational, deliberate, and systematic ways. They are fascinated by the world of concepts, ideas, theories, words, and analytic relationships. The range of behavior in this category runs from minimal thought to considerable depth in quality and quantity of thinking. Organization of thoughts ranges from random and scattered to highly logical and rational.
>
> Counselors with this orientation tend to focus on what clients think and the consequences of those thoughts. Special attention is paid to what the client says or does not say. Frequently, illogical, irrational thinking is seen as a major cause of client problems. A primary goal of this approach is to change irrational thinking, thus enabling the client to resolve problems logically and realistically. Counselors who use this approach are likely to be influenced by the work of Ellis (rational-emotive therapy), Beck (cognitive therapy), Maultsby (rational behavior therapy), and Meichenbaum (cognitive modification).
>
> *Feeling orientation.* People who have a feeling orientation tend to behave in emotionally expressive ways. They are likely to go with their feelings in making decisions: "If it feels good, do it!" The expression and display of emotions, feelings, and affect provide clues about people with a primary feeling orientation. A person's demeanor can range from angry, anxious, bitter, hostile, or depressed to one of elation, joy, or enthusiasm. One's emotional energy level can vary from low to high.
>
> Counselors with this orientation are likely to be regarded as especially caring persons. They tend to focus on the client's feelings, paying special attention to the emotion revealed in how the person talks. Knotted and tangled emotions are seen as a major source of the client's problems. These counselors help the client describe, clarify, and understand mixed-up and immobilizing emotions. As emotional incongruencies are straightened out, the client is frequently able to perceive things more clearly. Counselors using this approach are likely to be influenced by the work of Rogers (nondirective, client-centered, person-centered therapy), Perls (gestalt therapy), Maslow, and a host of phenomenological, humanistic, and existential writers.
>
> *Acting orientation.* People with an acting orientation are generally characterized by their desire to *do* something and by their drive to achieve goals.

They are frequently involved with others, and they tend to plunge into the thick of things. Action-oriented people get the job done, one way or another. To them, doing something is better than doing nothing; thus, they are frequently involved in a variety of activities. Their behavior may range from loud, aggressive, and public-oriented to quiet, subtle, and private.

Counselors with an action orientation tend to see client problems as arising from either inappropriate actions or lack of activity. These counselors focus particularly on what the client does or does not do, and they tend to encourage clients to begin programs designed to eliminate, modify, or teach new behavior. An action-oriented counselor is likely to be influenced by the work of Bandura (behavior modification), Wolpe (behavior therapy), Krumnoltz and Thoresen (behavioral counseling), and others espousing a behavioral approach to change. (p. 573)

THE NEW STANDARD OF CARE

Famed psychologist Arnold Lazarus (1990), one of the prolific foxes of modern psychotherapy, challenged the helping professions by asking whether we will be able to transcend the hold that psychological models and schools—what he deemed "therapeutic superstitions"—have on us. The best helpers, he asserts, will be those who are able to shift their orientations and techniques to fit client objectives and improve therapy outcomes. We believe that the convergence of the aforementioned forces on counseling and psychotherapy in the years ahead will either cause us to embrace or force us to yield to the dynamics that Lazarus proposes.

The transformation of psychotherapy to a more scientific enterprise is leading to significant change in the modern standard of counseling care. The simple twentieth-century standard (applying a preferred methodology in a one-size-fits-all approach regardless of client outcome) is quickly losing sway. As we have said, the twenty-first-century standard in psychotherapy will be driven by results and outcomes, and it will look much more like the specialized treatment protocols prevalent in the practice of medicine. This developing psychotherapeutic standard of care will ask which treatment and intervention or combination of treatments

- have been shown empirically to be clinically effective and are the most cost and time efficient;
- are delivered by the most competent therapist(s) in the most appropriate setting(s) with the best match to client values and goals;
- best fit the client (or couple, family, or group) with these specific problems, strengths, resources, and limitations at this particular time (and developmental stage) in his or her life.

Each of the three primary factors—treatment, counselor, client—has been discussed in the literature for years. A maturing profession is now developing the other distinguishing criteria that will likely become the mental health standard of care in the first quarter-century of the third millennium. All therapists, whether school-oriented or eclectic, will be increasingly evaluated across the above variables to determine effectiveness and expertise. Making a good-faith effort to achieve this standard of care will help maintain high-quality relations with licensure boards, courts, the church, third-party payers, and discriminating clients who have become sophisticated consumers.

THE TWENTY-FIRST-CENTURY CHRISTIAN COUNSELOR

If Doherty's prediction is correct—that fox therapists are the therapists of the future—we further this argument by stating that the Christian fox represents the best future of Christian counseling. By this we do not mean that modern hedgehog clinicians will be relegated to a secondary, even inferior, status. Rather, the effective Christian clinician will be a principled, biblically informed, and responsible eclectic who knows how to fit the right therapy with the right client at the right time and the right stage of living.

The Christian fox of the twenty-first century will be a Paracentric-type helper dedicated to the development of a universal (and unifying) superscience of Christian counseling. This is a supernatural science, one that is completely open to and dependent on the intervention of God in the counseling process. What's more, the effectiveness and efficiency of this God-centered approach will be empirically demonstrated.

The effective Christian counselor will be able to skillfully communicate to clients God's grace and covenantal plan as well as the authority of his Word. As Crabb (2001) states, "I am…convinced that God has provided us with everything we need to encounter Him, to enjoy community, and to experience personal transformation" (p. 6).

In fact, in the years ahead, the Christian counseling standard of care will incorporate this biblical orientation, and the question that will likely be asked will be, Which treatment and intervention or combination of treatments

- honors Jesus Christ and are grounded in biblical revelation, have been (or can be) shown empirically to be clinically effective, and are the most cost and time efficient?
- is delivered by the most competent therapist(s) in the most appropriate setting(s) with the best match to client values and goals?

- best fits the client (or couple, family, or group) with these specific problems, strengths, resources, and limitations, at this particular time (and developmental stage and level of spiritual maturity and commitment) in his or her life?

In the twenty-first-century paradigm, hedgehog models will be learned as needed, but they will be viewed within a larger fox context of eclectic therapies that counselors will use with high levels of clinical expertise. The counseling models that work for us as practitioners are those that are Christ-centered, intensely personal, embedded in the community of believers, and able to motivate people who seek comfort and healing. This orientation involves ongoing negotiation among counselor, client, community, and context while weighing the goals, values, beliefs, and means of accomplishing the therapeutic task.

Such approaches to Christian counseling parallel the general work of psychotherapy integration and common-factors definition—as well as the prescriptive therapies that tie diagnosis with treatment—in very specific ways. This essential (and creative) tension between diverse practice and common, unifying elements exists throughout our helping profession. We are convinced that the best twenty-first-century Christian counseling will follow this diversity-unity dynamic.

PART III

THE CHRISTIAN COUNSELING RELATIONSHIP

CHAPTER 8

THE ESSENTIAL HELPING RELATIONSHIP

Secrets to Counselor Character and Competence

GARY W. MOON AND FREDA CREWS*

Therapeutic relationships that foster healing are not formed merely from well-chosen techniques that can be relegated to one's professional identity, but grow out of the therapist's inner life.... In this sense, psychotherapy is both professional and personal.

—McMINN AND McRAY, 1997

Even a dog can judge character. At least that's what a columnist suggested in *USA Today* (Wilson, 2001). He presented his own mutt, Murphy, as living proof. Whenever a new guest visits their home, Murphy administers a quick character test. She positions herself next to the visitor, her head within easy reach. It's a simple scratch-and-pass test, really. If the guest fails, an immediate makeup exam is administered. Murphy places her nose under the person's hand in a not-too-subtle suggestion to extend a little love. If the second test is flunked, Murphy has identified a person of questionable character who may not be invited back. Character is important to dogs. It's about being others-focused and in loving relationship—at least in part.

It is essential that Christian counselors have impeccable character. A friend makes the humorous suggestion that he would be a much better therapist if he just had better clients. We've entertained similar thoughts when involved in the process of selecting clients or students for counselor training. The best way to

---

* Gary Moon contributed the first half of this chapter, and Freda Crews contributed the second half.

produce stellar graduates (effective counselors) is to select top-quality applicants. What should top the selection-criteria list, exceeding even grade-point average or undergraduate major? We believe the top criterion should be good character, generously sprinkled with the capacity for both selfless love and warmth in relationship. But without a good dog like Murphy, this can be hard to sniff out—and even harder to produce.

If the oft-said assertion is true—that good character is doing the right thing when no one is looking—then good character is largely unseen. Yet good character and its twin sister, ethical excellence, are counselor requirements for most clients who expect high levels of dedicated service. Character issues, then, are most visible when they are most dysfunctional, that is, when their lack or weak expression hurts clients. Weakened or lost character has ethical consequences, and it assaults the competence and excellence we wish to promote in this book. We look in this chapter at the person of the counselor—both personal character and relational dynamics—as a necessary condition to successful counseling.

BIBLICAL ANTHROPOLOGY

Biblical anthropology recognizes that humanity is the creation of God and that this creation includes traits made "in the image of God" (Genesis 1:27). Men and women are, in fact, the crown of creation. This God-image, in part, remains a mystery to us, but it is reflected in our ability to know God, to study and understand God's creation, to create, and to make moral choices. God also reveals that all of humanity and the whole of creation are flawed by sin, which breaks relations with God and produces death (Romans 3:10-18,23). This uniquely human condition can be redeemed and relations with God restored only by faith-acceptance of the death and resurrection of Jesus Christ, who gave himself as a love offering to atone for sin on behalf of all humankind (Romans 5:12-21).

The human person is a unitary being, comprising spiritual, psychological, social and interpersonal, and biological dimensions. The unitary nature of the human person reflects a systems understanding of reality, including the interconnectedness of our inner and outer realities. Hence, the reality of growth, suffering, healing, and sanctification affects the entire person. Experience for good or ill in any one dimension of life necessarily influences and is affected by all other dimensions.

Our created unity is assaulted by the struggle of the divided heart—the war between evil and good, darkness and light, sin and righteousness. This inner warfare of the heart is expressed externally in issues of character. It is an ancient, universal struggle that vexes everyone and, in truth, can be resolved only through personal relationship with Christ. God promises that in the act of redemption, "I will give them *an undivided heart* [italics added] and put a new spirit in them" (Ezekiel 11:19).

Christ is our perfect role model because he is both true God and true man, the first of his kind with an undivided heart wholly devoted to his heavenly Father. Because he is truly God-come-in-the-flesh, he reveals all the attributes of God that are being produced in us as we yield more and more to the sanctifying work of the Holy Spirit. As true man, he has experienced all the joys and vicissitudes of life just as we have, and he shows us how to cope with—even triumph over—the sufferings and challenges of life and death. In Christ, a divine anthropology is revealed: The undivided heart is swept away by the death of the conflicted way and by the creation and implantation of a new heart into the soul, a heart that is wholly devoted to God and is full of joy and peace.

THE GREAT DEBATE

The 1990s witnessed a great dispute within the counseling profession concerning what is most important in training mental health professionals—training in techniques versus developing the person of the counselor. The debate continues into the present millennium.

In 1993, at the request of David Barlow, president of Division 12 of the American Psychological Association, a task force was constituted to consider methods for educating clinical psychologists, third-party payers, and the public regarding effective psychotherapies. This task force championed the notion that it is much better if clinical treatment can be empirically validated. A host of recommendations were made, including the following:

1. A complete list of treatments of documented efficacy should be established and updated as new evidence is provided.
2. APA-site visitors for accreditation of doctoral programs were urged to make training in empirically validated treatments a high priority.
3. Once efficacy data is established, training manuals should be produced.
4. APA-site visit teams should make training in empirically validated treatments a criterion for APA accreditation.
5. Criteria for empirically validated treatments should be presented. (APoA Task Force, 1995)

The report of the task force was adopted in October 1993 and, with it, a gauntlet was thrown down. Technique was championed as more important than the person of the counselor. Counselor effectiveness was cast as strict compliance with standardized treatment procedures.

ON SECOND THOUGHT...

Garfield (1998), however, reviewed the developments that followed the task-force report. His article appeared as part of a special issue of the *Journal of Consulting and Clinical Psychology* that focused on the impact of the emphasis being placed on empirically validated therapies for specific psychiatric disorders. While acknowledging that the increased emphasis on empirical support is a positive, he raised many important concerns. Among them:

- The present emphasis on treatment procedures may overlook the possibility that the therapist may be more important than the manual.
- Is the validated importance of common factors, accounting for the preponderance of similar findings in the research on psychotherapy and outcome, to be ignored?
- With the large number of psychiatric disorders and the length of time it takes to demonstrate competency using only one of hundreds of different approaches to treatment, do we really want to become that specialized?

In other words, should we really become so specialized in our training practices as to produce graduates whose business cards no longer say *Psychologist* or *Professional Counselor* but *Expert in the Treatment of Bedwetting and Spider Phobias*? Those who are rightly concerned about the continuing fragmentation of psychology and the behavioral sciences should take note.

Garfield's perspective seems helpful to the field. We believe he provides a wonderfully mature both-and approach. Yes, techniques are important and should be empirically supported (he softened the word *validated*). Ethical obligations to our clients and practical realities of politics and payment demand nothing less than this level of accountability. But the importance of both the therapist and client must not be overlooked. Producing counselors whose lives reflect key common factors and uncommon character is also of vital importance.

COMMON FACTORS AND CHRISTIAN CHARACTER

Which is most important in producing effective counselors: theoretical orientation, therapeutic techniques, or the person of the helper? Many in our discipline have examined this question.

Combs, Avila, and Purkey (1971) promoted the idea of self-as-instrument and defined the character qualities of the counselor that correlated with constructive client change. The most effective counselors were those who

- were able to identify strongly with clients,
- perceived reality from an internal frame of reference,

- saw clients as capable and motivated,
- were oriented toward caring for others (not self-indulgent),
- were honest and open (not hiding),
- worked toward freeing others (not controlling them).

Truax and Mitchell (1971) conducted a review of more than one hundred studies on the effectiveness of counselors. They concluded that while therapeutic techniques can be useful, the person of the counselor (personality and character) is most important. Perez (1979) and Seligman (1995) concur and cite evidence that the counselor's personality is the single most important variable associated with effective therapy. It appears that capable counselors possess a cluster of personal qualities that transcend both their therapeutic techniques and their theoretical orientations (Small, 1990).

The Golden Triad

What are these personal qualities that are so important to the effectiveness of counseling? Perhaps the classic study in this area was conducted by Rogers (yes, that one), Gendlin, Kiesler, and Truax (1967). Their four-year investigation suggested that clients improved when counselors showed high levels of *warmth, genuineness,* and *empathy*—which became known as the "therapeutic triad"—regardless of their theoretical orientation.

Garfield (1994) points to research concerning common factors associated with effective counseling. By common factors Garfield is referring to those dimensions of the treatment setting (therapist, therapy, client) that are not specific to a particular technique—dimensions such as the client's expectation for improvement and the therapist's level of persuasion, warmth, attention, understanding, support, and encouragement.

The common threads that seem to run through these investigations are the importance of the person of the therapist and the ability of the therapist to foster a positive and compassionate relationship with the client. Perlman (1979) sounded a note that has rung true for many therapists. She even made it the title of her book *Relationship: The Heart of Helping People.*

Kottler and Brown (1996) compiled a list of desirable counselor traits gleaned from the works of numerous leaders in the field. Included in their list are self-confidence, high energy level, sense of humor, neutrality, flexibility, emotional stability, risk-taking experience, analytic thinking, creativity, enthusiasm, honesty, and compassion. Similarly, Parrott (1997) devotes a chapter to summarizing research on effective counseling. Regarding the personal qualities of competent counselors, he offers an annotated list of what he purports to be the eight most important qualities of an effective counselor:

1. psychological health
2. genuine interest in others
3. empathetic ability
4. personal warmth
5. personal power
6. self-awareness
7. tolerance of ambiguity
8. an awareness of values

Love and the Fruit of the Spirit

A former president of the American Psychological Association made a remarkable statement. Allport (1950) called love "incomparably the greatest psychotherapeutic agent...something that professional psychiatry cannot of itself create, focus, or

---

Box 8.1—A Case Study in Character Development

Sam was a good therapist and a dedicated Christian, experienced and respected by pastors and the professional community in which he practiced. Shortly after turning fifty, however, he developed a chronic medical condition and increasingly complained of "burnout and exhaustion" in his counseling ministry. He plowed ahead nonetheless, convinced of his duty to serve his needy caseload and anxious about his longstanding dependence on his counseling income. As a Christian, he had long struggled with the dilemma of knowing God versus knowing about God. For twenty-five years he had maintained his commitment to Christian counseling, to an exemplary ethical record, and to the control of his character flaws through the sheer force of his will. This dedication was facilitated by his keen intelligence, considerable energy, and broad-ranging practice abilities.

The onset of medical trouble and practice burnout was experienced as a major, though largely silent and unseen, crisis in Sam's life. More and more he felt overwhelmed by the complexity and intensity of client problems and crises. He found himself resenting and avoiding certain clients who aroused anger and disgust within him. He witnessed in himself the emergence of a passive-aggressive flaw that avoided some client contact by reducing sessions and refusing to return phone calls. In his secret thoughts, he fantasized ways to quit therapy and was confused about whether to try teaching or go into another career altogether. For the first time in his life, however, he did not have the courage to act. Sam was

release" (p. 90). Unfortunately, this lack of experimental control likely explains why for decades concepts such as *love* and *the soul* received so little attention from the "science" of psychology.

Collins (1988) references Allport's remark and suggests that Christianity offers "an approach to life that is based wholly upon love and thus is able to help where secular counseling fails" (p. 42). Collins then raises a thought-provoking challenge for the Christian counselor. If love and relationship are associated with effective people helping, he muses, why is it not appropriate for Christian counselors to ask God to love needy people through them? And why, as an ongoing part of our training as Christian counselors, should we not pray for God to transform our character in such a way that we become more loving?

After his own careful review of the common factors in effective counseling, Collins further suggests that the Christian counselor might summarize all of this

---

afraid; he believed he would fail because he did not have the motivation or energy to succeed at such a daunting change.

Aware that his symptoms suggested a growing depression, he consulted with his doctor, began a trial of antidepressant medication, and scaled back his practice to a more manageable level. Even so, he was convinced at times that he needed treatment more than some of his clients did. A variety of character flaws and ethical missteps, arising from problems that had been repressed rather than redeemed, were appearing and were even being noticed by some clients and colleagues.

Most alarming to Sam was the revelation, at a deeper level of his being, of his dependence on self rather than on God. This dilemma was exaggerated by the faulty belief that he had always done God's work in God's power. He now understood that he had largely done Sam's work in the name of God. When the sea of adversity struck, his self-made foundations were weak and washed away. Now, just when he needed to cleave intensely to God for refuge and renewal, he instead felt guilty, confused, and angry, and he wanted to avoid God.

Sam began praying desperately for a way out. For the first time in his life he knew he could not construct a solution on his own. At times he was seized by an inordinate fear. In his dreams he felt himself drowning in swift, cold, deep waters without the knowledge or stamina to save himself. Depressing though this was, this fear was the beginning of wisdom for Sam, and this revelation was also the seed of a new intimacy and reliance on God in Christ.

research on common factors by stating that the counselor's life should show evidence of the Holy Spirit's fruit as presented in Galatians 5:22-23: joy, peace, patience, kindness, goodness, faithfulness, gentleness, self-control, and—probably the most important ingredient in effective counseling—love. It is difficult to disagree. The fruit of the Spirit is the very character of Jesus Christ, and the goal of Christian formation is for our lives to become mirrors of the character of Christ.

IMPLICATIONS FOR CHRISTIAN COUNSELORS

Effective Christian counselors cannot ignore the present call for the use of empirically supported treatment approaches. But neither can we ignore the role of classic Christian transformation in producing positive character change in the life of the Christian counselor. Authentic Christian spiritual formation that produces the character of Christ (the fruit of the Spirit) within an individual may be the best way of enhancing the common factors within a counselor and facilitating an effective therapeutic relationship. And ultimately this process may become an established and legitimate part of the counseling process itself.

Carried along with the recent tidal wave of empirical validation of the value of counseling is a healthy focus on verifiable and effective counseling techniques. However, as has been pointed out by Worthington (1988, 1993, with Kurusu, McCullough, & Sandage, 1996) and Larson, Sawyers, and McCullough (1998), there is a growing sense of urgency for Christian mental health professionals to establish an empirically supported menu of treatment options that arise from Christian faith and practice.

Simultaneously, the past decade witnessed increasing interest in spiritual disciplines and the process of spiritual formation. According to Willard (1998), this derives from a "sense of our urgent need for mental and emotional health as well as spiritual depth, and from the simultaneous realization that recent standard practice of American Christianity is not meeting that need" (p. 101). In a 1996 interview for *Christian Counseling Today*, Willard asserted that

> [m]any counselors today are learning that for their own work, deep immersion in the [spiritual] disciplines is necessary, both for developing their own character and, beyond that, accessing special powers of grace for their work in counseling people. Many [counselors] are learning how to use techniques of prayer and various kinds of ministry to have a much greater effect than they could if all they had to go on were the things they learned in their clinical training programs. Graduate...training programs often are quite good, but they don't do very well in teaching counselors how to use prayer

in healing people, or how to use Scripture, or help people make wise decisions of various kinds about fellowship, worship, and so on, all of which might really bring a greater power into the healing process. (p. 19)

TRANSFORMATION IN LIFE AND PRACTICE

Let's be honest: The questions about the content and process of Christian counseling—whether spiritual formation activities are explicitly (or even implicitly) incorporated into one's counseling work—are becoming significant in the church. As shown earlier in this work, there seems to be a growing criticism of Christian counselors who possess a PhD education in psychology and human behavior but only a Sunday school education in Bible and Christian theology.

McMinn (1996) challenged us all to see that a crucial aspect of character development is training and living authentically as Christians in the realms of psychology, theology, and spiritual growth. And if we are to be equally honest with ourselves as Christian counselors, we should add that the growing interest of Christian counseling training programs in the process of spiritual formation perhaps reflects a realization that standard practice of American Christian counseling has not been fully meeting the need for mental, emotional, and spiritual health.

The recent interest in empirically validated techniques in counseling and the growing interest in Christian spiritual formation call for authentic transformation. As Clinton and Ohlschlager have shared, we are at a place of seeing spiritual transformation both as a uniquely Christian strategy for change and as a methodology for increasing the effectiveness of Christian counselors (by enhancing the ability of therapists to convey love and to participate in meaningful relationship in the church).

Toward these ends, we present Willard's (2000) model of the person (figure 8.1) as well as some of his observations concerning the process of authentic transformation as an illustration of a (character) change approach.

According to Willard (1998), "A soul is essentially the component of a person—as are mind and will, which are among the soul's essential parts—and does not exist without a person whose soul it is" (p. 102). Willard asserts that the soul is a component of a person—that aspect of the self that integrates all the other aspects into one life—and it is also the whole, the person. Therefore, the soul is simultaneously the most central component of a person (such as the central processing unit of a computer) and a representation of the whole (the entire computer set aglow). The soul is a part *and* the whole. "Granting significant dissimilarities, it is helpful to think of the soul as [that which] operates all dimensions of the human system by governing and coordinating what goes on in them. It has its own nature, parts, properties, internal and external relations" (p. 104).

As illustrated in figure 8.1, transformation is the process whereby the whole self is restructured from the inside out. Spiritual growth is the process of authentic transformation of each of the rings of the diagram—of each of the aspects of the person. Transformation is a matter of the heart and will, the mind (thoughts and emotions), the body, and interpersonal relationships all becoming a consistent reflection of the whole life of Christ. Character change is a form of will-alignment. It involves growth in the ability to surrender our will, as Christ did in the Garden of Gethsemane (Matthew 26:36-46), to the will of God—several thousand times each day. Character change in Christian formation begins in the heart (willing surrender), but it affects every aspect of the person including thoughts, emotions, behaviors, interpersonal relationships, and so forth. Willard's model represents the soul as the natural capacities of a person to choose or will, to represent or think, to feel (sensate and emotional), and to behave and interact with others.

FIG. 8.1 DALLAS WILLARD'S MODEL OF THE PERSON*

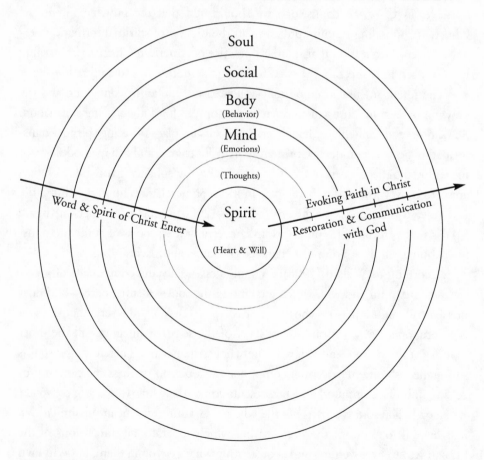

---

* Copyright © Dallas Willard, November 30, 2001. Used by permission.

Transformation of the soul means deep internal change, which is possible only through the mystery of Christ within (Colossians 1:26-27) and the evoking of faith in Christ to live and act through us. As part of the process, all aspects of the person begin to function as a whole and as a more focused reflection of the character of Christ. It is the soul—the whole of the person—that becomes transformed. But it is also accurate to say that the soul is deep within; it is the inmost part that unifies the whole. What was lost is being found.

Willard's model seems helpful for Christian counselors at many levels. The concept of the soul was all but lost to modern psychology, a fact that has been well documented (Boyd, 1998; Johnson, 1998). In light of Willard's uniting model of the various aspects of the person, it seems particularly interesting that psychology has, at times, become fixated on various parts of the whole—unconscious processing (psychodynamic approaches), body (behaviorism), mind (cognitive psychology), and interpersonal (interpersonal and social psychology). Willard provides a refreshing and integrative picture of the soul and an appealing methodology for facilitating transformation (character change) within the lives of clients and counselors. Psychology without consideration for the (whole) soul had been prone to compartmentalization—even fragmentation.

In addition to providing a larger and more inclusive focus, Willard's perspective on the soul and on spiritual formation offers Christian counseling a viable theory and methodology for authentic Christian transformation which, in our opinion, should become part of the training provided to Christian counselors as well as part of their practice of soul care among clients. What is offered seems nothing short of a uniquely Christian methodology for positive character development for counselors themselves. It is to that challenge that we now turn our attention.

CHARACTER SECRETS OF COMPETENT CHRISTIAN COUNSELORS

There is a desire within all of us to be the best we can be at whatever God calls us to do. For Christian counselors this means aspiring to competence and excellence in soul-care ministry.

An altruistic desire and a documented call, however, do not magically create competence. Competent counselors must discover and develop certain qualities, attributes, and skills. This discussion will focus on seven essential and identifiable characteristics of competent Christian counselors. Calling these traits "character secrets" gives them a mystique that we hope will arouse or perpetuate the yearning to realize your full potential as a person and counselor. As the apostle Paul said to us, "Whatever you do, work at it with all your heart, as working for the Lord, not for men, since you know that you will receive an inheritance from the Lord as a reward. It is the Lord Christ you are serving" (Colossians 3:23-24).

COMPASSION

Our desire to counsel must be fueled by *compassion* or it will lack a motivating force that cannot be compensated for even with well-learned skills and techniques. The most effective counselors will be driven by compassion for people struggling with the inequities and unfairness of life, the unanswered questions related to pain and suffering, and the habitual self-defeating behaviors they can't seem to break. Compassion enables counselors to perceive the anguish of soul that expresses itself through the distressed faces and tears of their clients.

According to Vine (1984), *compassion* refers to feeling distressed through the ills of, being affected similarly by, or suffering with others (p. 210). Hebrews 4:15 reveals that the compassionate Jesus feels and suffers with us when we experience distress and pain. Compassion gives the therapeutic process a life-changing force that must flow from the counselor to the client rather than the reverse.

Academic training alone cannot equip counselors with compassion. To be similarly affected, or to suffer with those we want to help, is not a skill that can be learned but is rather an internal dynamic that must be cultivated. We are exhorted by the Scriptures to "clothe [ourselves] with compassion" (Colossians 3:12). Our clients perceive more about us than we might be aware of, and they respond and react accordingly. If we exude compassion, it will exert a positive influence into the counseling relationship and will positively affect the outcome (Benner 1987, p. 39).

Psychotherapists Neuhaus and Astwood (1980) punctuate the value of compassion. They quote Rubin (1975) when they state that "compassion is defined as a 'feeling for another's sorrow or hardship that leads to help'. This is almost a definition of empathic therapy, for without the 'feeling for' the process becomes a technical exercise, and without the 'help' it is merely idle and disconnected pity or sympathy" (p. 67).

Let's reflect on the death of Lazarus, one of Jesus' closest friends. When Jesus learned from Mary and Martha, the two sisters of Lazarus, that he had died, Jesus was overwhelmed with grief—his own grief. He was also filled with *compassion* for Mary and Martha. As he watched them grieve, he knew their sorrow, and it led him to raise Lazarus from the dead. The shortest verse of Scripture says it all: "Jesus wept" (John 11:35). The competent Christian counselor is defined first by compassion.

CONSCIENTIOUSNESS

Competent counselors must strive to gain the trust of their clients, many of whom have been betrayed by significant others in their lives. We must regard the counseling relationship as sacred, to be protected from any and all contaminating influences or behaviors. It must be a safe place for those tormented souls who have turned to us for help.

To win our clients' trust we must prove to them that we can be trusted, that we are conscientious people of integrity who speak and model the truth. As conscientious counselors we will be honest about our training, our experience, and our credentials. We will be honest about what we know and do not know. Our lives will reveal us to be the persons we say we are. Counselors of integrity exemplify a consistency between what they say and what they do.

Neuhaus and Astwood (1980) warn, "If a patient should ever discover a therapist's deception...the likelihood of continued effective treatment would be greatly reduced or, more probably, totally destroyed" (p. 40). This is doubly true for Christian counselors. White (1987) asserted that "Psychotherapists who are reputed to be Christians carry a particular responsibility in view of [the fact that] clients tend to seek help from therapists who share their belief and value system. If that is true, clients who seek out Christian therapists will expect the therapist's Christianity to affect the counseling process" (p. 39).

Clients are entitled to ethical conduct in all areas related to the therapeutic interaction between counselor and client (Ohlschlager & Mosgofian, 1992). As competent Christian counselors we will readily admit that we are real and flawed people, but this admission will not let us off the hook regarding conscientiousness. Our goal is to be able to say with the apostle Paul, "Our conscience testifies that we have conducted ourselves...in our relations with you, in the holiness and sincerity that are from God" (2 Corinthians 1:12). This assertion points us toward the third secret of effective counselors.

CONFIDENCE

Imagine being a client and meeting a counselor who is nervous, fidgety, and sweating, and who speaks haltingly as he greets you. This wouldn't inspire much confidence in his (or her) counseling ability, would it? Insecure, timid, and passive counselors will not find themselves numbered among the competent. Competence demands that counselors have a healthy awareness of their ability, knowledge, and skills. Kottler (1993) asserts, "The ideal therapist is comfortable with herself and appears warm, tolerant, sincere, serene, tranquil and self-assured. This quiet confidence is counterbalanced by a contagious zest for life"

(p. 33). Confidence begins with a confirmation of our calling and is perpetuated by adequate training.

Am I confident I have been called to be a counselor? Every Christian is called to counsel in a general sense, but according to Collins, some are called and gifted specifically by God, and their calling can be confirmed. Collins (1988) alleges, consistent with the Paracentric focus of this book, "In Romans 12:8 (NKJV), we read of the gift of exhortation *(paraklesis)*, a word which means 'coming alongside to help' and implies such activities as admonishing, supporting and encouraging others.... Those who have and are developing this gift will see positive results in their counseling as people are helped and the church is built up" (p. 36).

You must be honest with yourself if there is reason to doubt your call. If God has called you to a counseling ministry, the search for confirmation will only make you a stronger and more confident counselor. If he does not confirm your call to be a counselor, then ask him to direct you to the ministry he would have you pursue (Jeremiah 33:3).

Is my academic or other training sufficient? When counselors exceed the limitations of their training and experience, an inner sense of inadequacy can erode their confidence. To grow in confidence, we must live and work with the tension of slowly stretching ourselves beyond our present comfort zones while, at the same time, refraining from seeing clients who present situations that truly exceed our capabilities. Our training and experience must match our counseling practice; incompatibility will rob us of the confidence we need to be effective, and clients can suffer additional emotional impairment in the process (see Cormier & Cormier, 1991, pp. 14-15).

Whenever the issue of training for Christian counselors surfaces, at least two questions arise: (1) What kind? and (2) How much?

What kind of training? The best kind of training is the kind that equips you for what you are already doing or what you plan to do in the future. Whether you are a lay helper, pastor, or professional counselor, there are basic skills to be learned and inner attributes to be refined. Whatever training is necessary to become knowledgeable and skilled as effective Christian counselors should be pursued within the confines of your resources. This should include training related to the "impact of spirituality on clients or with the individual spiritual issues of the counselors-in-training" (Hickson, Housley, & Wages, 2000, p. 59).

How much training? We would suggest "whatever it takes" to give you the knowledge, experience, and confidence you need to become a catalyst for change in your clients' lives. Clients expect their counselors to be knowledgeable and competent. Counselors must acquire the necessary academic, practical, and clinical skills to meet their clients' expectations. This should challenge all counselors to pursue the training course, supervision, and practical experience they need to match their distinctive counseling setting.

According to White (Benner, 1987), Christian counselors must derive three things from their training experiences:

1. They must possess a good level of clinical competence.
2. They must "identify and understand the beliefs and values inherent in their own worldview and how these affect them personally. For Christians this includes a concerted effort to grapple in depth with the Word of God to arrive at an ever-growing, integrated, cognitive and experiential understanding of the Scriptures" (p. 38).
3. They need "an understanding of self" (p. 38).

You must follow the maxim "Physician, heal thyself" when it comes to evaluating your own problems (Neuhaus & Astwood, 1980). These authors go on to urge therapists to admit to their own "intrapersonal conflicts and motivations and attempt to clarify and deal with them.... For this reason, personal therapy is viewed as a necessary part of professional training. Moreover, a continuing self-examination is also indispensable. The training of a capable therapist is never really complete" (p. 64).

The next secret will challenge counselors to look outside of themselves for a firm foundation upon which to build effectiveness.

CENTEREDNESS

Committing to walk through the dark caverns of adversity and despair with another person can test the limits of even the most proficient and competent counselors. Without solid moorings to hold us, we could easily be swept into the ocean of pain and distress that surrounds us day after day. Clinebell (1984) agrees that effective helpers can only be sensitive and responsive to the needs of others "to the degree that they possess this centered awareness of their own value and personhood. Persons who are not centered are out of touch with the only secure locus for stable self-esteem and identity" (p. 418).

The *centeredness* factor finds its strength in Christ. He is the One in whom we find our identity, the One who can keep us steady when the storms of our clients' lives are raging around us. Christ must work in and through us and be found at the center of our minds and ministries. As we reach out offering his message of hope, we must remind ourselves again and again that we are royal heirs and that we are loved unconditionally. As 1 John 3:1 says: "How great is the love the Father has lavished on us, that we should be called children of God! And that is what we are!" Promises and directions found in the Scriptures can help us keep our balance when the pressures appear to be closing in on us from every side.

It is not always easy to hold our own worlds together and at the same time to try to guide others to the Canaan rest they are so desperately seeking. The encouragement we need in order to persevere can be found in such promises as God gave to his unfaithful, yet unconditionally loved, Israelites millennia ago:

> Do not be fainthearted or afraid; do not be terrified or give way to panic before them. For the LORD your God is the one who goes with you to fight for you against your enemies to give you victory. (Deuteronomy 20:3-4)

BOX 8.2—BIBLE STUDY: BEING A CHRIST-CENTERED HELPER (EPHESIANS 6:10-18)

All the instructions needed for maintaining our center in God can be found in Ephesians 6:10-18. We are encouraged to be *strong* in the Lord and his mighty power (verse 10). Relying on God for strength will counteract our tendency to look either to (or within) ourselves or to our training and knowledge, and will make us the capable counselors we want to be. We will be strong when we

- put on the whole armor of God because we can expect to do war with the devil (verse 11);
- expect Jesus Christ to be a real presence in our counseling sessions;
- make sure that our armor is in place so that we will be able to stand our ground (verse 13);
- allow *truth* to guide us regarding ourselves and our clients. It was not an accident that the Holy Spirit placed the breastplate of righteousness (verse 14) over the heart area. Christian counselors are in both envious and risky positions of having to direct misguided people to the truth that can set them free;
- pursue the *peace* of mind and soul that our clients are looking to us to guide them to (verse 15);
- trust the *shield of faith* (verse 16), our defensive weapon that protects us from the evil one and enables us to persevere in the fiercest personal and professional battles. This shield also allows us to encourage clients to let our faith become their faith until their faith comes alive again. When they are unable to see God through their tears and are afraid to trust him or anyone else, we can ask them to trust us until they can trust him. Our

Centeredness in Christ opens a storehouse of resources available at all times to Christian counselors. When we are centered in him, he is the vine and we are the branches (John 15:1-8), and this life-giving connection flows from us to our clients. "The challenge that confronts each of us is to help release this potential by becoming *incarnational counselors*—persons whose imperfect relationships somehow enable the liberating Word to become flesh and dwell in and among us with healing power" (Clinebell, 1984, p. 430).

The first four character secrets of competent Christian counselors have focused on the *person* of the counselor (Bergin & Lambert, 1978). The fifth secret bridges the gap between the person and the *performance* of the counselor.

---

faith in the God who cannot lie enables them to carry on until they can believe for themselves (Hebrews 6:18);

- wear the *helmet of salvation* (verse 17), which serves as protection for our minds and provides hope for us and for our counselees that there is light at the end of the tunnel. Salvation is related to deliverance. Our clients come to us imprisoned by fear, anxiety, depression, abuse, lost relationships, and a spiritual darkness from which they seek deliverance. This piece of armor enables us to rise to the occasion;

- wield the *sword of the Spirit, which is the word of God* (verse 17). This is our offensive weapon when we engage in warfare against evil. The promises found in the Word will comfort and sustain us when it seems that our hearts will break or that we cannot carry the load any longer. They are a great counseling resource to use for comforting, encouraging, and even confronting our clients. The Scriptures are the key to living a God-centered life. McMinn (1996) says it well: "When Scripture is used creatively, spontaneously and confidently in counseling, it is only because the counselor is so close to God's Word that the ideas and principles in scripture have become contagious" (p. 118);

- *pray in the Spirit on all occasions with all kinds of prayers and requests* (verse 18). Praying in the Spirit denotes an intimacy with the Holy Spirit that helps us know how to pray regarding any and all situations in our lives at any given time (Romans 8:26-27). God-centeredness requires that we bathe every facet of our lives in prayer, including the competency we seek as counselors. Whatever deficiencies and inadequacies we discover in the process of becoming competent should be presented to God in prayer (Philippians 4:6).

COMMUNICATION

The central maxim of counselor training asserts that you are always sending a message by what you say or don't say, do or don't do. Counselors can be compassionate, conscientiousness, confident, and Christ-centered persons, but unless they become adept at communicating both verbally and nonverbally with their clients, they restrict their ability to effect change in clients' lives. When counselors are able to communicate effectively, they wield a potent *presence* in their counseling sessions that clearly says, "I care and I can help."

The task is to model and facilitate open and honest communication with our clients. Often clients will be reluctant to share their "deep, dark secrets" until they can trust the counselor. Many clients have never learned to honestly express how they feel or how they view their world. Fear of being betrayed may keep their tongues bound. The therapist must communicate that it is safe to talk openly, and this is not always done verbally. The therapist's *presence* can speak volumes of love, security, and acceptance to clients. It can build a bridge over which clients can cross into the interactive dialogue that is unquestionably crucial to successful counseling.

Placing great emphasis on the *person and presence* of counselors is not intended to discredit or underestimate the value of training, skills, and techniques. Competent counselors need all of these. Essence and performance go hand in glove, but communication skills such as active listening, attending, probing, and summarizing determine how effectively the two are synthesized (Egan, 1998). Counselors are like artists who express their personhood, their inner visions, and their creative abilities with paint and brushes. Counseling skills and techniques are the paint and brushes through which counselors communicate their inner visions for their clients. When the pictures of our clients are finally complete, they will bear our signatures.

CHANGEABILITY AND FLEXIBILITY

One constant in life is that everything changes. The same goes for counseling. Competent counselors must continue learning, growing, and adapting to an ever-changing world. Counselor growth and client change go together, for counselors cannot take their clients to heights they have not attained themselves.

Competent counselors must continue to "be engaged and evolving as human beings.... One can never be perfectly grown, but one can be continually growing" (Neuhaus & Astwood, 1980, p. 71). A counselor's life should model high levels of the enduring truth that, while the destination may be important, it is the journey that we must allow to teach and grow us.

COMPETENCE

Our last secret is the one we've been developing all along. *Competence* is the synthesis of character and performance, of Christ-centeredness and skillful communication.

Competence is not something magical that happens when a person decides or "answers the call" to be a counselor. Competence is gained by appropriate training, acquiring and practicing specific and basic skills, and allowing experience to help us trust our inner intuition and discernment (Neuhaus & Astwood, 1980, p. 47). Being too self-conscious about our performance as counselors will deprive us of self-confidence.

Like an accomplished artist who works masterfully but with effortless ease, competent counselors must learn to be accurately but loosely self-aware. Led by the Holy Spirit, they must allow their personhood, training, practice, and experience to do the work while observing enough of their own behavior to correct mistakes and grow toward maturity. Welter (1978) asserts that "persons who do anything very naturally are often people who have worked very hard at a skill" (p. 38).

Some people naively assume that because God has called them into the counseling ministry, he will take care of the training and competence. Benner (1987) disagrees. He relates that the distinctiveness of being Christian in the helping professions does not depend primarily on our psychology conforming to our theology, "but that it is the most superbly sound psychotherapy possible. To be a Christian therapist requires first of all that I be a thoroughly effective therapist" (p. 26).

Counselors must stay aware of what is happening in the world in general and keep pace with developing theories, pertinent technology, counseling ethics and legalities, and theological and psychological debates and challenges. All of this affects what goes on in the counseling office. Take advantage of all the great reading materials available, including counseling and marriage-and-family journals and books authored by experienced and knowledgeable practicing professionals. Attend seminars and workshops or even extend your academic education. Do whatever it takes to continue growing personally and professionally.

COUNSELOR DEVELOPMENT AND CARE

How do you rate yourself on those inner qualities and outward behaviors that demonstrate excellence in counseling? On a scale of one to ten, where do you fit?

In pursuing competence, you are not allowed the luxury of self-deceit. You must look yourself in the eye and ask hard questions. What about your personal life? Neuhaus and Astwood (1980) insist that if counselors' lives are not reasonably in order, their counseling will lack effectiveness. They do not suggest that counselors are superhuman or without problems of their own. However, competent counselors must be willing, at any given time in their lives, to give an account *of* themselves *to* themselves and, at times, to others.

CARING FOR ONESELF

To work excessively, obsessively, or in isolation puts additional strain on people deeply involved in the lives of troubled souls. Emotional health and professional growth are enhanced by contact with other counselors. Christian counselors have a colossal opportunity to learn, network, and grow by becoming members of professional organizations such as the American Association of Christian Counselors.

Some Christian helpers in particular seem prone to stretching themselves to the brink of exhaustion—all in the name of Christ and service to the church. This justification makes Christian counselor care such an important issue. Some writers have deemed this uniquely religious form of "compassion fatigue" to be a "messiah trap" (Berry, 1988). If it is true that 10% of the church does 90% of the ministry of the church, the issue of caring for oneself becomes especially pertinent.

Bugental (1987) speaks to the impairment issue when he asserts that "the therapist's first obligation in these instances is to do what is necessary to preserve her own well-being. Failing that, she will be less able to adequately serve all her patients" (p. 252). Collins (1980, p. 45) suggests some critical steps counselors can take to avoid burnout:

- Seek "the spiritual strength which comes through regular periods of prayer and meditation on the Scriptures."
- Have supportive people in our lives "who accept us for who we are rather than for what we do."
- Take "regular periods away from demanding, needy people."

Becoming our own counselor requires that we refuse to hide from ourselves and that we be willing to face the truth about what we find when we ask ourselves some of the following questions:

1. *Am I experiencing any physical, psychological, or spiritual impairments or relationship conflicts that can hinder my effectiveness or injure my clients psychologically?* Impairment, or the inability to continue functioning effectively, is a reality that all counselors must be willing to come to terms with. Counselors can become physically, emotionally, and spiritually bankrupt while trying to juggle their intimate work with anguished souls, other professional demands, and their own interpersonal conflicts, intrapersonal struggles, and domestic duties. A combination of exhaustion, depression, fatigue, lethargy, irritability, lack of compassion, psychoso-

matic complaints, and neglect of spiritual disciplines can signal counselors that changes need to be made.

2. *Do I enjoy the self-acceptance that I encourage my clients to seek?* Self-acceptance involves gaining and experiencing a sturdy inner sense of one's identity as a person (Clinebell, 1984, p. 418). Reaching this point in our lives means that we have doubted ourselves, examined ourselves, and learned that we can be trusted. It means we have ceased running from ourselves or hiding behind our self-woven masks; it means we have turned and embraced ourselves.

3. *Have I honestly dealt with my own pain—past and present?* In other words, have we done the work we are asking our clients to do? Unresolved conflict and pain will inevitably seep into the counseling process and will, without a doubt, distort a counselor's understanding and perspective of the client's world.

4. *Is my own neediness contaminating the therapeutic process?* This question requires us to sincerely examine our underlying motivation for being in a helping profession. If we find ourselves overly anxious to rescue and fix those who turn to us for help, then we have reason to suspect that we have a need to be needed that can be counterproductive for both counselor and client. Kennedy (1977) speaks to this phenomenon when he asserts, "Individuals determined to do something *for* their clients may actually be doing something through them for themselves.... They may counsel to meet needs of their own" (p. 30).

5. *Do I speak the truth when it is in the best interests of my clients?* Counselors need confidence in order to consistently confront their clients. Confrontation can be painful for both counselor and counselee. Counselors might lack the confidence to be truthful with their clients when they have not learned to be honest with themselves, when they fear losing their clients' approval, or when they fail to understand that the truth can be spoken in love (Ephesians 4:15).

Counselors cannot ignore their clients' self-destructive behavioral patterns. Sometimes they must heed the exhortation given in Proverbs 27:5-6: "Better is open rebuke than hidden love. Wounds from a friend can be trusted." The same can be said of confident counselors when they urge their clients to face the truth about themselves.

VISION, INTENTION, MEANS

Christian counselors must hold fast to the *vision* (a picture of life in the kingdom of God), the *intention* (increasing the desire to embrace the process of authentic transformation), and the *means* (spiritual disciplines) necessary for engaging in this process of transformation. Collins (1988) suggests that effective Christian counselors seek to develop counseling relationships based on love, strive to become proficient in the knowledge and use of basic counseling techniques, and show evidence of Christ's character (the fruit of the Holy Spirit) in their lives.

Apparently Collins was writing prophetically, for with these words he offered the best way to resolve the technique-versus-person debate: with a resounding "both-and." He also seemed to anticipate the role that Christian formation is beginning to play in the training of effective counselors (enhancing common factors through character transformation) offering a uniquely Christian approach to comprehensive change. Effective counselors are deeply surrendered to the process of authentic transformation of their own souls. Without a doubt they would pass the stiffest character test that Murphy the dog might offer.

CHAPTER 9

THE EMPATHIC CHRISTIAN COUNSELOR

Skilled Helpers Influencing Client Action

JAN HOOK AND GEORGE OHLSCHLAGER

They [who cared] made themselves infirm with those who were infirm, so that they might not be overcome with despair.... They wept with those who wept, and rejoiced with those who rejoiced.... They drew the imperfect ones out of imperfection, themselves becoming imperfect and infirm with them, as I told thee, with true and holy compassion.... For through love, they who gave...bore more pain than they who received it.

—CATHERINE OF SIENA, 1343–1380

One of the greatest challenges for the Christian counselor is to create a context where healing and growth can occur. The author of Hebrews wrote, "Let us consider how we may spur one another on toward love and good deeds" (10:24). The job of the Christian counselor is to do just that—to "spur" the client on toward change and growth, to encourage him or her to become a more whole and loving person, to become like Christ not only "with words or tongue but with actions and in truth" (1 John 3:18).

The Christian counselor is called upon to establish a relationship where the client is able first to trust and then to become aware of the issues and the ineffective ways he or she is dealing with problems. Within that context, the client is able to acknowledge the need to change, find the desire to do so, and take steps toward growth and development (Egan, 1998).

A major part of creating that healing context is the counselor's effective use of empathy, which, along with character, is key in formulating a high-quality therapeutic relationship (Cormier & Cormier, 1991). In this chapter we continue to discuss the counselor-client relationship as an important variable in the healing process. Then we will consider empathic communication to facilitate that relationship and, ultimately, to motivate client change.

THE CENTRALITY OF A HELPING RELATIONSHIP

Proverbs 20:5 asserts, "Though good advice lies deep within a person's heart, the wise will draw it out" (NLT). This concept is a cornerstone of the counseling relationship, and it highlights a great divide. Much Christian counseling is conceived of and practiced as a directive process of counselor advice-giving, often using the Scriptures and ecclesiastical authority to justify the direction given. The ideal client is expected to accept the counselor's directives and apply them to the growth process.

Sometimes this approach works, and sometimes it doesn't. Although brief therapy inherently pushes a more directive stance, and crisis intervention demands it, directive advice-giving has limited effectiveness as an exclusive strategy for counseling. The aforementioned proverb suggests that drawing out the truth from within the client is often preferred to merely *telling* the client what the truth is and what to do with it. Truth told to a person is less easily received and more easily defended against, and it sets up the counselor to take the blame when the advice doesn't work. This model of directive proclamation is often better done by preaching and teaching than by counseling and helping.

Truth drawn out of the client's own life tends to be more deeply understood and more actively embraced, and it motivates and sustains the change process. In essence, the counselor says, "Instead of telling you what to do, let's connect with the God whose Spirit lives within you and discover what you have learned, or need to learn, from him." The Spirit of God—who is the Spirit of truth—lives within every believer. Therefore, we, as Christian counselors, would do well to align ourselves with the Truth-teller rather than assuming too much of that role ourselves.

RESEARCH ON COUNSELOR-CLIENT VARIABLES

Beginning with Rogers's (1951, 1957) work on congruence, positive regard, and empathy, relationship variables have amassed a large body of data with nearly universal support for their value in counseling. Strong's (1968) now famous and oft-quoted study on the processes of social influence in counseling identified expertness, attractiveness, and trustworthiness as key perceptions of clients toward counselors that increase counselor influence and facilitate client change. Carkhuff

(1969, 1987) refined a counseling model—an integrated insight-action intervention system—based on these traits and skills that work across the primary theories.

Moustakas (1986) identified three principal ingredients that are necessary for optimal healing in therapeutic relationships:

1. *Being in.* This is the empathic ability to get into the client's world, understand it, and communicate that understanding back to the client. The client is able to say, "This counselor *does* know me and understand me, even though she hasn't exactly walked in my shoes."
2. *Being for.* Like unconditional positive regard, this refers to the ability to communicate and advocate a strong, unconditional commitment to your client, even when you challenge wrongdoing and maladaptive behavior. No matter how much you challenge clients, they know you are for them and have their best interests at heart.
3. *Being with.* This is the ability to connect with your client at a deep level while still maintaining your identity or differing perspective. Thus, a lack of intimacy as well as intimacy without boundaries are avoided as you and your client travel the road toward growth together.

The goal of the therapeutic process, as Egan (1998) asserts, is the development of a working alliance that increases the likelihood of achieving therapeutic goals. We agree with Egan that the counseling relationship, important though it is, is a means to an end, not an end in itself. (See Patterson, 1985, for an alternative view.) Counselors must win and maintain the client's trust, for without it the client too easily backs away from the difficult challenges inherent to change. High levels of empathy, acceptance, and counselor support operating in the therapeutic alliance correlate with the best client outcomes (Lambert & Bergin, 1994). In fact, across all schools of counseling, satisfied clients consistently noted counselor characteristics such as sensitivity, honesty, and gentleness as more important to their therapy than any techniques (Strupp & Binder, 1984). This has even been found to be true in behavior therapy, which has rarely emphasized the value of the therapeutic relationship (Lazarus, 1981).

The evidence confirms, then, the prominent place that the relationship between therapist and client holds in the success or failure of counseling (Dayringer, 1998; Whiston & Sexton, 1993). Squires (1986) states that "much of the healing in therapy may not be a function of theory, but of the trusting relationship between patient and therapist," and that "the strength of the relationship at the beginning largely determined the success of therapy" (p. 74). Hartley found that "the therapeutic alliance has two essential components. First, there's the *real relationship*—how patient and therapist interact. It should include an authentic liking, trust, and respect for each other. The second part is the *working alliance*—how well therapist and patient work together" (see Squires, 1986, p. 74). Gazda, Asbury, Balzer, Childers, and Walters (1984) insist that "the helper is the expert on the conditions necessary for change to occur and…must create an atmosphere of security and trust that is a prerequisite for the first step or goal in helping" (p. 20).

A successful counseling relationship also requires a "spiritual" bonding between therapist and client. Benner (1987) maintains that all psychotherapies include "a relationship between the client and the therapist which is personal, accepting, and perhaps even loving" (p. 17). A Paracentric focus may be understood as a psycho-social-spiritual influence process, one that not only uses the relational influence of the counselor but also invites the relational power of the Holy Spirit to effect deep and lasting change. Specific skills must be learned and perfected in order to cultivate this "mystical" relationship. The cardinal skill upon which all this is grounded is empathy.

WHAT IS EMPATHY?

Empathy is the skill that enables the counselor to really understand a client from his or her perspective (Carkhuff, 1969; Cormier & Cormier, 1991; Egan, 1998). The author of Hebrews wrote, "Remember those in prison as if you were their fellow prisoners, and those who are mistreated as if you yourselves were suffering" (13:3). Empathy is the ability to get inside a client's world and develop a sense of what that world looks like from her point of view. It is the ability to discriminate and perceive the client's world, especially her feelings, and to reflect that perspective back to the client to assure her that you understand.

Feelings are unique to each individual (Powell, 1969), and empathy is the ability to really connect and understand those feelings. When a client feels understood, he has an "Aha!" experience, which is a golden moment in the counseling session. The author of Proverbs said it very nicely: "A word aptly spoken is like apples of gold in settings of silver" (25:11).

Empathy connects the counselor with the client and deepens the counselor-client relationship. Through empathy the client is drawn deeper into relationship, a type of relationship where the client's need for "connecting" happens (Crabb, 1997). Through empathy, the client feels safer to focus on his story, to tell more of that story, and to go deeper with that story. The counselor is able to help the client focus on the issue or problem and increase his awareness of it (Gendlin, 1979). As the client's awareness develops, there is more freedom to acknowledge and, ultimately, to act on the issue. No matter what the theoretical framework of the counselor, the ability to be empathetic will be key for developing the facilitative conditions for effective counseling (Gazda et al., 1984).

WHAT EMPATHY IS NOT

Empathy can be easily misunderstood. We will give some clarity here by identifying five concepts that get confused with empathy.

Compassion. Since there is a fine line between empathy and compassion (a distinction we discussed in the previous chapter), we can differentiate between the two this way: *Compassion* is an emotional dynamic that provokes counselors to help their clients; *empathy* is a skill that can be learned and serves to bond therapists with their clients. Empathy says to our clients that we understand. Compassion tells them they are not alone, that someone who cares is with them and wants to help.

Sympathy. Empathy is not feeling "for" the client (Brammer & Shostrom, 1982) or feeling the same as the client (which might be called projection). It is possible that similar experiences may yield similar feelings, yet because people are unique, similar experiences often yield different feelings. Projecting one's feelings onto the client may not connect the counselor with the client's experience, and the client may feel misunderstood or overwhelmed.

Sympathy in the counselor-client relationship is sometimes like two people who do not know how to swim trying to save each other. Instead of saving each other, they will likely both drown. Instead of understanding the client's feelings and experience, the counselor might overwhelm him or her with sympathy. The counselor's own feelings—his own outrage, for example—might get triggered by the client's story, which could be counterproductive.

We do not want to imply that sympathy in counseling is bad or wrong. Sympathy has its place and can be an important part of the counseling relationship. In the book of Romans, Paul wrote that it is important for us to sympathize, to "rejoice with those who rejoice; mourn with those who mourn" (12:15). Sympathy is connecting and caring with the heart. "Loving with the head" is to analyze, which can be too objective and aloof. Empathy is the ability to love with both the heart and the head.

In chapter 26 of this book, Les and Leslie Parrott write that "empathy is deeper and stronger than sympathy. *Sympathy* is standing on the shore and throwing out a lifeline; *empathy* is jumping into the water and risking one's safety to help another. And the risk is real. In empathy we risk personal change" (p. 573).

Agreement. Sometimes counselors think that if they empathize with the client, they are somehow agreeing with the client or approving of his behavior. If a client is angry with his wife for rejecting him and is bashing her verbally, the counselor might think it is wrong for him to say such awful things about his wife. Empathy is not agreeing with the client's behavior but trying to *understand* the behavior.

The counselor can both empathize and disagree. As the counselor is empathetic with the client, the counselor will be viewed as helpful. Then the counselor will more likely be able to join the client and become a part of the solution. The empathy of the counselor will create a context where the client can accept disagreement or an alternative perspective.

Parroting. Empathy is not merely restating what the client has said. Rather, empathy is getting to the core of what the client has said and saying it in the counselor's own words. In attempting to understand everything the client says, sometimes the counselor may say too much and end up repeating what the client is saying.

Paraphrasing. Empathy is also not paraphrasing, though technically there is not really too much difference between empathy and paraphrasing. Paraphrasing does reflect back what the client is saying in his or her own words; however, it is more often focused on the content of what is being said. By paraphrasing, the counselor

---

BOX 9.1—EMPATHY AS THE NEUROTIC ALLIANCE: AN ALTERNATIVE VIEW

The classical psychoanalytic tradition eschews the use of empathy, asserting that such closeness between therapist and client can create a neurotic alliance. The therapeutic rule of abstinence prescribes minimal interaction with clients, which involves little or no self-disclosure, a deflection of personal questions, and an artful refusal to be sucked into the client's neurotic need for control and approval. This is done so that clients will be encouraged to project their feelings, wishes, angers, and fears onto the therapist. The picture of the client reclining on the couch, free-associating, while the therapist sits behind the client, silent and out of view, is the prototypic image of this viewpoint.

This view holds that empathic, therapeutic involvement contaminates this projective ability and that therapists, because of their own need for affirmation and approval, are seduced into affirming and aligning in unhealthy ways with a client's hidden agenda. Avoiding the creation of such neurotic alliances—honoring the rule of abstinence in therapy by being little more than a blank slate—is considered crucial to a client's understanding of the hidden and not-so-hidden forces in his or her own life.

makes sure that she has understood the content correctly. The focus of empathy is on making sure that feelings, and not just content, are being understood.

ATTENDING AND LISTENING

In order for the counselor to be empathetic, he or she must first be a good listener. And in order to listen well, the counselor must pay attention or *attend* to the client in a helpful way. The counselor must not only listen to the content of what is being shared but must also be aware of the process and how the client is sharing (Knapp, 1978). Researchers state that what clients say is not nearly as important as *how* they say it. Some research has shown that as much as 90% of communication is based on nonverbal cues. Of that 90%, approximately 40% of the message's believability involves tone of voice, with the other 50% involving other nonverbal cues, such as posture and facial expression (Egan, 1976).

Clients tend to talk about events, actions, and feelings. Their stories reveal, for the most part, what has happened to them, who was involved, what they did, and how they felt. As their story unfolds, the counselor needs to listen for and ask herself, What themes are being presented? What is the core message? What is most important to this person? What does this person want me to understand most of all?

NONVERBAL LISTENING

Kinesics is the study of nonverbal cues transmitted by the client's body language. The counselor must be able to pick up on these cues, especially those given off by the client's face and eyes. The eyes can give off an abundance of messages. For example, staring blankly or looking elsewhere might give the message, "I'm not paying attention." Looking away might indicate, "I'm uncomfortable." Looking down might indicate feelings of shame or embarrassment. Looking up might mean, "I am imagining or visualizing what I want to say."

Like the eyes, other parts of the face will express a variety of powerful meanings. Imagine the variety of messages that the mouth can give by smiling or grimacing, or the different kinds of messages that the eyebrows can communicate.

Think also of the variety of messages clients communicate using their hands and feet. Fidgeting, rubbing hands together, or tapping fingers or feet might say, "I'm impatient or anxious." Sitting with arms folded, legs crossed, and the body turned away might say, "I'm angry" or "I'm not comfortable." On the other hand, sitting with arms and legs crossed might indicate the opposite, "I am comfortable" or "I am relaxed." It is important to note that the same data can have different meanings (McKay, Davis, & Fanning, 1995).

Paralinguistics is the study of the tone of voice. Reflect on the possible meanings that your clients communicate as they speak. A flat monotone voice might communicate, "I'm depressed." Speaking in a loud or strongly inflected tone might mean, "I'm trying to impress you or overwhelm you." Speaking too softly might mean, "I'm not sure of myself." The challenge for the counselor is to listen to and empathize with how a client shares his or her story.

The Difficulty of Listening

Jesus said, "He who has ears, let him hear" (Matthew 11:15). Let us hope that Christian counselors are those who have ears that *truly* hear. In order to listen and to attend effectively, the counselor must be both physically and psychologically present (Egan, 1998). And to be most effective, the counselor must be healthy physically, emotionally, and spiritually. Only then can the counselor truly attend and listen.

Even though listening represents a large part of what counselors do, not all are skilled listeners. Consider the following ways that listening is done poorly:

- *Inadequate listening.* When we allow ourselves to be distracted, we rarely hear the whole message.
- *Evaluative or judgmental listening.* This kind of listening constantly evaluates good versus bad, right versus wrong, like versus dislike, and so forth. While evaluation does have an important place in counseling, the first priority should be to listen in order to *understand*.
- *Filtered listening.* Our cultural context creates filters that nearly always become screening devices by which we judge, label, and stereotype others. These filters prejudice our accurate understanding of the client. Furthermore, the language or lexicon used by mental health workers can easily become labels that distort and dehumanize our patients: all too quickly, people become "crazy," "neurotic," "depressive," "paranoid," "borderline," or "perpetrators" in our thinking.
- *Rehearsing instead of listening.* A prevalent failure is rehearsing what we're going to say next rather than listening to a client's entire message. We must train ourselves to listen to the end, to pause and think, and only then to respond. This tendency is a common issue with new counselors who are often self-consciously thinking about their next move or statement to a client.
- *Sympathetic listening.* This means distorting an accurate understanding by overidentifying and making one an accomplice of client concern. A common example is the counselor who hasn't resolved his or her own abuse victimization and overidentifies with abused clients by taking on their anger or their fight against the abuser.

- *Interrupting.* Possibly the most common failure at listening is interrupting another person—something we hear about consistently in marital therapy. When a counselor does it, however, that is a major gaffe. Even when clients stammer and stumble while searching for the right word, let them do it. Interrupting or finishing sentences for clients is doubly harmful because not only are you disrespecting them, you are also missing an opportunity to learn important information about them.

PHYSICAL ATTENDING

The acronym SOLER* can help the counselor be intentional about attending to the client (Egan 1998):

S—*Squarely facing the client.* Facing the client squarely—straight on, face to face—while listening helps the counselor stay focused. It also creates an environment where a client senses that he is the center of attention.

O—*Open posture.* The counselor's posture should give the message that she is receptive and available to the client. Although folded arms and crossed legs can be a comfortable way of sitting, such posture may indicate to the client that the counselor is closed and unavailable.

L—*Leaning forward.* The degree of leaning needs to be congruent with the degree of closeness and with the content of the counselor-client interaction. Leaning slightly forward will tend to send the message that the counselor is interested. If trust has developed and the interaction is intense, then the counselor might lean forward even more. If the counselor does not have a close relationship with the client and is leaning too far forward, the counselor may appear to be intrusive. Each client has a space bubble or comfort zone that must not be—or appear to be—invaded.

E—*Eye contact.* As with leaning, the degree and intensity of eye contact will vary with the closeness of the relationship and the content of the client-counselor interaction. Culture is an important consideration since eye contact can mean different things to different people. Steady, direct eye contact in our culture, however, generally indicates interest in what the other person is saying.

R—*Relax.* Being relaxed is key to attending effectively. Often the counselor who wants to listen well will get the first four parts right: face client

---

* From *The Skilled Helper: A Problem Management Approach to Helping, 6th Edition,* by G. Egan © 1998. Reprinted with permission of Wadsworth, an imprint of the Wadsworth Group, a division of Thomson Learning. Fax: (800) 730-2215.

squarely, keep posture open, lean forward, and maintain eye contact. But if the counselor is not relaxed, it will look as if the counselor is ready to wrestle. That kind of stance can feel overwhelming to the client.

Psychological Attending

As previously mentioned, a counselor who wants to be a skilled listener must be psychologically present and attentive. The counselor may be attending physically but be distracted and incongruent in the process. The following factors can diminish psychological attending:

1. *Physical concerns.* The healthier the counselor is, the more energy he will have for the counseling process. If a counselor is tired or hungry, it will be difficult to listen to her client. If a counselor is sick, it will definitely affect his ability to attend.

2. *Personal concerns.* The counselor's own life concerns can get in the way of effective listening. If, for example, the counselor gets an emergency call a few minutes before a counseling appointment, she will find it difficult to stay present with and attend effectively to her client. The counselor's mind will wander to the emergency and will distract her from her client.

3. *Psychological concerns.* A counselor's inability to deal with his own psychological and transference issues can also interfere with the attending process. Quite often a counselor's own experiences and interpretations get triggered by what the client says. A counselor's ability to work through his own issues will be key in being free to attend effectively.

During counseling sessions, our clients must sense that they are the center of our universe. To really hear our clients, we must give them our undivided attention. To do this we must

- shut out the world, including our own personal issues, and go inside our clients' worlds,
- suspend our agenda and preconceived solutions for our clients,
- allow our clients the freedom to talk,
- listen with all of our heart.

In the Old Testament, Job's friends failed to give him their undivided attention; they didn't stop talking long enough to hear what he was saying. They had their own agenda, believed they knew how to solve Job's problems, and told Job that his sin had brought on all his calamities (Job 4:7-21). Their solution was to coerce Job into coming clean with his sin (5:8,17-27). Job persistently defended his innocence (10:7; 27:5-6). He pleaded with his counselor-friends to "hear now my argument; listen to the plea of my lips" (13:6). Weary from trying to make them understand what he needed from them, he begged, "Listen carefully to my words" (21:2). Indeed, we can learn much about attentive listening and poor listening from the account of Job and his friends.

UNDERSTANDING FEELINGS

Accurate empathy involves a counselor's ability to discern and communicate the core feelings in what the client is saying.

As the counselor listens to the client's story, he must be asking, "What feeling or feelings is the client communicating? Is there a core feeling being expressed?" Then the counselor must reflect back to the client, in his or her own words, the feeling or feelings that were heard.

FEELINGS AND THE SASHET MATRIX

The acronym SASHET can help the counselor remember and identify feelings that the client is expressing (Carlson, 1988). SASHET stands for three negatively tinged feelings (**S**ad, **A**ngry, **S**cared) and three positively tinged feelings (**H**appy, **E**xcited, **T**ender).

If your client is not sharing feelings, you should ask, "What are you feeling?" Encourage the client to pick one of the six feelings. Have the client guess what she is feeling, if need be. What the client guesses will likely be what she is really feeling. Then observe. Feelings are accompanied by physical sensations. When appropriate, you can walk your client through the following emotions and their physical sensations.

Sad. Where in your body do you feel sadness? Stop for a moment. Try to remember a time you felt sad. Stay with your experience for a few moments. Now, as you reflect on your experience, where in your body does sadness appear and how does it feel? Do you feel some tightness? You probably feel some tightness in your throat, behind your eyes, and down in the center of your chest. Maybe you will sense tears coming to your eyes. And what about your heart? Your heart probably feels heavy or even broken. These are some of the physical sensations that will clue you in to sadness.

Angry. Where in your body do you feel anger? Think of a time you felt angry. Let that experience surface. Now, where and how do the physical sensations appear in your body? Are you clenching your fist? What else feels tight or constricted? Your jaw? Your neck? Your stomach? Are the veins starting to bulge in your neck? Do you want to hit or attack and yell? What is happening to your heart? Is it beating more rapidly? You may have tears, but angry tears are hot tears. These are the physical sensations that accompany anger.

Scared. Where in your body do you feel scared? Again, you will feel tightness, but you will feel a different kind of tightness than you experience with either sad or angry feelings. You will feel tightness down the back of your neck and into your shoulders. You will feel tightness across your chest, and your breathing will be constricted. Your heart will contract, and you will want to run and hide.

Notice the differences between feeling sad, angry, and scared. Sometimes they can be confusingly similar, but notice the differences. For example, a person may feel tightness in the chest when experiencing either fear or anger, but fear will tend to be higher up in the chest and anger will be experienced around the stomach area.

INTENSITY OF FEELINGS

Feelings are experienced on a continuum from mild to extremely intense. Feelings of anger can range from irritation to rage, frustration to fury. Feelings of sadness can range from numb to heartbroken, disappointed to distressed. All of these variations in intensity of feeling will have accompanying physical manifestations. The higher the intensity of a feeling, the greater will be the intensity of the accompanying physical response. (For more on the physiological impact of emotions, see Goleman, 1994).

There are thresholds, however, where the physical intensity may not match the intensity of the feeling. For example, the feeling may be so intense that the client reacts by closing down physically. If generalized, this closing down can become habitual, causing some clients to be out of touch with their feelings.

RESPONDING WITH EMPATHY

A counselor can attend, listen intently, and have great insight and understanding into a client's life, but if he does not communicate effectively, the client will not feel understood. It is, therefore, important to *communicate* empathy to the client. It is not enough to merely listen and understand.

To begin with, the counselor should reflect back or paraphrase the content of what the client is saying. The counselor might say, "I want to see if I've got this right. You said _____." Then the counselor might ask, "Did I get it right?"

The difficulty with much counselor-client communication is that counselors often assume they understand what their clients are saying when, in fact, they don't. When a counselor does not "get it right," misunderstandings occur.

In order to continue the empathy process, the counselor needs to keep trying to get it right by continuing to reflect back what the client is saying. The counselor will know that empathy is beginning to happen when the client's disclosure begins to make sense. The counselor then enters the client's world and understands what the client is experiencing from his or her perspective.

When a counselor thinks she understands, it will be important to say so at that point. The counselor may say something like, "What you are saying makes sense to me," or "I think I understand." This phrase is very important because it validates the client's feelings and experience.

Follow the validation with an empathy statement. The statement will essentially be a summary of what the counselor understands the client to be feeling and experiencing. The counselor can use the following phrase to convey the empathy: "When _____, you feel _____."

If the counselor is hearing more than one feeling and more than one piece of content, the counselor might say, "When _____ and _____, you feel _____ and _____." Shorter, however, is often better.

Sometimes it is best to stay with the feelings that one hears and leave off the content, especially if the counselor has been reflecting content all along. The counselor might just say, "You feel _____." This statement is short and to the point and lets the client know that the counselor understands.

The counselor will also want to empathize with the client's nonverbal communication. In response to the client's raised voice, for example, the counselor might empathize by saying, "Your raised voice tells me that you might be feeling angry."

The client will validate the accurateness of the empathy by how he responds. To the extent that the counselor gives empathy accurately, the client will feel free to continue with his story and go deeper in telling the story. Also, increased client awareness will be the result. The client will have an "Aha!" experience and will be challenged to do more work, even if the work is difficult.

If the counselor is not accurate, the client will tend to close down, and his story will become more superficial. The great thing about empathy, however, is that if the counselor truly wants to understand, the safety of the context that has already been created will enable the counselor to work through the misunderstanding, and the client will want to continue.

When the client finally does come to a stopping point, the counselor should ask if he would still like to say more. The counselor should not jump in with her own insights or interpretations until the client is finished.

By following this procedure, the counselor may not even need to intervene because a context has been created where the client is free to discuss any topic at whatever level he chooses. Many clients just need the space to explore an issue and come up with their own solutions. Accurate empathy can create that context for the client. If the client needs to be challenged further in order to grow, then the counselor can use the skill of advanced empathy.

WHAT IS ADVANCED EMPATHY?

As the name implies, advanced (also called level-two) empathy is a reflection of what the client is saying at a deeper level than basic (level-one) empathy. Early in the client-counselor interaction, advanced empathy may be perceived as too analytical or powerful and, therefore, not helpful, even if accurate. But when trust and rapport are established, this skill can be an excellent way for the counselor to challenge the client.

Advanced empathy is the ability to discriminate what is going on in the client at a deep, below-the-surface level and then to communicate that understanding. Advanced empathy might tap a feeling or an issue about which the client is unaware (Carkhuff, 1969; Egan, 1998). For example, if a client says she is angry with her husband because he forgot to buy her a gift for a special occasion, the counselor might first empathize by saying, "It sounds like you're upset with him because he forgot." The counselor intervention would be level-one empathy, and the client would probably respond by saying a resounding, "Yes!" and continue with her story.

Advanced empathy would be more of the same, only at a deeper level. It would tap into those feelings that may be hidden or beyond the immediate reach of the client's awareness. So the counselor might say to the client, "Maybe you are also feeling scared, like your husband is putting other things before you and maybe rejecting you." This empathic statement identifies feelings beneath those being expressed. Advanced empathy is challenging because it touches an area of awareness not previously recognized.

Advanced empathy uses the same formula that was used earlier for level-one empathy: "When _____, you feel _____." The counselor may turn the formula around and start with, "You feel _____ when _____."

We recommend that the counselor start with the content first. Reflecting back the content part first enhances the potential for connection because the content is typically easier for the client to hear. Saying the feelings first, especially at a deeper level, is more likely to trigger defensiveness. The client will more likely receive the statement "You're feeling scared, afraid that you are being rejected" after the counselor has heard and understood the content.

UNDERSTANDING CONTENT

Advanced empathy requires the counselor to understand the content of what the client is feeling at a deeper level. It takes an ability to understand what motivates clients to do what they do. Understanding content at a deeper level can happen in several ways (Egan, 1998):

Summarizing and concluding. After listening to the husband give all his good reasons for not buying his wife a present, the counselor could begin the advanced empathy by summarizing the content of what was shared. By summarizing and reflecting back to the client what he said, the counselor might conclude that the client's "reasons" actually sound like *excuses*. Doing so would go beyond what the client had said overtly and challenge him to consider a different possibility.

Looking for themes and implications. Identifying the underlying implication to what is being said will be challenging to the client. The counselor might say to the husband, "It seems like you are making all these other things—as important as they may be—more important than your wife."

Making interpretations. When making interpretations, be careful not to come across as judgmental. It may be inaccurate and disapproving for a counselor to assert, "You really don't care about your wife." A more accurate interpretation might be, "Perhaps you are so busy because work is a place where you experience success, as opposed to your marriage where you are experiencing failure." That would have been an interpretation that challenges him to look at himself and consider his motivations for his actions.

Presenting alternate frames of reference. Ultimately, advanced empathy is about pointing out alternative ways of viewing a particular situation, helping the client become more aware, and presenting a new way of seeing things. When the husband forgets to buy a present for his wife's birthday, he could be challenged to see the content of his behavior differently. He could be prompted to expand his awareness and see that his behavior may hurt his wife. The counselor might also challenge the husband to explore the motives behind his behavior, providing him with an opportunity to examine his own priorities, attitudes, feelings, and thoughts. Finally, advanced empathy could challenge the client to do things differently, to change his behavior toward his wife.

UNDERSTANDING FEELINGS

In order to help clients look at underlying issues and conflicts, the counselor must help them understand and acknowledge their feelings at a deeper level. It is important, therefore, for the counselor to realize that feelings are often layered and are experienced in combination, and that awareness of feelings often taps into underlying needs. With an understanding of his "thirst," the client can then seek to satisfy that thirst in healthy, godly ways.

In order to assess the thirst of the client the counselor should ask this question, "What emotion comes up most quickly?" Which of the three "negative" emotions—sadness, anger, or fear—is the client most aware of? Typically, the client will have one emotion that surfaces first.

A second question for the counselor to ask is, "What other feelings are you experiencing?" It is likely that the client may be experiencing more than one feeling and that the initial feeling identified may be covering other ones.

Anger-Sadness-Guilt/Shame/Fear. One common constellation of feelings involves anger that masks hurt or sadness prompted by an event, which then triggers feelings of guilt, shame, or fear (Teyber, 1992). For example, if the client experiences rejection, there is a good chance she will feel angry. Underneath that anger will be the hurt and sadness from being rejected.

If the client can accept or even embrace the hurt and sadness, she may discover an even deeper layer of feelings. The client may experience fear, the panic of isolation and abandonment, the agony of being alone with no one ever being there for her. Guilt will often accompany the fear, as if it were the client's fault that the rejection happened, as if the rejection occurred because of her bad behavior. Or shame may accompany the fear that the client not only behaved badly, but that the client *is* bad and that is the reason for the rejection.

Fear and the accompanying feelings of guilt and shame are very difficult emotions to experience. It is difficult to stay with those hurt feelings. It may be so much easier for the client to stay angry. It is a lot easier for clients to stay mad at someone for the hurt of rejection than to feel the loss, guilt, and shame that seem to suggest that something might be fundamentally wrong with them.

The counselor's ability to empathize with clients will help them feel the feelings and get in touch with the real needs that underlie their feelings.

Sadness-Anger-Guilt/Shame/Fear. Clients may respond differently, however. Instead of feeling angry about being rejected, for example, a client may first feel hurt and sad (Teyber, 1992). Feeling sadness is all about hurt and loss. Rejection is about loss, and it could be just as natural to respond to loss by feeling sad.

Clients might then need to explore other feelings, such as anger, that accompany their sadness. Most people who get stuck in sadness will have difficulty getting in touch with and expressing that anger. In that case, there is a good possibility that the stuck client has been the object of someone else's anger. Advanced empathy can help the client feel the anger and get unstuck and then move on to and through the guilt/shame/fear cycle.

Self-Disclosure and Immediacy

In order to empathize at the deepest levels, a counselor will offer some self-disclosures, some of his own observations and insights. Self-disclosure, however, should be an extension of empathic communication, done with the goal of making connection, communicating understanding, and assisting clients to further disclose their own issues and feelings. Self-disclosures should be brief and consistent with the content of client disclosure.

With regard to self-disclosure, two extremes need to be avoided. When counselors are too private and reserved, they can alienate their clients because of their lack of identity and openness. But if counselors are too open and self-revealing, they risk turning the focus onto themselves and diminishing their clients' importance (Kottler, 1993). Self-disclosure should be inaugurated into the counseling process "to create a more co-equal relationship, to communicate caring, to encourage more open disclosures on the part of the client, to acknowledge the therapeutic relationship as a fully human encounter, to validate client experiences and to illustrate key points through personal examples. But it is never, *never* to be used to meet one's personal needs" (Kottler 1993, p. 59).

When counselors provide more immediate feedback during sessions, their disclosures will be more powerful and challenging for their clients. Immediacy reflects back in the here and now the counselor's observations, insights, and feelings experienced in the client-counselor relationship (Egan, 1976). If, for example, the client is only aware of anger, advanced empathy might be stated in the form of immediacy: "You say that you're feeling angry. I can hear that. I do sense you're angry. I am also noticing your tears. I sense sadness as you talk. In fact, I feel sad when I hear your hurt." Such a self-disclosure might help the client get beneath the anger to the underlying hurt.

Because advanced empathy can be challenging to the client, it will be important for the counselor to be cautious in using it. Remember that each client is unique in how he or she feels, so how the counselor gives advanced empathy will be significant to the therapeutic process.

COMPETENT USE OF EMPATHIC COMMUNICATION

The counselor should use level-one empathy in conjunction with advanced empathy. Empathy with the surface feelings should be used before exploring deeper feelings. This will demonstrate to the client complete understanding and will lessen the client's need to be defensive. Accurate level-one empathy will help the counselor set the stage. That is, it shows the client that the counselor understands so that moving deeper will then be a natural next step. Also, the counselor should use level-one empathy in order to stay connected with the client after he or she responds to the challenge. If a client responds defensively, he may be sensing a need to protect against something the counselor has said. Level-one empathy will enable the counselor to stay with the client through the process. Ask yourself, Have I grounded what I am going to say in empathy? Am I ready to respond with empathy no matter how the client responds?

RESPONDING WITH ADVANCED EMPATHY

Since advanced empathy goes below the client's surface awareness, it will often be experienced as challenging and may throw off the client's equilibrium. It will, therefore, be important for the counselor to stay connected to the client in the process. The following guidelines are designed to help counselors use advanced empathy effectively.

Attitude. Essential to using advanced empathy will be the counselor's attitude. It is not okay for the counselor to use the skill to impress clients. As the counselor extends empathy, the skill must be congruent with the counselor's heart, which is characterized by grace and truth.

These are characteristics that Jesus embodied when he came to Earth. The apostle John wrote that Jesus "became flesh and made his dwelling among us...full of grace and truth" (John 1:14). Scripture asks that counselors embody the same characteristics, to imitate Christ (Ephesians 5:1) and to speak "the truth [advanced empathy] in [the context of] love" (Ephesians 4:15). The counselor's attitude must be one of love. Rogers (1961) called it "unconditional positive regard." Egan (1976) called it "respect." God calls it "grace."

Counselors must also respond to their clients with truth. The empathy statement is the truth part, and this implies that the counselor is a person of truth. Egan (1976) uses the term *genuine.* The apostle Paul wrote in Galatians 6:1: "Brothers, if someone is caught in a sin, you who are spiritual should restore him gently." Spiritual counselors are those who are able to respond with both grace and truth. Counselors should ask themselves, To what extent is my truth coming out of a desire to extend grace?

Trust. Has trust been established in the relationship? Does the client know that the counselor cares? Has the counselor's attitude of care and concern been proven? Here is where the previous skills of listening and basic empathy provide the basis for advanced empathy. It is important that a foundation of trust has been established, otherwise the counselor may be perceived as not caring. The more solid the foundation of trust, the greater the likelihood for success in using advanced empathy. Ask yourself, How solid is our relationship? Have I done the necessary work to create a context for advanced empathy?

Timing. It may not always be in a client's best interests to use advanced empathy, particularly if the client is unstable or is feeling overwhelmed. Ask yourself, Is the client ready or able to receive advanced empathy?

Awareness. This guideline is closely related to timing. Counselors may express empathy for feelings that are close to the client's conscious awareness. These feelings can often be addressed earlier than feelings that might be more deeply hidden. Ask yourself, How aware is the client of what I am going to say?

Tentativeness. In some situations, being tentative in counseling may be a weakness, but in advanced empathy, it can be a strength. It might help to avoid provoking a defensive response. Give the client room to deny the covert feelings or content and provide the freedom to make changes that lead to a better interpretation of the situation. Being tentative communicates openness and gives the client freedom to see things differently. It conveys respect for the client and acknowledges that the counselor does not know everything. Statements of advanced empathy are "skilled hunches." Clients are the final authorities on their inner experiences. Ask yourself, Am I giving the client room to disagree with what I'm going to say?

Concreteness. The counselor needs to be careful that empathy statements are not so tentative that they're vague and diluted. It is important for the counselor to state the empathy clearly and concretely. It will be helpful to support the interpretations with data. Where is your hunch coming from? The more data the counselor has to support advanced empathy, the easier it will be for the client to accept the interpretation. Data grounds the expression in reality. Ask yourself, Am I grounding my empathy with data?

Intuition and discernment. Learning to trust your own intuition and discernment requires that you learn to hear what clients *don't* tell you and that you be able to discern whether clients are being honest about what they *do* relate to you. When your "gut" prompts you to explore further, don't hesitate to listen and act. Simply express your hunch in a tentative way.

Egan (1998) writes, "To be an effective helper, you need to listen not only to the client but also to yourself.... Listening to yourself on a 'second channel' can help you identify...what you might do to be of further help to the client" (p. 78). Exploring with your clients what your "inner therapist" tells you can help them start uncovering the roadblocks to their healing. The process can open the door for you to confront your clients regarding contradictory and inconsistent behavior.

ENGAGING THE CLIENT

Effective counseling does not rest solely with the counselor. Clients must be serious and sincere about their involvement in the process, and empathic communication can help them engage more fully in therapy. Good counselors will not attempt to do the work for their clients. Instead, they will be there to facilitate and support them as they accept personal responsibility for positive change.

Therapy that effects positive change in our clients' lives is not a one-way street.

Both client and counselor must become involved in the process. For this to happen, there must be open and honest interaction between counselor and client. Competent counselors must become adept at engaging their clients in the interpersonal dialogue that is so critical to client improvement.

The ongoing attitude of grace and truth—along with the foundational skills of listening, attending, and empathy—will help clients move toward change and growth in the counseling relationship. Ask yourself, Am I willing to see this process through to the end? Am I willing to go deeper with my care for the client?

Regarding our example with the couple in counseling, advanced empathy helped the wife work through her constellation of feelings, from the anger of being rejected through the hurt and into the fear of being "rejectable." An important process for the husband was to be able to hear his wife's anger and hurt without being defensive and to recognize her underlying insecurity. Accurate empathy helped the husband work through his performance issues and into his fear of failure. In time, they were both able to understand each other's perspectives and were challenged to do things differently.

As the counselor uses empathy, speaking truth in the context of love, clients will be challenged to expand their awareness. Clients will acknowledge their need to be more like Christ (Ephesians 4:15) and then will begin to take the necessary steps to grow and change. Having created a safe context, the counselor will be in a position to help and encourage clients to make those changes. By using the skill of empathy, the counselor will "spur [the client] on toward love and good deeds" (Hebrews 10:24).

CHAPTER 10

THE EMPOWERED HELPING RELATIONSHIP

Fostering Client Change
Through Clinical-Spiritual Interventions

TIM CLINTON AND GEORGE OHLSCHLAGER

---

*God, grant me the serenity to accept the things I cannot change, courage
to change the things I can, and wisdom to know the difference.*
—THE SERENITY PRAYER, 1943

Change is so fundamental to the counseling enterprise that we often overlook how little we really know about it. We know that most individuals and families do change as a result of counseling. We also know that, in spite of our best efforts, a minority of stubborn cases do not improve. And we know that some even deteriorate. Yet we know very little about how change actually occurs (see Seligman, 1994).

Furthermore, some critics are questioning the nature and direction of therapeutic change. What are we changing exactly? For what purpose? If changing certain behaviors or reducing distressing symptoms are all we're about, so what? And if you go deeper and attempt to change attitudes and beliefs, should you? If the answer is yes, who decides which beliefs are to be changed and which attitudes need to be modified? Is the counselor playing God? Is the client? Speaking of God, are clients drawn closer to him as a result of therapy? Or is your definition of "successful therapy" tantamount to helping someone learn to live independently of God, as if God didn't matter? If so, what will you say to your clients on Judgment Day? What will you say to God?

Even if we forgo the heavy matters about goals, values, and eternity, the more mundane concerns about change still dog us. For some people, change is dramatic, sudden, and substantial, a hoped-for but often unexpected transformation or enlightenment that is miraculous (or at least described as miraculous). The rarity of such change, however, has been corrupted by our quick-fix, fast-food culture, which expects change to *always* be instantaneous ("If I can be on a plane flying to Hawaii this afternoon, why can't I have this problem solved today?"). What's more, many Christians carry this attitude and intertwine it with assumptions of miraculous and magic-like cures because they think God is committed above all else to their happiness.

For the majority of people, however, change is an incremental process—the proverbial three-steps-forward-two-steps-back experience that involves frustration, commitment, perseverance, and accountability. As Mahoney (1991) says, "Yes, humans can change—but doing so is much more difficult than many theories have admitted.... Significant psychological change is rarely rapid or easy" (p. 18). In fact, change planning—for treatment of addictions and other problems—increasingly factors in the likelihood of relapse (or recycling, as it is sometimes called) before sobriety can be consistently maintained.

Christians seem to be as susceptible to this slow, difficult process of change as anyone else, in spite of Christian media's penchant to promote the miraculous and dramatic instances of change as normative. The vast majority of Christian counselors believe miraculous change can occur; many pray for it, and some have witnessed it. The fact is, however, that most counselors and pastors say that dramatic, miraculous change is the *exception* rather than the *rule*. Furthermore, our experience has been that most Christians are motivated to change for less than the most honorable or godly reasons. As the old adage states (a truism for Christians and non-Christians alike): "Most people are willing to change, not because they see the light, but because they feel the heat."

The debate will likely go on forever about why this is so—whether it is because of our strong habitual behavior patterns, our lack of faith, the inherent limits of our humanity, God's design that things be that way, or some combination of all these factors. In this chapter we want to explore client change from biblical and clinical perspectives, and we'll examine how the Holy Spirit empowers change through the practice of spiritual disciplines.

Christian counseling, like all counseling, requires a proven strategy for moving from problem to goal, a way to consistently help people change and move from *where they are* to *where they want to be*. In order to carry out this strategy, Christian counselors must be able to function in the following roles:

- *an advocate for change*—able to motivate clients to move past their fears, comfort zones, and resistance to change (a subject we will address in chapter 16)
- *a teacher and planner of change*—able to show someone how to plan it and achieve it
- *a coach of change*—able to encourage, support, and challenge change when motivation wanes and surrender looks tempting
- *an evaluator of change*—able to help appraise and discern when goals are reached or when they need to be adjusted
- *a consultant for change*—able to help modify client plans when unexpected obstacles are encountered and to encourage clients to rest, reevaluate, and rev up for another period of sustained effort
- *a conduit of change*—able to call upon and be used by the Holy Spirit, appropriating his hope and power and wisdom

JESUS, THE GREAT PHYSICIAN

In the book of John, we read about Jesus' encounter with a man who had been blind from birth. The disciples said, "Rabbi, who sinned, this man or his parents, that he was born blind?"

> "Neither this man nor his parents sinned," said Jesus, "but this happened so that the work of God might be displayed in his life. As long as it is day, we must do the work of him who sent me. Night is coming, when no one can work. While I am in the world, I am the light of the world." (9:2-5)

The Great Physician knew the correct diagnosis of the blind man—an assessment that fell outside the sin-obsessed limits of the disciples' thinking. He also knew the reason for the man's suffering: A change was going to take place that would glorify God. Jesus healed the man, who then testified about the miracle before the Pharisees and worshiped Jesus as God.

As he did with his disciples, Jesus challenges us to look to him for answers, for healing, for everything good in life. He encourages us to see beyond our narrow frame of reference. He confronts our inaccurate and distorted thinking.

It is wise for Christian counselors to remain flexible, humble, and open to change and new learning from the Master. Let us be careful not to get locked into seemingly true theologies and brilliant psychologies. No matter how right and orthodox and elegant they seem now, getting rigid about them will only cripple our ability to know God's deeper truths.

CHANGE IN CHRISTIAN COUNSELING AND SOUL CARE

Human change—more specifically, change as promoted through counseling and psychotherapy—is a complex process that is best understood by viewing it from multiple perspectives.

CHANGE IN CHRISTIAN PERSPECTIVE

In 1998, I (Tim) spoke on change at an AACC conference. Advocating a biblical model of change, I asserted that Christ is both the end and the means to therapeutic change:

> If a person is in Christ, he is under new management. The Christian coun-
> selor must believe and steadfastly maintain that change is possible in Christ.
> Every change God desires and requires of us is possible in Christ.… The
> question has always been: Change people into what? I like the idea of grow-
> ing up into maturity in Christ, to put on the new man in Christ, and to
> teach people to think biblically, live authentically, and serve faithfully.
>
> Paul said in Philippians: "He who began a good work in you will carry
> it on to completion until the day of Christ Jesus.… One thing I do: Forget-
> ting what is behind and straining toward what is ahead, I press on toward
> the goal to win the prize for which God has called me heavenward" (1:6;
> 3:13-14). There is nothing else to give ultimately. In the end, it is about
> knowing the truth, and the truth shall set you free. As helpers, we become
> men and women of the Word. Seek him with your whole face. Turn your
> eyes upon Jesus. Your lives will never be the same. God's great desire is to
> know you intimately and to communicate himself through [you].

Adams (1986) likewise roots our potential for change in Christ—in his regenerative work in the hearts and minds of believers. In a brief, exegetical study of
Romans 6–8, Adams analyzes the struggle between the new nature that believers
receive in Christ and the old, sin-habituated patterns of wrongdoing embedded in
our souls. He argues that Paul's revelation of the struggle between good and evil
within himself is not a struggle between two natures in the heart, but between the
new nature that fully occupies the regenerate heart and the sin-lodged habits that
still infect body and soul. Adams (1986) concludes:

> The counselor has great hope for effecting change in truly regenerate per-
> sons. The Spirit and the Word, acting in concert with a new heart (nature),
> offer a remarkable potential for good. Not only is it possible for the regener-

ate person to put off old ways and put on new ones, he can even part way[s] with patterns that go back many generations (1 Peter 1:18). Let us see the picture clearly, maintain the proper emphasis, and take hope in the great potential for change that Christ has brought about in our counselees' lives. (pp. 13-14)

Craigie (1994) argues for recognizing an essential nexus between problem solving and Christian maturity. As people attain *freedom from* their problems, they increasingly realize the *freedom to* walk more intimately with God and to serve him. Craigie says,

Christian counselors promote healing as they help clients to solve problems.... They also promote healing as they help clients grow in faithfulness and vitality of Christian discipleship.... [Change in] Christian counseling...embodies the dual nature of freedom—*freedom from* condemnation, trauma, and other problems, and *freedom to* act as Christian disciples in the world. (p. 214)

This freedom-from/freedom-to relationship is mutual and complementary, and it may operate either sequentially or concurrently in the life of clients. Craigie encourages action on the freedom-to side of the equation—looking to the future and moving toward it in confidence and hope. He warns against excessive focus on past hurts and traumas, recognizing how obsession with problems can keep one stuck and feeling hopeless about possible change.

CHANGE AS A PSYCHOSOCIAL CONSTRUCT

Bandura (1982, 1986, 1989) has had a significant impact on our understanding of human change and learning. His social learning theory and work on self-efficacy in human expectation and change have received worldwide recognition. He sees expectations as revolving around outcomes and efficacy. *Outcome expectancy* refers to the belief one has (or doesn't have) that a particular outcome is capable of being achieved or will be effected. *Efficacy expectancy* refers to the belief one has (or doesn't have) with regard to certain actions aimed at producing an outcome. People will show different levels of confidence in these areas.

For example, a Christian who knows how to pray but fails to do so may reveal that he doesn't really believe his prayers will move God to change an outcome (high efficacy/low outcome problem). Anxiety and its attendant problem of avoidance also reflect this dynamic. Many people know *how* to face their fears and reduce anxiety, but they self-sabotage by believing their actions aren't going to accomplish anything and may even make things worse. The counselor may be challenged to show how prayer does move God—by reference to Scripture and to personal stories—and to discuss how much of the expected loss is in the believer's selective perceptions.

Addicts struggle with the reverse problem (low efficacy/high outcome). They may feel hopeless about ever controlling their compulsion (low efficacy), but they may also believe that their lives would improve if they could control their addiction (high outcome belief). Depression is so difficult to overcome for some people because they struggle with low efficacy as well as low outcome expectancy—another way of saying hopelessness and helplessness. Counselors are challenged to offer hope and facilitate action by helping clients set small goals that they can easily understand and achieve.

THE CHANGE PROCESS: A-B-C AND RECIPROCITY

Cognitive therapists have seized the old S-R (stimulus-response) model of behaviorism and have reinterpreted it as an A-B-C process: the **A**ntecedent (stimulus) event, feeling, or thought occurs, which calls into play **B**eliefs, thoughts, perceptions, and values, which influence the nature and direction of **C**onsequential responses of behavior and emotion.

When the mediating beliefs and thoughts are untruthful, unbiblical, and illogical, harmful behavior and negative emotions are often the consequence. The reverse also happens: truthful and logical beliefs will yield peace, right action, and harmonious relationships (Thurman, 1995; Vernick, 2000).

The key to the model is understanding and using the power of mediated beliefs and values, which are the true influence on our actions and emotions. Spiritually, the challenge is to replace illogical, untruthful thinking with the truths of God revealed in his Word. Clinically, the challenge is to overcome the common perception most people have, which asserts that A causes C ("The devil made me do it." "My teacher makes me so mad." "If only you'd change, I could love you more."). Clients are empowered when they understand that B causes C and that C will change as a result of changing B to align with God's truth. (This concept will be explained more fully in chapter 15.)

The A-B-C process is consistent with Jesus' revelation that sin and wrongdoing come from within, not without (Luke 6:45; 11:39-41). Hundreds of years before Christ, the ancient Greek philosopher Epictetus said, "We are not bothered by the things that happen to us, but by the view we take of them."

Family and social systems therapists have taken the A-B-C model even further by showing its reciprocal and cyclical nature. The feedback loop is a principle that reveals how a consequence of action often feeds back to the person or system to become a new antecedent for change. In other words, what happens when I change becomes a new stimulus that I react and respond to, sometimes for better and sometimes for worse. The key influence here is understanding that A-B-C is not the linear process it looks like on paper, but an ongoing spiral of interacting dimensions of living.

STAGES OF CHANGE AND COUNSELING READINESS

Research by Prochaska, DiClimente, and Norcross (1994) has revealed the universal stages of change and how a client's readiness for change requires the right counseling strategies. We have adapted their excellent model using biblical language (with Prochaska's terms in parentheses) to reflect the stages of change from a Paracentric perspective:

1. *The blind or unmotivated client (precontemplative).* These clients have little to no motivation to change. From teens dragged into counseling by determined parents to reluctant spouses who come to appease their partners, these folks deny or see no need for change. Often they think *someone else* needs to change, not them.

2. *The ambivalent client (contemplative).* These people may see the need for change but, for various reasons, do little or nothing about it. In light of Bandura's self-efficacy theory, they may see value in a different outcome but don't know how to achieve it or don't believe they can. They may know what to do, but aren't sure the outcome will be worth all the effort. For others, thinking about taking action "gives the illusion of actually doing something," and that is enough for them (Oliver, Hasz, & Richburg, 1997, p. 29).

3. *The intentional client (preparation).* This client is committed to change and has started to consider or even plan out how to accomplish it. If clients get stuck here, they are more like a *hearer* of the truth than a *doer* of it (James 1:22-25).

4. *The doer (action).* The client who takes action and begins to show the fruit of change is like a doer of the Word. This stage represents the heart of a Paracentric focus, and it is where the client actively pursues change (with the counselor's guidance). Change as a goal-directed undertaking should be specific in focus, but it is often broad in generalizing effect. According to accepted systems principles, changing one's behavior usually changes aspects of one's spiritual, emotional, and relational life as well.

5. *The persevering client (maintenance).* Helping clients maintain the gains of counseling is one of the biggest challenges of our field, one that is finally beginning to receive the attention it deserves. The persevering client is able to do exactly

that: sustain the new level of change and continue to grow in Christ without direct intervention. This step usually requires that counselor and client plan for post-treatment activity, including helping the client reestablish and rely on the assistance of his or her pastor and church community.

6. *The maturing client (termination)*. Termination of counseling comes when treatment goals are achieved and the client is living out what has been pursued in counseling. The maturing client is able to live well in Christ and, hopefully, is willing to teach others to do the same.

Prochaska et al. (1994) found that it is critical to first assess a client's stage of change readiness and then to tailor clinical interventions to that level. Mismatching client readiness and intervention is responsible for much of the failure that goes on in counseling. Prochaska's research found that "fewer than 20 percent of a problem population are prepared for action at any given time. And yet, more than 90 percent of behavior change programs are designed with this 20 percent in mind" (p. 15). Furthermore, "over 45 percent of clients drop out of psychotherapy prematurely, since treatments too often don't match the stage clients are in" (p. 16).

Therefore, while Christian counseling is action-oriented, it is also client-centered. Action should not be pushed on a client in stages 1 or 2 (unmotivated or ambivalent stages), or the client will be lost. Staying with and motivating clients in these stages means embracing an empathic, conversational, and client-centered focus—truly being with clients in their stuck or ambivalent or fearful places in order to motivate and encourage them to eventually act and change.

CONSTRUCTIVE CONFRONTATION

Counselors must be careful, however, not to allow their relationship development skills—empathy, listening, and acceptance—to interfere with the success of the counseling process. Instead, they must learn to build on and use the social and spiritual influence they have gained in the relationship to facilitate client action and to help carry out the change phase of counseling.

Many helpers are afraid to confront clients (while others do it excessively or exclusively), yet many clients welcome it when trust exists in the relationship. Trevino (1996) points out that a strong counselor-client relationship and compatibility of values foster growth-producing confrontation:

> Certain patterns of congruency and discrepancy…between client and
> counselor facilitate change. There is a significant body of research suggesting that congruency between counselor and client enhances the therapeutic relationship, whereas discrepancy between the two facilitates change….

[The] presentation of discrepant points of view contributes to positive outcome by changing "the way the client construes problems and considers
solutions." (p. 203)

Competent Christian counselors do well to learn and practice the art of doing
"tough-minded therapy [in] a tender-minded profession" (Weinrach, 1995, p. 296).
As counselors listen attentively and rely on their perceptions, they can become
adept at homing in on contradictions and inconsistencies revealed by their clients.
Counselors must lovingly yet firmly confront their clients concerning unhealthy
attitudes and behaviors they observe, such as the following:

1. *Dysfunctional, illogical, and unbiblical self-talk.* "I'm no good." "I don't
   have to follow the rules." "I should be the center of attention when I
   enter a conversation." "No one cares about me." "God can't be interested
   in this small problem." "God is probably too angry with me to listen."
2. *The shoulds, oughts, and musts of controlling and distorted beliefs.* "I must
   be in charge of this meeting or it will fail." "I shouldn't have to stand in
   line like everyone else." "He ought to be more considerate of my needs
   in this situation—what a jerk!"
3. *Unhealthy and damaging behaviors and speech.* "I won't talk to him until he
   comes and apologizes first!" "I'm just having a good time. What's wrong
   with that? If she wasn't so sensitive, she wouldn't feel hurt all the time."
4. *Faulty and exaggerated interpretations of the meaning of other people's
   behavior.* "I know she said that just to hurt me!" "He hates me. What
   other reason could there be for ignoring me like that?"
5. *Blaming others and failing to take responsibility for one's own problems.* "He
   started it. It's his fault I ended up hitting him. He should've kept his
   mouth shut!"
6. *Minimizing or exaggerating problems and stating goals in unrealistic ways.*
   "Sure, I can have this compulsion under control by next week." "No
   way. It's impossible to get that done by the deadline."
7. *The ongoing games, discrepancies, smoke screens, dishonesties, excuse making,
   and self-pitying that sabotage honest self-understanding.* "I was just joking. I
   didn't know your feelings would get hurt." "Yeah, I wanted the job. I
   didn't mean to oversleep and miss the interview. It's just one of those
   things." "I really do love my husband, but when other men flirt with
   me, I just can't help flirting back."

Egan (1998) notes that confrontation is difficult for many clients and that
some will not be receptive to it. Some clients, in fact, will turn the tables and

engage in counterchallenging actions that attempt to (1) neutralize or discredit you, (2) get you to change your view of things, (3) devalue or dismiss the importance of the issue, (4) seek support elsewhere for the issues being challenged, and (5) appease you during the session (but then do nothing afterward).

It is crucial, therefore, that the counselor gains the right to challenge so that the client is prepared to receive any confrontational messages. Egan (1998, p. 190) asserts that counselors should challenge clients only if the counselor

- has spent time with the client and has made an effort to build a relationship;
- is able to see the world through the client's eyes, because only then "can you begin to see what he or she is failing to see";
- is open to being challenged in return and is willing to model the kind of nondefensive attitudes and behavior that would benefit clients. Many times clients will drop their defenses when they see that you are not putting up any;
- is striving to grow personally and to live fully according to his or her own value system.

How you engage in confrontational behavior is also important to client receptivity. Egan (1998) suggests that one should be tentative but not apologetic. Counselors should challenge unused client strengths or gifts more than weaknesses and build upon successes (or near successes). Challenges should be specific, focusing on practical changes in behavior. The best confrontations, of course, are consistent with client values and goals, which can lead to *self*-confrontation. Such an interaction might go something like this:

Counselor: Everyone has some blind spots in their relationships with others. Imagine that you are invisible and your wife is sitting here. She doesn't know you're here. What might she tell me?

Client: Gee, uh, I don't know. I've never thought about it that way.

Counselor: I'll bet you have some hunches. You've probably heard her say some things, even if you weren't listening or paying attention.

Client: Well, yeah. I think she'd tell you that…that I don't listen or pay attention [laughs at the irony]. And she'd be right, of course.

Counselor: So all you'd have to do to make her more happy is to pay attention when she talks about something she wants to see change. All you have to do is face her, listen, nod your head from time to time, and let her know that you heard what she said.

Client: That sounds pretty easy, but it's not. She assumes that if I'm listening to her, I'm agreeing to what she says and that I'll do it.

Counselor: So instead of telling her you hear her but don't agree—and then discussing with her how to work out the disagreement—you ignore her and assume she'll understand. Is that right?

Client: Yeah, I guess so. That's not a really good way to do it, is it?

Counselor: What do you think?

Client: No, it isn't. She doesn't get my message. How could she? Then she gets mad about the message she *does* get: that I don't care about her. And that makes me want to ignore her all the more. It's pretty silly when I stop and look at it this way.

GOAL SETTING AND ACTION PLANNING

The goals of therapy claim a significant role in the outcome of the therapeutic process. As Christian counselors we are looked upon as experts in helping others define clear goals and achieve them. Competent counselors must know themselves and their clients, their theoretical road map, and how goals are shaped and pursued according to that map (McMinn, 1996, p. 58). Cheydleur (1999) asserts,

> It is important to remember that our big goal is one of restoring the broken-hearted person to a whole life. Reason, faith, and emotion should fit so well together that the person is able to deal effectively with his or her social environment in a responsible, moral and rewarding way. (p. 72)

Most clients come into counseling to be relieved of their suffering. In the midst of their pain, confusion, and disillusionment, they are looking to us for hope and guidance as they struggle to make sense of it all. Our compassion and confidence in believing that change is possible can calm their anxious souls and help them sort out their options. Clients must believe for themselves that positive change can take place, that recovery and healing are real possibilities. As they explore their options, they begin to gain a sense of control and efficacy. As they choose preferred directions in counseling, we can begin to formulate mutually agreed-upon therapy goals. The counselor's goal-shaping skills should fit the vision for the client's future. Crews (2001) asserts that a healthy and godly future for clients will involve at least five elements:

1. Clients will be able to sort out the past from the present and differentiate between old hurts and new ones. This is necessary so that they can identify what has been done to them by others and what they have done to themselves. This can enable them to eventually shed any victim mentality and start to take control of their own lives.

2. Clients will learn to accept responsibility for their self-defeating behavioral patterns in the present, envisioning how their lives will look and feel when they think and behave in more godly ways.

3. Clients will recognize the power of choices and become responsible for the changes they want to occur in their lives, renouncing the lie that their past binds them up with uncontrollable power.

4. Clients will have the ability to lay the past to rest, to make positive

---

Box 10.1—Structuring Change in the Christian Counseling Process

The following material shows the process of change in Christian counseling in the form of a progressive, step-by-step outline. This outline is adapted from unpublished information contained in the Christian Counseling Skills Training program, developed by George Ohlschlager and Peter Mosgofian.

I. *Setting Goals for Change:* Moving from Insight to Action
   A. The Importance of Setting Goals for Active Change
      1. Set goals to know what you want to achieve.
         a. "Where there is no vision, the people perish" (Proverbs 29:18, KJV).
         b. People don't plan to fail; they fail to plan.
      2. Take control of events in order to attain some end or objective.
   B. Five Criteria for Goal Setting
      1. Restate client problems as goals; fit treatment to assessment.
      2. Establish manageable goals with realistic time frames.
      3. Focus on accomplishments rather than on means or goal-related behavior.
      4. State goals that are specific and clear, with verifiable outcomes.
      5. Goals must match client values and priorities; clients must "own" goals.

II. *Planning for Action:* Think Before You Work, Then Work Smart!
   A. Advocacy: Why Planning Helps People Attain Their Goals
      1. Planning helps anchor goals in reality by specifying the time and personal costs required to reach a goal.
      2. Planning helps determine the resources needed to attain goals.

changes in the present, and to move forward with hope and confidence into the future (see Egan, 1998).

5. Clients will find and appropriate the "way, truth, and life" that come from a relationship with Jesus Christ. They will rely upon the power of the Holy Spirit to effect change. Christians have become new persons (2 Corinthians 5:17) and have within them an "incomparably great power" (Ephesians 1:19).

---

    3. Planning helps uncover obstacles to achieving goals.

    4. Planning helps identify areas of counselor support or challenge.

B. Help Clients Choose Change Strategies to Attain Their Goals

    1. Help clients engage in divergent (not convergent) thinking.

    2. Brainstorm to generate many ideas about reaching goals.

        a. Suspend judgments about ideas not working.

        b. "Let yourself go." List even far-reaching ideas.

        c. Encourage quantity.

        d. Piggyback ideas and clarify them.

III. *Taking Action to Reach Change Goals:* Work Out What You've Planned

A. Shape the Plan into a Guide for Behavior

    1. Break large goals into smaller subgoals or steps. (Key Rule: No step should be so large or difficult that the client can't understand it or take the action required to achieve it.)

    2. Discuss and negotiate action steps.

    3. Write out clear, specific, and measurable terms.

    4. Encourage the client to work toward the goal regularly and systematically.

    5. Emphasize the costs of avoiding action and promote the inclusion of rewards (and possibly some sanctions) toward desired behavior.

B. Finally, "Just Do It"

    1. Review progress frequently with limited revision of contract terms as actions and circumstances change.

    2. Help develop contingency plans: What will the client do if this step is not workable (or if he or she is not working it)?

    3. Encourage action, reinforce and celebrate every step taken, and serve as a helper, resource, comforter, and cheerleader.

Therapeutic goals should include short-term objectives (remedial change) and long-term direction (maintenance and prevention). Goals must be realistic and achievable for the client. Egan (1998) says, "If clients choose goals that are complex or difficult, then it is useful to help them establish sub-goals as a way of moving step by step toward the ultimate goal" (p. 303).

Two questions to ask clients when setting goals are (1) What is it that you want your life to look like when you've changed? and (2) What are you willing to do to make it happen? As clients answer these two questions, the therapist can begin to formulate a plan to move forward. These may seem like straightforward questions, but some clients will struggle to answer them, especially the second one. Many people are unwilling to pay the price and endure the pain necessary to achieve their goals (Egan, 1998, p. 333).

Clients who do accept the challenge to pursue their goals and who invest the time and effort to enact changes will eventually reap the rewards of their endurance. According to Dayringer (1998, p. 26), these rewards include:
- freedom from self-defeating behavioral patterns
- recovery and acceptance of the lost self
- ownership of personal power
- restoration of wholesome interpersonal relationships

In addition, clients will gain an inner contentment about their place in God's scheme of things so that life will hold new purpose and meaning for them. When this happens, the fragmented person becomes more of the integrated and whole person we envisioned.

There will be times when the goal is to help someone die peacefully. Suffering and pain are sometimes a prelude to death. You may someday work with dying clients who will whisper to you in fear and dread, "I don't want to die." Dying clients are searching for the same relief and hope as other clients, and Christian counselors can offer both. For God promises believers that heaven is certain and that "he will wipe every tear from their eyes. There will be no more death or mourning or crying or pain, for the old order of things has passed away" (Revelation 21:4; see also 1 Thessalonians 4:13-18).

THE ROAD MAP OF CHANGE:
STRATEGIES AND THEIR APPLICATION

The growth process involves two basic types of change: (1) *external* change or attempts to modify our environment, which may involve leaving or getting out of a toxic situation, and (2) *internal* change, which involves transforming our attitudes and views about a person or situation. Competent counselors are able to start with either type of change, depending on client need and readiness. Let's look briefly at some strategies for fostering both kinds of change.

BASIC PRINCIPLES OF BEHAVIORAL CHANGE

Clients most often enter counseling because they have failed to change a situation or deal with it effectively. Most people have a tendency to seek external change first, and they often view this as their only option. Helping them recognize and understand the wider range of change options available to them is a crucial component of competent counseling.

Reinforcement: The appropriate use of incentive and reward. Either by increasing reward (positive reinforcement) or by removing unpleasant barriers (negative reinforcement), this strategy always increases the strength of goal-directed behavior. Covert reinforcement teaches the client to generate and use pleasant images as a way to assist goal attainment. Competent counselors need to be able to praise, encourage, and celebrate client accomplishments whenever and however they happen.

Punishment: Used only in conjunction with reward. Although the effects are brief, and overreliance on punishment can produce negative consequences (such as rebellion or loss of interest in a goal), it is effective in suppressing unwanted behavior. Competent counselors work to help parents balance both reward and discipline (emphasizing the former) in child-rearing practices.

Avoidance: Never underestimate its power. Understand that avoidance behavior is paradoxical and hard to overcome because it is both rewarding (the client is relieved by avoiding the feared object) and increasingly frightening (fear of the object grows until it becomes overwhelming). Helping the client desensitize the fear—to feel the fear and face it anyway—is the preferred task.

Extinction: Behavior weakens when rewards stop. Usually, removing rewards will reduce goal-directed behavior and eventually stop it. Unless you intensively love your job, if your paychecks stopped, you'd likely stop showing up for work every morning.

Flooding: Behavior also weakens when you overwhelm someone with it. The cliché is true: "Too much of a good thing is no longer a good thing." When something is scarce, we want it more. When we have a lot of something, we no longer are so driven to get it.

Shaping change: Plan your work step by step and work your plan day by day. How do you eat an elephant? One bite at a time, of course. This witticism exemplifies the necessity of developing a well-shaped plan of goal attainment. Many treatment plans fail because the counselor or client tries to accomplish too much too quickly (or too little too slowly). Good goal-setting skills require properly balancing client resources and limitations and adjusting the plan as the client progresses.

Contingency contracting: Negotiate successful goal attainment with your client. These action-oriented contracts specify the behavior and rewards that are contingent on successful attainment of client goals. Good treatment planning should incorporate this principle into the process.

COGNITIVE CHANGE: ADJUSTING THE WAY WE THINK

Some clients enter therapy because they have been unable to change internally. They can't let go of a former lover, they are unable to forgive their parents, they can't control their anger, they are anxious, or they are troubled by a foreboding sense of doom. Some clients are caught in the stubborn refusal to shift from external to internal change: "No, I can't accept that about my spouse. He must change or our marriage is over."

Jesus taught that it's not external things that harm and corrupt us but those things that come from the heart (Matthew 15:10-11). A great amount of personal trouble and emotional distress flow from the faulty thinking—"stinkin' thinkin'," according to Twelve Step programs—that directly influences our judgment, behavior, and, ultimately, our mood. Bringing every thought captive to the will of Christ and renewing our minds to transform our nature are crucial to the process (Romans 12:2; 2 Corinthians 10:5).

FROM LIES TO THE TRUTH: TRANSFORMING OUR SELF-TALK

Christian cognitive (or belief-focused) counseling is a process of identifying and questioning the lies we believe, renouncing them, and replacing them with God's truth as it is revealed in the Scriptures. Although we will outline this process in greater detail in later chapters, here is a thumbnail sketch of the principles and practices:

I. Get the Right View: "My faith is right, but some of my thinking and beliefs are wrong."

II. Challenge and Change False and Distorted Thinking and Beliefs.

    A. What/so-what questioning technique.

        1. What's the evidence that your belief is true?

        2. What's the evidence against it?

        3. So what if it happens?

    B. What's another (less awful) way of looking at it?

    C. What does God have to say about this?

        1. *Apply if-then logic:* "If God tells me I'm completely forgiven, and he will never forsake me, then what does that mean for my fear that I'm unforgiven and that he will abandon me unless I measure up?"

2. *Practice as-if thinking:* Tell yourself the truth and act "as if" God were speaking the truth. Ask your clients to act out alternative and godly scenarios *as if* the true things they don't believe were actually true.

Transforming Imagery and Fantasy

The visual equivalents to self-talk (an auditory mental process) are imagery and fantasy. The process of daydreaming, the imagining functions of the mind's eye, sleep dreaming and nightmares, and various forms of memory recall (both healthy and traumatic) all involve the visual operations of the brain. Understanding and pinpointing disturbing imagery (hot cognitions) is a central task for people who have been shamed or traumatized to some degree.

Envisioning versus owning God's vision. We are visioning creatures who need to learn to use our imagining powers in ways that honor and glorify God. Consider the following points:

1. Let us discern and reject New Age practices, but let's not throw out the baby with the bathwater and reject how God would have us use the envisioning powers he's given us in order to solve problems and to attain spiritual maturity.
2. Use covert rehearsal strategies. Practice in detail in your mind what you're going to do or say, and rehearse it mentally as well as with a counselor or a friend.
3. Use biblical imagery to counter disturbed and distorted imagery. Imagery in prayer and in inner healing, or in the healing of painful memories and damaged emotions, can be a powerful tool when directed by the Holy Spirit.

Forgiveness

The challenge and practice of forgiveness is currently receiving a lot of attention in both Christian and secular counseling. Forgiveness is crucial in the process of relationship healing and restoration. Unforgiveness is also known to be a significant cause of anxiety and feelings of being threatened and prolongs trauma symptoms, social isolation, and the pain in interpersonal relationships. Helping clients give and receive forgiveness is an important objective in Christian counseling. We have adapted the work of McCollough, Sandage, and Worthington (1997) to facilitate this process:

1. *Engage in lamenting.* In the Scriptures, the call to lament was a challenge to emotional honesty and connection with God. Lamenting means

mourning the adverse effects of broken relationships and entreating God to bring divine healing and restoration. Permission to lament releases the raw power of anger, shame, sadness, and confusion. As Sandage (1998) says, "Through empathic therapist involvement, clients can feel the safety to relax anxious defenses and acknowledge [the pain]" (p. 22).

2. *Encourage humility.* Humility allows a person to move beyond simply feeling the pain and anger of victim status to being able to empathize with the "antagonist." It also helps clients see their own contribution to the relational trouble.

3. *Rehearse forgiving and apologizing.* During a counseling session, have your client engage in a forgiveness event or ritual that may or may not include the other person.

4. *Extend narrative horizons.* This work pushes the boundaries of the client's painful story outward to include God and others in a way that changes the meaning and purpose of the event. It allows the client to see God's larger purposes of character development and spiritual maturity in the suffering and in the forgiving. While attempts to do this too soon are usually resisted, using this technique at the proper time can give hope and Christ-centered meaning to a hurtful event.

It is important to discuss and work through client expectations, fears, and resistance to forgiveness before engaging in such intervention. Many false beliefs and expectations about forgiveness abound. For example, many people believe that forgiveness can't be done unless the perpetrator first owns the wrong and asks for forgiveness. Also, many clients have refused to forgive because withholding forgiveness serves a defensive, protective function. Lack of forgiveness allows people to maintain their protective anger and vigilance against the perpetrator; forgiveness will strip away that shield and expose them to further abuse. This is a significant issue for many victims that will take much time and patience to work through. The key is transferring trust to God as the One who will protect and defend. This can also be a major struggle since many victims do not trust God because he did not protect them from the original abuse.

INNER HEALING PRAYER

Inner healing prayer is different from encouraging and facilitating prayer as a spiritual discipline (see chapter 4). It is counselor-led and client-consented prayer intervention with the specific intent of healing and breaking the chains of past traumas. Tan (1996) developed a seven-step procedure for using inner healing prayer in counseling:

1. *Start the session with prayer* to ask for God's grace, power, healing, and protection during the session.
2. *Help the client relax* and get into a calm and receptive state that seeks God and anticipates that he will move in a curative way.
3. *Have the client return to the traumatic event and verbally recount what happened.* This may surface painful imagery or memories, so talk to the client soothingly and reassuringly, reminding him or her of God's presence. Allow the client to reexperience the emotions of the event and to describe them. Ask questions to keep the process moving forward. This procedure serves to shift the power of the trauma away from the perpetrator and into the hands of God.
4. *Pray aloud with your client.* After the client has described the event and is reliving some of the feelings, ask God to minister his love and healing grace in whatever way he chooses. Don't prescribe a certain pattern or structure to God or to the client.
5. *Wait for a time in quiet contemplation and silent prayer.* After a few minutes, ask the client what is happening internally, what she feels or sees in her mind's eye. Responses here will vary. Some clients will describe images of Jesus hugging or holding them. Others will recall an encouraging verse from Scripture, a hymn sung at church, or memories of happy and safe times as a child. Still others may describe a warm presence or feeling, as if they are being bathed in a radiant glow.

   In some cases, clients won't feel anything or have any imagery. It is important to reinforce that, by faith, we are assured of God's presence and intervention. While experiencing God is a wonderful result of this kind of prayer, it does not always happen and is not the goal of the exercise. "There is a letting go of control and [embracing] trust in God, who truly cares and works things out in good time" (p. 373).
6. *Close the intervention with prayer.* Encourage clients to pray as well, if they are so inclined. Give thanks to God and praise him for his love and power that are at work in our lives.
7. *Engage in a postintervention debriefing.* Make sure the client is okay emotionally, reinforce God's goodness and healing power, and explore any benefits of the experience. Also, there are often numerous ancillary issues such as forgiveness, dealing with anger or bitterness, reconciliation, and relationship restoration that should be discussed with the client at this time or in subsequent sessions.

Be careful that prayer is not presented as merely a technique, implying that God can be manipulated or that the right formula will bring results.

The Heavenly Reframe

One intervention that can encourage your clients' spiritual maturity is what we call the *heavenly reframe*. Some people, in fact, would consider it a spiritual discipline, and it certainly produces the best results when it becomes a daily, even hourly, habit in the life of the believer. It can also be seen as a clinical-spiritual intervention that follows the cognitive thought-stopping and replacement process.

The heavenly reframe involves stopping reactions from a worldly perspective and immediately praying and concentrating on a godly perspective of the issue. The goal is to reach a place of maturity where an individual is not controlled by events and other people but is able to bring a transformed, Christ-centered perspective to every problem and challenge in life. (The TRUTH model of intervention, which will be introduced in chapter 15, greatly assists with this process.)

Habermas (1998) calls this kind of reframing "top-down thinking" (p. 26). He says,

> The God of the universe invites believers to view the myriad details of life from his eternal vantage point.... God and his Kingdom are to be pursued above all else [so that life is viewed] from his eternal perspective. The result orders life so that it is single-minded: directed toward eternity [and] freed from many of its more painful aspects. Directed by God's power, this outlook should be thoroughly meshed with everything we think, say, and do. [It should] influence our worries and fears, finances, raising children, evangelism, assisting others, our approach to suffering, and our journey through life, even death. (p. 27)

Jesus presented this view in its most detailed form in Matthew 6:5-15,19-34, which records his teachings on prayer, money, possessions, and worry. He said that God should be our first love and desire in life. From this heavenly perspective, we will trust God for everything and use everything he gives us for his glory. Problems come and go, but they will never overwhelm us or divert us from our first love.

However, if God does not permeate your life like this—if you are earthly and not heavenly minded—you will fret about and selfishly hoard everything. Your life will be consumed with what you eat, what you wear, and when the next meal is coming. You'll worry if the roof is going to leak, how you're going to get enough money to retire, whether you have enough insurance, and what might happen if your health fails. In contrast to this earthly way of thinking, Jesus said:

Do not worry about your life, what you will eat or drink; or about your body, what you will wear. Is not life more important than food, and the body more important than clothes?… For the pagans run after all these things, and your heavenly Father knows that you need them. But seek first his kingdom and his righteousness, and all these things will be given to you as well. (Matthew 6:25,32-33)

The apostle Paul talked about this principle in 2 Corinthians 12:1-10. His thorn-in-the-flesh teaching has been transformative for saints throughout the history of the church. Caught up in heavenly visions, he was given a tormenting problem as a check against pride, one that he begged God again and again to remove. Jesus himself came to Paul and declined his pleas, telling him instead, "My grace is sufficient for you, for my power is made perfect in weakness" (verse 9). For on-fire Christians, this has been the paradoxical key to breaking through to empowered, heavenly living. For carnal Christians, this has been the ultimate "bummer" verse.

How did Paul respond? He was glad to boast about his weaknesses and delighted "in weaknesses, in insults, in hardships, in persecutions, in difficulties" (verse 10). This is certainly not the language of comfortable Christians in the modern age. It is the language, however, of Christians around the world who are growing up into maturity in Christ.

You have come a long way in your spiritual development when you are able to hold on to your joy and peace in Christ regardless of your circumstances. Practicing the heavenly reframe puts you in the same place where Paul lived, and it will move you toward the kind of maturity he had.

CHAPTER 11

THE ETHICAL HELPING RELATIONSHIP

Ethical Conformation and Spiritual Transformation

GEORGE OHLSCHLAGER AND TIM CLINTON

Politicians, scientists, physicians, business leaders, everyday citizens, and our clergy increasingly find themselves in situations where they really don't know what to do. As a result, ethics has become a boom industry, and moral failure a regular, front-page phenomenon.
—WIND, BURK, CARMENISCH, AND MCCANN,
Clergy Ethics in a Changing Society

Ethical decision making is mired in crisis and confusion in our values-relative and pluralistic world. The moral elasticity of our postmodern, post-Christian culture has even infected the church. Joe Trull of New Orleans Baptist Seminary and James Carter of the Louisiana Baptist Convention have written an excellent book, *Ministerial Ethics* (1993), in which they recount a sad story that has become all too common in some corners of the church:

> An article in a denominational paper…featured a…pastor of "one of the fastest-growing churches in Louisiana." Both of us know very well the small mission church where he pastors. The caption did not seem to fit. A check… verified our fears. The church membership numbered only a few more than one hundred. During a previous year church records reported a large percentage decrease, followed by a similar increase the next year. While this was "growth," overall attendance appeared about the same. (See Hart, 1988, p. 25)

These are not just the fumbling acts of ignorance or negligence; the wrongdoing is increasingly intentional. Whether it is pulpit exaggeration, printed hyperbole, the abuse of conferred power, sexual misconduct, or other serious forms of client and parishioner exploitation, too many church leaders and counselors today are losing the battle of moral purity and ethical integrity. As a result, Christians are ridiculed and besmirched, and the cause of Christ suffers.

In this chapter we reflect on this struggle as we define the contours of biblical and counseling ethics. We call on pastors and counselors everywhere—leaders of the church to whom most clients and parishioners still give unquestioned trust—to renew the pursuit of excellence and integrity in helping others change and grow up to maturity.

Accountability

Accountability is central to our consideration of what it means to be an ethical helper. Jesus practiced a divine accountability to his heavenly Father at every step of his public ministry. He asserted that his disciples were accountable in similar fashion to him and his Father as well. "All those who love me will do what I say. My Father will love them, and we will come to them and live with them.... And remember, my words are not my own. This message is from the Father who sent me" (John 14:23-24, NLT). The most powerful being in the universe was totally yielded to the One who had sent him. Imagine it. We are to do no less.

Getting Oriented to Christian and Counseling Ethics

Webster's New World Dictionary defines *ethics* as "the study of standards of conduct and moral judgment" and "the system or code of moral conduct of a particular person, religion, group, profession, etc." Christian ethics, we would assert, simply deals with distinguishing right and wrong behavior for a Christian." Corey, Corey, and Callanan (1998), leading authors on counseling ethics, further distinguish ethics and values: "Although *values* and *ethics* are frequently used interchangeably, the two terms are not identical. Values pertain to beliefs and attitudes that provide direction to everyday living, whereas ethics pertain to the beliefs we hold about what constitutes right conduct. Ethics are moral principles adopted by an individual or group to provide rules for right conduct" (p. 3).

A code of ethics is a systematic statement of ethical standards that represent the moral convictions and guide the practice behavior of a group—in this case, the various counseling disciplines. Every one of the primary counseling disciplines—psychiatry, psychology, social work, marriage and family therapy, and professional counseling—has an ethics code. These codes are revised and updated every few years to stay current with emerging issues and to develop a refined sense of ethical clarity and direction. Christian counseling groups have developed ethical codes, including the *AACC Christian Counseling Code of Ethics* (2001), parts of which are detailed in this chapter.

TWO KINDS OF ETHICS

Corey, Corey, and Callanan (1998) further discuss two basic kinds of ethics in professional counseling: *principle ethics* and *virtue ethics*. Principle ethics are the pragmatic rules that guide ethical behavior in particular situations. They cause us to ask the question, "What is the ethical course of action here?" Virtue ethics are the ethical ideals toward which all counselors should strive. Concerned more with counselor character than behavior, they lead us to ask, "What is in the very best interest of my client?" Principle ethics are specific and applied; virtue ethics are global and aspirational. Our dedication to maintain client confidences and respect for client privacy rights is an example of virtue ethics; concern for when and how to breach confidentiality in the case of a client's threat of suicide or homicide falls within the scope of principle ethics.

Ohlschlager (1999) followed this distinction—one that is rooted first in the Scriptures—in an article that revealed the zone of ethical behavior between conforming ethics and transforming ethics. Essentially, the article is a study of the differences and relationship between law and love. Conforming (or principle) ethics are the baseline standards, the floor below which no one should fall in counseling practice. Transforming ethics are the ethical ideals reflected in the law of love that Christ himself showed toward us by willingly going to a cross to die on our behalf. These are the perfect virtue ethics toward which all Christian counselors should strive. The relationship between the two kinds of ethics is described in box 11.1, "The Christian Counselor's Golden Rule."

ETHICAL FOUNDATIONS: THREE VIEWS

Rooted in questions about epistemology (the study of the origins of knowledge and the integrity, or truth-value, of the many ways of knowing), ethical decision making in the modern world is now influenced by three major orientations: (1) divine revelation yielding moral absolutes, (2) radical individualism yielding moral relativism, and (3) social constructionism yielding moral consensus.

Divine revelation yielding moral absolutes. For two millennia of church and Western history, most ethical systems have been rooted in the Bible and Judeo-Christian values flowing out of God's revelation in the Scriptures. This view asserts that the infinite, personal God of the Bible has revealed the perfect law—a transcendent and universal order of right and wrong—and has given us grace through Jesus Christ to know and attain it.

God's moral absolutes are held to be universal, not culture- or time-bound but applicable across all space and time. The Law of Moses and the ethics of Jesus Christ (revealed in their highest form in the Sermon on the Mount) are the basis of the ethical, legal, political, and economic principles that have shaped the development of Western history and culture. Honoring these ethics promises to bring order, peace, prosperity, and dignity to the people and culture that do so. Transgressing

---

BOX 11.1—THE CHRISTIAN COUNSELOR'S GOLDEN RULE

This Christian counselor's application of the Golden Rule is adapted from Romans 13:8-10, with apologies to all New Testament scholars out there. It is used by George Ohlschlager in his speaking and consulting with the AACC to synthesize and express the cardinal values and core rules of Christian counseling ethics.

Christian counselor, hear this:

- Do not be indebted to any client or parishioner, except the debt to *love them.*
- For if you *love your clients,* you honor all your professional and ministerial duties.

You know the rules of counseling and pastoral care:

- Do not engage in any form of sexual misconduct with your clients, whether current or past.
- Do not, as far as it possible with you, let them kill or harm themselves or anyone else.
- Do not steal your client's money or disregard your time with them.
- Do not harm or envy or look down on or manipulate or fight with or in any way exploit those Christ has sent to you for help.

In fact, to sum it up and state it conclusively:

- Practice the Golden Rule with all wisdom and grace.
- Love your clients as yourself.
- Don't do anything to your clients or those they love that you wouldn't want done to yourself.
- For love does no wrong to any client.

Therefore, to *love your clients as Christ loves you* is to fulfill all your obligations—all your moral-ethical-legal duties—as a Christian counselor.

these ethics is believed to result in personal distress, interpersonal conflict, political and cultural decline, and, if not halted and godly ethics restored, national anarchy and dissolution.

Radical individualism yielding moral relativism. The ethical history of the twentieth century reveals the incremental and systematic rejection of divine authority

---

BOX 11.2—BIBLICAL ETHICS: PURSUE AND HONOR SEVEN VIRTUES

We commend to you seven biblical ethics that flow out of this divine dedication that Christ revealed to us. These ethics shape the heart and the behavior of ethical pastors and Christian counselors in every form of ministry, and they incorporate some basic moral virtues that others have pegged as crucial to ethical case-handling. Biblical ethics are revealed ethics, rooted in the universal and timeless revelation of God in Christ (special revelation) and in nature (general revelation).

1. *Accountability to truth-telling.* Commit yourself to an active accountability to truth-telling in all that you do. Christian counselors should be accountable to their pastors and to at least one colleague or supervisor with whom discussions are as free and as confidential as humanly possible. Counseling is full of ethical dilemmas, moral temptations, and interpersonal quandaries, so it is imperative that helpers be committed to truth telling and be free to talk about every difficulty they face in the work of ministry. (See 1 Corinthians 12:12-27.)

2. *Responsibility to love one another.* Make a commitment to love others and to do them no harm—this is the principle of nonmalfeasance. If we love others with the love of Christ working in and through us, we will fulfill our gospel duties and not harm our counselees. We will also gain the wisdom to know when little to no intervention is the best course of action. (See Romans 13:8-10.)

3. *Fidelity to integrity.* Serve others with honesty and integrity. In recent history we have witnessed the national tragedy of too many fallen spiritual leaders and a dishonest president (who promised the most honest and ethical administration ever). There is simply no substitute for plain honesty and straightforward integrity in every kind of helping ministry. (See 1 Chronicles 29:16-18.)

4. *Trustworthiness in keeping confidentiality.* Always maintain client and parishioner respect by honoring their personal and family privacy. The

and the rise of secular humanism. Individual autonomy is supreme in this world-view, and moral relativism—which says, "Do your own thing. Just don't hurt me doing it"—is the result. The root value of this perspective is that "man is the meas-ure of all things," including his or her own judgment about right and wrong. Also known as *subjectivism,* or *situational ethics* as an applied practice, this view yields

secrets heard in counseling are the most personal and potentially devas-tating matters of a person's life. They must be zealously and consistently guarded at all times. In a church context, determining and consistently honoring the boundary between parishioner confidences and necessary disclosures is quite difficult and should be soaked in much prayer. (See Proverbs 11:13; 25:9.)

5. *Competent beneficence.* Work always for the good of others and only within the bounds of your competence. When needs arise beyond your competence or field of work, by all means consult or refer. Don't go it alone. Recognize that helping ministry is a corporate endeavor that involves the varied skills and dedication of many people in the body of Christ. (See Exodus 18:13-27.)

6. *Humility in justice.* Consider those you serve at least equal to, if not better than, yourself, and never show prejudice or favoritism toward anyone. Pride and arrogance are rampant and ugly character infections. Tragically, these dark traits have infected far too many in significant leadership roles in the church. Humility and consistent fairness toward others is attrac-tive, approachable, and honest, and they reflect the character of Christ. These traits should be sought after and worn with honor. (See Philippi-ans 2; 1 Peter 3:8-9.)

7. *Sufferability.* Stay with—don't abandon—your clients in the dark and painful places of their lives. We could argue that the ultimate empathy is not just *feeling* with your clients, but also *suffering* with them. Many helpers do not empathize because it is scary, draining, tempting, and just plain painful. Without Christ to identify with and to restore your strength, we don't believe counseling work can be done for very long without major counselor burnout, so this ethic may be more aspirational than the others. If you can, feel with and suffer with your clients, for such caring often transforms their lives. Such sacrifice can transform your own life with a Christian maturity and winsome attractiveness like noth-ing else in this world. (See 2 Corinthians 1:3-7; 1 Peter 3:13-17.)

an extreme form of moral relativism: "I will decide for myself what is right and wrong. Whatever is right for you may not be so for me."

Proponents of this view consider personal freedom to be the ultimate value and autonomous living the grand pursuit. Hence the value of individualism is radicalized—placed above and over all other values—and any recourse to social convention or moral absolutes is denied. Laws, custom, and social convention are held to be constraining, even oppressive forces that only serve to unjustly inhibit personal freedom. Politically, anarchy is the result of this view when pushed to its systematic conclusion, and so it has never found a solid constituency beyond radical freedom seekers.

The most disquieting expression of this view may be the politically correct campus rules gaining ground in many American universities. These rules squelch any speech that hurts the feelings of its hearers or disturbs them. There is no defense based on objective standards, no recourse to observed behavior that can be consensually evaluated. One is charged and judged guilty on purely subjective criteria: If the hearer is merely offended by the presentation, "wrongdoing" has occurred, and there is no rational basis for a defense.

Social constructionism yielding moral consensus. A third model currently gaining force is influenced by family and social systems theory and our democratic political tradition. The social constructionist view posits that ethics are forged in the interactive consensus-building process of people and systems in relationship. By means of negotiation, mediation, and arbitration—and as a result of political debate and democratic lawmaking—derived ethics reflect a group or social consensus, whereby the best values, as agreed upon by the participants in the process, are expressed as ethics and are codified into law.

Moral absolutes are not controlling in this approach because consensus values and ethics rule the day. According to this model, if biblical values survive the process, that is fine; if they don't, that is fine also. The group or the "body politic," whatever its size and function, is the creator of the moral consensus and the final arbiter of right and wrong. This view seems to be ascendant among those who recognize the social and political risks of a purely subjective and individualized ethic but do not want to adhere to the revealed ethics flowing from God's revelation.

ETHICAL DECISION MAKING IN
A PLURALISTIC WORLD

How one makes ethical decisions in situations where moral conflicts and dilemmas arise has been the subject of much theorizing and research, especially among the helping professions and in ministry.

The American Counseling Association (ACA; see Herlihy & Corey, 1996), for example, recommends the following steps in ethical decision making: (1) identify the problem, (2) apply the ACA ethical code, (3) determine the nature and dimensions of the dilemma, (4) generate potential courses of action, (5) consider the potential consequences of all options and develop a course of action, and (6) implement the action.

Corey, Corey, and Callanan (1998) have developed an eight-step procedure that is an amalgam of various approaches that include the client (who is the one ultimately affected) in the decision-making process:

1. identify the problem, including its ambiguity
2. outline the various elements and potential issues of the problem
3. review the relevant ethical codes that apply in the matter
4. know the applicable laws and regulations affecting the issue
5. consult with your client and with knowledgeable colleagues
6. consider possible and probable courses of action
7. define the consequences of various courses of action
8. decide on the best course of action for you and your client

THE AACC CHRISTIAN COUNSELING CODE OF ETHICS

Every professional discipline worth its salt has a code of ethics that codifies the aspirations of the discipline's members and regulates their behavior. The concept for the *AACC Christian Counseling Code of Ethics* was introduced in 1993 by the Law and Ethics Committee of the AACC, and the Code was completed in 2001— fifteen drafts and eight years later. The following excerpts from the introductory sections to the new Code describe the process, purpose, limits, and uses of a modern code of counseling ethics.

WELCOME

Welcome to the Y2001 revision of the *AACC Christian Counseling Code of Ethics* (Code). This edition of the Code revises the 1998 Provisional Code, and includes the new Procedural Rules section. The Y2001 Code supersedes the 1998 version of the Code in its entirety. This is the "final draft" code—the Y2001 Final Code in its completed form—which was presented at the AACC World Conference in Nashville in August 2001.

With the publication of this Code on our web site—www.aacc.net— we publicly present our ethics to our 45,000 members in all fifty states and nearly fifty other nations (as of May 2001). We also respectfully submit this document to the church and the helping professions, to the courts, legislatures, and licensure boards of America, to mental health and healthcare organizations everywhere, and to the world-at-large.

The 1998 Provisional Code has been adopted, in whole or in part, in over a dozen countries on every continent. It has been translated into Spanish, German, and Dutch languages. We at the AACC anticipate this Code becoming the basis of a worldwide statement of Christian counseling ethics

---

Box 11.3—Christian Values in Light of Radical New Age Ethics

In the eyes of unbelievers who have adopted various forms of a radical New Age ethic for living, many biblical Christians can rightly plead guilty to being judged negatively from this radical orientation and could be labeled as

- *Monotheists*, or *Christists*, by anyone who does not believe, as we do, in the infinite, personal, triune God who revealed himself in the Bible and continues to reveal himself today in the hearts and minds of regenerate believers;
- *Lifeists*, or *prolife activists*, by pro-abortionists, advocates of euthanasia and physician-assisted suicide, and anyone caught up in the seductive "lifeboat ethic" that calls for a major depopulation of planet Earth in order to create an optimally sustainable world. (The late Isaac Asimov thought the ideal world population was one billion, which would require a die-off of more than five billion people.);
- *Heteromarital sexists*, by gay rights activists, because we believe that sex should be restricted to one man and one woman in one heterosexual, holy, and lifelong union called marriage;
- *Speciesists* (or perhaps we would prefer *humanicists*), by godless bioethicists and animal rights activists who reject man as God's "crown of creation" and place animals, trees, and plants on the same moral plane as humans;
- *Churchists*, or *religionists*, by secularists or alternative religions who would deny religious freedom and even persecute and murder Christian believers because of their faith and the inherent threat that faith poses to despots, mass murderers, and authoritarian political regimes.

and, as it spreads further internationally, the foundation of a twenty-first-century, global standard of Christian care.

Work on this Code has been continuous since AACC created the Law and Ethics Committee in 1993. The primary mission given this group was to construct and manage a new, Christ-centered, interdisciplinary code of ethics for Christian counseling as it matures into the twenty-first century.

Committee members, AACC leaders, and other colleagues who helped me develop and write and survive this project through fifteen evolving drafts included: AACC President Tim Clinton, EdD; former president Gary Collins, PhD; Mark McMinn, PhD; Rosemarie Hughes, PhD; David Gatewood, MS; Peter Mosgofian, MA; W. L. Ryder, MD; Elizabeth York, MEd; Siang-Yang Tan, PhD; Chris Thurman, PhD; Ev Worthington, PhD; Tom Whiteman, PhD; Norm Wright, MA; Leigh Bishop, MD; Freda Crews, DMin; Gary Oliver, PhD; Bill Secor, PhD; Ron Hawkins, DMin, EdD; Diane Langberg, PhD; and Archibald Hart, PhD.

The Holy Scriptures and the AACC Doctrinal Statement are foundational to this Code. Other ethics codes, in alphabetical order, that were consulted as we drafted this statement included those from the:

- American Association of Marriage and Family Therapists (AAMFT), including portions of the California Association of Marriage and Family Therapists (CAMFT);
- American Association of Pastoral Counselors (AAPC);
- American Counseling Association (ACA), including the Association for Counselor Education and Supervision (ACES—ACA related), and the Association for Spiritual, Ethical, and Religious Values in Counseling (ASERVIC—also ACA related);
- American Psychiatric Association (APiA);
- American Psychological Association (APoA), including APoA General Guidelines for Providers of Psychological Services;
- Christian Association for Psychological Studies (CAPS);
- National Association of Social Workers (NASW), including NASW Standards for the Private Practice of Clinical Social Work; and
- The Society of Professionals in Dispute Resolution (SPDR).

Furthermore, some rules for procedure, for resolution of conflicted values, and the detail in this document were suggested by the legal profession's Code of Professional Responsibility. Finally, this code was also influenced by selected court cases, mental health license statutes, and licensure board administrative rules from California, Virginia, Texas, Colorado, Florida, Michigan, Minnesota, and New York.

INTRODUCTION AND MISSION

The Code is designed to assist AACC members to better serve their clients and congregants and to improve the work of Christian counseling world-wide. It will help achieve the primary goals of the AACC—to bring honor to Jesus Christ and his church, promote excellence in Christian counseling, and bring unity to Christian counselors.

A New Code for an Emerging Profession

The Code is a comprehensive, detailed, and integrative synthesis of biblical, clinical, systemic, ethical, and legal information. It was created this way because vaguely worded, content limited, and overly generalized codes are insufficient for the modern, twenty-first-century counseling environment. A more comprehensive and behavior-specific ethical code is needed for Christian counselors (and all mental health and ministerial professions, we believe) because of: (1) the mounting evidence of questionable and incompetent practices among Christian counselors, including increasing complaints of client-parishioner harm; (2) the largely unprotected legal status of Christian counseling, including the increasing state scrutiny, excessive litigation, and unrelenting legalization of professional ethics; and more positively (3) the vitality and growing maturity of Christian counseling—including its many theories and controversies—indicating the need for an overarching ethical-legal template to guide the development of biblical and empirically sound Christian counseling models.

This Code—beyond defining the boundaries of unethical practice—affirmatively educates counselors in the direction of becoming helpers of ethical excellence, capable of more consistently securing the best counseling outcomes. This Code shows four streams of influence. These include (1) the Bible (both Old and New Testaments) and historic orthodox Christian theology;[1] (2) accepted standards of counseling and clinical practice from Christian counseling and the established mental health disciplines; (3) codes of ethics from other Christian and mental health professions; and (4) current and developing standards derived from mental health and ministry-related law.

Mission, Uses, and Limits of the Code

The mission of the Code is to

1. advance the central mission of the AACC—to bring honor to Jesus Christ and promote excellence and unity in Christian counseling;
2. promote the welfare and protect the dignity and fundamental rights of all individuals, families, groups, churches, schools, agencies, ministries, and other organizations with whom Christian counselors work;
3. provide standards of ethical professional conduct in Christian counseling that are to be advocated and applied by the AACC and ABCC and that can be respected by other professionals and institutions; and
4. outline procedural rules for the fair hearing and adjudication of ethical complaints, the conciliatory resolution of disputes, the honorable discipline or just expulsion of erring members, and the compassionate restoration of AACC and ABCC members to counseling practice and ministry.

This Code defines biblically based values and universal behavioral standards for ethical Christian counseling. We intend this Code to become a core document by which Christian counselors, clients, and the church oversee and evaluate Christian counselors and counseling values, goals, process, and effectiveness. Furthermore, the Code asserts a Christian counseling standard of care that invites respect and application by the courts, the regulatory bodies of church and state, insurance and managed care groups, other professions, and by society.

This Code should be seen as normative but non-exhaustive. It provides a common definition of practice, but does not presume to be a complete picture of Christian counseling nor does it necessarily cover all ethical issues. This Code outlines a foundation of preferred values and agreed professional behavior upon which Christian counselors can shape their identity and build their work. It defines standards upon which practice diversity is acknowledged and encouraged as well as the limits beyond which practice deviance is not allowed.

The Code is both aspirational and enforceable throughout the AACC and ABCC. It consists of four major parts—Introduction and Mission, Biblical-Ethical Foundations, Ethical Standards, and Procedural Rules. It aspires to define, in the mission and the biblical-ethical foundations statements, the best ideals and goals of Christian counseling. The ethical standards and procedural rules are the codes of individual practice and organizational behavior that are to guide the membership of the AACC and ABCC. The mission and foundations statements are to be consulted in working out the problems and dilemmas of ethics application and procedural rules interpretation.

Concerning language, we have endeavored to avoid pedantic, legalese, and sexist language, but we also avoid a radical inclusivism that de-sexes the name of God. Unless denoted, we use the term "client" to refer to clients, patients, congregants, parishioners, or helpees. "Counseling" is usually a generic reference to clinical, psychiatric, pastoral, and lay helping.

Grace for the Task Ahead
This is a dynamic Code, one that will anchor the mission of the AACC and retain some elements without change, but one that will also live and grow with the life and growth of the Association and its membership. The Code calls us to a life-long commitment to ethical and excellent service; it challenges us to encourage ethical behavior in our colleagues, churches, organizations, and communities. May God give us the grace to own it professionally, the strength to live it honorably, and the hope to see it as a foundation of common identity and corporate unity.

BIBLICAL-ETHICAL FOUNDATIONS[2]

1st FOUNDATION: Jesus Christ—our wonderful Counselor and the Apostle of our profession—is the pre-eminent model for Christian counseling practice, ethics, and care ministry.

2nd FOUNDATION: Christian counseling maintains a committed, intimate relationship with the world-wide church, and individual counselors with a local body of believers.

3rd FOUNDATION: Christian counseling, at its best, is a Spirit-led process of change and growth, geared to help others mature in Christ by the skillful synthesis of counselor-assisted spiritual, psycho-social, familial, bio-medical, and environmental interventions.

4th FOUNDATION: Christian counselors are dedicated to excellence in client service, to ethical integrity in practice, and to respect for others.

5th FOUNDATION: Christian counselors accord the highest respect to the biblical revelation regarding human life, personhood, and the family.

6th FOUNDATION: The biblical and constitutional rights to free speech and religious freedom protects Christian counselor public identity and the explicit incorporation of spiritual practices in counseling.

7th FOUNDATION: Christian counselors are mindful of their representation of Christ and his church and are dedicated to honor their commitments and obligations in all social and professional relations.

THE MAJOR ISSUES IN COUNSELING ETHICS

We now proceed to outline some critical guidelines of ethical behavior that apply to the practice of Christian counseling. Under each section we have provided excerpted content from the *AACC Christian Counseling Code of Ethics* (2001), which gives a fairly full description of the content and the process of the ethical duty. Brief comments about recent trends and application issues accompany these Code excerpts.

ABOVE ALL ELSE, DO NO HARM

The overarching rule of ethics in any profession that serves human need (especially the counseling professions) is *do no harm*. At first this may seem absurdly obvious and simple, but on reading and reflection the depth and importance of this rule come to light.

Christian counselors acknowledge that the first rule of professional-ministerial ethical conduct is: *Do no harm* to those served.

1-101 Affirming the God-Given Dignity of All Persons
Affirmatively, Christian counselors recognize and uphold the inherent, God-given dignity of every human person, from the pre-born to those on death's bed. Human beings are God's creation—the crown of his creation—and are therefore due all the rights and respect that this fact of creation entails. Therefore, regardless of how we respond to and challenge harmful attitudes and actions, Christian counselors will express a loving care to any client, service-inquiring person, or anyone encountered in the course of

practice or ministry, without regard to race, ethnicity, gender, sexual behavior or orientation, socio-economic status, education, denomination, belief system, values, or political affiliation. God's love is unconditional and, at this level of concern, so must that of the Christian counselor.

1-102 No Harm or Exploitation

Prohibitively, then, Christian counselors avoid every manner of harm, exploitation, and unjust discrimination in all client-congregant relations. Christian counselors are also aware of their psychosocial and spiritual influence and the inherent power imbalance of helping relationships—power dynamics that can harm others even without harmful intent.

1-110 Avoidance of Client Harm, Intended or Not

Christian counselors strictly avoid all behavior or suggestion of practice that harms or reasonably could harm clients, client families, client social systems and representatives, students, trainees, supervisees, employees, colleagues, and third-party payors and authorizers.

1-111 Managing Client Conflicts

Christian counselors acknowledge that client conflicts are unavoidable. In fact, conflict and resistance are often a central dynamic of the helping process. We will attempt to resolve all counseling conflicts in the client's best interest. Counselors tempted to respond in harmful ways to clients shall seek out consultative and restorative help. If self-control is not accomplished—and client harm is not avoided—counselors shall terminate counseling relations and make referral in the client's best interest.

1-112 Action Regarding Clients Harmed by Other Helpers

Christian counselors take proper action against the harmful behavior of other counselors and pastors. We will act assertively to challenge or expose abusers and protect clients against harm wherever it is found, taking care to honor and support client decision-making regarding curative action against violators.

1-120 Refusal to Participate in the Harmful Actions of Clients

Christian counselors refuse to participate in, condone, advocate for, or assist the harmful actions of clients, especially those that imperil human life from conception to death. This includes suicidal, homicidal, or assaultive/abusive harm done to self or others—the protection of human life is always a priority value. We will not abandon clients who do or intend harm, will terminate helping relations only in the most compelling circumstances, and will continue to serve clients in these troubles as far as it is possible.

1-121 Application to Abortion

Christian counselors refuse to participate in, condone, advocate for, or assist the abortion activities of clients. All counselors will consider and inform clients of alternative means to abortion and, as far as it is possible, will continue to serve clients through the abortion crisis.

1-122 Application to Euthanasia and Assisted Suicide

Christian counselors refuse to participate in, condone, advocate for, or assist clients in active forms of euthanasia and assisted suicide. We may agree to and support the wish not to prolong life by artificial means, and will often advocate for hospice care, more effective application of medicine, and other reasonable means to reduce pain and suffering.

Regarding patients or clients who wish to die, we will not deliver, nor advocate for, nor support the use of drugs or devices to be utilized for the purpose of ending a patient's life. We recognize that the death of a patient may occur as the unintended and secondary result of aggressive action to alleviate a terminally ill patient's extreme pain and suffering. So long as there are no other reasonable methods to alleviate such pain and suffering, the Christian counselor is free to support, advocate for, and participate in such aggressive pain management in accordance with sound medical practice, and with the informed consent of the patient or patient's representative.

For many physicians, "do no harm" may translate into doing nothing medically or always considering the least intrusive action first. For example, the risks of a preferred medical intervention—invasive spinal surgery to alleviate a pain problem—may be so high that other less invasive, less risky interventions should be attempted first. Hence, the pain sufferer may be referred for physical therapy or exercise and movement training or for psychotherapy or biofeedback training to reduce pain as much as possible by noninvasive methods.

Christian counseling ethics also presume this all-encompassing rule of professional and helping ethics: To help others we must first ensure that we do not harm them. This is not as easy or as obvious as it seems. Understanding that harm is possible in any kind of human intervention yields an ethic enlightened and humbled by the following facts:

1. Even though saved by Christ and sanctified by the Spirit, humans remain susceptible to sin and wrongdoing (and do sin on a regular basis).
2. Research indicates that negative outcomes affect a stubborn minority of all counseling cases.
3. Unintended consequences are unyielding phenomena of human interaction, a core principle of social-systems theory, and a function of the feedback-loop mechanism in systems behavior.
4. Iatrogenic (harm-causing) medicine has an analogue for counseling as well. This potential for harm must be respected and avoided whenever possible.

INFORMED CONSENT

The need for obtaining client consent increases as the risk of the intervention increases or if a specialized kind of counseling intervention takes place. As an adjunctive, specialty application of the various mental health disciplines (which is merely one valid perspective among many), Christian counselors should take special care to ensure client-informed consent.

1-310 Securing Informed Consent

Christian counselors secure client consent for all counseling and related services. This includes the video/audio-taping of client sessions, the use of supervisory and consultative help, the application of special procedures and evaluations, and the communication of client data with other professionals and institutions.

Christian counselors take care that (1) the client has the *capacity* to give consent; (2) we have discussed counseling together and the client *reasonably understands* the nature and process of counseling; the costs, time, and work required; the limits of counseling; and any appropriate alternatives; and (3) the client *freely gives consent* to counseling, without coercion or undue influence.

1-320 Consent for the Structure and Process of Counseling

Christian counselors respect the need for informed consent regarding the structure and process of counseling. Early in counseling, counselor and client should discuss and agree upon these issues: the nature of and course of therapy; client issues and goals; potential problems and reasonable alternatives to counseling; counselor status and credentials; confidentiality and its limits; fees and financial procedures; limitations about time and access to the counselor, including directions in emergency situations; and procedures for resolution of disputes and misunderstandings. If the counselor is supervised, that fact shall be disclosed and the supervisor's name and role indicated to the client.

1-321 Consent from Parent or Client Representative
Christian counselors obtain consent from parents or the client's legally authorized representative when clients are minors or adults who are legally incapable of giving consent.

1-330 Consent for Biblical-Spiritual Practices in Counseling
Christian counselors do not presume that all clients want or will be receptive to explicit spiritual interventions in counseling. We obtain consent that honors client choice, receptivity to these practices, and the timing and manner in which these things are introduced: prayer for and with clients, Bible reading and reference, spiritual meditation, the use of biblical and religious imagery, assistance with spiritual formation and discipline, and other common spiritual practices.

1-331 Special Consent for More Difficult Interventions
Close or special consent is obtained for more difficult and controversial practices. These include, but are not limited to: deliverance and spiritual warfare activities; cult de-programming work; recovering memories and treatment of past abuse or trauma; use of hypnosis and any kind of induction of altered states; authorizing (by MDs) medications, electro-convulsive therapy, or patient restraints; use of aversive, involuntary, or experimental therapies; engaging in reparative therapy with homosexual persons; and counseling around abortion and end-of-life issues. These interventions require a more detailed discussion with patient-clients or client representatives of the procedures, risks, and treatment alternatives, and we secure detailed written agreement for the procedure.

CONFIDENTIALITY AND ITS EXCEPTIONS
Considering all the legal exceptions that have been created over the years, how managed care has eviscerated confidentiality of records, and the pervasive invasion

of human privacy in the interlocking electronica of the modern world, it is more than valid to ask now whether the exceptions and violations have overwhelmed the historic rule of client confidentiality.

1-410 Maintaining Client Confidentiality

Christian counselors maintain client confidentiality to the fullest extent allowed by law, professional ethics, and church or organizational rules. Confidential client communications include all verbal, written, telephonic, audio- or video-taped, or electronic communications arising within the helping relationship. Apart from the exceptions below, Christian counselors shall not disclose confidential client communications without first discussing the intended disclosure and securing written consent from the client or client representative.

1-411 Discussing the Limits of Confidentiality and Privilege

Clients should be informed about both the counselor's commitment to confidentiality and its limits before engaging in counseling. Christian counselors avoid stating or implying that confidentiality is guaranteed or absolute. We will discuss the limits of confidentiality and privacy with clients at the outset of counseling.

1-420 Asserting Confidentiality or Privilege Following Demands for Disclosure

Protecting confidential communications, including the assertion of privilege in the face of legal or court demands, shall be the first response of counselors to demands or requests for client communications and records.

1-421 Disclosure of Confidential Client Communications

Christian counselors disclose only that client information they have written permission from the client to disclose or that which is required by legal or ethical mandates. The counselor shall maintain confidentiality of client information outside the bounds of that narrowly required to fulfill the disclosure and shall limit disclosures only to those people having a direct professional interest in the case. In the face of a subpoena, counselors shall neither deny nor immediately comply with disclosure demands, but will assert privilege in order to give the client time to consult with a lawyer to direct disclosures.

1-430 Protecting Persons from Deadly Harm: The Rule of Mandatory Disclosure

Christian counselors accept the limits of confidentiality when human life is imperiled or abused. We will take appropriate action, including necessary disclosures of confidential information, to protect life in the face of client threats of suicide, homicide, and/or the abuse of children, elders, and dependent persons.

1-431 The Duty to Protect Others

The duty to take protective action is triggered when the counselor (1) has reasonable suspicion, as stated in your state statute, that a minor child (under 18 years), elder person (65 years and older), or dependent adult (regardless of age) has been harmed by the client; or (2) has direct client admissions of serious and imminent suicidal threats; or (3) has direct client admissions of harmful acts or threatened action that is serious, imminent, and attainable against a clearly identified third person or group of persons.

1-432 Guidelines to Ethical Disclosure and Protective Action

Action to protect life, whether your client or a third-person, shall be that which is reasonably necessary to stop or forestall deadly or harmful action in the present situation. This could involve hospitalizing the client, intensifying clinical intervention to the degree necessary to reasonably protect against harmful action, consultation and referral with other professionals, or disclosure of harm or threats to law enforcement, protective services, identifiable third-persons, and/or family members able to help with protective action.

1-433 Special Guidelines When Violence Is Threatened Against Others

Action to protect third-persons from client violence may involve or, in states that have a third-person protection (Tarasoff) duty, require disclosure of imminent harm to the intended victim, to their family or close friends, and to law enforcement. When child abuse or elder abuse or abuse of dependent adults exists, as defined by state law, Christian counselors shall report to child or elder protective services, or to any designated agency established for protective services. We shall also attempt to defuse the situation and/or take preventive action by whatever means are available and appropriate.

When clients threaten serious and imminent homicide or violence against an identifiable third-person, the Christian counselor shall inform appropriate law enforcement, and/or medical-crisis personnel, and the at-risk person or close family member of the threat, except when precluded by compelling circumstances or by state law.

When the client threat is serious but not imminent, the Christian counselor shall take preventive clinical action that seeks to forestall any further escalation of threat toward violent behavior.

1-470 Advocacy for Privacy Rights Against Intrusive Powers
Christian counselors hear the most private and sensitive details of client lives—information that must be zealously guarded from public disclosure. Rapidly expanding and interlocking electronic information networks are increasingly threatening client privacy rights. Though federal and state laws exist to protect client privacy, these laws are weak, are routinely violated at many levels, and the record of privacy right enforcement is dismal. Accordingly, Christian counselors are called to wisely protect and assertively advocate for privacy protection on behalf of our clients against the pervasive intrusion of personal, corporate, governmental, even religious powers.

Honoring confidentiality and dealing with its breach are part and parcel of being a therapist. Clients assume and rightly expect that whatever they reveal to a counselor will be kept confidential. Conscientious counselors will honor their commitment to this therapeutic law, but there are limitations that competent counselors must be aware of, and they have a responsibility to advise their clients of these limitations up-front. As you can see, we have incorporated *Tarasoff* principles into our ethics code. (*Tarasoff* refers to the now-famous California Supreme Court decision establishing a counselor's duty to warn the appropriate authorities of client threats of homicide.) We incorporated these principles in the Code because they are not only good law but also good biblical ethics. When the client's right to confidentiality and the need to ensure the safety of a client or others clash, human life takes precedence over confidentiality.

Competent counselors will need to familiarize themselves with (1) their respective state laws concerning counselor responsibilities related to suicide, child and elder abuse, and homicide threats; (2) the resources and procedures available in their areas for emergency action regarding suicidal and homicidal clients; (3) information regarding whom to contact and how to process child and elder abuse reports; and (4) information regarding AIDS reporting and limits.

COMPETENCE, CONSULTATION, AND REFERRAL
Becoming skilled and maintaining competence as a Christian counselor is a central theme of this book. Here is what it takes to do so ethically:

1-210 Honoring the Call to Competent Christian Counseling

Christian counselors maintain the highest standards of competence with integrity. We know and respect the boundaries of competence in ourselves and others, especially those under our supervision. We make only truthful, realistic statements about our identity, education, experience, credentials, and about counseling goals and process, avoiding exaggerated and sensational claims. We do not offer services or work beyond the limits of our competence and do not aid or abet the work of Christian counseling by untrained, unqualified, or unethical helpers.

1-220 Duties to Consult and/or Refer

Christian counselors consult with and/or refer to more competent colleagues or supervisors when these limits of counseling competence are reached: (1) when facing issues not dealt with before or not experienced in handling, (2) when clients need further help outside the scope of our training and practice, (3) when either counselor or clients are feeling stuck or confused about counseling and neither is clear what to do about it, or (4) when counselees are deteriorating or making no realistic gain over a number of sessions. Christian counselors shall honor the client's goals and confidential privacy interests in all consultations and referrals.

1-221 Consultation Practice

When counseling help is needed, and with client consent, consultation may be attempted first, when in the client's best interest and to improve helper's knowledge and skill where some competence exists. Counselors shall take all reasonable action to apply consultative help to the case in order to gain/maintain ground toward client objectives. The consultant shall maintain a balanced concern for the client discussed and the practice/education needs of the consultee, directing the counselor-consultee to further training or special resources, if needed.

1-222 Referral Practice

Referral shall be made in situations where client need is beyond the counselor's ability or scope of practice or when consultation is inappropriate, unavailable, or unsuccessful. Referrals should be done only after the client is provided with informed choices among referral sources. As much as possible, counselors referred to shall honor prior commitments between client and referring counselor or church.

1-223 Seek Christian Help, if Available

When consulting or referring, Christian counselors seek out the best Christian help at a higher level of knowledge, skill, and expertise. If Christian help is not available, or when professional skill is more important than the professional's beliefs, Christian counselors shall use the entire network of professional services available.

1-224 Avoid Counsel Against Professional Treatment

Christian counselors do not counsel or advise against professional counseling, medical or psychiatric treatment, the use of medications, legal counsel, or other forms of professional service merely because we believe such practice is, per se, wrong or because the provider may not be a Christian.

1-230 Duties to Study and Maintain Expertise

Christian counselors keep abreast of and, whenever possible, contribute to new knowledge, issues, and resources in Christian counseling and our respective fields. We maintain an active program of study, continuing education, and personal/professional growth to improve helping effectiveness and ethical practice. We seek out specialized training, supervision, and/or advanced certification if we choose to gain expertise and before we practice and advertise in recognized specialty areas of counseling and clinical practice.

1-240 Maintaining Integrity in Work, Reports, and Relationships

Christian counselors maintain the highest standards of integrity in all their work, in professional reports, and in all professional relationships. We delegate to employees, supervisees, and other subordinates only that work these persons can competently perform, meeting the client's best interest and done with appropriate supervision.

1-250 Protective Action When Personal Problems Interfere

Christian counselors acknowledge that sin, illnesses, mental disorders, interpersonal crises, distress, and self-deception still influence us personally—and that these problems can adversely affect our clients and parishioners. When personal problems flare to a level that harm to one's clients is realized or is highly likely, the Christian counselor will refrain from or reduce those particular professional-ministerial activities that are or could be harmful. During such times, the counselor will seek out and use those reparative resources that will allow for problem resolution and a return to a fully functioning ministry, if possible.

The counselor has the moral, ethical, and professional responsibility to admit to herself, and to her client, when the relationship fails or the client's situation exceeds her ability to help. Therapeutic relationships can experience failure when (1) the counselor and the client have incompatible personalities, (2) the counselor-client relationship involves transference or countertransference issues (such as sexual attractions) that could not be resolved, (3) there is an incongruity between the therapist's and the client's beliefs and values, or (4) the counselor is unable to break through the client's resistance to change. When any of these situations occur, the counselor must be willing to refer the client to someone who *can* help. This will require that the counselor be familiar with all resources and persons available for referral.

Sexual Misconduct and Dual Relationships

Nothing is more harmful to clients than being sexually exploited by a therapist they hired to respect and help them with their most sensitive and private issues. Sexual exploitation is betrayal unlike any other, and it is being criminalized across the board to reflect the seriousness of that kind of betrayal (Gabbard, 1989; Ohlschlager & Mosgofian, 1992; Pope, Sonne, & Holroyd, 1993).

1-130 Sexual Misconduct Forbidden

All forms of sexual misconduct in pastoral, professional, or lay relationships are unethical. This includes every kind of sexual exploitation, deception, manipulation, abuse, harassment, relations where the sexual involvement is invited, and relations where informed consent presumably exists. Due to the inherent power imbalance of helping relationships and the immoral nature of sexual behavior outside of marriage, such apparent consent is illusory and illegitimate.

Forbidden sexual activities and deceptions include, but are not limited to, direct sexual touch or contact; seductive sexual speech or non-verbal behavior; solicitation of sexual or romantic relations; erotic contact or behavior as a response to the sexual invitation or seductive behavior of clients; unnecessary questioning and/or excessive probing into the client's sexual history and practices; inappropriate counselor disclosures of client attractiveness, sexual opinions, or sexual humor; advocacy of the healing value of counselor-client sexual relations; secretive sexual communications and anonymous virtual interaction via the Internet or other electronic and informational means; sexual harassment by comments, touch, or promises/threats of special action; and sexual misconduct as defined by all applicable laws, ethics, and church, organizational, or practice policies.

1-131 Sexual Relations with Former Clients Forbidden

All sexual relations as defined in 1-130 above with former clients are unethical. Furthermore, we do not terminate and refer clients or parishioners, even at first contact, in order to pursue sexual or romantic relations.

1-132 Counseling with Marital/Sexual Partners

Christian counselors do not counsel, but make appropriate referral, with current or former sexual and/or marital partners.

1-133 Marriage with Former Clients/Patients

Since marriage is honorable before God, the lone exception to this rule is marriage to a former client, so long as (1) counseling relations were properly terminated, and not for the purpose of pursuing marriage or romantic relations; (2) the client is fully informed that any further counseling must be done by another; (3) there is no harm or exploitation of the client or the client's family as a result of different relations with the counselor; and (4) the marriage takes place two years or more after the conclusion of a counseling or helping relationship.

1-140 Dual and Multiple Relationships

Dual relationships involve the breakdown of proper professional or ministerial boundaries. A dual relationship is where two or more roles are mixed in a manner that can harm the counseling relationship. Examples include counseling plus personal, fraternal, business, financial, or sexual and romantic relations.

Some dual relationships are not unethical—it is client exploitation that is wrong, not the dual relationship itself. Based on an absolute application that harms membership bonds in the Body of Christ, we oppose the ethical-legal view that all dual relationships are, per se, harmful and therefore invalid. Many dual relations are wrong and indefensible, but some dual relationships are worthwhile and defensible (per 1-142).

1-141 The Rule of Dual Relationships

While in therapy, or when counseling relations are imminent, or for an appropriate time after termination of counseling, Christian counselors do not engage in dual relations with counselees. Some dual relationships are always avoided—sexual or romantic relations, and counseling close friends, family members, employees, or supervisees. Other dual relationships should be presumed troublesome and avoided wherever possible.

1-142 Proving an Exception to the Rule

The Christian counselor has the burden of proving a justified dual relationship by showing (1) informed consent, including discussion of how the counseling relationship might be harmed as other relations proceed, and (2) lack of harm or exploitation to the client.

As a general rule, all close relations are unethical if they become counselor-client or formal lay helping relations. Dual relations may be allowable, requiring justification by the foregoing rule, if the client is an arm's-length acquaintance—if the relationship is not a close one. This distinction is crucial in the applications below.

1-143 Counseling with Family, Friends, and Acquaintances

Christian counselors do not provide counseling to close family or friends. We presume that dual relations with other family members, acquaintances, and fraternal, club, association, or group members are potentially troublesome and best avoided, otherwise requiring justification.

1-144 Business and Economic Relations

Christian counselors avoid partnerships, employment relations, and close business associations with clients. Barter relations are normally avoided as potentially troublesome, and require justification; therefore if done, barter is a rare and not a common occurrence. Unless justified by compelling necessity, customer relations with clients are normally avoided.

1-145 Counseling with Fellow Church Members

Christian counselors do not provide counseling to fellow church members with whom they have close personal, business, or shared ministry relations. We presume that dual relations with any other church members who are clients are potentially troublesome and best avoided, otherwise requiring justification. Pastors and church staff helpers will take all reasonable precautions to limit the adverse impact of any dual relationships.

1-146 Termination to Engage in Dual Relations Prohibited

Christian counselors do not terminate counseling to engage in dual relationships of any kind. Some counselors and their former clients will agree that any future counseling will be done by someone else if, after legitimate termination, they decide to pursue another form of relationship.

MANAGED CARE: TERMINATION, ABANDONMENT, AND INEPT CARE

We will address how to properly relate to managed care in a clinical context in a subsequent volume. Here we address the problems of managed care in regard to how ethical patient care is adversely affected.

1-113 Managing Problems with Managed Care

Managed care has greatly expanded its influence in health and mental health service delivery. Widespread problems in client-provider-managed care relations are now being reported: breach of confidentiality, client abandonment, failure to maintain continuity of care, incompetent care, restriction of therapist choice and access, and even infliction of emotional distress. Christian counselors acknowledge these legal-ethical problems and will avoid and work to correct any unethical entanglement and unintended client harm due to managed care relations.

1-440 Disclosures in Cases of Third-party Payment and Managed Care

Christian counselors are diligent to protect client confidences in relations with insurance and third-party payors, employee assistance programs, and managed care groups. We are cautious about demands for confidential client information that exceed the need for validation of services rendered or continued care. We do not disclose or submit session notes and details of client admissions solely on demand of third-party payors. We will narrowly disclose information that the client has given written authorization [for] only after we have discussed and are assured that the client understands the full implications of authorizations signed or contemplated to sign.

1-560 Continuity of Care and Service Interruption

Christian counselors maintain continuity of care for all patients and clients. We avoid interruptions in service that are too lengthy or disruptive. Care is taken to refer clients and network to provide emergency services when faced with counselor vacations, illnesses, job changes, financial hardships, or any other reason services are interrupted or limited.

1-570 Avoiding Abandonment and Improper Counseling Termination
Christian counselors do not abandon clients. To the extent the counselor
is able, client services are never abruptly cut off or ended without giving
notice and adequately preparing the client for termination or referral.

1-571 Ethical Termination of Counseling
Discussion and action toward counseling termination and/or referral is
indicated when (1) counseling goals have been achieved; (2) the client no
longer wants or does not return to counseling; (3) the client is no longer
benefiting from counseling; or (4) counseling is harmful to the client.
Christian counselors shall discuss termination and/or referral with clients,
offer referral if wanted or appropriate, and facilitate termination in the
client's best interest. If crisis events alter, even end counseling prematurely,
the counselor, if it is safe and proper, should follow through with the client
to ensure proper termination and referral.

It is time to consider termination of counseling when clients (1) appear stable
emotionally, psychologically, and spiritually; (2) have achieved their therapeutic
goals; (3) have maintained the behavioral changes or goals for a reasonable amount
of time; (4) have a new perspective of their world as a whole; (5) appear to have
taken charge of their lives; (6) have improved in their personal relationships; and
(7) tell you they believe it is time to go. All of these factors indicate change, without which treatment is not yet complete or has failed.

Termination can be very much akin to shoving our children out of the nest. It
should be a gradual process when possible, and often it is not final. Some clients
return off and on for years. Others grow and soar to new emotional, psychological, and spiritual heights and never return. Kottler (1993) asserts, "There is nothing like that feeling of elation we sometimes experience when we know beyond a
shadow of a doubt that our efforts have helped redeem a human life" (p. 46).

MONEY AND FEE ISSUES
Charging fees for Christian service strikes some believers as near-heresy (especially
those who believe they should receive all benefits of ministry at no cost). But most
people in the church now accept the fact that charging for services is the way professional Christian counselors earn a living.

1-510 Fees and Financial Relationships in Christian Counseling
Professional Christian counselors will set fees for services that are fair and

reasonable, according to the services contracted and time performed, and with due regard for the client's ability to pay. We avoid all deception, confusion, and misrepresentation about fees and in our financial relationships with clients and client systems.

1-511 Disclosure of Fees and Payment History

Fee schedules and rules for payment shall be outlined clearly for client review at the outset of counseling. Moreover, agreement about fees and payment schedules will be made as early as possible in the course of professional relations. We will provide clients or their representatives with a full and accurate account of previous and current charges upon request.

1-512 Sliding Fee Scales Encouraged

Christian counselors are free, within the bounds of biblical, professional, and community standards, to set their own fees. Clinicians are encouraged, however, to use sliding fee schedules, scaled to clients' ability to pay, and other reduced payment methods to increase counseling accessibility to those of lesser financial means.

1-513 Pro Bono Work

Christian counselors are encouraged, beyond their fee schedule, to make a portion of their time and services available without cost or at a greatly reduced fee to those unable to pay.

1-514 Avoiding Self-Serving Financial Relations

Christian counselors avoid financial practices that result or appear to result in greedy and self-serving outcomes. We do not select clients or prolong therapy based on their ability to pay high fees, nor do we quickly terminate counseling with low-fee clients. When making referrals, we do not divide fees with other professionals nor accept or give anything of value for making the referral. We do not exaggerate problems nor refer exclusively for specialized services to get clients into special programs or institutions in which we have a proprietary interest.

1-515 Financial Integrity with Insurance and Third-Party Payors

Christian counselors maintain financial integrity with client insurers and other third-party payors. We do not charge third-party payors for services not rendered, nor for missed or cancelled appointments, unless specially authorized to do so. We do not distort or change diagnoses to fit restricted reimbursement categories. Any special benefits or reductions in client fees must also be extended in full to third-party payors.

Values Conflicts with Clients

We have shown, in a variety of ways, that counseling is a values-laden experience requiring that a counselor's values be made known to the client at the start of counseling. Having to address values and role conflicts somewhere in the middle of a sticky issue in a client's life suggests that preventive work done up-front is the wiser and ethically preferred action.

1-543 Avoiding and Resolving Role Conflicts

If/when Christian counselors are asked to perform conflicting roles with possible unethical consequences (i.e., pressure to keep "secrets" or called to testify as an adverse witness in a client's divorce), we will clarify our therapeutic, neutral, and mediative role and/or decline to serve in a conflicted capacity, if possible. Some counselors will contract for professional neutrality at the beginning of professional relations, securing client agreement not to have oneself or one's records subpoenaed or deposed in any legal proceeding.

1-550 Working with Persons of Different Faiths, Religions, and Values

Christian counselors do not withhold services to anyone of a different faith, religion, denomination, or value system. We work to understand the client's belief system and always maintain respect for the client. We strive to understand when faith and values issues are important to the client and foster values-informed client decision-making in counseling. We share our own faith only as a function of legitimate self-disclosure and when appropriate to client need, always maintaining a humility that exposes and never imposes the way of Christ.

1-551 Action if Value Differences Interfere with Counseling

Christian counselors work to resolve problems—always in the client's best interest—when differences between counselor and client values become too great, adversely affecting counseling. This may include discussion of the issue as a therapeutic matter, renegotiation of the counseling agreement, consultation with a supervisor or trusted colleague or, as a last resort, referral to another counselor if the differences cannot be reduced or bridged.

We recognize a continuum of Christian counselors who emphasize varying degrees of inclusion of Christ and Christian practices in counseling. At one pole is the helper who plans and practices every session as a discipling experience, praying overtly with clients in every session, referencing Scripture, encouraging yieldedness to Christ, exhorting confession and forgiveness, and reinforcing any movement toward Christian growth. At the other pole is the helper who, although he or she confesses Christ, believes that including Christ in therapy is an unjust imposition of religious values that violates client self-determination. Although some counselors may engage in Christian practices—especially the practice of prayer—with Christian clients who ask for it, these brothers and sisters emphasize a psychological practice where evangelism and overt forms of spiritual exhortation and advocacy of Christ are not done.

While our bias is clearly toward Christian counseling that incorporates spiritual disciplines and helps clients mature spiritually, we take an inclusionary approach and see all believers as welcome within Christian counseling's "big tent." We suggest that excellence and positive outcome are better correlated with an active inclusion of Christ and Christian principles, but an inclusion that respects the limits, capabilities, learning styles, and readiness of clients. Of what benefit is it to present Christ to every client, or to do so when the model calls for it, when our words sometimes fall on deaf ears? Then again, what good is mere psychological adaptation if one adapts better to evil ways? Both polar extremes are likely too doctrinaire, putting ideology, absolute ethics, and rigid theology above people. Nonetheless, we recognize all practitioners who name the name of Christ as citizens of God's kingdom, and we welcome them into the Christian counseling fold.

BASE STANDARDS FOR SUPERVISORS AND EDUCATORS

Some Christian counselors serve in senior professional roles as administrators, supervisors, teachers, consultants, researchers, and writers. They are recognized for their counseling expertise, for their dedication to Christ and the ministry or profession to which they belong, and for their exemplary ethics. These leaders are responsible for the development and maturation of the Christian counseling profession, for serving as active, ethical role models, and for raising up the next generation of Christian counselors and leaders.

2-110 Ethics and Excellence in Supervision and Teaching

Christian counseling supervisors and educators maintain the highest levels of clinical knowledge, professional skill, and ethical excellence in all supervision and teaching. They are knowledgeable about the latest professional and ministerial developments and responsibly transmit this knowledge to students and supervisees.

2-111 Preparation for Teaching and Supervision

Christian counseling supervisors and educators have received adequate training and experience in teaching and supervision methods before they deliver these services. Supervisors and educators are encouraged to maintain and enhance their skills through continued clinical practice, advanced training, and continuing education.

2-120 Supervisors and Educators Do Not Exploit Students and Trainees

Christian counseling supervisors and educators avoid exploitation, appearances of exploitation, and harmful dual relations with students and trainees. Students and trainees are taught by example and by explanation, with the mentor responsible to define and maintain clear, proper, and ethical professional and social boundaries.

2-121 Sexual and Romantic Relations Forbidden with Students and Supervisees

Christian counseling supervisors and educators shall not (1) engage in any form of sexual or romantic relations with their students and trainees; (2) subject them, by relations with others, to any form of sexual exploitation, abuse, or harassment; nor (3) pressure them to engage in any questionable social relationships. The standards of sections 1-130ff, "Sexual Misconduct Forbidden," shall apply fully here.

2-122 Dual Relationships Cautioned

Integrity and caution shall be the hallmark of dual relationships between supervisors and supervisees and between teacher and student. Those relations that harm or are likely to harm students and trainees, or that impair or are likely to distort the professional judgment of supervisors and teachers shall be avoided. The standards of sections 1-140ff, "Dual and Multiple Relationships," and those stated below shall apply here.

2-123 Supervisors and Educators Do Not Provide Psychotherapy

Christian counseling supervisors and educators do not engage in psychotherapeutic relations with supervisees or students. Personal issues can be addressed in supervision and teaching only insofar as they adversely impact counselor supervision and training. Students and supervisees needing or wanting counseling or psychotherapy shall be referred to appropriate resources.

2-124 Acknowledgment of Professional Contributions

Christian counseling supervisors and educators shall fully acknowledge the contributions of students and trainees in any creative professional activity, scholarly work, research, or published material. This shall be done by co-authorship, assistance in speaking or project presentation, or other accepted forms of public acknowledgment.

ETHICAL RELATIONSHIPS WITH THE STATE AND OTHER SOCIAL SYSTEMS

Christian counselors, as individual members and as an Association, will strive to maintain ethical relations with the worldwide church and the local church, with the state in its various forms, with the mental health professions and associations to which some of us belong, with other professions and organizations, and with society-at-large.

1-810 Ethical Relations with Other Professions and Institutions

Christian counselors recognize and respect that we are part of larger networks of Christian ministry and of mental health care. To borrow a metaphor, we envision church-based ministry and professional mental health care as the two tracks on which runs the Christian counseling train—tracks with different rather than opposing objectives.

Within the AACC are representatives of many different mental health and ministerial disciplines—we invite and welcome them all in the name of Christ. We will honor and preserve these relations, will challenge value differences with respect, and will build the best relations we can with all these professions and institutions that intersect with us as Christian counselors.

1-820 Working for a Caring Church, a Just Government, and a Better Society

Christian counselors are dedicated to build a more caring church, a more just government, and a better society in which to live. We will honor the laws and customs of our culture and will challenge them when they threaten or abuse our freedoms, dishonor our God, or deny the rights of those most powerless. When critical, we will strive to offer a better alternative—model programs to govern our ecclesiastical, socio-cultural, and governmental life.

We will support the cause of Christ and advocate for Christian counseling in the church, in our ministries and professions, and in society. We will work to shape laws and policies that encourage the acceptance and growth of Christian ministry generally and Christian counseling in particular. We will facilitate harmonious relations between church and state and will serve and advocate the best interests of our clients in church, community, and governmental relations.

1-830 Being Salt and Light in a Post-Christian Culture

Christian counselors acknowledge that we live in a post-Christian and pluralistic culture that no longer shares a common Judeo-Christian value base. We are called by Christ to be "salt and light" throughout our culture, a call of engagement with our culture and the world-at-large. Hence, the AACC and its members are encouraged to engage in active and honorable relations with the world around us—relations in which the world can see the light and taste the salt of Christ.

1-831 Christ and Culture: Diversity over Conformity

We accept that there are differing views within our Association on the proper relationship of the Christian life to a modern culture that no longer substantially honors Christ. Our Association includes those who are largely apolitical—acknowledging a receding religio-cultural status as Christians but dedicated to building up the church and our profession. There are also those who believe it is necessary to retain a vibrant Christian value base in society and seek to return our culture to these roots, including by political and legal action. We wish to support this diversity and encourage this ongoing debate, respecting the validity of these different views as the healthy evidence of a living church and a vibrant and growing profession.

Remember that when a counselor is dedicated to fully revealing the love of Christ, there is no law against this kind of love. In this love no harm is done to another person. Because of this love, people's lives are transformed into something beautiful and holy. This is the love of Jesus, and the Holy Spirit thrives on pouring it out to those who seek it.

LAW AND ETHICS

While developments in the law and in ethical codes regulating the mental health professions are becoming increasingly similar, there are and will always be particular issues of conflict between law and ethics. Corey, Corey, and Callanan (1998) stated this about the distinction between the two fields: "Ethical issues in the mental health professions are regulated by both laws and professional codes.... Law defines the minimum standard that society will tolerate; these standards are enforced by government. Ethics represent aspirational goals...[the] ideal standards set by the profession, and they are enforced by professional associations, national certification boards, and government boards that regulate professions" (p. 4).

Counselors are wisely advised to defer to the law in such cases, while attempting to honor the ethical prescription as much as possible (American Counseling Association, 1995; American Psychological Association, 1995; Ohlschlager & Mosgofian, 1992; Remley, 1996).

Conflicts between the law, ethical codes, and agency or clinic policy are so common, in fact, that we developed a special section (Section V, "Standards for Resolving Ethical-Legal Conflicts") in the *AACC Code* (2001) to guide Christian counselors in resolving these dilemmas.

ES5-100 BASE STANDARDS FOR ETHICAL CONFLICT RESOLUTION

5-110 Base Rule for Resolving Ethical-Legal Conflicts
Christian counselors acknowledge the sometimes conflicting responsibilities to clients, to colleagues and employing organizations, to professional ethics, to the law, and to Christ. If a higher obligation to Christ or to the client's best interest suggests or requires action against legal, ethical, or organizational rules, we will act peaceably and humbly in its outworking, in a way that honors God and our role as Christian counselors.

5-111 First, Attempt to Harmonize Conflicting Interests
When caught between legal-ethical demands and the way of Christ or the best interests of the client, we will first attempt to harmonize biblical, clinical, legal, ethical, and client interests, if possible. We will secure proper consultation and take action that defines and offers a better and harmonious standard of professional conduct.

5-112 When Conflicts Cannot Be Harmonized

Christian counselors' fidelity to Christ sometimes calls us to respectfully decline adherence to non-Christian values and behavior. When such conflicts cannot be harmonized, some counselors will stand firm or act on Christian principle against the law of the state, the ethics of one's profession, or the rules of one's employing organization. Such action should be (1) defensible biblically and ethically, (2) according to the client's best interest, (3) done without self-seeking purposes, (4) done with sober consideration after consulting with informed colleagues and Christian counseling leaders, and (5) done with a willingness to pay any adverse consequences. Such action must never be done to hide wrongdoing or to justify an obscure or self-promoting position.

The AACC suggests that priority values in the resolution of these conflicts be (a) integrity to Christ and the revelation of Scripture, then (b) the client's best interests, then (c) fulfilling our legal, ethical, and organizational obligations in a way that is least harmful to Christ or our client's interest.

ES5-300 RESOLVING PROFESSIONAL AND ORGANIZATIONAL CONFLICTS

5-310 The Higher Ethics of Jesus Christ

Christian counselors are bound to honor the ethics and rules of one's profession, church, or employing organization in every way possible. However, when these ethics and rules are in direct opposition to God, and if unable to harmonize the mandates of Scripture with these rules, we declare and support the right of Christian counselors to elect nonadherence to those ethics and rules that offend the way of Christ.

5-311 First, Act to Resolve Conflict with Church or Profession

Christian counselors always first seek peaceable and biblically defensible resolution of disputes. After proper consultation with colleagues and Christian counseling leaders, we will define and advocate for a new ethical standard as an alternative to the offensive rule—one that honors Christ, protects the client's interest, and attempts to fulfill the policy behind the ethical rule.

5-312 When Ethical Harmony Is Not Reached

If ethical harmony is not possible, and after all attempts at resolution have been exhausted, Christian counselors may elect to violate the offending rule for the sake of Christ or the client. The violative action should be defensible biblically, logically, and clinically and, if possible, in accordance with the ethic's intent.

Counselors shall (1) define the rule that cannot be respected in the narrowest form possible, (2) declare to honor all other ethical mandates, (3) consult with other colleagues and soberly count the cost of such action, and (4) be prepared to face any consequences for breach of ethics or rules.

ES5-400 RESOLVING CONFLICTS WITH THE STATE AND ITS LAWS

5-410 The Higher Law of Jesus Christ

Christian counselors are bound to honor the law in every way possible. However, when the law is in direct opposition to God, and if unable to harmonize the mandates of Scripture and the law, we declare and support the right of Christian counselors to elect judicious nonadherence to those laws that offend the way of Christ.

5-411 First, Act to Resolve Legal Conflict

Christian counselors always seek first the peaceable and biblically defensible resolution of disputes with the state and its laws. After proper consultation, including consulting with an attorney and with Christian counseling colleagues and leaders, we will attempt to define and advocate for a new and harmonious legal standard as an alternative to the law-offending rule at issue. This newly proposed standard will honor Christ, protects the client's best interest, and shows how the action of the new rule fulfills the intent or policy behind the law.

5-412 When Legal Harmony Is Not Reached

If harmony is not possible with the state and its laws, and after all attempts to resolve the issue have been exhausted, Christian counselors may elect action that violates the law for the sake of Christ or the client. The violative action should be defensible biblically, logically, clinically and, if possible, by the law's intent or policy.

Counselors shall (1) define the law that cannot be respected in the narrowest form possible, (2) declare to honor all other legal mandates, (3) consult with other colleagues, including lawyers, and soberly count the cost of such action, and (4) be prepared to face any consequences that may be imposed for violation of the law.

Other Important Ethical Issues in Christian Counseling

Ethical Practice in Christian Counseling and Evaluation

1-520 Casenotes and Proper Record-Keeping

Christian counselors maintain appropriate documentation of their counseling activities, adequate for competent recall of prior sessions and the provision of later services by oneself or others. Records used in legal and other official capacities will show the quality, detail, objectivity, and timeliness of production expected by professionals who practice in these arenas.

1-521 Records Maintenance and Ownership

Records of professional activities will be created, maintained, stored, and disposed of in accordance with the law and the ethical duties of the counselor, especially maintaining client confidentiality. Ordinarily, client records belong to the employing organization or to the therapist in a private or group practice. However, in view of the expanding right of client record access and the ethic of continuity of care, client records should follow the client. Therefore, in any dispute about record access or ownership at the termination of professional employment, the records will stay with the employer if the therapist is leaving the area and his or her clients, or they should go with the therapist if he or she is staying in the area and the clients are staying with the therapist.

1-530 Ethics in Testing, Assessment, and Clinical Evaluation

Christian counselors do clinical evaluations of clients only in the context of professional relations, in the best interests of clients, and with the proper training and supervision. Christian counselors avoid (1) incompetent and inaccurate evaluations; (2) clinically unnecessary and excessively expensive testing; and (3) unauthorized practice of testing and evaluation that is the province of another clinical or counseling discipline. Referral and consultation are used when evaluation is desired or necessary beyond the competence and/or role of the counselor.

1-531 Use of Appropriate Assessments

Christian counselors use tests and assessment techniques that are appropriate to the needs, resources, capabilities, and understanding of the client. We apply tests skillfully and administer tests properly and safely. We substantiate our findings, with knowledge of the reliability, validity, outcome results, and limits of the tests used. We avoid both the misuse of testing procedures and the creation of confusion or misunderstanding by clients about testing purposes, procedures, and findings.

1-532 Reporting and Interpreting Assessment Results

Christian counselors report testing results in a fair, understandable, and objective manner. We avoid undue testing bias and honor the limits of test results, ensuring verifiable means to substantiate conclusions and recommendations. We recognize the limits of test interpretation and avoid exaggeration and absolute statements about the certainty of client diagnoses, behavior predictions, clinical judgments, and recommendations. Due regard is given to the unique history, values, family dynamics, socio-cultural influences, economic realities, and spiritual maturity of the client. Christian counselors will state any and all reservations about the validity of test results and present reports and recommendations in tentative language and with alternative possibilities.

1-540 Working with Couples, Families, and Groups

Christian counselors often work with multiple persons in session—marriage couples, families or parts of families, and small groups—and should know when these forms of counseling are preferred over or used as an adjunct to individual counseling. In these relationships we will identify a primary client—the group as a unit or the individual members—and will discuss with our client(s) how our differing roles, counseling goals, and confidentiality and consent issues are affected by these dynamics.

1-541 Safety and Integrity in Family and Group Counseling

Christian counselors will maintain their role as fair, unbiased, and effective helpers in all marital, family, and group work. We will remain accessible to all persons, avoiding enmeshed alliances and taking sides unjustly. As group or family counseling leaders, Christian counselors respect the boundary between constructive confrontation and verbal abuse and will take reasonable precautions to protect client members from any physical, psychological, or verbal abuse from other members of a family or group.

1-542 Confidentiality in Family and Group Counseling

Christian counselors do not promise or guarantee confidentiality in family and group counseling, but rather explain the problems and limits of keeping confidences in these modes of therapy. We communicate the importance of confidentiality and encourage family or group members to honor it, including discussion of consequences for its breach. Christian counselors do not share confidences by one family or group member to others without permission or prior agreement, unless maintaining the secret will likely lead to grave and serious harm to a family member or someone else.

ETHICAL RELATIONSHIPS IN THE PROFESSIONAL WORKPLACE

1-610 Honorable Relations Between Professional and Ministerial Colleagues

Christian counselors respect professional and ministerial colleagues, both within and outside the church. We strive to understand and, wherever able, respect differing approaches to counseling. We strive to maintain collaborative and constructive relations with other professionals serving our client, in the client's best interest.

1-611 Solicitation of Clients Under Another's Care

Christian counselors do not solicit clients nor do we knowingly offer professional services to those under the care of another mental health professional or pastor, except with that provider's knowledge or when someone is in crisis. When approached by clients being served by other counselors, due regard will be given that relationship with a commitment to encourage client resolution with the other counselor before starting professional relations.

1-612 Maintaining Honor Toward Others When in Conflict

If a counselor learns that a current client is receiving therapy from another pastor or mental health professional, reasonable steps will be taken to inform the other helper and resolve the situation. Professional relations in this case are to be maintained, as much as is possible, with a priority of Christian love and peace.

Any action to challenge or confront the wrongdoing of other service providers will be done with accuracy, humility, and protecting the dignity and reputation of others. Behavior that slanders, libels, or gossips about colleagues, or uncritically accepts these things from others about other service providers will be strictly avoided.

1-620 Maintaining Honorable Professional and Employment Relations

Christian counselors create and preserve honorable relations in the professional workplace, whether church, counseling agency, or other setting. We maintain the utmost honesty, respect, and integrity in all employment and collegial relations. We shall contract relations that balance the best interests of clients, colleagues, and our organizations, and will honor all contractual obligations, even if it is costly for us to do so. We will avoid all actions and appearances of greed, fraud, manipulation, and self-serving action in all collegial and employment relations, and will disclose and discuss all reasonably foreseen problems to our colleagues before they enter into relations with us.

1-621 Toward Clear Role Boundaries and Work Definitions

All professional/employment relations should be mutually understood and described in sufficient detail by work agreement. Administrators and staff should reasonably understand (1) required work behavior, expectations, and limits; (2) lines of authority and responsibility; (3) bases for and boundaries of accountability; and (4) procedures for voicing and curing disagreements and substandard work performance. When such guidelines do not exist, Christian counselors encourage development of sound collegial and employer-employee rules and relations.

1-630 Christian Counselors as Employers

Employers of Christian counselors shall provide a personnel program that honors the dignity and promotes the welfare of employees. Information will be given about the mission, goals, programs, policies, and procedures of the employing person or organization. Employers should deliver regular programs of in-service training, supervision of staff, and evaluation and review of employee work performance. Employers do not coerce, manipulate, threaten, or exploit employees or colleagues.

1-631 Employers Avoid Discrimination and Promote Meritoriously

Employers hire, evaluate, and promote staff meritoriously—based on staff training, experience, credentials, competence, responsibility, integrity, and ethical excellence. We do not discriminate in hiring or promotion practices on the basis of age, race, ethnicity, gender, disability, medical status, socio-economic status, or special relationship with employer or other staff.

1-640 Christian Counselors as Employees

Counselors accept employment only when they are qualified for the position—by education, supervised training, credentials, skill, and experience. We will honor and advance the mission, goals, and policies of employing organizations. Employees have duties to both employers and clients and, in the event of conflict between these duties, shall strive to resolve them in ways that harmonize the best interests of both.

1-641 Employees Serve with Integrity and Dedication

Employees serve with dedication, diligence, and honesty, maintaining high professional and ethical standards. We do not abuse our employment positions, nor presume excessive demands or rights against an employer.

1-642 Moving from an Agency to Private Practice

While employed in a counseling agency, and for a reasonable time after employment, we do not take clients from an employing organization to develop a private or group practice of a competing kind. Any part-time practice while employed must be kept strictly separate from the clients and resources of the employing agency. If we develop a full-time private practice with intent to resign employment and take current clients, each client shall be apprised of their right to choose to stay with the employing organization or go with the therapist.

ETHICS IN ADVERTISING AND PUBLIC RELATIONS

All advertising and public communications by Christian counselors shall be done with accuracy and humility, with a primary goal of assisting clients to make informed choices about counseling services.

1-710 Unethical Statements in Public Communications

Christian counselors make only factual and straightforward public communications and avoid statements that (1) are false, inaccurate, exaggerated, or sensational; (2) are likely to deceive or mislead others because they are partial or taken out of context; (3) are testimonials by current clients; (4) exploit others' fears or distressing emotions; (5) note the inferiority or negative characteristics of another counselor; and (6) express unique or unusual helping abilities outside the range of accepted Christian counseling practices.

1-720 Communication of Association with the AACC and Other Groups

Public communication of AACC or other professional membership should adhere to all the requirements of this section and should not express or imply that such membership confers special status, expertise, or extraordinary competence in counseling.

1-721 Communication About Professional Status and Credentials
Christian counselors do not state that professional credentials—state licenses, graduate degrees, specialized training, church, professional, or governmental certifications, or any other credentials—confer greater status or power than the credentials actually represent. Advanced credentials shall be communicated with accuracy and humility, adhering to the guidelines of the credential itself.

1-722 Communication of Unaccredited and Unrelated Credentials
Christian counselors avoid public communication of degrees or credentials received from schools and organizations (1) not holding or maintaining a reputable and widely known national stature; (2) not accredited by state, regional, or national authorities; or that (3) are not substantially related to counseling, pastoral counseling, or mental health services. Holders of religious licenses or credentials only for church ministry shall not state or imply that they are counseling professionals or that they hold a mental health practice license.

1-730 Communication of Work Products and Training Materials
Christian counselors ensure that advertisements about work products and training events adhere to these ethics. We take care to avoid undue influence and respect informed consumer choice in promoting our work to anyone under our professional influence or authority.

1-740 Ethical Guidelines in Public Statements by Others
Christian counselors ensure adherence to these ethics by third parties we engage to create and make public statements about our work—employers, publishers, producers, sponsors, marketers, organizational clients, and representatives of the media. We do not pay for or compensate the news media for news items about our work. We are responsible to correct, in timely fashion, any misinformation by third parties regarding our work.

ETHICAL STANDARDS FOR CHRISTIAN COUNSELING SUPERVISORS

2-210 Counselor Supervision Programs
Christian counseling supervisors ensure that supervision programs integrate theory and practice and train counselors to respect client rights, promote client welfare, and assist clients in the acquisition of mutually agreed goals in the counseling process. Supervision programs in Christian counseling

shall adhere to these ethics, to those of other applicable professional groups, and to all applicable state and federal laws.

2-211 Baseline Program Standards

Counseling programs shall only accept supervisees who are capable of professional practice, are fully informed about the program, and are committed to engage in counselor training following (1) mutual agreement that the supervisee meets base standards of education and experience; (2) disclosure of the training goals, supervisory site policies and procedures, and theoretical orientations to be used; (3) understanding of program relationship to national accreditation and credentialing organizations; (4) understanding of the standards, procedures, and time of evaluations of supervisee skill, professional-ethical awareness, and clinical effectiveness; and (5) disclosure of the manner and expectations regarding remediation of professional deficiencies and substandard performance.

2-220 Supervisors to Provide a Varied Experience

Christian counseling supervisors will provide a varied counseling experience, exposing the trainee to different client populations, clinical activities, and theoretical approaches to counseling. Supervisees should gain experience in direct counseling practice, clinical evaluation, treatment planning, record-keeping, case management and consultative presentation, legal and ethical decision-making, and the development of professional identity.

2-221 Supervisors Are Responsible for Services to Clients

Christian counselor supervisors ensure that supervisee work with clients maintains accepted professional and ministerial standards. Supervisors do not allow supervisees to work with clients or in situations where they are not adequately prepared. Supervisors retain full professional-clinical responsibility for all supervisee cases.

2-230 Supervision Evaluation and Feedback

Christian counseling supervisors meet frequently and regularly with supervisees and give timely, informative feedback about counselor performance and effectiveness. These evaluations shall minimally require supervisor review of casenotes and discussion or brief check of each client case. Evaluative feedback is given in both verbal and written forms, covering counseling content, process, and ethical-legal issues of counselor training.

2-231 Supervisors Are Aware of Licensure and Certification Requirements
Christian counseling supervisors are aware of and honor the legal, ethical, and professional requirements of supervisees who are pursuing state licensure and specialized certification standards.

Ethical Standards for Christian Counseling Educators

2-310 Counselor Education and Training Programs
Counselor education programs are dedicated to train students as competent practitioners using current theories, techniques, and ethical-legal knowledge. Christian counseling educators ensure that prospective students and trainees are fully informed, able to make responsible decisions about program involvement.

2-311 Baseline Program Standards
Christian counseling educators accept students on the basis of their educational background, professional promise, ethical integrity, and ability to reasonably complete the program. Program information should clearly disclose (1) the subject matter and coursework to be covered; (2) program relationship to national accreditation and credentialing organizations; (3) the kinds and level of counseling skills necessary to learn; (4) personal and professional growth requirements and opportunities; (5) the requirements and kinds of supervised clinical practicums and field placements offered; (6) the kinds and quality of research opportunities, including thesis/dissertation possibilities and requirements; (7) the basis for student evaluation, including appeal and dismissal policies and procedures; and (8) the latest employment prospects and program placement figures.

2-312 Student and Faculty Diversity
Christian counseling educators ensure that their programs seek and attempt to retain students and faculty of a diverse background, including representation by women, minorities, and people with special needs.

2-320 Student and Trainee Evaluation
Christian counseling educators provide students and trainees with periodic and ongoing evaluation of their progress in classroom, practice, and experimental learning settings. Policies and procedures for student evaluation, remedial training requirements, and program dismissal and appeal shall be

clearly stated and delivered to student-trainees. Both the method and timing of evaluations are disclosed to students in advance of program involvement.

2-321 Overcoming Student Limitations

Educators help students overcome limitations and deficiencies that might impede performance as Christian counselors. Student-trainees will be assisted and encouraged to secure remedial help to improve substandard professional development. Honoring student due process, supervisors and educators will retain and fairly exercise their duty to dismiss from programs student-trainees who are unable to overcome substandard performance.

2-322 Student-Trainee Endorsement

Educators and field supervisors endorse the competence of student-trainees for graduation, admission to other degree programs, employment, certification, or licensure only when they have adequate knowledge to judge that the student-trainee is qualified.

2-330 Integration Study and Training

Christian counseling educators ensure that programs include both academic and practice dimensions in counselor training and integrate biblical-theological study with learning in the bio-psycho-social sciences, however these are emphasized. Students, if not producing research, should learn to be effective research consumers.

2-331 Exposure to Various Counseling Theories Encouraged

Educators develop programs that expose students to various accepted theoretical models for counseling, including data on their relative efficacy, and will give students opportunities to develop their own practice orientations. If a program adheres to or emphasizes one particular theoretical model, that fact should be clearly stated in all public communications without asserting that the model is superior to all others.

2-332 Teaching Law, Ethics, and the Business of Practice

Training programs should teach students about the legal, ethical, and business dimensions of Christian counseling. This includes study of these issues through didactic and clinical training. Students should be able to make competent ethical judgments and assess their own practice limitations, learn how to analyze and resolve ethical-legal conflicts, and do consultation and referral competently.

2-340 Field Placement, Practicum, and Intern Training

Educators develop clear policies and procedures for all field experience, practicum, and intern training experiences. Roles and responsibilities are clearly delineated for student-trainees, site supervisors, and academic supervisors. Training sites shall meet required training standards, including national accreditation standards if applicable. Field supervisors shall be competent and ethical in their clinical and supervisory work. Educators do not solicit and will not accept any form of fee, service, or remuneration for the field placement of a student-trainee.

2-341 Clients of Student-Trainees

Academic and field supervisors ensure that clients of student-trainees are fully informed of trainee status and the trainees' duty to honor all professional obligations. Trainees shall secure client permission to use, within the bounds of confidential duties, information from the counseling work to advance their counseling education.

ETHICAL STANDARDS FOR CHRISTIAN COUNSELING RESEARCHERS

2-410 Respecting Standards of Science and Research

Christian counseling researchers honor accepted scientific standards and research protocol in all research activities. Research is ethically planned and competently conducted. Researchers do not undertake nor do they let subordinates conduct research activities they are not adequately trained for or prepared to conduct.

2-420 Protecting Human Research Participants and Human Rights

Researchers maintain the highest care for human participants and respect human rights in all bio-psycho-social-spiritual research activities. Researchers plan, design, conduct, and report research projects according to all applicable state and federal laws, ethical mandates, and institutional regulations regarding human participants.

2-421 Special Precautions to Protect Persons

Researchers take special precautions and observe stringent standards when (1) a research design suggests deviation from accepted protocol, or (2) when there is any risk of pain or injury to participants—whether of a physical, psychosocial, spiritual, reputational, or financial nature. In all such cases, we will obtain appropriate consultation that apprises participants of these risks and secures informed consent.

2-422 Minimizing Undesirable Consequences

Researchers reasonably anticipate and diligently work to minimize any adverse or undesirable consequences of the research on human participants. This includes a commitment to minimize any possible long-term research effects, including those on the participants' person, family and family life, spiritual beliefs, moral values, reputation, relationships, vocation, finances, or cultural system.

2-430 Informed Consent and Confidentiality in Research

Researchers obtain informed consent from research participants using language that the participant can understand. This consent shall disclose (1) a clear explanation of research purposes and procedures; (2) any risk of harm, injury, or discomfort that the participant might experience; (3) any benefits that the participant might experience; (4) any limitations on confidentiality; (5) a commitment to discuss all concerns of the participant about the research; and (6) instructions on the right way to honorably withdraw from the research project. Researchers shall honor all commitments made to research participants. Data and results shall be explained to participants in ways that are understandable and that clarify any confusion or misconceptions.

2-431 Consent from Those Legally Incapable

Researchers obtain consent from parents or a participant's legal representative when the research participants are minors or adults incapable of giving consent. Researchers inform all participants about the research in understandable language, seeking the participant's understanding and assent.

2-432 Concealment and Deception in Research

When a research design requires concealment or deception, the researcher shall apply these methods most narrowly and will inform participants as soon as possible after the procedure. The research value of a deceptive practice must clearly outweigh any reasonably foreseen consequences, especially how such deception may reflect adversely on Christ and the church.

Normally, we do not use methods of deception and concealment when alternative research procedures are available to accomplish the project objectives.

2-433 Protecting Confidentiality and Voluntary Participation
Researchers ensure participant confidentiality and privacy and that subjects are participating voluntarily in the project. Any deviation from these ethics shall (1) be necessary to the project and justifiable upon panel review; (2) shall not harm the participants; and (3) shall be disclosed to the participants, ensuring their consent.

2-440 Reporting Research Results
Researchers report research results fully, accurately, and without alteration or distortion of data. Data and conclusions are reported clearly and simply, with any problems with the research design fully discussed. Researchers do not conduct fraudulent research, distort or misrepresent data, manipulate results, or bias conclusions to conform to preferred agendas or desired outcomes.

2-441 Protecting Participant Identity
Researchers are diligent to protect the identity of research participants in all research reports. Due care will be taken to disguise participant identity in the absence of consent by participants.

2-442 Reporting Challenging or Unfavorable Data
Outcomes that challenge accepted policies, programs, donor/sponsor priorities, and prevailing theory shall be reported and all variables known to have affected the outcomes shall be disclosed. Upon formal request, researchers shall provide sufficient original data to qualified others who wish to replicate the study.

ETHICAL STANDARDS IN WRITING AND PUBLICATION
2-510 Integrity in Writing and Publication
Christian counselors maintain honesty and integrity in all writing and publication ventures, giving full credit to whom credit is due. Christian counselors recognize the work of others on all projects, avoid plagiarism of others' work, share credit by joint authorship or acknowledgment with others who have directly and substantially contributed to the work published, and honor all copyright and other laws applicable to the work.

2-520 Submission of Manuscripts
Christian counselors honor all publication deadlines, rules of submission of manuscripts, and rules of format when submitting manuscripts or agreeing to write invited works. Articles published whole or in major part in other works shall be done only with the acknowledgment and the permission of the previous publisher.

2-521 Review of Manuscripts
Christian counselors and editors who review manuscripts for publication shall consider the work strictly on its merits, avoiding prejudice for or against a particular author. Reviewers will diligently protect the confidential, reputational, and proprietary rights of all persons submitting materials for publication.

2-522 Encouragement of New Authors
Christian counseling editors and publishers will be diligent to call forth, encourage, and help develop new writers and materials from among the growing community of Christian counselors.

2-530 Avoiding Ghost Writers
Christian counselors shall resist use of ghost writers, where the name of a prominent leader-author is attached to work substantially or wholly written by someone else. Instead, in accordance with section 2-510 above, Christian counseling authors will give due authorship credit to anyone who has substantially contributed to the published text. Order of authorship should reflect the level of substantive contribution to a work.

FINAL ENCOURAGEMENT

May God be exalted, the Holy Spirit be invited, and Jesus Christ be seen in all of our counseling and helping endeavors. If that happens, our clients and parishioners will be blessed and not harmed, their wounds will be healed, their sins will be forgiven, and they will be given hope for the future. By acting ethically in all things, we will participate in a wonderful adventure that will likely never grow old or stale, and we will fulfill our call to excellence and integrity in Christian counseling.

PART IV

THE PROCESS AND PRACTICE OF CHRISTIAN COUNSELING

CHAPTER 12

INTAKE AND ASSESSMENT

Global Evaluation of Bio-Psycho-Social-Spiritual Life

TIM CLINTON AND GEORGE OHLSCHLAGER

The inclusion of spiritual issues in the latest revision of the Diagnostic and Statistical Manual of Mental Disorders (DSM-IV) *is indicative of a growing recognition of their importance in mental health assessment and treatment.*

—FROMA WALSH, *Spiritual Resources in Family Therapy*

George: *The woman was angry, and her anger barely concealed a nervous suspicion that silently screamed, "You're a man, and I don't know if I can ever trust a man again!" It was her first session, just forty-eight hours after her husband stopped lying to her and confessed to being "in love" with his secretary. The couple had had a huge fight that night, after which he packed and left. Now she was in my office, after two mostly sleepless days and nights, and her emotions were raw.*

After she haltingly told her story, I asked why she had picked me instead of a woman. She admitted she wasn't sure now and wondered aloud whether she should have seen a woman for counseling. She had heard from a friend that I had been helpful when her friend's "lout of a husband" also had cheated. We discussed the pros and cons of gender role and choice in counseling, and at the end of that interchange, I realized that she was still unsure. I then reached for my secret weapon—one that I've used for years with many clients, both male and female.

I pulled off the shelf my well-used and slightly faded copy of Everything Men Know About Women, *written by Dr. Alan Francis, "America's foremost psychologist." The cover quotes the* Daily News *as saying that the book "fully reveals the shocking truth." On the back cover the* Chronicle *noted that the book "says it all!"*

I gave it to my client and told her that we'd learn why her husband did what he did by studying this book. She snorted—a common reaction of most clients—looked warily at the cover, and then opened it. As usual, she started flipping pages and, with her eyes flaring in surprise, she burst out in a contagious laugh that also got me going. The tension was completely broken. From that point on, we worked constructively in counseling.

Every inside page of that little classic, you see, is completely blank—not a word— nothing but clean white pages!

Humor—and its surprising delivery—doesn't work with every client, nor is it always appropriate. Every counselor, however, must learn how to break the ice in a variety of ways with nervous, angry, and insecure clients. Every counselor must evaluate whether the client should be seeing someone else. This is just one of the challenges of the first counseling session.

ATTENDING TO YOUR CLIENT

According to *Webster's New World Dictionary, to attend* means "to give heed to" and "to stretch toward." We like the idea of "stretching toward" your client in a way that focuses every sense and instinct you have to know and understand the person before you. Previously presented in chapter 9, the SOLER acronym identifies a set of skills for high-level attending behavior (Egan, 1998). In brief review, remember that you are to

S—Face the client SQUARELY

O—Adopt an OPEN posture

L—LEAN toward your client on occasion

E—Maintain appropriate EYE contact

R—Stay RELAXED in the interaction

The real art of attending is achieved by maintaining a relaxed style in the midst of these rather intense interactive skills. Attending is meant to communicate a serious attention to your client's needs. It is *not* meant to overpower or put the client on edge. So relax and be yourself in the exchange. High-level attending means you are engaged in artful questioning without prying, intensive assessment without being judgmental, and graceful responses without ever shifting the focus to yourself.

Listen to and respect the admonition of Proverbs 18:2: "Fools have no interest in understanding; they only want to air their own opinions" (NLT). Furthermore, Proverbs 20:5 says that "the purposes of a man's heart are deep waters, but a man of understanding draws them out." Embrace wholeheartedly the challenge of Isaiah 40:27-31, for it reveals that God is always in an attending posture toward us:

Why do you say, O Jacob, and complain, O Israel, "My way is hidden from the LORD; my cause is disregarded by my God"? Do you not know? Have you not heard? The LORD is the everlasting God, the Creator of the ends of the earth. He will not grow tired or weary, and his understanding no one can fathom. He gives strength to the weary and increases the power of the weak.... Those who hope in the LORD will renew their strength. They will soar on wings like eagles; they will run and not grow weary, they will walk and not be faint.

FIRST-SESSION OBJECTIVES

The first session in counseling is unique to the entire helping endeavor. It is not only the first session of counselor-client contact (a major issue in itself), but in many cases, it is the only session that will take place. In fact, a helper does not really know whether counseling will develop into an ongoing, multisession relationship until the client shows up for the second and third sessions. Hence, some counselors assume that one session with a client is their only opportunity to be of help.

Such an assumption may seem cynical to some. But there is wisdom in believing that, in case this client doesn't return, I must do all I can to influence him for the better while he is here. Therefore, the first session in counseling should be viewed as a microprocess for the entire counseling relationship. If multisession counseling is like a video of an ongoing relationship, then the one-session intervention is a snapshot of the counseling work.

This means that counselors must do assessment, tentative diagnosis, initial intervention, and implicit termination in the first hour or two they have with their clients. They must also operate with an inherent (but best unfelt and unexpressed) tension between using the first session as the prelude to an ongoing relationship and as the only session they may have with new clients.

Your goal in initial sessions is to accurately learn everything you can about your clients in order to understand their frame of mind, their way of perceiving and evaluating things. This is what creating a therapeutic alliance is about. To the degree that you accurately and deeply understand your clients—and can effectively communicate that understanding to them—you will be given permission to enter and influence their lives in the goal direction on which you both agree. Hence, you learn to notice

- how they dress and present themselves in a public sense,
- how they position and shift their bodies in relation to verbal and emotional cues,
- how they hold your gaze and deflect it, and on what topics,

- how the pitch and tone and decibel level of their speech confirms or questions things,
- what their overall mood is and how they express or suppress any emotions.

Balancing these numerous and sometimes conflicting demands is both a challenging science and an accomplished art. For most counselors, it may take many hundreds of hours of counseling to learn to do this well.

In the first session, then, the counselor must listen to the client's *verbal messages, nonverbal messages* (tone of voice, facial expressions, posture), *context* or social setting of living, and *"sour notes"*—the things that will eventually need to be challenged.

Clients tend to talk about events, actions, and feelings. Their stories reveal, for the most part, what has happened to them, who was involved, what they did, and how they feel about it today. As clients' stories unfold, counselors need to be asking themselves the following questions:

- What themes are being presented here?
- What is the core issue?
- Is this person aware of and telling me the core issue or hiding it?
- What is most important to this person?
- What does he or she want me to understand most of all?

CREATING THE THERAPEUTIC ALLIANCE

In order to join with and understand your client, it is necessary to establish a good working relationship—to construct the beginning of a therapeutic alliance. An alliance is established when your client risks opening up his or her life and allows you to influence him or her for good—however you two have defined that goal. Putting your client at ease and establishing trust are accomplished by (1) communicating your ease with the client and your confidence about goal attainment; (2) affirming confidentiality and spelling out its limits; (3) telling the client a little bit about yourself, your training, your experience, and your reliance upon the Lord; and (4) staying attentive—asking few but focused questions and assuring the client on occasion that you understand.

The therapeutic alliance is not a therapeutic end but a means to better goal acquisition by the client. At this beginning stage, the goal is to gather as much information as possible about client problems, goals, and resources by facilitating the client's story-telling process as well as avoiding potential blocks and detours. Therefore it is important in the first session to focus on the following objectives:

1. *Suspend criticism and judgmental talk.* Confronting clients about their sins, distortions, denials, and evasions may be necessary as counseling proceeds (and sometimes this is done very early in crisis intervention), but it is crucial to convince

most clients early in this first session that you are their friend, that you are there for them, and that you are committed to understanding them—before you evaluate or challenge them. You want to discern how much clients know about themselves and how willing they are to admit their own culpability without your charging them with wrongdoing. The simple truth is that most people will not allow you to challenge or evaluate them until they are convinced that you know them and care about them.

2. *Listen actively and avoid pat answers, simplistic solutions, and minimizing or exaggerating the seriousness of the problem.* This is merely an extension of the first principle—listening and understanding must come before evaluation, judgment, and direction. Remember the one-mouth-two-ears rule: If you aren't listening at least twice as much as you are talking to your clients, you're missing the purpose of this stage.

3. *Stay client-centered.* Don't tell your story; facilitate the telling of your clients' stories. You may engage in some self-disclosure, but only reveal tidbits of your own life in order to encourage your clients to reveal their own stories.

4. *Begin a global assessment of client problems, strengths, and resources.* Use questions that gather information around the bio-psycho-social-spiritual spectrum. Conduct only a cursory assessment (one that you will complete in the second session) because you must leave time for interaction around solution-directed action.

5. *Ground your counseling in prayer and expect God to help.* As you are able, and with your clients' consent, invite them to join you in praying aloud for guidance, protection, and success in the search for answers to the problems they bring to you. If you discern that this would not be appropriate, pray silently, giving each client's situation to the Lord and asking him to guide you in providing help.

First or Only Session?

All of this discussion assumes, of course, that you will be engaged in an ongoing counseling relationship in which your client will return for additional sessions and work to achieve his or her goals. However, clinical experience and much research tell us that this presumption does not always fit the facts. Many clients stay with a counselor for only one or two sessions, no matter how good the counselor may be.

Therefore, it is crucial to work to help bring about change at the same time that you are assessing what is going on. In fact, the skilled helper is adept at achieving both objectives in the first session, regardless of whether the client returns for additional counseling. We believe that any constructive change clients engage in and are aware of increases the likelihood that they will see you as an expert who is able to help them and will return for more counseling.

The skilled helper is able to accurately (but not exhaustively) assess client issues and promote limited (though maybe not enduring or substantial) change in that first session. We add these qualifiers so you won't feel overwhelmed with unrealistic expectations of the first session. We would also assert that while these goals of assessment and change may not be sufficient for the client, it is necessary in the first session.

THE ASSESSMENT PROCESS

George: *After my family doctor had finished listening to my chest and back, I queried, "What's wrong, Doc? Is it my heart?" I was suspicious of the worst for some reason. "Maybe," he replied, "but I'm not sure yet. Tell me more about what's been going on." So I reviewed in more detail the way I'd been feeling the past few days—dizziness, headaches, shortness of breath, quick fatigue, and fluttering feelings in my heart. "I think the first thing we need to do is an EKG, then we'll figure out where to go next," said the doctor, deferring a premature judgment.*

After the EKG came an immediate referral to a cardiologist, who set me up with a treadmill/stress test that same afternoon. In less than two minutes on the treadmill, I was exhausted, done in. As I cooled down, the cardiologist came in and started reviewing the output tape. Within twenty seconds he looked up at me and paused, eyeing me up and down, assessing my readiness to hear what he had to tell me. Then he stated quite matter-of-factly, "George, you've had a pretty serious heart attack."

Every day, in virtually every situation, we are constantly assessing ourselves and others. McReynolds (1975) simply defined *assessment* as a process in which we attempt to know, understand, or size up another person or situation. All of us are engaged in informally sizing up someone else; people everywhere are engaged in an ongoing evaluation and judgment and prediction of other people. No doubt you can remember evaluative judgments you made today about yourself, your spouse, your children, your parents, your colleagues and coworkers, and even strangers on the street. Were they good judgments, honoring of self and others? Were they critical, even abusive? Was there some of both?

Counseling, like medicine, begins with *accurate assessment.* Maloney and Ward (1976) see assessment in professional counseling as an indispensable link in the chain of treatment, a process of solving problems in which tests are often used as a method of collecting important information. As with the assessment of a heart problem, formal clinical assessment and diagnosis in medicine, and increasingly in counseling and psychotherapy, usually means using interviews, tests, and clinical logic in an experienced process that entails the following activities:

- gathering relevant information about the problem, its history and behavior, patient resources, and action to ameliorate it
- looking for clinical patterns and relationships in the data
- synthesizing the data into clusters of symptoms
- making tentative diagnoses
- testing diagnostic questions and impressions
- ruling out related diagnoses or doing differential diagnosis
- gathering more information
- doing more questioning, testing, and ruling out
- consulting with others
- arriving at a confirmable (and often consensus-based) diagnosis

The Christian counselor must learn to accurately evaluate both the visible and invisible elements of a person's life—the intrapsychic and interpersonal processes—and to discern and communicate how God evaluates us. Knowing your client well and having a full and accurate picture of his or her life make your intervention more focused, more helpful, more potent, and more accepted by the client.

ASSESSMENT AND ALIGNMENT

Client assessment with a refined sense of clinical judgment is invaluable because you can't treat what you don't see, and if you can't see it accurately, you can't treat it properly. Furthermore, the work done to create a therapeutic alliance between counselor and client—to *align* with clients so that they believe you understand and are for them—is not an end in itself. Like a good doctor-patient relationship in medicine, the purpose of a good counseling relationship is to (1) facilitate an accurate and comprehensive evaluation of the problem(s) and the resources available to cure or manage it properly, and (2) devise an effective and efficient treatment plan that is achievable and can be understood and owned by the client.

Consider Jesus Christ's assessment of Nathanael and how that evaluation affected their relationship:

> Philip went off to look for Nathanael and told him, "We have found the very person Moses and the prophets wrote about! His name is Jesus, the son of Joseph from Nazareth."
>
> "Nazareth!" exclaimed Nathanael. "Can anything good come from there?"
>
> "Just come and see for yourself," Philip said.

As they approached, Jesus said, "Here comes an honest man—a true son of Israel."

"How do you know about me?" Nathanael asked.

And Jesus replied, "I could see you under the fig tree before Philip found you."

Nathanael replied, "Teacher, you are the Son of God—the King of Israel!" (John 1:45-49, NLT)

The transformation of Nathanael's attitude and mood is remarkable during this encounter. He moves from skeptical sarcasm to quizzical wonder to excited belief. Nathanael's skepticism is familiar to all helpers who consistently face client resistance, cynicism, and fears about change. The ability of Jesus to see supernaturally—perceiving the fig tree vision and the best nature of Nathanael's heart—challenges all helpers to assess with eyes that see both externally and internally.

Jesus aligned himself with Nathanael's honest self—something Nathanael must have cultivated and was known for in the community. This is an excellent strategy for affirming the best in others and acknowledging those resources that will be necessary for constructive change to take place. Christian counseling is as concerned with evaluating client strengths and positive character in order to encourage and reinforce their development as it is with assessing problems. Doing so certainly helped win Nathanael over to Christ. Likewise, it will help you win over your clients and better prepare them for the tough work that is yet to be done.

WHAT IS CLINICAL ASSESSMENT?

In the twenty-first-century paradigm, clinical assessment works to accomplish the following five objectives in counseling:

1. to identify and understand the client's complaints and problem issues
2. to gather data on and understand the client's world and way of seeing things
3. to learn about family history, developmental events, and significant relationship issues
4. to identify client strengths and weaknesses across the bio-psycho-social-spiritual range of living
5. to begin the case formulation process that leads to goal definition and treatment planning

ASSESSMENT SUBJECTIVITY AND OBJECTIVITY

On a broad scale, clinical assessment is divided into subjective and objective forms. Subjective assessment is the process of making evaluative inferences—educated and experienced hunch making, if you will, based on data from interviews or observation. Objective assessment is a more formal process that usually involves standardized tests and better controls the variability of subjective evaluation. All counselors use subjective methods of assessment—especially direct-interviewing procedures—but not all use more objective and standardized tests and measures.

Psychological testing. A standardized psychological test is one that controls various conditions of testing that can otherwise adversely affect the "truth value" of an assessment. "Standardization implies uniformity of procedure in administering and scoring the test" (Anastasi, 1998, p. 25). For example, instead of asking a lot of open-ended questions in an interview and allowing the client a wide latitude to answer them, a standardized test will ask the same question repeatedly to force the client to choose an answer.

It is important to understand that these different approaches to testing are simply that: different ways to gather information about people. Each way, each method, each test, has its value. The competent clinician usually has a variety of assessment tools and procedures and often uses more than one of them with any given client in order to get a more complete and unique portrait of the person being helped.

Technically, assessment is neither diagnosis nor treatment. Yet assessment, diagnosis, and treatment should be experienced as a continuous stream of case formulation where change is taking place and where the competent counselor is thinking about all three dynamics and how they interrelate. As clinical assessment expands, assessment and knowledge of the client increases, a counselor's diagnosis becomes more accurate, and treatment becomes more focused and refined. And as treatment brings about change, the treatment plan is continually reevaluated. The entire process keeps recursively spiraling upward into an ever-greater intervention that should bear wonderful fruit in the life of the client.

TYPES OF ASSESSMENT

In this section we will overview various types of assessment procedures, from the more subjective to the more objective.

The clinical interview is the most common assessment tool used by nearly all counselors with clients (see Cormier & Cormier, 1991; Morrison, 1995). Whether conducted in a formal office setting or over a cup of coffee, the interview is a "conversation with a purpose." Clinical interviewing involves asking a series of systematic questions designed to elicit as much information about the client as pos-

---

BOX 12.1—BRIEF OUTLINE OF THE CLINICAL INTERVIEW

1. Presenting Problem(s)
Symptoms and onset
Course and severity
Previous episodes
Hospitalizations
Impact on patient/family

2. Review of Current Symptoms
Eating/appetite disorders?
Sleep disorders?
Seizures/head injury?
Chronic pain?
Other medical disorders?
Past medical problems?

3. Substance Use/Abuse
Current meds/substances?
Duration of use?
Quantity and cost?
Consequences of use?
Abuse and consequences?

4. Suicidal Thinking/Behavior
Attempted suicide?
Thought about seriously?
How done/thought about?
Seriousness?
Consequences?
Hospitalized?
Need help now?

5. Homicidal Thoughts/Behavior
Assaulted anyone?
Jail or other consequence?
Thought about homicide?
Anyone currently targeted?
Revenge or hurt someone?
How controlled?
Difficult to control?
Need help now?

6. Childhood and Family History
When and where born?
Siblings/birth order?
Raised by both parents?
Parent relations?
Adopted?
Blended family?
Health as child?
Any abuse/neglect?
Problems in puberty?
Loner or friends?

7. Education History
Last grade completed?
Education complete or may
return?
Scholastic problems?
Behavior problems?
Quit or kicked out?

sible in the time you have and to work toward the goals of rapport building and client change (Morrison, 1995).

All the while the counselor is directing and organizing the interview, recording

8. **Adult History**
    Marital status?
    Times married?
    Sexual problems?
    Who lives with?
    Children/ages/sex?
    Marital/family trouble?
    Current work?
    Like it or not?
    Any trouble at work?
    Financial stress?
    Legal trouble?
    Veteran? (describe)

9. **Religion and Spiritual History**
    Active in church or other...?
    What religion/denomination?
    How frequent?
    Born again?
    How important in life?
    Incorporate in counseling?

10. **Mental-Status Exam**
    Client appearance
        Apparent age?
        Race?
        Health/hygiene?
        Clothing?
    Behavior
        Eye contact?
        Posture?

Activity level?
Tremors?
Unusual mannerisms?
Smile and laughter?
Accent?
Mood
    Type?
    Lability?
    Appropriate?
Cognitive
    Oriented to person,
        place, and time?
    Memory—immediate,
        recent, and remote
    Attention and concentration
        serial sevens
        count backward
    Abstract thinking
        similarities
        differences
    Insight and judgment
Flow of Thought
    Word associations
    Speech rhythm
    Fluency
    Comprehension
Content of Thought
    Anxiety/phobias
    Obsessions/compulsions
    Delusions
    Hallucination

client answers as well as the nonverbal and behavioral context in which answers are delivered.

A good clinical interview—whether done in one sitting or over two or three sessions—explores the client problem and what has been done to resolve it. You want to know what doesn't work and what does, even if only partially. The interviewer also reviews other current and related issues and key people affecting the problem; assesses drug abuse and suicide and homicide risks; and gains some historical information related to problem etiology and process (Cormier & Cormier, 1991).

The full clinical interview also does an initial mental status exam to red-flag any other areas of concern that may not be presented. Some of the most helpful assessment devices that are commonly used to expand the range of concern and identify related issues in clients' lives are the Symptom Checklist–90, SCID–II, Beck Depression Inventory, and the multimodal Life History Questionnaire.

The best interview questions at this stage are open-ended, focusing on what, when, where, and how, but not on why. They elicit information about how the *client* judges things, not on how *you* judge them. The best open-ended interview questions include the following:

- "How are you feeling?" not "Are you feeling depressed?"
- "What brought you in for counseling?" not "You must have felt pretty desperate to come, huh?"
- "Where were you when you felt the panic coming on?" not "Why do think that happened?"
- "How often does that happen in a day or a week?" not "How come it seems so severe?"
- "What is it you don't like about doing that?" not "You know doing that is wrong, don't you?"
- "Let's think about what kind of payoff there might be if you continue doing that," not "Why do you keep hurting your wife that way?"
- "What do you think your boss will do if he finds out about that?" not "You know he's going to go through the roof when he learns about that, don't you?

The clinical assessment interview and mental status outline on the previous pages (box 12.1) can be used in any counseling setting. It is a traditional outline that has been revised and updated to reflect life in our modern culture.

Client observation is an ongoing clinical process whereby the counselor observes and assesses client behavior in context. Most often this is in context of the client's own behavior—both verbal and nonverbal cues—but it also involves observing the client interpersonally. Seeing the client actually live with spouse and family or being able to observe the client at work, in the classroom, or at church provides valuable information to the counselor. Sometimes what a counselor sees in context is quite different from what the client describes in session about that context.

Secondhand reports are a useful corollary to client observation and comprise reports about the client given by those in closest relationship to the client—family, friends, employers, colleagues. These reports can provide valuable insights about client behavior and can confirm or disconfirm client reports. On the other hand, secondhand reports can be just as biased and inaccurate as a self-serving client report might be. Therefore, while secondhand reports are often quite valuable to the counselor, they must be accepted with some skepticism owing to the inherent bias of subjective reporting about others.

Self-assessment is a skill counselors can teach clients to do through journaling, autobiographies, self-coding reports, self-report questionnaires, and narrative reports. The key difference between self-assessed descriptions and client reports elicited by interview is that in self-assessment the client is trained to write down events and self-evaluations soon after the events take place. Clients are trained to maintain a log of their experiences around problem events or people and to do it in a way that produces insights and resources for change that aren't often recalled in an interview. We encourage counselors to train clients in self-assessment, since self-monitoring is often the left hand to the right hand of counselor assessment. Client self-assessment accomplishes four crucial goals:

1. It helps clarify distortions about problem behavior and significance. Since there is often some degree of exaggeration or minimization in all interviews and self-reports, client self-assessment helps a counselor gain a more accurate picture of what is actually going on.

2. It better reveals the process of problem occurrence, noting antecedents and consequences. This empowers the client to intervene more often and at different places in the problem flow in order to increase the likelihood of change.

3. It reveals important clues that are often missed in self-reports and are sometimes central to unlocking the puzzle of change. A sex addict was surprised by the influence of lunchtime girl watching that often fueled his masturbation fantasy later in the day. He would not have made the connection without close self-assessment.

4. It monitors change in a concrete fashion, allowing for the development of more realistic expectations regarding change. It also provides a tangible reward as the client sees the small changes that indicate problems are being resolved and desired goals are being achieved.

Acted-out or expressive tools provide a nonverbal assessment alternative for clients who are so angry, so withdrawn, so regressed and afraid, or so young and nonverbal that you will not get good data using verbal, sit-down assessment methods. The best way to learn about and connect with these special folks is to have them draw pictures, paint with hand and brush, play in a sand tray, use the house-tree-person tool, play with toys, run through a ropes-and-obstacles course, or use a variety of other active modes of expression. In fact, these methods are often the preferred course of interaction with many children and adolescents, with highly regressed and fearful trauma victims, and with certain psychotic patients. When you can't connect by talking with someone, find another mode of communication. It works!

Checklists and questionnaires are nonstandardized question-and-answer tools that can give quick and useful information about a client in a particular area. These tools are simple to administer in order to confirm client crises and assess client depression, anxiety, stress levels, hyperactivity, risk of suicide or threats of violence against another person, and many other issues. Every counselor should keep on hand a variety of checklists and questionnaires to immediately assess client problem issues.

Genograms are a family-systems assessment tool that indicate the interactive web of family relationships as well as the strengths and weaknesses of those interactions.

Multimodal inventories are global assessment inventories that reflect the technical eclecticism that Lazarus (1981) has promoted. Multimodal assessment systematically collects a great deal of information across a variety of life issues. Our BECHRISTLIKE multimodal assessment for Christian counselors, presented later in this chapter, follows the pattern of the metamodel that Lazarus developed.

Standardized Psychological Tests

Standardized psychological tests (SPTs) are considered to be the cream of assessment tools because they have been refined to the point where they can measure behavior, aptitude, ability, or personality with a high degree of objectivity and consistency (Anastasi, 1988). As a result, they are used whenever it is important to predict a person's outcome in a particular area. The Scholatic Aptitude Test (SAT), for example, has long been used to predict the academic success high-school students will have with a particular course of study in college.

Some Common Standardized Tests

While tests can be a rich source of information, most require extensive training to administer, score, and interpret. For more information about standardized tests see the Buros Mental Measurements Yearbook, a comprehensive source of consumer-oriented test reviews. Some of the most common standardized tests include the following:

Vocational
CISS (Campbell Interest and Skill Survey)
SDS (Self-Directed Search)
SII (Strong Interest Inventory)

Achievement
SAT (Scholastic Aptitude Test)
WIAT–II (Wechsler Individual Achievement Test–II)

Behavioral and Mood Assessment
ADDBRS (ADD Behavior Rating Scale)
Adult ADD Behavior Rating Scale
CRS–R (Conners' Rating–Revised)
BDI–II (Beck Depression Inventory–II)

Intelligence
K-Bit (Kaufman Brief Intelligence Test)
Stanford-Binet Intelligence Scale, Fourth Edition
WAIS–III (Wechsler Adult Intelligence Scale–III)
WISC–III (Wechsler Intelligence Scale for Children–III)

Personality
CPI (California Psychological Inventory)
Jackson Personality Inventory
MBTI (Myers-Briggs Type Indicator)
T-JTA (Taylor-Johnson Temperament Analysis)
MMPI–2 (Minnesota Multiphasic Personality Inventory–2)
Millon Clinical Multiaxial Personality Inventory–II

Developmental
BINS (Bayley Infant Neurodevelopmental Screening)
CDI (Child Development Inventory)
DASI–II (Developmental Activities Screening Inventory,
    Second Edition)

Misusing Tests and Assessment

One graduate-school professor essentially believed that "you are your MMPI." Since this instructor seemed to put more faith in that well-validated personality inventory than in the redeeming power of Christ, he argued that, due to one student's atypical profile, the student should never have been admitted to the counselor training program. Fortunately, in spite of the instructor's evaluation, the student stayed in the program and graduated with honors. The instructor was gone after one year. While this is one of many personal controversies in our culture over the right use and application of test data, let us put this controversy in context.

Test validity and reliability. SPTs are useful for predicting human behavior and performance because they have been tested to a high level of validity and reliability. A valid test is one that actually measures what it says it does; likewise, a reliable test is one that scores consistently and accurately, as different scores represent differences in knowledge or ability or whatever is being tested. Kuhn (1970) has shown us that absolute objectivity is a myth. We can discuss only approximations of perfection in anything but the attributes of God. We now understand that every test and its interpretation is a value-laden and culturally conditioned exercise.

Humility in testing and interpreting tests. Any test results must be accepted with humility, balancing their power to reveal with the knowledge that no test ever equals the dignity or reveals a complete picture of any one person. The *AACC Christian Counseling Code of Ethics* (2001) states the following with reference to assessment and testing:

1-530 Ethics in Testing, Assessment, and Clinical Evaluation
Christian counselors do clinical evaluations of clients only in the context of professional relations, in the best interests of clients, and with the proper training and supervision. Christian counselors avoid (1) incompetent and inaccurate evaluations, (2) clinically unnecessary and excessively expensive testing, and (3) unauthorized practice of testing and evaluation that is the province of another clinical or counseling discipline. Referral and consultation are used when evaluation is desired or necessary beyond the competence and/or role of the counselor.

1-531 Use of Appropriate Assessments
Christian counselors use tests and assessment techniques that are appropriate to the needs, resources, capabilities, and understanding of the client. We apply tests skillfully and administer tests properly and safely. We substantiate our findings, with knowledge of the reliability, validity, outcome results,

and limits of the tests used. We avoid both the misuse of testing procedures and the creation of confusion or misunderstanding by clients about testing purposes, procedures, and findings.

1-532 Reporting and Interpreting Assessment Results

Christian counselors report testing results in a fair, understandable, and objective manner. We avoid undue testing bias and honor the limits of test results, ensuring verifiable means to substantiate conclusions and recommendations. We recognize the limits of test interpretation and avoid exaggeration and absolute statements about the certainty of client diagnoses, behavior predictions, clinical judgments, and recommendations. Due regard is given to the unique history, values, family dynamics, sociocultural influences, economic realities, and spiritual maturity of the client. Christian counselors will state any and all reservations about the validity of test results and present reports and recommendations in tentative language and with alternative possibilities.

Testing abuse. Maybe you or someone you know has been a victim of testing abuse—discriminated against because of an IQ score, the results of a polygraph test, or a personality profile that is less than stellar. As a Christian counselor, be a human rights advocate: *Never confuse the person in front of you with his or her test score on anything.* Tests can reveal important clues and dynamics about someone, but they can never fully reveal an accurate composite of the entire person. (Every test score includes True Score and error.) So be extra cautious about:

- labeling others and creating self-fulfilling prophecies
- assuming the absolute accuracy of any test
- racial, ethnic, and gender bias
- the "tunneling" effect of testing
- violating client privacy

GLOBAL ASSESSMENT IN CHRISTIAN COUNSELING

In the schoolist, hedgehog models that dominated the twentieth century—where a counselor was dedicated to a particular school of therapy—assessment and treatment were largely unrelated (see chapter 7). In fact, assessment mattered little because a schoolist therapist largely did the same thing regardless of diagnosis or individual client factors. The cognitive therapist always placed great weight on identifying and changing or stopping the distortions and lies that were embedded in the client's beliefs and thoughts. The psychoanalytic practitioner consistently worked to facilitate greater client insight through analysis and interpretation. The gestalt or experiential therapist always sought to evoke a more honest and expressive emotional awareness.

It is little wonder why psychotherapy was seen by many as little more than shamanism or the practice of magic. The weakness of assessment and the disconnect between diagnosis and treatment were major criticisms of the mental health field. However, two developments mark the sea change from twentieth-century to twenty-first-century clinical assessment and treatment: (1) *the integrative development of a comprehensive evaluation*—a bio-psycho-social-spiritual assessment of a client's life, and (2) *the linkage between assessment and treatment*—with treatment planning that flows logically and clinically from comprehensive client assessment.

In this new paradigm, multilevel assessment-treatment linkage is a central dynamic of the foxlike, short-term prescriptive therapies of the twenty-first century. The hedgehog thinker will likely remain stuck viewing just one or two factors as all that is necessary to understand a person. The fox thinker will recognize that many factors are influential and that all must be assessed both distinctively and interactively. (For a detailed discussion on the "hedgehog" and "fox," see chapter 7.) A comprehensive evaluation in the twenty-first century will consider social relationships, family influences, cultural and environmental contexts, and one's relationship to God. An integrated view of modern assessment incorporates the following five modalities that once were (and to some true believers, still are) competing conceptualizations of mental disorders (APiA Task Force, 1993):

1. *Psychodynamic causation.* This modality emphasizes the role of drive states and the inability of the ego to properly regulate conflicting inner tensions. It is reflected in psychoanalytic approaches to therapy and was the dominant mode of influence through the middle part of the twentieth century.

2. *Social causation.* This views people as enmeshed in dysfunctional interpersonal and social structures and with deficient resources to facilitate structural change. It is reflected in the social and family-systems approaches to therapy, approaches that have been largely championed by the social work and marriage and family therapy professions.

3. *Behavioral causation.* Problem behavior is seen as primary (not symptomatic) and operates as poor interactions and dysfunctional judgments with one's environment. This view is reflected in the behavioral and cognitive-behavioral approaches to therapy.

4. *Biological causation.* This view, becoming ascendant in psychiatry consonant with the biological revolution in medicine and the strictures of

managed care, points to genetic anomalies and bio-chemical-structural disorders as the root of mental disorders. This approach is seen in the pharmacotherapy treatment of mental illness.

5. *Spiritual causation.* In the past quarter-century, Christian counseling has helped advance the spiritual dimension—a fifth causal factor—and one that has been sorely overlooked by the mental health professions for most of the twentieth century. This realm recognizes the spiritual dimension of life, especially for Christians as revealed in the Old and New Testaments. It includes the reality of both the *imago Dei* and the sin nature of humans, and the necessity of a reconciled and intimate relationship with the infinite and personal God of the Bible. Christian counseling, especially that which incorporates salvation and growth in sanctification, is a primary approach in this realm.

COMPETENT ASSESSMENT IN CHRISTIAN COUNSELING

As a brief prescriptive therapy in its first stage, competent Christian counseling is tied to client assessment in a substantial way. We commend to you a global client assessment that is narrowed to specific issues and targets doable change strategies. This process shapes the direction of differential treatment—the counselor judiciously chooses procedures that have shown promise in ameliorating the particular client problems shown.

So then, the client's presenting problem and understanding (or lack of understanding) of problem dynamics takes on a greater degree of importance. Counselors must, at a high level of agreement with clients, find common ground in the assessment of client problems so the client will more fully receive and implement the prescription for change. Remember, most clients come to counseling not so much because they are unaware of their problem (even though they may often be confused and ignorant of its causes and influences) but because the remedies they have attempted are not working.

We must, therefore, be able to substantially agree with our clients about their self-assessments in order to increase their trust in us when we prescribe solutions. Even when clients' self-assessments are deficient, substantially distorted, or self-serving (and they often are), and when the goal of correcting these distortions becomes an essential prerequisite to lasting change, counselors must find ways to listen respectfully and withhold early judgment in order to win trust. Clients' trust in counselors is facilitated when they believe that they are understood and are seriously accepted no matter how a counselor views their description of the problem.

Emotive Assessment: Dark Feelings and Hot Cognitions

Human emotional life is a central variable in the pursuit of help because it is often a felt disturbance—a persistent distress that cannot easily be overcome and may, in fact, be intensifying—that motivates a personal crisis that can lead to salutary change. Out of the invitation to express charged emotions such as fear, anger, confusion, impotence, and ambivalence, can come both limited relief for the sufferer and crucial knowledge for therapist and sufferer alike. The client is infused with hope and is empowered finally to gain ground against a problem that has heretofore defeated him or her. Both counselor and client gain invaluable knowledge about hot-button issues in the client's life—hot cognitions—that command attention in the definition of client problems that need to be addressed.

The right role for our emotional life—to say nothing of the proper respect for it—has had a difficult history in the conservative church. The emotional or affective life has been generally denigrated in evangelical circles, where the priority is placed more often on cognitive processes: transformed minds and propositional truth. One reason for this may be the (sometimes necessary) theological-institutional response to a feel-good culture that worships the ecstatic. Another more personal reason is that our emotional system is not as easily swayed by our divided selves, that is, our tendency to lie to ourselves about our spiritual struggles and to present ourselves as being more perfect than we really are. Allender (1996) states:

> I find three sorts of assumptions about emotions in my work with
> Christians:
>   1. Emotions are amoral (we can't do anything about what we feel, but
>   we can change our thinking and our behavior).
>   2. Emotions are nearly impossible to predict or understand, therefore
>   it is better to ignore them.
>   3. Spiritual maturity means having few, if any, dark emotions.
>   All three assumptions are incorrect and dangerous to true spiritual
> growth. A more biblical perspective on emotions reveals how they can
> deepen our intimacy with God. (p. 33)

Our clinical experience teaches us that our emotions, along with nonverbal cues and behavior, reveal our struggles with God and others. To deny these struggles and to suppress the feelings that go with them is to admit that we don't pursue God with our whole heart, mind, and strength. To deny these struggles also leads us astray from a central truth about growing up in Christ: At times our struggle is dark and painful, taxing us and forcing us beyond the limits of our ability. Again, Allender (1996) states it well:

> God subjected the world to frustration (Romans 8:20-23).… We are left in a world that will inevitably leave us frustrated—that is, experiencing the kind of pain that reveals we are not home. God intends for us to struggle. The dark emotions that come with the pain propel us toward God or toward greater self-sufficiency.… Denial of emotions…is…related to our flight from God. Feeling the effects of living in a fallen world compels us to wrestle with God.… When clients see their darker emotions as related to their hunger to possess what only heaven can provide, a new wrestling match begins. (pp. 34-35)

At first blush, Allender's proposition may sound heretical to some believers. But we agree with Allender that the honest confession and expression of our dark emotions toward God may be more desirable to him than the mere recitation of our propositional faith. We believe that God loves passion, even when at first the passion is directed against him. (On the other hand, we must not get stuck in our negative emotions.) Could God be saying that he wants passion more than pronouncement? As the book of Revelation states, "I know all the things you do, that you are neither hot nor cold. I wish you were one or the other! But since you are like lukewarm water, I will spit you out of my mouth!" (3:15-16, NLT).

Therefore, if we depend only on the formal recitation of client problems by a client in tight control of his or her passions, we will usually get an insufficient or distorted picture of client issues. Let the feelings flow in counseling, and learn some deeper truths about your client's life.

SINGLE- AND DUAL-TRACK ASSESSMENT

Single-track assessment by all Christian counselors is called for across the bio-psycho-social-spiritual dimensions of those seeking help. Assessment is a quasi-formal process of structured interviewing at the inception of counseling as well as an ongoing dynamic where the counselor is constantly asking (mostly internally) how the client is doing and what it will take to help the client move in the desired direction.

Professional clinical assessment, on the other hand, is a dual-track procedure, combining psychiatric assessment with a global assessment of client problems and strengths. Psychiatry's diagnostic "bible," the latest edition of the *Diagnostic and Statistical Manual of Mental Disorders* (DSM-IV-TR), is used consistently and is

BOX 12.2—ASSESSING PATHOLOGICAL RELIGION

Religious and spiritual pathology—lies and distortions about God and self that are believed to be true—confront every Christian counselor and pastor at times. These lies and half-truths, whether subtle or glaring, are used by different people as the pursuit of true religion, as covers for sin, and as defense mechanisms that protect fragile personality structures. No matter how they are used, they yield both personal and cumulative trouble for those who hold them and operate their lives by them. The following "Dirty Dozen" are distortions that all Christian helpers must face.

1. *Self-worship* is the substitution of self for God, even though God is consciously admitted as the object of worship. Religion and spiritual behavior are on display, giving is self-promoted as sacrificial and cross-bearing, and religion is used to meet the narcissistic compulsions of the believer. Biblically, self-worship suggests resistance to God's transforming power or failure to allow his power to penetrate deeply.

2. *Sin focus/avoidance* is an intense preoccupation with sin and with avoidance of God's punishment. Often in the religious dimension of an obsessive-compulsive disorder, there is some correlation with a history of abuse, disabling perfectionism, and concern about committing the unpardonable sin. Biblically, this attitude suggests a failure to understand Christ's substitutionary sacrifice or to appropriate God's forgiving grace.

3. *Sin denial/substitution* is a close corollary to the above dynamic, in which the sin-denier refuses to take responsibility for wrongdoing at some crucial levels, and the sin metastasizes like a cancer that eventually threatens the entire organism. The refusal to take personal responsibility for one's life and actions is the core of this problem. Whether the client blames the devil, the pastor or elder, the spouse or boss, one's past or one's parents, blame-shifting is a central dynamic.

4. *Religious pride* is often revealed by the consistent public expression of religious and moral accomplishments: "I lead the largest church in the city." "We are the premier Christian counseling clinic in America." "I've never looked at another woman in thirty-two years of marriage." Attempts to challenge the pride and call for humility are often met with anger, as if God himself is being challenged.

5. *Religious hostility* is unresolved anger, bitterness, and unforgiveness that is repressed, denied, and veiled by religious fervor. It is seen in the tendency

toward interpersonal aloofness and is often expressed by calling down God's judgment on sinners and unbelievers. Such hostility is shown by some liberal Christians toward "right-wing fundamentalists" and by some conservative Christians toward abortionists and homosexuals. Bitterness and resentment toward God are often present but are usually vigorously denied.

6. *Loveless truth-telling* is a tactic of the emotionally detached (and often tactless) believer who understands and applies only half of the Ephesians 4:15 injunction to "speak the truth in love." The sole focus is on truth and truth-telling no matter what the social context, no matter how much it might hurt others. The ability to empathize with others—to speak the truth at the right time and seasoned with grace—is poor or nonexistent.

7. *Blame-shifting* is characterized by the obsessive focus on a person or event in the client's history, which is the *sine qua non* for why "religion stinks" or why "all Christians are hypocrites." "My pastor told me I was going to hell twenty years ago, and I still think he's a jerk for saying so."

8. *Divisive dogmatism* stems from a divisive spirit obsessed with imposing dogmatic truth on people and churches. While most Christians agree on the essential doctrines of our faith, the dogmatist often displays a rigidity on relatively minor issues that never backs down or seeks to find a resolution that could be seen as a compromise. *Compromise* is a dirty word to the dogmatist, a red flag that signals defeat to the evil forces. The dogmatist is often well-versed in the Scriptures and projects an air of authority, disguising his or her beliefs as holiness and doctrinal purity.

9. *Experiential excess,* the opposite of controlling dogmatism, describes a person who continually seeks to be lost in God's presence. The EE client often pursues and goes beyond legitimate charismatic expression to the point of becoming a source of confusion and divisiveness in the church. Though often breaking away from and denouncing dead religious formalism, the person susceptible to excess has no clear biblical boundary on the other side to evaluate which "spirits" may be at work in various phenomena.

10. *Church detachment disorder* describes the loner Christian—an uncommitted, often demoralized believer who eschews church and Christian fellowship for a variety of reasons (usually unresolved past hurts experienced in church). It could also describe the person who shops around in a consumerist search for the perfect church without ever finding it or committing to one.

(continued)

11. *God-talking* refers to the tendency to say the right things—to spout God-words at the appropriate moments—but to show little evidence of God's transforming truth or sanctification in one's life. God-talking is often used by the client in counseling to deflect, dodge, and deny dealing with uncomfortable issues.

12. *Health-and-wealth religion* views the Christian faith as an exchange-reward contract with God wherein he rewards us for our goodness with health and wealth. This view denies the reality of suffering and trials in life as well as the fact that God uses them as a means of spiritual growth. It also denies or minimizes the role of God's sufficient grace and of our completely un-merited reception of blessings that God always gives us. This distorted view assumes that God is little more than a cosmic "Santa Claus" who is avail-able to give you what is really most important in your life—not himself, but lots of money and the health and longevity to enjoy it as you please.

respected—especially as a common diagnostic language between helping profes-sionals. It may well be the single most influential volume in the common-factors challenge. It certainly is shaping the various mental health disciplines around a common diagnostic procedure and is a key reason why the counseling process looks more and more like medical practice.

However, DSM's value as a global, comprehensive assessment tool is limited. Its medical-model structure and process have been widely criticized as being too individualistic, too psychopathologic (denying or overlooking analysis of strengths and resources crucial to modern brief therapies), more political than scientific in its definitions and criteria defining mental disorder, and too weak in its assessment of social, familial, and environmental factors.

Even though DSM-IV is an improvement over DSM-III (Axis 4 assessment) in social- and environmental-factors analysis, it is still soundly criticized as being too simplistic across this variable. Since DSM diagnosis is a professional clinical exercise, and since we believe it is a system that need not, even should not, be uni-versalized beyond its already excessive reach, we address it in a later chapter on pro-fessional clinical practice.

THE CHRISTIAN GLOBAL ASSESSMENT SYSTEM

Out of our own study, practice, and interaction, we have developed a global assessment system that derives useful diagnostic information—data that points toward applying the best treatment to bring about the desired change. This system—the Christian Global Assessment System (C-GAS)—is designed to help Christian counselors become competent in evaluating clients for twenty-first-century practice. We use an acronym—BECHRISTLIKE—to describe the many modes of human experience across which assessment is done. To "be Christlike," or to be "in Christ," is a phrase that Paul used extensively in his New Testament writings, and it reflects a primary goal in Christian counseling.

We have been influenced in this model by Lazarus (1981) and his multimodal therapy, by social work's development of the global Person-in-Environment (PIE) system of assessment, and by our commitment to prescriptive therapies that tie client assessment to specific treatment planning and practice. We find this C-GAS assessment eminently usable in clinical practice, having both substantial parsimony (Occam's razor: A theory or model is descriptively accurate, avoiding excessive simplicity and excessive complexity) and heuristic value (usable for teaching and learning).

BECHRISTLIKE: Christ-Centered Multimodal Assessment

B—*Behavior:* Focus on observable behavior and assess whether it is helpful or harmful. Define key behavior patterns around problem issues. Is there any addictive behavior? Assess antecedents and consequences of behavior. Note behavioral strengths and deficits.

E—*Emotions:* Assess primary emotional disturbance and the emotional patterns. Describe desired feelings. How does the client value emotions in relation to beliefs, thoughts, and behavior? Does pleasure or emotional relief reinforce addiction? How do emotional themes reveal the client's relationship with God?

C—*Cognition:* Assess thought content and process. What are the lies and distortions that animate this client? Reasoning ability? Psychotic or delusional symptoms? How is self-talk or client imagery helpful or traumatic? What is imagery content, intensity, and frequency? Is a neuropsychological exam indicated?

H—*Health:* What is the client's overall health status? Note medical problems and whether the client is under a physician's care. Note sensory or somatic complaints and psychosocial interactions, whether for better or for worse. Assess sleeping, eating, and exercise habits and conditions. Is physician referral called for?

R — *Religion:* Where is the client in Christ? Saved or not? Maturing or not? Stuck with God about something? Assess church life and Christian practices. Conduct a biblical analysis of problem behavior. Assess receptivity versus resistance to spiritual interventions.

I — *Idols and false beliefs:* What desires and values compete with God or with God's priorities? What values line up biblically and need strengthening? How is the client's problem related to value conflicts and discrepancies? How can the problem be biblically understood?

S — *Substances:* Assess what drugs the client is taking, both prescribed and illicit, if applicable. What are drug interactions? Does the client need physician referral for psychotropic meds? Is client resistant to taking such meds? Does the client need a program for detox and substance abuse treatment?

T — *Teachability:* Is the client motivated or resistant? Is his or her teachability global or specific, dependent on problems or other variables? Does the client exhibit hope or hopelessness? Does the client trust the counselor? Are there racial, ethnic, or gender differences that need to be bridged?

L — *Law and ethics:* Is the client a danger to self or others? If so, is the danger serious or imminent? Any current legal trouble? Any other red-flag issues that demand immediate attention? Does the client need to be referred to a lawyer?

I — *Interpersonal relationships:* Describe current issues and history with family and friends—rich web or deficient? Who is the best and the worst family member? best and worst friend? What are the best and worst traits in father and mother? Describe spousal relations, satisfying and dissatisfying. Describe sexual behavior and problems.

K — *Knowledge:* Does the client have sufficient knowledge or skill to change? Assess skill strengths and deficits. Note formal education and what, if anything, the client does to improve knowledge. Consider resources for further learning, formal and informal.

E — *Environment:* What are the external obstacles and reaction triggers? What strengths and resources are available to the client? What is the client's locus of control? Does the client perceive him- or herself to be controlled by events or free to influence events?

BOX 12.3—THE CHRISTIAN GLOBAL ASSESSMENT SYSTEM (C-GAS)

The following global assessment matrix frames the entire clinical process in a single page. It is a heuristic device that focuses on key issues and actions that lead to constructive change. It is useful for the practicing counselor, for the client's self-knowledge, and for supervisors and colleagues consulting with helpers.

	Problem	*Goal*	*Intervention*	*Evaluation*
B – Behavior				
E – Emotions				
C – Cognition				
H – Health				
R – Religion				
I – Idols				
S – Substances				
T – Teachability				
L – Law/ethics				
I – Interpersonal				
K – Knowledge				
E – Environment				

CHAPTER 13

CLINICAL DIAGNOSIS AND TREATMENT PLANNING

Uses and Limits of the DSM System

MIRIAM STARK PARENT AND TIM CLINTON

A unique contribution a theistic strategy makes to a multi-dimensional approach is that it provides therapists with a rationale and approach for assessing and conceptualizing the religious and spiritual dimensions of their client's lives.

—RICHARDS AND BERGIN,

A Spiritual Strategy for Counseling and Psychotherapy

Although the story of Daniel in the lions' den is familiar to us, we don't often contemplate its application to our professional lives. Yet that is precisely the focus of the story. Daniel 6:4 reveals the crux of the matter: "The administrators...tried to find grounds for charges against Daniel in his conduct of government affairs, but they were unable to do so."

He stood out because he was trustworthy, honest, and upright in a time and place that expected bribery and corruption. It was not only Daniel's personal or spiritual life that made him noteworthy. The manner in which he conducted his professional life also revealed the integrity of his character.

Could the same be said of our professional practice as Christian counselors and therapists? If administrators or officials came looking for something to hold against us, would they be confounded by the integrity of our professional work? Would they be forced to look at our personal faith practices in order to find anything against us? What a testimony that would be! Sadly, that is not always the case. Too often we hear of counselors legally sanctioned for inept care, sexual misconduct, inadequate recordkeeping, or insurance fraud.

Years ago, in not-for-profit Christian counseling settings, lack of professional structure was a simple fact of life. Casenotes were sketchy, diagnoses were nonexistent, and treatment planning was often limited to intense prayer prior to counseling sessions. Even in professional clinical practice, new professionals waited for someone to offer a practical plan for gathering, organizing, and using all the information clients seemed to spill forth. Eventually someone did devise a plan, but by that time most therapists had already adjusted to the trial-and-error pragmatism that was often typical in the mental health field. Such a process, however, lacks the essential core value of integrity.

Today, we practice in a changed and changing environment. The socialservice model that developed after World War II and flowered in the '50s and '60s has been replaced by a far more professional business model. While we may not like it—particularly as we see it being defined by the insurance industry—the truth is that it's not all bad. Responsibilities, both in ministry and professional counseling, have changed significantly. Today's expanding use of services, greater consumer awareness, increasing litigation issues, professionalization of practice, and the growing severity of client problems all demand a greater degree of competence and quality in our counseling work.

In the past, much of Christian counseling has been legitimately criticized as being unprofessional and unbusinesslike. For many counselors, the fear of being seen as secular and mercenary by the church made it difficult to combine professionalism and good business practice with the call to a people-helping ministry that brought us into this field. However, there is nothing spiritual about sloppy work. The ambiguity involved in helping individuals in a spiritual context is not a valid excuse for not articulating the counseling process or meeting appropriate professional standards.

This chapter addresses and outlines those standards, especially for professional Christian counselors and specialized pastoral psychotherapists working in professional environments. Though many chapters in this book address assessment, this is the only chapter that discusses how to build on assessment to form an accurate clinical diagnosis and then construct a competent treatment plan, which are baseline clinical tasks for all professional clinicians.

The fact is, astute treatment planning is essential for providing quality care. "For all practical purposes, treatment planning is in fact the ultimate avenue to quality assurance" (Woody, 1991, p. 20). Most practitioners find treatment planning the most tedious and difficult part of the counseling process. For someone geared to helping people and ameliorating pain, taking time for paperwork and planning is often seen as wasteful, not to mention costly.

Even in pastoral or church-related counseling, it is good practice these days to keep appropriate counseling records. Professional structure and planning allow for greater accountability in ministry and an appropriate flexibility in meeting a parishioner's need. Rigid structures may protect a reputation, but they also limit ministry effectiveness and the expression of biblical compassion. Lack of structure may facilitate relationships, but it may also foster inappropriate vulnerability and loss of ministry integrity and opportunities.

Any structure must be adapted to the setting and the individual, but having a framework to start from can be helpful. Such a framework ought to include the components covered in this chapter (see also Stark, 1997).

PART ONE: DEFINING AND DIAGNOSING THE PROBLEM

> Do not judge, or you too will be judged. For in the same way you judge others, you will be judged, and with the measure you use, it will be measured to you. (Matthew 7:1-2)

Making judgments about people is a fearful and humbling task that should not be taken lightly. Every day we make informal judgments about the people we meet. Formal assessment, as the previous chapter showed, requires even more painstaking attention to the issues. Biblical integrity demands that we make those judgments with as much compassion and understanding as we can bring to the situation. While lack of diagnostic training, professional turf disputes, or theoretical bias may tempt us to bypass diagnostic assessment, we no longer have that luxury. Even pastors who counsel are increasingly called upon to articulate and define the specific issues of concern they are facing in counseling.

In the mental health arena, psychiatry and clinical psychology have long owned the diagnosis of mental disorders as part of their professional heritage. Many social workers and counselors, on the other hand, have historically steered clear of the medical-model diagnosis, using instead a systemic or developmental orientation while maintaining a professional skepticism concerning diagnostic practice (Hohenshil, 1996).

In recent years, licensure, legal liability, insurance companies, and third-party reimbursement have changed the diagnostic picture and forced licensed professionals to learn individual diagnosis in therapy and counseling. The ethical codes of both the American Psychological Association (APoA) and the American Counseling Association (ACA) state the clear need for proper diagnosis: "Counselors take special care to provide proper diagnosis of mental disorders" (ACA, 1995).

A strong case can be made that every counselor diagnoses, either formally or informally, by making judgments about the nature of the problem, the possibilities for effective intervention, the client's motivation, and other crucial issues. It is not *whether* we do it, but *how* we do it, that becomes the critical concern. Good diagnostic assessment is the cornerstone of individualized treatment planning in mental health. Without good assessment, treatment plans may be ill conceived, often resulting in a week-to-week crisis modality (Woody, 1991).

It is a challenge to be a good diagnostician. It requires understanding, knowledge, and, more than anything, wisdom and discernment. Whether we use clinical terminology or pastoral judgment, it is crucial that we clearly and concisely determine the concerns of our counselees. The process of diagnosis, treatment planning, and treatment evaluation is outlined in the remainder of this chapter, which highlights twelve principles of competent clinical practice: five diagnostic principles (DxPs), four treatment principles (TxPs), and three treatment evaluation principles (TEPs).

DxP 1: A formal diagnosis is a necessary but not a sufficient condition of accurate mental health assessment. For licensed professionals, this involves arriving at an accurate DSM diagnosis. Diagnostic assessment is not the same as diagnostic labeling.

Making a valid diagnosis is a necessary and essential part of modern mental health assessment and planning. And we will emphasize again that *how you see the issues shapes what you do to treat them.* Hinkle (1994) stated, "At the foundation of effective mental health care is the establishment of a valid psychodiagnosis" (see Seligman, 1996, p. 55). Without the establishment of reasonably precise areas of concern or potential growth, counseling can proceed no further than an ambiguous, feel-good relationship that can lead to an inappropriate self-focus.

As we consider the problems that people face, the need for a common language and approach to defining symptoms becomes evident. DSM-IV (1994) represents an ongoing attempt by the mental health professions to systematize and clarify diagnostic categories and criteria. DSM-IV criteria provide a common set of symptoms and behaviors, which serves to facilitate professional communication, provide common ground for research, and allow for consensual diagnosis (Clarkin & Kendall, 1992). One major benefit to the practitioner is in providing a consistent framework that provides insight into the typical symptoms, the course of a disorder, and the language to use when making a referral or consulting across disciplines. "Although the DSM-IV does not provide information on treatment...

this manual is the stepping stone to determining effective treatment strategies" (Seligman, 1996, p. 59).

However, any system of diagnostic classification is, by definition, both arbitrary and limited. DSM-IV diagnoses are arbitrarily limited to addressing individuals rather than addressing family or social systems. They are also limited to observable behavior, focusing on the *what, when,* and *where* rather than the *why.* Any classification system is also limited by its determination and definition of health and illness, as well as by the specific criteria chosen for observation. Therefore, societal and cultural definitions play heavily in the underlying assumptions (Sue & Sue, 1999).

With increasing consumer awareness, psychological terminology and categories are being used by the general population, often with disastrous or confusing results. There are understandable concerns about diagnostic labeling. The possible pejorative effects of misused diagnostic labels have ranged from self-fulfilling prophecy to social and political discrimination. Christians have legitimately been concerned about the application of a disease or medical model to address problems that might be better addressed spiritually (or from the standpoint of moral responsibility and sin). Likewise, our increasing understanding of the interaction of biological and psychological components in many problems has raised new concerns and has multiplied our potential interventions.

If we view diagnosis primarily as the classification of symptoms and personality patterns, resulting in the labeling of emotional disorders, we limit the therapeutic opportunities available to the client. Such a process of diagnosis can be dehumanizing and reductionistic. The process can, however, be approached in a comprehensive way that enables counselors to develop a good understanding of their client, to formulate a valid diagnosis, and to devise a thorough treatment plan, while it also serves to enhance the counseling relationship (Seligman, 1996). Good diagnosis, therefore, requires far more than simply applying a diagnostic label.

Counselors and therapists with grave concerns about the categorical diagnosis of the DSM system have often been guilty of compassionate diagnosis. One clinical psychologist is quoted as saying, "I diagnosed everyone with 'adjustment reaction' because I didn't want to hurt them" (Wylie, 1995, p. 23). Such actions, although well meaning, can constitute insurance fraud. Not only do they damage the individual counselor's credibility and competence, but they also undermine the integrity of the mental health profession. As Christians, we know that dishonesty never honors God, but we may underestimate our own capacity for rationalization, particularly when it comes clothed in biblical compassion.

Inadequate assessment and sloppy diagnostics can also lead to a subtle erosion of professional competency. Sometimes poor diagnostics are the result of colorful professional fads and trends. Like most human beings, we have a strong tendency to see whatever it is we're looking for. It can be far more exciting and interesting to deal with the exotic rather than the mundane, and if we look hard enough, we may find some signs of such things in most people. Consequently, we may over-look simple answers in our desire to deal with the complex and intriguing. Personal prejudices and theoretical biases may also work against our objectivity and create a one-size-fits-all approach or a single-diagnosis practice where everyone comes out wearing the same label despite their unique concerns. Perhaps the largest reasons for poor assessment lie in more pragmatic areas.

Unfortunately, mental health diagnosis has all too frequently become a commercial issue, driven not by professionalism and competent planning, but by economics and client demand for insurance coverage. Despite biblical and professional ethics, managed care review, legal liability issues, and informed consent, some therapists still openly confess that they tend to put down diagnostic labels that they believe will be reimbursed.

An article in *The Family Therapy Networker* (now *Psychotherapy Networker*) highlights the issue by describing a client who questioned the code placed on an insurance form because she was uncomfortable with the definition of "dysthymia." In response, she was laughingly given a diagnostic manual and told to select a more appealing diagnosis. After leafing through it, she decided on "anxiety disorder, NOS" as she occasionally experiences some anxiety and, after all, the number is easier to remember (Wylie, 1995). If a nonspecific anxiety disorder can be successfully approached with the same understanding and interventions as dysthymia (chronic, mild depression), then perhaps oranges really are apples.

While the licensed counselor or therapist has to deal with the complexities of formal diagnosis involving the DSM-IV categories, the unlicensed or pastoral counselor is not bound by such concerns. Yet the overall issue of formally assessing and articulating the problem cannot be avoided. To adequately determine an appropriate counseling approach, the issues must be clearly stated in commonly understood language. For a pastor to simply say, "I'm going to do marriage counseling," with no awareness of the situation, is analogous to his saying, "I am going to preach a sermon," with no awareness of what the text, passage, or topic will be. It is astonishing that some ministry leaders who would not preach a sermon or teach a class without hours of preparation will broach people's most sensitive and intense issues with little more than casual reflection. Such an approach to shepherding

God's flock cannot ultimately please God, although his ever-abundant grace is often displayed.

DxP 2: Every assessment should be multidimensional across four spheres: physical, psychological, social, and spiritual. People's personalities, perceptions, aspirations, reactions, and responses to life circumstances are all unique and individual. While mental health problems may have a common element or even a common core, each person's experience with them remains uniquely his or her own. Every diagnostic assessment should involve the individual as a whole person rather than as a simple (or complex) collection of observable behaviors. Human beings are multidimensional and need to be assessed across physical, psychological, social, and spiritual concerns. While one concern may take precedence in any given situation, a holistic understanding of the individual is necessary to evaluate the impact and to consider possible resources.

Understanding the contexts in which individuals exist is critical to accurate assessment. One of the major challenges in the twenty-first century is to become

---

Box 13.1—Using the Multiaxial Diagnostic System of DSM-IV

Classification of mental disorders according to the five-stage multiaxial system began with DSM-III and continued through DSM-III-R, DSM-IV, and now DSM-IV-TR. This system is also consistent with the International Classification of Diseases (ICD) system, which has standardized medical and psychiatric diagnoses on a worldwide basis. The axes include

Axis I—Clinical Syndromes, including V Codes

Axis II—Personality and Development Disorders

Axis III—Medical or Physical Disorders and Conditions

Axis IV—Psychosocial Stressors and their Severity

Axis V—GAF Score: Global Assessment of Functioning

The heart of the DSM system, these five axes list the psychiatric disorders and their symptoms, which provide diagnostic clarity and are needed for treatment planning, research, and prediction of clinical outcomes. Most professional counselors use the DSM system in their ongoing clinical practices.

Axes I and II are used to describe the client's present condition. Sometimes multiple diagnoses are necessary as well as diagnoses on both axes. Axis I covers most of the DSM codes that list the clinical disorders and subdisorders (V codes)

multiculturally competent (Sue & Sue, 1999). Most counselors, whether in professional practice or in a ministry context, will need to develop an awareness of the cultural dynamics of their clientele. Few will work in monocultural settings. Social and especially familial relationships vary significantly in our culturally diverse society, and they profoundly affect the success of potential interventions. Multicultural awareness has increased significantly in the counseling field, often mandating curricular changes and facilitating training experience in diverse settings.

Generally, professional counselors have done well in assessing and referring for physical and medical concerns. When someone comes in with complaints of deepening depression, practitioners ought to be careful to ask about—and, if necessary, refer for—medical evaluation. Cognitive, emotional, relational, and other areas of functioning that fall broadly into the psychological and social dimensions are, of course, the counselor's forte.

However, when it comes to the spiritual dimension, counselors are far too

---

of the diagnostic system of psychiatry. Axis II covers the personality and developmental disorders—those problems that are more ingrained and enduring.

Axis III is designed to list physical and medical conditions and disorders. These may be either causative (the basis for Axis I disorders) or informative for treatment. Examples are hyperthyroidism, cancer, diabetes, kidney failure, liver cirrhosis, heart disease, chronic back pain, and so on. Only medical doctors are qualified to diagnose Axis III disorders; however, this information is helpful to counselors when deciding whether to refer a client, particularly if they suspect a client's problem may stem from a medical condition.

Axis IV involves the description of psychosocial stressors and their severity in adults and adolescents. Using clinical judgment, the counselor can make a determination as to the degree of stress present in the client's life, including global stressors, disability, and activity toward change. Examples are separation, divorce, loss of a loved one, bankruptcy, arrest, relocation, unemployment, rape, illness, surgery, and so on.

Axis V gives an estimate of the client's level of functioning at the time of evaluation and/or the highest level of functioning during the past year. The Global Assessment of Functioning (GAF) scale considers psychological, social, and physical functioning on a continuous scale from one (severe illness with near total debilitation) to ninety (excellent health).

often inclined to over- or underreact, and objective assessment is rare. Often Christian therapists feel exposed and vulnerable to charges of "imposing our values" if even the slightest mention of spirituality is raised. Historically, the counseling professions have challenged any discussion of spirituality. In recent years, however, the pendulum has swung in the opposite direction. Professional ethics in psychology now mandates respect for religion as part of the diversity of client beliefs and values (see Principle D and Standard 1.08 of the APoA *Code of Conduct,* 1995). Major ethics texts now cite numerous studies indicating that it is essential to understand and respect the client's religious beliefs and to include such beliefs in assessment and treatment practice (Corey, Corey, & Callanan, 1998). Today, including spiritual and religious dimensions as a regular part of the intake process is an ethical and essential component to considering the client's problems from a holistic perspective.

Many researchers (see Bergin, 1991; Worthington, 1986) agree that "spirituality is an important component of mental health, and its inclusion in psychotherapy renders the treatment process more effective.… Spiritual and religious values play a major part in human life and in an individual's search for meaning. Exploring these values with clients may help them find solutions to their struggles. Spiritual and religious values can be integrated with other therapeutic tools to enhance the therapy process" (Corey et al., 1998, p. 82). A well-rounded assessment involves taking an appropriate look at all the aspects of how an individual functions—especially the spiritual dimension—and making a diagnosis that considers the holistic perspective presented in this volume.

DxP 3: Proper assessment demands clear, accurate, and objective data to back up the intuitive hypotheses of a diagnosis. Most counselors tend to rely upon qualitative assessment, generally found in the clinical interview process. Sometimes simply listening long enough to hear what the client really wants to say, while not being misled by surface issues, is the hardest part of the diagnostic process. Counselees rarely present with neatly articulated and conceptualized concerns. Generally, they are looking for help in working through some measure of chaos and ambiguity. When what was foggy and overwhelming can be described and made clear, hopelessness is often replaced with hope and renewed motivation for change.

However, *quantitative* assessment, usually in the form of self-report inventories or standardized testing, is sometimes necessary to back up diagnostic hypotheses (Fong, 1995). Good diagnosis should never be based on a single piece of data, whether from standardized testing or diagnostic interview. While no test can or should determine a diagnosis, the right testing can provide additional objective data. Tests should be viewed as tools to add data to a developing picture rather than as prescriptive or determinant answers. One of the benefits of using a diagnostic classification system such as the DSM-IV is the valuable link that it provides to standardized testing.

The APoA *Code of Conduct* (1995) states, "Psychologists' assessments, recommendations, reports, and psychological diagnostic or evaluative statements are based on information and techniques (including personal interviews of the individual when appropriate) sufficient to provide appropriate substantiation for their findings" (Standard 2.01b). While assessment based on personal interview is often sufficient, in many other cases, additional assessment data is crucial to a complete picture.

The adequate assessment of risk and liability areas, such as suicide and violence, can also be facilitated by quantitative assessment. When qualitative assessment indicates potential for harm, it is wise to add objective data that may increase insight into the level of severity, allowing you to assess potential risk of lethality with greater precision. Using a simple self-report inventory (such as the Beck Hopelessness Scale) when suicidal ideation is present can contribute greatly to the assessment of risk. When screening for serious pathology, more objective data from standardized testing such as the MMPI or Millon inventories are helpful (Fong, 1995).

Of course, using such testing without adequate training and knowledge is both unwise and unethical. Professionals and ministry counselors who use various forms of quantitative assessment, whether in risk assessment or in areas such as premarital counseling, need to closely monitor their competence in general testing principles as well as their understanding of the specific test. While computer assessments can be helpful, they often provide only broad interpretations of an individual's data. Accurate determination of the usefulness of such interpretations depends largely on the counselor's good conceptual knowledge of the test being used. Testing provides data; it is the therapist and the client who ultimately provide the interpretation.

DxP 4: Your theory of intervention defines the diagnostic and treatment planning process and is also essential to understanding how you approach soul care. A clear theoretical orientation is necessary to give meaning to the diagnosis. As we asserted in chapter 7, everyone has a theory of therapy or counseling. Theories are based on worldview—each with its own values, biases, and assumptions of how best to bring about change in the therapeutic process (Collins, 1993). The goals emphasized in therapy, the techniques and methods used, the division of responsibility, and various other issues all reflect one's counseling theory. As Corey, Corey, and Callanan (1998) say, "Practicing [counseling] without an explicit theoretical rationale is somewhat like flying a plane without a map and without instruments" (p. 197).

A clear understanding of your theoretical foundations and assumptions is a necessary prerequisite to articulating your approach to counseling. Often we hear that the only important factor in providing professional soul care is the personal life of the counselor or therapist. While a clear personal commitment to Christ is essential, it is not enough to provide quality soul care. As our relationship to the Christ of Scripture grows, it is important that we also grow in our understanding of the assumptions, biases, and presuppositions upon which our healing work is based and how those apply to the various situations we confront in counseling. Knowledge and experience must walk hand in hand if we are to provide a wise foundation for the competent practice of Christian counseling.

As both a primary fact of the mental health field and a major premise of this book, the days of rigid adherence to one school of therapy or one theorist's approach to counseling have passed. Most of us would like to say we are theoretically eclectic—meaning that we carefully draw compatible pieces from various approaches and form them into a coherent whole, which becomes our unique model of personality, change, health, and dysfunction. While counselors at all levels often list themselves as eclectic on surveys, the truth is that few of us are responsibly eclectic (Jones & Butman, 1991). Karoly (1993) asserts,

> Unfortunately, the vaunted union of physical, psychological, interpersonal, and environmental attributes suggested by advocates of eclecticism and multimodal assessment is not always readily achieved. In many quarters, the only tangible result of so-called systems thinking is the implicit endorsement of a "more is better" philosophy of data collection and treatment planning. (p. 273)

For many of us, pragmatism—doing whatever seems to work—rules the day. The problem with neglecting the use of a coherent theory in favor of pragmatism is that it is analogous to traveling from Nashville to Chicago simply by using a compass and heading north. Eventually you might get there, but you could also miss it entirely and end up in Lake Michigan! Good clinical theory serves as our road map, helping us identify the various possible routes available. Sometimes the journey calls for a scenic route that inspires learning. Other times the need for speed mandates a direct, shortest-distance route. Without theory, both client and counselor may end up wandering in the right direction but uncertain of both destination and process.

Technical eclecticism is a vital attribute in arriving at an accurate diagnosis. While each of the major schools of therapy is primarily associated with certain techniques, most are not rigidly exclusive. Counseling interventions and techniques serve as tools. An electrician may certainly use a hammer, but it is generally associated with carpentry.

Technical eclecticism differs from theoretical eclecticism. For example, a psychodynamic therapist may still be able to assist a client demanding simple symptom relief, although the prognosis and conceptualization may differ dramatically from a pure behaviorist's assessment. Good clinicians, much like a good handyman, are familiar with a variety of tools, but they are more adept at the use of some than others. A well-constructed theoretical orientation, then,

- gives meaning to symptoms,
- provides a way to conceptualize the presenting issues,
- provides a forum within which to find the elements of change,
- helps to determine interventions and strategies but allows for flexibility.

DxP 5: Making an accurate DSM diagnosis follows well-practiced principles that evaluate and organize assessment data in systematic and hierarchical ways. The information derived from the assessment phase of counseling is the raw data from which a diagnostic impression must be fashioned by the professional clinician. With this data, the clinician must continually search for clusters and groupings of behavior that suggest tentative diagnoses on Axis I (all DSM codes except personality disorders) and Axis II (personality disorders) of the five-stage multiaxial system. Medical diagnoses and the less likely disorders must be ruled out by medical personnel.

In sorting through and arriving at a diagnosis, the following seven rule-out-and-priority principles have been well tested by clinical experience and research (Morrison, 1995).

1. Client history is better than cross-sectional data. The longitudinal data of a client's history with a disorder is more reliable than merely viewing it at a particular point in time. A client who presents complaining of depression and proceeds to tick off the classic symptoms could easily mask a history of substance abuse or a grief reaction, which tells you very little to help differentiate between major depression, dysthymia (milder depression), or a manic-depressive illness.

2. Recent history is better than ancient history. Change is ongoing, and the data from one's long-ago past is less valid (more likely to have changed over time) than more current data.

3. Information from others may confirm or disconfirm information from the client. Clients often present themselves as better or worse than they actually are (and they do so in both intentional and unintentional ways). So information gathered from spouses, family, friends, and others often helps construct a more accurate picture of the issues and dynamics

involved. The key caution here is that collateral information is system-biased, just like information from your client, so information from multiple sources is better than from just one other source.

4. Observable signs are better than reported symptoms. Your clinical observations are generally more reliable than reported symptoms, which are influenced by client perceptual distortions and value biases. (Following the logic of the point above, what you see is only filtered through one set of biases—your own—instead of two.)

5. Objective assessments are better than subjective judgments. Similar to the above principle (and owing to the added value of doing standardized testing for a fuller database), this principle challenges reference to DSM criteria and objective data rather than relying exclusively on intuitive hunches and diagnostic impressions, no matter how good one may be at them.

6. Be cautious about extrapolating personality and behavior from crisis-generated data. Such data usually says more about a person's response to

BOX 13.2—CASE VIGNETTE

Henry is a forty-six-year-old married man who just relocated with his family to a new state. His wife has brought him to you for therapy and tells you about their recent dotcom business bankruptcy, their move to take a new job, and Henry's "depression." He has been sleeping and watching television excessively, has been complaining of chest pains, is lethargic and unmotivated, and has been avoiding people. However, over the last couple of weeks he has slept less and less, seems full of energy, and talks incessantly. The last couple of days he's been talking about taking what little family savings are left and investing it in a "can't-miss scheme." This is how they got started in their business venture that failed, so the wife pressured her husband to come see you.

Henry talks rapidly and jumps from subject to subject. He is testy and suspicious, and he tells you he is seeing you "just to humor my wife" and "get her off my back." He says he was "kind of depressed" and gets that way from time to time, but now he "feels better than he has in years." He denies any drug use or suicidal thoughts, though he admits to a history of alcohol and marijuana use in his late teens and early twenties. He's convinced he now knows what led to his previous business failure and tries to convince you that he can't fail this time. He even asks if you want to invest now before his stock goes wild. Family history is crisis than it does about how he or she thinks and acts during normal circumstances. Keep this information conformed to the crisis event rather than projecting it to create and assert a clinical profile of the client.

7. Honor these rule-outs of the clinical diagnostic-treatment hierarchy. A diagnostic-treatment hierarchy helps direct further and more complex diagnostic work if it is needed. A hierarchy also helps you determine what issues should be treated first. It is an essential bridge in the case formulation process because it helps to focus your diagnostic effort and prioritizes your treatment decision making. The simplest diagnostic-treatment hierarchy contains five basic rules:

   a. The *cognitive-disorder rule* trumps all other diagnoses of the same symptoms. This is due to the sometimes life-or-death reality of certain cognitive disorders. Hallucinating patients may be psychotic or abusing drugs, or they may have a brain tumor (or head trauma,

positive for depression, and his mother has been treated for bipolar disorder for many years.

DISCUSSION

Although depression exists in the family and is reported by both husband and wife, the collection of symptoms doesn't point to a primary depressive diagnosis. Henry presents in a manic episode and shows the overall symptoms of a bipolar disorder with some delusional features. He may have been in the manic phase when he launched his prior business venture. His mother was diagnosed bipolar—a disease with a strong genetic link. There is a question of a possible organic or medical problem, which should be ruled out as a factor in the disorder.

DIAGNOSIS

Axis I: Bipolar disorder, manic phase, moderate severity, possibly recurrent, with some mood congruent psychotic features, code 296.4x

Axis II: Diagnosis deferred, code 799.90

Axis III: Rule out medical problems with appropriate medical personnel

Axis IV: Occupational and financial stressors, moderate

Axis V: GAF: 55 currently, 60–70 over the past year

exposure to toxins, rapidly progressing dementia, or a dozen other diseases) that must be treated immediately. A neurological or neuropsychological exam should always follow the appearance of substantive cognitive disorders in order to rule out more serious medical illness.

b. The *parsimony rule* dictates that the simplest diagnosis is the best one. A close corollary rule is that fewer diagnoses are better than many. If your patient is abusing drugs and complains of depression, anxiety, and paranoid feelings (seeing cops on every corner), see if these mood and perceptual problems fade away once he or she sobers up before you choose to treat all four symptoms.

c. The *chronology rule* places priority on the disorder that has been present the longest. The logic of this rule is that the longer the disorder, the more likely it is a primary (and not secondary—not a function of some other) disorder. A long history of depression suggests that prioritizing and treating depression is the wiser choice as it is unlikely to be a function of some other problem.

d. The *crisis rule* gives priority to resolving crisis issues first. The nature of crisis is such that it consumes nearly all the time, attention, and energy of the people embroiled in it. Some crises are also life-threatening and demand attention. Therefore, helping to resolve the crisis and stabilizing the client's life is a priority in diagnosis and treatment.

e. If nothing else rises in the hierarchy, honor the *safety or outcomes rule*. All the psychiatric disorders can be placed within a rough safety or outcomes hierarchy. To generate success and motivation to tackle the more difficult problems in a client's life, the rule suggests that treating the safest problem first—the one with the best prognosis—is the wisest choice.

PART TWO: DEVELOPING A TREATMENT PLAN

To man belong the plans of the heart, but from the LORD comes the reply of the tongue. (Proverbs 16:1)

Solid diagnostic assessment makes managing even the most difficult case easier. Without it we are left wandering, as if we were trying to help someone get to Chicago without any idea of his starting location. Once we know where we are starting from, we are able to move ahead and deal with the more concrete, practical management issues involved in planning interventions and outcomes. If we have done our homework, we can confidently expect the Lord to guide our participation in the ebb and flow of the counseling relationship.

Planning is never a static process. A good plan is always changing, developing, and maturing. Even as diagnostic assessment continues throughout the process of counseling, so plans must continually be reevaluated in light of new or changed data and outcomes (Karoly, 1993). It is a dynamic process, which should be reflected and updated constantly in the progress notes (Jongsma & Peterson, 1995).

TxP 1: Client and counselor matching is essential to excellence in therapy. Careful consideration of counselor/client variables is a necessary component of good treatment planning. Excellence in counseling demands high self-awareness (and accurate awareness of others if you are a supervisor) in order to match the right counselor with the right client. We must also remember that human beings do not arbitrarily relate well to every other human being and that counseling is, above all, a relational process. You need to know what issues and client problems you work well with and which ones you don't, as well as what kinds of people you work well with and what kinds you don't. Counselors working with abuse victims, for example, may not work well with perpetrators. In addition to licensure and practice domains, the explosion of data in the mental health field in the past few years has mandated a certain amount of specialization.

Also, client and counselor resources and responsibilities need to be evaluated to determine an appropriate match. Spiritual, psychological, financial, and other resources must be considered. For Christian counselors, the assessment of spiritual resources, both internal and external, may significantly change the direction of the treatment plan. In addition, practical commitments in terms of time and social and occupational responsibilities need to be factored into the counseling process. Potential conflicts in values need to be carefully considered, evaluated, and discussed if there is to be good rapport and understanding. Diversity issues involving gender and culture, among others, require awareness and critical evaluation of competency (Sue & Sue, 1999).

All of these components are often assessed up front, intuitively and internally, by experienced clinicians. However, occasionally even the most experienced clinician should actively and consciously assess what he or she is doing at this level of treatment planning. It is too easy and too costly to allow everyone to be pigeonholed into the same diagnostic categories or to begin to believe that we can truly do good work with every person and every problem. The mature counselor knows that sometimes the best plan is to make a referral before treatment begins.

TxP 2: Clear treatment goals, matched with achievable objectives, are a critical part of the strategic planning process. One of the most difficult areas in treatment planning has historically been the art of writing effective and appropriate goals and objectives. Clinicians have long shied away from being tied to specific, measurable outcomes. Goals were often verbally articulated, broadly defined, and arbitrarily changed. Measurable objectives were rarely found in casenotes, and therapy terminated when everyone had a vague sense of resolution. Third-party payers have changed the way we work in this area more than any other. They require objective, measurable goals and objectives written in a concise format.

In response, we have been inundated with books, treatment manuals, and computer programs that have the potential to ease this part of the treatment process. However, reliance on scripted objectives and interventions cannot substitute for understanding and being personally involved in the process. The right tools can wonderfully facilitate the use of the right terminology and can aid in writing, but the program is only as good as the user. Without the balance of an individualized treatment plan, any assistance tool will fall short in assessing human complexity and uniqueness. No diagnostic or treatment program will relieve the counselor of the necessity of understanding what is happening and the implications of it for the client. Likewise, no computer can relieve the need for professional and personal integrity.

Let's briefly consider goals and objectives. Treatment goals are stated in global terms, indicating the positive outcome desired, and they usually employ *increase* or *decrease/reduce* language. Clients want to increase feelings of satisfaction, or pro-social behaviors, and decrease anxiety, stuttering, and angry outbursts or reduce depressive symptoms. Consumer awareness and informed-consent issues have encouraged all mental health practitioners to develop mutually acceptable and understandable goals. Clients need to understand and believe in the potential outcomes if they are to adequately participate in the process (Seligman, 1996; and review goal setting in chapter 10).

Goal statements need to be *realistic* and *doable.* Many times either the counselor or the client wants more than can reasonably be accomplished in therapy, given time and the personal constraints of the client. Who hasn't met the parent who wants the clinician to transform their difficult teenager into a perfect young adult overnight?

Regarding objectives, Jongsma and Peterson (1995) state, "In contrast to long-term goals, *objectives* must be stated in behaviorally measurable language. It must be clear when the client has achieved the established objectives" (p. 5). Objectives represent the step-wise *progression* toward a particular goal. They need to be *achievable*—small enough to be accomplished and set up for success. Target dates need to be built into the objectives along with some measure of *accountability.*

The most difficult thing for some clinicians is that objectives must also be *concrete* rather than abstract. A simple way to operationally define a goal is to add the words "as evidenced by" in order to create appropriate objectives. Objectives must also be *measurable,* which usually means specifying conditions and timing, as well as prioritization. Objectives focus on specific thinking, emotions, or actions. They represent the link to interventions and are reflected in the progress notes in light of the stated goals.

While an appropriate goal for a suicidal client might be to decrease depression and increase hope, objectives would need to state clearly and measurably how this will be accomplished. A decrease in depression might require an increase in physical self-care and grooming. An increase in hope might be measurably stated as being able to visualize oneself taking part in specific future pleasurable activities.

TxP 3: Change strategies and techniques need to be tied to clear treatment objectives and dictated by issues of competency and informed consent. Competent counselors are able to be creative and eclectic in their choice of strategies and interventions for change. Technical eclecticism, as we asserted earlier, is a necessary fact of clinical life these days. It may have been possible to build a log cabin with just an ax once upon a time, but today's builder must be able to call upon a significantly larger toolbox. As Thorpe (1987) states, "There are no easy answers to the question of which treatment is best for which patient. As a result therapists have turned toward eclecticism and model-building.... These models can serve as guidelines for any form of therapy, since they transcend particular schools of theory and technique" (p. 729).

Movement toward theoretically oriented goals may be accomplished through a diversity of technical interventions and objectives, often limited only by the counselor's creativity. While some techniques may not fit a particular theoretical orientation, most can be adapted appropriately. Understanding and being able to articulate the connection is a necessity of competent counseling. In addition, a Christian counselor will build this sensitivity under the leading of the Holy Spirit and from an understanding and application of Scripture.

Each treatment objective should be tied to at least one intervention. Simple questions to ask are, "How will this client accomplish this objective?" and "What can be done to help this person accomplish the objective?" This is the most flexible part of the treatment plan. Some things will work; others won't. As counseling progresses, casenotes need to reflect modifications and variations along with the rationale for those changes.

Cognitive, affective, behavioral, relational, or other areas may be tapped in assisting particular clients with particular difficulties. For one client, a decrease in depression might be evidenced by a greater understanding of the grace of God, which might be facilitated through study and memorization of Scripture. For less cognitive clients, that might best be facilitated through specific interactions with the church as the body of Christ where they can experience that grace affectively and relationally.

Determining appropriate counseling strategies requires personal assessment of the client by the counselor. Assessment of *skill*, *training*, and *comfort level* with various techniques is essential. Aggressive, confrontational techniques may not be well suited to quieter, more relational personalities. For some Christian counselors, certain techniques are in opposition to core values or may raise theological questions. Lack of technical expertise may also dictate a referral or supervision. In addition, a Christian counselor must fully address client concerns about therapeutic interventions and not shuffle them away under the guise of expertise. Clinical research is increasingly showing which intervention techniques are most effective with various types of client problems (Seligman, 1990; see box 13.3). This issue must now be carefully considered as part of the developing treatment plan.

Appropriate intervention also includes making decisions regarding modality, intensity level, setting, duration, and frequency as well as adjunct resources and referrals (Stark, 1997). Some therapeutic modalities work better for certain problems. Family, group, or individual modalities of counseling need to be considered in light of the client's best interests rather than based solely on what the therapist offers. Different situations also require differing levels of intensity in counseling. Some clients are insightful and need only minimal levels of support to be able to take effective action. Others, particularly in the confusing fog of traumatic crisis, may need far more directive intervention.

While the setting may already have been dictated when the client comes in, the therapist must also keep in mind that treatment plans are ongoing formulations. A depressed but stable client may become overwhelmed by additional crises and need to be hospitalized for self-protection. *Duration* and *frequency* of counseling may also require renegotiation at various stages of the treatment plan. Appropriate limits on the time and frequency of meeting need to be set and then reevaluated when objectives are reached or when difficulties arise.

TxP 4: Counselors must be aware of the resources available in their communities and be willing to make appropriate referrals, when necessary, as part of the treatment plan. Taking a holistic approach in counseling requires working with a team orientation, even if a counselor is in solo practice. This includes knowing and evaluating the resources available within the professional and spiritual community. The use of referral sources is often difficult for counselors, as there may be legitimate concerns about expertise, orientation, and faith issues. The decision whom to refer a client to may be influenced by the need for specialty work, technical competency issues, medical concerns, or ethical or boundary issues, among others. Working with other professionals, including clergy, often necessitates getting an appropriate release of information from the client. This information can greatly facilitate communication and provide a common ground for the client's specialty work.

Interventions may also necessitate the use of *adjunct* services. Recovery groups, church-based support or fellowship groups, hospital programs, and community and social services all need to be part of the competent counselor's repertoire. Biblical stewardship requires us to make wise use of the client's resources as well as our own. This is particularly true as termination approaches. While some goals and

---

BOX 13.3—EMPIRICALLY SUPPORTED TREATMENTS THAT ARE BRIEF AND COGNITIVE-BEHAVIORAL

Consider the list of preferred—that is, empirically supported—treatments promoted and recommended by the American Psychological Association (Tan, 1995) as important tools in modern Christian counseling practice. Nearly all of these practices are both brief and cognitive-behavioral in nature. They are therefore easily assimilated into the brief intervention phase of a Paracentric focus. The recommended treatments include the following:

- behavior therapy for headaches and irritable bowel syndrome
- behavior therapy for male and female sexual dysfunction
- behavior modification and token economies for developmentally disabled individuals and other programmatic applications
- behavior modification for enuresis and encopresis
- cognitive-behavioral marital therapy
- cognitive-behavioral therapy for chronic pain
- cognitive-behavioral therapy for generalized anxiety
- cognitive-behavioral therapy for panic disorder
- cognitive therapy for depression
- exposure therapy or systematic desensitization (both forms of behavior therapy) for phobias
- exposure therapy for post-traumatic stress
- exposure therapy/response prevention for obsessive-compulsive disorder
- cognitive-behavioral group therapy for social phobia
- parent training (mostly behavioral) programs for oppositional children

objectives may have been reached, others may still be valid but no longer require specific counseling intervention. Knowing what is available in the client's larger world and making appropriate use of those resources may serve to continue the client's progress toward his or her goals.

PART THREE: TREATMENT EVALUATION AND TERMINATION

It is difficult to genuinely evaluate what transpires in the life of a human being who has worked with and been in relationship with another human being. Difficult or not, it needs to be done. If integrity demands that counselors provide the best possible care, then we must constantly evaluate that care against the standards of our field and biblical principles.

TEP 1: Evaluation of treatment outcome and the effectiveness of the counseling process is an essential part of the entire client record. Both client and counselor need to know what will constitute success and what an effective outcome will look like. While that picture may change during counseling, it is essential that it be articulated as it develops. A treatment plan with no point of outcome leaves one floating in a vacuum, uncertain what to expect. If goals are well stated, then knowing when they are accomplished follows naturally and is understood by both counselor and client. This assessment may lead to renegotiating the counseling process and the formulation of other goals and objectives, or it can move naturally to an effective termination of services. Such a process challenges and encourages all involved.

Increasingly, formal outcome measures must be applied and recorded as part of the treatment plan. Major insurance reporting standards have recommended for a number of years that treatment plans be updated every six sessions in order to accurately evaluate progress. The Joint Commission on Accreditation of Health Organizations (JCAHO) standards now requires that outcome measures be included in mental health records (Jongsma & Peterson, 1995).

Whatever formal or informal outcome assessment is used will depend largely on the type and nature of practice. Books and articles are beginning to proliferate as the profession addresses various options. As Woody (1991) states, "There is no way for the contemporary therapist to avoid accountability, measured in part by the outcome of treatment" (p. 74). Utilization review boards, peer supervision, and other modalities are becoming the norm as we enter a new age of accountability based on outcome. When the diagnostic and treatment planning process is clear and well documented, outcome assessment demands can be more easily satisfied.

TEP 2: Providing appropriate termination and follow-up planning brings closure to the process and facilitates redefining counseling issues and roles. Ending a counseling relationship is often the most difficult part of the counseling process. The art of ending a relationship well is not one that many of us have mastered. Many counseling terminations are unplanned and premature. Clients "fire" their therapists or fail to return for many reasons, ranging from economic concerns to lack of therapeutic readiness to unresolved therapist-client conflicts. Occasionally, clients may even be "fired" for appropriate reasons, such as threatening violence against or sexually harassing a therapist. Sometimes they are simply referred to someone better able to facilitate the next step toward growth.

Both the rationale and the procedures for successful termination of the therapeutic relationship should be part of the treatment plan. "Regardless of the therapist's theoretical orientation, clients have a right to expect that their therapy will end when they have realized the maximum benefits from it or have obtained what they were seeking when they entered it. The issue of termination needs to be openly explored by the therapist and the client, and the decision to terminate ultimately should rest with the client" (Corey et al., 1998, p. 121).

Ending counseling should include a follow-up policy specifying continuing contacts or procedures for making further contacts. With the increasing need today to manage multiple role relationships, it is essential that counselors wisely and clearly define the new relational boundaries. Care must be taken to leave openings for future counseling, to define or reestablish noncounseling roles and expectations, and not to undermine the work done. While in some situations this will require minimum effort, in others it will be complex and critical if client gains made in counseling are to be maintained.

Human beings require closure. While we may not always get it, we work better when we have it. Counseling closures will be as individualized as the client. Some clients require an incremental closure that follows a longer, more intense relationship; others require little outward closure, content that they have accomplished their goals and objectives. Mutually agreeing to the way to end counseling leaves both counselor and client more satisfied and helps the client better maintain the gains made in counseling when it is over.

As part of the complete client record, then, write a closing summary that addresses the successes and failure of treatment and the follow-up recommendations.

TEP 3: Self-evaluation is essential to continued growth as a counselor and as a human being. As a part of the process, termination of a counseling relationship should also provide time for self-evaluation by the counselor. If we are to continue learning and growing, we need to do significant self-assessment. For some counselors, saying good-bye over and over again after deeply investing in a counseling relationship may lead to depersonalization, a key component in professional burnout. "Compassion fatigue" is a reality that must be assessed. Counselors who work with emotionally draining clients may need to process their sessions with a supervisor, colleague, or consultant. Difficult issues raised in counseling may necessitate further study or continuing education.

Maintaining one's emotional balance and a healthy distance in counseling relationships are essential to continuing health and productive practice for every counselor. Self-evaluation on a continual basis is part of good professional practice. Even as we provide good closure for our clients, we must take responsibility to do so for ourselves.

BEING GOOD STEWARDS

The man [or woman] of integrity walks securely. (Proverbs 10:9)

Competent Christian counseling requires enough structure to balance the often ambiguous nature of the healing work to which we aspire. Too rigid a format will stifle both creativity and the counseling relationship. Too little and we may find ourselves wandering randomly through another human being's soul, acting as psychological and spiritual voyeurs.

As we strive for integrity in our professional lives (and in our personal lives), it is important that we choose to be proactive in meeting and exceeding the world's standards for counseling care. As competent Christian counselors, we must be good stewards of the ministry opportunities God has given us. If we are to competently meet the responsibilities placed before us, we must use our resources well. Careful planning and thoughtful practice should be our hallmarks.

This chapter has attempted to provide a simple and practical framework for working through some of the issues involved in counseling diagnosis and treatment planning. With a bit of practice, planning, and perseverance, most of the time-consuming paperwork can be avoided. With a bit of creativity, the important elements can be developed into a simple form that can be adapted to each unique counseling practice. The hard part, of course, is getting started.

CHAPTER 14

CHANGE BY SOLUTION-BASED BRIEF THERAPY

Basic Principles and Beginning Treatment

GARY J. OLIVER AND JOHN CARMACK

Only true Christian ministry can put grace in the heart so that lives are changed and problems are really solved. The best thing we can do for people is not to solve their problems for them but so relate them to God's grace that they will be enabled to solve their problems and not repeat them. People may not cause their own problems, but if they relate to their problems the wrong way, they will make the problems worse. What life does to us depends on what life finds in us, and that is where the grace of God comes in.

—WARREN WIERSBE, *On Being a Servant of God*

I n the last decade, a revolution in mental health care has accelerated the popularity and growth of brief approaches to therapy. Brief therapy is demanded by managed care and preferred by an increasing number of clients. Whether by design or default, brief treatments are becoming the norm of counseling practice. Though some material on this subject was presented in previous chapters, here it is applied to *solution-based brief therapy*.

Research indicates that the mean number of sessions attended by clients is between five and six (De Shazer, 1991; Garfield, 1986; Hampson & Beavers, 1996). Research on treatment outcome consistently shows that short-term treatment is as effective as long-term therapy (Hampson & Beavers, 1996; Howard, Kopta, Krause, & Orlinsky, 1986; Koss & Butcher, 1986). A twelve-year study

---

We gratefully acknowledge the contribution of Melissa Peck to the literature review in this chapter.

published by the Menninger Clinic showed that clients receiving brief therapy profited as much from that approach as those who received extensive, long-term, psychoanalytically oriented treatment (Garfield, 1986).

Traditional approaches to psychotherapy assume that the presenting problem is not the *real* issue but is a symptom of deeper psychological problems that must be uncovered, interpreted, and treated. Therapy takes a lot of time and must be intensive, reconstructive, and problem-focused. In some cases, long-term therapy might be indicated for treating problems such as sexual and physical abuse (Hampson & Beavers, 1996), health-related illnesses, and panic disorders (DeJong & Berg, 1998). But in fact, many traditional treatment modalities are applying brief therapy assumptions and principles to their framework (Donovan, 1999).

Brief therapy isn't the treatment of choice for everyone, but it can be a powerful and effective tool in one's therapeutic tool chest. In the following pages, we will highlight some of the distinctives of what we call solution-based brief therapy (SBBT). We will also share with you where we are in our process of understanding one of several effective ways God can use counselors to help people change. Whether you are a pastoral counselor or a professional clinician, the SBBT approach can be helpful to you. Whether you would consider your primary therapeutic orientation to be analytic, object relations, family systems, nouthetic, or cognitive-behavioral, you will find SBBT useful.

We want to emphasize our belief that there is no *one* way to do counseling. There isn't one set of techniques or interventions that can be applied in every situation. Truth doesn't change, but the type of clients we see does. Their presenting problems, ethnicity, age, and backgrounds are diverse. These variables affect the ways in which the therapist can help clients apply truth to their unique and specific situations. This dimension of counseling is well illustrated in the life of Christ. Jesus would change his interactions and approach depending on the individual, whether a thirsty Samaritan woman, a paralytic by a pool, or a rich young ruler. There is a constant need for flexibility in clinical decision making. Counseling must be tailored to the individual.

Effective counseling is more than just a "truth dump." That approach could appropriately be called "Pharisee counseling." The Pharisees were the ultimate truth dumpers, yet they were unable to experience true spiritual change in their own lives, much less facilitate it in the lives of others. Jesus pointedly told the Pharisees, "You diligently search the Scriptures because you think that by them you possess eternal life. These are the Scriptures that testify about me, yet you refuse to come to me to have life" (John 5:39-40). Jesus gives life—he is the *living* Word.

Solution-Based Brief Therapy

Contrary to popular opinion, brief therapy isn't new. In the 1950s entire books were devoted to the topic of brief therapy. Today, the publication of numerous books and the growing attendance at workshops worldwide suggest that the most popular brief therapies are those that emphasize helping people find solutions. Even this is not a new idea. Solution-based approaches grew out of the brief and strategic therapy movements that gained prominence about twenty years ago. Much of the early work was pioneered at the Brief Therapy Center at the Mental Research Institute (MRI) in Palo Alto, California.

This approach was also influenced by Erickson, who emphasized the value of narrative—the stories people tell about themselves—in the change process. He believed the therapist could utilize the language, beliefs, resources, and sense of humor that clients brought to therapy to construct therapeutic tasks. Much of solution-focused therapy involves the application of Erickson's utilization principle.

Some of the most significant work was done by De Shazer (1991) and Berg (Berg & Miller, 1992) at the Brief Family Therapy Center in Milwaukee, Wisconsin. What they called solution-focused brief therapy has been expanded by others (O'Hanlon & Weiner-Davis, 1989; Quick, 1996; Walter & Peller, 1992; Walter & Peller, 2000). Sometimes called solution-focused, solution-centered, or solution-oriented therapy, this approach focuses on discovering solutions to problems rather than endlessly discussing them.

When therapists learn to look through the lens of solutions, problems become filled with new possibilities for change. There is encouragement, hope, and fresh motivation. The therapy process moves beyond mere insight, blame, and analysis to helping people discover that problems can be solved and that change can begin in the first session. This approach can be effective with individuals, marriages, and families dealing with a wide range of presenting problems.

The therapist stance is active, directive, and solution-focused. One of the therapist's main tasks is to help a client learn how to recognize times that the problem is not occurring. Central to a solution-based therapy is the hypothesis that no problem happens all of the time. There are always exceptions to the problem. This is then used as the basis for developing a more enduring change, which is found by helping clients capitalize on their existing strengths and resources. This emphasis enables and empowers clients to take responsibility for change and makes future changes more likely.

The basic principle appears simple: Increase what works and decrease what doesn't work. What are the exceptions to the problem? What are clients doing differently at those times when they aren't anxious or depressed? What has worked before? What strengths can clients apply? What would be a useful solution? How can we help achieve it?

SBBT: OUR FOUNDATION

In our practice, we try to make sure that our techniques are consistent with sound psychological principles. However, that's not the foundation on which our approach is based. We believe that sound psychology is at best limited, and at worst useless, unless it is based on sound theology. The key to effectively speaking God's truth into people's hearts and lives is an intimate knowledge of who he is, what he has revealed to us, and who he has designed us to become. Who we are in Christ precedes what we attempt to do for him.

Colossians 2:8 tells us not to allow philosophy and deception to take our thoughts captive. It's easy for Christian counselors to become so fascinated by or enamored of the theory and technique of different psychological schools of thought that we forget what is most important. While some aspects of psychology can provide helpful insights and tools for the counselor, what it means to be a whole person can only be understood within the context of a personal, life-changing relationship with Jesus Christ. Our vertical relationship with him defines, informs, and instructs our horizontal relationship with others.

We value science and psychological research and utilize those aspects that we find consistent with the Bible. But we believe that divine revelation in Scripture is more reliable, dependable, and authoritative than the discoveries and theories of science. We believe that the Bible is the sufficient and final authority for faith and clinical practice. While some approaches to brief therapy are superficial and offer little more than a Band-Aid approach, we have developed an approach to brief therapy that builds on a solid biblical anthropology and utilizes some of the insights of family-systems, cognitive-behavioral, and solution-focused brief therapy. Since it isn't a pure solution-focused model, we have chosen to refer to it as solution-based brief therapy.

KEY ASSUMPTIONS

We are not presenting solution-based brief therapy as the one and only way to help people grow, and we are not presenting an apologetic for brief therapy. We are saying that, at the very least, there is a way of beginning the counseling process that accelerates the change process and saves the client time, money, and, most important, unnecessary pain.

Before going into detail about the process of solution-based brief therapy, we must outline some key assumptions underlying this approach:

1. All people are created in the image of God and, as his image-bearers, have infinite value and worth.
2. All have sinned and fall short of the glory of God (Romans 3:23).
3. For God so loved the world that he gave his one and only Son, that whoever believes in him shall not perish but have eternal life (John 3:16).
4. The most effective treatment takes into account the whole person: body, soul, and spirit.
5. Different approaches can be helpful with different kinds of people struggling with different kinds of problems.
6. People have various strengths and resources to help them solve their problems.
7. Small changes are all that are necessary. Small changes lead to large changes. A change in one part of a system usually leads to a change in other parts of the system.
8. Problems are solved; people are not cured.
9. Change is inevitable, growth is optional.

Learning SBBT by Case Study

Let's take a look at how these assumptions might apply to an actual case. Jim and Carol had been married for seven years. Jim was a rising executive with an electronics firm, and Carol was a stay-at-home mother with two preschoolers. Jim and Carol were both active in a local evangelical church. Carol was the one who called to make the appointment to begin therapy. They'd had some counseling several years earlier, but Jim had decided it was a waste of time because the therapist didn't make many suggestions and never gave them anything specific to do.

Presession Distinctives

SBBT began before the first session. It started with a phone call to make the appointment. Even before the first session, Jim and Carol were challenged to consider their goals for counseling and what change will look like to them. Here is a sample of an initial phone conversation.

Carol: My husband and I need some help with our marriage.

Therapist: How are you hoping I might be able to be of help to you?

Carol: Well, we don't communicate very well, and we argue more than I like.

I've wanted to get some counseling for a long time, and Jim finally said he'd be willing to come.

Therapist: So Jim wants to come for counseling too.

Carol: Well, he doesn't really want to, but he is willing to.

Therapist: Carol, there are two things I'd like you and Jim to do before our first session. Doing these two things will help the counseling process be much more effective. First, ask yourselves what would have to happen for you to know that our work together has made a positive difference in your marriage. Another way of looking at it is to ask yourself when you will know that you no longer need counseling. Do you think you can do that?

Carol: Sure. What's the second thing?

Therapist: In the past several years, I've had many couples tell me that they experienced some small improvements between the time they made the phone call to arrange for therapy and their first session. Between now and our appointment, I'd like you and Jim to notice anything that happens in your relationship that is positive and pleasant. You may want to write it down and bring your notes with you.

FIRST-SESSION DISTINCTIVES

The first session is an essential part of successful SBBT. This is when clients discover that they will be the ones to determine if, how much, and when they change. In addition to the usual first-session tasks (such as establishing rapport), one of the therapist's primary tasks is to establish the termination criteria. Answering the question "What do you suppose needs to happen for you to no longer need counseling?" often contributes to the treatment plan.

When Jim and Carol came in for the first session, they were pleasant and appropriate, but they sat on opposite ends of the couch.

Therapist: When we talked on the phone, I asked you to think about what would need to happen for you to know that our work together was helpful. Jim, what did you come up with?

Jim: Well, one of the main things is that we wouldn't argue so much. Sometimes I come home from work, and as soon as I walk in the door, I feel attacked.

Carol [with a disgusted look and a sarcastic tone of voice]: If you'd come home when you say you will, maybe you wouldn't feel so attacked. I'm sick and tired of working hard to have dinner ready and then you waltz in at least a half-hour late.

Therapist: So, Carol, one way you would know that Jim is really committed to making your marriage work is by coming home when he says he will?

The Use of Questions

Another important aspect of the SBBT model is the use of questions. A distinctive component of Jesus' approach to helping people change involved questions. In fact, he asked questions to help people even though he knew the answers to their problems. In our approach, we strategically use questions to discover solutions. This process is both intentional and collaborative. We seek to find the appropriate question that will lead to solutions to the problem (intentional), and we elicit the clients' participation in the discovery (collaborative). This approach builds a degree of competency and responsibility necessary for change to occur.

The Use of Scaling Questions

According to this model, one of the most helpful tools applied to a variety of counseling concerns is the use of scaling questions.

The scaling question in assessing progress. Ask the couple to use a scale of 1 to 10, with 1 being when the problem is at its worst and 10 being when significant change has occurred. Then ask them, "Where on the scale are you now?" Their answer can be followed with a question such as, "What would need to happen for you to be 0.5 higher on your scale?" Scaling uses language to create a kind of visual image, a spatial component that provides a way to notice change while reinforcing the idea that no change is too small or insignificant. Even small steps can be measured by scaling their progress. This simple technique can confirm for the client, and inform the therapist, if change is occurring. This builds hope and encourages more positive change in the future.

The scaling question in assessing satisfaction. Another use of scaling questions is to assess satisfaction in the relationship:

Therapist: I'd like you to imagine a scale between one and ten. A one means that you are discouraged and dissatisfied and have little hope for your marriage. A ten means that most of the time you are pleased with your marriage. You enjoy high levels of satisfaction, good conflict resolution, and deep levels of love and affection. How would you rate your marriage?

Carol [responding immediately]: I'd give it about a three. I know that compared to some other couples, our marriage isn't horrible. I mean, Jim doesn't beat me or anything. But he always wants to go to Canada and fish for northern pike. When I compare our marriage to what it could be, to what God would have it to be, I'm discouraged. At times I think that if things don't change, it's not worth going on.

Jim [with a surprised voice]: I didn't have any idea you thought it was that bad. I was going to say a seven.

In the first session, we established that there is a tremendous difference between their perspective on the health of the relationship.

The scaling question in assessing commitment. Another valuable first-session task is to determine the commitment level of your clients. Some are visitors who are there only because someone has made them come. Others are complainants who are there because someone they know has a problem, and they are convinced that everything else will be fine if you can just fix that other person. Finally, there are some clients who are committed to making changes to improve the relationship. In our experience, when therapists get stuck in therapy, it may be because they have not adequately assessed the status of the client and they may be treating a visitor or complainant as if he or she were a customer. Consider the following example:

Therapist: I'd like you to imagine a scale between one and ten. A one means you have virtually no commitment to making your marriage work. A ten means that you would be willing to do almost anything to make your marriage the best it can be. How would you rate your level of commitment?

Jim: Carol may not believe this, but I'm at a ten. I know I've been slow in realizing how bad things are, but I am committed to making our marriage all that God wants it to be.

Carol: Well, in spite of how discouraged and frustrated I am, I would say that I'm at about an eight.

As the session continued, it became clear that, while they loved each other, Jim and Carol had become emotionally estranged. Three years earlier, Jim had been given a big promotion that involved extended travel. Carol had given up a successful sales career to be at home with their two children who were only nineteen months apart. Though Jim and Carol were committed Christians, they rarely read the Bible or prayed together. What's more, they rarely went on a date together. Toward the end of the session, they revealed that they hadn't enjoyed physical intimacy for over a year.

THE MIRACLE QUESTION

Probably the most talked about technique developed by De Shazer and Berg is the miracle question. It begins with asking the client to imagine a future in which the problem has been solved: "Suppose you were to go home tonight, and while you were asleep, a miracle happened, and the problem that brought you here was solved. How will you and those around you know the miracle happened? What will be different? What would you do differently? What would your spouse notice you were doing differently?" The miracle question not only gives the clients hope, it also helps the therapist determine how realistic their goals are and what change will look like.

> *Therapist:* I want to ask you both an unusual question. Suppose you go home tonight and you go to sleep. Sometime in the night a miracle happens, and the problems that brought you here are solved. You have changed and your partner has changed. Of course, you don't know a miracle has happened because you were asleep. When you wake up in the morning, what might be the first small thing that would tell you that a change had taken place?
>
> *Carol:* That's easy. Jim would touch me before we got out of bed. And then maybe he would smile.
>
> *Therapist:* So you're saying that if Jim touched you and smiled, that would let you know something had happened? If Jim did that, what might you do differently?
>
> *Carol:* Well, after I got over my shock, I'd probably look him in the eye, smile, and say good morning.
>
> *Therapist:* Jim, if this happened, how would it be helpful?
>
> *Jim:* That would be the most positive start to a day that we've had in months.

We have found that the miracle question is most effective when you help clients draw out the descriptions and make them specific, realistic, detailed, and achievable. Encourage them to describe inner feelings as well as outward signs.

EXCEPTION-FINDING QUESTIONS

As we mentioned earlier, it is assumed that no problem happens all the time, twenty-four hours a day, seven days a week. So exception-finding questions are used to discover when the problem is not occurring with the same degree of severity or frequency. Discovering exceptions leads to solutions to the problem.

The miracle question is a form of exception-finding in the future, when the client no longer experiences the problem. Other forms of exception-finding questions include: "There are times when you thought the problem would happen, but it didn't. How do you get that to happen? When over the past week did the problem not occur? What was different about that time? Who was involved and what did they do?" Sometimes clients exaggerate and claim "the problem happens

24/7." At such times, the therapist might use humor to address the exaggeration with another question, such as, "Even when you are asleep?"

Sometimes the client has difficulty identifying when the problem is not occurring. In these cases, we encourage the clinician to shift to exception questions that find times when the problem is not as severe or when it is happening less frequently. For further study of exception-finding questions, see DeJong and Berg (1998) and De Shazer (1988).

DEVELOPING WELL-FORMED GOALS

By now you understand that solution-based treatment begins by immediately delving into the discovery of solutions. Just sitting around and talking about what change might look like is of limited value. The next step is to move past a discussion of possible solutions to implementation.

The formation of realistic, achievable, and highly specific treatment goals is critical to solution-based therapy, and these goals are determined by the client. De Shazer (1991) believes that if therapy is going to be brief and effective, both the therapist and client need to know where they are going and what life will look like when they get there. A picture of "life after successful therapy" can guide the work of both therapist and client.

Well-formed goals are small, concrete, specific, and behavioral. They are in the here and now and are indicated by the *presence* of something rather than the *absence* of something. They emphasize what the person *will* be doing or thinking rather than what they will *not* be doing or thinking. Clearly articulated goals describe and encourage the first small steps the patient needs to take rather than the end of the journey. The scaling question can also be used to help the couple set realistic goals.

Therapist: Jim, at the beginning of our session you said you would rate your marriage at about a seven and, Carol, you said you'd give it a three.

Jim: Well, that was at the beginning of our session. After what we've talked about, I think I'd probably give it a five.

Therapist: Okay. Carol, what would need to happen between now and our next session for you to rate your marriage at a 3.5?

Carol: There are two small things Jim could do that would make a big difference. If he would call once a day to see how we were and if he would come home on time.

Therapist: How would that be helpful?

Carol: It would let me know that he is thinking of me, that I count, that I am important to him.

Therapist: Jim, are those requests realistic? Are they too much? Would it be better to do just one of them?

Jim: No. They're easy.

Therapist: How many times have you done those in the past month?

Jim [after a pause]: Once or twice.

Therapist: Jim, what would need to happen between now and our next session for you to rate your marriage at a 5.5?

The first session ended by summarizing some of Jim and Carol's individual strengths as well as the strengths of their relationship. Then the therapist assigned them some homework. Due to Jim's travel schedule, they would not be able to come back for two weeks. In addition to the specific behaviors they suggested, the therapist recommended they go on a date by themselves and do something enjoyable. They were told that they could not discuss anything conflictual during their date. They also agreed to spend at least five minutes a day praying for their spouse and to read chapters 4 and 5 of *How to Change Your Spouse Without Ruining Your Marriage*, which deal with male-female differences (Wright & Oliver, 1994).

SECOND-SESSION DISTINCTIVES

The second session might begin with a question such as, "What's been a little bit better since the first session?" The therapeutic task is to discover, amplify, and reinforce any changes that have taken place. Many people will focus on what *hasn't* happened rather than on what *has* happened. Jim and Carol answered the therapist's question.

Carol: Well, the past two weeks have been okay except for last Sunday.

Therapist: What was better about them?

Jim: We had a great date night on Saturday. We went to an early movie and then had dinner afterward. It was a lot of fun.

Therapist: Carol, what do you think you did that made Saturday night go so well? Positive changes rarely just happen, so you must have done something differently. What was it?

As the discussion continues focusing on changes, it is important to link the current success with the future. Asking "What will you do to make this happen again?" or "What will make it easier to happen again?" raises the level of hope and expectation. It can be useful to target the exact time for the next occurrence by asking, "When are you planning on having another good day? How about setting the time now?"

At the beginning of the session, it was clear Jim and Carol wanted to focus on the one bad day rather than the thirteen good days they had enjoyed. Our solution-based approach does not ignore problems or concerns. At the same time, it is our belief that positive change is more likely to take place when we focus on what *does* work, on what has gone well, and on what positive changes did take place.

Because of people's tendency to focus more on the negative than the positive, it is usually helpful to teach them new criteria for measuring success. If their partner makes a 10% or even a 5% change in a week, that is a significant change. It may not appear that way when contrasted with the remaining negative patterns, but considering how long these patterns have been in place, a 5% or 10% improvement is significant. The natural tendency is to concentrate on the remaining negative responses, but doing so only reinforces "bad behavior."

A basic principle of learning is: *Whatever behavior gets rewarded or reinforced tends to be repeated.* In the SBBT approach, we try to refocus a couple's attention on growth and help them discover which behaviors they are reinforcing, the old or the new, the negative or the positive.

Toward the end of the session, Carol mentioned that when they got home from their date, they enjoyed their first sexual intimacy in over a year. Given the significance of this event, one might think they would have answered the first question with an enthusiastic, "You'll never guess what happened!" But they didn't. It took most of the session for them to reveal this breakthrough. Why? Most people in conflicted relationships are conditioned to dwell on the negative, the deficits, the weaknesses, and the pain.

One of the goals of brief therapy is, obviously, to facilitate meaningful change in a short time. Some assume that this approach requires less of the clinician—less training, less experience, and less skill. In reality, the opposite is true. Quality brief therapy requires the therapist to analyze, evaluate, and then make sometimes complex and difficult decisions rapidly. This approach actually takes *more* skill rather than less skill.

SOLUTION-BASED ASSESSMENT

An invaluable part of doing time-effective therapy is utilizing a breadth of information in a short period of time. We have found that the limited use of psychological testing early in the process can give us six to eight sessions worth of information. The Taylor-Johnson Temperament Analysis is an assessment tool we have found helpful. We also utilize the Myers-Briggs Type Indicator, the Beck Depression Inventory, the SCL-90-R, and, when appropriate, the Minnesota Multiphasic Personality Inventory.

Homework

The use of homework (out-of-session work) is commonplace within an SBBT framework. Because the assumptions discussed earlier emphasize change and action on the part of the client(s), out-of-session work is very important. Several types of homework assignments are utilized, such as bibliotherapy, formula and surprise tasks, attending seminars and conferences, pretending part of the miracle, focusing on small change, and repeating an activity that has brought about improvement.

We use bibliotherapy especially when clients are experiencing a particular problem (such as ACOA issues, sexual addiction, and depression) and they want to know more about the condition and solution. In the case of bibliotherapy, abundant resources are available for therapists to choose from. Whatever you choose, make sure that you have read it first, that it applies to the specific goals the client has set, and that you help the client make some practical application of the information in the context of their therapy. We frequently use Scripture, not to be superspiritual but because we believe that God's Word is relevant, practical, and powerful for the real-life needs of people.

We also want to emphasize the importance of determining whether the client is a reader before using this type of homework. Clients who do not complete homework assignments are not necessarily resistant to change or therapeutic directives; it may be that the therapist suggested an inappropriate and unachievable homework assignment for that particular client.

The most meaningful and significant assignments are those connected to the goals of therapy. It is important to work with the client to create an assignment that can be accomplished. Therefore, the change in the client's pattern must be small and concrete. Some clinicians refer to homework tasks as "video descriptions"—what an observer could see that would indicate change in the client (Preston, Varzos, & Liebert, 2000).

Homework assignments are used with clients to build success and competency. Clients experiences change and a different way of handling their problems. We make it a habit to always attribute the homework successes to the client, not the therapist. We believe in the client's ability to change.

Sometimes homework assignments flop or fail. We insist that assignments that are successful should always start with the client's ideas, past attempts, and exceptions to when the problem occurred. If the client still is unsuccessful, we look at whether the tasks were small enough or concrete enough. We believe a homework assignment can be discovered that *any* client can successfully accomplish with *any* problem. In the event of an unsuccessful assignment, the therapist should collaborate with the client to keep searching for one that will be successful, usually beginning with the client's ideas and goals, and thinking in smaller units of change.

We often use the surprise-task assignment at the conclusion of a couple's first session. The surprise task sends the couple home with a challenge for each partner to think of "something you could do this week, as many times as you want, that would turn your partner's head" (for good, of course). These are things that would make the person's partner think, *I wonder if that is the surprise task.* We ask the couple to not disclose to each other whether they have done a surprise task; they are simply to take note of what the partner is doing to get their attention. We also ask them not to talk about this until the next session. This assignment usually distracts couples from the negative aspects of the relationship and gets them focused more on positive actions and exchanges. The negative gets little attention during this time, which helps to create hope and encouragement.

RECENT RESEARCH ON BRIEF THERAPY

One of the challenges in evaluating any new therapeutic approach is the time it takes to conduct meaningful research. Several clinical researchers are utilizing and testing the effectiveness of brief therapy even with problems that have been traditionally assumed to require long-term treatment (DeJong & Berg, 1998; DeJong & Hopwood, 1996; Miller, Hubble, & Duncan, 1996; O'Hanlon, 1993; Trute, Docking, & Hiebert-Murphy, 2001). It is also interesting to see the widespread application of brief therapy within a variety of settings and populations, such as the following:

- difficult adolescents (Selekman, 1993; Sells, 1998)
- adult addictions (Berg & Miller, 1992; Stanton & Todd, 1982)
- domestic violence (Bogard & Mederos, 1999; Lipchik, 1991; Lipchik & Kublicki, 1996)
- schools and groups (Durrant, 1995; Metcalf, 1998; Murphy, 1997; Sklare, 1997; Webb & Webb, 1999)
- depression and anxiety disorders (Kung, 2000; O'Hanlon, 1993)

It is also encouraging to find brief therapy, especially solution-focused models, being utilized within pastoral settings (Kollar, 1997; Stone, 1993; Stone, 2001; Thomas & Cockburn, 1998). We believe such application is a trend of the future, and that more and more Christians will be trained in the brief therapy modalities. We also believe that the use of brief therapy in Christian settings will increase dramatically.

While additional research is needed to examine its strengths and limitations, the existing literature demonstrates that solution-based approaches can be effective ways to help people change (Oliver, Hasz, & Richburg, 1997). In our experience, SBBT is a pragmatic approach that can be used in a variety of church, parachurch, and clinical settings. It can be especially helpful in situations where the pastor or clinician has a limited amount of time.

A PARADIGM SHIFT

Space has not permitted us to discuss some of the limitations of solution-based brief therapy. For example, a pure solution-focused model says that solutions can be pursued with very little or no attention to the nature of the problem. However, in our experience, there are times when an understanding of what hasn't worked has been essential to developing effective solutions.

The constraints of this chapter also haven't allowed us to focus on some of the implications of this approach from a biblical perspective. (This issue is addressed more fully in Oliver et al., 1997.) That is a question we ask ourselves about *everything* we do on a regular basis. We believe that the Bible is the sufficient and final authority for faith and clinical practice. The solution-based brief therapy model involves a fresh combination of techniques and tools for helping people change that are consistent with what we understand to be an orthodox biblical and theological foundation. However, its pragmatic focus is on how people change, and we have added our dedication to fostering maturity in Christ.

Solution-based brief therapy is more than a collection of questions and techniques. We believe that it represents a major paradigm shift in looking at how people can change. The therapist and client work together to create solutions for what is problematic and what needs to happen so that the situation can improve. Some theories start by focusing on what is wrong and how to fix it. This approach seeks to be aware of and sensitive to what is wrong but chooses to focus on what is right and how to use it. The focus is more on the strengths and resources that clients bring to therapy than on their weaknesses or limitations. It's an approach that positively asserts that our God "causes everything to work together for the good" (Romans 8:28, NLT).

We've seen the solution-based approach effectively used by and used with a variety of people from a variety of theological persuasions. It doesn't matter whether you are charismatic or fundamental, dispensational or Reformed; whether you use only the *King James Version* or prefer the *New Living Translation;* whether you worship on Saturday or Sunday, or like the old hymns or contemporary praise music; whether you believe in sprinkling or dunking; or whether you hold to a pre-, mid-, or post-tribulation view of the Rapture, solution-based brief therapy can be a powerful tool in your therapeutic tool chest.

We don't believe that all problems can be solved in a short period of time. We agree that good questions and an optimistic, solution-based approach are not magic. Some people have complex problems that take a longer period of time and greater work to solve, even when counselors ask good questions. We believe and have experienced that most problems can be solved in twenty sessions or less and that many people can receive meaningful help in fewer than ten sessions.

CHAPTER 15

CHANGE IN PROCESS

Working from a Biblical Model of TRUTH in Action

LESLIE VERNICK AND CHRIS THURMAN

Man is not disturbed by events, but by the view he takes of them.
—EPICTETUS, A.D. 55–135

Whatever one's clinical or theoretical orientation, the overarching goal of counseling is to help people change. For counselors who embrace a Christian perspective of counseling, the goal is to help people change in the direction of Christlikeness.

Christian counseling relies on, and fully expects, the Holy Spirit to intervene and cause supernatural change in the life of the client. Most Christian clients desire and expect a Christian counselor to invite God to be present and to be experienced in spiritual intervention. Counseling that does not welcome and request God's involvement can't honestly be called Christian.

This type of counseling affirms that God is faithful to equip the client with all that is necessary to be transformed in spirit and soul—and to learn how to think, act, and judge biblically in any situation. Deficits of character, knowledge, or skill can be assessed and remedied through Christ and the resources of his church.

This counseling is present-focused and future-oriented. Most people come to counseling not primarily to understand their past, but because they are unhappy now and desire a better future. They want something to change today in order to live a more satisfying life tomorrow.

This counseling is brief. It is typically conducted over two to twenty sessions with specific goals and targeted interventions to accomplish them. If counseling evolves into a long relationship—six months or more—it is either depth psychotherapy, maintenance therapy, or a different kind of association altogether: mentoring, discipleship, coaching, or consulting.

In this chapter, we address the action phase of counseling by exploring the middle stage where the work of change is engaged in most strenuously. This phase moves logically from and builds on the initial stage of counseling as shown in the previous chapter. It also emphasizes a slightly different aspect of the process of change—working from a biblical TRUTH model that each of us has developed (Thurman, 1995; Vernick, 2000).

The professional Christian counselor will be challenged to think in parallel and concurrent ways to DSM diagnosis and treatment advances, and the pastoral counselor should feel right at home with this focus. This chapter reveals common elements of brief Christian therapy—of a Paracentric orientation—as well as the distinctives that each counselor shows in its application.

THE CASE OF GINA

Using a case study to describe the action stage of competent Christian counseling, we will show the entire process—from intake to assessment to intervention—that it entails (Vernick, 2000).

Gina came for counseling clinically depressed and struggling with low self-esteem. She described her life as "a mess." Gina was deeply in debt, the result of impulse spending. She reported difficulty managing her time, and she never seemed to be able to schedule regular exercise or devotions with God, which she said were important to her. Gina's health was deteriorating, but when her doctor recommended a special diabetic diet, she found it impossible to follow.

"I just can't seem to do it," she cried. "It's too hard."

Gina's interpersonal relationships were superficial, and she avoided going out with friends from church. She claimed to be "just too depressed." Gina wanted something to change, but she wasn't sure how to define it and was even less sure how to go about it.

ASSESSMENT AT TWO LEVELS

What were Gina's troubles? Initially, we would define them in terms of her presenting issues: money problems, health concerns, time-management difficulties, and unsatisfying personal relationships. Gina stated that she felt overwhelmed and depressed most of the time. She regularly told herself that change was too hard and that she was too weak. Gina believed in God and said she wanted a better relationship with him, but she often expressed disappointment in God and didn't understand why he allowed her life to be so difficult. She shopped impulsively, watched too much television, and ate excessively as a way of coping with her unsatisfying life.

Any one of these areas would give a counselor plenty to work on to help Gina change. Should we have begun by helping Gina feel better about herself so she wouldn't be so depressed and would perhaps be empowered to tackle some of her problems? Should we have helped her learn time-management techniques so she could get more done, or should we have focused on money-management skills so she could control her spending? Perhaps we should have started by exploring Gina's family background and personal history for abuse or addiction problems.

Before we could develop a treatment plan to help Gina change, we had to make sure we understood her properly. Why did Gina think the way she did about herself and God? What was going on in her heart? What did she love? What did she fear? What were the deepest desires of her heart?

Jesus tells us that our outward behaviors are directly linked to what is in our heart (Luke 6:45). Therefore, it is important as Christian counselors to understand the deeper motives of clients' hearts, all the while helping them tackle the presenting problems. Freeman, Pretzer, Fleming, and Simon (1991) state, "A therapist who is able to develop an accurate understanding of his or her client and then think strategically will be able to develop effective interventions even if he or she knows few established techniques" (p. 79).

THE PURPOSE AND DIRECTION OF CHANGE

Before we continue our discussion on the process of change, we must be acutely aware of what our purpose is in helping people change. When defining what needs to change, we must first evaluate what criteria we will use to determine a successful therapeutic outcome: better functioning? happier feelings? improved relationships? all of the above? Mahoney, Norcross, Prochaska, and Missar (1989) found agreement among psychologists regardless of theoretical orientation that "development of the self-system is an important element in psychological change" (p. 255).

Yet as Christian counselors, we are called to something more. Johnson and Johnson (1997) remind us that in addition to the reduction of distressing symptoms, "Christian counselors typically have counseling goals that are fundamentally distinct. Beyond mere alleviation of discomfort—often the sole focus of their secular counterparts—Christian counselors recognize their work as redemptive and restorative in character" (p. 52). Change, then, involves both symptom reduction and transformed beliefs, both external obedience and inner redemption, both behavior change and the adoption of a new thought life.

When Jesus calls people to repentance *(metánoia)*, he doesn't just ask for an outward change; he requires a change of heart (Zodhiates, 1991). God desires to transform a *natural* person's heart into a *spiritual* person's heart. Powlison (1993) says, "In biblical anthropology, *heart* has to do with man's relationship either to God or to false gods of the world, flesh and devil.... The issue of the heart is the question, 'Who or what rules me?'" (p. 27). Tillich (1951) believed that "whatever concerns a man ultimately becomes god for him" (p. 211).

We all worship something, either God or god-substitutes (Powlison, 1993). The apostle Paul confirmed this idea when he said that human beings have made a terrible exchange. We have exchanged the truth of God for a lie and have worshiped the creature or creation instead of the Creator (see Romans 1). As worshipers, we assign ultimate worth to those things we are passionate about—or what we center our heart on (Vernick, 2001). Therefore, understanding Gina's desires and passions, her loves and fears—gaining an accurate picture of her heart—was an important part of the overall assessment.

Gina believed in God, but her heart was not centered in him. As Christian counselors, we must be careful not to separate dysfunctional, sinful, or irresponsible behavior from the deeper heart issues at work. The ultimate goal of the Chris-

---

Box 15.1—The Lies We Believe

Following is a list of the more common lies and falsehoods that people often believe and live out (with varying degrees of commitment)—usually with painful consequences (Thurman, 1989):

- I must be perfect.
- I must have everyone's love and approval.
- It is easier to avoid problems than to face them.
- Things have to go my way for me to be happy.
- My unhappiness is caused by other people and events.
- I can have it all (and if I don't, life is not worth living).
- I am only as good as what I do and accomplish.
- Life should be easy; life should be fair.
- I want it now; I shouldn't have to wait for what I want.
- People are basically good; it's society that corrupts us.
- My marriage problems are my spouse's fault.
- My spouse should meet all my needs.
- My spouse owes me for what I've done for him or her.
- If marriage takes hard work, we must not be right for each other.

tian counselor is not to help clients achieve better functioning, although that should be the result of good counseling. We are aiming for a deeper change— nothing less than the transformation of the heart.

The apostle Paul told us in Ephesians 4 that various gifts are given to those in the body of Christ, and by exercising these gifts we build up one another so that we will grow in Christlikeness and become mature (meaning God-centered worshipers). Therefore, as Christian counselors who have been given gifts to help hurting people, we must be cautious when looking at secular definitions of what constitutes healthy change.

Gilligan (2001) said, "By one count, there are well over one hundred distinct psychotherapy approaches, each asserting its own version of 'truth'" (p. 54). We may find that certain secular approaches provide good ideas that can help us implement strategies for change, but ultimately those approaches may define healthy change in a way that's inconsistent with a Christian worldview. As we have learned so far in this book, God's Word must be our authoritative guide about what needs to change and how change occurs.

- My spouse should be like me, think like me, and believe like me.
- I shouldn't have to change to make my marriage/relationship better.
- I refuse to admit being wrong; I often make mountains out of molehills.
- I tend to take things too personally.
- Most issues are black and white for me.
- The past predicts the future; people don't really change.
- I tend to reason with my feelings rather than with the facts.
- God's love can be earned.
- God hates the sin and rejects the sinner.
- If I do the right thing, God will protect me from pain and suffering.
- All problems in life are caused by sin.
- It's my Christian duty to meet all the needs of those around me.
- Painful emotions—anger, anxiety, depression—are signals that my faith is weak or that sin exists somewhere in my life.
- God can't or won't use me unless I'm spiritually strong.
- If I can't *be* good, at least I can always *look* good.
- I've arrived; most of these ideas do not apply to me.
- I'm hopeless; all of these lies plague my life.

ARRIVING AT A BIBLICAL DIAGNOSIS

In order to help Gina mature and experience a spiritual transformation, we had to understand what ruled Gina's heart. The *NIV Study Bible* (Barker, 1995) defines the *heart* as the "center of the human spirit, from which spring emotions, though, motivations, courage and action" (p. 783). Although Gina said she believed in God and wanted a better relationship with him, her heart was not controlled by love for him. Rather, it was ruled by lies and other loves. Instead of loving God with all her heart, mind, soul, and strength, Gina loved an easy life. She valued pleasure over discipline and hard work, and she clung to the misguided view of a God who was her servant.

Gina had no understanding of the concept that her greatest purpose in life was to love and serve God. Instead, she believed the lie that God existed to meet her needs first and foremost, that she was helpless, that life should be easy and fair, and that God was disgusted with her because of her failures (Thurman, 1999).

Gina's outward behaviors and presenting problems were largely a reflection of what was in her heart. In fact, this is a central way of analyzing and arriving at an accurate diagnosis of the heart: to inferentially reason backward from the observed behavior to form biblically defined hypotheses about one's inner beliefs and values. These heart hypotheses should then be expressed tentatively and humbly to the client so the individual will take responsibility and make a commitment to change. This principle sometimes works as simply as we state it here. Often it is a complex struggle between counselor and client, one that takes perseverance and dedication by both to overcome.

Mahoney (1991) found that "regardless of theoretical leanings, most therapists agree that healthy growth involves changes in self and that such changes are facilitated by a safe and caring human relationship" (p. 16). Gina definitely needed to make some changes in her self, particularly in the way she thought and how she viewed herself, the world, and God.

Since the importance of building a therapeutic relationship is covered elsewhere in this book, we will focus on the process of change assuming a good therapeutic alliance. It is imperative that we not neglect this important aspect of counseling because Sexton and Whiston (1994) found that the "quality of the counseling relationship has consistently been found to have the most significant impact on successful client outcome" (p. 6).

Helping Gina experience repentance involved a change in Gina's heart and in her habits (Willard, 1998). If we focused only on Gina's outward behaviors without an awareness of what ruled her heart, we may have inadvertently helped her become a more functional idol worshiper. (See 2 Kings 17:40-41 for an example of the Israelites who worshiped both God and idols.) How we help clients like Gina will be the focus of the rest of this chapter.

THE PROCESS AND METHODS OF CHANGE

Albert Ellis (1958), the founder of Rational-Emotive Behavior Therapy (REBT), discovered that clients' fundamental or core beliefs about themselves and about adverse events were the most critical components in understanding their self-defeating behavior or neurotic upsets. Gina's core beliefs influenced the way she thought and felt and contributed to her dysfunctional and sinful behaviors. She believed that she was helpless and incapable of significant change, and she believed that God was distant and unresponsive to her situation.

These beliefs, although untrue, contributed to her negative view of herself and of life. Freeman et al. (1991) state that "One of the major premises of the cognitive view of human functioning is that automatic thoughts shape both individual's emotions and their actions in response to events" (p. 4). They then say that "a second premise of cognitive therapy is that an individual's beliefs, assumptions, and schemas (terms used interchangeably) shape the perception and interpretation of events" (p. 4).

HOW OUR THOUGHTS MEDIATE OUR FEELINGS

Let's look at these ideas more systematically. When most of us are faced with an adverse event, such as a traffic jam, we react with unpleasant feelings. We might conclude—and often talk as if—the traffic jam is making us upset.

Adverse Event	Feeling
Traffic Jam	Anger
	Irritation
	Frustration

However, it is not the traffic jam itself that is causing our angry and frustrated feelings. Our *thoughts* about the traffic jam are actually generating our emotional upset. These thoughts are often automatic and unconscious, but they usually mediate what we experience emotionally.

Adverse Event	Automatic Thought	Feeling
Stuck in traffic	This is terrible.	Anger
	Why does this always happen when I'm in a hurry?	Frustration
		Irritation
	I should have left earlier.	
	This isn't fair!	

Mahoney (1991) also found strong consensus that good psychotherapy involves self-examination (p. 16). Scripture also encourages self-examination (Lamentations 3:40; Proverbs 14:15; Haggai 1:7; 1 Corinthians 11:28). An important part of change is helping a client "see" what the problem actually is. Gina wanted to change but was stuck in a pattern of lies that kept her from seeing herself, her troubles, or God truthfully. Most of our emotional struggles, relationship difficulties, and spiritual setbacks are caused by the lies we tell ourselves (Thurman, 1999). Peck (1978) concurred when he said, "One of the roots of mental illness is invariably an interlocking system of lies we have been told and lies we have told ourselves" (p. 58).

Gina told herself that her difficult life situation was causing her depressed feelings. If we were going to help Gina see herself differently, we had to help her discover the link between her unbiblical beliefs and her negative feelings. During one session, Gina shared something that happened at church, which she believed caused her to feel very upset. We used this incident to help Gina understand the source of her negative feelings.

Adverse Event	Automatic Thought	Feeling
Friend didn't say hi at church.	She's mad at me.	Hurt
	I must have done something wrong.	Confusion
	Nobody wants to be friends with me.	Sadness

The first step in Gina's growth was to help her examine what she thought in response to her situation and to evaluate whether those thoughts and beliefs are true. Reading through the Old Testament gives us good examples of this phenomenon. In Deuteronomy 9, for example, the Israelites had just succeeded in conquering nations that were much stronger than they were. God told Israel not to interpret this victory incorrectly. He said, "Do not say to yourself, 'The Lord has brought me here to take possession of this land *because of my righteousness* [italics added]' " (verse 4). He then went on to warn them on the basis of an accurate—that is, God-centered—view of the issue: "No, it is on account of the wickedness of these nations that the LORD is going to drive them out." God understands that the way we think about something or interpret a situation will largely determine how we feel about it. God warned the Israelites against interpreting their victory incorrectly so that they would not feel proud and self-confident.

As the previous chapter showed, one effective strategy for helping a client examine his or her thinking is through the use of questions. Saltzberg and Dattilio (1996) state "it is essential to help clients begin to question the evidence for their ideas or beliefs, rather than simply viewing their thoughts as facts. Furthermore, clients need to examine the quality of the evidence on which they base conclusions in order to form a foundation for rational thought" (p. 27). Beck, Rush, Shaw, and Emery (1979) suggest three questions that help a client examine his or her thoughts:

1. What evidence do you have that these thoughts are true?
2. What is another way of looking at what happened (adverse event)?
3. If it is true, then what does that mean?

Let's consider how a Christian counselor would explore Gina's judgment using this strategy:

Therapist: You say that when your friend didn't say hi to you in church yesterday, you felt bad. We've now looked at why you were feeling so bad—you were thinking that she was angry with you for something. What evidence do you have to support this idea?

Gina: Well, she didn't even look my way. She must be mad about something. She is the one person I can always count on to come up to me at church, and now she doesn't want to be bothered with me either.

Therapist: Gina, I can understand why you may have thought she was angry, but is there another way of looking at your friend's behavior? Is there another explanation as to why she ignored you yesterday?

Gina: I can't imagine any other explanation as to why she would purposely ignore me. Unless…well, maybe she just didn't see me. I know she's had a lot on her mind lately. It's possible that she was thinking about something else and didn't notice me. Maybe she's not mad at me. Maybe she didn't know I was there.

Therapist: Gina, since you know your friend regularly says hi to you and doesn't ignore you, do you suppose you could give your friend the benefit of the doubt until you check with her about what happened? Perhaps it's true that she was preoccupied about something and just didn't see you.

Gina: Yeah, maybe…

Therapist: Let's think about it as if that is what happened. How would that change your view of the event?

Gina: Well, I probably wouldn't be so angry or so worried that she is mad at me about something.

It was important to affirm Gina's slight shift in thinking and reinforce the possibility that although her thoughts were understandable, they might not have been true. And if not true, then she wouldn't have been as upset either. Part of our counseling task was to systematically help Gina examine her thoughts in response to difficult situations so she understood that her thoughts contributed a great deal to how she felt and responded to unpleasant events. Consider this process in box 15.2.

OVERCOMING COGNITIVE DISTORTIONS

"A third premise of cognitive therapy is based on Beck's (1976) observation that errors in logic, or 'cognitive distortions,' are quite prevalent in clients suffering from a number of different disorders. These cognitive distortions can lead individuals to erroneous conclusions even if their perception of the situation is accurate" (Freeman et al., 1991, pp. 5-6).

These lies of distortion include (see Thurman, 1999):

- *Magnification*—making a mountain out of a molehill
- *Personalization*—taking someone's behavior as a personal affront or as if we caused their actions

---

Box 15.2—The TRUTH System: Developing the Mind of Christ

The acronym TRUTH is used for analyzing the dysfunctional process of unredeemed living and for learning a new process of biblical, Christ-centered evaluation and right living (Thurman, 1995). It works this way:

T—*Trigger event:* something that happens to you. (Your child spills milk in your lap at breakfast.)

R—*Reckless thinking:* unredeemed and automatic self-talk. ("I can't stand and will not tolerate any mess interfering with my morning routine.")

U—*Unhealthy response:* pain-causing behavior to you and your relationships. (You scream at your child, who breaks down and cries. Your spouse intervenes, angry about your reaction. Exasperated, you blame it all on spilled milk, as if perfect behavior by your child is the right cure.)

T—*Truthful thinking:* God-honoring beliefs and biblical thinking that replace the lies you believe. (You tell yourself, "I don't like my routine being interrupted, but my relationship with my child is more important.")

H—*Healthy response:* right actions and controlled emotions maintain right relations. (You feel the flash of anger, stop and pray to control it without erupting, and tell your child, "Oops, we've got a mess to clean up!"

- *Polarization*—seeing something in black-or-white, all-or-nothing extremes when it was really some shade of gray
- *Selective abstraction*—focusing on a detail at the expense of the bigger picture
- *Discounting*—denying or dismissing evidence that challenges your distorted perspective
- *Overgeneralization*—predicting the future from a given event
- *Emotional reasoning*—believing something is true just because you strongly feel it is true

Let us suppose that no amount of persuasion could convince Gina that her interpretation of the events on Sunday was wrong. We asked her what the evidence was, and in her mind she came up with evidentiary proof. She generated no alternative way of thinking. It would be most helpful at this juncture to turn to our third question:

Therapist: Well, Gina, suppose it is true. Your friend *was* mad at you on Sunday and didn't want to talk with you. What would that mean?

Then you jump up to get a rag for cleanup with that angry energy properly redirected.)

In a nutshell, it simply works like this:

1. Recognizing the T-U fallacy: Our false belief that one's unhealthy behavior and ugly feelings are caused by unwanted trigger events. ("Spilled milk makes me angry.")
2. The T-R-U train: Our unhealthy reactions are actually a function of reckless thoughts and wrong beliefs that mediate our responses—what we call self-talk. ("My intolerance of morning messes makes me angry.") These mediating beliefs are usually automatic and unconscious—one reason most of us get trapped in the T-U fallacy.
3. TRUTH therapy intends to make us aware of the lies we believe so we can evaluate them biblically, renounce them, and replace them with God's truth. ("I love my kid and can't control spilled milk—it happens. I can control my attitude and change my demand for a perfect morning.")
4. T thinking (developing the mind of Christ) will yield life in all its variety—the H healthy responses desired and worked for in TRUTH therapy. ("I still don't like spilled milk, but it no longer makes me go ballistic. In fact, I'm more relaxed in the mornings and enjoy them more. That's good for me and my children.")

Gina: That I can never do anything right *[polarization]*. I will never be able to keep a good friend *[overgeneralization]*, and I'm so stupid I don't even know what I do to make them so mad at me *[personalization]*.

Each of Gina's statements reveals errors in the way she thought and shows distortions in her beliefs about herself. Part of helping Gina change would involve helping her identify and label these distortions and replace them with the truth.

Therapist: Gina, is it true that you *never* do *anything* right?

Gina: Yes.

Therapist: What about the time you told me that you got praised for your progress at work?

Gina: Oh, that. Well, that doesn't count.

Therapist: Really? I'm counting it, and I don't see any reason why you shouldn't count it as well. I also remember your telling me that you recently took the initiative to reach out to that elderly woman in your apartment building who was sick. Sounds like you did something right then.

Gina: Yeah, but now I've just messed up an important friendship.

Therapist: Perhaps you're right. Maybe you've done something that has led your friend to be angry with you, but that doesn't mean you've never done anything right, nor does it mean that your friendship is over. I'm sure that there have been times when you were angry with a friend but it didn't end your friendship. It may mean, however, that you need to talk with her about what happened.

Gina [beginning to weep]: I can't. It's too hard. I wouldn't know what to say.

Therapist: We might need to work on your communication skills in such encounters. But, Gina, I've noticed that you seem to react to difficulties by telling yourself that you can't deal with them and that life is just too hard for you to cope with. Something that I want you to think about right now is this: It sounds like whenever you think you may have done something wrong or made a mistake, your first thought is that you are a failure and your response is to give up and stop trying. How do you think that approach to your difficulties is hurting you now?

This dialogue is given to demonstrate the actual way a counselor might help a client work through his or her distortions, negative thoughts, and lies. Jesus often used questions as a means of zeroing in on a person's heart. As we do this, it can also reveal the larger themes in a person's life that need to be addressed in order to make changes. In addition to the use of well-formulated questions, we can also utilize teaching, metaphor, story, and humor as ways of helping our client change (Neilson, Johnson, & Ridley, 2000). Scripture is replete with examples of metaphor and story, as well as direct teaching, in order to help move God's people toward change.

TEACHING TRUTH AND SKILLS

Instructing a client how to change can be done directly through dialogue within the session, but most often it is more effectively done through bibliotherapy and homework. Assigned readings and audiotapes can be an important adjunct to therapy. Reading the Psalms, for example, can help normalize clients' feelings and help them know they're not alone. The book of Proverbs can be used to help someone understand the consequences of foolishness or a bad temper and why God calls us to change.

Notice also the way false beliefs create patterns of avoidance with a lot of fear attached to corrective and remedial action. It is vital to assess skill deficits as a result of these dysfunctional patterns. Training in personal and relational skills (e.g., assertiveness, negotiation, planning and time management, study skills, presentation skills) may be necessary. Christian counselors should be adept at role-playing and simulation-work, acting out with clients the critical interactions that are planned between sessions.

The work of therapy occurs not only in the therapist's office, but it also must be exercised in the client's everyday life if it is to have lasting effect. Gina's homework began after her first counseling session with instructions to write down her painful feelings and the situations that triggered them. This was an important first step in helping Gina assume responsibility for her problems and make changes. Seligman (1994) stresses how important this component is to the change process when he points out that "all successful therapy has two things in common: It is forward-looking and it requires assuming responsibility" (p. 241).

As Gina began to understand the connection between her thoughts and feelings, she was instructed to write down her automatic thoughts and notice how they contributed to her emotions. Next she was taught how to dispute her untrue thoughts using God's Word. Each session built upon the previous one, teaching Gina to think truthfully about herself, her difficulties, and God. These homework assignments provided much of the content that was addressed during Gina's sessions. It is crucial that we work collaboratively with the client in creating homework assignments that will be within his or her skill level and be relevant to the problem (Saltzberg & Dattilio, 1996).

In addition to written homework or bibliotherapy, we can assign behavioral tasks, which can be helpful for a client seeking to make specific changes. Freeman et al. (1991) report that "a well-designed behavioral experiment can be very effective, particularly when the client accepts the therapist's point of view intellectually but is not yet convinced 'on a gut level'" (p. 77).

One particular assignment helped Gina comprehend more fully that she was not helpless over her problems. She was instructed to act as if she already had some of the social skills she needed to interact with people. We defined those skills as maintaining eye contact, smiling, and responding to small talk by nodding her head. Her homework was to act in a friendly way at church and notice the responses of others, then to report her observations during our next session. Gina was amazed that "people were friendlier to me." We discussed how she might maintain and build upon those small changes in order to experience an improved social life.

NARRATIVE WORK: THE POWER OF STORY AND METAPHOR

Metaphor and storytelling were an integral part of the teaching tools of Christ and are generously woven throughout the Scriptures. Gordon (1978) says that "Metaphor is ever present as a tool for changing ideas and affecting behavior" (p. xi). The editors of *Futurist* magazine assert that storytellers will be the most valuable workers in the twenty-first century.

Metaphor can be a way of bypassing the "watchdog" left brain, or getting around the resistance to change, to confrontation, or to a new idea (Barker, 1996). When we use story or metaphor, we often find that we are working with our client at a deeper emotional level. Hill et al. (1988) found that clients report therapeutic verbal interventions most helpful when they are involved in a high level of emotional processing. Barker (1996) holds that metaphor and stories are particularly useful to do the following:

- illustrate a particular point
- suggest possible solutions to a problem
- promote insight or awareness
- motivate or plant ideas in a counselee's mind
- overcome and bypass resistance (the subject of the next chapter)
- reframe or redefine the problem
- remind people of their resources

When using this therapeutic technique, it is important that we connect it with our client's interests (Ottati, Rhoads, & Graessar, 1999).

Leslie: *Recently, I used a metaphor with a client who was struggling with self-image issues. She always felt inferior to an older brother and was envious of his power and position in the family. She described herself as small and insignificant, and she resented her parents' affirmations of her brother, and believed, by comparison, that she was inadequate. We examined her untrue thoughts, yet what helped her feel differently about herself was a well-timed metaphor.*

Over several weeks, I noticed that when we began our sessions, she often commented about the flower garden outside my office. With this in mind, I asked her if she'd like to see two of my favorite flowers. She agreed, so we went outside and I pointed to a bush filled with red roses. It was big, bold, and dramatic. She was impressed, and I said, "Yes, it is lovely, but it could hurt you when you get too close to its thorns, and it requires a lot of upkeep in order to look so beautiful." But we agreed it was gorgeous and demanded to be noticed.

Off in a more secluded and shady spot was my other favorite, a beautifully delicate specimen—a bleeding heart. This small bush had tiny, paper-thin, heart-shaped pink flowers that dangled from their stems like a tear that's about to fall. I remarked, "The bleeding heart is a very different flower than the rose but equally as lovely." My client nodded silently. Then I asked her to think about something. "What if the bleeding heart thought it was not as beautiful or as important just because it was not big and showy like the rose? Do you suppose my garden would be as beautiful if all the flowers were roses?"

She began to cry and I knew that she received the truth behind the story. We then processed her feelings during the session, and a shift in her self-perception occurred. Greenberg and Korman (1993) suggest that when we fail to pick up on in-session affective experiences, we neglect a crucial element of bringing about therapeutic change in our client's lives.

UNCOVERING THE HIDDEN THINGS

As we help clients make small changes through the use of metaphor and story-telling, we will also uncover what they believe, love, worship, fear, and trust in. This is where we can address the deeper heart issues. Wilson (1995) says that "We don't always live what we profess, but we always live what we believe."

As we work with our clients on the immediate concerns they bring us, we will see repetitive patterns of thoughts or responses to life's difficulties that are based on lies. As Christian counselors, we must be alert to these lies and address them not only with human truth, but also with God's truth.

A fundamental lie in Gina's heart was that God was supposed to come through for her and give her a great life. In her mind, he existed to serve her and to make her happy. From Gina's perspective, he wasn't doing such a good job. Gina would never have stated this so directly, but this lie was exposed by her reactions to life's difficulties.

Jesus once said, "Out of the overflow of [the] heart [the] mouth speaks" (Luke 6:45). As Gina revealed her automatic thoughts, feelings, and responses to problems, her misconceptions about God were exposed. As counseling progressed, it was important to help Gina look at her struggles in light of God's truth. God tells us that our troubles in life are often meant to mature us, to develop our character, and to strengthen our faith (see James 1 and Romans 5).

Throughout counseling, Gina was confronted with the truth that God says he uses the hardships we experience in our life to develop something in us. A verse that was especially helpful to Gina was Proverbs 15:32, "He who ignores discipline despises himself." Could it be that Gina's depression and low self-esteem were the result of inadequate self-discipline to deal with her problems maturely rather than the result of her troubles themselves? Could it be that God, in his faithful love toward Gina, was working to develop in her the very discipline that would help her to mature and, ultimately, to see herself as a priceless child of God?

As Gina began to absorb and believe what God's Word was teaching her, her heart began to respond in faith. Her picture of God changed from an errand boy who served her into that of a loving Father who disciplined her so she would not continue to hurt herself. Her heart began to repent of the sinful, self-destructive ways in which she thought, acted, and lived.

She also began to recognize that she loved pleasure more than God. To her, avoiding pain was a higher priority than living close to God. As an outgrowth of her heart change, Gina took small steps toward self-discipline, which would eventually help her stop old patterns and develop new ones (Ephesians 4:20-24). As she began to practice these steps and develop self-control, her depression lifted.

The apostle Paul said that we are transformed by the renewing of our minds. This occurs when we become aware of who God is and all he has done for us, and then make a personal response to him, offering ourselves back to him as our spiritual form of worship (Romans 12:1-2). Transforming one's mind doesn't occur without engaging one's heart. The Bible tells us to take every thought captive to the obedience of Christ (2 Corinthians 10:5). Genuine and lasting change involves repentance in our hearts whereby we allow God to be God and his truth to become our deepest reality.

MAINTAINING CHANGE AND GROWING INTO MATURITY

Growth and change continue beyond the therapist's office and the counseling time frame. People continuously change. In fact, many people report that their most significant changes happen after treatment has ended (Frank, Hoehn-Saric, Imber, Liberman, & Stone, 1978; Reynolds, 1980). Both of us give our clients tools to help them maintain and reinforce the changes gained in counseling.

As Christian counselors, we have the unique privilege and responsibility to be God's instruments in the restoration of one another. Thomas à Kempis (1981), in his classic work *The Imitation of Christ,* reminds us, "We must diligently search into and set in order both the outward and the inner man, because both of them are important to our progress in godliness" (p. 40).

CHAPTER 16

CHANGE AS PARADOX

Overcoming Client Resistance and Fear of Change

GEORGE OHLSCHLAGER AND TIM CLINTON

One of the paradoxes of psychotherapy is that no matter how strongly patients want to overcome their problems, and no matter how much time and money they invest in therapy, they also persistently engage in efforts to fight the treatment, to avoid facing their pain, to resist growth, and to hang on to their maladaptive patterns.

—BRUCE NARRAMORE, 1994

Alicia came in for her counseling session and sat down, nervously perched on the edge of her seat. This was her eighth session, and for the last two weeks she had been pursuing a good action strategy—becoming more assertive with her invasive male boss. She was different this session, however, and her therapist zeroed in on it.

"Am I detecting something wrong?" asked the therapist. "You seem uneasy today."

"Well...I *am* uneasy," replied Alicia, haltingly. "I, uh, I didn't realize this change thing would be so hard."

"Hard...how?"

"Well, not hard really," she said. "I can be more assertive. I *was* assertive with my boss—in a respectful way, I thought. But the consequences are hard."

"In what way?" the therapist asked.

"My boss's reaction," Alicia replied. "He's really been cold toward me—real angry, I think—since I told him his behavior was inappropriate and unwanted. I know we talked last week about expecting something like this, but I didn't realize how uncomfortable the situation would become. Maybe I should have just kept quiet and hoped it would stop."

"Yes, that was an option—it still is. But you yourself said that simply *doing nothing* hadn't changed anything. In fact, his comments and pressure had only gotten worse."

"I know," said Alicia, exasperated, "but right now it seems to be the lesser of two evils."

"It does seem that way in the thick of the reaction and all the turmoil it causes. But keep in mind the reaction curve we discussed. Eventually, things will likely return to normal—only with clearer boundaries between you and your boss."

"I guess so. But there's something else I didn't count on."

"What's that?" asked the therapist, leaning forward in his chair.

"There's something about his attention that I really miss," Alicia said softly. "I feel stupid saying it, but he made me feel special and attractive. I think a part of me was hoping that he would start treating me better and then something would happen between us. Can you believe what I'm saying?" Apparently, she could hardly believe it herself.

"Yes, I can believe it," the therapist replied. "And I wonder if there was a part of you that subtly played to his attentions. I also believe that these kinds of conflicting dilemmas are common to most people, even if many people deny them. Though it feels crazy when you're living the contradictions, it is good that you are aware of what's going on."

THE PERVASIVENESS OF HUMAN RESISTANCE

Resistance is endemic to counseling and helping relationships. At a conscious level, people who come voluntarily for counseling are expressing a desire to change. But at another, often subconscious level, many people fear and resist change. And, in a variety of ways, they resist you and your efforts to help.

Likewise, people frequently come into counseling and point to the resistance of their spouse, child, colleague, or friend as the primary problem, and they want your help to overcome it. Some of these requests are legitimate reflections of the problems; some are not. Sometimes in asking you to help someone else change, a client can actually be masking the need to address change in his or her own life.

Client resistance strains the helping relationship in significant ways, and it reinforces the need for a strong therapeutic alliance to deal with resistance and fear. As we noted in chapter 10, clients who resist change during counseling will respond in different ways. They may discredit the counselor and question whether he or she can understand them. Some clients devalue the importance of the issue, dismissing it as tangential to the real concerns. Others will try to persuade the counselor to change his or her views and agree with their assessment and revised plan of action.

If these strategies don't work, they will often quit counseling and seek support elsewhere. Or, afraid to end counseling, they adopt a passive-aggressive approach, agreeing with the counselor without really changing their behavior.

Here are some common client responses that communicate resistance:

- "I don't need help. I only came because my wife [or husband, dating partner, or whoever] brought me here."
- "She [or he] is the problem! Fix her, not me."
- "I don't [or am not sure I can] trust you."
- "I don't like you [but may be too timid to tell you]."
- "Are you a born-again [or committed or Spirit-filled] Christian?"
- "You can't help me. You haven't been through what I have."
- "I don't believe in counseling."
- "This must be done my [or God's] way or I won't do it."
- "Yes, but…"
- "I can't."
- "I'll have to pray about it first."
- "I'll have to talk to my spouse [pastor, parents, children, and…] about it first."
- "But I've already done that, and it doesn't work."
- "This is hopeless. Nothing is going to help."
- "This is too hard. Just tell me what to do."
- "No sweat. This will be easy."

Indeed, client resistance is nearly always present at some point in counseling and is something every counselor must learn to handle (Egan, 1998; Weeks & L'Abate, 1982). Many counselors resist this challenge in their training as well as in their counseling practice, seeing it as an unpleasant reality, an unwanted side effect of choosing to become a therapist. In this chapter, we hope to help you overcome any resistance *you* may have to dealing with the resistance of those you are called to help. We will define resistance, describe some common ways it is expressed in counseling, and outline various strategies for overcoming it.

DEFINING RESISTANCE BIBLICALLY AND SPIRITUALLY

After Adam and Eve had eaten the forbidden fruit in the garden, their eyes "were opened, and they realized they were naked" (Genesis 3:7). When God approached them, they ran and hid from him (verse 8). And when God called, Adam replied in a manner universal to all of us when we encounter a holy God who is confronting our sin: "I was afraid…so I hid" (verse 10). When questioned about their actions, Adam and Eve responded in classic blame-shifting fashion. Adam blamed both God and Eve ("the woman *you put here* [italics added] with me" [verse 12]), as if the desired blessing of a companion had become an instant curse. And Eve, of course, blamed the serpent (verse 13). Adversity in the form of human resistance and hiding has been around from the very beginning.

In the New Testament, the call of the disciple Nathanael reveals Jesus' wonderful way of dealing with resistance (John 1:43-51). The prejudiced and skeptical Nathanael said, "Nazareth! Can anything good come from there?" (verse 46). The Son of God then peered into his heart and revealed the good man inside, the one who aspired to a pure righteousness.

"How do you know me?" a psychologically disarmed and now curious Nathanael queried.

Jesus then, with stunning supernatural authority, revealed his divinity to Nathanael, who immediately praised Jesus as God and the King of Israel (verses 48-49). It was a transformational encounter that changed the man from a skeptic to an enthusiastic believer.

Another time, Jesus instructed his disciples about facing adversity in ministry:

> I am sending you out like sheep among wolves. Therefore be as shrewd as snakes and as innocent as doves. Be on your guard against men; they will hand you over to the local councils and flog you in their synagogues. On my account you will be brought before governors and kings as witnesses to them and to the Gentiles. But when they arrest you, do not worry about what to say or how to say it.… Anyone who does not take his cross and follow me is not worthy of me. Whoever finds his life will lose it, and whoever loses his life for my sake will find it. (Matthew 10:16-19,38-39)

Two things stand out about the revelations of Jesus regarding the work of ministry. First, adversity is built into the process as a primary dynamic. Those who expect or hope that trouble won't come need to realign their expectations with God's truth. Second, every adversity is an opportunity for the gospel to be revealed.

In his book *Shattered Dreams,* Crabb (2001) develops the thesis that we are so attached—so desperately dedicated—to our life dreams that God must allow them to be shattered so they will lose their idolatrous appeal. Unless our dreams are shattered (or lost or broken or stolen), we are in danger of never being set free to pursue our first call in life: to love God and others with our whole selves.

If we would simply give up those things that obsess and enslave us, it would not be necessary for God to shatter them. But we resist giving up the things we love. We fight, claw, scratch, and scream to hold on to the things that we believe will fill up the holes in our souls. We try to create heaven on earth, deluding ourselves that these things are either God ordained or God honoring. This addiction dynamic may well represent the greatest threat to our call to love God first and to put him above all else.

DEFINING RESISTANCE PSYCHOLOGICALLY

Resistance is any behavior or impediment—whether from the client, the therapist, or the environment—that interferes with or retards the achievement of mutually agreed upon counseling goals. Resistance can be overt and apparent to all, or it can be covert, subtle, and hidden from view. As our earlier list of excuses implies, clients can resist by being silent, by talking too much, by talking around an issue, by praying about it, by appearing to cooperate but doing nothing about it, and so on. There are as many different ways to resist as there are personalities.

Resistance is one way to understand and define sin as "missing the mark"; however, not all resistance should be deemed pathological. Every counselor must accept that fear, hiding, and blame-shifting are normal and inevitable dynamics involved in helping clients. Confronting clients with the challenge of change can elicit guilt, confusion, and shame, in addition to a wide variety of fears. Clients hide behind masks because they believe that to expose themselves honestly will lead to great pain and suffering. Giving up familiar and comfortable patterns of living, no matter how toxic or dysfunctional, is difficult. Most clients, to some degree, resist and deflect counselor intervention because they have learned not to trust another person, or they give their trust sparingly over a long period of time in order to test the helper.

Resistance was first defined and addressed in counseling and psychotherapy by Freud (1900) and other practitioners of the psychoanalytic approach. In fact, a central tenet of classical psychoanalysis is working through client resistance and bringing avoided issues into the client's conscious awareness. Freud conceived it as a defensive reaction, a self-protective symptom used to ward off unwanted anxiety and psychic conflict. Clients hold on to these defense mechanisms because of their protective function in helping the client avoid anxiety and maintain an internal or psychic equilibrium.

Freud (1920) also wrote about *thanatos,* a "death wish" type of existential-like despair that he believed drove many people to engage in aggression toward others and in a variety of self-destructive behaviors. Experienced counselors and physicians can attest to the frustration and fear of serving patients who are more than merely resistant or noncompliant to following prescribed treatments. They are self-destructive, whether consciously or subconsciously. We have referred to this trend as "slow suicide," for without a halt and change of direction, self-destructive behavior will eventually result in death. An ancient axiom has long been shared among physicians: "Man does not die. He kills himself." Resistance in the form of self-destructive behavior therefore requires an active yet delicate form of intervention, as the counselor is often confronted with the paradox of a powerful counterforce at work, masked by the client's strong denial and negation.

Resistance is not just an individual phenomenon. Family and systems therapists understand collective resistance as a way to maintain system stability or family homeostasis. Change is perceived as a loss, a threat to the order and stability of the family or the organization. It is therefore resisted and sabotaged, as in the dynamics of the classic alcoholic family. Some systems therapists, in fact, assert that most families come into therapy not for the purpose of changing for the better, but because they want to return to "the way things were." They have lost their homeostatic stability as a result of unplanned or unwanted change that has forced the family out of their comfort zone.

The similarities between analytic and systems therapists should be noted here (Anderson & Stewart, 1983). Both see resistance to change as a function of perceived or anticipated loss of the stable operations of clients' worlds—the internal world of the individual or the multiperson world of the family or social system. Change is seen as the enemy, not the goal, and maintaining the stability and order of one's world is the highest good. If resistance is a universal phenomenon, then, to some degree, we must all view change as a threat. The more it is perceived as a threat—the more we cling to our comfort zones—the greater the resistance, and the tougher it will be to achieve the change goals of counseling.

INERTIA AND ENTROPY: UNIVERSAL BATTLES

Egan (1998) points out additional reasons why change is so difficult and so often resisted. He borrows two core concepts from the physical sciences—*inertia* and *entropy*—and makes strong analogies of their applicability to human and social change.

As in the physical world where the amount of energy needed to move a body at rest is substantial, the principle of *inertia* when applied to human change suggests that it is quite difficult to leave our comfortable, though dysfunctional ways because the demands of change are so great. In other words, the hardest part of changing for many people is getting started.

The sources of inertia range from pure sloth to paralyzing fear. In trying to help clients act, we will encounter the many faces of inertia. We should not be too quick to blame our clients for their passivity. After all, inertia permeates life, and it is one of the principal mechanisms for maintaining stability and order as well as for keeping individuals, organizations, and institutions mired in the "psycho-pathology of the average."

Entropy, the corollary to inertia, is the tendency to give up action that has been initiated. Programs for constructive change, even those that start strong, often dwindle and disappear. Not only is it hard to help some clients get started, but it is also hard to assist nearly all of them to persevere and attain their goals. The universal tendency for things to wind down is as true for humans and social structures as it is for machines and nature. Egan (1998) asserts that most helping efforts are not characterized by successful goal acquisition; rather, "attrition, noncompliance, and relapse are the name of the game" (p. 332). Nearly forty years of combined clinical practice has taught us that this is no less true for Christians than for anyone else.

Evidence for these dynamics is strewn across the terrain of counseling, medicine, and change programming. Just consider the multibillion-dollar weight-loss industry in America and the claims it makes. Consider as well how many times a New Year's resolution must be repeated year after year before a commitment to change truly happens? Futhermore, noncompliance with medical treatment is one of medicine's dirty little secrets that rarely, if ever, gets addressed as a public policy issue.

CHANGE DOES NOT COME EASY

Christian counselors face the full range of common client resistances as well as some that are unique to the Christian identity. Resistance is expressed both verbally and nonverbally by clients, and the varieties of resistance encountered in counseling are as myriad as the differences in gender, age, values, personality, beliefs, and history. Learning ways to combat, deflect, persuade, work through, and ultimately overcome client fear and resistance is imperative in order to attain goals.

THE ETIOLOGY OF CLIENT RESISTANCE

Client resistance is the most commonly understood form of resistance in counseling. As we have asserted, most clients are resistant to counseling to some degree, and they tend to be held responsible even when the resistance is due to the therapist or other factors. A few common components of client resistance are low motivation, learned helplessness, genetic blame, extreme self-sufficiency, and transference and countertransference.

Low motivation. Lack of motivation is often attributed to clients. In fact, this may be the most common complaint from counselors about client resistance, whether it is true or not. Similar to the blind or precontemplative client referred to in chapter 10, unmotivated clients are usually steeped in denial or are apathetic about the need for change. Helpful counselors will attempt to gain clear understanding of the behavior and of the reason for low motivation. A common reason why clients get labeled this way is due to an expectation on the part of therapist or client (or both) that counseling will fail—they simply don't believe it will work. A close variant of this pessimism is the view that counseling *will* work, but the client will end up in a worse place.

Learned helplessness. Understanding how people learn and become conditioned to helplessness and hopelessness will aid our understanding of the dynamics of resistance and depression (Seligman, 1994). The language of learned helplessness permeates our culture and shapes our attitudes and behavior. This mind-set is evinced by such phrases as: "That's just how it is"; "He's done it for so long that he'll never change"; "You can't teach an old dog new tricks"; "I'm addicted to it"; "It's genetics—my parents did it and so do I"; and "What's the use?"

Genetics blame. Closely related to learned helplessness is the growing emphasis on genetics, addictions, and disease as the cause of supposedly insurmountable problems. The implication is that people have no control over these forces. Indeed, our culture is perilously close to believing that biology is destiny. Biological determinism is replacing behavioral determinism in science. It is a pernicious ideology without basis in fact, but it is a powerful type of self-fulfilling prophecy when ingrained into our thinking.

Extreme self-sufficiency. In contrast to those who "blame it on genetics," are people who go to the opposite extreme. The autonomous, self-sufficient person is touted as the antidote to assembly-line culture and the deterministic coercion of thought. The self-made man or woman—a prominent ideal in American history and literature—is a beast of a different sort, however, in view of the call to change and grow as a follower of Christ. To the self-sufficient person, who may resist help because it indicates weakness and is seen as the first step to giving up freedom and autonomy, mutual support and interdependence are difficult to embrace.

Transference and countertransference. In the language of classical psychoanalysis, *transference* is the emotional transfer onto the therapist (or counselor or pastor) of a client's unresolved feelings for significant people in his or her life, especially parents or others who are major sources of trauma. *Countertransference* is transference operating in the opposite direction. In other words, unresolved counselor issues are transferred onto a client.

Ignorance or denial of these dynamics can create significant confusion, distress, boundary violations, and resistance in the counseling relationship. The novice or uninformed counselor can easily misread expressions of excessive anger or sexual seduction and may handle them poorly (giving anger back or playing to the seduction). A good supervisory experience for the therapy intern will address these issues as an ongoing part of therapist training.

Cavanagh (1982) proposed three major reasons why clients resist change and growth during the counseling process:

1. *Growth is painful.* This statement echoes the introductory sentence in Peck's (1978) classic book *The Road Less Traveled:* "Life is difficult." There is a familiarity, even a perverse pleasure, in our sins and dysfunctions that we don't want to give up. Leaving a long-practiced habit—possibly something that has become addictive—for a healthy new regimen is a good thing. But when that means giving up late-night movies with a bowl of ice cream for a 6:00 A.M. workout at the health club... Well, it just proves the assertion that transitions to better living can often be painfully difficult.

BOX 16.1—A CASE OF RESISTANCE: WHAT WOULD YOU DO?

Tom and Amy enter counseling and explain to you their ongoing conflicts about money and the way they decide to spend it. Unlike many men who are "dragged" into therapy by their spouse, Tom is enthusiastic about counseling. Amy, however, is reluctant to be there.

As you discuss Amy's lack of motivation in group supervision, her reasons for it become clearer. Tom presses her to submit to his leadership on money issues, and both Tom and Amy expect that you, as a Christian counselor, are going to support that admonition. Amy complains that Tom is spending way too much money on eating out and on his thrice-weekly golf outings. She says that they have no savings and are getting into credit trouble. Tom retorts that he needs to have his outlets due to the stress of his job and that they would be fine if she would just budget the money better.

- When you see this couple the next session, how would you address this situation and remain true to the Scriptures?
- What would you say or do if either one of them got angry and threatened to quit counseling?
- How would you address Amy's reluctance toward therapy and low motivation to change the situation?

2. *Secondary gain is hard to give up.* This refers to some payoff or outcome that the client experiences by maintaining dysfunctional patterns. The client resists giving up a harmful behavior because it fills a need for attention, provides an escape from unwanted thoughts or feelings, maintains a desired persona, or offers any number of other rewards.

3. *Clients have hidden agendas.* A wise and experienced counselor once said that all clients have two agendas in counseling: the one they think they came for and tell you about, and the one they do not know or don't tell you about.

COUNSELOR RESISTANCE

Many counselors, especially those with little experience, underestimate how pervasive client resistance is in counseling. Consistently expecting the ideal client response—that the client will carefully examine the issues and make a genuine commitment to change—will only frustrate counselors and promote burnout. It is important for Christian counselors to expect—dare we say, embrace—client resistance. It is also important to find ways to effectively respond to resistance so counseling goals can be achieved.

Resistant clients tend to violate counselors' deeply held convictions about people's inherent goodness and their positive expectations about the helping endeavor. When this happens, counselors often react as they try to cope with their own feelings of confusion, frustration, anger, and hurt. A classic double bind sets in that quickly grinds therapeutic gain to a halt: The counselor begins to resist the client's resistance.

Perhaps one of the last deficits to be overcome in the course of a counselor's career is the negative response to client resistance and fear of change. Counselors can improve in this area by confronting some misconceptions and misbeliefs about themselves, their clients, and the therapy process:

- I must succeed with every client; I'm no good as a helper.
- The success of this case is entirely on my shoulders.
- The success of this case is entirely on the client's shoulders.
- Every client must like me and trust me, or counseling will fail.
- Every client will be helped no matter how resistant he or she is.
- No client can be helped if he or she is the least bit resistant.
- Most clients will fight me as soon as I put the slightest demand on their life.
- Most clients are too weak or fragile for me to challenge them to change significantly.
- Most clients' habits and addictions are too strong to overcome.

- All a client needs to do to turn his or her life around is pray more.
- This client is not achieving his or her goals because he or she doesn't have enough faith.
- Resistance is a predictor of failure: Only motivated people change.
- All resistance is sin: Confrontation and confession is all it takes.
- Resistance is all my client's fault; this case is hopeless.
- Resistance is all my fault; I've blown it and I should refer the person to another therapist.

Christian counselors should not be surprised to see themselves reacting and behaving in unhelpful ways to some degree with resistant clients. In fact, counselors who are unaware of such responses or who insist they do not behave this way need to do some soul searching to identify their blind spots.

Unhelpful reactions to client resistance include:

- taking a client's resistance personally and assuming that the client is retaliating for something;
- reacting to client opposition with frustration and anger as well as with direct or indirect hostility;
- attempting to coerce, guilt-trip, or manipulate client behavior in the "right" direction;
- ignoring client resistance in the hope that it will pass, so you can get on with the work of change;
- adopting a guilty and placating strategy, as if client resistance is justified;
- disengaging from the client to some degree, assuming that failure is inevitable;
- increasing warmth and acceptance in order to overwhelm resistance with love;
- blaming the client and attaching labels such as "unmotivated," "resistant," "hostile," or "game-player;"
- washing your hands of the case and abandoning the client.

HELPFUL WAYS OF MANAGING RESISTANCE

Understanding your own resistance will not only increase your empathy for clients, but it will also help you recognize and change counterproductive responses. The following attitudes, strategies, and behaviors can help you and your clients overcome resistance.

1. *Look squarely at the issue.* Some concerted self-reflection, collegial feedback, and meditative prayer will likely reveal at least one or two of the misconceptions

listed in the last section. The existence of such blind spots is not shameful, but denying them will surely spell trouble. The following principles are also important in handling resistance:

- Accept and address the reality of resistance: Lean on God's strength and pray your way through every obstacle.
- Understand that some resistance is avoidance and that the payoffs of avoidance often outweigh the pain.
- Remain flexible: Retreat and approach the issue from another angle at another time.
- Start small: Expect and respect the path of least resistance.
- Bring in others to help: Create a network of key people for support, accountability, and encouragement. (This applies to both you *and* your client.)

The best you can say (and should pray) is, "Oh Lord, I hope my blind spots as a helper are smaller and less consequential than they were a year ago. Please increase my awareness of them and help me shed them further so that they will be even smaller and less harmful to my clients a year from now." This request is honest and achievable—God is able to help you do it, and you will be a better helper if you do.

2. *View resistance as a friend, not an enemy of either you or your client.* Recall the psychodynamic view of resistance: It is a mechanism of protection for your client. Protection, in and of itself, is a good thing. Therefore, you can restate the goal of *overcoming* resistance (just getting rid of it) to *working through* it.

3. *Reframe resistance as necessary to your client's sense of safety.* From a client's frame of reference, to overcome or even work through something that "protects" them is inherently threatening and will naturally induce even stronger resistance. That is why directly fighting client resistance is usually so useless and counterproductive.

4. *Free your client to act by becoming the defender of your client's resistance.* Here, you are applying a paradoxical strategy, a counterintuitive approach that disarms and even works with resistance in order to break through the impasse it creates. This strategy requires thinking and behavior that operate counter to what the perceived logic of the case would demand. If you become the defender of the resistance, you set your clients free from the need to defend it themselves. They are literally freed to challenge their own resistance by becoming, in effect, their own counselor. This requires some reprogramming on your part, training yourself to think therapeutically or counterintuitively.

5. *Consider "spitting in the client's soup."* The intention of this Adlerian technique is to metaphorically "kill" the power of sabotaging client behavior by exposing it and

taking away its hidden power. Such exposure emasculates the meaning behind the behavior, and as a result, it becomes unattractive to the client. A classic example of "spitting in the soup" of victimhood is exposing the payoffs of the codependent victim in an alcoholic marriage—how victims often sabotage change by covertly working to maintain family uproar and hang on to their sympathy-attracting roles.

OTHER WAYS TO OVERCOME OR MANAGE RESISTANCE

Counselors can work to overcome or manage client resistance in some of the following ways:

- Discuss client resistance in a humorous or matter-of-fact way.
- Give new meaning or interpretation to the resistance.
- Admit you are stuck and ask your client for help.
- Tell stories and use metaphors to break through.
- Solicit client directives and suggestions instead of giving them.
- Reframe the goal in terms of "client position."
- Use direct skills training or a detailed rehearsal strategy.
- Give suggestions when the client is most relaxed and open.
- Better arrange cues and reinforcement and reduce competing stimuli.
- Help the client make a small change from his locked-in routine.
- Concentrate on changing a small, workable, easier problem.
- Ensure strong rewards for new and goal-directed actions.
- Add or take away rewards.
- Find new rewards and give new meanings to client payoffs.

THE STRANGE LOGIC OF PARADOXICAL INTERVENTION

The goal of the last two ways to manage resistance is paradoxical: You are challenging resistant clients in order to increase, not lessen, their symptomatic behavior. In essence, you are urging them to willfully avoid trying to get better. By resisting these paradoxical and seemingly upside-down directions, clients begin to behave in the direction of the "real" or intended goals. When resistance cannot be worked through by conventional and logical means, you reverse the power dynamic that is opposing goal attainment by reframing and joining it, and even embracing it. In doing so, you rob the resistance of its antipower and transform it to work on the clients' behalf.

Adler (1963) and Frankl (1965) were the early masters of paradoxical instruction. Adler often "prescribed the symptom" and encouraged his resistant clients to exaggerate it, to practice doing it until they became "experts." Pushing the resistance to its extreme expression often reveals the absurdity and sabotaging nature of it as nothing else can—even a counselor's futile attempts at verbal persuasion. Jackson (1963) encouraged paranoid patients to be as suspicious as possible of everyone, which quickly revealed the foolishness of their paranoid thinking and behavior.

Jackson's approach also showed why paradoxical instructions should not be the interventions of first resort. In fact, their use is cautioned against altogether in cases

---

BOX 16.2—RESISTANCE AND PARADOX DONE POORLY

You've come to understand your client as a quiet, passive, unhappy person who allows his family, friends, and boss to control his life and even run over him at times. It frustrates you that he has not taken charge and used the assertive communication strategies you have taught him. In fact, the only thing that seems to be strong in his life is his resistance to your suggestions! His boss has been coercing him into some shady accounting practices that not only worry him but could also lead to legal trouble. Yet he still refuses to confront his boss.

During today's session, you attempt to prod him into action by suggesting you go with him to provide support while he confronts his boss. (You think—and hope—that maybe he'll agree to confront his boss himself in order to avoid having you go with him.) Alarmed, your client begs you not to even contemplate such a horrible thing. Then he runs out of the session, yelling that he is through with counseling.

Your well-intentioned but poorly planned paradoxical strategy has just backfired. What happened? What now? Common sense dictated a fight-fire-with-fire approach in the face of resistance, but it simply did not work. In fact, it produced the opposite effect, and you may have lost your client.

This strategy failed because a more-of-the-same approach rarely works in the face of resistance. Your client will outlast you, dig in his heels, and fight you "to the death." Simply put, it's his life, and he's much more invested in it than you are. You can't win. So run up the white flag, happily surrender your useless common-sense tactics, and start learning how to join your client and help him achieve his goals by using paradoxical strategies competently.

In the common vernacular, this approach is called reverse psychology, negative practice, or "working against the grain." Although some people find paradoxical strategies troubling because it seems deceptive and underhanded (when judged from a position of conventional logic), they have a sure, though upside-down, logic to help achieve client goals. That is, when clients won't yield their resistance, you must learn to use that power on their behalf—or you are forced to declare failure as a counselor.

involving suicidal or homicidal threats, crisis, delusions, extreme dependence, or emotional vulnerability. In addition, paradox can sometimes backfire with clients who are paranoid or have borderline personality disorder since paradox tends to increase fear. Using paradox with sociopathic clients is also discouraged as they are likely to use it to manipulate situations to their own ends (Weeks & L'Abate, 1982).

These interventions are best used when (1) client resistance is so persistent and pervasive that therapeutic progress is blocked, (2) the resistant behaviors are not overcome using more direct interventions, and (3) the possible downside consequences either are well-controlled (inpatient settings) or present a low risk of occurring based on patient history.

USEFUL STRATEGIES WITH RESISTANT TEENAGERS

Some counselors consider the adolescent client as the epitome of resistance. While we believe this evaluation unfairly prejudices the counseling endeavor with teens, we would agree that resistance is normative, not exceptional, with adolescents. Hence, it behooves any counselor working with teenage clients to be able to call upon a diverse repertoire of skills to help make counseling a success. Consider the following suggestions for dealing with teen resistance:

- Get out of the office and be active while interacting.
- Reduce the trappings and behavior of authority.
- Have food and snacks available.
- Laugh, especially at yourself.
- Be courteous and respectful.
- Put on some rock music and discuss it if the client notices it.
- Avoid showing off your expertise.
- Use and allow for different mediums for expression.
- Pursue behavior change, *then* consider working on insight and meaning.
- Reframe drug use as avoidance of pain.
- Highlight hidden and positive personality aspects.
- Encourage resistance and join your client in reviewing how it's done.

WORKING WITH POTENTIALLY DANGEROUS ADOLESCENTS

The most difficult counseling cases involve hostile and potentially dangerous clients, especially impulsive, angry, and drug-abusing adolescents. Consider the following guidelines for working with these clients:

1. *Stay in control; be clear about boundaries.* Establish minimal rules and be clear in letting your adolescent client know what they are: No smoking in session, no violence or threats, no physical contact, no coming to sessions high. If helpful,

write out the rules and post them. You must be able to work with a sense of safety, especially when counseling risky clients. Do not be shy about speaking with your supervisor about your work environment if you do not feel that you can maintain control with certain clients. Here are some ways you can stay in control:

- Avoid power struggles as much as possible.
- Acknowledge intense anger.
- Validate, then correct client misperceptions.
- Seek out the hurt beneath the client's anger.
- Acknowledge and reframe shock statements.
- Admit your confusion and need for further information.

2. *Draw the line and respond when it's crossed.* If your rules are broken, give a clear and assertive warning, noting the consequences of the second breach. If the rules are ignored or broken again, end the session immediately and instruct the client that you will consult with parents or guardians before the next session is scheduled.

3. *Speak briefly and directly.* Some counselors start to ramble when they feel out of control. They keep talking until they regain a sense of control. This may be helpful for therapists, but it almost certainly is not for clients since it can increase their frustration and diminish their respect for you. It's better to learn to speak honestly, briefly, and directly to the client, using physical gestures to reinforce your message.

4. *Be able to address tough issues.* Acknowledge racism and sexism. Identify victimization and the call for justice. Address abuses of authority when it's appropriate. Don't shy away from discussions of death, suicide, heaven and hell, and the meaninglessness of life.

CHALLENGE AND PARADOX WITH RESISTANT CHRISTIANS

While most of the previous ideas are somewhat paradoxical in nature, working with resistant believers requires an experienced wisdom and careful handling. Overcoming resistance in committed Christian clients is doubly difficult because it is often supported by reference to Scripture and God or reliance on spiritual practices (Kehoe & Getheil, 1984; Lovinger, 1979). Thus, when you challenge a client's resistance, you are challenging God and religious beliefs, fighting all that is right and good in the view of your client. As a result, client resistance often increases, and your influence can quickly plummet. As an alternative approach, consider using paradox, metaphor, and storytelling as a way to deflect and disarm the religious resistance that cannot (and in clients' eyes, *should not*) be fought.

A BIBLICAL EXAMPLE OF "PARADOXICAL CONFRONTATION"

In 2 Samuel we read how Nathan confronted King David about his misdeeds:

> When [Nathan] came to him, he said, "There were two men in a certain town, one rich and the other poor. The rich man had a very large number of sheep and cattle, but the poor man had nothing except one little ewe lamb he had bought. He raised it, and it grew up with him and his children. It shared his food, drank from his cup and even slept in his arms. It was like a daughter to him.
>
> "Now a traveler came to the rich man, but the rich man refrained from taking one of his own sheep or cattle to prepare a meal for the traveler who had come to him. Instead, he took the ewe lamb that belonged to the poor man and prepared it for the one who had come to him."
>
> David burned with anger against the man and said to Nathan, "As surely as the LORD lives, the man who did this deserves to die!..."
>
> Then Nathan said to David, "You are the man! This is what the LORD, the God of Israel, says: 'I anointed you king over Israel, and I delivered you from the hand of Saul. I gave your master's house to you, and your master's wives into your arms. I gave you the house of Israel and Judah. And if all this had been too little, I would have given you even more. Why did you despise the word of the LORD by doing what is evil is his eyes? You struck down Uriah the Hittite with the sword and took his wife to be your own....' "
>
> Then David said to Nathan, "I have sinned against the LORD."
> (12:1-5,7-9,13)

Had Nathan directly confronted David's sin with Bathsheba—a confrontation with the king of Israel—it would likely have triggered a defensive denial and a counterreaction in David. In fact, many men throughout history have lost their heads for less when confronting a king with a pointed or undesirable message.

By telling a story, Nathan completely bypassed David's defenses and, on an emotional level, drew him into the injustice of the situation from the Lord's perspective. As a result, David's assimilation of guilt and confession was profound, as was his acceptance of the serious penalties that God exacted as a consequence of his sin (verses 10-23). Could a direct confrontation have worked as well? Probably not. Nathan's use of a paradoxical story was a brilliant, God-directed approach that bore the best fruit that could possibly come from such a tragic incident.

OTHER STRATEGIES FOR WORKING WITH RESISTANT CHRISTIANS

Narramore (1994) was especially insightful about this process, and we have adapted his work in the development of the following outline on using paradoxical interventions to help overcome religious-based resistance.

1. *Affirm and support religious and spiritual practices before you challenge any behavior that is tied to them.* "Yes, it is a blessing to study God's Word as much as you do, but I wonder if you use your Bible study at times to avoid talking with your wife about your marital problems."

2. *Affirm the truth in any statement of resistance before going on to the challenge.* "Yes, I agree with you that Scripture is very clear about the primacy of our relationship with God, but what did he do when he saw that Adam was alone? He didn't berate Adam for desiring someone besides God. He created woman and gave her to Adam as a blessed gift. We need God, and we need other people as well."

3. *Return to the emotional state of the client when you acknowledge biblical truth—even while you are challenging the client's attempt to intellectualize the discussion and escape emotional discomfort.* "Yes, you're right about the need for children to obey their parents. Believe me, I know how tough but necessary it is to strike that balance between granting your teenagers certain freedoms and requiring that they obey the rules. Still, I notice how your children's disobedience hurts you and produces a lot of anger. How do you deal with those feelings when you're challenging your kids' misbehavior?"

4. *On occasion, it is better to concede the fight over interpretation of a particular text or doctrine in order to defuse the resistance and return to the real issue.* "Yeah, I suppose the church will be debating how much the congregation should know about a church disciplinary matter until the Lord returns. I see your point and know there's much support for that view. Even if your committee agrees with you, how are you going to heal the hurt feelings in your church that this fight has created?"

5. *If clients refer to Philippians 3:13-14 to justify their refusal to look at painful issues from the past, note that Paul is calling people to avoid pride over past accomplishments, not suggesting that we avoid past issues and hurts.* "In my counseling work, I don't spend a lot of time dwelling on the past either, but it is important to deal with any unfinished business, like confessing what has happened, giving it to God, and forgiving those who hurt us."

6. *If clients cite Philippians 4:8 to justify focusing only on the positive and denying anything painful, remind them that the verse starts out by calling*

us to think on whatever is true. "Let's not dwell on the painful event, but let's do acknowledge it and deal with it in a godly way because it is a true event in your history."

7. *If Ephesians 5:22 (regarding wifely submission) is used by either husband or wife to justify control or abuse, point out that the section on marital instructions actually begins with verse 21 (husbands and wives should submit to one another).* State categorically that what you see is "unjust and that there is no biblical justification for abuse or coercive control in marriage."

8. *When Ephesians 4:26 is used to deny anger because "good Christians don't get angry," note that the Bible gives room for anger and only challenges sinful anger.* Furthermore, consider reframing anger in terms of the fear of loss or abandonment and address the root issue.

Narramore (1994) wisely reflects that

[w]hen patients utilize biblical passages or Christian concepts to reinforce their resistances, therapists need to find ways of interpreting those resistances without undermining or challenging the healthy aspects of patients' faith.... This can be done by affirming the healthy aspects of a patient's faith while offering balancing biblical passages or alternative scriptural interpretations that challenge the defensive use of Scripture. Like any other confrontation...this must be done in a manner that preserves or heightens the patient's affective awareness and contact with the therapist rather than in a way that leads to a defensive, intellectualized discussion. (p. 258)

Resistance in counseling and psychotherapy is, at another level, grist for the argument that all helping should take place in the context of a supportive and growing church community. By its very nature, counseling is a temporary and somewhat alien experience that will never be fully synonymous with the personal friendships and loving relationships that should be normative in the church.

It is amazing (and humbling) to observe how a client's determined resistance (toward you as a counselor or toward some issue) can completely disappear when it is addressed in the context of a group of caring friends and respected church leaders who join a session to consider how to be a support system for the individual in crisis. While a good counseling or helping ministry should be part of every church's outreach, it will never take the place of the church.

PART V

THE MAJOR
MODALITIES
OF CHRISTIAN
COUNSELING

CHAPTER 17

PASTORAL CARE AND COUNSELING

Soul Care Centered in the Church

RON HAWKINS, EDWARD HINDSON, AND TIM CLINTON

Do not run from [him who gives good counsel] for never in your life will you esteem anyone like him.... Two are better than one, says Scripture.... He who deprives a blind man of his leader, a flock of its shepherd, a lost man of his guide, a child of its father, a patient of his doctor, a ship of its pilot, imperils all. And he who attempts unaided to struggle with the spirits is slain by them.

—JOHN CLIMACUS, *The Ladder of Divine Ascent*

Steel beams covered the ground, each bearing numbers that, although beyond comprehension, were clearly of great significance to some master builder. In the midst of the rusting steel stood a massive crane seven stories high with a boom more than one hundred feet in length. One look and you knew that when connection was made between steel and machine, each piece of rusting steel would leave the ground, make its way to an appointed place in the superstructure of the building yet unformed, and fulfill its preestablished role in bringing to completion the intentions of the master architect. The university community whose life would be enriched by the presence of this huge new edifice watched with excitement as each part was placed into the fabric of the soon-to-be academic structure.

This scene may serve as a metaphor to enhance our understanding of the church and the provisions God has set within her to empower competent Christian counseling as a ministry rooted in the church.

THE ROLE AND PURPOSE OF THE CHURCH

Ask for a definition of the church today and you will get a variety of answers:
- the building on the corner
- the people who have accepted Jesus Christ as Lord and Savior
- a place to meet friends and share common interests
- a place to serve the community
- a place to meet with and worship God
- a place (cynics might say) where they always ask for money; a place rigid in its rules and full of hypocrites

Barna (1998) emphasizes the role of the church in contemporary culture: "In the end the Church must address the contradiction between what the Bible exhorts us to pursue spiritually and what Americans have chosen to pursue, based upon cultural assumptions and preferences" (p. 21).

Let's return to our construction metaphor to help us see the church's role and purpose. In Adam, we are like the steel girders lying in the dirt, settled and comfortable in the niches and vices we have cut for ourselves. Comforted by the impressiveness of our mass and weight, we are only moderately aware of the deadly process that is consuming us (Ephesians 2:1-2; Romans 5:12). Occasionally, in more sober moments, we long for someone with the power to lift us to a place of meaningful purpose and with the compassion to use a grand superstructure designed to transcend our temporality.

Jesus said, "I will build my church" (Matthew 16:18). He is the Architect, the Master Builder. Colossians 1:18 reveals that he is the head of the body, the church. The biblical account of the birth and growth of the church demonstrates the existence of this compassionate Master Builder (Ephesians 1:1-3; Romans 9:10-29; 1 Corinthians 12:4-27). Sitting exalted in the heavens, Jesus has might and power far beyond that of a massive construction crane. He sees the markings on each corrupted piece of steel that speak clearly to his ownership. He has appointed each piece a place in the superstructure of the church, the blueprints for which have existed from the foundations of eternity (Ephesians 1:4-5).

Through the church's two-thousand-year history, the Master Architect has employed many "subcontractors" to accomplish his purposes (2 Corinthians 5:14-21). Paul said, "By the grace God has given me, I laid a foundation as an expert builder" (1 Corinthians 3:10). Pastor Rick Warren (1995) believes "the church exists to edify, encourage, exalt, equip, and evangelize. To bring people to Jesus Christ and membership in His family, develop them into Christlike maturity, and equip them for their ministry in the church and life mission in the world in order to magnify God's name" (p. 106).

The church is the visible expression of God's compassion for humanity, his passion for connection with a people, and his will to create a community through whom he might reveal his love and glory to a fallen world (Hosea 3:1-2; 1 John 3:1-24). By means of the gospel working through the Son and the Spirit, God frees us from sin and death, lifts us out of our resting place in the earth, and connects us to himself for his heavenly purposes (Galatians 4:1–5:18; Hebrews 10:25).

THE CHIEF METAPHORS FOR THE CHURCH

The Bible uses many metaphors to describe the church, and each captures some unique element of the nature and character of the body. An examination of several metaphors can sharpen our competency in pastoral care and counseling centered in the church.

A BUILDING, A DWELLING PLACE FOR GOD

Writing to the church, Peter said, "You also, like living stones, are being built into a spiritual house to be a holy priesthood, offering up spiritual sacrifices acceptable to God through Jesus Christ" (1 Peter 2:5). Paul likewise employed the metaphor of a building to describe the church: "Don't you know that you yourselves are God's temple?" (1 Corinthians 3:16). These passages relate the spiritual nature of the church and designate it as a dwelling place for God.

Many have written of the need people have for an anchor in their lives. The need to *belong* is at the heart of the human struggle. Peter offered grounds for everyone in the church to feel moored to something permanent, to feel anchored to God himself. Beyond that, Peter provided an argument for every believer to feel a sense of significance. Members of the church are connected to the God of the universe. We were once dead, but we are now living stones. We have a purpose. Life is different for us.

Pastoral care and counseling that is centered in the church delivers a message of life, significance, and purpose for all who embrace the gospel and come alive in the church. The well-being that people experience through embracing these realities must be recognized by caregivers as an essential component of physical, spiritual, relational, and psychological health (Benson, 1975; Hart, 1999).

A LIVING BODY

The apostle Paul wanted the members of this "spiritual house" to know that theirs is not just a corporate identity. Who we are as individuals—and our providential placement in the building—is a matter of great importance. Consistently, Paul used the metaphor of the body to convey this message. He told the Corinthians that they were all baptized into one body by the Holy Spirit (1 Corinthians 12:13). Then he reminded them, "There are diversities of gifts.... But one and the same Spirit works all these things, distributing to each one individually as He wills.... Now God has set the members, each one of them, in the body just as He pleased" (1 Corinthians 12:4,11,18, NKJV).

The Ephesian believers were told that there is one body, that Christ is the head of the church, the Savior of the body, and that he gave himself for it. He designated some to be apostles, prophets, evangelists, and pastor-teachers for the equipping of the saints for the work of the ministry. The whole body is to "grow up in all things into Him who is the head—Christ—from whom the whole body, joined and knit together by what every joint supplies, according to the effective working by which every part does its share, causes growth of the body for the edifying of itself in love" (Ephesians 4:15-16, NKJV).

The body metaphor conveys a sense of connection with community, a family identity. It conveys, like the building metaphor, a sense of belonging, an anchor point that is of vital significance for individual health and growth. Individual contributions to the larger body are rooted in personal giftedness, and they impact others for good. This ability to make an impact validates personal significance and is inherently therapeutic. It calls for the establishment of personal boundaries, contributes to a sense of healthy uniqueness, and calls forth the confessional praise, "I am fearfully and wonderfully made...and that my soul knows very well" (Psalm 139:14, NKJV).

Equipping people in the church to make such a confession should be a high priority in the delivery of competent pastoral care. It equips people with a testimony infused with celebration that is catalytic in the conversion of the unregenerate (Cloud & Townsend, 1999; Crabb, 1999).

THE PEOPLE OF GOD, A HOLY NATION

The church is also described in the Bible as the people of God. Peter, commenting on the nature of the church, said followers of Christ "are a chosen generation, a royal priesthood, a holy nation, His own special people, that you may proclaim the praises of Him who called you out of darkness into His marvelous light; who once were not a people but are now the people of God, who had not obtained mercy but now have obtained mercy" (1 Peter 2:9-10, NKJV).

It is impossible to fully comprehend Peter's words without understanding their source. In the Old Testament book of Hosea, we see the heart and holiness of God as it unfolds in the life of a family. Hosea comes home from a hard day in the life of a prophet to find that his wife is gone. She has taken to playing the harlot and has abandoned Hosea and his children. The children bear the names *Lo-Ruhamah* and *Lo-Ammi,* which translated mean "no love" and "not my people." Hosea's tragic family situation is a metaphor for Israel's abandonment of God and subsequent harlotry.

In Hosea 3 we discover something that is of inestimable value for pastoral-care ministry. God instructed Hosea, "Go, show your love to your wife again, though she is loved by another and is an adulteress. Love her as the LORD loves the Israelites" (verse 1). In obedience to God's command, Hosea redeemed his wife for fifteen shekels of silver, half the going rate for a slave.

Clowney (1976) remarks, "The people of God are not an already existing nation brought into relationship with him. They are constituted by God's assembly and God's dwelling" (p. 15). It is God, in the mystery of his own willfulness, who is the designer of the church's composition as well as the stipulator of its structures (Ephesians 1:1-6). No matter how far we may run away from God, our life as a covenanting people is shaped by the directives received for the Master Architect in his Word.

The assembly of God's people is not, however, an end in itself. Rather, "the church as a people-in-covenant is related to God's larger intention" (Grenz, 1994, p. 614). The definitions that shape our mission and build our character are not derived from earthly regents, but rather from One who reigns supreme and has chosen us for a place in the church. Our view of the church must always be understood within the larger context of the reign of God. We are a people of his choosing, formed for his purposes to bear the marks of his kingdom. As the people of his kingdom, we are people with a future. This sense of purpose and connection to the future is vital to our emotional and physical health (Frankl, 1984; Moltmann, 1993).

This is a powerful message, one that is at the heart of pastoral care. It is a message of unfathomable love and grace that speaks of a God who pursues the fallen sinner and rebellious saint to the darkest corners of our escape attempts. It is a story of God's insistence and pursuit, and of his refusal to surrender us to our sins (Hosea 11:9-11). Hosea informs us that God really does love us, really can heal us, really can make his way to where we are.

Pastoral care requires a heavy emphasis on the nature of God as invasive in his compassion, invested in the creation of a godly seed, and highly intentional in his resolve to use that seed for the accomplishment of his purposes (Genesis 1:27-28; Hosea 3:1-5; 11:9-11; Malachi 2:11-15). It further requires that we portray God as sovereign and beyond human attempts to frustrate his purposes (Ecclesiastes 3:11; Romans 8:28-30).

THE FELLOWSHIP OF THE SPIRIT

The church is also the fellowship of the Spirit. The people of God are possessed by the Spirit of God, renewed, assembled in the body under the headship of Christ, and destined for full maturity in Christ (John 3:3-8; Galatians 5:22-23). The Spirit brings a power for transformation that surpasses what is normal. His supernatural empowerment provides Christian counselors a level of competence that revolutionizes our optimism regarding potential for change.

Paul spent major portions of his writings exhorting believers to fulfill the truths embodied in the above metaphors and confronting them regarding their failures to do so (Galatians 4–6; Ephesians 4–6). Additionally, he prescribed a structure to oversee and direct the worship and ministry of the church. Paul's counsel in the New Testament is still totally appropriate for our context today. We will now develop that structure and move on to examine where the church of the third millennium finds itself.

THE ROLE AND PURPOSE OF THE PASTOR

People still seek pastoral care in life's darkest hours and grandest moments. Central to the work of the church is the caring pastor (Hart, Gulbranson, & Smith, 1992; Miller, 1985; Warren, 1995). The Master Builder has placed in the church "some pastors and teachers, for the equipping of the saints for the work of ministry, for the edifying of the body of Christ, till we all come to the unity of the faith and of the knowledge of the Son of God, to a perfect man, to the measure of the stature of the fullness of Christ" (Ephesians 4:11-13, NKJV). Pastors are vital to the success of the program Jesus has committed to his church and are God's gift to the church (Murren, 1999; Warren, 1995).

Hart, Gulbranson, and Smith (1992) describe the power of the preaching and counseling work of a pastor to bring about the transformation of individuals and families:

> Because a preacher got close enough to understand what was going on and
> help us through the struggles, we made it. I can't imagine my preaching apart
> from being involved with people in counseling. To get close and wrestle with
> the human condition and to explore the depths of God's Word, to speak to
> people's situations from the pulpit and in the counseling setting—these are to
> me the perfect, indispensable complements of pastoral ministry. (p. 51)

Hurting people who make their way into our churches need a pastor who, in his shepherding ministry, imitates the Good Shepherd. As Isaiah 40:11 says, "He tends his flock like a shepherd: He gathers the lambs in his arms and carries them close to his heart." Adams (1975) states:

> Pastoral counseling is a special, not separate, area of pastoral activity; indeed it is close to the heart of shepherding. It involves the extension of help to wandering, torn, defeated, dispirited sheep who need the restoring mentioned in Psalm 23:3. Restoration here means refreshment. It constitutes the work of putting new life into one by convicting and changing, encouraging and strengthening after trial, defeat, failure, and/or discouragement. (p. 14)

The apostle Paul appointed caring shepherds and elders in every town where he planted a church, and he carefully prescribed their duties (Titus 1:5; 3:9). He reminded Timothy that "elders who direct the affairs of the church well are worthy of double honor" (1 Timothy 5:17). Paul affectionately described his engagement of the pastoral task (Acts 20:22-31) and offered an example of a discipling relationship (2 Timothy).

Addressing the counseling challenges in a local church can benefit the overall effectiveness of pastoral ministry. As MacArthur and Mack (1994) write, "When a pastor neglects the ministry of counseling others, crucial areas of his ministry suffer. For example, his preaching is dramatically affected. He loses touch with the people's difficulties and the thought processes and habits that lead to problems. Thus he is not prepared to provide the spiritual weapons they need to overcome those problems" (p. 303). Counseling provides preachers with real-life illustrations, keeps them in touch with the emotions of their people, and makes their preaching more applicable to the challenges their listeners confront in daily life.

Because of the multiple demands of ministry, however, pastors should keep in mind the following guidelines for counseling:

1. Pastors should limit the amount of time they spend in counseling. They have many responsibilities and must jealously guard the time they give to their counseling ministries.
2. Pastors should pursue training for their counseling ministry and seek to become as effective as possible in the fulfillment of this aspect of their ministry.
3. Pastors should structure their counseling ministry and be clear with leadership and care-seekers regarding schedules, setting, time constraints, referrals, and so on.
4. Pastors should assure that counseling takes place in a protected environment where any possibility of impropriety is ruled out.
5. Pastors should limit both the number and the length of sessions.

6. Pastors should spread out responsibilities for the management of parishioners' problems. In addition to the support offered by pastor-counselors, it is best to pair every care-seeker with a spiritual director, a friend, or a confidant. In more difficult cases, it is best to pair care-seekers with a professional counselor and have the pastor act as spiritual director and team manager.

7. Pastors should manage confidentiality issues well.

8. Pastors should guard against trying to meet needs beyond their level of training, and they should be prepared to refer parishioners to well-qualified agencies and professionals.

9. Pastors should learn to weigh the personal impact of their engagements with hurting people and be willing always to live with the fallout of their decisions.

10. Pastors should oversee the development of groups to meet specific needs (divorce recovery, for example) as well as the training of lay caregivers and staff members.

THE ROLE OF LAY HELPERS

At least two considerations motivate a pastor's concern to develop lay caregivers. First, if he attempts to fulfill the ministry of caregiving alone, he will be overwhelmed. "Our pastors cannot lead alone. They need others to come alongside to assist and encourage" (Wagner & Martin, 1998, p. 55). Second, it is the pastor's responsibility to train church members to use their gifts for the edification and growth of the body (Ephesians 4:15-16).

Pastors understand that "as the members of the body minister to each other, speaking the truth in love, the church is built up. The strengthening of each member results in a collective growing up to the fullness of the stature of Christ. Thus the entire body is matured as the members minister to each other according to their giftedness" (MacArthur & Mack, 1994, p. 312).

Counseling is therefore to be conducted by the entire body. Each member is filled with goodness to counsel (Romans 15:14). The church is brought to maturity only as every Spirit-gifted member serves God, one another, and those outside the church (1 Corinthians 12:1-31; Ephesians 4:7-16). The assembly gathers for instruction and worship, but equally important is their commitment to encourage one another toward love and good works. This commitment often requires that members exhort one another in light of the calling that rests upon the assembly and of the approaching day of Christ's return (Hebrews 10:24-25).

The call to collective ministry in the body and the need to fulfill the biblical mandate to make disciples mean that all new Christians should be engaged with a "triangle" of caregivers (see figure 17.1). Although this arrangement might involve any number of people, three roles are critical: (1) an elder or shepherd, who acts as a team coordinator overseeing a discipling process; (2) a caring confidant, who offers acceptance and encouragement no matter what; and (3) a spiritual director, who provides guidance and accountability (Ecclesiastes 4:12).

FIG. 17.1. TRIANGLE OF CAREGIVERS

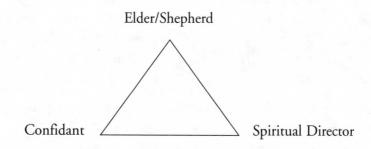

Elder/Shepherd

Confidant   Spiritual Director

When a disciple gets stuck on a personal issue, the help of a well-trained pastoral or professional Christian counselor should be inserted into the growth triangle. The professional joins the team for as long as it takes to get the disciple healthier and then transitions to a consultant role as the church-based discipleship team continues its work.

WHO'S COMING TO CHURCH IN THE THIRD MILLENNIUM?

Determining precisely who is coming to church is vitally important as pastoral and professional Christian counselors seek to deliver the most competent and helpful care in a ministry context (Backus, 1987; Barna, 1998; MacArthur & Mack, 1994; Murren, 1999).

SOME ARE DEAD AT THE CORE OF THEIR PERSONALITIES

Hart et al.(1992) describe the tragic condition of those men and women who are in Adam: "God's image is encapsulated by a fallen sinful core that becomes surrounded by stiff defenses. But before it can be adequately contained, sin will have contaminated the rest of the self, both ego- and self-system, leaving us tainted by evil, replete with many bad habits and tendencies" (p. 180).

Paul urged the Ephesian assembly with strong words when he said, "Awake, you who sleep, arise from the dead, and Christ will give you light" (Ephesians 5:14, NKJV). Horton (1994) admonishes the church to beware of attempting to bring about transformation in the lives of people who have never received a new nature. He issues a sobering challenge to those called to pastoral care and counseling:

> The liberating power of grace is not found first in its transformative charac-
> ter—important as that is—but in its imputational character. We not only
> want to appeal to God's grace as something that converts and improves, but
> as something that declares. It declares the individual righteous even while
> he or she is still sinful, even before grace has begun its work of moral trans-
> formation. Apart from justification of the sinner before the face of God
> even as sinner, the guilt and just fear of condemnation cannot be dealt
> with. (p. 240)

At the center of the evangelical call to pastoral care and counseling in the church is the issue of regeneration. Hart et al. (1992) write, "Every evangelical Christian ought to hold dear the doctrine of regeneration which simply means 'rebirth.' No wonder so many people are suspicious of all therapy. As commonly practiced, it often lacks any recognition of the divine work of grace in the heart, or any recognition of how this work can be fostered and developed" (pp. 170-171).

Pastoral counseling centered in the church is rooted in the good news of the gospel. Grenz (1994) asserts,

> Conversion occurs as an individual responds to the gospel. In repentance
> we see ourselves as sinners: as alienated from God, justly condemned, and
> enslaved by sin. We acknowledge that our life's direction is misguided, we
> feel remorse for this condition, and we desire to follow a new direction. But
> we know that we are ultimately helpless. We are unable to begin anew and
> powerless to remedy our situation. (p. 534)

Faith awakens as we embrace what God has done for us in Christ. Central to regeneration and the experience of baptism is the desire to embrace repentance. Repentance begins with recognizing sin. Paul wrote, "Godly sorrow produces repentance leading to salvation" (2 Corinthians 7:10, NKJV). Godly sorrow results in conviction. People are set free from the power of sin only through repentance. According to Jeremias (1971), "Repentance means learning to say 'Abba' again, putting one's whole trust in the heavenly Father, returning to the Father's house and the Father's arms.... In the last resort, repentance is simply trusting in the grace of God" (p. 156). Romans 7:7-25 makes clear that Christians will still struggle with sin, but they are able to recognize their sin, repent, and restore their relationship with God.

SOME ARE LIVING "IN THE FLESH"

The apostle Paul said there was something inherent in his natural self that was at odds with God's purposes and plans for him (Romans 7:14-25). This indwelling evil tears at the fabric of the people of God individually, and it severely hinders their fellowship in the Spirit. We call it by different names, but this old sin nature, flesh, or sin principle hates God and everything he seeks to do in our lives. The flesh goads us, as it did Adam and Eve, to rebel against God's Word and the ministry of the Holy Spirit in our lives (Galatians 5:13-26).

The impartation of new life in Christ generates a desire for God, a bent toward pleasing God. "However, as long as [Christians] are exposed to the influence of the sin principle, which is resident in the body's flesh, they, as well as the unredeemed body, are as susceptible to sin's domination as they are to the Holy Spirit's control" (Barackman, 1981, p. 197; see also Romans 7:17-18,23; Galatians 5:19-21). The people who come to our churches live in unredeemed bodies and feel the pull of the indwelling sin principle called *the flesh*. They often struggle with appetites that desire satisfaction by means contrary to the laws of God and the life of the Spirit. These individuals are in need of our counsel as they seek in their everyday lives to discipline the "self and its flesh" (Hart et al., 1992, p. 145).

SOME HAVE THOUGHT PATTERNS THAT NEED RENEWAL

Most Christians have spent many years developing thought patterns based on a high degree of error and absorption with self (Backus, 1987; Thurman, 1995; Wilson, 1990). It would be wonderful if God would do a "mind-wipe" as a companion to regeneration, but it doesn't work that way. As Hart et al. (1992) state, "Being born anew is a vital and necessary experience, but it is only the beginning work of grace. Its focus is on healing the core of our being, not our whole being in one fell swoop" (p. 171). Obeying the truth of the Bible and pursuing behavior in harmony with the Holy Spirit are responsibilities of Christians who seek spiritual maturity (Romans 6, Romans 12, Galatians 5, and Ephesians 5).

Renewing our thought life is hard work. Thurman (1995) reminds us that our "brain is like a tape deck. It has access to a personal library of thousands of tapes ready to play at a moment's notice. These tapes contain beliefs, attitudes, and expectations recorded during your life. Some of the tapes are truthful...some of the tapes are filled with lies. Your emotional and spiritual health hinges on these tapes. The challenge in life is to make our mental tapes as truthful as possible so we can maturely handle whatever circumstances come our way" (pp. 2-3). Paul promoted the same process when he discipled Timothy (2 Timothy 2:15). By replacing error-based thinking with the truth found in God's Word, Timothy would gain the wisdom necessary to overcome his fears (2 Timothy 3:15-17). Paul encouraged the Philippians to renew their thought life and confront their anxieties by choosing to think about things that were "excellent" and "praiseworthy" (Philippians 4:8).

The people who come to church often have minds filled with errors that have been absorbed through years of dialogue with the world, the flesh, and the devil. They may be ignorant of the truths found in God's Word. Their minds are filled with attributions rooted in hurtful memories, with broken relationships, with failed promises, with impossible fantasies, with shattered dreams.

Some Are Addicted and Need to Be Set Free

Some people who come to church are addicted to drugs, sex, money, or the things of the world. They need help learning to dehabituate behaviors that hinder growth in Christ and to habituate new behaviors that build relationship with God and others.

Truthful thinking is only part of the struggle faced by people who want to walk in the ways of Christ. Part of the old walk in Adam involved the habitual practice of behaviors that were contrary to walking in the Spirit. Paul reminded the Philippians that, in addition to renewed minds, they should imitate him if they wanted to move to maturity (Philippians 4:9).

When it comes to Christlikeness, one of the main objectives is to break the power of patterns of wrongdoing and evil that govern our lives because of our long habituation to a world alienated from God. "We must learn to recognize these habitual patterns for what they are and escape from their grasp" (Willard, 1998, p. 341). Paul presented a representative list of these evil habits in Galatians 5:19-21 and Ephesians 4:17-32. Adams (1979) reminds us that it is the process of *dehabituation* and *rehabituation* that moves the immature toward maturity in Christ. He said, "Paul not only exhorts, he explains how change can be effected. Change is a two-factored process. These two factors always must be present in order to effect genuine change. Putting off will not be permanent without putting on" (p. 239).

Humans show a marked preference for behaviors that God condemns, but he condemns these behaviors because they are destructive. The management, dehabituation, and ultimate disempowerment of these habits occur when people receive the transforming presence of the Spirit of life in their core self. They can then take responsibility for rehabituating thoughts and behaviors that are contrary to the truth, filling their minds with the Word of God, faithfully practicing the disciplines that support this radical commitment to obedience, and maintaining an attachment to the body of Christ that fosters accountability.

SOME ARE TROUBLED WITH TRAUMA AND POST-TRAUMATIC STRESS

Some people who come to church have been abused and traumatized in the past (or are being abused and traumatized in the present) and may struggle daily with desperation and despair. They need help understanding and managing their feelings. Paul counseled comfort and patience as the approach for those ministering to the timid ("little of soul") and weak in the church (1 Thessalonians 5:14). He spoke with terms of endearment while seeking to help Timothy rise above his fears (2 Timothy 2:1).

Many who enter our churches struggle with depression, anxiety, fears, anger, and a host of other negative emotions. People are sometimes stuck in hurtful emotional cycles, and they seem unable to free themselves in spite of the fact that they are sincerely engaging the challenges to believe and behave well. Ignorant of the body-mind connection, they don't understand that negative feelings often find their derivation in stress, overwork, lack of sleep, metabolic and biochemical imbalance, and other causes having little to do with thoughts or behaviors.

Such people require counseling to ferret out what is at the root of their hurtful feelings (Hart, 1999; Stoop & Masteller, 1996). The simple discovery that emotions are the consequence not of events but rather of our beliefs about those events can be a revelation for some people.

Additionally, it is helpful to view emotions as indicators and motivators. Emotions provide invaluable assistance in identifying thoughts and behaviors not rooted in truth. Much of our motivation for moving ahead in this life is drawn from positive emotions. Those struggling with understanding, managing, or coping with hurtful emotions are frequenting our churches and are in need of counsel (Hart, 1999; Stoop & Masteller, 1996; Wilson, Wilson, Friesen, Paulson, & Paulson, 1997).

SOME ARE WALKING WOUNDED

Some people who come to our churches may be struggling with wounds experienced during hurtful relationships in the past. Murren (1999) states:

> People today are much more wounded. They suffer from relationship
> wounds (consider the high percentages of marriages that end in divorce);

emotional wounds (broken, dysfunctional families leave long trails); the wounds of abuse (sexual abuse alone has been perpetrated upon one-quarter of all female baby boomers); the wounds of drug and alcohol addiction and so much more. (p. 220)

People coming from hurtful environments have formed attachments that are often extremely unhealthy for themselves and others. They enter relationships as codependents or predators. These practices do not disappear with spiritual regeneration, and they can be hidden for a time under the initial transformation and healing influence of the Spirit. They often reemerge, however, during periods of high stress and low spiritual vitality. Deliverance for most will not be magical or instantaneous but will require discipline and counsel. Crabb (1997) observes, "Beneath what culture calls psychological disorder is a soul crying out for what only community can provide" (p. xv).

SOME ARE BESET BY EVIL POWERS

Not surprisingly, the struggle between light and darkness continues today and seems to be intensifying. Anderson (1995) reports that a great many "professing Christian young people are hearing voices or struggling with bad thoughts" (p. 15). Since the Garden of Eden, the war for the soul of man has raged. We must train some believers in spiritual warfare to help free and insulate the soul.

Paul reminds us that "We do not wrestle against flesh and blood, but against principalities, against powers, against the rulers of the darkness of this age" (Ephesians 6:12, NKJV). Peter admonishes us to "be self-controlled and alert. Your enemy the devil prowls around like a roaring lion looking for someone to devour. Resist him, standing firm in the faith" (1 Peter 5:8-9). We read that when Daniel prayed for help, the moment the prayer left his lips, God sent an angel to help him. The angel couldn't get to Daniel for a period of time because "the prince of the Persian kingdom resisted me twenty-one days. Then Michael, one of the chief princes, came to help me, because I was detained there with the king of Persia" (Daniel 10:13).

THE PRESENT INADEQUACY OF THE CHURCH

So how are we doing with the hurting multitudes? How are we helping those already in the church and the masses yet to come? What are we offering them? Is the church able to fulfill its healing mission and its call to make disciples?

Many pastors and counselors are rightfully concerned about the church's state of preparedness to meet the needs of those in our congregations. We rely too much on the preaching and teaching ministries of our pastors. We are far too cognitive and propositional in our approach to maturing people in Christ. We are fairly good at being the "spiritual school," but we are failing to be the "spiritual hospital" that so many need.

Anderson (1995) shares this concern: "I was deeply committed to preaching and teaching God's Word, and I still am. But I had just given a person the best possible teaching on the attributes of God, which she listened to three times, and the effect was zero" (p. 110). Sweet (1999) asks, "Can the church stop its puny, hack dreams of trying to make a 'difference in the world' and start dreaming God-sized dreams of making the world different?" (p. 16).

Crabb (1997), too, is concerned about our response to the wounded people who are in our churches: "It is time to go beneath the moralism that assumes the church's job is done when it instructs people in biblical principles and then exhorts them to do right" (p. xvi). He believes that "the greatest need in modern civilization is the development of communities—true communities where the heart of God is home, where the humble and wise learn to shepherd those on the path behind them, where trusting strugglers lock arms with others as together they journey" (p. xvi).

Such is the vision of God for his church. Our challenge is to create a church with global impact that manifests equal regard for winning people to Christ and for maturing people in him (Matthew 28:18-20). This vision can be achieved only if the church is highly intentional in both evangelism and discipleship.

One pastor we know has often said, "The goal at our church is to make disciples." When asked how many converts have been made as a result of his church's ministry, he glowed with gratefulness for the large number who have come to Christ. When asked how many of those people have been discipled and were discipling others, he confessed his desire to see a great improvement in those numbers. When questioned further about his strategy for achieving better results in fulfilling his expressed mission "to make disciples," he confessed that he had no plan.

PASTORAL CARE AND COUNSELING IN AN INTENTIONAL MODEL FOR CHURCH DISCIPLESHIP

Barna (1998) makes the following observation: "Our approach [to growing the church] must be strategic and intentional. The plan will work best if it incorporates a vision for what we hope to achieve, a strategy for getting there, specific steps we may take to advance toward our vision, and ways of objectively evaluating how well we are doing" (p. 196). What would the church's program look like if we agreed with the goal of making disciples? How would the insights gained from biblical counseling and data from the bio-psycho-social sciences contribute to an intentional plan for making disciples?

Figure 17.2 illustrates the current state of disciple making in the church (evaluating both intention and action) and provides an intentional model for disciple making. Each element should be considered critical to achieving this goal and should therefore be approached with a high degree of intentionality and commitment to action.

In this model, the church is a multifaceted fellowship of believers who minister together to evangelize the lost, provide restorative counseling for them, help them grow in spiritual formation, equip them as the saints of God, and disciple

FIG. 17.2. DISCIPLE MAKING IN THE CHURCH

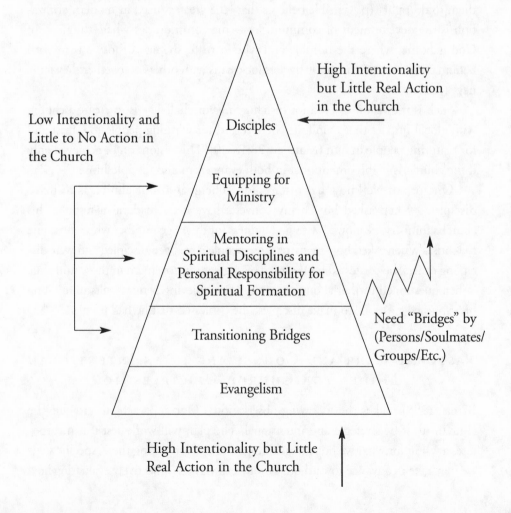

High Intentionality but Little Real Action in the Church

Low Intentionality and Little to No Action in the Church

Disciples

Equipping for Ministry

Mentoring in Spiritual Disciplines and Personal Responsibility for Spiritual Formation

Transitioning Bridges

Need "Bridges" by (Persons/Soulmates/ Groups/Etc.)

Evangelism

High Intentionality but Little Real Action in the Church

them into mature believers. In these processes, caregivers of all kinds are needed to help resolve personal and relational issues that affect spiritual growth and to prepare the hearts of believers for maturity. Thus we equip caregivers for practical ministries that are an outgrowth of their own spiritual progress. In so doing, we enhance the qualitative growth of the members—helping them grow into true disciples—in order to more effectively assimilate the quantitative growth of the church through outreach.

EVANGELISM MINISTRY

God's passion for evangelism and redemption of the lost is documented consistently throughout the Old and New Testaments. (See the book of Hosea and Luke 19:10.) He commissioned the church to carry out this mission, and he calls believers to share the gospel of reconciliation (Matthew 28:18-20; Romans 1; 2 Corinthians 5:11-21).

Yet we are failing in the call to evangelize because so few churches are intentional and purposeful in their approach to reaching the lost (Bakke, 1997). Warren (1995) laments this lack of intentionality: "The concept of targeting is built into the Great Commission. Each people group needs an evangelistic strategy" (p. 159).

When we come alongside the people of this world, we often discover deep wounds and seeking hearts. Indeed, ours is a generation thirsty for spirituality (Barna, 1998; Horton, 1994). We should view these needs as an open invitation to evangelism, but not as an invitation to slam people with the gospel. Murren (1999) adds, "When broken and disenfranchised people first start coming to church services, they want to feel welcome, yet also remain anonymous. These two desires are not as antithetical as they may seem. Postmodern men and women often require an extended preconversion phase in which they're allowed to simply sit, watch, and listen for a while. It does no good to force the pace" (p. 219).

People called to be healers must learn to listen well, connect through serving, build trust, and meet tangible needs. We must always be ready to speak to the greatest need, which is a personal relationship with Jesus Christ. Aldrich (1981) insists that Christians be ready to cross traditional boundaries and become the good news of the gospel as Christ ministers through our serving hearts. When people see Christ in our caring, they are more open to our proclamation of the words of the gospel. Aldrich asserts, "Once a thriving church is established, the starting point for evangelism increasingly shifts from proclamation (confrontational) to presence (relational)" (p. 81). Presence is about understanding, acceptance, hope building, and acts of service that validate true love for people where they are.

This kind of presence is not normal for people in love with self and dominated by a quest for self-fulfillment. The people of God who are trained in communication and listening skills, and who practice loving service that meets real needs, will find the soil fertile for sharing the life-changing hope found in the gospel.

We cannot begin to engage this challenge unless we move beyond the pulpit and our professional offices and involve the people in the pews. However, most parishioners are not ready for this challenge. They require intentional training to come alongside people who have oft-unspoken spiritual questions. They need to learn how to match their life message, the Scriptures, and the gospel call to their immediate context (Ecclesiastes 12:9-10). The wounded of every generation are comforted and encouraged through the stories of healing that come from recovering sufferers empowered by God's love. Evangelism is foundational to any model of intentional discipleship.

Counseling for Assimilation

Barna (1998) indicates that the average newcomer attends church for approximately eight weeks and is not seen again. Other research illustrates the sporadic nature of most people who attend church. "Nearly one-fifth of all churchgoers now attend more than one church and the most committed church people only allocate two blocks of time in their week to church-related activities, down from four blocks twenty years ago" (p. 18).

This tenuous connection with a local church makes most Americans unwilling to be held accountable for their beliefs and behaviors. To use Barna's metaphor, church for the average American has become a place where Christians can make a "pit stop." And we are commanded to make disciples out of such a transient crowd? How are we to accomplish such a worthy goal? What elements should be kept in mind as we seek to assimilate people into the life of the church?

Purposeful assimilation. We must become highly intentional about moving people from a positive response to the gospel into a discipleship situation where they can grow and mature. As Warren (1995) says, "Assimilate new members on purpose!" (p. 138). Assimilation must anchor them in the Scriptures and in a vital relationship with God's people.

Attractive bridges. Bridges must be securely in place in the church across which these people can safely move to explore opportunities for growth and discipleship. The rationale for these bridges and the call to cross them must be explained in a manner that appeals to and makes sense to the new convert. The benefits of crossing into areas that will stimulate maturity—as well as the disadvantages of doing so—must be clearly set forth.

Coming alongside. There must be helpers in the church who are willing and equipped to provide direction and encouragement to new converts. The relationships will be intense, but they will also be a source of fun and joy to the people on both sides. These helpers will assist people in crossing bridges and in developing spiritual disciplines that promote the imitation of Jesus Christ.

Skilled communications. Helpers who disciple others must be thoroughly trained, and, at a minimum, they must understand how to do the following:

- Communicate a biblical worldview.
- Utilize their life messages to bring encouragement and comfort.
- Listen carefully and connect with personal needs.
- Pray for people's needs.
- Share God's love and the gospel message.
- Offer biblical direction on matters of spiritual concern.
- Know when to refer to a pastoral or professional counselor.

Counseling that renews minds and reshapes behavior. We must be thoroughly prepared to assist people with the resolution of conflict that is rooted in error-based thinking and destructive behaviors. This is a process of helping others put off the ways of sin and put on new life in Christ.

Patience and perseverance. People who are being discipled sometimes get stuck because of unresolved issues in their past. We must be prepared to lead them through the process of repentance, forgiveness, and the biblical resolution of these issues. We must also make a relational investment that builds trust, encourages a healthy identity in Christ, and engages the disciple in acts of service in Jesus' name.

Small groups. It is necessary to structure opportunities for small-group involvement that allow new converts to experience appropriate levels of transparency, intimacy, and accountability with fellow believers. Small-group ministry undertakes reparative tasks in the lives of the children of God that should have been accomplished in the family of origin (Erikson, 1950; Stoop & Masteller, 1996; Wilson, 1990). We must help our church families acquire the skills necessary to develop healthy, Christ-centered relationships.

Fitting the approach to the person. Remember that Jesus challenged the Pharisees when he said that the Sabbath was made for people, not people for the Sabbath (Mark 2:23-27). Paul counseled flexibility in people helping (1 Thessalonians 5:14). One size does not fit all. The faint of heart require large doses of encouragement. The arrogant who have an idolatrous relationship with their own ideas need to be challenged. Those struggling with addictions need a mixture of support, compassion, and instruction. Effective caregivers are "flexible—that is, they are not tied to a single methodology that they use for all clients.... Flexible counselors adapt. The behavior is always mediated by the question, 'Which technique will work best for this particular client with this set of problems?' " (Cormier & Cormier, 1991, p. 12).

Expect setbacks. Growth doesn't follow a consistently upward trajectory. With all its ups and downs, it looks more like a stock market graph. That is why Paul counseled, "Be patient with everyone" (1 Thessalonians 5:14). Sanctification does not occur in one glorious moment; it requires one who walks alongside another to show patience and endurance (Erikson, 1950; Grenz, 1994; Hart et al., 1992).

The small number of genuinely mature believers is due in large part to the lack of mentor-disciplers who facilitate the assimilation of people into the life of the church. People will continue to spill out of our churches—or, worse yet, to stay and sabotage much of the Lord's mission—unless we help individuals move from *convert* to *disciple*. We are not fulfilling the commandment of our Lord to make disciples who can in turn disciple others. We get clobbered in our churches because these undisciplined and immature people then serve on our governing boards, compromise the church's integrity, and often become the pastor's worst nightmare.

SPIRITUAL DISCIPLINES: FORMING THE LIFE OF CHRIST WITHIN

The idea of becoming intentional with regard to examining values, beliefs, virtues, attitudes, attributions, and developmental histories strikes fear in some pastors and church leaders. Is it really necessary? Who is prepared for such an undertaking? Most pastors are not negative regarding the advisability of such care, but they're fearful because so few in the church are prepared to undertake the challenge. It was Paul who told the Roman believers of his great confidence in their ability to handle such a ministry of transitional care. He was confident that they were "full of goodness, complete in knowledge and competent to instruct one another" (Romans 15:14).

It is our privilege to share the gospel message that redeems people from sin and to engage people intentionally in the process of sanctification. Is training desirable? Yes. Is it available? Yes. Will we still need professional counselors to back us up? Certainly. However, it is amazing to witness the power of a simple testimony wrapped in love and awe to impact another person for powerful life change.

Assimilation into the body of Christ requires growth in the spiritual disciplines, forming the life of Christ within individuals and leading them to mature discipleship. Developing these disciplines will foster in new converts a fuller experience of the Holy Spirit. This experiential spirituality will overwhelm and render powerless many of the wounds that have troubled people in their preconversion days. Connecting with a pastoral or peer-level caregiver, experiencing intimate connection with caring people in the church, and practicing Spirit-empowering activities will promote transformation for individuals. Spiritual disciplines that must be taught include prayer, worship, Bible study, evangelism, meditation on Scripture, fasting, serving, and solitude (Foster, 1988; Willard, 1998).

An important consideration in teaching the disciplines is modeling for new converts how these are done. We often tell our parishioners to read the Bible, pray, and worship. But the old nature doesn't know how to do these things and really doesn't want to. We must model the spiritual disciplines and encourage new believers until, like children learning to ride a bicycle, they "get it." Accountability is critical, for it alone provides the proper environment for mastering the inner world, the place where deception and compromise are everyday occurrences.

Spiritual formation should never be separated from discipleship. The disciplines alone will prepare the believer for the Spirit's filling, for a lifestyle that reveals personal integrity, and for the spiritual warfare that confronts those who move toward maturity. Failing to address either the training of the caregiver or the disciple may result in an aborted mission: the drifting away of the new believer and the loss of all he or she could have brought to the church. Indeed, many Christians may have a spiritual epitaph that reads, "Died in childhood."

DISCIPLESHIP MINISTRY

Since the process of spiritual formation in the transition phase focuses extensively on reworking the inner life of the new convert, it is an exercise in futility to assume that we can be part of a magnificent superstructure without carefully attending to the foundation.

We are now ready to train for leadership positions those believers who are aware of their internal issues, have experienced healing, and consistently practice the spiritual disciplines. Counselors have gained some interesting insights regarding the demands of certain positions and the qualities individual believers offer to meet those challenges (Bradley & Carty, 1991). Many new converts have poor experiences with assimilation into the body because they are ill-trained and ill-suited to accomplish the tasks assigned to them. Being intentional about equipping people for ministry will include an emphasis on the following six points:

1. *All believers are gifted by the Holy Spirit for ministry* (1 Corinthians 12:1-31). The church cannot be effective unless all believers utilize their gifts to serve the body and Christ (Ephesians 4:1-16). Spiritual gifts can be discovered through the use of assessment inventories, the accuracy of which can be confirmed through feedback from mentors. The process of equipping should be highly personalized.

2. *Believers have unique and varied personalities.* Human personality is the result of nature and nurture and their mutual interaction—and it is not easily changed. Sometimes there is a high degree of similarity between spiritual gifts and personality and sometimes not. Assessing personality type should always be utilized as a precursor to equipping for specific tasks in the church. Some personalities fit the demands of certain ministry situations better than others.

3. *Believers have different gifts and leadership styles.* Leadership style can also be determined through assessment. Every gift and style has its own weaknesses and strengths and requires the presence of balancing team members to assure ultimate team effectiveness. Leadership training should always include careful attention to team development and a clear explication of how each person contributes to the overall effectiveness of the team.

4. *Believers have varying degrees of planning ability.* These abilities can be assessed and a team can be formed in a way that allows planners and nonplanners to balance one another. This arrangement will also foster an appreciation for how each individual fits into the overall ministry plan and contributes to its accomplishment.

5. *Frequent retreats for team building are essential.* Retreats serve to build trust, unity, and cooperation. The unique contributions of each individual should be celebrated, and the equipping and encouraging of servants should be a continual process.

6. *Believers should have a designated mentor-coach.* Everyone dedicated to becoming a disciple needs a mentor-coach to confide in and consult with. Training these coaches should be a high priority for church leadership. No equipping ministry should go forward without growth partnerships in which someone (clearly designated) bears the responsibility for the consistent development of those being equipped for and engaging in ministry. Mentors should contract with each recruit and should look for evidence of growth during the recruit's time of service.

POISED FOR INFLUENCE

The tasks associated with blending evangelism and discipleship in the local body are large indeed. Think about how we began this chapter: the image of all those steel girders on the ground with their mysterious numbering and the mighty crane in their midst. By the power of his grace, God lifts us individually from our earthbound places and positions us in the great superstructure of the body of Christ.

This structure into which he places us is magnificent beyond words. God has ordained it and configured it to achieve the fullness of his purpose. He is a highly intentional God. In his church are all the gifts necessary to meet the challenges related to reaching, teaching, and discipling.

Our greatest challenge is to admit our need for the full participation of the people God has placed in the superstructure of his church. We must seek counsel from those whose gifts are different from our own, promote the building of the team, and strive to balance and blend individuals' giftedness. As we honor God by honoring one another, we may focus better on the challenges of evangelism and discipleship that lie before us.

A church that is highly intentional about evangelism and discipleship—and fully equipped to meet the counseling challenges that help people mature spiritually—is a church that is poised for great influence in the third millennium. Pastoral counselors, peer-level caregivers, and professional Christian therapists are uniquely positioned to significantly contribute at every level to this mission of the church.

CHAPTER 18

LAY HELPING

The Whole Church in Soul-Care Ministry

SIANG-YANG TAN

The purpose of the church cannot be to survive or even thrive, but to serve. ...
The church cannot live when the heart of God is not beating in her.
—ERWIN MCMANUS, *An Unstoppable Force*

As a church grows, so do the congregation's needs for pastoral care and counseling. Many pastors are realizing that they are unable, by themselves, to provide all of the soul-care services that their parishioners may need (see Steinbron, 1987, 1997; Tan, 1991). Lay pastoral care and counseling, as well as small-group ministries, have mushroomed in order to meet this ever-increasing demand in churches and parachurch ministries.

Lay helping can be broadly defined as caregiving by nonprofessional or paraprofessional helpers who have limited or no training in counseling skills. Lay helping has become a significant part of both Christian ministry, especially in local churches, and the contemporary mental health scene (Tan, 1991, 1997b). This service will take on even greater prominence in the years ahead as managed health care continues to grow in the United States, with the possible results being less coverage for mental health services and fewer people able to afford costly long-term psychotherapy (Tan, 1999b). Consequently, increasing numbers of people will seek counseling from lay helpers, particularly in local churches and parachurch organizations that typically provide these services free of charge.

Several well-known Christian leaders and authors have also recently emphasized the need for lay helpers, shepherds, spiritual directors, or elders to be involved in caring for people in local churches. Crabb (1996) in particular underscores his central concern of seeing more of God's people shepherded. He proposes that the deep wounds of the soul can be healed in the context of biblically based church communities where deep, personal relationships can be developed (Crabb, 1997, 1999). He challenges us to go beyond even biblical counseling to create true Christian community. The biblical basis for both lay helping and deeply connecting in a community can be found in passages such as Romans 15:14, Galatians 6:1-2, John 13:34-35, 1 Thessalonians 5:14, and James 5:16.

The apostle Peter emphasized the priesthood of all believers, implying that the work of ministry is not only for pastors and church staff but also for every Christian (1 Peter 2:5-9). Appropriately gifted laypeople with relevant spiritual gifts should be involved in various church ministries, including lay helping and pastoral care (see Romans 12; 1 Corinthians 12; Ephesians 4; 1 Peter 4:8-11). All Christians are also called by God to be involved in building biblical communities of love by connecting with one another in the Spirit. In addition to such biblical support for lay helping ministries, there is also research support for the general effectiveness of lay or paraprofessional helpers.

EFFECTIVENESS OF LAY HELPING

In both secular and Christian contexts, a crucial question regarding lay helpers is whether they are effective in their counseling or helping endeavors. There has been some debate about this issue in literature reviews of studies that have evaluated the comparative effectiveness of paraprofessional and professional helpers (Durlak, 1979, 1981; Nietzel & Fisher, 1981) as well as in the meta-analyses of such studies (Berman & Norton, 1985; Hattie, Sharpley, & Rogers, 1984; Stein & Lambert, 1995). However, most of the results obtained in the secular research literature have indicated that lay helpers are generally as effective as professional therapists for most common problems (see Christensen & Jacobson, 1994; Lambert & Bergin, 1994; Tan, 1991).

Nevertheless, Beutler and Kendall (1995) still advocate training in psychological therapy because an updated meta-analysis of relevant therapy outcome studies by Stein and Lambert (1995) favors professionally trained therapists over paraprofessionals, especially in outpatient settings where they tended to have fewer drop-outs than therapists with less training. Similar results favoring professional experience have also been found by Kendall, Reber, McLeer, Epps, and Ronan (1990), but their specific focus was on the use of manualized interventions with conduct-disordered children.

Bickman (1999) reviewed the relevant research literature and critiqued Stein and Lambert's (1995) conclusions. He applied more stringent criteria to evaluate the studies they included in their meta-analysis and noted: "I found that eleven of the forty-seven studies measured outcome by using therapist-reported assessments, which may be biased. Of the remaining studies, only eight involved consumers' mental health outcomes (as opposed to their satisfaction ratings), along with clear distinctions between degreed and nondegreed therapists. Only one of these studies had effect sizes significantly different from zero (Burlingame, Fuhriman, Paul, & Ogles, 1989)" (p. 971).

Shadish et al. (1993) found that therapy treatment effects were not moderated by the presence or absence of a degree among the therapists. Shadish's research was one of the most rigorous meta-analyses to date evaluating the effects of family and marital psychotherapies. It covered 163 studies, including many unpublished dissertations. Bickman (1999) therefore draws the following strong conclusion:

> Thus, even many years after the publication of Strupp and Hadley's (1979) controversial study, it appears that whatever improvements are made, whatever studies are included or excluded, findings still indicate no clear differences in outcome between professionals and paraprofessionals who lack an advanced degree. Until additional research demonstrates consistent results, we should consider the belief that degree programs produce better clinicians a myth. (p. 971)

It should be mentioned that Bright, Baker, and Neimeyer (1999) more recently evaluated the relative efficacy of professional and paraprofessional therapists in conducting group cognitive-behavioral therapy and mutual support group therapy with ninety-eight depressed outpatients. They found that the paraprofessionals were as effective as the professionals in reducing depressive symptoms and that clients in both kinds of group therapy improved equally. However, at the six-month follow-up, more patients in the cognitive-behavioral therapy groups led by professionals were classified as nondepressed and alleviated than in similar groups led by paraprofessionals. These findings, however, do not negate the general conclusion made by Christensen and Jacobson (1994) in their review of the research literature: Paraprofessional helpers are generally as effective as professional therapists in terms of therapeutic outcome produced. They also found positive effects from other nonprofessional psychological treatments, such as self-administered materials and self-help groups.

Christensen and Jacobson (1994) challenge professional psychologists to "give psychology away" saying,

> The research summarized in this article suggests that the psychology that is given away (or at least sold much less expensively) through paraprofessional,

self-administered and mutual-support group treatment may be as effective for some problems as the professional psychology that is sold. A second body of research summarizing the current prevalence of psychological disorders and the available resources to provide treatment suggests that if psychology is not given away, most people in need will not get it, because they cannot afford it. The first body of research encourages us in our efforts to give psychology away. The second body of research demands it. (See Miller, 1969, pp. 1063-1075.)

The research literature evaluating the effectiveness of Christian lay helping is much more scarce. In a ten-year review of empirical research on religion and psychotherapeutic processes and outcomes, Worthington, Kurusu, McCullough, and Sandage (1996) cited a few studies that have generally shown the effectiveness of Christian lay helpers. All of the studies, however, had serious methodological limitations (see Boan & Owens, 1985; Harris, 1985; Walters, 1987).

Two other studies have been completed in the area of outcomes research. Toh, Tan, Osburn, and Faber (1994) found positive results in a preliminary evaluation of a church-based lay counseling program, but no control groups were employed. In a later controlled outcome study, Toh and Tan (1997) reported that clients who received ten sessions of Christian lay helping in a local church had significantly more improvement on all outcome measures (target complaints, brief symptom inventory, spiritual well-being scale, and global ratings of client's psychological adjustment) compared to a no-treatment, waiting-list control group. Therapeutic gains of the treatment group were also maintained at a one-month follow-up. Clients were randomly assigned to either the treatment (lay helping) or control (waiting list) group.

Empirical or research support for the effectiveness of Christian lay helping is growing, but more and better research in this area is still greatly needed.

BIBLICAL MODELS AND PROGRAMS FOR LAY HELPING

Several Christian lay helping models and training programs are available and have been previously described (see Tan, 1991, 1993, 1999c). They include:

- Jay Adams's (1970, 1973, 1981) nouthetic counseling
- Larry Crabb's (1977; Crabb & Allender, 1984) biblical counseling
- Gary Collins's (1976a, 1976b) people helping
- William Backus's (1985, 1987; Backus & Chapian, 1980) misbelief therapy

- Charles Solomon's (1975, 1977) spirituotherapy
- Kenneth Haugk's (1984) Stephen Series for training people in lay caregiving

(For a description of these and other programs, see Tan, 1991, pp. 115-134).

A few other models and training programs for Christian lay helping ministries have been made available (Tan, 1999c). In the basic area of lay pastoral care, Steinbron (1997, p.16) describes his Lay Pastors Ministry model using the PACE framework:

P—PRAY for members of five to ten households

A—Be AVAILABLE to them in times of need or celebration

C—CONTACT them regularly, at least once a month

E—Be the best EXAMPLE possible as a lay pastor

He has also noted that there are other training models for lay caregiving, such as the Stephen Ministries, Befriender Ministry, and People's Ministries (Steinbron, 1997, p. 169). Rapha Resources has developed The Shepherd's Staff, a training program for lay counselors or lay helpers that includes five videotapes with fifteen weeks of training. Turning Point Ministries has a number of published training materials, and this organization conducts a nine-hour weekend seminar called the Turning Point Seminar, which focuses on helping those who hurt as well as on small-group ministry.

CENTER FOR BIBLICAL COUNSELING

Most recently, the American Association of Christian Counselors (AACC) has made available three significant and substantial distance learning training programs through its Center for Biblical Counseling.[1] These five-part, thirty-lesson videotape training programs focus on teaching church members how to care. Program topics include:

1. "Caring for People God's Way," which focuses on educating and equipping a community of helpers within the church to provide biblical encouragement, direction, hope, and personal growth to hurting people.
2. "Marriage Works," which focuses on enriching the marriages of individuals and equipping a community of marriage mentors.
3. "Extraordinary Women," which focuses on encouraging women to improve faith, marriage, family, church, and community service life.

Those who successfully complete these training programs receive certificates of completion; however, such certificates do not certify those individuals to conduct counseling. This would require a decision by a person's pastor or counseling minister or director.

AACC plans to make available a shorter series of videos that would provide training in lay helping or lay counseling skills and in setting up a lay helping ministry in a church or parachurch context, based on Tan (1991). It should also be noted that Cheydleur (1999) and Sweeten, Ping, and Clippard (1993) have written books that are useful for lay helping skills training.

TAN PROGRAM

Drawing from several well-known models for Christian lay helping that have already been mentioned, I have developed an integrated, biblically based model for effective Christian lay counseling or lay helping. The model is based on the following five points about human nature (Tan, 1991):

1. The need for security (love), significance (meaning or impact), and hope (forgiveness) are among the basic psychological and spiritual needs or longings of human beings.
2. The basic problem of human beings is sin; however, not all emotional suffering is due to personal sin. Suffering may be due to the effects of other people's sins on us, or it may come simply because we live in a fallen world. Paradoxically, it may also be due to obedience to God's will (such as the sufferings of Jesus in the Garden of Gethsemane and eventually on the cross).
3. The ultimate purpose of humanity is to know God and to enjoy him forever (i.e., to enjoy spiritual health).
4. Problem feelings are usually due to problem behavior and, more fundamentally, problem thinking. But biological and demonic factors should also be considered.
5. A holistic view of people must include the physical, mental-emotional, social, and spiritual dimensions (see Luke 2:52).

The following are biblically based principles for effective lay counseling or helping (Tan, 1991):

- The Holy Spirit's ministry as Counselor is crucial (see Tan, 1999a).
- The Bible is a basic and comprehensive (though not exhaustive) guide for counseling and helping people.
- Prayer is an essential part of biblically based counseling, although it can be implicitly or quietly practiced and not necessarily done verbally with a client.
- The ultimate goal of lay helping or counseling is the client's maturity in Christ as well as fulfilling the Great Commission.
- The personal qualities—especially spiritual ones—of the lay helper or counselor are important.

- The client's attitudes, motivations, and desire for help are important.
- The relationship between the lay helper and client is significant.
- Effective lay helping is a process involving exploration, understanding, and action phases, with a focus on changing problem thinking.
- The style of, or approach to, lay helping should be flexible.
- Specific techniques or methods of helping should be consistent with Scripture. With certain qualifications, cognitive-behavioral strategies may be especially helpful.
- Cultural sensitivity and cross-cultural helping skills are required.
- Outreach and prevention skills developed within the context of a biblical, caring community are important.
- Awareness of limitations and referral skills are crucial.

EVALUATION OF PROGRAMS

With so many biblical models and training programs now available for Christian lay helping, it is essential to critically evaluate them from both biblical and psychological perspectives. It is also crucial to differentiate the various levels of lay helping ministries, which range from basic (general caring or encouragement skills for all Christians in interpersonal relationships) to sophisticated (specialized helping or counseling skills for some gifted Christians to use with people experiencing significant problems).

It is also important to clearly describe different ways of providing lay helping ministries. I have categorized service delivery into three major models (Tan, 1991):

1. *The informal, spontaneous model.* Christian lay helping is provided spontaneously and informally in relationships already present in the church. Friendship or peer helping is a good example of this approach. Helpers may or may not receive some basic caring skills training, but they do not have any ongoing supervision.

2. *The informal, organized model.* Lay helping is still provided in informal or natural settings (homes, hospitals, restaurants, and other community meeting places), but it takes place within the context of a well-organized system of training and with the ongoing supervision of lay helpers. A good example of this model is the Stephen Series of lay caring ministry developed by Dr. Kenneth Haugk.[2]

3. *The formal, organized model.* Lay helping is provided in more formal settings (in a church counseling center or in a community counseling clinic or agency), and it takes place within the context of systematic training and continued, regular supervision of the lay helpers.

It is important to choose an appropriate model or models for delivering lay helping services in a local church or parachurch context. It will then be easier to select specific training programs and materials for use with lay helpers. The informal, organized model of providing lay helping ministries may be the most appropriate and helpful for many local churches, especially for some ethnic churches where there may be a stigma against both professional counseling and formal lay helping.

A biblical model for Christian lay helping will also put such helping in the wider context of the manifold ministries and mission of the church, with a focus on loving God and loving people. It must therefore not elevate lay helping above other ministries of the church (Bufford & Buckler, 1987).

STARTING A LAY HELPING MINISTRY IN A LOCAL CHURCH

Starting a lay helping ministry in a local church is not as easy as it may seem. There are many decisions to make and challenges to overcome. The following five guidelines for starting a lay helping ministry can make it easier to get such a ministry under way (see Tan, 1991, 1995):

1. *Choose an appropriate lay helping model for your church (or parachurch organization).* Some churches will prefer the informal, organized model for delivering lay helping services. Other churches, particularly bigger ones, may want to adopt the formal, organized model, where clients will need to make an appointment to see a lay helper and where formal sessions will usually be held at a church counseling center. Some churches that are large enough may choose to use both an informal, organized model (such as the Stephen Series) as well as a formal, organized model (such as a church lay counseling center) to provide lay helping services to people.

2. *Obtain full support for the idea and model(s) of lay helping ministry from the pastor, pastoral staff, and church board.* Such a ministry should be regarded as an extension of pastoral care and counseling in the church as well as an essential part of the priesthood of all believers (1 Peter 2:5,9).

3. *Screen and select appropriately gifted and qualified Christian lay helpers from the congregation.* Important selection criteria should include:

- spiritual maturity
- psychological and emotional stability
- love for and interest in people (empathy, genuineness, warmth, or respect)
- appropriate spiritual gifts for helping relationships (the gift of encouragement or exhortation mentioned in Romans 12:8)

- previous training or experience in people helping (this is helpful but not essential)
- age, gender, socioeconomic, and ethnic or cultural background relevant to the needs of the congregation
- availability and teachability
- the ability to maintain confidentiality

The selection of a lay helper can be either closed (based on nominations or recommendations) or open (anyone can apply for possible selection as a lay helper). In either case, potential lay helpers should be interviewed.

4. *Provide an adequate training program for the lay helpers.* Many lay helper training programs are available, and some have already been mentioned in this chapter. The programs vary from a minimum of several hours of training to fifty or more hours of training, usually spread over a period of several weeks to several months. The number of lay helper trainees is usually limited (from a few to twenty-five or thirty), and regular training sessions are conducted weekly or bi-weekly for two to three hours each time.

According to Collins (1980), a training program should include instruction in the following areas:

- basic Bible knowledge relevant to lay helping
- counseling and helping skills with opportunities to practice such skills (through role-playing and other activities)
- understanding common problems such as depression, anxiety, stress, abuse, and spiritual dryness
- understanding law and ethics as they relate to people helping as well as awareness of the dangers inherent to helping
- the importance of referral and the techniques involved

Lay helpers need to know their limits and their limitations, and they need to know when and how to refer clients to professionals. They should also be aware of the limits to confidentiality and should know how to obtain informed consent from clients before they begin a lay helping ministry. They should inform clients of the limits of confidentiality as part of obtaining informed consent from them. Such limits usually include situations where there is danger to the client or to others or the possibility of child or elder abuse. (This is discussed in more detail in the next section.)

In addition, a good training program will incorporate (1) clear and practically oriented lectures, (2) reading assignments, (3) observation of good counseling or helping skills demonstrated or modeled by the trainer or professional counselor, and (4) experiential practice, especially through role-playing. Professional counselors can help by being involved in the training and supervision of lay helpers.

5. *Develop programs or ministries in which trained lay helpers can be used while they receive regular, ongoing supervision.* It is preferable that ongoing training and supervision be provided by a licensed mental health professional or at least by a pastor or church leader who is experienced in people-helping ministries. Regular supervision of the lay helpers, usually in small groups or dyads, should be conducted weekly or biweekly. Individual supervision of lay helpers should also be made available where necessary.[3]

If you choose to use a formal, organized model for providing lay helping services in your church, the following ten guidelines should prove helpful (see Partridge, 1983):

1. Determine clear objectives for the lay helping center.
2. Establish the distinctive character or ethos of the center by giving it an appropriate name.
3. Carefully select, train, and supervise the lay helpers.
4. Obtain suitable facilities and office space for the center.
5. Establish operating hours for the center.
6. Set up a governing structure that will guide the center's operation and functioning (such as a director and a board of advisors).
7. Publicize the lay helping services offered by the center.
8. Clarify what services the center will and will not provide.
9. Include the financing or funding for the center in the annual church budget.
10. Decide on the center's affiliation with the church.

It is advisable to start a church lay helping or counseling center modestly. For example, open the service facilities two or three evenings a week rather than five days a week. The range of services offered and the times they are available can be expanded over the course of months or even years. This gradual development of the center's activities may not be necessary in a large church, where staff, finances, and facilities may be more readily available. In such a church, the center can often begin functioning on a bigger scale immediately.

LEGAL AND ETHICAL ISSUES IN LAY HELPING

The key legal and ethical issues pertaining to lay helping in the local church will be presented in a subsequent volume (see also Ohlschlager & Mosgofian, 1992;

Tan, 1991, pp. 212-226; 1997a), but they will be briefly reviewed here. Becker (1987) emphasizes that trust is the essence of the counseling or helping relationship and that it should be developed in three major areas: the confidentiality of the helping relationship; the competence of the lay helper; and the client's freedom of choice.

Confidentiality. With regard to confidentiality, it is wise to follow the legal and ethical standards of professional counselors and to require that lay helpers report child or elder abuse and the potential danger to the client or to others as these constitute the legal limits to confidentiality. Such limits to confidentiality should be disclosed to clients at the beginning of the first session as lay helpers obtain informed consent in order to engage in lay helping. There are further limits to confidentiality when minors are receiving services provided by lay helpers.

Some churches, especially those who follow the nouthetic counseling model advocated by Adams, may require their lay helpers to be involved in administering church discipline, a practice Becker (1987) advises against. Lay helpers in such churches should inform their clients at the beginning of the first session that limits to confidentiality will include church discipline situations.

Competence. Adequate screening, training, and ongoing supervision are essential to ensure the competence of lay helpers. Scanish and McMinn (1996) provide the following guidelines for assessing the competence of lay Christian counselors or lay helpers (p. 29):

1. They are not living in blatant sin.
2. They and their families are spiritually and emotionally healthy.
3. They understand and use Scripture wisely.
4. They represent themselves accurately.
5. They refer when appropriate.
6. They practice within their level of training.
7. They request help for their own problems.
8. They maintain current awareness of pertinent new developments.
9. They use care when speaking in public.
10. They are sensitive to human diversity.

Client choice. With regard to the client's freedom of choice, Becker (1987) maintains that for proper informed consent to be freely given by the client, the lay helper should provide accurate and adequate information about his or her qualifications (or lack of them), training, and values, as well as the goals, process, and possible results of the lay helping that will be provided. The lay helper should not represent himself or herself as a trained professional, so terms such as *psychologist* or *psychotherapist* should not be used. In some states, even the term *counselor* cannot be used by lay helpers or lay counselors because of licensing laws that limit the use of that term only to those who are licensed professional counselors. Hence, the term *lay helper* (or lay caregiver) is a more appropriate and acceptable term to use.

Becker (1987) also recommends that lay helpers follow the ethical codes or guidelines of professional counseling organizations. While most of the ethical guidelines followed by professional counselors do apply to lay helpers (such as avoiding romantic or sexual relationships with clients and helping within the limits of the lay helper's competence, for example), some do not. An obvious example is the guideline to avoid dual relationships, which cannot be applied to lay helpers in general because many of them are involved in friendship counseling or peer helping relationships in the church. It may be helpful for lay helpers to consult the *AACC Christian Counseling Code of Ethics* (2001).[4]

Becker (1987) also describes eight high-risk situations that lay helpers should avoid in order to minimize possible malpractice lawsuits or litigation:

1. charging fees or asking for donations
2. using psychological tests without proper training or supervision
3. having simplistic beliefs that can lead to superficial treatment, misdiagnosis, and harm
4. helping those with severe problems that require professional intervention
5. giving advice against medical or psychological treatment
6. ignoring statements of intent to harm or signs of violent behavior
7. helping or counseling with a relative or employee
8. developing a romantic or sexual relationship with the client

Legal advice should also be obtained regarding whether malpractice insurance is necessary for the lay helpers. If client records are kept, clients should be made aware of this as part of the informed-consent process. Such records should be kept safe and secure in an appropriate place. Clients should also be informed that they and their problems will be discussed, albeit confidentially, in supervision sessions that the lay helpers regularly attend.

FUTURE EMPHASES OF LAY HELPING MINISTRIES

A distinctively Christian approach to lay helping that is biblically based, Christ-centered, and Spirit-empowered will have these future emphases (Tan, 1994, 1999c):

- healing and deliverance ministries
- evangelism and discipleship training
- missions
- small-group ministry

- peer helping
- cross-cultural helping

The role of professional counselors and psychologists in lay helping ministries will also be important. They can assist in the following ways (Tan, 1997b):

- training and supervising lay helpers
- serving on boards of directors of lay helping organizations
- educating groups and churches about the positive contributions of mental health or psychological services
- consulting with churches or organizations interested in establishing lay helping services
- serving as a referral source when professional counseling is needed (but avoiding any conflict of interest)
- conducting outcomes research and evaluation of the effectiveness of lay helping
- educating other mental health professionals and psychologists about the key role they can play in the development of lay helpers

Finally, the specific needs of rural communities—many of which lack adequate mental health services—and how the church can function as an agent in rural mental health, including providing Christian lay helping services, have been addressed by Voss (1996).

BEARING ONE ANOTHER'S BURDENS

The Lord Jesus has called us to carry each other's burdens (Galatians 6:2) and to reach out to one another with his agape love (John 13:34-35). The ministry of lay helping is an integral part of the manifold ministries of the church and an important adjunct to the practice of professional counseling. Lay helping is, therefore, a crucial manifestation of the whole church in soul-care helping ministry, and it will become even more important in the years ahead.

CHAPTER 19

GROUP WORK

Counseling and Church-Based Discipling in Small Groups

JOSEPH A. KLOBA

*I see a healing community as a group of people who place connecting at
the exact center of their purpose and passion...connecting with God
(worship), others (loving service), and ourselves (personal wholeness).*
—LARRY CRABB, *The Safest Place on Earth*

In his best-selling book, *Sharing the Journey*, Princeton sociologist Robert Wuthnow (1994) reported that four out of ten Americans belong to a small, organized group that meets regularly and provides caring and support for its members. Furthermore, those who joined these groups testified that their lives had been deeply enriched by the experience. Such groups occur in a variety of settings, including treatment facilities, churches, outpatient counseling centers, schools and colleges, the business world, and the community.

Concurrent with this dramatic interest in small groups is a significant trend within the field of mental health: the advent of managed care. Clear specification of outcomes, a limited number of counseling sessions, cost containment, and similar constraints have led to an increased demand for the use of groups in counseling—groups that are solution-focused (Spitz, 1996). Groups can provide effective service for a lower cost over an extended period of time.

Wuthnow (1994) found that churches are the primary proponents of small groups, with nearly two-thirds of all small groups having some connection to churches. Those churches across the country that are growing and meeting the needs of people are those that provide a variety of small-group opportunities such as home fellowship groups, Bible study groups, support groups, and lay or professional counseling groups (Donahue, 1996).

GROUP DEFINITION, DIFFERENCES, AND DATA

A *group* is a collection of two or more individuals who interact and relate with one another (Lifton, 1972). According to Loeser (1957), six elements differentiate a group from a mob, a crowd, or an aggregate of people. Members of a group

1. interact face-to-face
2. share a common goal
3. are present by their own consent and volition
4. have the capacity for self-direction
5. establish a group structure (spoken and unspoken)
6. have a sense of group identity

All groups have three things in common: content, process, and goal (Lifton, 1972). *Content* is the "what"—the subject matter or focus of deliberation within a group. The subject matter varies on a continuum from external topics (such as planning a building) to internal topics (such as loneliness). *Process* is the "how" or the way in which content is handled within the group. Process includes such variables as the structure and ground rules of a group, interaction and communication patterns, cohesion, stage development, and leadership style. *Goal* is the "end" or destination toward which the group is moving. Generally, groups are designed for one of three purposes: (1) to accomplish a task (e.g., developing a mission statement), (2) to provide a structured learning situation (e.g., a seminar on marital communication), or (3) to develop or change the way participants think, act, or feel (e.g., through a counseling group for recently divorced individuals).

DIFFERENT KINDS OF GROUPS

Groups may be classified into eight broad categories (Conyne, 1999; Corey & Corey, 2001; Dibbert & Wichern, 1985):

1. *Task groups* are designed to enhance or resolve performance and production goals in work or organizational groups.
2. *Psychoeducational groups* are designed to transmit, discuss, and integrate factual information and skill building through the use of semistructured exercises and group process with the goal of educating members or developing their skills.
3. *Counseling groups* are designed to improve skills for coping with problems by focusing on interpersonal problem solving, interactive feedback, and support methods within a here-and-now framework.

4. *Psychotherapy groups* are designed to reduce psychological or emotional dysfunction by exploring the antecedents to current behavior using intrapersonal and interpersonal assessment, diagnosis, and interpretation and by connecting historical material with the present. As with counseling groups, psychotherapy groups focus primarily on the needs of the individual members, and the leader serves as a facilitator, teacher, or counselor.

5. *Self-help groups* are designed to be mutually supportive groups led by paraprofessionals or group members themselves. Through self-help, group members improve and increase their self-esteem and self-identity, realize they are not alone, and feel empowered by sharing ideas, giving help, and receiving aid (Wheeler, 1989). Examples of these groups are any of the variety of Twelve Step groups such as Alcoholics Anonymous (AA). The assumption about the leadership of self-help groups is that "fellow sufferers" or "wounded healers" are able to deal most effectively with each other by coming together in a group and sharing through disclosing, listening, and learning.

6. *Fellowship groups,* which usually occur in a church setting, are designed to stimulate the development of spiritual maturity through edification and discipleship and to provide support, encouragement, and fellowship for group members. Fellowship groups can provide outreach to the community as well as a means of ministry to a large number of people in a personal manner.

7. *Growth groups* are designed to more actively challenge members to grow than other kinds of groups, so they tend to have greater commitment requirements, more honesty, more openness, and more involvement with group members outside of meetings. In a sense, a growth group is a fellowship group that emphasizes spiritual maturity, fellowship among members, and contacts or meetings outside of the group meeting per se. Leaders of these groups lead by modeling and sharing themselves. An attempt is made to encourage group members to use their spiritual gifts to build up each other and to mentor one another and others outside the group.

8. *Sensitivity, encounter, and T-groups* (training groups) are generic groups that are more educational than therapeutic. They are geared to the acquisition of interpersonal competence, communication skills, and constructive personal or organizational change. T-groups help members of an organized body function more effectively as a team.

RESEARCH ON THE EFFECTIVENESS OF GROUPS

The kind of research being reported in the professional literature of a discipline is often an indication of the maturity of that discipline. According to Zimpfer (1970), four generational stages are involved in discipline research. First-generation research simply describes, in anecdotal fashion, the kind of treatment program that has been developed. Group research in the 1960s and 1970s was of this type.

Second-generation research, often using self-report data, examines whether people who are exposed to a treatment are any different after treatment than before treatment. A review of group research in the late 1970s reveals a preponderance of these kinds of studies. As researchers move on to examine the difference between various types of treatment and nontreatment control groups, they then become involved in third-generation research, the research found in the literature of the 1980s. Fourth-generation research occurs when it is generally accepted that the treatment is effective, and efforts are initiated to vary different aspects of the treatment in an effort to determine how to make treatment more effective.

According to Zimpfer's (1970) model, group work is in its fourth generation of research. It is generally accepted that group work is extremely effective (Fuhriman & Burlingame, 1994; Smith, Glass, & Miller, 1980; Toseland & Siporin, 1986). Present-day fourth-generation group research is examining ways to enhance the effectiveness of groups by studying such variables as:

- matching certain individuals to specific groups
- member selection criteria and group composition
- styles of group leadership
- interventions at various stages of groups (Riva & Smith, 1997)

In his description of the history of group work, Gladding (1995) states that the effectiveness of group work has less to do with a specific theoretical orientation than with finding an optimum combination of pregroup training, member characteristics, therapeutic factors, group structures, and stages of development.

THE BIBLICAL BASIS OF GROUPS

Coleman (1989) states that human beings have three basic needs that can be dealt with most effectively in the context of a Christ-centered group: (1) the need to be, (2) the need to belong and to have goals, and (3) the need to do something with regard to these goals.

Each of us has the need to be in touch with reality—aware of our own uniqueness and our fears regarding rejection or not having value. A Christ-centered group can help members see the nature of God's love and forgiveness through the love and care of fellow group members as they bring their concerns to the Cross. The need to belong is nourished by social interaction where members move out of self-sufficiency into a relationship with God and fellow believers in the context of a covenant experience. The need to have goals and to do something with regard to these goals is worked out within the group, which serves as a laboratory for doing theology—for exploring the principles of the faith in the group itself and in areas outside the group (such as work and play) while using the group as a place to process and reflect on what happens outside of the group.

GROUPS ARE GOD'S WAY

From the beginning, God set in motion certain divine and human realities that are uniquely imaged and reflected where two or more people come together in his presence (Icenogle, 1994). Small groups had their beginning right after creation. God often worked through family groupings and other forms of small groups to establish his purposes (McBride, 1995). He used Noah's family of eight to demonstrate his desire for the people to be righteous (Genesis 6:18), and it was through this family group that God established his covenant with his people (Genesis 9:8-9). Later, after God delivered his people out of Egypt, he established a new nation structured around small groups. In Exodus 18, God, through Moses, divided the people into groups of tens, fifties, hundreds, and thousands (verse 25). The division into small groups enabled individuals to receive better care.

Other parts of the Old Testament reveal this same pattern (McBride, 1995). In Numbers 2, the different tribes of Israel were lined up in family groups. In Joshua 4:12, groups of armed men were sent ahead by Joshua to cross the Jordan River. Nehemiah organized the people into groups to subdivide the tasks associated with rebuilding the wall (Nehemiah 3).

In the New Testament, Jesus incorporated small groups as the heart of his ministry. From the many, he chose twelve disciples to form a core group. He drew this group around himself to eventually prepare them to be sent out to do his work. Three tactics seem evident in Jesus' use of small groups (Olsen, 1973):

1. *Jesus demonstrated how needs are supplied by an intimate small group.* He valued the disciples' love, reflection, and support in the midst of suffering, hurt, disappointment, and anger. His relationship with the disciples was a beautiful portrait of giving and receiving in relationship. How else could we know about his forty days in the wilderness or his agony in the Garden of Gethsemane? God could supply Jesus' every need, but one of the channels he used was other human beings.

2. *Jesus was able to teach in greater depth in a small group than he could with a larger following.* When speaking to crowds he often used parables; when he was alone with his disciples he would explain everything to them in greater detail. He used action-reflection teaching: Acknowledging the disciple's fear of storms, their anxiety over the lack of bread, and Peter's anger over Jesus' washing his feet, Jesus used these occasions to teach who he was and who God was.

3. *Through the use of a small group, Jesus built a model of corporate faith and living.* He tried to put to rest the assertion that faith is private. One of his prayers emphasizes the crucial nature of the corporate composition of the Christian community. In John 17:21 he prayed "that all of them may be one, Father, just as you are in me and I am in you. May they also be in us so that the world may believe that you have sent me." Somehow the mystical in-with-God relationship was connected to the disciples' unity. This unity resulted from the small groups and energized their witness (Olsen, 1973).

As a result of Peter's Pentecost speech, the church grew in one day from 120 people (Acts 1:15) to more than 3,000 (Acts 2:41). In order to help these new believers grow in their faith, the church was divided into smaller groups. Acts 2:46 tells us that the Jerusalem church was divided into two mutually supportive groups: (1) a large group that met in the temple, and (2) small groups that "broke bread" in homes. Believers experienced unity by meeting regularly as an entire fellowship, and they developed more intimate community by meeting in smaller groups.

THERAPEUTIC FACTORS IN GROUPS

Change is an enormously complex process and occurs through an intricate interplay of various *therapeutic factors*. Group leaders recognize the importance of these factors and try to maximize them within the group (Corey & Corey, 2001; Yalom, 1995). These factors include:

- *universality*—knowing that others share similar issues, problems, concerns, or feelings
- *instillation of hope*—knowing that people in situations similar to yours do improve and get better
- *altruism*—giving to others unselfishly with no expectation of return or gratitude
- *imitation of behavior*—modeling effective ways of relating and communicating
- *development of socializing techniques*—learning how one is perceived by others and practicing new ways of relating and communicating

- *information impartation*—learning new and unfamiliar material related to oneself
- *interpersonal learning*—becoming more aware of personal issues through feedback from others
- *cohesiveness*—trusting other group members enough to engage in important and appropriate self-disclosure and to care for, support, and encourage one another
- *catharsis*—venting of emotions, expressing deeply held, intense feelings that have been pent up, repressed, or denied
- *corrective recapitulation of the family of origin*—to replay group members' family-of-origin roles and to experience different and more desirable responses and outcomes
- *issues of meaning and purpose*—addressing such issues as aloneness, death, responsibility, and freedom

Acknowledging these factors openly helps members realize that their feelings can be understood or addressed. Brown (1988) believes that group leaders need to recognize the value of these therapeutic factors, accept that they enhance the group process, and identify them when they appear. In addition, leaders need to openly bring attention to these factor(s) in appropriate ways, paying attention to timing.

MEMBER SELECTION CRITERIA

What kinds of people should be in a group? The answer is, "It depends." It depends on the kind of group, the goals of the group, the age or stage of development of the participants, the setting, and the amount of time available (for each group session as well as for the overall period during which group sessions will be held).

According to Corey and Corey (2001), the type of group should determine the kind of members accepted. A person who can work well in a short-term psychoeducational group may not be ready for an intense therapy group. A person who is presently psychotic may not benefit from a counseling group but might do well in a weekly outpatient group at a mental health center. The key question to consider is, "Should *this* particular person be included in *this* particular group at *this* time with *this* group leader" (Corey & Corey, 1997, pp. 1-2).

Certain members can sap the energy from a group and make the experience nonproductive for others. This includes people who are hostile, people who monopolize conversation, people who are extremely aggressive, and people who act out (Corey & Corey, 1997). Before starting a group, it is a good idea, if possible, to have an individual session or at least a pregroup meeting of all potential members to clearly explain the goals of the group, the ground rules, expectations for member involvement, and the kind of involvement the leader will have.

If a prospective member is unable to identify and personalize his or her own goals relative to the overall group goal, or if he or she does not agree with or feel comfortable about other aspects of the group, this person may not be a viable candidate for that particular group. If a pregroup individual or group meeting is not possible, the first group meeting may be used to review the aforementioned issues and give prospective members the opportunity to decide whether to commit.

Brochures, posters, and informed-consent documents that specify as much as possible about the group may help prospective members in self-screening. Written documents should include information on goals and purposes, entrance procedures, time limits, termination procedures, rights and responsibilities of members and leaders, techniques and procedures that may be used in group meetings, leader qualifications, fees and expenses, follow-up services provided, personal risks, and confidentiality parameters.

Other considerations in selecting members: Should the group be homogenous or heterogeneous by age, problem, gender, or other criteria? What size should it be? How often should the group meet and for how many total sessions? How long should each session be? Should the group be open or closed? Where should a group meet? Again, "It depends." It depends on the goals, the members, the setting, and a host of other factors. (See Corey and Corey [2001] and Jacobs, Harvill, and Masson [2000] for an extended discussion of these questions and the issues involved in answering them.)

GROUP LEADERSHIP ATTRIBUTES AND SKILLS

Leadership is the art of promoting interest in people and influencing them to work together toward common goals (Glanz & Hayes, 1967). According to Corey and Corey (2001) and Brown (1998), group leaders ideally should exhibit a number of attributes including the following:

- courage
- willingness to be an example or model for the group
- presence (fully experiencing the emotions being experienced by others)
- goodwill and caring
- belief in the group process
- openness toward the people and the process
- nondefensiveness in coping with attacks
- personal power and self-confidence

- stamina and perseverence
- willingness to seek new experiences
- self-awareness
- a sense of humor
- inventiveness and creativity
- personal dedication and commitment
- an awareness of one's own culture (background) and how it influences decision making
- ability to admit mistakes
- organizational skills
- flexibility, ability to tolerate tension and ambiguity

No leader possesses all of these characteristics at a high level, but the more one does possess, the more effective he or she will be (Brown, 1998; Corey & Corey, 2001). The leader's general tasks in small-group work are to focus discussion toward goals, to regulate (facilitate) discussion, to guide (direct) discussion if it bogs down, and to draw together and link what is being discussed (to help the group draw conclusions) (Corey & Corey, 1997).

Structuring. This key leader skill involves the leader either stating or demonstrating (by modeling) the rules of the helping process. At the onset of a group, structuring may involve a review of group goals and of ground rules such as confidentiality and starting and ending on time. According to Corey and Corey (1997), structuring continues throughout the group process as situations arise. An example of leader-guided structuring might be that when a member cries, the leader doesn't immediately go sit beside and embrace him or her. Rather, the leader should let the tears flow for a while and simply hand the member a tissue.

Linking. This leader skill involves seeing and pointing out commonalities and similarities among members. Its purpose is to link one person's verbiage with that of another (Corey & Corey, 1997). In a sense, group members have similar "musical themes" in their lives with different "words to their songs." The leader will point out the similarities and differences in feelings and content among members and keep relating these similarities and differences to what is happening in the group and what the members want to happen outside the group.

Helping members formulate and work on goals. This skill is closely related to structuring and linking. How do leaders know when a group is successful? It is successful if members reach the goals they set. These goals must be precise, measurable, or observable. If they are not, a leader may never know for sure if the group is successful. (See Corey & Corey, 2001.)

Traffic-director or blocker. Much like a police officer at an intersection, a group leader must direct the flow of the actions of group members. According to Corey and Corey (2001), specific behaviors that a leader must block and redirect include:

- *inappropriate or unhelpful questions*—those that narrow the range of options, put someone on the spot, involve privacy, are disguised statements, hide a person's wants or needs, or are rhetorical
- *gossip*—talking about people who are not present
- *circular and nondirected storytelling*—long-winded diatribes
- *there and then*—extreme focus on a past event in a member's life
- *supermothering*—someone who tries to make everyone happy or feel good by behaviors such as hugging a crying person

The literature on group leadership includes a number of skills necessary for effective group counseling as well as for individual counseling. These skills include active listening, open questions, reflection of feelings, confrontation, silence, paraphrasing, feedback, summarizing, interpreting, reality testing, and self-disclosure (Jones, 1993). A goal of every effective group leader is to *not* be needed by the group.

By *modeling* appropriate leadership skills, by *teaching* (such as telling the group what is being done and why), and by *coaching* the members (such as letting them proceed with the group and jumping in occasionally to help them improve upon what they are doing), leaders help members learn how to function effectively in the group.

THE PROCESS OF GROUP DEVELOPMENT

According to Lifton (1972), groups are living clusters of people that grow, change, mature, and die. Like any living organism, groups also go through stages of development and growth. Stages are labeled differently depending on the nature of the group, although the common theme is that each type of group has a beginning, a middle, and an ending stage. Following, we will review some stage models for *task groups, psychoeducational groups,* and *counseling therapy and support groups.*

Among the stages for *task groups* are preparatory, incubation, illumination, and verification (Krech & Crutchfield, 1959); orientation, evaluation, and control (Bales & Strodbeck, 1951); and forming, storming, norming, performing, and adjourning (Tuckman 1965).

Stages for *psychoeducational groups* include experience, identify, analyze, and generalize; initiation, identification, and integration; and hook, look, book, and took (Lifton, 1972).

Stages for *counseling therapy and support groups* include involvement, transition, working, and ending (Mahler, 1969); and initial, transition, working, and ending (Corey & Corey, 2001).

Member needs and leader tasks are present in each of the different stages. As one reviews the stages for a *task group,* the common leader theme is that the leader must help the group accomplish a task and thus promote movement toward a tangible outcome or decision, with minimal attention to process and feeling issues.

The stages for a *psychoeducational group* seem to have common themes of precipitating members' awareness that the content is needed, providing members with a certain type of experience, and connecting the experience in order to develop a cognitive framework and understanding about the experience. This understanding serves as a catalyst to get the member to apply the concepts learned within the group to life outside of the group.

COMMON PROCESS ACROSS GROUPS

Counseling, therapy, and support groups have, as a commonality, members who start out with mistrust, transition to trust and to serious personal working, and end with a tapering off and an application of lessons learned within the group to one's life outside of the group.

A simple example from Corey and Corey (1997) illustrates the importance of understanding the leader intervention interaction at different stages. In a counseling group, a member may say, "I'm afraid people here think I'm foolish." If this statement is made in the *initial stage,* the leader will attempt to get all members to identify with this emotion and to share similar emotions.

If this statement is made in the *transition stage,* the leader focuses on how that emotion is experienced in the group's "here and now." The leader might invite members to explore who in the group may be causing the member's fear and then ask the other members to provide feedback to the individual.

If such a statement is made in the *working stage,* the member may be asked to look at historical causes for the feelings or thoughts and to engage in a role-play with another group member to work through the issue.

At the *ending stage,* the leader may respond to the comment by having the member review the insights he or she has learned and think carefully about how these insights can be continued and utilized successfully in life after the group.

TECHNIQUES IN GROUPS

Technique refers to a leader's explicit and direct request of a member to focus on material, to augment or exaggerate effect, to practice behavior, or to solidify insight

(Corey, Corey, Callanan, & Russell, 1992). It is important that a leader have a reason to use a technique. Variables that need to be considered include:

- time available
- familiarity of members with one another
- experience of members
- number of people to be involved
- expected outcome
- follow-up plans
- the training and skill of the leader

Experienced leaders know that a technique used effectively with one group may not work as well with another group. Processing and analyzing the group experience are much more important than the actual experience of using the technique. The technique should generally be structured to last for a short time, whereas the processing of the experience may take up the majority of the session time. Take, for example, a role-play between Member A and Member B. Member B plays Member A's boss, with whom he is having difficulty being assertive. The role-play might last six minutes while the discussion and implementation of action may take forty minutes.

After a role-play, leaders may process the use of the technique in different ways. I prefer to use the following procedure:

1. Carefully think out a set of questions relating to a member's present state. In the previous example, the question may be "What do you feel right now?" or "What did you see yourself doing?"

2. A leader may insert a descriptive observation of what he or she saw and ask what it meant to the member. For example, the leader may say to Member A, "I noticed you failed to make eye contact with your boss and your voice was very low."

3. Ask others in the group to provide direct feedback to Member A about what they observed. A group member may say, "You didn't make eye contact in the role-play, but you don't a lot of time in the group either."

4. Link the observations to see if they apply to other group members, then develop procedures to work on any issues identified. In our illustration, the leader may say to another group member, "You indicated that you, too, have difficulty being assertive with those in authority over you. How can you help one another with this in group?"

It is important to note that a series of techniques or structured exercises do not make a group. Techniques are not ends in themselves. A technique is a means to an end, aimed toward a goal that the leader should have in mind before using the technique. There are a number of excellent materials, such as Corey et al. (1992); Coleman (1989); and Brown (1998) to help the group leader further develop techniques with a wide variety of groups.

ETHICAL ISSUES IN GROUPS

Ethical refers to doing the right thing. In counseling, *ethical* refers to following the guidelines of one's professional peers (whether a professional association or a governmental body such as a state licensure board) and one's employing organization in doing what is generally perceived to be proper and correct. Ethical guidelines or codes, in themselves, are never able to guide all situations that a counselor may encounter. Knowledge of ethical codes and relevant statutes is essential but not sufficient to help counselors know exactly what to do in any given situation. Therefore, counselors must also develop a basis for making ethical decisions relative to their work with clients.

The American Counseling Association (ACA) recommends the following steps in ethical decision making (Herlihy & Corey, 1996; see also chapter 11):

1. identify the problem
2. apply the appropriate ethical principle
3. determine the nature and dimensions of the dilemma
4. generate potential courses of action
5. consider the potential consequences of all options and develop a course of action
6. implement the action

The ACA (Herlihy & Corey, 1996) also recommends six moral principles that should undergird the counselor's rules of conduct:

1. autonomy—a client's independence and self-determination
2. nonmaleficence—doing no harm
3. beneficence—promoting good
4. justice—fairness
5. fidelity—honoring commitments
6. veracity—being truthful

Although the ethical guidelines of many professional organizations have standards that apply to group work (AACC, 2000; Herlihy & Corey, 1996), the Association for Specialists in Group Work (ASGW) has developed a document titled *Best Practices in Group Work* to replace its former *Ethical Guidelines Document* (Rapin & Keel, 1998). Following are some of the salient ethical issues that need to be implemented by group practitioners (Rapin & Keel, 1998):

- Members must be in a group voluntarily.
- Members should be provided informed consent. (They should know what they are agreeing to be involved in—techniques, goals, procedures, fees, and so forth.)
- Members have the freedom to withdraw.
- Members should assess and review the psychological risks of group process.
- Members should be clear about confidentiality and its limits at the beginning of group sessions and on a continuing basis.
- Techniques should not be abused.
- Leaders should not impose their values on clients.
- Dual relationships should be avoided, if possible.
- Members must be properly screened.

Small Groups in the Church

For those wishing to minister to the felt needs of the greatest number of people, there is no organization to better meet these needs than the church. Nowhere else are people from all ages, all stages, and all walks of life gathered together within a common framework. Within this context are some people who need remedial assistance; some who want to prevent problems from occurring; some who desire to develop their hearts, minds, and skills in new areas; and others who just want to participate in planning and administration.

Types of Small Groups
The church can uniquely combine professionals and lay persons to lead a wide variety of groups in a manner and intensity matched by no other organization (Dibbert & Wichern, 1985; Galloway, 1995; Price, Springle, & Kloba, 1991). These groups include the following:

1. *Task groups* exist to accomplish a certain project (such as organizing a retreat, selecting furniture, planning a service).

2. *Teaching groups* communicate knowledge and information largely through the lecture method of discussion (as in Sunday school classes and educational programs).

3. *Growth groups* encourage and challenge members in areas such as marriage, family and work life, Bible mastery, discipleship, self-esteem, codependency, community outreach, or social justice. (In the secular world, many of these groups are called psychoeducational groups.) Growth groups combine content with the unique needs of group participants in such a manner that the content stimulates personal

application in members' lives. In such groups it is important that content not be disseminated to a passive audience; the recommended leader-to-member "talk ratio" is 20:80.

4. *Support groups*, offered by progressive churches, focus on specific emotional or relational needs. Generally, members attend because they feel stress in coping with life's problems. People need support and perspective in dealing with issues such as job loss, marriage breakup, single parenting, and codependency.

5. *Counseling/therapy groups* are offered by an increasing number of churches that are hiring professional counselors to provide leadership for these groups or to train and supervise others to lead similar counseling groups. These groups are similar to support groups, except that the leaders are trained in a variety of techniques to provide assistance in many different problem situations. Such groups focus on content similar to that of support groups, but the leaders are more skilled in process application.

One helpful way to understand the similarities and differences between these types of groups is to examine them in the context of four major activities of groups and the focus of each: (1) giving information, (2) encouraging discussion, (3) facilitating process, or (4) planning action. Table 19.1, developed by Price, Springle, and Kloba (1991), summarizes these activities.

TABLE 19.1

Activity	Focuses On	Examples
Giving Information	public lectures, what you should know	Sunday-school classes
Encouraging Discussion	what you think	home Bible studies, town meetings
Facilitating Process	what you feel	counseling groups, grief support groups
Planning Action	what you do	committee meetings, workshops

Table 19.2, also by Price, Springle, and Kloba (1991), describes the five main categories of groups used in churches with reference to the degree of emphasis these groups place on the four activities mentioned in table 19.1.

Table 19.2

Activity	Types of Groups				
	Task	Teaching	Growth	Support	Counseling/ Therapy
Giving Information	medium	high	low	low	low
Encouraging Discussion	medium	low	high	high	high
Facilitating Process	none	none	medium	high	high
Planning Action	high	low	medium	medium	high

Blessings, Cautions, and Other Considerations

According to Dibbert and Wichern (1985), there are a number of advantages to small groups in the church context:

- People are easily assimilated into church life because they have a sense of belonging.
- Spiritual growth usually occurs because of the high degree of participation.
- A small group is an effective vehicle for pastoral care.
- With the right focus and training, a small group can easily become an instrument of evangelism.

Crabb and Allender (1984), however, do raise a number of problems that can occur if churches slowly begin to trust the group process more than commitment to the Lord within the context of a group. They express the following eight concerns:

1. The Bible can become less a stimulus for belief and behavior and more a stimulus for fevered fellowship.
2. Members can shift from belief and truth to feelings and emotions.
3. Sharing one's faith can become more important than knowing one's faith.
4. Bible study can become less a study and more a discussion of needs, experiences, and opinions.

5. The truth of Scripture can gradually be replaced by the theology and anthropology of those who try to comfort hurting people with the affirmation that "man is good, so you are good" and "the real you is perfect."

6. Participants can wallow in victimization, blaming others for their failure and absolving themselves from personal responsibility.

7. People can begin to believe that Jesus came to make us happier.

8. Sharing can begin to place pressure on emotional honesty without a framework of commitment to God and to the welfare of others.

For a small-group program to be effective in the local church, there must be careful planning and organization (Galloway, 1995; George, 1997). A leader or coordinator of small groups should report directly to the pastor and be a proven spiritual leader with good relational and organizational skills. According to Jones (1993), a good leader or coordinator does the following:

- selects group leaders (with input from the pastor)
- participates in training
- spearheads the ongoing development of leaders
- participates in problem solving
- shepherds and encourages leaders
- serves as an example of love, faith, strength, and prayer
- arranges referrals for those who need help beyond the group
- serves as a liaison to the pastor

Jones (1993) also believes small-group leaders should be faithful (prepare for meetings, pray for members, and lead with love and strength), be available to group members (honest and vulnerable), and be teachable (willing to learn from other small-group leaders, trainers, members, and the Lord).

There are many different formats that can be used for the varying types of groups that are held in church. The reader is referred to Price, Springle, and Kloba (1991), George (1997), Galloway (1995), and McBride (1995) for a more thorough discussion of formats. The following format works well for many church-based groups:

- arrival and socializing (mixing)
- praise and worship
- opening prayer
- development or reminder of ground rules
- a teaching on the Holy Spirit
- study of the Bible-related material
- praise reports

- prayer requests
- prayer
- socializing and departure

AN EXCITING OPPORTUNITY

God's historical use of small groups and the research demonstrating their effectiveness provide ample justification for us to be involved with group work. It is my hope that this brief overview of the place of groups in competent Christian counseling will motivate the reader to step forward and risk using small groups to minister to people. The opportunity to lead others in exploring God's truth as well as seeing what it can mean in their lives is exciting and fulfilling.

CHAPTER 20

CHRISTIAN MARRIAGE AND MARITAL COUNSELING

Promoting Hope in Lifelong Commitments

EVERETT L. WORTHINGTON JR. AND JENNIFER S. RIPLEY

When marriages achieve the ideal of soul friendship, the mutual care they provide affords the possibility of a constancy of soul care that is seldom possible in other human relationships.

—DAVID BENNER, *Strategic Pastoral Counseling*

Christians believe marriage is a sacred institution ordained by God until one partner dies. However, there is a puzzling lack of professional literature on Christian marriages and marital counseling. In 1993 Worthington, Shortz, and McCullough concluded that the professional field was essentially at the toddler stage still taking its first fumbling steps. Five years later, Ripley and Worthington (1998) also concluded that the field lacked direction, empirical support, and theories that are distinct from the general field of couples counseling.

As a result, in some areas Christian marital counseling is a weak shadow of the broader field of secular couples counseling. It lacks a body of important professional literature to help Christian marital counselors practice, leaving most to try to Christianize secular approaches. It lacks guidelines for integration. It lacks empirical support for specifically Christian, integrated therapies or even for biblically based approaches that make no effort to integrate theology and psychology (Worthington, 1996).

Four Types of Marital Interventions

In this chapter we will provide encouragement that some support is beginning to accumulate for Christian-tailored and Christian-consistent interventions that promote better marriages. We will briefly consider (1) preparation for marriage; (2) marriage enrichment; (3) church and community-based interventions, including Christian education for marriage, marriage mentoring, and lay marriage counseling; and (4) marital therapy (we do not look solely at marriage counseling). After summarizing the status of the field, we will describe one flexible intervention to strengthen marriages and attempt to provide empirical support for this intervention. Hope-focused relationship enhancement (Worthington, 1999) can be used for couple enrichment, prevention of problems, and therapy for strengthening marriages. While we will review some literature on this approach, our emphasis will be on practical techniques for counselors.

Preparation for Marriage

Christian authors who have written perhaps the most about preparation for marriage are Les and Leslie Parrott and H. Norman Wright. The Parrotts' (1995) program, Saving Your Marriage Before It Starts (SYMBIS), has been described in a number of books and articles. The Parrotts draw eclectically from a variety of sources including Bowen's (1994) systems theory as well as behavioral therapy (Gottman, 1994) and cognitive therapy (i.e., expectations and myths of marriage, Beck, 1988). An initial investigation of the effectiveness of Parrotts' SYMBIS preparation-for-marriage program has shown it to have some effectiveness at helping troubled engaged or newlywed couples feel more hopeful and adjusted (Ripley, Parrott, Worthington, & Parrott, 2000).

Wright (1992) has written more than fifty books on marriage, family, and related topics. Most often he has written of preparation for marriage (Wright, 1992, 1995, 1997, 1999a) and remarriage (1999b). Wright's roots are firmly established within cognitive-behavioral therapy, and his programs focus on providing information and changing partners' marital beliefs. He uses many interactive premarital exercises to help prospective partners explore their beliefs, attitudes, and behaviors. At present no published research has evaluated Wright's preparation-for-marriage programs, though book sales indicate his written counsel has been popular among churches and practitioners.

A third program for helping prepare couples for marriage—and by far the most scientifically sound program—is conceptualized more as a problem-prevention program than as a marriage-preparation program. The Prevention and Relationship Enhancement Program (PREP), developed by Markman, Renick, Floyd, Stanley, and Clements (1993), was revised and tailored for the Christian population by Stanley and Trathen (1994). However, Trathen's 1995 dissertation found that no difference was detected between the Christian PREP participants and a control group. This result was not out of line when compared with research on the secular version of PREP (Hahlweg, Markman, Thurmaier, Engl, & Eckert, 1998; Markman et al., 1993; Stanley & Trathen, 1994). Typically, PREP and control couples differ more as time goes on, which is consistent with its emphasis on prevention of marital difficulties.

Stanley, Trathen, McCain, and Bryan (1998) have described Christian PREP in a book for married partners titled *A Lasting Promise: A Christian Guide to Fighting for Your Marriage*. In addition, Stanley et al. (2001) received federal funding to investigate the effectiveness of Christian PREP as applied among congregations. Using Denver University leaders or pastors as facilitators for 138 couples, Stanley et al. (2001) found PREP superior to what churches usually provide for premarital counseling.

A survey of the cutting edge of Christian premarital intervention reveals that this is an area shaped by the expertise of a few leaders in the field. These leaders propose that their approaches will prevent divorce and promote better marriages. Pastors, practitioners, and couples express high satisfaction with these programs. However, this foundation is a shaky one at best, and there is scant direct research and study of the theories and interventions proposed by these leaders.

MARRIAGE ENRICHMENT

Marriage-enrichment interventions attempt to promote better relationships among couples whose marriages are essentially normal. The targeted population comprises (1) those who function well, (2) those with an average number of problems, and (3) those who have subclinical problems. Self-help books on marital enrichment exist in absolute profusion, including those aimed at the following:

- enriching troubled relationships (such as Clinton, 1999; Parrott & Parrott, 2001)
- improving the spiritual side of marriage (such as Thomas, 2000)
- helping couples improve already good marriages by reading about marriage (such as Wright, 2000)
- helping couples work on relationship-building exercises together (such as Clinton & Clinton, 2000)

This is just a sampling. The amount of writing aimed at improving Christian marriages is staggering.

A good deal of research on marriage enrichment has been conducted over the years. Most research has focused on secular marital-enrichment programs; however, two Christian approaches have begun empirical investigations of their methodology. The general research in marriage enrichment has shown encouraging efficacy, as demonstrated by recent meta-analysis by Hight (2000). He found an effects size between 0.3 to 0.5 of a standard deviation, relative to control groups (mean effect size = 0.35). That is, couples receiving marriage enrichment improved substantially, on average, across a large number of programs.

Consistently, the highest effect size for a marriage-enrichment program has been for the Relationship Enhancement (RE) program (Guerney, 1977). This eclectic program focuses on empathic listening and communication skills and is typically scheduled for twelve to eighteen hours. In reviewing research from the last fifteen years, Hight (2000) found that the mean effect size of RE was around 0.6, lower than that reported by Giblin, Sprenkle, and Sheehan (1985) for the period of 1970 to 1985. By contrast, the Couples Communication Program by Miller, Wachman, Nunnally, and Miller (1988) is another eclectic program with a history of efficacy supported by research (Butler & Wampler, 1999). Miller's program has been conceptualized as being consistent with Christian theology (Oliver & Miller, 1996). However, neither of these programs—RE or Couples Communication— has been tested in a published study involving Christian couples.

Recent studies by Combs, Bufford, Campbell, and Halter (2000) have investigated a cognitive-behavioral program of marital enrichment aimed at Christian couples. A strong effect size was reported in one study (Norval, Combs, Wiinamak, Bufford, & Halter, 1996) and a more moderate effect size in a second study (Combs et al., 2000). This program shows promise for additional investigation.

In 1997 Worthington et al. developed "hope-focused relationship enhancement," the principles of which are consistent with theologically conservative Christianity. This approach, however, has not been investigated in a specifically Christian setting. We will discuss this approach in detail in the following section.

While marriage enrichment is generally effective and may be effective in Christian contexts with Christian couples, there is a ceiling effect with enrichment settings. Couples who are already satisfied with their relationships can benefit only to a limited degree. Also, some evidence suggests that troubled couples might get worse if they are not directly supervised when they employ communication exercises and interventions (Doherty, Lester, & Leigh, 1986). In addition, marriage-enrichment investigations have rarely attempted to distinguish between those couples who will benefit and those who may get worse as a consequence of this approach. Therefore, some couples who may be utilizing Christian marital enrichment might be better advised to seek other marital assistance.

CHURCH AND COMMUNITY-BASED MARITAL INTERVENTIONS

Pastoral counseling. Arguably, pastors may do more marriage counseling than any other helping professionals; however, there is little or no empirical study of the effectiveness of pastoral counseling for marital difficulties. Benner (1992) found that 84% of pastors surveyed noted marriage problems as among the five top problems they address. Typically, parishioners report high degrees of satisfaction with the pastoral counseling that they receive (Gurin, Veroff, & Feld, 1960; Miller & Jackson, 1995). This finding does not imply that the counseling is effective, merely that it meets people's expectations.

Most of the information that has been disseminated professionally about pastoral marital counseling has been through books. For example, Worthington and McMurry (1994), writing in Benner's series on strategic pastoral counseling, presented a three-stage model of brief pastoral counseling for marital difficulties. Other examples of marital counseling approaches for pastoral counselors include Wimberly's (1997) approach for African American churches and Wright's (1995) approach for church leaders.

Christian education. Despite the consensus in many churches that building stronger marriages is a valued function of the church, few congregations enter into systematic programs of Christian education to promote better marriages (Worthington, 1995). At the congregational level there are many opportunities to educate members, including sermons, classes, seminars, libraries, and audiotapes. As of this writing we are unaware of systematic studies of the effectiveness of such interventions—a topic worthy of investigation.

Marriage mentoring. Marriage mentoring involves pairing newly married couples with more experienced married couples who serve as models and are sources of advice and interaction. One such program was originated by the Parrotts (1995). Ripley, Parrott, Worthington, Parrott, and Smith (2001) have investigated the effectiveness of training for coordinators of marriage mentoring programs. They found that the coordinators improved their own marriage and self-efficacy beliefs as a result of marital training and exposure to mentoring.

Lay marriage counseling. Lay marriage counseling provides trained paraprofessional counselors who advise and counsel troubled couples. Worthington (1994) has written a book on lay marriage counseling; however, despite the growing lay counseling movement, relatively little attention has been given to this area of lay counseling. The American Association of Christian Counselors (AACC) is now distributing a video training program for church-based marriage mentoring and lay counseling titled Marriage Works,[1] but it is too soon to evaluate the program's effectiveness.

Another program that has received attention is McManus's (1993) widely disseminated Marriage Savers program, which includes marriage mentoring. This program has not been evaluated scientifically, although some case studies about its effectiveness in local application are informally available.[2] Both McManus's and the Parrotts' programs seem, in theory, to provide promising models for community-based Christian marital interventions; however, they have not received close empirical scrutiny to date.

Marriage Therapy

Although a huge number of volumes have been written on Christian marriage (and many by Christian therapists), surprisingly few books have been published on Christian marital therapy. Wright (1981) put forth a biblical and cognitive-behavioral therapy (CBT) model. Worthington (1989) followed with an approach heavily influenced by CBT and family-systems therapy (namely from Haley and Minuchin). Friessen and Friessen (1989) also put forth a CBT model.

As managed care began to dominate therapies during the early 1990s, marital therapies were influenced by brief approaches, even though problems of a strict marital nature were not usually diagnosable (and thus were not reimbursed by third-party payers). Oliver, Hasz, and Richburg (1997; De Shazer, 1988) published a solution-based Christian model influenced heavily by solution-focused therapy (SFT). Worthington (1999) wrote of hope-focused marital therapy, which drew eclectically from CBT, SFT, family-systems therapy, emotion-focused couple therapy (Greenberg & Johnson, 1988), integrative behavioral couple therapy (Jacobson & Christensen, 1996), hope theory (Snyder, 1994), and pastoral counseling (Worthington & McMurry, 1994).

The paucity of books explicitly about Christian marital therapy (as distinct from enrichment, pastoral counseling, preparation for marriage, marriage mentoring, marriage dynamics, and marital self-help approaches) reflects one of the two paradoxes within this general area. Christians value marriage highly, yet (1) relatively little research has been conducted on Christian marriage or marital interventions, and (2) few books explicitly lay out a clear system of how to do marital therapy with people who have troubled marriages.

Hope-Focused Marriage Enhancement

Worthington et al. (1997) present a hope-focused relationship enhancement model, which focuses on increasing hope as the key to enhancing marriages.

Hope-focused relationship enhancement has been used as the basis for the following activities:
- one-hour lectures
- thirteen-week Sunday-school classes
- yearlong couples' groups
- weekend marriage retreats
- Saturday morning workshops
- three-hour group discussions of videotaped talks
- five-, six-, and eight-hour marriage-enrichment workshops
- six-week (two hours per week) discussions and support groups
- variable-length consultations between counselor and couple

The approach has been implemented by psychologists, counselors, pastors, and lay church leaders throughout the United States as well as in Singapore, Malaysia, Brazil, and South Africa. In all settings, leaders testified informally that couples experienced high satisfaction, substantial learning, and a willingness to refer their friends. Most couples estimated not only that they would use the information in their marriages, but that the marriage-enrichment experience would positively affect their marriages.

Testimonies of satisfaction and perceived effectiveness are essential for a program's success as well as for its widespread use. However, such testimonies do not tell whether a program really will help people build better marriages. Also, testimonies cannot tell which elements of a program, if any, are effective. To build a strong foundation of support for an approach, therefore, it is necessary to conduct a systematic study of its effects on participants.

Published Studies of Hope-Focused Relationship Enhancement

Efficacy of the whole model. In 1997 Worthington et al. published an outcome investigation of the hope-focused marriage-enhancement intervention model as presented in six hours of enrichment consultation with individual couples. They found that the intervention was highly effective in helping couples increase their satisfaction with their relationships. Whereas Hight (2000) noted a mean effect size of 0.35 for all marital enrichment intervention investigations since 1985,

Worthington's group found that the hope-focused intervention had a greater mean effect size of 1.2 in increasing relationship satisfaction.

Effects of skilled group leaders. So which parts of hope-focused relationship enhancement contribute to its success? Different aspects of hope-focused relationship enhancement have been investigated in group settings. In 1985 Hammonds and Worthington examined how marriage-enrichment interventions are discussed among groups of couples. They found that the group facilitator's leadership style is crucial to effective intervention. The topics that facilitators introduce typically initiate discussion and focus the attention of the group. When group facilitators follow up a group member's statement by asking for other comments, discussion typically increases.

Effects of being in a group with other couples. In 1989 Worthington, Buston, and Hammonds investigated the effects of providing videotaped information to groups of couples or to individual couples in a consultancy setting. The couples watched ten-minute videotapes on topics such as communication, conflict resolution, and intimacy, then they discussed their own marriages either within the group or with a marriage consultant. Worthington et al. found that providing brief information alone did not help couples improve their relationship. However, they found that couple participation in discussions about their marriage promoted modest increases in marital satisfaction. The confounding variable in the study is that when individuals participated in group discussion, their intervention took four times as long as when couples met with consultants. Nonetheless, we believe that there is power in having couples discuss their marriages in groups.

Effects of assessment and feedback. Worthington et al. (1995) investigated the effects of another component of hope-focused relationship enhancement: completing questionnaires and receiving feedback. The consultants were typically first-year or second-year graduate students in a counseling program, so the level of technical counseling expertise was not exceptionally high. Nonetheless, it was determined that meeting with a consultant to receive written feedback about the marriage was responsible for approximately one-fourth of all gains that couples typically experience in marriage-enrichment interventions.

Ripley et al. (2000) again investigated the assessment and feedback portion of the hope-focused model of intervention. This study was different from Worthington et al. (1995) in several ways. First, the study by Ripley et al. (2000) was specifically targeted to Christian married couples, and it added a religious component to assessment and feedback. Second, the study was conducted through telephone interviews and mail questionnaires; written reports were mailed to the couples in lieu of in-person feedback. Third, written questionnaires eliminated a long, open-ended self-report inventory as well as videotaped discussion. Consultants were first- or second-year graduate students in a clinical psychology program. In this format, smaller gains were reported by couples. In addition, the study tended to attract more couples who had lower levels of baseline marital adjustment in their marriage. Ripley et al. proposed that the loss of some of the written assessment inventories and videotaped discussion, as well as the loss of the in-person assessment and delivery of feedback, accounted for the lower effects of distance intervention. This finding suggests that, despite time and cost pressures, hope-focused counselors should not cut corners on the in-person assessment and feedback portions of their intervention.

Effects of training in communication, conflict, and forgiveness. Ripley and Worthington (2001) compared two six-hour group interventions. The first intervention helped couples learn communication and conflict-resolution skills and then gave them the opportunity to practice those skills within a group. The second intervention taught couples how to forgive their partners for having hurt them in some way. Thus, in Ripley and Worthington, the intervention studied in Worthington et al. (1997) was split apart. The material on forgiveness was expanded by drawing from other research on forgiveness (McCullough & Worthington, 1995; McCullough, Worthington, & Rachal, 1997; Worthington et al., 2000). Transgressions between the partners were discussed, and partners practiced an early version of Worthington's (1998) Pyramid Model to REACH Forgiveness. Thus, Ripley and Worthington (2001) investigated two halves of the hope-focused intervention and compared findings to each other as well as to a test-retest control group of couples. Although approximately 40% of participants reported that they attend church once a week, the groups were conducted in a secular format.

The *communication and conflict resolution* intervention produced a substantial change in the way partners communicated with each other, which substantially increased the ratio of positive interactions to negative interactions. That ratio is thought to be crucial to the long-term success of marriages (Gottman, 1994). The *forgiveness* intervention did not produce comparable changes in the way partners communicated with each other, nor did it affect the way partners rated their marriages. Partners did experience a moderate amount of forgiveness. Ripley and Worthington (2001) concluded that partners need to be taught how to discuss transgressions, not just how to forgive.

Burchard, Yarhouse, Worthington, Berry, and Canter (2001) have investigated the effectiveness of the *communication and conflict resolution* portion of hope-focused marriage enhancement versus the *intimacy, forgiveness, and reconciliation* portion versus a repeatedly retested *control condition*. Their study was a pilot test for an ongoing clinical trial. The pilot test used only twenty-four couples (eight in each condition) who met individually as couples with consultants for nine hours of enrichment consultation. Both interventions resulted in self-reports of improvements in marriage quality. Given the low number of participants per condition, the findings suggest that both parts of the overall hope-focused method could benefit marriages.

Conclusions from research. Overall, then, based on these studies of components of the hope-focused relationship-enhancement model, we can draw several helpful conclusions:

1. The amount of time spent focusing on the marriage is important.
2. It is important to have leaders who are active (but not overly active) as facilitators of the marriage groups.
3. Providing thorough, in-person, written feedback—based on objective assessment—to partners about their marriages will likely increase marital satisfaction.
4. Explicit training in communication and conflict resolution is important in helping people change their actual marriage communication—though it is less clear that such training produces an immediate change in marital satisfaction.
5. Simply training couples how to forgive each other is not likely to help their marriages apart from explicit training in how to communicate their requests, explain transgressions, and ask for and grant forgiveness.
6. It is important to allow couples to discuss their marriages, whether with other couples or with a consultant.
7. Hope-focused relationship enhancement is effective in helping married couples build better relationships.
8. No single part of the method can be thought of as *the* crucial part; rather, each portion contributes to overall effectiveness.

Hope-Focused Marital Counseling

Worthington (1999) has described hope-focused marriage therapy as one aspect of the general method of hope-focused relationship enhancement. To enhance training, several resources are available. These include written case studies by Hight (see Worthington, 1999) and Worthington (1991) in Collins's collection of case studies on Christian counseling.[3]

Building Hope

At the center of hope-focused marriage counseling is the concept of hope. Hope is defined by Snyder (1994) as consisting of two parts. The first is called "willpower to change," or motivation to strive for a goal. The second is called "waypower to change," for the multiple pathways needed to attempt to achieve the goal. Snyder summarizes this in an equation:

$$Hope = Willpower\ to\ change + Waypower\ to\ change$$

Worthington adapted Snyder's (1994) equation to incorporate the idea from theologian Marcel (1962) that hope is needed even when one cannot sense movement toward a goal. That is, we can have hope by knowing that God is with us, even though progress toward a desired goal is not apparent. Worthington (1998) calls this "waitpower for change."

The goal in hope-focused relationship enhancement is to make the marriage relationship better. This might involve (1) solving marital problems through therapy, (2) learning information and skills to enhance an already good relationship (enrichment), and (3) learning skills that can prevent future problems (prevention). Therapy, enrichment, and prevention are often blended through intervening with the same couple. In the final half of this chapter, we describe over twenty counseling techniques to promote willpower to change, waypower to change, and waitpower for change.

BUILDING WILLPOWER TO CHANGE

Willpower involves the belief—in the heart, not just in the head—that people can make their marriages better. Most married couples have been exhorted to work on their marriage, to persevere when the going gets tough, and to stay committed to their relationships. By the time a couple gets to counseling, such exhortations by the therapist are rarely helpful and can even be counterproductive. The couple wants a counselor to acknowledge their effort, not pound on them to do what they have already tried for years to accomplish. By this time, failure has taken its toll, and the husband and wife may believe additional efforts are likely to fail. They may have little willpower to change. Thus the counselor's first objective is to build willpower.

Build willpower by enhancing belief in the counselor. Partners want to believe that a counselor can help. Counselors can enhance this belief by emphasizing their strengths. An experienced counselor should provide information about his or her experience. For inexperienced therapists who cannot draw on a wealth of clinical experience, the couple needs to know that the counselor is committed to helping, has boundless energy, and is enthusiastic about working with them.

Counselors can also enhance this belief by providing professional feedback that the marriage is flawed yet redeemable. Partners want to know that if they work hard and trust God, they can redeem their relationship. They do not want to be encouraged to return to an old relationship; instead, they want the counselor to help them build a *new* relationship. Couples need to know that there are no miracle cures, but at the same time they need assurance that there is a cure.

Build willpower by providing written feedback. To help build the couple's willpower, do an initial assessment session that culminates in a written report. Give the report to each partner at the beginning of the second session. That report should not gloss over problems, but it should identify at least as many positive characteristics of the marriage as negative characteristics. If the road to an improved marriage is likely to be long and rocky, partners want to hear that the counselor is astute enough to perceive that. A Pollyanna solution should not be proposed in the assessment report. The counselor should write an assessment report that grounds the hopeful evaluation either in specific events that occurred in the first session or in the inventories that the couple completed. We have found written inventories especially helpful in this regard since questionnaires are more difficult for partners to discount or ignore than what they say aloud. In a similar way, despite how busy you may be, we recommend that you write your assessment. A written assessment will likely be your single most powerful intervention.

Build willpower by helping partners successfully change. Willpower to change grows as couples notice success in changing their relationships. It is important, therefore, to help partners experience some initial successes at effecting change, which makes the first two counseling sessions crucial (De Shazer, 1988). Hope-focused marriage counseling is brief counseling, usually occurring in one session for assessment, one session for feedback, and no more than six to eight therapy sessions. While the first two sessions are technically described to couples as assessment-and-feedback sessions, many of the gains of therapy happen during these initial meetings. During assessment and feedback, focus on (1) aspects of the marriage worth fighting for, (2) strengths of the marriage, (3) efforts the couple has made to improve their situation, and (4) the couple's willingness to come to counseling. Use solution-focused techniques such as the "miracle" question: "If a miracle occurred and your marriage were perfect, what would others see?" (De Shazer, 1988).

Build willpower through a realistic choice of the initial target. When counseling proper starts, wisely choose the topic that will be considered first. If the couple is highly conflicted and cannot inhibit negative communication and arguing, then begin with communication and conflict resolution. If they are going to argue anyway, they may as well do so in session because you are working specifically on how to resolve differences. If assessment reveals low intimacy, you may begin by discussing how to make their marriage more intimate. Address how to communicate positively to build that intimacy.

Build willpower by drawing out of the couple a positive vision of marriage. Couples can boost their willpower to change by developing a clear, positive vision of marriage. They may have begun their marriage with a dream, but by the time they get to counseling their vision has become a pipe dream. Now they must build a new vision that reflects their maturity, their resilience, and their acceptance of their history of marital problems. Engage partners in speaking about what their marriage ought to be by using some variant of the miracle question, a technique advocated by many counselors (see Hasz, Oliver, & Carmack, 2000; Oliver, Hasz, & Richburg 1997; Oliver & Wright 1997; Worthington, 1999). Hope-focused marital counseling uses the miracle question during the couple's first assessment session.

Build willpower by using technology to help create a positive vision of the marriage. Say to the partners, "Between sessions, I will evaluate your questionnaires and think about the strengths and weaknesses of your marriage. As I write an assessment report for you, would you spend more time thinking about your vision of marriage? Would each of you bring me a description of the way you would like your marriage to be? Don't use this time to make points with your partner. Don't criticize. Merely describe your ideal marriage. Write, audiotape, or videotape your description."

You will use variations of this "technology" task at several points during counseling For instance, at various times you could ask partners to make video- or audiotapes to describe ideal communication, ideal intimacy, ideal child rearing, or a perfect date. At the beginning of the feedback session, ask partners to describe highlights of their written, audiotaped, or videotaped description of the ideal marriage. Play portions of their tapes so they can hear each other verbalizing their thoughts and dreams.

Build willpower by affecting the Gottman ratio. Early in counseling, tell the couple that their marriage will improve if they increase the ratio of positive-to-negative interactions to greater than five-to-one, simultaneously decreasing negative interaction and increasing positive interaction (Gottman, 1994). Use analogies, often shaped by people's experience, to get this point across. You might say that positive interactions are like stockpiling love and that negative interactions are like removing five times the weight of a positive interaction from that stockpile. Challenge partners to build a huge stockpile of love because that stockpile provides a reserve from which they can draw when they disagree or hurt each other. In his books *His Needs, Her Needs* (1994) and *Love Busters* (1997), Harley used the analogy of a love bank and encouraged people to add to it.

Build willpower through homework. The effectiveness of counseling can be dramatically enhanced if couples work on their marriage several hours each week outside of therapy. Therefore the counselor should assign regular homework and should repeatedly emphasize its importance. At the beginning of each session, ask about the homework and determine how much homework the couple actually did. Couples either complete homework fully and correctly, complete it fully but not correctly, complete it partially, or do not make the attempt. Do not shame or scold them for incomplete or incorrect homework; instead, treat their inability to complete their homework as a problem that you can work with them to solve. Even complete and correct completion of homework requires discussion about what actually happened when the homework was attempted and what the couple learned from the homework.

One way to motivate couples to do their homework is to ask them how much time, energy, and emotional investment they have put into their marriage. Then ask whether they are willing to invest the equivalent of one workweek—forty hours of their time—in their marriage. Because counseling sessions may require only six to ten hours, approximately thirty hours are available for them to invest at home in rebuilding their marriage. Get them to agree that they will invest those additional thirty hours before counseling ends.

Build willpower by providing a final evaluation. The final task in counseling is to provide a final written evaluation of the marriage. Write the report before the final session. Highlight the positive aspects of the couple's marriage and the gains they have made through counseling. Describe a plan to help them continue to make progress. Because the plan is written and comes from a professional counselor, it is likely to motivate the couple to continue to work on improving their relationship even after counseling is complete. In addition, your final report will help the couple transfer their willpower to change from the therapy sessions to their home life.

BUILDING WAYPOWER TO CHANGE

Partners often believe that only one solution exists for their problems: "My partner must change." However, because they themselves can't bring about that change in their partner, they're frustrated and angry. They believe "My partner has become calcified. He [she] will never change." Hope is at low ebb. Snyder (1994) addresses this mind-set by emphasizing the importance of helping clients discover the waypower to change, or what he calls "pathways to change."

Build waypower by keeping partners focused. It may be tempting to believe that your job as a counselor is to provide five hundred techniques a couple can use to make their relationship better. Such behavior, however, would result in disorganized counseling. Keep partners focused on the topic being discussed in the current session.

Build waypower through strategy. A strategy is a general plan that helps you decide where to put limited energies and how to focus tactics in order to promote change. The overarching hope-focused strategy is to teach couples to build love, work, and faith in their relationship. This is based on the apostle Paul's discipleship strategy of promoting "faith working through love" (Galatians 5:6, NKJV).

The first part of the strategy is *love*. *Love* is defined as being willing to value and not devalue your partner. Partners are told repeatedly throughout counseling to "value your partner." (Counselors may say these words at least ten times over the course of counseling.) Partners should not put down, criticize, belittle, or devalue their mate in any way. Instead, they are to treat the other person as a pearl of great value (Matthew 13:45-46). This way of expressing love is supported by research, which finds that high amounts of positive interactions (valuing) and low amounts of negative interactions (devaluing) are likely to be the strongest indicators of marital health (Gottman, 1994).

The second part of the strategy is *work*. Couples must set aside time to work on their marriage if it is to improve. They must also exert the effort to make specific changes in their behavior toward each other. This is another reason why homework is so important.

The third part of the strategy is *faith*. Faith always has an object. The objects of faith in hope-focused marriage counseling include God, the counselor, counseling itself, interventions, and each partner.

Couples should have faith in God and in his ability to redeem their marriage, regardless of how broken their relationship is. Help couples build their faith in God by encouraging them to invite Jesus Christ into their marriage. Ask them to imagine vividly what would happen if Jesus were to enter their marriage. Suggest that each partner invite the Holy Spirit into his or her imagination. Implore God to change the couple's vision of their marriage from negative and hopeless to positive and hopeful. Acknowledge that the primary work of healing is being done by the supernatural intervention of God, with psychological processes occurring simultaneously.

Couples can also benefit as they develop faith that the counselor can help. By being optimistic (without being unrealistic), focused, insightful, and perceptive, you can maximize a couple's belief that you can help. Their faith in you will also grow as you recommend interventions that make a difference in their behavior.

Likewise, couples need to develop faith in the counseling itself. People come to counseling for many reasons. Some people try counseling, not because they believe it can help their marriage, but because they want to be able to say they tried everything prior to divorcing. Such people have little faith that counseling can help. It may be possible to help them build faith in counseling by pointing out the positive—even small—changes you see both initially and along the way.

Help partners build faith in each intervention, whether it is an in-session intervention or a homework assignment. Describe candidly what partners might get out of doing their assignments. After completed assignments, discuss with partners what they got out of each assignment.

Finally, help partners restore their faith in each other. If partners are to maintain their gains after counseling ends, they must regain such faith. This is usually the most difficult aspect of counseling. You can help build a couple's faith in each other by calling attention to each partner's efforts to make the marriage better. Ask each partner to express appreciation for the efforts the other person is making.

Build waypower to communicate better. Teach partners STEPS to Better Communication. Our acrostic, STEPS, is similar to one element of the Couple Communication Program called the Awareness Wheel (Miller et al., 1988). Miller's program involves systematic training in both the Awareness Wheel and the Listening Cycle.[4] The STEPS to Better Communication are as follows:

S—*Situation:* Each person describes what occurred.

T—*Thoughts:* Each person describes what he or she is thinking.

E—*Emotions:* Each person describes past and present feelings. Couples often need coaching here to use "feeling" words instead of describing their thoughts again.

P—*Plans:* Each person describes his or her plans. Plans include what people are doing, have done, or intend to do to deal with a situation.

S—*Statement of valuing love:* Partners say explicitly that they care for the other person, that they value what the other person thinks, and that they want to hear what the other person is experiencing. For example, one partner might say, "I care for you more than I care about getting my own way in this situation." The final *S* can make a big difference in helping couples be less defensive so they can maximize their love.

Another pathway we encourage to increase waypower for communication is to teach partners *leveling* and *editing* (Gottman, Notarius, Gonso, & Markman, 1975). *Leveling* is saying what is on one's mind "on the level." In the apostle Paul's words, leveling is "speaking the truth in love" (Ephesians 4:15). *Editing,* on the other hand, is knowing that one does not have to say everything that is on one's mind. A partner can choose not to hurt the spouse. Valuing a partner, regardless of what that person says or does, is the key. Because *love* is defined as valuing the partner and not devaluing the partner, "speaking the truth in love" means speaking the loving truth after deciding whether a particular statement will value and not devalue the partner.

Teaching couples methods of effective listening has proven helpful in many approaches to marital counseling (Hahlweg & Klaan, 1997; Jacobson & Addis, 1993); however, counselors should be aware that researchers have been debating whether listening interventions are actually helpful (see Gottman, Coan, Carrere, & Swanson, 1998; Stanley, Bradbury, & Markman, 2000). We propose that the truly beneficial effects of teaching listening skills to couples are found in three specific actions:

1. breaking entrenched patterns of self-interest
2. teaching partners to cease negative communication patterns (such as negative reciprocity, a sucking vortex in which negative communications are reciprocated with more negative communications until a small disagreement turns into a hurtful interchange)
3. increasing the number and quality of valuing interactions

Build waypower to better resolve differences. Pathways to resolving differences involve teaching partners another acrostic: LOVE.

L— *Listen and repeat.* People usually *feel* misunderstood because they *are* misunderstood. When a person feels misunderstood, he or she stops listening to the other person and focuses instead on how to make the other person understand. That failure to listen usually results in misunderstanding the other person. When such misunderstandings develop, both partners are usually caught in a cycle in which neither partner listens to the other. To break out of this cycle, one partner must begin to listen and reflect both content and feeling until the other person feels that he or she is understood. Then the listening partner can ask whether the other person would like to know what he or she is thinking. This is a simpler version of the active listening skills commonly taught in marital therapy.

O—*Observe your effects.* Tell the couple to be vigilant to cues that indicate that the other partner does not understand. When one partner does not seem to understand, the other partner is to stop talking and ask, "What did you understand me to say?" If a misunderstanding has indeed occurred, the speaker should say, "I'm sorry I came across that way. I didn't mean to convey that. What I was trying to say was…"

V—*Value your partner.* As partners work to resolve differences, they must continually strive to value and never devalue one another.

E—*Evaluate the interests of both partners* (Fisher & Ury, 1981). When part-ners get locked in a dispute, it is common for each to focus on a solu-tion that he or she has decided is the *only* solution. It is as if each person has chosen one path and refuses to consider alternative pathways. To break such impasses, you may need to help couples examine their underlying interests. For example, a husband may adamantly refuse to buy a new dining room set because he is seeking to become more finan-cially secure. The wife may demand the purchase because she wants to help their dinner guests feel more welcome and comfortable in their home. Once underlying interests are uncovered, solutions can be worked out that meet both people's interests.

Build waypower to grow in spiritual intimacy. Spiritual intimacy is not a mere mechanical adherence to having devotions or attending Bible studies together. Spiritual intimacy grows from the ability and willingness of partners to share their ideas and discoveries about their individual relationships with the Lord. You can help partners build spiritual intimacy by encouraging them to describe recent faith experiences, talk about speakers they have heard, or share exciting insights they have discovered while reading God's Word. Another way to facilitate spiritual inti-macy is to encourage each partner to daily ask what he or she can pray about on behalf of the other. The asking partner then listens and notes the issues with which the other partner is wrestling and follows up with silent prayer for that partner. Of course, if partners wish, they can pray aloud together. The important thing is to persist in prayer for one another, which helps keep partners connected spiritually with each other and with the Lord.

Build waypower to emotional intimacy. An effective intervention to promote emotional intimacy has been demonstrated by Worthington (1990, 1991) on a videotape available through the Liberty University School of Life-Long Learning.[5] This method uses the physical space in the counseling room as a metaphor for emotional closeness or distance. The goal is to help couples become alert to their level of intimacy and then discuss their hopes for greater intimacy. In the inter-vention, partners stand facing each other and imagine that the distance between them represents levels of intimacy. Hugging each other in the middle of the room represents the closest emotional intimacy they could possibly experience, and standing against opposing walls represents the least.

At the counselor's instruction, partners place themselves at a distance that rep-resents their sense of how emotionally intimate they currently are. Then the coun-selor encourages partners to move to where they would like to be. (This step often reveals an emotional *distancer-pursuer* pattern where one partner wants to be extremely close emotionally and the other partner does not desire as much closeness [Guerin, Fay, Burden, & Kautto, 1987].) Partners then return to where they feel they are right now, and the counselor has them talk about a topic they believe would help them feel closer to each other. When the mood shifts, partners actually move to where they feel they are at the present time. Couples thus learn that they can change their emotional closeness by how they interact.

BUILDING WAITPOWER FOR CHANGE

Even with the large collection of practical, sensible interventions recommended by Worthington (1999) and sampled in this chapter, change is not always apparent to married partners or to the counselor. The counselor must prepare the couple to persevere when change is not seen, and that takes *waitpower.*

Build waitpower during relapse by explaining the surge-euphoria-relapse (SER) cycle. The SER cycle is a waitpower strategy. At the beginning of counseling, couples frequently *surge* ahead. They feel *euphoric.* Some couples want to terminate, and the counselor must help them decide to remain in counseling. Then a *relapse* occurs, usually prompted by a heated argument or a breach of trust. Again the counselor must help the couple remain in therapy to find ways to deal with their disappointment and negative feelings during sessions as well as at home.

Build waitpower when expectations are not fully realized. Hope-focused marriage counseling is brief (six to ten sessions), which means that each partner has to give up the dream that they will have a perfect marriage when they say good-bye to you as their therapist. Some couples become demoralized and want to declare counseling a failure. A primary task of counseling for waitpower, then, is to help the couple process their disappointment and its significance—and not to extend the counseling sessions indefinitely simply because they are disappointed that their marriage is not perfect. A good time to address unrealized expectations is in the next-to-last session.

Build a memorial to enhance future waitpower. Have couples initiate a "Joshua memorial" between their next-to-last and final sessions. In the next-to-last session, remind them of the memorial of stones Joshua built after leading the Israelites over the Jordan River (Joshua 4:8). Then ask the couple to reflect on their counseling experience and to prepare a symbol of the work God has done in their marriage. Some couples are very creative, making amazing works of art. One couple bought a special box to put objects in that reminded them of their time in counseling. Another couple had a professional photographer take their picture together, which they framed and put on their wall at home.

Build waitpower by providing a final report. Finally, write a final assessment report (described earlier) during the week prior to the last therapy session. A professional *written* assessment report testifies to progress. It builds hope for the future by providing tangible evidence of the couple's ability to change. This report will help the couple build waitpower for those times in the future when they might struggle.

STRENGTHS OF THE HOPE-FOCUSED APPROACH

While many programs have been created to enhance marriages, few have received much attention from researchers. Those that have include Stanley's (1994) Christian PREP; Miller's Couples Communication Program (Butler & Wampler, 1999); Combs's Marital Enrichment Program (Combs et al., 2000; Norval et al., 1996); and Worthington's (1999) hope-focused relationship enhancement.

In this chapter we have surveyed the field of marital counseling with special attention paid to the research and implementation of the hope-focused relationship enhancement model. We conclude that the hope-focused approach utilizes many of the essential aspects of marital intervention to help couples improve or rescue their marriages. These aspects, and some of the means of intervention, include:

1. *Maximizing hope* through initial written feedback, the counselor's hopeful attitude, an articulated vision for marriage, early success in counseling, realistic choices of targets, increased positive interactions, regularly completed homework, and final evaluation.

2. *Using a strategy* that involves conceptualizing the marriage relationship in terms of love, work, and faith.

3. *Enhancing love* through the use of valuing as a theme in practically all interventions, an increased Gottman ratio, videotaped ideal communications, STEPS intervention, leveling and editing, LOVE intervention, and space as a metaphor for change.

4. *Promoting faith* through building spiritual intimacy, the surge-euphoria-relapse (SER) cycle, the Joshua memorial, and a final assessment report.

5. *Inviting supernatural intervention* by building spiritual intimacy, inviting Christ into the marriage, the use of faith-based explanations for interventions with couples, a vision for marriage, the therapist praying for the couple, and partners praying for each other.

6. *Breaking negative reciprocity cycles* through STEPS intervention, LOVE intervention, the use of valuing statements during conflict, and the use of homework.

It is our prayer that the hope-focused approach to couples counseling will be used to accomplish God's goals of helping couples create and maintain happy, healthy marriage relationships that last a lifetime.

CHAPTER 21

THE SECOND-HALF MARRIAGE

Helping Couples Transition into the Empty-Nest Years

CLAUDIA ARP AND DAVID ARP

Persons [age 50 to 64] are a high-energy group. Many have skills and wisdom that are unsurpassed. This group [is] poised to make a major contribution to the betterment of U.S. society...if its members can abandon the mindset that they should be winding down and instead grasp the concept that their lives and careers are only a prelude of what is to come...[which is more than] ticking off miles in an RV or spending time at the golf course. At retirement, they can move from success to significance.

—GEORGE GALLUP JR., *The Next American Spirituality*

Aging baby boomers. The phrase seems like a contradiction in terms, but the fact is that in the United States someone turns fifty every seven seconds. According to Waldrop (1991), when all of the baby boomers pass their forty-fifth birthday in the year 2010, 37.7 million people will be in their peak income years (ages 45–54). Probably for the first time in history, they will be able to live those years in good physical health. But the question is, Can couples in the second half of life keep their marriages healthy as well?

Yes they can—if Christian educators, counselors, and clergy are prepared to help them transition into the empty-nest years. This period can be a difficult passage for even the most stable of marriages. Few people are prepared for the changes they will experience; their course is uncharted, and their needs will be great.

Concepts for this chapter are taken from the book titled *The Second Half of Marriage* as well as from seminar and video curriculum by Marriage Alive International, Inc. (www.marriagealive.com).

CRIES FOR HELP

More and more frequently we hear stories of midlife marital upheaval:

- The phone rang. A stockbroker from Chicago was on the line. "My wife says she doesn't love me anymore, that our marriage is boring, and that with our last child leaving for college, she wants out of the marriage. I had no idea my wife was so unhappy. Is there something you can do to fix my marriage?"
- A recent e-mail message brought a cry for help from a wife whose husband of twenty-five years just walked out. She was a great mom, and he loved the way she cared for the kids—but now their daughter was leaving home and he was filing for divorce.
- Ruby and George have a great marriage, so they had few problems adjusting to the empty nest because they had stayed emotionally connected during their children's trying adolescent years. But now Ruby is facing cancer.
- Rob and Nancy are facing the empty nest. Their daughter has finished one year of college, and their son has one more year of high school before he leaves home. Nancy shares, "When my daughter, Julie, left home, I missed her terribly. We were best friends—and then she was gone." Rob continues, "While our children were growing up, we concentrated on them. Now that we're facing the empty nest, we're going to have to figure out how we can reconnect. Most all of the time we spend together is centered around our family. I'm concerned about how we're going to handle this."

For Rob and Nancy, the empty-nest transition is proving to be a challenge. But the first emotion many other empty-nesters feel is relief—until life becomes confusing. For many couples, the empty nest is almost like a new marriage. And like newlyweds, the empty-nest couple can take one of several different paths.

THREE PATHS TO THE EMPTY NEST

In *Fighting for Your Empty Nest Marriage* (Arp, Arp, Stanley, Markman, & Blumberg, 2000), we described three ways in which many couples enter this transitional time: *drift, crash,* and *charge.*

Drift. Some couples *drift* into the empty nest without much thought or awareness. They wake up one day and realize the kids are gone and that they have done nothing to prepare for this next stage of marriage. If their relationship is basically healthy, they will probably manage, but if they are disconnected emotionally, troubled times may be just ahead.

Crash. Some couples *crash* into the empty nest with a period of unexpected crisis. Remember the stockbroker whose wife wanted out and the wife whose husband surprised her by asking for a divorce.

Charge. Other couples, like Ruby and George, *charge* into the empty nest with a sense of celebration only to find that other issues, such as health problems, are waiting for them.

The empty-nest syndrome starts at different times for different couples. Some couples, like the drifters, are so overwhelmed with their children's teenage years that they don't see the empty nest coming until the last child leaves or gets married. Other couples, like the chargers, begin talking about the empty-nest syndrome when the first college catalog arrives. And still others find that their nest never really empties— or it empties only to refill with adult children, grandchildren, and aging parents.

THE SECOND HALF OF MARRIAGE

In the mid-1990s we coined the term "second half of marriage" to describe the empty-nest years. It is purposely ambiguous because this is an ambiguous time of life, uncharted and undefined.

How can you know if you or your clients are in the second half—or are getting close? Maybe you realize that your active parenting years are coming to a close. Perhaps your own parents are aging and experiencing health problems. Or perhaps you recently attended a twenty-fifth high-school or college reunion. Maybe you exercise more but burn fewer calories. Perhaps you notice that suddenly your arms aren't long enough to hold your reading materials, or that the golden oldies station is playing all your songs.

OUR OWN EXPERIENCE

We realized we were empty-nesters when, out of the blue, Domino's Pizza called us. A concerned voice on the other end asked if we were okay because it had been weeks since we had ordered pizza! (That was probably a hint right there—the pizza kid checking on the "old folks.") Dave assured the caller that all was fine. Actually we were enjoying our brand-new diet of lima beans, broccoli, and Brussels sprouts—all the vegetables our youngest child had hated.

Why the menu change? Several weeks earlier we had dropped Jonathan off at college. Now we could eat what we wanted to eat when we wanted to eat it. Finally, our time belonged to us. No more junior tennis tournaments or soccer practices. No more impromptu teenage parties. Our house—and the kitchen—were ours again, and menu planning was once again delightful.

Please don't misunderstand us. We love our three sons and enjoyed the active parenting years (well, most of them), and yet our initial reaction to the empty nest was one of relief. Parenting three adolescent boys was not easy, but with a few good parenting principles, a sense of humor, God's grace, and more than twenty years of forced labor, we made it through our children's teenage years.

Now it was *our* turn to enjoy life! After all, we were once again in control of our home, our schedules, and ourselves. Or so we thought. It didn't take us long to realize that transitioning to the empty nest wasn't the breeze it first appeared to be. Instead, it was more of a tornado.

After binging on vegetables for a while, we struggled just to eat regular meals. Without Jonathan's demands to be fed, we found ourselves working and doing other things until nine or ten at night and then suddenly realizing we had not eaten dinner. Our late-night gourmet dinners of Frosted Mini-Wheats threatened to become an empty-nest tradition.

Claudia: *Changing roles also confused the landscape of our lives. I had been more involved with our children and running our home than Dave had been. So now was my time to do what I wanted to do with my life—but what was that?*

I still remember a conversation we had the first year of our empty nest. In the middle of a fitness walk around our block, Dave shocked me by saying, "Claudia, for the first half of our marriage we've lived wherever I have needed to be professionally. For the second half let's live wherever you need or want to be."

That was quite impressive. But the problem was, I didn't know exactly where I wanted to be or exactly who I was. I knew I was a writer. And I knew I had enjoyed the times we had traveled and spoken together during our active parenting years. But now what?

Suddenly I realized that all those things I had delayed until the kids left home were now possibilities. Children had definitely moderated my workaholic tendencies. So with my urging, Dave and I accepted too many writing projects, speaking engagements, and seminars—which left us with little time and energy for each other. It took time for us to gorge on all the opportunities and then search for the right balance.

Sitting at our breakfast table one morning over coffee, we agreed something had to give. We realized we needed help; we needed to regroup, refocus, and refresh our own relationship. So to help us retool our marriage, we decided to research the passage into the empty nest and beyond.

That day we began what would become a ten-year journey. And in the last decade we have learned how to reinvent our own relationship, how to refocus on each other, and how to renegotiate and resolve issues in new and fresh ways that build our marriage. But then, nearly all boomers are facing these same issues.

QUICK QUIZ: TO WHAT DOES AARP REFER?

If you know the answer to that question, you probably belong to AARP or are on the cusp of receiving your invitation. The postwar baby-boomer generation is turning fifty and has begun receiving invitations to join this most influential group in America, the American Association of Retired Persons. Most boomers are not thinking of retiring soon, but they can no longer deny that they are facing old age.

At seventy-six million members strong, the boomer generation is shaping and reshaping American politics, commerce, demographics, and values. This generation now holds most of America's leadership positions, and it will soon comprise the largest population of elderly in our nation's history (both in total numbers and as a percentage of the population). An extremely diverse group, boomers have grown up with television and instant communications bringing life and the banalities of life into their world from across the globe.

Baby busters, GenXers, and the millennial generation—the children and grandchildren of boomers, primarily—are also developing their own demographic "bulges" in American society, and these age groups will exert a significant influence on national life early in the twenty-first century. Understanding and responding to the challenges of these demographic "bulges" will be central to the success of any business, educational, or service program in twenty-first-century America. Our focus here, however, is on the boomer generation and how it lives out its second half of life and marriage.

Boomer values. Boomers, especially those nurtured on the upheavals of the 1960s, may be rightly described as the transition generation to the post-Christian culture (Collins & Clinton, 1992; Gallup & Jones, 2000). The pursuit and accumulation of wealth, pleasure, and influence are the dominant values of many boomers, who are passing these values on to future generations. Some of the other driving values of many boomers in America are:

- *Relevance.* Boomers are constantly concerned with the relevance of things and how it will affect "me and mine."
- *Participation.* More active than passive in groups of all sizes, boomers want to and do participate in a range of activities that they can directly influence.
- *Flexibility and informality.* Boomers like relational fluidity, flexibility, choices, informality, and temporary commitment. They eschew rigidity, tradition, rules, formalistic applications, and appeals to authority as key factors that influence choice.
- *Questioning.* Wary of authoritarian pressures, boomers maintain idealism as well as skepticism about the world. They are not afraid to challenge prevailing views and conventional wisdom about what is considered right.

- *Enthusiasm for causes.* Boomers led the myriad movements that have brought significant change in the past thirty to forty years—the antiwar movement, Civil Rights movement, feminist movement, men's movement, environmental movement, transnational democratic movement, and, yes, even the Jesus movement of the 1960s and the world evangelization movements of today.
- *Acceptance and tolerance.* Tolerance of diversity in values, behavior, politics, and religion is a hallmark of the boomer generation. Likewise, boomers are most intolerant of perceived intolerance, especially in its judgments of intolerance in religious, racial, political, and values spheres.
- *Lack of enduring commitment.* Flexibility and informality often translate to a general lack of commitment, one of the many downsides of boomer values. As record divorce rates, job changes, geographic moves, shifting political allegiances, and fluid church attendance and membership suggest, boomers often lack long-term commitment to those things that earlier generations valued.
- *Instant remedies.* Wanting fast cures and instant remedies, boomers reject many things that take time and patience to attain. From get-rich-quick schemes to miracle health cures to psychic network hotlines, boomers are influenced by—even enamored with—the fast-food mentality that shapes much of America's pace of living.

Boomer religion and spirituality. Much has been said in recent years about the return of baby boomers and their families to the church. Lost in the hoopla, however, is a closer examination of what boomers expect and value in church life. In *Baby Boomer Blues,* Collins and Clinton (1992) note that boomers appreciate the following:

- a consumerist orientation over traditional denominational loyalty
- experience and relationship over dogma and membership
- participation and active involvement over passive receptivity
- challenge in ministry over comfortable religion
- contemporary worship over traditional forms
- peer leadership and accountability over authoritarian control

There is surely a combination of promise and danger in these values. Churches of the twenty-first century will be constantly challenged to strike a godly balance between cultural relevance and God's timeless truth. Churches will increasingly offer counseling and caring ministries to their members, and those churches that flourish will be those with helping programs that are grounded in Christ and faithful to his Word.

Why the Empty-Nest Transition Can Be Difficult

In the midnineties we conducted a national survey of long-term marriages that took us to the very heart and soul of many empty-nest marriages. The statistics and findings from our survey are found in our book, *The Second Half of Marriage* (Arp & Arp, 1996).

Through a kaleidoscope of more than six hundred written survey responses, we saw many unique marriages. Some were beautiful to behold: healthy, loving, and warm. Others were distressing: hurtful, bitter, isolated, and lonely. Most marriages were somewhere between ecstasy and despair. The common theme this survey revealed was how difficult it is to maintain quality marital relationships during the empty-nest years. While our survey did not have the scientific rigor of a controlled group, Gottman, the well-known marital researcher at the University of Washington, confirmed that our findings were consistent with his research (J. Gottman, personal communication, Smart Marriage Conference, Washington, D.C., July 1998).

As we compiled our survey results, we discovered that couples who successfully made it through the empty-nest transition achieved a higher level of satisfaction later in their marriage. For example, when their twin daughters left home, Ted and Sally threw themselves into their careers. Suddenly, and thankfully, they realized that they were spending less time together rather than more, so they decided to do something about it. They took up golf together and found ways to develop other common interests. They became each other's best friend. Because of their adjustments, what had begun as a dangerous passage for their marriage resulted in an even closer relationship.

In the sections that follow, we will share some of the things we have learned from couples like Ted and Sally about the transition to the empty nest.

A Time of Insecurity

When children leave home, they take with them their energy and vitality. Parents are left to rattle around in houses that now feel too big. With kids on their own, parents have more time to be introspective. For the first time ever, many spouses take a serious look at their marriage. Understandably, this can be a risky time for couples who have not maintained a close relationship during the parenting years. Mothers who have chosen to stay home with their children, for instance, struggle to find their identity. Jill, a friend who homeschooled her two children, told us as she sent her young-est off to college, "Now I have to decide who I want to be when I grow up."

Compounding this challenge is a shift that takes place across gender lines as we age. Many men become more nurturing and begin to turn their focus back toward home (Sheehy, 1995). They are ready to slow down and enjoy life more. Work becomes less important to them than it was in previous years. At the same time, women can become more focused, assertive, and independent. Now it's their time to go out and make an impact on the world, especially if they dedicated the first half of their marriage to nurturing and parenting the children.

These changes are developmental, and they occur across different cultures. If they are not managed well, they can threaten the health of any marriage. Handled wisely, however, these kinds of changes can enhance a second-half marriage. Couples can move closer to each other and may actually have more in common than they had during their active parenting years.

MISLEADING TERMINOLOGY

The empty nest is not always completely empty, however. In fact, more than one-third of unmarried American men between the ages of twenty-five and thirty-four still live at home. In addition, many adult children return home to mom and dad, often bringing grandchildren with them.

One survey participant wrote, "Really, we never had an empty nest. My widowed mother lived with us in her own apartment in our home for twenty-five years. One son left home, lived on his own for a while, and then returned to live with us. My mother died about a year ago at ninety-two, and my son, his wife, and their baby moved into her apartment. Consequently, we've never experienced an empty nest. For years we've been members of the sandwiched generation" (Arp & Arp, 1996, p. 154).

Also at this stage of life, many couples are in second marriages—with his children, her children, and younger children from the present marriage. The increasing number of blended families adds to the ambiguity of the empty-nest stage.

CHANGING DEMOGRAPHICS

As the baby-boomer generation ages, more couples are becoming empty-nesters today that at any time in history. Empty-nesters have become a major target in our market-driven economy. Viagra couples dance through the pages of shiny, four-color magazine ads. The AARP is restructuring itself with new looks, products, and services to cater to aging boomers.

RISING DIVORCE RATES FOR LONG-TERM MARRIAGES

At the same time that America is graying, long-term marriages are breaking up in record numbers. Conventional wisdom indicates that many couples stay together as long as their children are the focus of the relationship, but when the children leave home, so do the reasons for staying together.

According to the National Center for Health Statistics (1991), although divorce in the United States declined 1.4% from 1981 to 1991, divorce among couples married thirty years or longer increased 16%. A wife married twenty-two years wrote in our survey, "If my husband's anger and critical spirit remain after our children leave, then divorce is inevitable. It seems hopeless."

LONGER LIFE SPANS

Today it is not unusual to hear about couples celebrating their sixtieth or seventieth wedding anniversaries. In one century the average life span has increased by thirty years; people today are living longer than those just one generation ago. The empty-nest years may now comprise the biggest part of a marriage. In the past, couples married, raised their families, and then died. Now it's as if you have a second marriage!

The empty-nest marriage can actually be far more rewarding and enjoyable than the first half of marriage. But before the children leave is the time to prepare to embrace the second half. We're convinced that in the second half of marriage, couples can build a more personal and fulfilling relationship than was ever possible during the parenting years. During the first half of marriage, couples live largely in response to their circumstances, parenting their children and building their careers. So much of life's demands are a given. But in the second half, couples have the opportunity to reinvent their marriage relationship. Husbands and wives have a new freedom to choose, to change, and to seek the fulfillment of their hopes and dreams. Unfortunately, however, our survey revealed that the practical help to make these changes is not readily available.

LIMITED RESOURCES

As couples enter the second half of marriage, they enter uncharted waters. Most marriage curricula, books, and seminars are focused on premarriage, early marriage, or marriage with children. When we hit the empty nest a decade ago, we were amazed at how few resources even mentioned empty-nest marriage, so we decided to research the subject ourselves.

EMPTY-NEST ISSUES IN THE TWENTY-FIRST CENTURY

Since researching and writing *The Second Half of Marriage* in 1996, we have conducted an additional survey and found that the issues remain basically the same: In the empty nest, without parenting responsibilities, couples find that past unresolved issues are likely to resurface and perhaps loom larger on the marital landscape.

Following are the top ten issues revealed by our survey and discussed in *Fighting for Your Empty Nest Marriage* (Arp & Arp, 2000). On a scale from one to ten, one represents the most severe marital issue and ten represents the least severe issue:

1. conflict
2. communication
3. sex
4. health
5. fun
6. recreation
7. money
8. aging parents
9. retirement planning
10. children

Interestingly, the top three issues in the empty nest—conflict, communication, and sex—are also the three major problem areas for younger couples. Clearly, even as we transition through the different seasons of a marriage, we tend to take our issues along with us. The survey revealed no overall gender differences that are very strong. However, females tended to rank communication as more problematic than males did, and males tended to assert that sex is more of a problem than did females. (Are you surprised?)

At the empty-nest stage of life, money issues do not rank as high as they do among younger couples, but not surprisingly, health issues rank higher. The fact that fun and recreation rank so high indicates that perhaps empty-nest couples are having trouble figuring out what to do together for fun. For years their shared recreational activities may have been centered around their children, and now they don't know how to have fun as a couple.

How would you rank these issues in the empty-nest marriages you observe? Box 21.1 shows a sample of our survey. You may want to use it as a way to help couples facing the empty nest look at issues and discuss them.

COUNSELING WITH BOOMERS IN SECOND-HALF MARRIAGES

Successful ministry to the baby-boomer generation requires truth and relevance as well as some general values that are important in any counseling ministry. In your interventions with second-half marriages, be sure to

- honor the centrality of Jesus Christ in all counseling ministry, be true to the Bible's teaching, and rely upon the Holy Spirit in your work;

- emphasize brief and time-limited interventions while supporting the need for and role of long-term counseling in certain cases;
- respect the diversity of cultures and values in our post-Christian world without abandoning the tenets of your evangelical heritage;
- emphasize the most innovative interventions promising the best helping outcomes—those that are the best fit for the client-parishioner according to his or her needs and abilities—rather than emphasizing theory and psychological dogma;
- regard the client-parishioner as a fount of wisdom, a valued coworker in the helping process rather than a passive recipient of expert help;
- place a high value on the protection of human life, the preservation of marriage and family life, and the promotion of biblical values throughout the culture.

Box 21.1—The Second Half of Marriage Issues Inventory

Consider the following list of issues. Please rate how much of a problem each area currently is in your relationship by writing in a number from 0 (not a problem at all) to 10 (a severe problem). For example, if money is a slight problem in your relationship, you might enter a 2 or a 3 next to *money*. If money is not a problem, you might enter 0, and if money is a severe problem you might enter 10. If you wish to add other areas that aren't included, please do so in the blank spaces provided.

_____ money	_____ grandchildren
_____ in-laws	_____ religion
_____ recreation	_____ household responsibilities
_____ communication	_____ health and physical fitness
_____ conflict resolution	_____ retirement planning
_____ friends	_____ ministry and community service activities
_____ extended family	
_____ aging parents	_____ friendship with spouse
_____ careers	_____ fun and leisure activities
_____ alcohol and/or drugs	_____ other issue:
_____ sex	_____ other issue:
_____ children	

EIGHT KEY COMMITMENTS

Our surveys as well as the research of our colleagues and coauthors at the University of Denver have helped us identify the major challenges facing couples who want to make a successful transition into the empty nest and beyond. The good news from our combined research is that couples who hang together through the empty-nest transition and who risk growing in their relationships will find marital satisfaction increasing and staying that way.

In *The Second Half of Marriage* (Arp & Arp, 1996), we presented the following eight challenges to those entering the empty-nest years.[1] We are convinced that if counselors help couples prepare for and work together on these eight challenges, empty-nest marriages will be enriched. However, if older couples do not overcome these challenges, then their marriages will not be as fulfilling as they could be.

1. *Let go of past disappointments and unmet expectations, forgive each other, and commit to making the rest of your marriage the best.* Spouses must let go of their unmet expectations and unrealistic dreams. That may mean accepting the missed promotion or giving up the dream of having a condo on the ski slope. Or maybe they must realize that their child is never going to be a Rhodes scholar or a professional baseball player. The other person's irritating habits may never disappear—and, at this point, they probably are here to stay. Extra pounds, graying hair, the lack of hair, and slower bodies may be other things to deal with. Giving up lost dreams and dealing with each other's imperfections is a positive step toward forgiving past hurts and moving on in a marriage.

You may want to have the husband and wife you are working with each make a list of things they are letting go of or things they will never do again. Follow this assignment by having them make lists of things they *will* do in the second half of their marriage, such as being willing to forgive each other and committing to make the rest of their marriage the best.

2. *Move from a child-focused marriage to a partner-focused marriage.* When children leave the nest, it's easy for couples to move from a child-focused marriage to an activity-focused marriage. Community or church activities may take up the time and energy formerly devoted to children. Unfortunately, even positive activities such as these may actually get in the way of a healthy, partner-focused marriage.

Remember that in the second half of marriage the dynamics of the relationship change. Roles and functions that previously worked no longer do. Without children as distractions, though, spouses have the opportunity to refocus and redefine their marriage. So marriage in the second half can be more personal and more fulfilling as spouses make their relationship with one another their top priority.

3. *Maintain an effective communication system and learn to express your deepest feelings, joys, and concerns.* What can spouses do when the communication patterns that seemed to work during the first half of marriage are inadequate for the second half? With the children absent, couples may find more spaces of silence and less to say to each other. Couples may ask themselves, *We made it this far. Why is communication so difficult now?* A husband, married thirty-four years, wrote of his "hope for a renewal of the kind of communication experienced during courtship."

Midlife is a time when spouses need to develop interpersonal competence, the ability to talk on a personal level and to share their deepest feelings, joys, and concerns. But when we begin to talk about really personal matters, it's easy to feel threatened. Finding a healthy balance between intimacy and autonomy is critical for healthy relationships during the second half of marriage.

4. *Use anger and conflict to build your relationship, not to tear it down.* Anger is often a real issue in many empty-nest marriages because many problems may have gone unresolved through the years. The fact that they were not properly dealt with fuels anger.

Both love and anger play a role in building a marriage, but anger must be processed in an appropriate way. We challenge you to help couples learn not only to process anger appropriately but also to face the more difficult issues of marriage in a whole new manner, which will allow them to grow closer in the years ahead.

5. *Build a deeper friendship with your spouse.* In our research we found that the greatest indicator of a successful long-term marriage is the level of the couple's friendship. Indeed, in the second half of marriage, spouses can and should deepen their friendships with each other. One benefit of a long-term marriage is that the husband and wife are more familiar and comfortable with each another. We know we aren't perfect, so we can relax and enjoy each other.

Here are some questions you can ask the couples you are counseling:

- What are you doing to build your friendship with your spouse?
- What are you doing to take care of your health?
- What can you do to stretch your boundaries and prevent boredom?
- How many "couple friends" do you have?
- What can you do to put more fun in your marriage?
- In what ways can you use humor to diminish the effects of an already-too-serious world?

Friendship and fun in marriage—especially during the second half—is serious business! In our work in marriage education, we continually stress the importance of friendship and dating. Empty-nest couples can benefit from a structured dating program such as *10 Great Dates to Energize Your Marriage* (Arp & Arp, 1997a, 1997b), which is both a book and a video curriculum.[2] They can also energize their own marriage by getting involved with and mentoring younger couples.

6. *Renew romance and revitalize your sexual relationship.* Most people believe that as people grow older they lose interest in sex, but research shows otherwise. In fact, our survey results suggest that sexual satisfaction increases rather than decreases the longer a couple is married. So as couples enter the second half of marriage, it is important that they renew romance even as they acknowledge the inevitable changes in their bodies. The quality of one's love life in this season of life is not so much a matter of performance as it is a function of the quality of relationship. A husband, married thirty years, wrote of the best years in his marriage: "We enjoy each other. We like to do similar activities. We are good friends. We are in good health and we exercise. We enjoy good, healthy sex. We do know how to party and celebrate life."

7. *Adjust to changing roles with adult children and aging parents.* Just as parents need to release their children into adulthood, they also need to reconnect with them on an adult level. At the same time they must balance relationships with their own parents. If an empty-nester couple's parents did not successfully handle this challenge in their own marriage, the new empty-nesters may have difficulties handling it as well. Whatever the situation, the relationship with elderly parents and adult children definitely has an effect on a marriage. None of us can go back and change our family history, but what we do in the future is our choice and our decision. You can help empty-nest couples choose to forge better relationships with both their parents and their adult children.

8. *Evaluate where you are on your spiritual journey, work on growing closer to God and to each other, and, together, serve others.* Couples who come to counseling bring with them many different perspectives on faith, religion, and belief systems. You may be working with spouses who are at very different places spiritually. Regardless of their individual beliefs, couples need to realize that this is an important time to draw together spiritually. Most people, as they age, become more interested in spirituality. Researchers speculate that this is because people think more about the meaning of life as they get closer to death. Your challenge is to help empty-nest couples consider this time of transition as a great opportunity for the two of them to talk more openly and regularly about how they view life: what it means, what matters, where it all leads, and what all of this means for their marriage.

For the Christian couple, shared faith in God should make a difference in the quality of their marriage—especially during the second half. After all, the marital relationship tests and validates one's own relationship to God, and praying together offers couples a unique closeness. Couples in the second half often have more time to draw closer to each other spiritually and to get involved in serving others. It's also a great time to mentor younger couples who need healthy role models for marriage.

STICK OR BECOME STUCK

People are living longer, so the possibility of a long-term marriage is now the norm instead of the exception. But more people are ending their marriages than ever before, perhaps because they don't want to face the next forty or fifty years in a less-than-satisfying union. The glue that held them together (the children) is gone, and now they don't know how to stick together.

As Stanley (1998) notes, couples who stay together long-term either stick or become stuck. Decisions couples make at the beginning of the empty-nest phase have a lot to do with what path they will be on in the years ahead. You, the counselor, can help couples make wise commitments so that these can be the best years of their lives.

The apostle Paul wrote, "Forgetting what is behind and straining toward what is ahead, I press on toward the goal to win the prize for which God has called me heavenward in Christ Jesus" (Philippians 3:13-14). Applying this passage to the empty-nest marriage, let us seek to help couples live out their marriages—and let's personally live out our own marriages—in such a way that glorifies God. As we grow older, we can renew our zest for our marriage and focus on the second half with hope and anticipation of all that God has in store for us.

BOX 21.2—TAKING STOCK OF YOUR EMPTY-NEST MARRIAGE[3]

Use these questions to help couples begin to think carefully about the key issues in empty-nest relationships:

1. What major transitions are you presently facing? (Is your first or last child leaving the nest? Are you or your spouse changing roles? relating to new in-laws or to new grandchildren?)
2. What do you want your marriage to look like when you're in your eighties?
3. What are your financial goals? your educational plans? your retirement plans?
4. How healthy and physically fit are you? What lifestyle changes, if any, do you need to make in order to lead a healthier life?
5. What do you do together just for fun?

CHAPTER 22

SEXUALITY AND SEXUAL THERAPY

Learning and Practicing the DEC-R Model

DOUGLAS E. ROSENAU, MICHAEL SYTSMA, AND DEBRA L. TAYLOR

Eighty percent of couples seeking marital therapy [are] sexually dissatisfied. Even in very happy marriages, about half of the couples report some sexual problems or sexual dysfunctions.

—EVERETT WORTHINGTON JR., *Marriage Counseling*

Mention sex in any conversation and heads turn. That's because sexuality is an important part of our lives and relationships, especially in marriage. God's Word affirms this truth and reveals God as the creator of gender and sexuality (Genesis 2:18-25; Proverbs 5:15-19; Song of Songs; 1 Corinthians 7:1-5; Hebrews 13:4). Within the church, however, we often have been unable to create comfortable conversation or offer open and godly teaching about sexuality. Unfortunately, this discomfort found in the church frequently extends to the counseling arena. In the area of sexuality, the Christian counselor has often failed to be "a workman who does not need to be ashamed and who correctly handles the word of truth" (2 Timothy 2:15).

This failure becomes tragic since people today desperately need God's truth about sexuality. God's gift of sex is badly distorted and misused, and many people are deeply wounded in their sexuality. Ten years after Worthington's (1989) research, data from the landmark University of Chicago sex survey revealed that 43% of the women and 31% of the men in America reported experiencing sexual dysfunction (Laumann, Paik, & Rosen, 1999). These sexual problems can be compounded even more in marriages.

Of critical concern is that most counselors and counselors-in-training have little education or experience in dealing with sexual issues. They can easily be intimidated when clients need to deal with the sexual aspects of life and relationships. This chapter contends that every Christian counselor can and must learn to become comfortable and effective at counseling in the sexual area. The DEC-R model, a simple and practical approach to sexual counseling, has been developed to assist counselors in beginning to work with sexual issues.

THE DEC-R MODEL

The DEC-R model (pronounced "deck-are") is a four-step counseling process for helping clients begin to deal with their sexual concerns. The therapist starts by introducing the subject and creating a *Dialogue*. Dialogue progresses to *Education* as needed information is shared. The therapist's *Coaching* guides the couple through basic self-help steps to address more specific problems. Finally, as in any counseling situation, the therapist needs to know when and to whom to make a *Referral* for specific professional treatment that he or she cannot offer. Throughout the process, referral is a crucial part of sex therapy—probably more so than in any other type of therapy.

It is important to note that these four steps are all part of a continuous counseling process. Each of them—dialogue, education, coaching, and referral—is a different and vital aspect of counseling. In almost any counseling session these four tasks are often utilized, but they are especially important for dealing with sexual issues. Each of the authors of this chapter utilizes the following tasks many times throughout the entire therapeutic process:
- starting a discussion to ease anxiety and to normalize sexual issues and concerns
- offering psychoeducation, because nearly all people have either incomplete or some distorted sexual knowledge
- assigning and coaching homework for self-help and maintenance of change
- referring to a physician for specialized assistance or medication

For ease of presentation, the DEC-R model is taught sequentially. In reality, you will find yourself jumping from one step to another throughout the counseling. For example, while helping a couple dialogue, you might do some coaching by assigning them an exercise and then returning to dialoguing about a specific issue they raised. In other words, this is a dynamic model that will help you map out what you need to be covering with a client.

Those who counsel, and especially those who work with marriages and families, should be competent at basic sexual assessment and counseling skills. If you are willing to carefully understand and utilize the four interrelated tasks discussed in this chapter (and if you read at least three books from the bibliography), you will be pleasantly surprised by how much more skilled you will become as a therapist and by how much more comfortable you will feel when you address issues of sexuality with your clients.

DIALOGUE

A vital element of therapy and marriage counseling is giving clients permission to talk about the sexual part of their lives. Creating dialogue is truly the beginning task of sexual counseling. Therapists will sometimes say that they don't seem to get many sexual problems or issues in their counseling practice. This is not necessarily a commentary on the population therapists are working with but on their inability to create dialogue about sexual topics with their clients.

We are appalled by the number of clients who have been to several other therapists but have never addressed a deep sexual concern. One client with a history of sexual abuse said that when she raised the issue with her first therapist, the therapist dealt briefly with it and then moved on to other topics. Consequently, the client believed that the abuse wasn't crucial to her issues. Her second therapist didn't even pick up on it.

Failure to address issues like rape, sexual abuse, sexually transmitted diseases, painful intercourse, and lack of sexual desire is a commentary on the counselor. Professional and pastoral counselors gloss over these issues.

It is the therapist's responsibility to directly initiate comfortable sexual dialogue. If you don't, the client often won't bring up the topic of sex or will do so only indirectly. So how do you begin such a dialogue? We will discuss this skill, but first note that the necessary foundation for dialogue about sexual concerns is a therapist who has personally prepared to engage in sexual discussions.

PREPARING FOR DIALOGUE

When we talk about sexuality, we are on sacred ground. Therefore, we must prepare ourselves for this journey into an intimate part of our clients' lives. In sex therapy, as in so many areas of therapy, it is difficult for a therapist to help a client grow beyond the level to which the therapist has grown. We recommend that therapists spend time sorting through the following crucial areas in order to comfortably engage in sexual dialogue.

1. *Possess and make peace with your own sexuality.* Be a Caleb, who asked for the part of Canaan in which the giants were, and then went in and possessed it (Numbers 13:30–14:38; Deuteronomy 1:36). The sexual aspects of ourselves and our relationships are some of the most daunting "giants" we face in our lives. When teaching sex counseling to developing therapists, one of our major goals is to get students to deal with their own sexual issues. The first step is encouraging them to process their own sexual history:

- How did they learn about sex?
- What messages about sex did their parents and others communicate?
- What are their own sexual experiences, and how have those experiences shaped or distorted their view of sex and sexuality?

Just as you ask your clients to process these issues, you may find it helpful to process your own history. When you do so, be strong and courageous as you face the ignorance, guilt, shame, pain, pleasures, and joys of your sexual past. Too many Christian leaders, pastors, and counselors have fallen into sexual sin. You can't counsel and dialogue on these topics safely or effectively until you have dealt with your own issues. Get wise counsel, therapy, and, if needed, supervision as you work through your own wounds, questions, and values. Accept and understand your own sexuality. Learn to set good boundaries. Deal with your own curiosity through reading and coursework in sexuality. If you do not take time for this growth, your counseling questions will too easily become voyeuristic and invasive.

2. *Desensitize yourself about sexual topics.* Helping your clients feel safe to reveal their sexual thoughts, hopes, and fears requires that you be somewhat desensitized to sexual discussions. It is fascinating to note how clients watch for a therapist's reactions to their comments, especially comments about sexual topics. Clients often use slang or children's language when trying to discuss sexual issues. Sometimes they begin talking and suddenly realize they have told you more than they intended. Statements like "We love doing it in the shower" or "I've always thought my boobs were too small" must be received calmly and professionally with no reaction (and certainly no glances at her chest).

Desensitizing can be accomplished in many ways. Take a human sexuality class. Learn about the common sexual disorders and be comfortable discussing them. Read *aloud* from sexual books and engage in conversations with either your spouse or an appropriate same-gender friend. Practice teaching the basic facts of life as you trace the path of the sperm to the egg. Say aloud the terms used when talking about sexuality until you are comfortable with them.

While working to desensitize yourself to this subject, remember to keep a holy balance and maintain healthy boundaries. Seeking to desensitize yourself is not a license to explore sexual depravity and risk damaging your own moral purity. Just as a skilled therapist can work effectively with cocaine addiction without trying cocaine, you can handle sexual issues with sensitivity and professionalism without having firsthand knowledge.

3. *Remember that sexual responses can be reflexive and that countertransference will occur.* When you dialogue with a client about sexual topics, you may experience some personal sexual arousal. This can be troubling to a beginning therapist, especially if this arousal occurs during a client's erotic retelling of sexual history. Some sexual arousal in these situations does not make you abnormal. Your response should be to take mental note of this sexual surge, evaluate its appropriateness (perhaps after the session), and manage it in a godly way by moving on with therapy.

You can choose not to feed this sexual arousal and to process it later with a colleague or supervisor. Don't waste your client's time and interrupt the therapeutic process with internal recriminations. Focus on your client's needs. When you proceed with the dialogue, your arousal will become unimportant. However, don't just ignore it; deal with your sexual response later. It's critical that you talk about your response *in supervision or consultation* and grow from your experience.

You may also experience some sexual attraction and countertransference with a client. Don't—and we repeat, *don't*—ever process your own issues with a client. Avoid discussing your own sexual feelings, even if your client asks, "Do you feel attracted to me?" or "I think we have some real sexual vibes, don't you?" You can carefully process *your client's* transference, but your own countertransference should be processed outside of therapy and only with a trusted colleague or supervisor.

4. *Begin to define your own theology of sex.* Christian therapy is unique because Christian therapists integrate faith into the therapeutic process. Preparing yourself to conduct sex therapy entails knowing what you believe God says about human sexuality. What does Scripture say about (or what scriptural principles can be applied to) premarital sex? masturbation? pornography? oral sex? anal sex? sex toys? frequency? fantasy? These are common sexual issues, and even if you do not specialize in sex therapy, you will likely need to address them at some point as you help people deal with their sexual history, behavior, or relationships.

Scripture often doesn't give specific guidelines or instructions about sexual behaviors and issues. On some issues, we have to understand God's character and apply general biblical principles to sexual behavior. The circle in figure 22.1 describes what this process looks like as we move from God and his principles to creating our heart attitudes, which in turn shape our behavior. We work from the inside out as theology influences our heart.

When clients come to us for help with sexual issues, it is common for counselors to immediately zoom in on sexual behavior. Often, however, the behavior is

Fig. 22.1. Process of Applying Biblical Principles

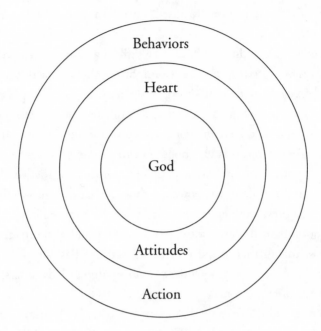

only the symptom. When a client asks what we think about oral sex or masturbation, we should first seek to understand what oral sex or masturbation means to the client's motivations and relational values.

Consider, for example, the issue of masturbation. Start with God's principles: " 'Everything is permissible for me'—but not everything is beneficial. 'Everything is permissible for me'—but I will not be mastered by anything" (1 Corinthians 6:12) and "Each of you should learn to control his own body in a way that is holy and honorable, not in passionate lust like the heathen" (1 Thessalonians 4:4-5). Ideally, our heart attitudes will be shaped by what God wants for us sexually, and we will discipline our lusts, our thought life, and our behavior. This process obviously affects the behavior of masturbation.

The basics of God's sexual economy will be developed more throughout this chapter. As counselors, we need to continually be working on our personal sexual values and heart attitudes, always thinking through behaviors from the inside out. This process is a crucial part of defining our personal and professional boundaries.

SETTING BOUNDARIES IN SEXUAL DIALOGUE

We have already stated two crucial boundary principles:

1. You *will* have reflexive sexual reactions. Acknowledge them only to yourself during the session, learn to manage them, and then move on in your counseling.

2. *Never* discuss your own sexual countertransference with your client.

Both of these issues can be processed outside the session with an appropriate person.

The following are additional boundary skills that counselors need to develop.

Maintain personal sexual integrity. An important skill to practice is the ability to stop personal sexual fantasies both during and after your counseling sessions. Sometimes on your way home from a counseling session, an attractive client or some sexual activity that was described will come to mind. Put into practice the technique of thought-stopping: Immediately choose not to pursue or dwell on that thought, but instead set your mind on Scripture or some other constructive idea. God has given both us and our clients the power to choose what thoughts to dwell on.

Apply God's power and guidelines for maintaining sexual integrity. This ability comes from a basic understanding of God's principle of covenant monogamy. (We will cover this further in the Education section.) Basically, God's guidelines are clear and simple. Sexuality—gender sexuality (moms, dads, sisters, brothers) as well as romantic or erotic sexuality—was given to us by the Creator to enable intimate connection and relationship. For every Eve there is a possible Adam, and for every Adam there is a possible Eve. We don't engage in lovemaking with any person other than our own Adam or Eve.

Practice simple skills like staying three-dimensional with clients: Choose to remember that each of God's children is body, soul, and spirit, not merely a body or body parts. This perspective allows us to see an attractive body yet choose to focus on that person's soul and spirit. Our clients are precious lambs that God has entrusted into our care. They are hurting, and their needs must be our primary concern. For some clients, counseling will be their first safe opposite-gender relationship.

Create a safe environment. State to your clients that you maintain professional boundaries in the counseling session, then follow through and maintain those boundaries. A written commitment from you can be especially reassuring to abuse survivors who think most relationships or sexual discussions are not safe. Here are other ways to increase your clients' sense of safety:

- Pray with your clients. Inviting God's presence and power into the session reminds you as well as your client that God is in charge and that he wants to minister to his child through you.
- If you are married, mentioning your spouse or children during a session can ground your life in intimate relationships that are important to you. Doing so will in turn give your clients a sense of safety and a real-life perspective.

- Learn to skillfully back off from a sexual topic if transference is getting too strong. Questions can strategically do this, helping you move from the emotionally and erotically charged to the more rational. A question like "How did these sexual experiences in college affect your ability to respect men?" can take the dialogue from personal erotic stories to the more constructive point of processing content. Always remember that you control the session and can keep it safe. You can start and direct the dialogue.

- Be very careful about any physical contact such as holding hands during prayer or hugging after sessions. We encourage counselors not to engage in *any* touching, especially with opposite-gender clients.

INITIATING SEXUAL DIALOGUE AND HISTORY TAKING

It is the counselor's responsibility to initiate dialogue. You can make this dialogue part of the flow of counseling and general history taking.

Begin the dialogue as simply and naturally as possible. When we are training therapists to initiate dialogue, we often jokingly tell them that we have a magic question that instantly opens up clients and frees them to pour out their sexual issues. They eagerly wait for something profound, but the question is: "How is the sexual part of your life?" Simply inviting clients to talk about their sex life is usually sufficient to start the dialogue. As you model a comfortable handling of the topic, your clients will become more comfortable as well.

This opening dialogue is essential to effective sex therapy. Many couples have never talked openly with each other about their sex lives. Remember that sexual activity is a powerful form of nonverbal communication. Unfortunately, like other forms of nonverbal communication, it is often misunderstood. A wife who thinks her husband is just "using her body" may be surprised to hear him talk about how meaningful that experience is to him. Helping them talk about what they like, dislike, fear, and dream of, as well as the significance of their actions, is in itself a powerful counseling intervention. You will be surprised how many couples with good sex lives don't talk easily or effectively about sex. Couples with sexual issues *must* be able to talk with each other about the problem or concern. This discussion often begins during your session as you model open sexual communication. Couples often learn enough new information as they listen to each other talk with the therapist that options for change become obvious.

In addition to dialogue during the session, certain exercises can help clients become more comfortable with sexual language and dialogue. Have them read aloud from a book like *A Celebration of Sex* (Rosenau, 1994) or *The Secrets of Eve* (Hart, Weber, & Taylor, 1998). Give them homework, such as writing out their ideal sexual encounter. Encourage them to give details and share with each other how the details of this ideal encounter create mood, feelings, and arousal within them.

Include several key pieces of information in the assessment of the client's history. Don't be intimidated by discussing the topic of sex so that you fail to make an accurate assessment of your client's sexual history. Assessment of sexual issues is similar to an assessment of depression or anxiety. Individuals will rarely volunteer all the important information you will need.

As you begin an assessment, it may be helpful to think of taking a sexual history as simply enabling clients to tell their sexual stories. You might start with their present experiences and then explore their history, or you might begin with how they learned about sex and their early sexual experiences and then work your way to the present.

SIX KEY PIECES OF HISTORICAL INFORMATION

When beginning to explore clients' sexual histories, you must be sensitive to their safety and level of comfort. While all of our sexuality is a private arena, some sexual issues are more private than others. For example, asking clients how frequently they engage in sexual activity is less threatening than asking if or how frequently they masturbate.

Sensitivity to the private nature of sexuality is especially important when working with couples. Take special care when asking questions with spouses in the room. Often you will be asking for information the couple has never discussed with each other. It can be valuable to have each partner fill out a written sexual history questionnaire or to meet with each one separately. You can follow the individual sessions with a couple session in which each partner summarizes his or her individual session for the other.

However you choose to move forward, assessing sexual issues requires the ability to answer several key questions that fall into six main categories.

1. *"What is the problem as you see it?"* Listen to the client's language and clarify important words. "I'm impotent," for instance, can mean a variety of things. Reflect back what you hear your client saying or ask gentle probing questions to help him elaborate and define the problem specifically for you. Knowing that he believes he climaxes too quickly identifies the problem as he sees it. However, how you intervene will be determined by whether he is attempting to maintain an erection for forty minutes of active intercourse so he can climax with his wife, or whether he indeed becomes aroused so quickly that he consistently climaxes before penetration.

2. *"How long has this problem been present?"* Knowing the onset of the sexual problem and the surrounding circumstances is critical for accurate diagnosis and treatment. A similar question would be "Does this problem seem to be related to any specific circumstances?" Finding out that a wife cannot reach orgasm when she is with her husband but can with masturbation makes a difference in interventions. Knowing that sex hurts during deep penetration may indicate a physiological problem (e.g., ovarian cyst) whereas pain at the very opening of the vagina (even when she isn't engaging in sexual activity) may be a sign of vestibulitis. "How often does the problem occur? For how long?" and "What have you already tried?" are related questions that can help define the problem and determine your intervention.

3. *"Describe a typical sexual experience for you."* Examine other areas of your clients' current sexual functioning. What is their level of sexual desire? Do they have difficulty achieving arousal? Do they experience orgasms? Do they experience pain during sex? Do they engage in any sexual behaviors they do not want to engage in? These questions can help you identify other issues that your clients didn't realize were related to their presenting issue.

One important area to assess is possible masturbatory practices. As mentioned above, this is one of those very secret topics that usually calls for an individual session. Explore the person's history of masturbation and current practice. It is not uncommon to learn of compulsive or paraphilic behaviors when you begin to ask specific questions.

4. *"What health issues might be complicating this sexual issue?"* Are there any other physical issues like obesity, menopause, diabetes, or hypertension? Are there currently, or have there previously been, STDs (sexually transmitted diseases)? Have STDs been tested for and successfully treated? When clients have been exposed to STDs through multiple partners or by having a mate who has had sex outside of marriage, *always* discuss testing, including how to ask the family physician for testing.

Have community resources available for referral if your clients prefer not to discuss STDs with their personal physician. Do not pass over this area quickly— your clients' health, fertility, and even life may depend on it. We recommend that you contact the Centers for Disease Control for up-to-date information for yourself and your clients.[1]

Another critical question is "Are you taking any medications?" Most medications have the potential for sexual side effects. Discovering complicating physical issues may mean referring clients back to their physician after coaching them about how to discuss this issue with their physician.

5. *"How are things in the rest of your life?"* Explore other relational and emotional issues. Anger, anxiety, guilt, and depression have all been linked to sexual

disorders. You must assess and treat these issues if you are to effectively resolve the sexual issue. Think systemically here. A client's sexual issue may be tied to many external issues.

6. *"What is your sexual past?"* Briefly explore sexual behaviors and attitudes from the client's past. What were the family's attitudes about sex? What are your client's earliest sexual memories? These questions can give valuable insight into the etiology of sexual issues. A careful way to learn about past sexual abuse or traumatic experiences is to ask, "Has there ever been a time when you were in a sexual situation you thought you were not in control of or one in which you couldn't say no?"

EDUCATION

Psychoeducation is a crucial part of any counseling relationship. In the sexual arena, it is often the key to helping a client resolve sexual concerns. Education is critical to changing sexual attitudes as well as building needed skills. In this section, we outline four primary areas of psychoeducation, and we show how to utilize it to help a client achieve sexual wholeness.

This one section, however, won't prepare you to answer all your client's questions. Read several of the books we have included in the bibliography. You'll be greatly encouraged when you see how reading strategic chapters in a couple of good sex manuals will increase your teaching skills. Clients appreciate therapists who can be great sex educators.

CREATING A THEOLOGY OF SEXUALITY AND INTIMACY

The church has neglected to create and communicate a clear and practical theology of sexuality. As a result, myths abound such as "the more we talk about sex, the more we will lust and cross boundaries." The opposite is usually true. Many Christians also believe that sexual sins are more sinful than others, that they produce greater guilt, and that they will (or should) haunt a person forever. We must never minimize the true godly sorrow (2 Corinthians 7:10-11) that motivates vital change. First Corinthians 6:18-20 does point out that sexual sins affect our deeper personhood and can never be committed without consequence to ourselves and our intimate relationships with God and others. Our goal in educating clients is to help them better understand their forgiving and merciful heavenly Father, who removes our sins—all sins—as far as the east is from the west, as we eliminate false guilt and shame.

Viewing sex as God's good creation. We are often asked, "Why did God create sex?" The answer is that he wanted to teach us about intimate relationships, which are so dear to his heart. He wanted us to understand his very makeup and image. It's no surprise that a God who calls us to reflect him in characteristics such as holiness, love, and forgiveness would also call us to reflect him in intimacy and oneness. As the doctrine of the Trinity demonstrates, God is an intimate *one*. He created us male and female—distinctly different—and he called us to be one. Sexuality is the Almighty's grand metaphor, providing special insight into himself. "So God created man in his own image...male and female he created them" (Genesis 1:27). In doing so, he provided both vision and boundaries to his gift of sex. Understanding his vision and boundaries form the basis for a theology of sex.

Connecting as soul mates and knowing one another intimately. Scripture introduces sex with the phrase, "And Adam knew Eve his wife; and she conceived" (Genesis 4:1, KJV). If you read popular modern translations, you might find the term "laid with" instead of "knew." While some scholars suggest that the scriptural use of "knew" is euphemistic, we would disagree. *Yada,* the Hebrew word used here, is an experiential and reflexive knowing. It is knowing, being made known, perceiving, and learning. It reflects a God who knows himself and us intimately and who desires that we know him intimately as well.

This word *yada* sets the vision for a powerful theology of sex, a kind of sex that is focused on intimately knowing and revealing one's self as well as exploring, learning, and knowing one's spouse. Part of Christian sex therapy is helping clients discover this intimacy in their own lives. For hundreds of years the enemy has successfully distorted God's gift. Sex is often seen as an animalistic and hedonistic urge for physical pleasure, and the goal is a bigger and better buzz. When the focus is solely on physical pleasure, God's boundaries are often quickly broken for the promise of greater pleasure.

Clearly, God designed sex for physical pleasure. Our bodies are wonderfully made to respond to sexual stimulation with great delight. Denying this reality is not any more true to God's design for sex than acting as if sex is only about physical pleasure and not also about deeply connecting with one's spouse. Sex with one's husband or wife provides a unique opportunity to explore each other physically, emotionally, mentally, and spiritually. However, doing so requires that sex be experienced as an intimate connection.

Honoring covenant monogamy and becoming soul virgins. God created the covenant and relationship of marriage to be the place for expressing erotic sexuality: " 'The two will become one flesh.' This is a profound mystery—but I am talking about Christ and the church" (Ephesians 5:31-32). A covenant is a formal contract between two people that binds them together in courageous commitment. The marital sexual union, with its emotional bonding, passion, orgasmic excitement, and loving nurture gives us a picture of the special redemptive covenant relationship that Jesus has with his bride, the church.

In covenant monogamy, spouses are choosing to be sexually intimate with only one other person in their lifetime: their mate. This exclusivity is reflected in the concept of being a soul virgin. Soul virginity is not based upon past experiences or whether we have had intercourse outside of marriage. It is an attitude of chastity and purity that God wants us to practice. Becoming a one-woman or one-man person involves continual choice and a disciplined fantasy life (Song of Songs 8:6-10; Proverbs 5:15-19).

Understanding and disciplining sexual desire and lust. It is interesting that the scriptural concept of desire is God-given and not inherently evil. We can lust after and deeply desire our spouse as well as deeper spiritual growth. *Lust* is used to refer to good and strong desires in Luke 22:15, Philippians 1:23, and 1 Thessalonians 2:17 (Vine, 1996). In psychology, *lust* is often used as a term for sexual feelings, again with no negative connotations. However, Scripture passages such as James 1:14-15 teach that desire can become evil, which gives birth to sin, which eventually causes death—separation from God.

Our clients need to hear that sexual desire is normal and that each of us is given responsibility for disciplining our sexual desires so they don't cross over into evil lust and sin. Teach clients the behavioral intervention of "thought stopping" to help them choose not to mentally pursue an inappropriate fantasy. If a neighbor's wife comes to mind in a sexual way, one can choose to switch thoughts to something else. You cannot keep environmental cues from coming into your thinking, but you can choose not to give them free rein in your mind; you can choose not to allow those images to develop into sinful lust.

Recognizing sensuality and human eroticism. We are all sexual, sensual, and erotic beings. We were created male or female with the accompanying sexual feelings of arousal and attraction. Not accepting or expressing and enjoying these feelings can severely limit who God created us to be. Our clients need to understand that, contrary to some of the church's historical teachings, there is a healthy, God-reflective nature to their sensuality and erotic propensities.

Human sensuality is the capacity for taking in data through the senses: touching, hearing, seeing, tasting, and smelling. This sensuality is an important aspect of marital lovemaking. Eroticism is that sexual and romantic part of us that is attracted to another person and that ultimately, in a God-given way, yearns to become one flesh. We distinguish this eroticism from gender interaction that is typical of healthy brother-and-sister, parent-and-child interactions. Eroticism, like lust, needs to be disciplined and brought into God's plan, recognizing that it is designed for complete expression only within the covenant of marriage.

Disputing common myths, stereotypes, and assumptions. Far too many people operate on incorrect assumptions, myths, and false expectations as they live out their sexual lives. The following are examples of some of the myths and false assumptions you will encounter:

- Women seldom fantasize about sex and are less sexual than men.
- Men are always ready to go and can have instant erections with little stimulation.
- All men want is to get lucky and score.
- Sex will create instant intimacy.
- Sexual chemistry and being in love are constants.
- Erections and lubrication indicate that the partner is fully aroused.
- Intercourse is the ultimate form of sexual fulfillment.
- If you wait until marriage, you will automatically have a great sex life.
- The sexual switch will instantly flip on when you are married, and you will become wild and crazy.
- Most couples naturally have a great sex life.
- My husband will know all about sex and be the primary initiator.
- My wife will think about sex frequently and keep sex on the front burner.
- The size of my penis [my breasts] makes a real difference in how great a lover I am.
- Romance comes easily if you are in love.

These and many other myths, false assumptions, and unrealistic expectations can wreck a sex life. Counselors have the opportunity to gently educate and correct these myths. Lovemaking requires being comfortable and learning skills. This takes time. Those who come to marriage as virgins will have fewer scars and bad habits to overcome, but they still have to *learn* to make love. Most couples struggle with some aspect of sexuality and must work together to overcome these problems, whether it is performance anxiety, body image problems, premature ejaculation, or any of a host of other issues.

Correcting misinterpretations. Helping clients recognize misinterpretations and clear up false expectations is crucial to education and sex therapy. We suggest that Christian counselors undertake a conscientious personal Bible study of passages related to sexuality and engage in discussions with a mate or colleague to think through scriptural corrections of counterproductive interpretations.

Couples will bring these and other issues to you and interpret them in many different ways:

- "The wife's body does not belong to her alone but also to her husband" (1 Corinthians 7:4). The key to this passage is that making love is not about demand but about giving.

- "Anyone who looks at a woman lustfully has already committed adultery with her in his heart" (Matthew 5:28). Consequences may be different between having a fantasy and not acting upon it and actually having a physical affair. However, in this passage, Jesus warned that fantasy does have consequences: It not only demeans our sister or brother but it can also lead to actions.
- "Men give love to get sex, and women give sex to get love." Men misunderstand the role of sex when they expect the sex act to meet their wife's needs for physical affection, emotional vulnerability, and quality time. Men, too, need love and not just sex. Women can actively desire sexual connection, although perhaps not with such an emphasis on intercourse and orgasm. Women need sex expressed with both caring love and respect for marital companionship.

APPRECIATING MALE AND FEMALE DIFFERENCES

It is difficult to teach or write about the sexual differences between men and women without sounding as if we are stereotyping. Yet one of the greatest myths in our culture is that men and women are or should be the same sexually. Our culture only knows one model of sexuality: male sexuality. Unfortunately, this ignorance causes women to feel inadequate and keeps them from discovering, experiencing, and enjoying their own sexuality. Much misunderstanding, frustration, and anger between husbands and wives could be avoided if all of us better understood female as well as male sexuality.

A good picture of how different and yet how similar men and women can be is found in their anatomy. The genitals of both female and male fetuses develop out of the same tissue. Yet due to genetic codes and hormones, male and female genitals look and function differently. Likewise, genetics, hormones, family influence, and emotional and sexual experiences produce a different sexuality in men and women.

The most common difference between men and women is how frequently they think about sex. Men usually think about sex much more frequently than women do. Another difference between men and women is what is valued most about sex. Women like the closeness—whether physical or emotional. And men? As one man said, "What do I like most about sex? *The sex!*"

Yet another key difference lies in our energy for sex. For most men, tiredness is not as much of an inhibitor of desire as it is for most women. In fact, in one study of two thousand Christian women, nearly half of those who acknowledged a sexual problem said their problem was "finding the energy for sex" (Hart, Weber, & Taylor, 1998). Also, women's sexual desire is strongly influenced by their body image and menstrual cycle. Men, however, do not tend to lose their desire for sex when they feel overweight or don't feel or look particularly fit. Other areas of difference between men and women include how often each gender desires to have sex as well as how each expresses connection or uses sex to connect.

To become more familiar with these differences, we recommend reading *The Secrets of Eve* (Hart et al., 1998) or *Men and Sex* (Penner & Penner, 1997). We also encourage couples to read these books together and discuss how the information does or does not fit them.

Understanding Sexual Response

Much of the education stage of DEC-R sex therapy involves teaching about "normal" sexuality. While this standard is still a debated topic in the field, some generally accepted models of normal sexual response have been developed by authors such as Masters and Johnson (1966), Kaplan (1974), Walen and Roth (1987), Schnarch (1991), Zilbergeld (1999), and McCluskey (2001). These models are especially important as the therapist seeks to understand and diagnose problems, but they're often valuable as teaching tools for the client as well.

Each of these authors use different models, but we recommend that the beginning therapist explore McCluskey (2001). This model is based on Masters and Johnson (1966) and includes the four stages of atmosphere, arousal, apex, and afterglow. It is simply outlined, quickly grasped, scripturally integrated, and easily taught to couples.

Acquiring Important Data

Obviously, one chapter cannot contain all the information you need for the educational task of sexual counseling. As in all therapy, the counselor will need to be able to find information in textbooks and on the Internet. We have listed a bibliography to help you build a knowledge base. The outline in box 22.1 details important information that counselors should know. Take the time to do the research you need to enhance your understanding and knowledge.

Information from the DSM-IV or about sexually transmitted diseases will be constantly updated. Presently, for instance, the DSM is looking to modify the definition of hypoactive sexual desire in women because it is very different from the male-driven definition. With women, it may not be a sexual-desire disorder but simply fatigue or distractions. Some sex therapy research is questioning the concept of female arousal disorder and what constitutes the condition of vaginismus. Sex counselors must keep updating their information if they are to be wise and helpful teachers.

COACHING

In counseling, the therapist is often called upon to guide or coach the process toward a desired outcome. This is the third task of the sex counselor. This part of the counseling process should not be confused with the new discipline, life coaching. Life coaching does not involve training in counseling or psychotherapy, and it is not centered on problem solving; thus, it is truly different from the therapeutic coaching that we will develop in this section.

The metaphor of coaching is very appropriate for sex therapy. We aren't on the

---

BOX 22.1—A BRIEF OUTLINE OF SEXUAL DISORDERS IN DSM-IV, WITH STDS AND AIDS INCLUDED

Disorders of sexual dysfunction are disturbances of the sexual response cycle: desire, excitement, orgasm, and resolution. The phrase can also refer to pain associated with sexual intercourse.

1. Sexual desire disorders include:
   a. *Hypoactive sexual desire*—lack of (or absence of) sexual desire, including a paucity of thoughts, fantasy, and desire for sex in the relationship.
   b. *Sexual aversion disorder*—extreme aversion to sexual contact with partner, including the avoidance of all sexual behavior.
2. Sexual arousal disorders include problems that arise during (prior to cessation of) sexual activity:
   a. *Female arousal disorder*—recurrent failure to attain or maintain swelling and lubrication in response to sexual excitement.
   b. *Male arousal disorder*—recurrent failure to maintain erection (impotence).
3. Orgasmic disorders include:
   a. *Orgasmic disorders in both male and female*—delay or absence of orgasm during normal sexual response cycle.
   b. *Premature ejaculation*—occurrence of ejaculation before it is desired, either prior to, upon contact with, or shortly after insertion.
4. Sexual pain disorders include:
   a. *Dyspareunia*—persistent pain experienced by either male or female during and after sexual intercourse.
   b. *Vaginismus*—recurrent, persistent, involuntary muscle spasms of the

playing field with our clients. In fact, we are not even on the sidelines. Instead, we are in the locker room with dialogue, education, and helpful instructions. We then respectfully send the couple back to the privacy of their own homes and lives to play the game.

In our DEC-R model for beginning sex therapy, *coaching* refers to guiding couples beyond education into a growing sexual intimacy as well as to assigning *self-help exercises* to address specific problems. It is a given that some couples' problems will require intensive therapy, and you will need to refer them to an experienced sex therapist.

---

outer part of the vagina that makes penetration painful, difficult and, for some, impossible.

5. *STDs or STIs* (sexually transmissible disease or infections)—any of a number of infections and diseases that are spread by sexual contact. The Centers for Disease Control provides up-to-date information on these problems.[2]

Sexually transmissible infections and diseases pose a huge public health problem, worldwide as well as in the United States. The human immunodeficiency virus (HIV) is the most threatening of the STIs, but all of them can be a source of physical and emotional suffering. Many STIs are epidemic, particularly among younger Americans, but the vast majority of people remain poorly informed about them.

Each year, approximately 15.3 million Americans acquire an STI, and one in three sexually active Americans will have contracted one by age twenty-four. Some of the most common STIs in the United States are chlamydia, trichomoniasis, gonorrhea, PID (pelvic inflammatory disease), HPV (human papilloma virus, or genital warts), herpes, hepatitis B, syphilis, and the HIV or AIDS virus (Centers for Disease Control, 1998).

6. *AIDS* (acquired immunodeficiency syndrome)—an incurable and usually deadly disease caused by the human immunodeficiency virus (HIV). It is characterized by destruction of the immune system, which leaves the infected person susceptible to a wide range of serious diseases.

Today, AIDS is considered the world's leading threat to public health. It has claimed the lives of more than 420,000 Americans; another 271,000 Americans have been diagnosed with it; and up to 1,000,000 Americans are believed to have been infected with HIV (Centers for Disease Control, 1998).

Many times, clients have already bought a self-help book and read about their problem. They may even have begun trying some exercises. It is our experience, however, that most of these couples will still need a coach-therapist to explain the exercises and guide them through them and to provide accountability. An initial step in coaching is finding a helpful layman's book. There are a variety of excellent resources mentioned in the references section of this book, including *A Celebration of Sex* (Rosenau, 1994), *The Secrets of Eve* (Hart et al., 1998), and *Restoring the Pleasure* (Penner & Penner, 1993).

In addition to providing important information, Rosenau (1994) and Penner and Penner (1993) also provide couples with specific exercises. Sex counselors need to familiarize themselves with the information and counseling skills these exercises require. Practice going over the instructions for common sexual exercises until you are comfortable and can communicate them clearly. Sexual issues are complex and require a variety of intervention strategies. The first area we will examine below is behavioral interventions. Although helpful, behavioral methods alone are not enough. For example, working on an erection problem medically—with Viagra—or behaviorally does not address the relational or emotional concerns that must also be considered.

BASIC SKILLS REQUIRED FOR SELF-HELP EXERCISES IN SEX THERAPY

Sex therapy exercises require counselors to use many basic skills repeatedly. Some of these are common to any cognitive behavioral therapy, and you may find that you are already using many of these in other areas of counseling. This section considers interventions that are often used with specific sexual problems such as impotence, premature and delayed ejaculation, vaginismus and pain in intercourse, poor body image, performance anxiety, or difficulty achieving orgasm.

Conditioning and desensitizing. Effectively changing behaviors often involves pairing a positive experience or reward with a desired behavior. Sexual activity paired with anxiety is changed to sexual activity paired with relaxed massage and pleasuring. Desensitizing means helping the client take the negative thoughts and feelings—such as anxiety—out of a sexual experience and become more comfortable with a thought or activity. This is usually accomplished by slowly exposing the person to the negative (fear of premature ejaculation) while pairing it with a pleasant experience (penis lying quietly in vagina without ejaculation).

Building in small increments. People change more effectively by taking small steps toward their end goal. Going too fast can retraumatize and create more anxiety, so keep clients encouraged with slow steady changes. Learning new skills and changing attitudes (e.g., "Don't worry about erections now, just start to play and touch sensually") takes time.

Utilizing cognitive restructuring. This builds upon the excellent scriptural principle of renewing our minds and changing destructive attitudes. It may begin with education and encouragement: "The size of your penis isn't crucial in your lovemaking. The outer third of your wife's vagina is the most sensitive. Your penis will easily reach that area." The mind is the most important sexual organ, and any sexual change typically requires an adjustment here.

Deeper attitude changes will occur only with more in-depth therapeutic work over time, often involving assigned reading and homework assignments. Clients suffering from poor body image, for example, can be coached through the "mirror exercise" (see Rosenau, 1994) in which they stand in front of a mirror and try to accept their body without making judgments about themselves. This may help *begin* to change attitudes—but it is only a first step.

Encouraging sensate focus. This classic sex therapy technique encourages relaxing with sensual touching and takes the focus off performance. Many sex therapy books, including Kaplan (1974), describe this technique in detail. The sex counselor can also use Rosenau (1994) or other sex self-help books that give couples clear directions on how to do this.

The goal of sensate focus is to give and receive pleasure rather than to achieve arousal or orgasm. The couple is instructed not to have sexual intercourse during the week(s) they do sensate focus. Some honor this injunction, but others respond paradoxically—becoming sexual as a violation of a no-sex rule. Either outcome can be worked with as the sexual dynamic between the couple is slowly changing. The sensate focus exercise begins with caressing, where one person is the toucher and the other is the touchee. Then roles are reversed and the couples run through the exercise again.

As they coach, counselors should explain some of the rationale behind the exercise: "God gave us feelings; we need to relax and gently tune in to them." Counselors should also discuss how sensate focus can help with performance anxiety: "When we worry about how we will 'perform,' we mentally 'get up on the bedpost' and become a spectator and judge. Sensate focus can help us to stop watching and instead reinvolve us in the process of sensual feeling and making love."

Sensate focus can be used in several ways. You can, for instance, prescribe no communication while the one giving the massage touches the partner's body in ways that feel good to the giver. This decreases performance anxiety and allows the one touching to tune in to his or her own sensuality and to the partner's body. You can also prescribe that the one being touched coaches the other on what feels good to him or her.

Promoting Kegel exercises. In the 1950s Arnold Kegel worked to alleviate urinary incontinence by helping women to strengthen the PC (pubococcygeal) muscle. These exercises are described in most self-help books. The PC muscle stops urine flow and can be easily strengthened by exercising daily in the car while driving, before going to sleep, or at whatever time is convenient for the client. Exercising this muscle can increase awareness of the genital area and improve sensation in the vagina for women. For men, these exercises can help with premature ejaculation.

Processing sexual accelerators and brakes. Another way counselors can coach couples is by helping them identify the factors that enhance their sexual functioning (accelerators) and those that detract from healthy sexual functioning (brakes). All couples have genetic and personal factors that increase their sexual awareness and excitement as well as factors that turn them off sexually. One great coaching technique is to talk with couples about their typical sexual encounters, helping them identify these brakes and accelerators.

A CASE STUDY

In sex therapy, Jim and Susan listed the brakes and accelerators that affected their sexual desire. Susan identified a list of brakes, including being tired and feeling pressured. Accelerators included items such as Jim's being romantic, feeling good about her physical appearance, and hearing a romantic story. Jim realized that his brakes and accelerators were less complicated than Susan's. One of the brakes he identified was feeling criticized by Susan and one of the accelerators was anything that made him think about her in a positive way.

Simply taking this first step helped Jim and Susan recognize things they were doing to sabotage their partner's desire and what they could do to help increase that desire. Susan also realized that she spent very little time thinking about sex compared to Jim. This meant that he stayed at a higher level of sexual arousal than she did. Taking time to allow herself to recognize her sensuality and sexuality helped increase her overall desire and receptivity.

Next, Jim and Susan explored their typical sexual encounters. What types of sexual initiation were accelerators, and what types of sexual initiation were brakes? They were able to talk through a variety of ways they could let each other know they were in the mood, and they even came up with some new ideas to try.

Once they began openly talking about their typical encounter, Jim and Susan began to learn valuable information about each other and about themselves as a couple. Both laughed as they realized that one of their common foreplay practices was neutral to both. Jim did it because he thought Susan enjoyed it; Susan did it because she thought Jim enjoyed it. In reality, neither viewed it as an accelerator. At the same time, Jim shared with Susan some fantasies he had that he thought would be accelerators for both of them. Susan talked about how her accelerators and brakes often seemed to jump categories.

Sometimes having Jim kiss her breasts was an accelerator, and sometimes it was a brake. This was confusing to Jim, who felt that the same things always worked for him. They continued to process ways she could tell him what was and wasn't working *during* sex without her feeling critical or guilty and without him feeling hurt or frustrated.

Over the course of a couple weeks, Susan began to realize that one major brake happened when they began intercourse before she felt emotionally or physically ready. As Jim moved toward climax, Susan often experienced the same feeling she had had in early dating in which she had felt pressured and "used" by others. This brake was strong enough to inhibit her sexual excitement with Jim. Jim was aware that this sometimes happened, but they had never before talked about why. As they discussed it, they were able to come up with ways to avoid this brake and continue adding accelerators for both.

Jim and Susan also talked together about fantasies, new techniques, undesirable positions, desires, and frustrations. They didn't always agree or understand why something was a brake or an accelerator, but realizing how certain behaviors affected the other partner allowed them to increase each other's excitement and pleasure.

Part of the beauty of this coaching technique is that the counselor doesn't have to know all the intimate details of the couple's sexual encounters. Helping them talk about some of the common brakes and accelerators identified above and in other writings is often enough to get a couple well on their way to a healthier and happier sexual relationship. Occasionally, when one or both partners is controlling, unaccepting, or having difficulty with the introspection required in this technique, the therapist may need to take a more active role.

COACHING FOR DEEPER EMOTIONAL CONNECTION

Finally, since sex is more than just a physical experience, you may need to coach some couples to a deeper emotional connection. Here are some ideas to get you started with this important counseling task:

Help the couple focus on the context of their sexual connection. What type of atmosphere is a couple creating in their marriage? Many therapists recommend that married couples spend *at least* ten minutes each day connecting emotionally with each other. Regularly revealing our hurt, anger, disappointment, hope, and joy to each other is crucial to setting a good atmosphere for connecting sexually. This is especially true when the verbal communication happens in a context of acceptance, commitment, apology, forgiveness, and celebration. Often the best sex therapy happens when we focus on developing a good atmosphere for deep emotional connection.

Help the couple learn to keep their partner present during sex. While this might sound obvious at first, many husbands or wives begin by having sex with the spouse but, partway through the process, they focus exclusively on their own physical sensations. The focus moves to the buzz and away from connecting with the spouse. Coaching them to keep their partner present can temporarily short-circuit their arousal and ability to achieve orgasm, but as they get comfortable connecting with their spouse, the arousal and orgasm will return with the added power of connecting.

Help the couple make their connecting time sacred. Something that is sacred is something set aside as special and holy. For married couples, connecting sexually can be a way to reflect on and learn about God and each other, and it deserves to be set aside as special and holy. Learning to set boundaries to protect this time from the pressures of life, parenting, and career is a start. Just as Scripture points out that we aren't to enter into worship with unresolved conflict, so should we keep our sexual connecting sacred by first working to resolve conflict. We also keep our connecting sacred by protecting it from any sexual focus or sexual behavior outside our marital relationship. Helping couples explore how well they are doing in these arenas enhances the emotional connection during lovemaking.

REFERRAL

Like dialogue, education, and coaching, referral might happen strategically within the other parts of this counseling model. As you begin to dialogue, you may discover sexual abuse or a medical condition that needs immediate referral to an appropriate specialist. As you educate or coach a couple through some self-help exercises, you may see that you have exhausted your skills and need further resources. Skillful referral is obviously a crucial task in sex therapy.

When to Make a Referral

Several factors should be kept in mind when deciding whether to make a referral. Not only do we need to recognize when we are beyond our training or experience, we also need to take other factors into consideration.

Accessing medical or other professional help to assist therapy. Though many sexual difficulties can be psychological, always begin by ruling out any physical and medical issues. This guideline is especially important in treating problems like impotence or pain. You will need to refer to a physician to determine hormonal deficiencies, vascular problems, drug interactions, or the cause of pain. You may also find it necessary to refer the client to any of a variety of other professionals. (A physical fitness trainer, for example, can help a client who has problems with body image.) These professionals will be an important adjunct to sex therapy and can help your client reach his or her goals.

Referring when additional training and skill level is warranted. While this chapter is designed to help skilled therapists address sexual issues by using some of the skills they already have, reading a few books on sex therapy doesn't make one a qualified sex therapist. You will run into client issues that are beyond your ability to address. To continue with those clients would be unethical. At these points, it is imperative that you refer them to someone who does have additional training and experience in sex therapy. Sometimes it is fairly obvious when additional expertise is needed. However, that determination is more difficult when what seems to be a straightforward case of impotence or a desire discrepancy becomes complex and progress is not being made.

Maintaining boundaries. There are certain sexual issues that therapists have no business treating because of their own wounds or lack of boundaries. A male therapist may find that a seductive woman involved in an affair is triggering his own lust. A female therapist, perhaps an abuse survivor herself, may discover that a selfish man demanding an increase in his wife's desire is triggering an emotional response in her own heart. Don't believe you are above being ensnared! Recognize your vulnerabilities and put in place professional and personal boundaries to protect yourself and your clients—and refer!

WHERE TO REFER
Several important types of resources must be considered when making a sex therapy referral. You will find it helpful to create a list of the specific options in your community and geographic area. These resources include, but are not limited to, the following:

Physicians. Urologists work with male issues like impotence and penile or prostate problems. Gynecologists work with female concerns. You may need someone who specializes in dermatology problems to work with specialized problems like vestibulitis. A general physician or gynecologist can check for hormonal deficiencies, but an endocrinologist may also be required.

Adjunct professionals. We have mentioned that someone struggling with body image may need a physical trainer or nutritionist. Chiropractic or physical therapy may also be helpful.

Specialized psychotherapy professionals. Sexual problems can be symptomatic of other issues such as an extramarital affair or a severe marital conflict. In those cases, your client may need a skilled marital therapist. A sexual abuse survivor may be dealing with major issues that profoundly impact lovemaking and marital intimacy and may need a therapist who specializes in abuse. Sex addiction can destroy a sex life and marriage in many ways. A specialist in this area can save hours of sex therapy time.

Professional sex therapists. An increasing number of counselors-in-training are required to, or have the opportunity to, take some basic sex therapy training. This basic training, however, is different from what is offered by those counselors who have chosen to specialize in the area of sex therapy, have received specialized training, have become certified, and, above all, have worked in supervision with a professional sex therapist.

Groups and church or community resources. As in other areas of counseling, a good group can be both financially and therapeutically efficient. A men's growth group to teach intimacy skills or an abuse survivors group can be crucial to a client's growth. In sex addiction, a group is often the mode of choice for therapy. Spiritual growth groups and couples community groups are also helpful in some situations. All of these inexpensive or free resources help clients keep working on their issues while staying within their budget.

How to Make a Referral

Don't assume that simply giving a professional's name and phone number to a client will be enough. If necessary and appropriate, help your client make contact and call the professional to apprise him or her of the client's situation. Coach your client as to why you are making this referral. Help the client know what information is important to tell the professional so that he or she can get the help needed. If the client is coming back to see you, be sure to follow up in the next session. Assure the client that you will help find the right person if this referral is not a good fit or if it does not promise to foster needed changes or healing.

A "Missionary" for Sexual Wholeness

This is an exciting and challenging time in the history of the church. We are poised to tackle issues that have never been comfortably dealt with before. We appreciate a comment by Hart, Weber, and Taylor (1998): "We believe that one of the most critical issues facing the church as we enter the twenty-first century is the whole issue of sexuality" (p. 6). We are finally ready to develop a practical theology of sexuality for the twenty-first century, a theology that will provide helpful, scriptural guidelines and better answers for struggling individuals and marriages.

The goal of this chapter is to help and encourage each person who counsels to learn to "correctly [handle] the word of truth" (2 Timothy 2:15) within the context of sexual dialogue, education, and coaching. If we as counselors are willing to learn and grow, we can use God's Word in a skilled and wise manner that honors Christ and increases intimacy for couples.

We conclude this chapter by encouraging you to become a "missionary" for sexual wholeness. Initiate a conversation, write an article, coach a client, give a book, or preach a sermon. Join others in bringing education and healing to the important sexual part of individuals and their relationships.

CHAPTER 23

FAMILIES AND FAMILY THERAPY

Understanding and Growing a Christian Social System

DAVID STOOP

Among family therapy pioneers, Virginia Satir stands out as one of the few who openly embraced a transcendent spirituality in her practice.... More recently, a number of family therapists, most from a Christian orientation, have begun to break down barriers to explore ways to bring spirituality into therapeutic work.

—FROMA WALSH, *Spiritual Resources in Family Therapy*

When the word *counseling* is spoken, the typical image that comes to mind is that of a counselor and a counselee, one-on-one, in a room together. Most professional counselors and pastors prefer to work this way. In fact, much of what you read in this book is oriented to this one-on-one, individual type of counseling, which deals primarily with intrapsychic conflicts and the interaction of a person's inner world with his or her external environment.

But there is another way to look at counseling, and it starts with the premise that an individual is much more than just one person. He or she is a part of a social system that begins with the family of origin and that can expand over time to include other significant people. To understand the individual, then, one must see the individual in the context of his or her system of relationships (Bowen, 1978; Framo, 1982; Guerin, 1976; Haley & Hoffman, 1967; Madanes, 1981; Minuchin, 1974; Napier & Whitaker, 1978; Satir, 1972; Watzlawick, 1978).

Marian: A Case Study

Marian was a twenty-two-year-old female who had been hospitalized four times for depression. Each time, prior to her hospitalization, she had been suicidal; one of those times she attempted suicide with her mother's sleeping pills. She was the younger of two children with a brother four years older. Her father was a police officer, and he and her mother had been married for almost thirty years.

In each of Marian's first three hospitalizations, she had responded well to in-patient treatment and was sent home with instructions to stay on her medications and continue working with a therapist. Eventually, by mutual agreement with her therapist, treatment was terminated. But within six months, Marian was suicidal again. She was readmitted to the hospital, given a new therapist, and after a week or ten days, she stabilized and was discharged.

At her fourth admission, a clinical social worker was struck by her pattern of hospitalization. She spent additional time with Marian, working with her therapist, but asking questions about her family dynamics. For the first time, Marian's treatment team began to see her in the context of her family system. What they discovered was a pattern of relationships that assigned to Marian the very rigid role of family scapegoat.

About six years earlier, Marian's brother had attempted suicide using his father's service revolver. He failed in his attempt but ended up permanently handicapped because of his self-inflicted injuries. The treatment team at the hospital discovered that the family blamed Marian for her brother's suicide attempt, based on the fact that a week before he shot himself he had talked with her about his feelings of emptiness and his belief that life was futile. Marian was only fifteen at the time and didn't know what to do with the information. Unfortunately, she didn't take it seriously until after her brother shot himself.

Gradually, as the family processed this tragedy, they began to shift the blame for what had happened to Marian. Though this was not a conscious, deliberate decision by anyone in the family, Marian nonetheless became the family scapegoat. She was the one who carried the family's burden of shame and guilt over this tragedy.

Because this information had not come up in her three previous hospitalizations, no one was concerned about her returning home after treatment. This time, however, the team helped Marian make arrangements to move into her own apartment after she was discharged, and she was referred to me for follow-up therapy. When I met her, she was stabilized and not suicidal. One of the first things we did was to arrange a series of sessions with her and her parents.

Marian and I also set up a schedule for when and how she would interact with her family. She agreed to limit her contact with her family to our in-session meetings for approximately six months. During that time, we worked on helping the family understand and articulate some of the family rules, especially some of the covert rules—the hidden, unspoken but powerful ways her family communicated with each other. One of our primary goals was to create new ways for Marian to interact with her family, particularly with her father.

After about three months of working with the family (the brother was institutionalized so he did not attend), Marian and I worked together for another year. Eventually, we agreed to terminate therapy. About six months later, I received a panicky call from her. She told me that she had just stood up to her father in a lengthy phone disagreement and that she had held her own with him. After hanging up from talking with him, however, her doubts returned and she wasn't so sure of herself. I advised her to just wait and see what her father would do.

The next day she called and joyfully reported that she had just had another conversation with her father and that "for the first time, he treated me like an adult!" I was pleased, of course, and congratulated her on the new way she was interacting with her father. A two-year follow-up revealed that Marian had maintained this new and better way of interacting with her family, and that she was still living on her own and functioning well.

Family Systems: A New Way to See and Think About Family

The difference between my treatment of Marian and her earlier therapy was that I first saw her and treated her within the context of her family. Later, when I worked with her alone, I was still thinking of her within the context of her family system and how it would react to any changes in her. Earlier in therapy, counselors had looked only at how Marian could experience healing within herself and then unknowingly sent her back home where the powerful forces of her family system undid everything that had been accomplished. This is quite common in working with children in many contexts (just ask your youth pastor). While working with Marian individually, we still did "family therapy" in the sense that we were thinking systemically. We worked on her issues within the context of her family and their probable reactions to any changes she would make in herself.

As Marian's situation suggests, when we consider working with families in counseling we are confronted by two fundamental questions: (1) What is the family? (How do we define it?), and (2) What does it mean to think systemically? (What does it mean to approach family therapy from a systems orientation?)

WHAT IS FAMILY?

According to Goldenberg and Goldenberg (1985), "Family is a natural social system, with properties all its own, one that evolved a set of rules, roles, and power structure, forms of communication, and ways of regulation and problem solving that allows various tasks to be performed effectively" (p. 3). Demographically, the two-parent family with biological children, all living together, has nearly reached minority status as a family type in America. Single-parent, blended, multigenerational, and other alternative family types continue to increase (see Barna & Hatch, 2001). The family is considered by most to be the basic socialization unit of any society, the linchpin of civilizing culture. The axiom, "As goes the family, so goes the community, the church, and the nation," is often quoted because it is largely true.

Families are also defined and evaluated by their boundaries, those invisible but very real lines of distinction that separate one family from other families as well as from the rest of the world. These boundaries regulate both the degree of influence the world will be allowed to have on the family and the influence the family will have on its surrounding world (the flow across boundaries is usually two-way in any system). A *closed family system* has tight boundaries and allows very little interaction with and influence from the outside world; it is often described as an insulated or enmeshed family system. The Mormon man with five wives and twenty-nine children who was prosecuted in Utah for polygamy ruled over a closed family system.

In contrast, an *open family system* has loose family boundaries, with much back-and-forth flow between family members and the outside world. Families who live together in a communal or community relationship, with mutual flow of people, ideas, and influence between families and among its individual members, are an example of more open family boundaries. Healthy families usually enjoy a good balance between open and closed boundaries: distinctive and supportive of its individual members, yet able to grow with and adapt to the surrounding culture.

This boundary evaluation is important in assessing the family's ability to function, to regulate itself, and to effectively accomplish the tasks that families do. Grunlan (1984), in a Christian perspective on family life, noted that the family serves basic functions in living, functions that both individuals and families depend on for survival and meaning:

1. *Regulation of sex and reproduction.* The bio-psycho-social-spiritual dimensions of these gifts are given by God to function wholly within the bounds of marriage and family life.

2. *Socialization and identity.* The family is the primary tool by which individuals learn the roles and rules of living in society that shape personal and family identity.

3. *Companionship.* The family meets needs for love and affection, for solace and comfort, and is the place to discuss and test out new ways of interacting and relating with the larger world.

4. *Conferred power or status.* The family is the vehicle for learning and testing the powers and limits of living in the social web of relationships, understanding the influence of gender, birth order, size, assigned roles, age, and developmental status, and is a significant influence on day-to-day living.

KEY PRINCIPLES

Synthesizing these definitions and perspectives on the family emphasizes the importance of the following four basic principles when a helper approaches any family:

1. *The family, in its social dimensions, reflects God.* The social nature of the family imitates the sociality of the triune God. The Father, Son, and Holy Spirit have distinctive identities, yet they are also one together as God, existing in relational communion with one another, with other created beings, and with the entire creation. Similarly, the family is one, but it also has distinctive members: father, mother, and children interact out of love for each other and with the outside world.

2. *Family health, individual health, and maturity are inseparably entwined.* A corollary principle is that the power of family identity and socialization is critical for optimal individual development and maturity. Increasingly, the helping professions are recognizing that the degree of health and maturity that people display is often a function of their exposure to healthy family living. The social and behavioral sciences are replete with data on the costs to individuals, communities, and society that are brought about by individuals who have not been raised in healthy family systems. It is not simply the massive costs of maintaining a huge criminal justice and penal system or the enduringly high divorce rates or the perverse abortion industry in America. It is also the pervasive and multiplying costs of people everywhere living primarily for themselves, living in a society that has lost a primary dedication to being other-centered as opposed to self-centered. God has created and ordained the family as the primary social unit for learning to live well and to love others. Everything that people have engineered to replace or substitute or stand alongside as an "alternative" to God's way should be seen as

having a loss/cost factor attached that will bring eventual grief to the culture that admits them.

3. *The family is also like the church.* Similar to the vertical analogy with God noted above, the family also has a horizontal analogy as the church, the family of God, the body of Christ on this earth. Systemically, the identity, boundary, and relational functions of the church—both within it and in relation to the outside world—operate almost synonymously with family dynamics. In fact, a good argument could be made from Scripture that the primary purpose of family life is to be socialized into the life of the church and to learn the interpersonal skills necessary to be a loyal and productive member of the church. From an eternal perspective, the biological imperative "Be fruitful and multiply" will eventually cease. But God's people, and relationships among them, will go on forever.

4. *Trouble is reproduced, but can also be stopped, in families and in generations of families.* There is an undeniable psychosocial and spiritual dimension to family reproduction, for "the sins of the fathers are visited unto the third and fourth generations." Whether literal or metaphorical, it is accurate to speak of "generational curses" existing in alcoholic families, violent families, or depressive families. We now know, of course, about the growing evidence that biology and genetics influence these inherited traits, but let us be careful not to fall prey to the biological reductionism of a godless culture that sees the physical transmission of these troubles as the only culprit. (And let us not succumb to the countererror of spiritual reductionism, believing that one must just pray and be delivered from such curses.) This fourth principle also magnifies the redemptive effects of Christ's transforming power, for the promise of new life is not just for individuals but for the entire family—and the blessings travel down through the generations just as the sins and their consequences do.

WHAT IS SYSTEMS THINKING?

Beginning in the 1930s and 1940s, mathematicians and engineers developed systems concepts to apply to the increasing complexity and demand of their work. Then in the 1950s and 1960s, general systems theory became the basis for computer development and caused that technological field to mushroom. Interdisciplinary thinkers and scientists in the 1960s and 1970s began to transfer these concepts to the living world. A biologist (von Bertalanffy, 1968) and an anthropologist-ethnologist (Bateson, 1972) took systems concepts and applied them for the first time to human interaction processes. Now instead of looking only at the historical facts and inner dynamics related to a person's problems, we look at the pattern of transactions going on among family members and the world around them. Following are five systems concepts.

FIRST CONCEPT: CIRCULAR OVER LINEAR CAUSALITY

When we focus on the historical sequence of events in a person's experiences, we are operating in a linear frame of reference related to causation. We begin with *A,* which we believe causes *B,* and then we move to *C,* which was caused by *B.* When using this linear logic, this straight-line pattern of causality, we are looking for a "real" or primary cause—as if finding it will create a solution. Parents use this type of thinking when they ask their children a question like "Who started this argument?" What follows from the children is the blame-shifting search for the primary cause. One child says, "*He* started when he said..." That remark will be followed by "I said that because *she* said...," and round and round it goes, in useless circles of argument and frustration and with little resolution of the problem.

Circular causality recognizes the fruitless circularity of many of our arguments and *looks more at the process of what is going on in the relationships.* This way of thinking takes a metaview of issues: It looks more at how we consider and attempt to resolve a problem than at the actual content of the problem (e.g., "Maybe I need to step back and take a different look at how I'm trying to solve this"). Recognizing that you could cut a circle at any point or focus on any link in the chain and come up with a false cause, systems thinking skirts this useless search for "Who started it?" realizing that this will do nothing to help change the situation for the better.

In Marian's case, the family regarded her failure to report the conversation she had had with her brother as the ultimate cause of his suicide attempt. This was her parents' way of denying that any other issues in the family may have contributed to the problem. Basically, her parents had cut the circle at that inaccurate point and said they had found the cause. But cutting the circle around Marian was no different, in family process, than cutting it around her brother. A different person sat in the role of the identified problem (see next section), but the family dynamic was the same.

Circular causality, however, would look at that as only one piece of information among many others. A multitude of other factors feed in to counseling, and finding one grand and simple ultimate cause is usually impossible and almost always distorted or inaccurate. Other obvious factors in this case would include her brother's depression and the faulty communication patterns within the family. The list of factors would also include issues and tensions in her mom and dad's relationship, job tensions for her dad, and the sense of isolation felt by each of the children and perhaps by each of the parents. Eventually, as these other factors are acknowledged and considered, an honest and accurate picture of the complex pattern of functioning within the family can be identified.

SECOND CONCEPT: FAMILY HOMEOSTASIS AND THE IDENTIFIED PROBLEM

Another factor in Marian's problems was that the family needed her to be the scapegoat, so she became the identified problem (IP) in order to maintain family homeostasis (the balance or equilibrium of forces within the family). Prior to his suicide attempt, Marian's brother was the IP. In adapting to the changes brought on by their son's suicide attempt and his resulting handicaps, the family had to do something radical in order to maintain its homeostasis, which literally means "same status."

The best solution the family could come up with was to transfer blame to Marian, because that continued to keep the focus off her mom and dad's chronic problems and the injuries to her brother. Each time Marian was hospitalized, she temporarily broke free from those secretive and dysfunctional family patterns. But whenever she returned home, the family system pushed her back into the problem role, which resulted in her decompensating and being readmitted to the hospital.

Homeostasis, an idea borrowed from biology and ecology, refers to the process that keeps a system in steady-state functioning. The human body, for example, maintains homeostasis by keeping a steady temperature of 98.6 degrees. Whenever some outside factor (such as hot or cold weather or a virus) creates change in body temperature, the body begins to fight back, to restore and maintain the steady state of 98.6 degrees. We perspire, we shiver, we fight off the infection.

In the same way, a family will fight back and resist change in order to maintain a steady state even when the change is desirable and the homeostatic state is highly dysfunctional. But in crisis, even a dysfunctional state is attractive because it is familiar. It looks like a safe place from which the family can operate. Family systems theory asserts that the more dysfunctional the family, the more rigid and inflexible the family system and the harder that system must work to maintain homeostasis.

In Marian's case, the family sessions revealed that, prior to his suicide attempt, her brother was the IP, the problem child in the family. Such roles develop as marital and parental conflicts become stuck and unresolved. Rather than allow the tension and conflict to build to a point where family integrity is threatened—where divorce and family breakup become likely—the family operates unconsciously to concentrate the problem and all its harmful tension on a different object, a child who is anointed to assume the role of the IP. The parents, who may not be able to agree on anything, begin to agree and collude together that this or that child is the problem; the child naturally begins to resist and to act out, which becomes a self-fulfilling cycle of trouble. This is how the cursed family dance of dysfunction—a dysfunction that helps maintain homeostasis—is put into play.

The conflict between Marian's brother and father was probably a key factor in her brother's depression and suicide attempt. Now that he was handicapped and unable to live at home, he couldn't play out his IP role, especially since the other family members felt so much guilt. So the IP role was assigned to Marian. When she went to the hospital and got healthy, she stopped playing that role, so the family system worked to restore their steady state, which required a problem child. The pressures to maintain the IP role were powerful and unrelenting, and Marian would eventually let herself fall back into the role of the problem child.

The key to Marian's treatment following her fourth hospitalization was to develop strategies she could use to pull herself out of the family dynamics and break free from the role she had been assigned by the family. She had to become strong enough to resist the pull back to the old homeostatic state within her family.

THIRD CONCEPT: FAMILY ROLES

One of the forces that help families maintain homeostasis is role assignment for different family members. A family role is an assigned place in the family constellation where an expected pattern of behavior and emotion is played out. That role hides the family pathology and serves to maintain family equilibrium. The more rigid these roles are in a family, the more difficult they are to break free from.

Much of the research on family roles has been done with alcoholic families. In the alcoholic family, someone (usually one of the parents) has a problem with alcohol. However, other family members are punished if they confront the problem person, so eventually no one is willing to face up to the problem. Once the other parent gives up confronting the problem directly, he or she tends to become the chief enabler, codependent and in collusion with the drug-dependent partner, and helps to maintain the facade that there is no problem.

The children will take on specific roles as well, roles that vary depending on the number of children in the family. In intelligent and highly active families, the enabling parent and some of the children learn multiple roles (some of which are detailed below), switching back and forth as the situation demands. Many times these roles are so well learned and practiced that the family becomes confused and unaware of the real problem(s) until treatment is started.

The scapegoat. This key role is often assigned to the firstborn child. Rather than the parents assuming responsibility and confronting the real issues in their marriage and family, they tend to lay blame for all the family trouble or badness onto one person. All the family energy is then focused on this child and on his or her "problem." Marian's older brother had been the family scapegoat, but when he bailed out of the role by attempting suicide and becoming incapacitated, Marian's parents needed someone else to blame and assigned her the role.

The hero. This child makes the family look good to outsiders. I recall working with one dysfunctional family: the dad never worked, the mom held down temporary jobs, and most of the kids were in and out of trouble. But the parents were proud of the oldest son, who had "held down a job for over twenty years at a good company and even been promoted several times." This oldest son was the family hero. If a neighbor complained about this family, someone would probably say, "Yes, but they can't be that bad—look at their older son!" The hero serves the desired family image well.

The comic. If there are enough children in the family, a child may step into this role and offer comic relief when tensions get too high. This role is perfectly revealed by many professional comedians who describe their families of origin as being highly dysfunctional and painful. While much of the family dysfunction is exaggerated in their comic routines, much is not, and such dysfunction is in fact played out as bizarrely as the professional comics describe it. Comedians are usually telling the truth when they say that they learned their comedy within the family as a means of coping with pain.

The lost child. Another common role is that of the lost child, sometimes known as the perfect child. This child, usually the youngest, gets lost in all the family chaos. The lost child does fairly well in life, seldom makes any waves in the family, and often is insulated from the parental chaos by the older children. In many ways this child is raised by older siblings as well as by the parents. Because the lost child isn't a problem, he or she is often overlooked by the parents. Like the enabler-in-training (see next paragraph), the lost child often ends up repeating the patterns of the parents in his or her own marriage and family.

The enabler-in-training. This child supports and helps out the adult enabler, learning to hide, lie for, and excuse the problem parent whenever such cover is needed. This child's role kicks in especially when the enabling adult is too tired or too angry to fulfill the adult role. Typically the enabler-in-training learns this role well as a child and, as an adult, often repeats the pattern of the enabler parent, marrying someone just like the problem parent.

The violent child. A form of the scapegoat or problem child, the violent child is an angry child who learns to act out in aggressive and violent ways, both within and outside the family. Often diagnosed with a conduct disorder, the violent child may be a fire starter, may enjoy inflicting pain on people and animals, and may be socially isolated and inept. The violent child is almost always male and is often picked on and bullied in school. He often shows an inordinate interest in guns, bombs, violent video games, and blood-and-gore horror movies; possibly the most telling examples of this role are the school shootings by children in recent years. The violent child reveals how insufficient any use of dysfunctional roles is in maintaining family homeostasis. While no doubt sustaining the attention and concern of the rest of the family, this child's acting out threatens to blow the family cover and tear the family apart.

FOURTH CONCEPT: FAMILY SECRETS, MYTHS, AND LIES

Other factors that help a family maintain dysfunctional homeostasis are family secrets, myths, and lies. Family secrets are those shameful things that "good families" never acknowledge or talk about. Secrets may involve drug abuse or alcoholism, incest, or a loveless or previous marriage. Secrets can be as seemingly innocuous as the "crazy uncle in the institution" that the nephews and nieces never learned about until adulthood, or they can spring from an unspoken rule that certain emotions, such as anger, are not acceptable in the family.

Families are as sick as their secrets. In the classic metaphor, family secrets are like an elephant in the living room that no one ever talks about. Eventually the elephant grows and takes over the living room, spraying its waste on everyone and making it impossible for anyone to be in the living room. Still, no one ever talks about the elephant. Guests come to the house and have to walk around the elephant and its waste, but they somehow quickly learn that they are not to ask about the elephant, perhaps because they themselves have an elephant in their own living room and don't want you to ask about it.

Family myths. Like secrets, all families have myths that are used to project and exaggerate a picture of family goodness or perfection. When asked about their family of origin, family members often start and end by saying, "We're very close as a family." But in between those statements, they describe a family that is anything but close. Other common family myths include how much the family enjoys get-togethers and reunions; how harmonious family relations are; how much the family members respect one another; and how selfless, godly, and ungreedy family members are.

Family lies. Family lies are the corollary to family myths, except that lies are told to exaggerate the ugliness or badness of certain families or family members. Family lies operate when families fail to resolve their problems or to forgive the pain that has been caused. Like the ugly-but-funny exaggerations comics use when talking about their family of origin, family lies are used to contrast good and bad members of the family. Commonly seen in divorced and blended families, much conflict in remarriage and blended family therapy revolves around family lies. Lies and exaggerations are common between stepparents and stepchildren or concerning ex-spouses. Stepparents will often contrast their own or favored perfect child with the black sheep stepchild, and stepchildren will contrast their perfect but lost-to-divorce natural parent with the mean and hateful stepparent.

The important idea here is to recognize how both family roles and the behavior surrounding family secrets, myths, and lies help maintain homeostasis in a dysfunctional family. The circularity of these dynamics suggests that maintaining family equilibrium helps reinforce the roles that different members of the family play and the various secrets, myths, and lies that family members tell. All members are thoroughly convinced of their truthfulness, of course. These systems dynamics are to be seen and understood as the ways families live in denial and resist change, and they are a major part of the family's system of overt and covert rules.

FIFTH CONCEPT: FAMILY TRIANGLES

According to Bowen (1978), the basic building block of a family's system is the triangle, a relationship made up of three people. By definition, a triangular pattern of relationship is more stable over time and gives us all kinds of information about the system. In contrast, a dyadic family relationship is relatively unstable and gives less relational information. In Marian's case, for example, if we had met only with Marian and her father, we would have gotten very little helpful information about the patterns within the family. The same would be true if we had met only with Marian and her mother. But when we had meetings with Marian and both her mother and her father, we were able to learn a lot about the family dynamics. We learned how the parents had colluded to scapegoat Marian, how they had triangulated her into their marital mess because her older brother was now lost to that role, and how the scapegoating allowed the parents to deny and skirt the issue of their own dissatisfying and unworkable marriage. We can best understand relationships by looking at patterns of threes in families and other relationships.

During family therapy with Marian and her parents, we learned that the relationship between Marian's mother and father had been tenuous over the previous ten years. The anxiety the mother felt about her marriage was transferred to her relationship with Marian's brother, where she communicated her distress with her husband to her son. This separated Marian's mother even more from her father emotionally as he resented his wife's confiding in their son. As a result, conflict intensified between the father and the son, which added to the tension between Marian's mom and dad. Because the son was in a no-win situation—taking sides with either parent would create conflict with the other—he rebelled and acted out, becoming a problem for both parents. This, of course, would serve to perversely pull the parents back together as an emotional unit, which became their sad substitute for true marital intimacy.

When the son's handicap prevented him from emotionally engaging with either parent, the tensions between her mom and dad started to pull in Marian, who took on the scapegoat's role. With the added tension of having a severely handicapped son, the earlier pattern with the son quickly repeated itself with Marian. Mom started to lean on Marian emotionally, which created problems between Mom and Dad again. But rather than act out and get into trouble as her brother had, Marian withdrew into herself and became more and more depressed. But her depression fulfilled the same role as her brother's acting out had: It drew the parents back together emotionally in response to her neediness.

Marian's story is an excellent example of how we can get to the bottom of relational issues by looking at the various triangular relationships within the family. (See Stoop and Masteller [1991] for a more detailed explanation of triangular relationships both in a biblical family and in modern-day families.)

One of the tools often used to help people the triangular patterns of relationships in their family is the *genogram* (McGoldrick & Gerson, 1985), which pictorially portrays family relationships over several generations. Since family patterns tend to be repeated over several generations, a genogram helps both the client and the therapist see some of these patterns. Moses reminded God in his prayer that God had visited upon the children "the sins of their parents to the third and fourth generations" (Numbers 20, NLT). A genogram often shows the patterns of the "sins of the parents." It's interesting that dysfunctional patterns tend to increase in intensity for three or four generations until someone finally becomes strong enough to be the transitional person and break the pattern. Often this happens because of an encounter with Christ and a personal spiritual renewal that reverberates throughout an entire family system.

Family Systems Pioneers and Background

Family systems thinking started to come together in the early 1950s, at a time when it was unacceptable for therapists to work with anyone other than the individual. The early work was research-based, which gave it credibility, and it has been generally focused in four different geographic locations.

In Palo Alto, California, a group that eventually became the Mental Research Institute (MRI) focused on communication patterns between clients with schizophrenia and their different family members (see Fisch, Weakland, & Segal, 1980; Watzlawick, Beavin, & Jackson, 1967; Watzlawick, Weakland, & Fisch, 1974). Bateson, Haley, Jackson, Watzlawick, and Weakland (see Haley, 1981) articulated the concept of the double bind in communication between a parent and the client with schizophrenia. A double bind occurs when an individual receives contradictory messages from the same person on a continual basis. Forbidden to comment on the contradiction, the individual feels doomed to failure, unable to make any safe response to the contradictory messages. The recipient of the double-bind message, often a child, is forced into an impossible situation that eventually leads to a break with reality.

At about the same time, Bowen (1978), first at the Menninger Foundation in Kansas and then at the National Institute of Mental Health near Washington, D.C., began to hospitalize not only the person diagnosed with schizophrenia but also the family members. He did this so he could study the patient alongside the patient's family unit.

Meanwhile, Whitaker, first at Oak Ridge, Tennessee, during World War II, and later at Atlanta and the University of Wisconsin, also worked with families of schizophrenic patients (see Napier & Whitaker, 1978; Whitaker & Bumberry, 1988). He used innovative techniques that he later described as "psychotherapy of the absurd." Sometimes he would escalate a symptom to the point of its being absurd, even to the patient. He regarded everyone in the room, each member of the family, and even himself and his cotherapist, as both patient and therapist.

In New York City, Ackerman (1966) started working with the family as a social and emotional unit as early as the 1930s. He was trained as a child analyst, but rather than seeing the child himself and having a colleague see the parent, he started seeing the family together. By the 1950s Ackerman worked only with whole families together.

These four groups are generally recognized as the founding fathers of family therapy and family systems thinking, which at that time was considered a radical approach to treatment.

SIX SCHOOLS OF THOUGHT

Since those early days, family therapy has become a professional field of study and practice in the United States and around the world. The field has basically divided into six different schools of thought regarding the family as the patient.

1. *Psychodynamic approach to family therapy.* The first school of thought, which was headed by Ackerman (1966) and included Framo (1982), Borzormenyi-Nagy and Spark (1973), Scharff and Scharff (1991), and Slipp (1988), considers the most important information in therapy as coming from the past. By looking at a history of earlier experiences through a psychodynamic lens, unresolved family conflicts from the past are brought into the open so that these insights can lead to new understandings. Family problems are seen as the product of persistent, unresolved conflicts both within the person and between persons within the family. Ackerman was an active therapist who moved right into the midst of the family's conflict, directly influencing the interactional process and supporting positive moves while blocking negative ones.

Framo considered the most powerful obstacles to change to be the person's attachments to the internalizations of their parents. These attachments were often unconscious material that needed to be brought out into the open. Borzormenyi-Nagy felt that, when treating the family, the context of past, present, and future interconnections that bind families together must be considered. The context—what he called "invisible loyalties"—was the inevitable intergenerational consequences that we all experience. Each family member is viewed as part of a multigenerational pattern that a client needs to identify and understand in order to experience change.

2. *Experiential approach to family therapy.* The experiential school of thought represents Whitaker's legacy and also includes the work of Satir (1964, 1972), who helped found the Mental Research Institute. The focus is on the present, the here-and-now information that can be observed in the therapy room with the family, rather than on the covert, unconscious material. For that reason, Whitaker preferred to work with a cotherapist, probably because at times he acted as "crazy" as the patient.

Like Whitaker, therapists working in this school of thought use a wide variety of techniques as they seek to create new experiences for the family. These "new experiences" may seem random, but in fact, they are carefully designed to help family members make better choices and take responsibility for those choices. The focus is on the relationship between two people. Humor, indirection, seduction, indignation, boredom, and even falling asleep are all considered appropriate techniques to use with the family. The goal is to create a better balance within the family system.

Family roles, communication styles, and even seating arrangements in the therapy room become tools to help facilitate change. Techniques such as family sculpting, where family members are molded into characteristic poses representing one family member's view of the family, have been developed by those working in this school of thought by therapists who also are strongly influenced by gestalt techniques.

3. *Bowenian approach to family therapy.* Bowen's (1978; Kerr & Bowen, 1988) approach is similar to the psychodynamic school, but it has several differences that warrant separate discussion. Bowen looked primarily at the present while remaining within the context of family-of-origin issues. He felt that emotional problems in the present were maintained by current relational binds with others. He saw the family as an emotional unit from which the individual must be differentiated. The individual must find a way to get unstuck from the *undifferentiated family-ego mass,* which is defined as an intense, symbiotic family system that blocks the development of the individual sense of self.

Prior to differentiation, family members know each other's feelings, thoughts, and dreams. But they don't really know their own feelings, thoughts, and dreams. Once differentiated, a person knows who he or she is and can express clear convictions and beliefs. To differentiate, one must understand generational patterns and unhealthy triangular relationships. Bowen used family genograms to help himself and the clients see what they needed to work on.

Bowen liked to work with two adults, even when the presenting problem was with a child. Therapists trained in Bowen's method work in a calm, neutral manner as they seek to reduce anxiety, resolve symptoms, and ultimately help adults differentiate from their family of origin.

4. *Structural approach to family therapy.* Minuchin (1974, 1984), at the Philadelphia Child Guidance Clinic, developed the structural approach. He describes his viewpoint as being based "on the concept that a family is more than the individual biopsychodynamics of its members. Family members relate according to certain arrangements that govern their transactions. These arrangements, though usually not explicitly stated or even recognized, form a whole—the structure of the family" (1974, p. 89). This structure is quite different from the reality that each individual member sees.

Structural family therapists work with both the present and the past, looking primarily at habitual behaviors and roles within the family. They are quite active in sessions and use *enactments* to help change family actions. These enactments attempt to actually bring family conflicts into the therapy session and act them out. During the enactments, specific behaviors are changed in an attempt to create a better understanding of the underlying family structure. Boundaries, coalitions, and hierarchical issues are all studied as part of treatment and help identify the family's covert rules.

Another technique is that of *reframing*. This is where the original meaning of an event or situation is placed in a new context to give it new meaning. Everything is done with the purpose of unbalancing the family's homeostasis and then mapping out ways for the family to make constructive changes.

5. *Strategic approach to family therapy.* The strategic approach is primarily credited to the MRI group and even more to Haley (1973, 1984). These therapists look primarily at what is going on now, choosing to put the intrapsychic material into what they call the "black box" (see Watzlawick et al., 1967). To them, problems manifest themselves in faulty communication. One concept has to do with "punctuation": What you say has different meanings depending on how it is punctuated. Not only is causality circular, but communication can be circular as well, depending on how one punctuates what is being said.

To the MRI group, all behavior is communication. Communication takes place at two levels. There is the surface content, and then there is what is called *metacommunication,* which qualifies what is said on the first level. Body language is a form of metacommunication. If I say I want to be with you but I walk away from you, my communication is saying one thing, but my metacommunication is saying something else. Therapists from this school of thought often use therapeutic double binds or paradoxical interventions. Rather than allow homeostasis to continue, therapists carefully plan these and other interventions to create changes in the system.

One of the groups in this school of thought is the Milan group of Selvini-Palazzoli, Cirillo, Selvini, and Sorrentino (1989). This group, which has been successful in treating eating disorders, uses a technique they developed called *circular questioning.* One of their significant contributions is to treat a family system not as truly homeostatic but as evolving. They believe information will change family dynamics.

6. *Behavioral approaches to family therapy.* The behavioral school of thought is among the more recent approaches to family therapy, due to the fact that most behaviorists or cognitive-behaviorists usually work with individuals to deal with current issues. But in recent years, those therapists working with marital and parenting issues from a behavioral perspective have used systems thinking. They have focused on learned behaviors and have sought to modify those behavioral patterns. The therapist is seen as a teacher or trainer who is seeking to change behavioral sequences between persons.

Bedrosian and Bozicas (1994) added the cognitive component to this school of thought, focusing on the source of family patterns of cognitive distortions. Faulty belief systems are learned from families of origin and must be identified;

knowing the source can help to neutralize them. One of the unique features of this type of family therapy is that it operates on linear causality as opposed to circular causality.

The MRI group has developed a behavioral approach, which they call the Brief Therapy Project. Another approach is solution-focused brief therapy, described by De Shazer (1980). (See chapter 14.) These approaches are time-limited, pragmatic, step-by-step approaches that focus on behaviors in the family. They seek to change the homeostatic setting of the family through direct, often paradoxical, interventions. Often the therapy is done by a team, with one person leading the therapy and others watching behind a one-way mirror.

So What's Christian About Family Systems?

Like family systems theory, the church supports the importance of viewing the individual within a larger context. The apostle Paul talked about our being members of the body of Christ (see especially 1 Corinthians 12). Peter referred to individual believers as "living stones" that are being placed with other Christians as building blocks in God's spiritual temple (1 Peter 2:4-10). One can see that biblical themes tend to support the family systems approaches described in this chapter.

Family Systems in the Bible

We've already commented on the "sins of the parents" as an example of generational patterns. We can clearly see these generational patterns when we look at biblical families.

Abraham's family over four generations. Genesis provides information about four generations of Abraham's family, which allows us to clearly see some of the patterns that repeat themselves.

For example, Abraham lied about his relationship with Sarah, calling her his sister. This happened twice. (See Genesis 12:10-20 and Genesis 20.) In Genesis 26:1-10, Isaac did the same thing, calling Rebekah his sister. In each generation there was a pattern of a mother who was overinvested in the life of a son. Sarah was too involved with Isaac; Rebekah was enmeshed with Jacob; and Rachel was totally involved only with Joseph. Three generations of mothers doting on their sons.

In addition, favoritism toward one child is probably the most dysfunctional pattern in Abraham's family. Both Abraham and Sarah clearly favored their son Isaac over their son Ishmael. The pattern changed a bit in the next generation as Isaac favored his son Esau, while Rebekah favored her son Jacob. In the third generation, Jacob changed the situation but ended up with the same result. He had two wives, one of which he clearly favored. Both he and his preferred wife, Rachel, clearly favored their son Joseph over all the other children in the family.

In each of these three generations, one of the sons ended up being sent away due to the parents' favoritism. In Abraham's family, Ishmael was sent away because of Sarah's jealousy of Hagar. In Isaac's family, Jacob was sent away due to his mother's fear that Esau would kill him. In Jacob's family, Joseph was sent away by his brothers, who at first meant to murder him. (It is interesting to note that there was a progression of intensity with each generation: Ishmael was sent away due to jealousy, Jacob was sent away due to fear, and Joseph was sent away through a hatred that almost led to murder.) Joseph became the transitional person in the family lineage, stopping this dysfunctional pattern in the fourth generation and maintaining the hope of the Promised One to come (Stoop & Masteller, 1991).

Saul and David. Another example has to do with the father issues in the life of King Saul. These issues led to authority problems with the prophet Samuel, which fed into Saul's fears and led to his disobedience and the loss of his anointing by God as king.

Disobedience in David's life—taking too many wives and committing adultery—directly led to problems with his children. Amnon raped his sister Tamar; Absalom sought revenge by killing Amnon; and David emotionally cut off Absalom to the point that Absalom attempted a coup to unseat his father as king.

Jesus and the use of paradox. Another technique for change in family systems theory is the use of paradox. Relationships between people often operate on paradoxical principles. The paradoxical nature of relationships is seen in Jesus' teachings: "Whoever tries to keep his life will lose it, and whoever loses his life will preserve it" (Luke 17:33). Think of the many ways he used paradox to teach the disciples and change the group dynamics:

- Imagine Jesus hunched over and drawing in the dirt while a terrified woman and her Pharisee accusers stand around him (John 8:3-11). Those ready to throw rocks must have been smirking in the knowledge of the no-win double bind they had deliberately set to entrap Christ. Jesus' behavior suggests that he felt the pressure of the bind and was searching his heart and mind for the right response. He stood up and said, "He who is without sin among you, let him throw a stone at her first" (verse 7, NKJV). *Bang*—he nailed them with the paradoxical truth of their own law, for only the perfect One—only God—truly has the right to judge. They slinked off, and Jesus said to the adulterous woman, "Neither do I condemn you; go and sin no more" (verse 11, NKJV).

- Remember the disciples' squabble about who would be greatest in Christ's kingdom? (Look at Luke 22:24-27 and John 13:2-9 for a complete picture of the incident.) How did Jesus respond? He got down and washed the disciples' feet to demonstrate that the lowly servant is the greatest of all. What an object lesson—and what a powerful, paradoxical response!
- How about Philippians 2 and Isaiah 53 as paradoxical portraits of God? Rather than hold to his all-powerful, throne-seated majesty, Jesus yielded to flesh, suffering, and death. He allowed himself to be tortured and wounded for our sakes. His bloodied and broken appearance on the cross would more likely repel than attract those who witnessed the event.

THINKING SYSTEMICALLY

Learning to think beyond the individual and to work with clients within the context of their families—in particular, the context of their family of origin—takes training. Many counselors prefer to work with individuals because, as several therapists have said to me, "I get confused when there is more than one other person in my counseling room." It can be confusing until one learns how to listen more to process than to content and how to process systemically instead of by linear logic.

Many family systems teaching programs use cotherapists during the training phase to give confidence to the new therapist as he or she works with a group of people. This partnership encourages the new therapist to focus more on process than on content. The cotherapist is sometimes in the room with the family, but at other times views the process through a one-way mirror. Reading the transcripts of family therapy sessions can also be helpful as well as entertaining (many of the early theorists were quite unpredictable).

When counselors work with couples, they benefit from being able to see a couple within the context of their own system as well as within the family systems in which they grew up. One can learn to think systemically whether working with an individual, a married couple, or a family. Many organizational counselors also have learned to view the workings of an organization through the eyes of systems thinking. Church staffs as well as congregations often can best be understood through the lens of family systems thinking. Its theories shed light on all types of relationships.

CHAPTER 24

CHILD THERAPY I

The Mandate to Work with the Next Generation

GRANT L. MARTIN AND DANIEL S. SWEENEY

Of all the needs (there are none imaginary) a lonely child has, the one that must be satisfied if there is going to be hope and a hope of wholeness, is the unshaking need for an unshakable God.

—MAYA ANGELOU, *I Know Why the Caged Bird Sings*

Perhaps the greatest tribute to any society—or the greatest indictment—is its response to the call to care for its children. Children, as the next generation and as our legacy, deserve the priority that God intended. Children are indeed a "heritage from the LORD" (Psalm 127:3), and they should not be hindered, "for the kingdom of heaven belongs to such as these" (Matthew 19:14). Clearly, the Creator holds children in high esteem.

Few would argue with these truths. Since actions speak louder than words, however, it appears that our society does not always place a priority on the well-being of children. Further, it is unfortunate that the priority is not always reflected in the Christian community. We are disappointed about this, and we're frustrated and dismayed to see that the Christian counseling community also does not seem to consider this a priority.

This chapter is not meant to harangue or indict Christian counselors. Additionally, this chapter is not (and indeed cannot be) a comprehensive examination of child psychology from a Christian perspective. Rather, we see this as an opportunity to educate counselors about the crucial need to work with children and the need for more Christian therapists to take up this calling.

THE CHILD'S WORLD

Childhood today is significantly different from what it used to be. Bennett (1993) noted that in 1940 teachers identified the following behaviors as the primary concerns in America's schools: talking out of turn, making noise, cutting in line, chewing gum, littering, and violating the dress code. The picture in 1990 was much different, as teachers reported the top concerns to be drug and alcohol abuse, suicide, pregnancy, rape, robbery, and assault. According to the U.S. Department of Health and Human Services (2000), there were an estimated 903,000 victims of child maltreatment nationwide in 1998. This report also noted that during this time, the highest victimization rates were for the zero- to three-year-old age group. An estimated 1,100 children died of abuse and neglect, and 144,000 child victims were placed in foster care. Children must grow up in a frightening world, and mental health difficulties are a devastating consequence.

The World Health Organization indicates that within twenty years, "childhood neuropsychiatric disorders will rise proportionately by over 50 percent, internationally, to become one of the five most common causes of morbidity, mortality, and disability among children" (National Institute of Mental Health, 2001, p. 1). The U.S. Surgeon General's Report on Mental Health (U.S. Department of Health and Human Services, 1999) reports that almost 21% of children in this nation have a diagnosable mental or addictive disorder. The Center for Mental Health Services (CMHS, 2001) reports this same percentage but notes that the majority of children do not receive appropriate mental health services. Studies cited by the surgeon general's report indicate that approximately 70% of children and adolescents in need of treatment do not receive mental health services.

Therapists dedicated to working with children still remain a significant minority, and the availability of quality training in child psychotherapy is limited (Culbertson, 1993; Illback, 1994; La Greca & Hughes, 1999; Roberts, 1994). According to Tuma (1989), a little more than 10% of psychiatrists and less than 1% of psychologists have a commitment to work primarily with children. While this statistic is somewhat discouraging, our experience is that interest in child therapy and childhood issues in general may be growing.

Unfortunately, the obstacles faced by children and families are complicated by the general culture in which we live. For example, the influence of the media contributes significantly to childhood and family problems. Media should not replace family relationships, yet children spend an average of six and a half hours per day with various electronic media, such as television, movies, and video games

(Roberts, Foehr, Rideout, & Brodie, 1999). Children need the direction of parents, not the diversion of television.

The effects of this cultural obsession are seen routinely. The National Television Violence Study found that nearly two-thirds of today's television programming contains violence, that children's shows contain the most violence, and that the portrayals of violence are normally glamorized (Federman, 1998). Body image and self-esteem are also influenced by the media. Field et al. (1999) report that the majority of girls (59%) expressed dissatisfaction with their body weight, and 66% expressed the desire to lose weight.

The statistics on substance abuse and its effects on children are also alarming. According to the National Clearinghouse for Alcohol and Drug Information (2001):

- There are an estimated 26.8 million children of alcoholics (COAs) in the United States, 11 million of whom are under the age of eighteen.
- Children of alcoholics are four times more likely than non-COAs to develop alcoholism.
- Studies of family violence document high rates of substance abuse, and children in these homes are much more likely to be the targets of abuse and to witness domestic violence.
- Substance abuse is reported to be a major problem in 81% of abuse and neglect cases handled by state child protective service agencies.
- Children of substance abusers exhibit more symptoms of depression and anxiety, more behavioral problems, and more learning problems than do other children.

The many challenges facing children in our nation are just as prevalent inside the church as outside of it. It might be argued that childhood problems are compounded within religious circles, fed by doctrinal rigidity as well as the need to maintain a proper appearance. Sadly, when the church should be a place of refuge for children and adults alike, the prevalence of abuse and emotional turmoil in the church is as unhealthy as it is in the secular realm. In fact, in some areas the problems may be worse. According to Barna (1999), a national survey shows that Christians are more likely to experience divorce than non-Christians. Additionally, rates of domestic violence may be higher in the church and, sad to say, may be covered up (Alsdurf & Alsdurf, 1998; Ellison, Bartkowski, & Anderson, 1999). Hurting Christian children must have places to turn to. Secular mental health services may be excellent for many cases, but for the family searching for Christian services, the paucity of trained and committed therapists makes the quest challenging.

CHILDHOOD PROBLEMS

The etiology of childhood problems is not unlike that for adult psychopathology. There is credible evidence that both biological and psychosocial factors influence the development and perpetuation of childhood disorders. It is often not possible to fully explain the specific cause of childhood problems, but it is crucial to briefly look at predisposing factors.

There are established biological factors for many childhood disorders. Strong indications and substantial consensus point to biological factors in pervasive developmental disorders, obsessive-compulsive disorder, tic disorders, and early-onset schizophrenia. Genetics play a significant role in disorders such as autism, schizophrenia, ADHD, and bipolar disorder (National Institute of Mental Health, 1998). It is important to note that biological elements of etiology may be inherited, but they may also develop in other physiologic manners. Some of these include the effects of injury, exposure to toxins, infection, or nutritional imbalance on the brain and central nervous systems. Prenatal exposure to any of these is also involved in childhood disorders, perhaps most obviously seen in fetal alcohol syndrome and the associated mental retardation.

Psychosocial contributors to childhood disorders may be either linked to, or independent from, biological influences. Many environmental factors, including parental conflict, family psychopathology, economic hardship, abuse and neglect, and attachment problems, can affect a child's mental and emotional health. A comprehensive list would be much longer. The effects of parental depression or substance abuse also can be substantial, sometimes resulting in serious neglect or abuse or creating anxiety or depression in children. For example, research has found that children of depressed parents are more than three times as likely as children of nondepressed parents to experience a depressive episode (Birmaher, Ryan, Williamson, Brent, & Kaufman, 1996a, 1996b). What's more, parental depression increases the risk of anxiety disorders, conduct disorder, and alcohol dependence in children (Wickramaratne & Weissman, 1998).

Stressful life events, such as loss (e.g., parental death or divorce) or even typical developmental changes, may be emotionally disabling for some children. Children exposed to these environmental stressors tend to engage in various risk behaviors themselves. Flisher et al. (2000) studied risk behaviors in children and found a strong relationship between children engaging in risk behaviors and those with various psychosocial stressors, inadequate resources, and psychopathology.

Children of any age may be impacted by mental health challenges. Although advances in age and development do bring more complex challenges, even young children can experience emotional and behavioral difficulties. Lavigne et al. (1996)

demonstrated that the prevalence of psychiatric disorders for preschool children was consistent with rates for older children. Most childhood problems persist into adulthood without intervention (Hofstra, Van Der Ende, & Verhulst, 2000). Prevention and intervention at earlier stages of childhood may save a person a lifetime of difficulties.

It is not possible to discuss the full range of childhood disorders in the scope of this chapter. The diagnostic criteria for these disorders are outlined in the DSM-IV-TR (APA, 2000). Some experts divide childhood disorders into two primary categories: internalizing disorders and externalizing disorders. *Internalizing disorders* involve "acting in" and include such problems as depression and anxiety. *Externalizing disorders* involve acting out and include disruptive behavior disorders. In many ways, internalizing disorders are of greater concern, as these children are less likely to be noticed and given appropriate attention and intervention.

Child Assessment and Treatment

The assessment and treatment of children and their problems carry several inherent challenges. Although childhood disorders often present similarly to adult psychopathology, there are several distinctive considerations.

1. Children normally do not self-refer. They are usually brought into treatment by family members, whose investment in the process should be assessed. As such, children are basically involuntary clients, which is an issue that the therapist must be aware of and overcome.

2. Children do not have the cognitive or language facility adults have and thus have limited abilities to provide historical information or to process intrapsychic issues verbally. Children should not be expected to perform beyond their developmental capabilities.

3. Children have limited control over their family and school environments. This points to the need for a systemic approach to treating childhood problems.

4. Historical information is generally provided by significant others, frequently a parent or parents who are under considerable stress at the time of referral. History should be obtained from all available sources to confirm or rule out diagnostic and treatment options.

5. Developmental issues must be kept in mind. Children are psychologically and physiologically different from adults. Before diagnosis and treatment, therapists must consider what the normal and appropriate behaviors are for children of varying ages.

6. Childhood assessment results may be less reliable than adult assessments. The validity and reliability of any assessment instruments should be considered, and therapists should be adequately trained to administer all evaluation tools.

7. The age limits for childhood and other DSM-IV-TR (2000) disorders are not consistent and not firm. Chronological and psychological age should be considered in light of the time of onset of symptoms.

8. Multiple diagnoses are often possible for a child client. The appropriate diagnosis must be made, recognizing that this facilitates treatment planning and avoids mislabeling or overlabeling a child.

9. There are few consistent and established standards of practice for treating children and childhood disorders. It is imperative that child therapists stay current with research and theory in the field of child psychopathology and psychotherapy.

10. Symptom lists for many childhood disorders are broad "laundry lists." Differential diagnosis is a key element in sorting through a child's presentation.

11. The focus of child treatment is too often on the symptoms rather than on the underlying cause. Etiology must be considered, and the individuality of the child client should never get lost in the diagnosis and treatment process.

ASSESSMENT OF CHILDREN

The treatment process naturally must begin with assessment. Martin (1992) states,

> To accomplish the goals of assessment, it is helpful to work within an established framework: a method of systematically collecting and organizing information to assimilate the formal and informal data gathered during the assessment process. The assessment structure also helps the counselor choose the tools or techniques for gathering, interpreting, and summarizing the data. (p. 8)

Following, in greater detail, are the elements of the assessment process:

- Assessment begins with a *clarification* of the reason for the referral. The therapist and the referral source (usually the parents) must agree on the issues to be investigated. This results in a statement of the *presenting problem*.

- The next step is to determine what assessment process is appropriate to answer the questions being asked. If the initial interview does not yield sufficient information to define the problem, assessment instruments may be used. Some examples include cognitive and achievement measures, behavior rating scales, and various questionnaires. It must be determined whether or not the therapist has the skill and competence to ethically utilize these tools.

- As assessment proceeds, the therapist must determine the child's *developmental status* in the emotional, social, intellectual, and spiritual areas. It is important to note that children's chronological ages may or may not equal their developmental ages.

- Based upon the conclusions from this process, a *diagnostic description* is made and types of intervention are determined. This final step essentially culminates in the development of a treatment plan.

TREATMENT PRINCIPLES

Treatment must often be multimodal and multidisciplinary. Working with children, however, must fundamentally begin with the therapist's recognition that there is a developmental difference between children and older clients. Sweeney (1997) asserted that children do not communicate in the same way that adults do; adult communication requires both verbal abilities and abstract thinking skills. Children interact through play, their natural medium of communication. Child therapy should, therefore, include some element of play therapy.

Landreth (1991) defines play therapy as a "dynamic interpersonal relationship between a child and a therapist trained in play therapy procedures who provides selected play materials and facilitates the development of a safe relationship for the child to fully express and explore self (feelings, thoughts, experiences, and behaviors) through the child's natural medium of communication, play" (p. 14). There are crucial elements contained within this definition, which apply to most modalities of child therapy. This is discussed in greater detail in a later chapter.

Once the therapist has assessed a child client's developmental level, interventions can also include behavior management, pharmacotherapy, family therapy, cognitive-behavioral therapy, group therapy, art therapy, animal-assisted therapy, residential care, and parent training. (Many more interventions could be added to the list.) The child therapist utilizing any of these or other interventions must receive adequate training and supervised experience.

Martin (1995, 1998) described the process of implementing a multimodal intervention with a child who has attention deficit hyperactivity disorder. A careful assessment must be done, involving the child, parents, school personnel, and a medical evaluation. Treatment should involve interventions and accommodations within the home, at school, and within the child. Treatment of ADHD may also involve prescription of some type of medication.

Several types of medication have been demonstrated to have significant positive effects for the hyperactivity, impulsivity, and inattention that are characteristic of the disorder. Medication, however, is not enough. Often, parents must be trained in simple behavior management techniques, and adaptations in the school setting may need to be made.

Children with ADHD may have coexisting learning challenges, and special education programs may need to be established. ADHD children have also frequently been ostracized by peers and family members. Their self-esteem and self-control have been affected, for which a psychotherapeutic intervention may be needed. Play therapy should never be considered completely adequate for the child with ADHD, but it should be considered as a part of the treatment plan. Medications are often a necessary component of treatment, but they should never be considered to be completely adequate for the ADHD child. Parent training is a critical component when working with an ADHD child, but it is unnecessarily complicated if a child needing medication is denied a pharmacological intervention.

Since no childhood problem develops and exists in a vacuum, it is important to take a systemic approach to the treatment of children (Martin, 1995). Parents and family should always be involved in the therapy process, but even this may not be adequate. Other persons and organizations may also need to be involved, including school personnel, medical practitioners, child protective service agencies, law enforcement and probation, courts and attorneys, and foster care.

Ackerman (1970) noted that "without engaging the children in a meaningful interchange across the generations, there can be no family therapy" (p. 403). Many therapists working with children and families, however, exclude children (particularly young children) from participation in family therapy sessions (Chasin, 1989; Gil, 1994). In our work with children and families, we have found that the inclusion of children in family therapy greatly enriches the therapeutic process. We would assert that therapists working with families who want to actively engage children must be intentional about the process. A study conducted by Korner and Brown (1990) found that family therapists who had received specialized training with children, or who felt that their training with children was adequate, were those who were more likely to include children in the therapy process. The process and the training must be intentional.

Parent education and training is a key element in the treatment process. It may be that parent training is the primary intervention. Sweeney, Homeyer, and Pavlishina (2000) recommend filial therapy (which is a relationship-focused and play therapy–based intervention) as an effective parent training method:

> Many available parent training programs focus on behavior management or control. Behavioral interventions for children who act out can be useful. However, if a child's behavior is primarily a reflection of emotional turmoil and unmet needs, behavior controls will not have a lasting impact. It becomes necessary to provide a therapeutic experience that touches the child at emotional and relational levels while empowering the parent to be the change agent for the child, themselves, and their relationship.... As parents look to Christian therapists and to Christian parenting literature, they are often met with a focus on the child's behavior and the need to provide appropriate discipline. Discipline, while biblically and psychologically appropriate, is incomplete.... With some popular parenting approaches, there is potential to equate discipline with behavioral control or punishment. The concept of discipline as a relational or teaching process can easily get lost. Labeling a child as "strong-willed" or a "problem" may in fact be an accurate interpretation. Nevertheless, such labeling may result in the justification of the use of force to bring about compliance. This leads to adversarial parent-child interactions, not relationships noted for understanding, valuing and honoring of one another....Parents can employ the most researched, effective, and developmentally appropriate rules of parenting and behavior management; but if the parent-child relationship is poor, the result will involve minimal compliance and potential rebellion. It is relationship that creates the environment for emotional expression and problem solving. Filial therapy provides this opportunity. (pp. 239-240)

Parental self-care may be another crucial therapeutic intervention. After all, it is a simple truth that stressed and sleep-deprived parents are not often effective parents. It may be that the most expedient intervention for a child is individual or marital therapy for the parent(s). Respite care is often a simple yet effective intervention for many child cases.

Pharmacological treatment is also an important intervention when working with children. As noted above, medications may be the primary element in a multimodal treatment plan, but they should never be the only intervention. It is certainly wrong to medicate a child who does not need to be medicated, but it is equally wrong to deny medications to a child in legitimate need of this intervention. Nonmedical child therapists should educate themselves about psychotropic medications and should cultivate useful relationships with medical personnel. Their efforts will benefit children in need. (The interested reader is encouraged to investigate chapter 27 "Child Psychopharmacology.")

LEGAL AND ETHICAL CONSIDERATIONS

Several legal and ethical issues are important to consider when working with children. It is imperative to remember that while the child may be the focus of treatment, the legal guardian is essentially the client from a legal and ethical perspective. This is because the law presumes minors to be legally incompetent. Therefore, children are not considered to have the legal capacity to consent (or refuse) services, nor do they have the right to obtain and retain privilege in regard to confidential information. The legal guardian (most often the parent) is the holder of these rights.

CONFIDENTIALITY

Confidentiality is a foundational ethical issue. In most circumstances, parental consent is required to authorize treatment for a child. Because of this, parents have the right to obtain information about their child's treatment from the therapist. As a result, confidentiality generally cannot be promised to a minor. Sweeney (2001) noted that this may present a challenge to the therapist wanting to establish a therapeutic relationship. The child therapist cannot promise his or her client that everything shared, whether verbally or nonverbally, will not be shared with the parents.

Furthermore, all therapists should be aware of the basic exceptions to confidentiality. Although these may vary slightly from state to state, these exceptions include the following: disclosure of child or elder abuse, disclosure of an intent to commit harm to self or others, written authorization by the parent or guardian, a legal action brought against the therapist that is initiated by the client, and a court order to release information.

Sweeney (2001) discussed the importance for the child therapist to consider confidentiality issues in light of the increasing use of technology. Records stored on a computer should be encrypted and preferably not stored on the computer's hard drive. Electronic mail should also be encrypted and fax machines closely monitored. Phone conversations with clients should not be made over wireless phones, as these employ airwaves that can be accessed or monitored. If parents use a nonsecure means to communicate with the therapist, it is the therapist's responsibility to make the necessary adjustments that ensure confidentiality.

INFORMED CONSENT

To satisfy the principle of informed consent, which is essentially a legal doctrine, the consent of clients must be given in a knowledgeable, competent, and voluntary state. This issue becomes complex for child clients. Because of their minor status, children are not considered to be knowledgeable, competent, and voluntary. Since children are considered legally incapable of consenting to the process of child therapy, an appropriate substitute must do so. Normally, this person will be the parent or legal guardian. In cases where the parent is not involved, the therapist must ensure that the person providing the consent is legally able to do so.

Grandparents or other relatives who are not the legal guardians generally cannot provide consent. Additional exceptions to the requirement for parental consent for treatment vary from state to state. These exceptions may include emergency treatment situations; the case of an emancipated minor; drug and alcohol treatment for children (generally aged twelve or older); counseling for birth control, pregnancy, or sexually transmitted diseases; and other specific situations as outlined by state law.

DIVORCE AND CUSTODY CONFLICTS

With the high incidence of family conflict and divorce today, child therapists may be called upon to conduct custody evaluations (Martin, 1992). Usually, the question at issue will be what is in the best interests of the child. This is not an uncomplicated issue for either clients or therapists. Child therapists may frequently find themselves in the awkward position of dealing with competing family members while still attempting to promote the best interests of the child. There is also the question of whether child therapists can engage in the dual roles of therapist and evaluator for the family.

Child therapists may appear in court on custody matters as fact witnesses, expert witnesses, or both. Fact witnesses may provide simple testimony to the court regarding client history, diagnosis, treatment, and so on. Custody evaluators, however, often operate in the capacity of expert witnesses, providing the court with professional opinions on issues of custody and visitation.

RECORDKEEPING

All therapists are responsible for the production and maintenance of records, which include: intake information; professional disclosure statements; release forms; client histories; psychological tests; progress notes; treatment plans; and basic office forms, such as informed consent, billing information, and cancellation fee policy. A reasonable standard to consider in the maintenance of client records is whether you would feel comfortable having the file subpoenaed and reviewed by a court and professional peers.

Records should be properly secured and maintained for an appropriate length of time (most states and professional organizations have established minimums). Therapists should be well acquainted with these laws in the states where they practice. A conservative recommendation would be to maintain records for ten years following termination of therapeutic services. Additionally, it is recommended that records for child clients are stored for four years beyond the age of majority.

While the focus of treatment in child therapy is most often the child, exclusion of the parents from the process is both impractical and unethical. In most cases, the parents are not only the significant caretakers for the child but are also legally responsible for the child. Only the parent or guardian can authorize treatment and can obtain information about the diagnosis, prognosis, and treatment plan. Any therapist who works with children should be aware of state and local statutes regarding parental rights.

When Attention Is Needed

Part of the challenge for therapists involves knowing when children and parents need intervention. Christian therapists can educate their clients, churches, and communities about the need for child intervention. As with adults, the psychological health of a child may be measured by change. Although we can't provide a comprehensive list here, some of the significant changes that would indicate a need for psychotherapeutic attention include marked changes in the following areas:

- school performance (academic performance, behavioral difficulties)
- sleep habits (including insomnia, nightmares)
- behavior patterns (increased anger or aggression, self-destructive behaviors, hyperactivity, and acting out, including oppositional and criminal behavior)
- mood (both dysphoria and euphoria)
- levels of anxiety and fear
- appetite and eating behaviors
- withdrawal
- unusual or bizarre behavior (including strange thoughts or feelings)
- child stressors, including losses or changes such as parental divorce, serious illness or death of a family member, financial crisis, or any major trauma

The presence of any of these behavioral and emotional changes in and of themselves may not indicate the need for professional intervention. It is important, therefore, to consider the basic factors of intensity, duration, and frequency. Many childhood expressions of emotion and behavior are challenging at times. If the intensity becomes extreme, intervention may be warranted. Likewise, many of these challenging issues are short-lived. If the duration becomes excessive, intervention may be warranted. Many of these challenging childhood problems may occur only infrequently. When the frequency increases, intervention may once again be warranted.

We have established the need for more child therapists. In addition to the calling, the personality, and the training, some other fundamental qualities are needed for this special work. While there is no set mold for an effective child therapist, Martin (1992) discussed some of the basic characteristics a child counselor needs to have. These include:

- the ability to establish a good relationship with the child
- the ability to convey interest, warmth, and respect for the child
- the ability to balance childlike freedom and playfulness with professional objectivity and self-control
- the resolution of the counselor's own childhood issues
- the desire to relate to, talk to, and find out about children
- an interest and appreciation for creative expression
- the ability to use all channels of learning, including auditory, visual, and kinesthetic

Working with children is both a calling and a lifestyle. Landreth and Sweeney (1997) suggest that "child…therapy is not a cloak the…therapist puts on when entering the playroom and takes off when leaving; rather it is a philosophy resulting in attitudes and behaviors for living one's life in relationships with children" (p. 17). This calling is an important one that too few have answered. We encourage readers to see God's priority in working with his little ones as well as the way such work will benefit current and future generations.

CHAPTER 25

CHILD THERAPY II

Treating Traumatized Children
with Play Therapy

DANIEL S. SWEENEY

Whoever humbles himself like this child is the greatest in the kingdom of heaven. And whoever welcomes a little child like this in my name welcomes me. But if anyone causes one of these little ones who believe in me to sin, it would be better for him to have a large millstone hung around his neck and to be drowned in the depths of the sea.

—MATTHEW 18:4-6

One of the greatest pains human beings can experience is loneliness. Children who have experienced trauma routinely struggle with this feeling. Boys and girls, already searching for autonomy and identity in this world, are cruelly oppressed when trauma strikes from any source, and they are left feeling isolated and disconnected. Few, if any, of these children have an advocate who will dare to invest in and care for them.

In his discussion of loneliness, Moustakas (1974) poignantly states, "It is the terror of loneliness, not loneliness itself but loneliness anxiety, the fear of being left alone, of being left out, that represents a dominant crisis in the struggle to become a person" (p. 16). It is in this lonely place that so many child victims of trauma reside, and Christian therapists must be willing to enter this place and be instruments of healing.

Children today live in an unsafe world. According to the U.S. Department of Health and Human Services (2000), in 1998 there were an estimated 903,000 victims of abuse and neglect nationwide, some 2,806,000 referrals to child protective agencies, 1,100 child deaths from abuse and neglect (77.5% of whom were less than five years of age), and 144,000 child placements in foster care.

Statistics compiled by the Children's Defense Fund (2000) give us a picture of what a single day is like for the children of America: 2 children under the age of five are murdered (10 children and adolescents total); 6 children and adolescents commit suicide; 218 children are arrested for violent crimes; 399 children are arrested for drug abuse (5,044 are arrested in general); and 17,297 students are suspended from school. That's every single day!

Where does the therapist begin? Some counselors and psychologists insist that these children need to *talk* about what has happened to them, that they must verbalize their pain as part of the healing process. My experience as a psychotherapist, as a child advocate, and as a play therapist does not entirely support this conclusion. An increasing body of research literature also points to a different approach (Association for Play Therapy, 1999; Landreth, Homeyer, Glover, & Sweeney, 1996). I would like to discuss therapy with traumatized children from a play therapy perspective.

How Children Communicate

A fundamental truth about children is that they do not communicate in the same way that adults do. Adult communication requires both verbal abilities and abstract thinking skills. Children, on the other hand, communicate through play. It is their natural medium of communication. The basis for doing play therapy, therefore, is to honor children by entering their world of communication rather than forcing children to enter our adult world of verbalization and to fit into adult models of counseling. This is empathy—the core counseling skill—in action.

The greatest demonstration of empathy in the history of the world was shown by the Creator in the Incarnation. If it was not below God to humble himself and enter our human world through Christ, it is not below those of us who work with children to enter their world (Sweeney, 1997).

Do people need to talk about their issues in order to process them? Yes. *Children, however, talk through play.* The toys become their words. Is this the same as verbalization? No. When I conduct training on play therapy, I often ask for a volunteer in the audience to stand up and share with us his or her most embarrassing and traumatizing sexual experience. After the nervous laughter has subsided, I point out: "Isn't this precisely what we do to sexually abused children when we say, 'Tell me what happened to you'?" This is unfair and potentially retraumatizing. As a community of Christian helpers, we need to rethink how we approach the traumatized child.

I attended a conference several years ago where the keynote presenter stated that he requires his sexually abused child clients to draw a picture of the perpetrator during the first session. *Requires?* Hasn't the child already been *required* to participate in enough trauma?

Other therapists suggest using toys and play as a means of leading children to talk about what happened to them. The idea is to use the toys as a way to build rapport so that the trauma will be discussed. We should be careful about this. Doesn't a common pattern of molestation involve the offender using games, candy, and toys to establish trust with the potential victim before abuse begins? Do we want the therapeutic process to follow the same pattern? I don't think so.

I am not suggesting that talking to children is wrong. Talking is an essential part of assessment, family therapy, psychoeducational interventions, and so on. (The need for a multimodal approach to treating traumatized children will be commented upon later in the chapter.) It has been my experience that traumatized children who participate in play therapy will begin to verbalize about traumatic events; however, this is never my requirement (which is not fair to the child) nor my expectation (which will cause me to control the healing process rather than facilitate it).

THE NATURE OF TRAUMA

Among the many sources of trauma that affect children are physical or sexual abuse, chronic neglect, death, natural disasters, war, divorce, injury or illness, and social discrimination (e.g., racism). The common result of these experiences is some level of psychic trauma. Gordon and Wraith (1993, p. 561) discuss the characteristics of this phenomenon, noting that trauma

- is beyond normal experience,
- causes a massive quantity of emotion to be generated,
- violates normal psychological assumptions,
- ruptures expectations about the future,
- ruptures preexisting adaptations,
- ruptures meaning,
- is placed outside time, constantly repeated in the present,
- has an existential dimension.

In his description of childhood victimization, Shengold (1989) reminds us that trauma not only damages children's bodies and emotions, but it also wounds their souls. He uses the graphic and appropriate term *soul murder,* "the dramatic term for circumstances that eventuate in crime—the deliberate attempt to eradicate or compromise the separate identity of another person.... Sexual abuse, emotional deprivation, physical and mental torture can eventuate in *soul murder*....

Children are the usual victims. For the child's almost complete physical and emotional dependence on adults easily makes for possible tyranny and therefore child abuse" (p. 2).

Traumatized children often have views of self that are far from the self-image intended by the Lord. We know that "the thief comes only to steal and kill and destroy" (John 10:10). When children are stolen from and destroyed by traumatizing experiences, the enemy not only robs them of their childhood, but also potentially steals from their adulthood, thus weakening the effectiveness of the church. It is part of our job as Christian counselors to be spoilers of the enemy's plan.

How Children Experience Trauma

It is important to recognize that children experience and view trauma quite differently from the way adults do. Adults generally have greater coping mechanisms as well as established defense mechanisms with which to defend against and process traumatizing experiences. Children are no different from adults when it comes to fearing and being adversely affected by trauma. But the limited understanding and developmental immaturity of children decreases their ability to deal with pain. Understanding the child's world and the child's perspective becomes all the more important when counselors deal with traumatic issues.

Several authors have identified various traumagenic states or conditions in the evaluation and treatment of traumatized children. James's (1989) categorizations of traumagenic states include self-blame, powerlessness, loss and betrayal, fragmentation of bodily experience, stigmatization, eroticization, destructiveness, dissociative or multiple personality disorder, and attachment disorder.

Self-blame is common among children who have been traumatized. When children experience trauma, their inherent egocentrism leads them to believe that they are responsible. Since they instinctively wonder if they caused the trauma, it is crucial that children come to understand and believe the traumatic event was not their fault.

Traumatized children also feel a strong sense of *powerlessness*. They must regain a sense of power and control in their lives. Trauma is overwhelming, and the physiological and psychological immaturity of children exacerbates the effect. Many children hold on to the powerlessness they experienced when they were traumatized. As a result, they develop significantly impaired self-images.

Loss and betrayal greatly affect children who have experienced trauma. Children lose a sense of safety and may feel a loss of security because people have not protected them from trauma. Betrayal, which is essentially a loss of trust, shakes the very foundation of childhood development. Children who experience betrayal view the world as a threatening place and often believe that they do not deserve any better than the traumatizing experience.

The *fragmentation of bodily experience* is very real for many child trauma victims. Children may encode the traumatic event through sensory and muscular memory as well as affective memory. These children do not trust, respect, or feel mastery over their bodies. One reason play therapy is helpful in treating this aspect of trauma is that children have the opportunity to engage all their bodily senses in the therapeutic process to express themselves nonverbally and actively. The psycho-biological effects of trauma are analyzed by van der Kolk (1996).

Stigmatization also marks children who have endured such trauma. They feel an internal sense of shame as well as an external categorization and labeling. These children experience pronounced shame and alienation from others because of the trauma. It is also common to encounter children who have based an inordinate portion of their identity on the trauma. Despite their own efforts to compensate, such children are often stuck in a relentless pursuit of acceptance. Group therapy, both for stigmatized children and the parents of these children, can greatly facilitate the abatement of shame and alienation.

Children who have experienced sexual trauma may experience *eroticization,* which can be quite disturbing to parents, teachers, and even counselors. Through the experience of molestation and rape, children may perceive that their value comes primarily from being sexual; thus, they often become eroticized. In fact, their entire personality may be grounded in the perspective that they are valued only for their sexuality. Social-skills training about appropriate and inappropriate touching may be an important adjunct intervention.

Destructiveness is another hallmark of traumatized children. Many children lose their impulse control, establishing a self-defeating cycle of aggression and destructiveness. This cycle may lead to frightening displays of temper and release of rage. This destructive behavior often causes people to dislike or punish the traumatized child. This, in turn, can cause the hurting child who is acting out to internalize shame and anger even further, which leads to greater displays of destructive behavior. It is important for parents and counselors to work together on behavioral strategies and to provide a play therapy experience for the child.

Dissociative disorders can provide an efficient way for a child to cope with traumatic events. Although defense mechanisms such as denial, repression, and dissociation are seen as dysfunctional, they realistically serve a valid function for the child who experiences trauma. The only way for a child to cope with an uncontrollable situation may be to dissociate. Fragmentation and depersonalization can help protect the child from the overwhelming emotions that come from traumatizing experiences. Although counselors should not reinforce dissociation, they should accept it so that the child may integrate it within the counseling process.

Attachment disorders are also possible responses to trauma. Attachment is vital for survival, so it is understandable that threats to attachment are life-and-death issues for children. They may experience attachment disorders either from repeated traumatizing events or from a single event, such as parental abandonment, the death of a parent, or removal from the home. It is crucial for children who have endured trauma to experience safety and a place to develop positive attachments. The important relationship that is established in play therapy forms a foundation for this to occur.

PLAY AND PLAY THERAPY

Play is the most important and most natural activity of childhood. Throughout history, children have played, and children in all cultures play. For children, play is not just *what they do;* it is an expression of *who they are.* Scripture recognizes play as a natural activity for children: "The city streets will be filled with boys and girls playing there" (Zechariah 8:5). Landreth (1991) notes,

> Children's play can be more fully appreciated when recognized as their nat-
> ural medium of communication. Children express themselves more fully
> and more directly through self-initiated spontaneous play than they do ver-
> bally because they are more comfortable with play. For children to "play
> out" their experiences and feelings is the most natural dynamic and self-
> healing process in which children can engage. (p. 10)

Adult communication is abstract by nature, whereas children are, by their very nature, concrete. Play and language are, therefore, relative opposites, as they are contrasting forms of representation. With cognitive verbalization, children must translate thoughts into the accepted medium (talk). An inherent limitation of most adult therapies is that children must fit their world into this existing medium. Play and fantasy, however, do not carry this limitation. Children can create without the restriction of making their creation understandable.

PLAY THERAPY DEFINED

What is play therapy? This is an important question because many who work with children describe their work as play therapy when it is little more than adult cognitive therapy with the presence of toys. Landreth (1991) defines play therapy as a "dynamic interpersonal relationship between a child and a therapist trained in play therapy procedures who provides selected play materials and facilitates the development of a safe relationship for the child to fully express and explore self [feelings, thoughts, experiences, and behaviors] through the child's natural medium of communication, play" (p. 14). There are a number of crucial elements contained within this definition (Sweeney, 1997):

1. Play and child therapy involve a *dynamic interpersonal relationship,* which is the basis for the Christian faith as well as for therapeutic healing. Without question, therapeutic relationships should be dynamic and interpersonal.

2. The child therapist should be *trained in play therapy procedures.* Providing play media and using talk therapy does *not* turn the process into play therapy. Utilizing adult theory and techniques while sitting on the floor and speaking in a childlike voice does not turn the process into child therapy. Neither does attending a brief workshop or reading a book about child therapy make someone a child therapist. Training is essential.

3. *Selected play materials* should be provided, not just a random collection of toys. The selection should be purposeful and intentional. Several resources provide helpful lists (Landreth, 1991; Martin, 1992; Sweeney, 1997).

4. The child therapist *facilitates the development of a safe relationship.* This is not achieved by following the prescribed agenda of the therapist. Safety grows out of a facilitated process more than a directed one. Growth cannot occur where safety is not present.

5. Children also need to be given the opportunity to *fully express and explore self.* Healthy self-exploration enables children to discover a healthy self-image. Since the healthiest self-image may arguably be to recognize in whose image we have been made, this process moves children closer to their Creator. And, as already noted, child therapy should allow children to use their *natural medium of communication—play.*

THERAPEUTIC RELATIONSHIP

Play therapy focuses on the child rather than on the nature of the child's problem; thus the therapeutic relationship becomes the key to healing. The alliance between the child and the therapist is the single most creative force in the healing process. This connection reflects the Christian life, which is also all about relationship. It is our relationship with the Son of God that brings redemption and wholeness, and we are called as Christians to be in relationship with each other. The counseling techniques and the play materials, as well as other related issues, are important, but they should be considered subordinate to the therapist-child relationship.

When we are willing to enter the world of children, especially the world of traumatized children, we are honoring them. We are also honoring their Creator. Since Scripture reminds us to be like little children in order to enter the kingdom of God, perhaps we learn more about God when we enter the "kingdoms" of our child clients "as little children." We must remember that although we, as adults, may have "put away childish ways," our child clients have not. Our child clients talk like children, think like children, and reason like children. Let's allow them to continue doing so in counseling.

COUNSELING TRAUMATIZED CHILDREN

As previously suggested, children who have been traumatized need a therapeutic experience that is safe and empowering. It should involve their senses and provide them with an opportunity to gain the mastery and control that have been stripped away by the traumatizing experience. I believe that the sensory and kinesthetic quality of play is key in this regard.

This perspective makes both practical and diagnostic sense. The diagnostic criteria for post-traumatic stress disorder (see DSM-IV, APA, 2000), which is frequently diagnosed in cases of trauma, are largely sensory-based. This makes sense because trauma itself is sensory-based. It would seem logical, therefore, that treatment also be sensory-based. Talk-based counseling approaches do not meet this need. Terr (1990) suggested that "children show a healthy tendency to cope with external difficulties and inner feelings through play. Post-traumatic play, however pathological it is, can be effectively used therapeutically. It is, in fact, the most potent way to effect internal changes in young, traumatized children" (p. 299).

Landreth et al. (1996) further emphasize this point:

> Psychological trauma is an extremely stressful event or happening that is usually atypical in the life experiences of the child and is remarkably distressing to the child to the point of being overwhelming and causing the child to be unable to cope. Young children should not be expected to verbally describe such experiences because they do not have the verbal facility required to do so, and such experiences are usually too threatening for the child to consciously describe. The natural reaction of children is to re-enact or play out the traumatic experience in an unconscious effort to comprehend, overcome, develop a sense of control, or assimilate the experience. This repetitive playing out of the experience is the child's natural self-healing process. (p. 241)

Consider the following key points regarding traumatized children and play therapy:

1. *Working through the pain.* For the child who has been traumatized, being placed in a room with a strange adult who is asking questions about the trauma is yet another disempowering experience. Furthermore, since questions inherently cause a person to think and thus to remain in a cognitive realm, the issues of the heart might not even be adequately dealt with. (As Proverbs 4:23 says, the heart is "the wellspring of life.") Allowing children to "talk" on their own terms and at their own level provides a forum where the issues of the heart can be safely addressed. Through play, the traumatized child can process intrapsychic pain in a safe and therapeutically distant way.

2. *Working through painful memories.* The therapeutic distance of play therapy provides children with the opportunity to abreact in order to resolve traumatic experiences. *Abreaction* is a process in which memories of trauma are brought to the surface with a corresponding release of emotion. Schaefer (1994) suggests several properties that allow play to provide the sense of distance and the resultant sense of safety that children experience:

- *Symbolization:* Children can use a toy (e.g., a predatory animal) to represent an abuser.
- *"As if" quality:* Children can use the pretend quality of play to act out events as if they are not real life.
- *Projection:* Children can project their intense emotions onto puppets or toy animals, which can then safely "act out" those feelings.
- *Displacement:* Children can displace negative feelings onto dolls and other toys rather than express them toward family members.

Children need to have the freedom to use this therapeutic distance without the therapist's probing questions and interpretations. I do not believe that interpretation of the play behavior is essential to the healing process. I often need to remind myself that when I interpret, I do so with an adult's mind and experience, not a child's. We need to be careful in interpreting a child's expression of an experience, and we need to remember that sharing the interpretation is meant to serve the client's need and not the therapist's. Therapeutic progress for traumatized children does not come through the therapist's interpretation of the play, but through the *process* of the play.

3. *Regression in play therapy.* Traumatized children will often experience regression in the play. The child who was hurt at age four and enters therapy at age seven will often regress to age four in the play while acting out the trauma. It is also possible that this child will regress to an age earlier than the age of the trauma in order

to experience within the fantasy of the play what life was like before the trauma. It is also common for the traumatized child to regress a little bit in the play to test the therapist's level of acceptance. When children find that it is safe to regress a little bit, they will feel safe to go further and further, until they are able to bring the play back to the trauma itself.

Following this regression and abreaction, traumatized children often will further test limits in play (which, in fact, is testing the relationship) and, in doing so, will often be able to gain the impulse control that is a problem for many traumatized children. Additionally, many traumatized children experience some level of developmental arrest. As the children have the opportunity to process the trauma through play, they will be able to progress to the appropriate developmental level. Quite simply, after the *re*gression comes *pro*gression.

Play is simply a child's way of making sense of the traumatic event. In children's efforts to make sense of what happened to them, they often act out after a traumatic event. Post-trauma reactions can be seen in their behavior, their affect, and certainly their play. Children's wounds begin to heal as they build a relationship with a counselor who understands and accepts them, as they experience the therapeutic distance of the play therapy setting, and as they process issues in their natural medium of communication. Piers and Landau (1980) assert,

> Children actually heal themselves of emotional injuries through play, coping with and mastering potentially devastating occurrences.... Without the chance to experience the natural healing power of imaginative play, the emotional wounds caused by such events might never close, leaving the child with a lifelong residue of anxiety and insecurity. If children did not play, they could not thrive, and they might not survive. (p. 16)

SUMMARY OF PRINCIPLES

As previously noted, children who have experienced trauma often need a multimodal approach to treatment. With play therapy as a foundational element in the treatment process, the counselor should consider the need for any and all available resources. Some of these include social support, parent training, behavior management, pharmacotherapy, sensory integration therapy, recreational therapy, psychoeducational interventions, group play therapy (see Sweeney & Homeyer, 1999), inpatient care, and various other adjuncts.

Finally, therapists must consider many issues when counseling children who have experienced trauma. Although not a complete list, I propose the following summary as some fundamental considerations when working with this challenging population:

- Traumatized children, like all children, naturally communicate through play. Effective counseling of these children should, therefore, take a play therapy approach.
- Trauma is extraordinarily intrusive. Therefore, the therapist's interventions should be nonintrusive, allowing the child sufficient freedom to explore, process, and grow.
- While children must explore and work through their pain in the therapeutic process, verbal acknowledgment is *not* always necessary.
- Trauma most often occurs within the framework of the family. Thus, family therapy and parent training may be crucial elements of the therapeutic milieu.
- Additionally, because of this relational framework, children can benefit from the experience of building a safe, appropriate, and affirming *relationship* with a trusted helper.
- Children who have been traumatized may be vulnerable to secondary trauma related to the original experience because of psychological and physical maturation. Treatment of these children may need to be ordered and cycled over time to respond to these development vulnerabilities.
- Positive and affirming therapeutic messages should be frequent and passionate if the wounded and hypervigilant child is to hear and feel them. The low self-esteem and lack of self-acceptance that traumatized children feel must be actively worked against.
- Abused children are often forced, shamed, or threatened to keep the abuse secret. The therapist must be intentional about allowing and promoting self-expression.
- Traumatized children often employ elaborate or bizarre defense mechanisms in order to cope with the trauma. While this should be addressed, these defenses should not be torn away by professionals. Indeed, such defenses must be given a place for full expression.
- The needs of the child may not be entirely met by a therapist working without the support of others involved with the child. A treatment team, including medical, legal, agency representatives, and, perhaps most important, the child's caregivers, is frequently necessary.
- Treatment must attend to a continuum of issues, including physiological, cognitive, psychological, and spiritual. Trauma may involve damage to any and all of these areas.

- Because of the developmental process of therapy and the developmental change of children in therapy, ongoing assessment is crucial.
- Trauma is an experience that may be sudden, chronic, or forced. Counseling should, therefore, be gradual and facilitative instead of forced by therapeutic prescription.
- Children who have experienced trauma frequently evidence damaged or distorted boundaries. These children should benefit from learning skills to employ in both difficult and everyday circumstances. Group psychoeducational work may be helpful.
- Clinical work in the area of trauma often involves direct encounters with horrible and horrifying circumstances. Never underestimate the professional and personal impact of this on the therapist.
- The focus of treatment should never be the trauma or the child's symptomatic response to the trauma. The focus of treatment should always be the child.

THE CURATIVE POWER OF PLAY

Consider how Christ would have ministered to the needs of the hurting and traumatized child during his time on earth. He was clearly a busy man with many demands placed upon his time and attention. Yet so often we see in the Gospels how Jesus took time to make individual contact with people in need. We know that he did not shy away from people with all manner of pain and disease. He brushed aside the objections of his disciples (even rebuking them) when they tried to prevent children from making contact with him. Jesus ministered to children and he touched them, laying on his hands of blessing.

Following Jesus' example, we need to enable wounded children to work through their pain through play. If traumatized children do not have the opportunity to experience the curative power of play, the emotional wounds might never heal. We as Christian counselors must not allow a generation of hurting children to live out their lives in fear and anxiety. Despite what the adage says, time does not heal wounds. Rather, it is the power of relationship that heals wounds—relationship with God and with his children. Neale (1969) wrote: "Consider the play of the child, and the nature of the Kingdom will be revealed. Christ is that fiddler who plays so sweetly that all who hear him begin to dance" (p. 174).

For the sake of the children, let's join in the play.

CHAPTER 26

COUNSELING ADOLESCENTS

Serving the Struggle for Identity and Place in the World

LES PARROTT AND LESLIE PARROTT

The physical and emotional tumult of the teen years has always presented multiple problems and challenges. But today's youth struggle with many issues that most of their parents would find difficult to bear. Many teens show incredible resilience in the face of difficult circumstances. Some cope admirably, against all odds. Others, however, become casualties of the dangerous road to adulthood.

—JOSH MCDOWELL AND DICK DAY,
Why Wait? What You Need to Know About Teen Sexuality

During World War II, Erik H. Erikson coined a phrase that stuck: *identity crisis*. He used it to describe the disorientation of shell-shocked soldiers who could not remember their names. Through the years this phrase has become a useful tool to describe the struggle of growing up.

Achieving a sense of identity is the major developmental task of teenagers. Like a stunned soldier in a state of confusion, sooner or later young people are hit with a bomb that is more powerful than dynamite: puberty. Somewhere between childhood and maturity their bodies kick into overdrive. With this acceleration of physical and emotional growth, they become strangers to themselves. Under attack by an arsenal of fiery hormones, the bewildered young person begins to ask, "Who am I?"

THE CHALLENGE OF IDENTITY FORMATION

While achievement of a meaningful answer to this question is a lifelong pursuit, it is the burning challenge of adolescence. According to Erikson (1968) having an identity—knowing who you are—gives adolescents a sense of control that allows them to navigate through the rest of life.

Without identities, awkward adolescents carry a How'm-I-doing? attitude that is always focused on their concern about the impressions they are making on others. Without self-identities they will be or do whatever they think others want. They will flounder from one way of acting to another, never able to step outside a preoccupation with their own performance, and genuinely ask others, "How are *you* doing?" Erikson (1968) calls this miserable state "identity diffusion."

The successful formation of self-identity follows a typical pattern. Teens identify with people they admire. Whether in real life or through magazines and television, they emulate the characteristics of people they want to be like. By the end of adolescence, if all goes as it should, these identifications merge into a single identity that incorporates and alters previous identifications to make a unique and coherent whole.

The quest for identity is scary. Somewhere between twelve and twenty years of age adolescents are forced to choose once and for all what their identity is to be. It is a formidable task. Uncertain which of their mixed emotions are really their true feelings, they are pushed to make up their minds. Their confusion is complicated further when they begin to guess what others, whose opinions they care about, want them to be.

Four Fundamental Views of the Self

Arkoff (1980) postulated four fundamental ways in which adolescents view themselves:

1. *The subjective self* is the private view adolescents have of who they see themselves to be. Although this self-view has been heavily influenced by parents and has been hammered out in interactions with peers, it is still one's own assessment.
2. *The objective self* is the way others see adolescents. It is what others think they are.
3. *The social self* is the perception adolescents have of themselves as they think others see them. It is what they think they look like to others.
4. *The ideal self* is the concept adolescents have of who they would like to become—their ultimate goal for themselves.

For adolescents who never achieve an integrated identity, "All the world's a stage." In their adult years they will play the part of human beings who change roles to please whoever happens to be watching. Their clothes, their language, their thoughts, and their feelings are all a part of the script. Their purpose will be to receive approval from those they hope to impress. Life will become a charade, and players will never enjoy the security of personal identity or experience the strength that comes from a sense of self-worth.

How Adolescents Search for Identity

Young people look for identity in countless ways. In this section, seven common paths are examined: family relationships, status symbols, grown-up behavior, rebellion, others' opinions, idols, and cliques.

1. *Through family relationships.* Adolescents' families have significant impact on identity formation. To assert individuality and move out of childhood, teenagers will wean themselves from their protecting parents. But individuality may also be found in reaction to the identities of one's brothers and sisters. If the first child, for example, decides to be a serious intellectual, the second may seek individuality by becoming a jokester. Seeing these places already taken, the third child may choose to be an athlete. In some cases, when young people feel they possess no distinctive talents, they may rebel by separating themselves from the accepted standards. They may become delinquents or prodigals and gain identity by causing trouble.

2. *Through status symbols.* Adolescents try to establish themselves as individuals through prestige. They seek out behavior or possessions that are readily observable. They purchase sports cars, hairstyles, letter jackets, skateboards, guitars, stereos, and designer clothes in hope of being identified as people who belong. Their status symbols help teens form self-identity because they are the trappings of the groups the teens aspire to be part of: the jocks, the brains, the party types, the gearheads, the rockers. Owning status symbols, however, is not enough to achieve identity. Adolescents quickly recognize a struggling peer's attempts to carve out an identity by buying the right status symbols. In fact, they enjoy detecting these imposters and reinforcing their own identities by labeling them as "wannabes" or "posers."

To be authentic, appropriate behavior must accompany the status symbol. A "party girl," for example, must not only wear the right clothes, have the right hairstyle, and buy the right music, but she must also do the things a party girl does. Soon the behavior will earn the adolescent a reputation, something she must live up to if she is to maintain her identity and something she must live down if she is to change it.

3. *Through grown-up behavior.* Adolescents have a strong desire to be like adults. The more mature they appear, the more recognition they receive, and the closer they get to feeling that they have achieved an identity. Because real maturity is not always visible, young people often resort to behavior that is symbolic of adults. They engage in taboo pleasures—the things parents, preachers, and teachers say they are too young to do.

The most common of these taboo pleasures are tobacco, alcohol, drugs, and premarital sex. By the time adolescents reach high school, smoking is a widespread practice. Drinking is a status symbol for girls as well as for boys, often beginning in the junior high school years. And as with drinking, doing drugs usually begins as a group activity.

Statistics on the number of sexually active adolescents are staggering (McDowell & Day, 1987). Teens engage in these behaviors to gain independence from family restrictions, to increase their social acceptance, to experience adventure, or to satisfy curiosity (Smith & Fogg, 1974). Nearly every adolescent will experiment with these "adult" behaviors at some point, but certain adolescents will struggle intensely in these areas.

4. *Through rebellion.* Rebellion is a logical consequence of young people's attempts to resolve incongruent ideas and find authentic identity. Rebellion results from a desire to be unique yet still maintain the security of sameness. "But, Dad, I gotta be a nonconformist," the teenager says to his father. "How else can I be like the other kids?"

A rebellious attitude is frequently accompanied by an idealism that prompts adolescents to reject the values of family, school, society, and church. However, their oversimplified and unrealistic ideals often are found to be impractical and are rarely held for any significant duration.

5. *Through others' opinions.* Essential to identity formation is the validation of one's self-image by other people. Adolescents' perceptions of themselves change

---

Box 26.1—Helping Adolescents in Their Quest for Identity

- Ask teens to write "Who am I?" at the top of a sheet of paper and then quickly to write twenty answers to the question. Analyze the answers and discuss the process as well as the content. Did the teens self-censor any responses?
- Using old magazines, ask teens to create collages—one titled "Who I Am" and another titled "Who I Would Like to Be." When the collages are completed, ask teens to write a description of each, indicating the meaning of the pictures they selected. Ask what they learned about themselves.
- To help adolescents discover what is most stable and enduring about their identity, have them draw a set of three concentric circles. In the innermost circle, have them list or describe those aspects of themselves—qualities, behaviors, values, and goals—that are most important and resistant to change. In the outermost circle, have them identify the least important and least stable aspects of themselves. The middle circle is for those aspects of intermediate importance.

depending on what they believe others think about them. For example, if a young person sees himself as a talented actor but is not offered the lead role in the school play, his identity as an actor may be weakened, and he may try to find his identity in academics or sports. If, however, he hears that others believe it was a mistake not to cast him as the lead, his identity may be maintained.

Adolescents do not always fall in line with what others think of them. In fact, because adolescent identity is shaped by their perception of how others see them, they may change in order to contradict their perceptions, even if those perceptions are positive. It may be harmful to tell young people they won't have any problems, that they are the best, or that they will someday be the greatest. Aware of their weaknesses, they feel uncomfortable with an affirmation that leaves no room for error. They will go out of their way to prove parents and counselors wrong and to relieve themselves of the burden of being perfect. For some, relief will come only in identifying with what they are least supposed to be, not in being something that is unattainable (Erikson, 1968).

6. *Through idols.* Especially in their early years, adolescents often overidentify with famous people to the point of apparent loss of their own individuality. In our star-conscious society, literally thousands of rock stars, professional athletes, movie actors, and television personalities are available for teenagers to idolize. Celebrities become models because adolescents are looking for ways to experiment with different roles. In their search for identity, they latch on to notable personalities in order to explore different aspects of themselves. Idols allow them to test new behaviors and attitudes before incorporating them into their own identities. Idolizing celebrities does not necessarily mean that adolescents endorse their idols' lifestyles or values.

7. *Through cliquish exclusion.* In their search for identity, adolescents may become remarkably intolerant and even cruel as they exclude others on the basis of minor issues such as dress. They persistently try to define, overdefine, and re-define themselves in relation to others. If they see something in peers that reminds them of what they don't want to be, they will scorn and avoid those people and feel not an ounce of remorse. Teens strengthen their sense of self through ruthless comparisons and persistent exclusions. Erikson (1965) sees the cliquishness of ado-lescence and its intolerance of differences as a defense against identity confusion. Usually, in the late teens, adolescents realize that it takes a well-established identity to tolerate radical differences.

WHY ADOLESCENTS STRUGGLE WITH IDENTITY DEVELOPMENT

The establishment of a personal identity is not easy. The danger of identity con-fusion lurks around every bend. Erikson (1965) points out that some confused young people, as in the case of Hamlet, take an excessively long time to reach adulthood. They may regress into a childish state and thus avoid having to make decisions on confusing issues. Other adolescents express their confusion through premature commitments and impulsive actions. They give in to poorly thought-out ways of being and end up fighting needless battles.

Adolescence is a period of stress and turmoil for many young people (Arnett, 1999). While the difficulties that occur in adolescence are due in part to lack of experience, at least five common changes may exacerbate or create significant struggles: physical, sexual, social, religious, and moral.

1. *Physical changes.* A fourteen-year-old tried to excuse his poor report card by saying, "My problem is not tests, but testosterone." He had a legitimate argument. The biochemical changes in adolescence may cause more apprehension than studying for an exam. Waking up with pimples, having your voice crack in public, wearing new jeans that are already too short, and growing new facial hair or beginning menstruation and breast development—all of these are traumatic. As hormones set in motion the chain of physiological events that usher in adulthood, nice kids seem to turn into moody, rebellious adolescents. In fact, some parents with well-behaved teenagers worry that their kids aren't developing properly.

2. *Sexual changes.* As the adolescent's body begins to take on the characteristic shape of his or her gender, new behaviors, thoughts, and physiological processes occur. Each adolescent reacts to the cultural stereotype of sexual changes. The adolescent boy encounters locker-room comparisons and wonders if his genitals are too small and why he hasn't begun to shave yet. If he gets an erection while dancing with a girl or while reading or merely thinking, he may suffer from a sense that his body has betrayed him. He might resent the lack of control he has over his body and feel he is doing something wrong.

The adolescent girl also experiences confusion and shame about her sexual maturation. Menstruation is a serious concern, often compounded by fear and ignorance. It may cause physical discomfort, weight gain, headaches, mood swings, and other discomfiting events. Because it is commonly referred to as "the curse," a girl's period may encourage her to play the passive role of a martyr. It is not surprising that even the anticipation of this change contributes to other common struggles.

3. *Social changes.* While the biological changes of puberty are dramatic, they are no more significant than the social changes that occur during adolescence. Between the sixth and eighth grades, the structure of school becomes quite different. Most young adolescents move from a relatively small neighborhood elementary school to a much larger, more impersonal junior high school. This move has

many social ramifications. It disrupts the old peer-group structure, exposes students to different achievement expectations by teachers, and provides new opportunities for different extracurricular activities.

Family relations also shift as boys and girls become teenagers. Conflicts in family discussions increase. Male adolescents become more dominant in conversations, especially with their mothers. Feelings of affection toward their parents decline from the sixth to the eighth grades. This does not mean it necessarily becomes negative, but that the change is from very positive to less positive.

4. *Religious changes.* Contrary to popular opinion, adolescents are genuinely interested in religion and feel that it plays an important role in their lives. However, adolescence is a time when young people question the religious concepts and beliefs of their childhood. They may become skeptical of religious forms, such as prayer, and later begin to doubt the nature of God. This is sometimes mistakenly interpreted as skepticism or doubt when, in reality, it is sincere questioning. Adolescents investigate their religion in a quest to make their faith their own rather than that of their parents. They question not because they want to become agnostic or atheistic, but because they want to accept religion in a way that is meaningful to them. Still, this quest is often frightening to parents, as their adolescent's search for faith may lead to involvement in destructive religious cults or to other problems.

5. *Moral changes.* An important change occurs in adolescents when they realize that their behavior must conform to social expectations without the constant guidance, supervision, and threats of punishment they experienced as children. To become adults, they must replace specific childhood rules with their own moral principles. Mitchell (1975) identifies five basic changes that occur in the moral thinking of adolescents:

1. They become more abstract and less concrete.
2. They become more concerned with what is right and less concerned with what is wrong.
3. They become more cognitive and less emotional.
4. They become more altruistic and less egocentric.
5. They become more willing to exert emotional energy on moral issues.

During adolescence, according to Kohlberg (1969), teens reach a stage of moral development that is based on respect for others rather than on personal desires. While adolescents are intellectually capable of making this change and creating their own moral code, the task is difficult (Piaget, 1969). Every day adolescents see inconsistencies in moral standards. As they interact with peers of different religious, racial, or socioeconomic backgrounds, they recognize that people have different codes of right and wrong. Some fail to make the shift to adult morality during adolescence and must finish the task in early adulthood. Others not only fail to make the shift but also build a moral code on socially unacceptable moral concepts.

Physical, sexual, social, religious, and moral changes all contribute to the adolescent struggle for identity and may contribute to potential complications and possible problems.

WHAT ADOLESCENTS DO WITH THEIR STRUGGLES

It is difficult to predict exactly how a specific adolescent will attempt to manage his or her problems. A number of personality traits and environmental factors influence the struggling adolescent's coping style. There are, however, at least three common ways young people contend with their struggles. They (1) hold them in, (2) act them out, or (3) work them through (see Olson, 1984).

Hold them in. Many adolescents cope with their difficulties by keeping them to themselves. Like Adam and Eve hiding in the bushes, these adolescents camouflage their struggles, hoping they will eventually disappear. Some conceal their anxiety by *blocking,* allowing unconscious conflicts to interrupt thoughts. Tony, for example, is troubled by sexual fantasies about a girl he was assigned to work with in his social studies class. At the dinner table he begins to tell his parents about the project. He suddenly gets confused and "forgets" what the project is.

Another way adolescents hide their problems is through *sublimation,* transforming unacceptable impulses into behaviors that are more socially acceptable. Angry at his alcoholic father, a young man might disguise his hostility by pouring a tremendous amount of energy into basketball.

Adolescents who feel hurt sometimes hide their struggles through *emotional insulation,* keeping potential pain at bay. For example, Carla, a junior in high school, has just been asked to the prom by the boy of her dreams. In order to avoid any possibility of being disappointed, she feels no excitement or joy. She becomes numb for fear that he might drop her at the last minute.

Related to emotional insulation is *intellectualization,* interpreting a situation only at a cognitive level in order to avoid dealing with uncomfortable feelings. When asked how he was doing after being cut from the school drama tryouts, Kevin, who actually feels deeply hurt, responds, "I think it's all for the best. God is in charge, and he's really teaching me to be a better person through this. It's probably the best thing that could have happened to me."

Perhaps the most common form of hiding one's struggles is through *repression,* pushing thoughts, feelings, impulses, desires, or memories out of awareness. Take Mike, who has grown up in the church and is sincerely seeking answers to some of life's difficult questions. He begins to doubt God's existence but quickly forces this questioning from his awareness because it is "bad." Later this repressed doubt shows up as an inability to be genuine with other feelings. He fails to show normal emotions, and he becomes legalistic.

Act them out. Some adolescents cope with struggles by *acting out,* expressing their feelings through impulsive actions in order to reduce tension. The anxiety they feel about failing a class, for example, is temporarily released through truancy, harassment of other young people, or vandalism. The tension they feel over not being accepted by their peers may be acted out through sexual promiscuity.

Adolescents act out in several ways. They sometimes act out their struggles by *displacement,* transferring feelings to a more neutral object. The fifteen-year-old who is angry at his mom might kick over a neighbor's garbage can on his way to school. The payoff is obvious. Telling off one's parents may have costly side effects, but kicking garbage cans vents the hostility for free.

Another way of acting out comes in the form of *regression,* retreating to an earlier developmental period that was less stressful. If Wendy, fourteen, is denied her desire to stay out with her friends past midnight, she may regress to childish behavior and relieve some of her frustration by sulking, crying, or throwing temper tantrums.

Adolescents who are afraid of their own thoughts or impulses may act them out through *projection,* putting them onto another person. Neal, a sixteen-year-old jock, becomes convinced that Craig is a homosexual. To ward off fears of his own sexuality, Neal transfers his sexual confusion onto Craig and acts out his anger by ridiculing him in front of other teammates.

Another common way of warding off uncomfortable emotions is through *denial,* refusing to accept reality. Wayne does this by partying. Regardless of the problem—poor grades, a broken home, depression, anger, and so on—Wayne denies the reality of his pain with two words: "Party, dude!" He avoids having to face up to his struggles by simply pretending they don't exist, "celebrating" through truant behavior, hanging out at the park, and drinking.

Work them through. Adolescents who hide their struggles and the ones who act them out have at least one characteristic in common. Both are avoiding *responsibility,* the freedom to consciously choose their actions and attitudes. Both are hung up at some level in their thinking and suffer from a tendency to wonder why others do not fix their problems. Glasser (1972) sees this lack of responsibility as the central cause of adolescent struggles and even juvenile delinquency. He claims that young people have problems in proportion to the degree that they avoid taking responsibility for their actions or attitudes.

By holding their struggles in or acting them out, adolescents avoid having to confront them head-on. It's not that they do not have the capacity to take responsibility. Most psychologists agree with developmental expert Piaget (1969) that, by adolescence, young people are moving beyond concrete thinking and reaching a stage he calls "formal operations." They are able to look past what seems unchangeable, weed out irrelevant issues, and consider ramifications of choices they were unable to distinguish as children.

Adolescents are capable of understanding the present and imagining the future. They can think abstractly and consider the consequences of their actions. Adolescents have the capacity to say, "The trouble with me is *me,* and I am going to do something about it."

Like most abilities, responsibility is best seen on a continuum. In extreme cases of psychosis, people are simply unable to recognize that they have a choice. For example, the paranoid schizophrenic, who believes someone is out to get him, believes he can do absolutely nothing to change his situation. At the other extreme, some people take on too much responsibility, feeling guilty about things for which they have no responsibility (the teenager, for example, who feels guilty about her father's death because she was away at school when he died).

The majority of young people are somewhere between these extremes. The competent Christian counselor or youth worker will help them understand that they are sometimes responsible for the things that happen to them and that, even when they are not, they are free to choose attitudes that will help them transcend debilitating struggles.

This chapter is designed to help you guide the adolescents with whom you work to a place where they squarely face their struggles and choose to work through them. The techniques outlined in the sections that follow will help you allow adolescents to become their own counselors. When adolescents are able to solve their problems with reasonable success and to feel increasingly confident in their abilities to cope, their periods of struggle gradually become less frequent and less intense. Only then will fulfillment begin to outweigh struggle.

Characteristics of Effective Helping with Adolescents

As has been shown in this book, the single most important factor in effective counseling is the personhood of the counselor, regardless of education, training, theoretical orientation, or counseling technique. It is now widely accepted that if certain qualities are not brought to the helping relationship by the counselor, little chance of successful intervention exists (Brenner, 1982). The self-inventory in box 26.2 will help you determine the degree to which these traits are present in your approach.

The Effective Counselor

The most important instrument you have to help adolescents is *you* (Parrott, 1997). Who you are as a person is critical in determining the effectiveness of your

---

Box 26.2—A Self-Inventory on Counseling Effectiveness

For each statement, indicate the response that best identifies your beliefs and attitudes. Keep in mind that the "right" answer is the one that best expresses your thoughts at this time. Use the following code:

> 5 = I strongly agree
> 4 = I agree
> 3 = I am undecided
> 2 = I disagree
> 1 = I strongly disagree

1. Giving advice has little to do with good counseling.
2. I can accept and respect people who disagree with me.
3. I can make a mistake and admit it.
4. I look at everybody's side of a disagreement before I make a decision.
5. I tend to trust my intuition even when I'm unsure of the outcome.
6. I don't need to see immediate and concrete results in order to know progress is occurring.
7. Who you are in counseling is more important than what you do.
8. My presence frees others from the threat of external evaluation.
9. In a tense emotional situation I tend to remain calm.
10. I know my limits when it comes to helping others.

Total your responses to determine the degree to which you have the qualities necessary to be an effective counselor:

40–50: You are well on your way to being an effective counselor; take special care to maintain the qualities you have.

30–39: You have what it takes to be effective, but you will need to exert special effort to groom the traits described in this chapter.

Below 30: Seek out an occupational counselor who can assess your strengths more accurately.

counseling. This understanding, however, does not diminish the importance of the Holy Spirit. The point is that your attitude and behavior either help or hinder any healing work the Holy Spirit is prepared to do through you.

Many researchers have attempted to identify the qualities that contribute to successful counseling. They have discovered the importance of sensitivity, hope, compassion, control, awareness, and knowledge. The list could fill several pages. However, Rogers, Gendlin, Kiesler, and Traux (1967) conducted a four-year study that has been supported by subsequent research and is cited in nearly every text on counseling. The findings are unequivocal: People are more likely to improve when their counselors are (1) warm, (2) genuine, and (3) empathic. (See also chapters 8, 9, and 10.) If the counselor does not embody these traits, a client's condition may actually worsen regardless of the counselor's technical knowledge.

Warmth. Paul Tournier, the renowned Swiss counselor, said, "I have no methods. All I do is accept people." The key to nonpossessive warmth is acceptance. It is an attitude that does not evaluate or require change; it simply accepts the thoughts, feelings, and actions of the client. This warmth helps a teen develop a base of self-worth: "If my counselor cares about me, maybe I am valuable."

Nonpossessive warmth is not necessarily approving of everything a client does. Collins (1988) recounts how in John 4 Jesus showed warmth to the woman at the well: "Her morals may have been low, and he certainly never condoned sinful behavior. But Jesus nevertheless respected the woman and treated her as a person of worth. His warm, caring attitude must have been apparent wherever he went" (p. 168).

Nor is this warmth a kind of smothering sentimentality. It does not skip through the counseling session whistling a happy tune and tossing out platitudes and contrived emotion. Through unconditional warmth we invite struggling adolescents to catch glimpses of God's grace. And grace is the bedrock of growth. When adolescents feel sure they will not be condemned for who they are and that the counselor will make no judgment of them, the power of God's grace begins to turn the wheels of change. Unconditional warmth frees adolescents from attempting to win your approval. Young people no longer wonder whether they are loved for who they are or for what they do. Why does this matter? Because teenagers who feel a need to perform to get approval will be troubled by a nagging uncertainty over whether you genuinely accept them. And in their relationship with God, they will continually chase the carrot of divine approval.

Nonpossessive warmth provides a springboard for struggling adolescents to accept themselves and become strong individuals who do not compulsively conform their personalities to what others wish them to be.

Genuineness. Without honesty there is no way to touch hurting teenagers.

Adolescents have built-in radar that spots phoniness even at a distance. They are experts at detecting fabricated feelings and insincere intentions. To every overture of help they apply their own polygraph test. Honest thoughts and authentic feelings may be verbally expressed at appropriate times, but it is just as important for genuineness to come through in all its subtle forms such as your body language, eye contact, and facial expressions.

Genuineness cannot be faked. Either you sincerely want to help, or you are simply playing the sterile role of a "helper," hiding behind masks, defenses, or facades. Authenticity is something you *are,* not something you *do.* Genuineness has been described as a lure to the heart. Jesus said, "Blessed are the pure in heart." Or to put it another way, "Consider the counselor in whom there is no guile." When genuineness is present, a hesitant and skeptical adolescent is likely to stay with you and invest energy in the counseling process.

Empathy. The best way to avoid stepping on adolescents' toes is to put yourself in their sneakers. I don't know who said that first, but it's surely true. Empathy lets struggling adolescents know that you hear their words, understand their thoughts, and sense their feelings. This does not mean that you necessarily understand all that is going on in their lives; it means you understand what they feel and think. Empathy is void of judgment and says, "If I were you, I would act as you do; I understand why you feel the way you feel."

Two important distinctions about empathy are helpful.

1. Empathy is not identification. You don't need to wear faded jeans and blare rock music on your car radio to enter the adolescent's world. In fact, teenagers want to be seen as unique and complex. They resent blatant attempts by adults to identify with them. To say "I know exactly how you feel" to a struggling adolescent is like telling a Vietnam veteran that his post-traumatic stress is easy and simple to understand.

2. Empathy is deeper and stronger than sympathy. *Sympathy* is standing on the shore and throwing out a lifeline; *empathy* is jumping into the water and risking one's safety to help another. And the risk is real. In empathy we risk personal change. Understanding the aching heart of a struggling adolescent *will* change you in spite of the human tendency to resist change. Yet when we have the courage to enter the pain of a hurting teenager, we begin to build a relationship in which healing can occur.

Maintaining Warmth, Genuineness, and Empathy

Stop and assess. To maintain the qualities of warmth, genuineness, and empathy, routinely ask yourself these questions:

- Do I honestly accept this adolescent without requiring change? Do I value her in spite of her thoughts, feelings, or behavior?
- Am I more concerned about doing the right things as a counselor than with being who I am as a person? Am I aware of my emotions when I am with others?
- How would I act, think, and feel if I were in this adolescent's situation? Do I understand her so accurately that I have no desire to judge her?

Necessary but not sufficient. Although warmth, genuineness, and empathy are critical for effective counseling, they do not assure success. They are necessary but not sufficient. Persons who possess these qualities will still vary in their effectiveness as counselors. Also crucial to effective counseling is the practice of active listening, which we address later in this chapter, as well as a working knowledge of when and how to use practical techniques that have proven helpful in alleviating specific struggles.

Beware of excessive emphasis on techniques. We counselors are not technicians with boxes of gimmicks and quick fixes. The methods and techniques recommended in this book must be enhanced by counselors' warmth, genuineness, and empathy. The result will be meaningful expressions of love and more effective outcomes for our clients.

LEGAL AND ETHICAL CONCERNS

Adolescents present unique practice considerations because of their dependency upon parents or legal guardians. Parent(s) or guardian(s) must be consulted or related to as an integral part of counseling minors, which is one of the foremost reasons for using family- and systems-oriented psychotherapies.

PRIVACY RIGHTS AND REPORTING DUTIES

Generally, parents have the right to control private information regarding their minor children; this includes the right to know certain information. For example, a mental health professional normally must advise parents when treating minors for sexual assault or substance abuse. In fact, most counseling situations involving a minor require parental notification and consent.

However, in some situations the parents do not control the child's private information or decisions regarding treatment help. A child over age fourteen (or fifteen or sixteen, depending on your state) can be treated for a time without the parent's consent if, in the professional opinion of the counselor (1) the child is mature enough to participate intelligently in outpatient counseling, (2) it is not in the child's best interests to contact the parents (high abuse risk, for example), and (3) the child meets one or more of the following conditions. The minor must

- present a danger of serious physical harm to self or others, or
- have been the victim of child abuse or neglect, or
- have been sexually active and be pregnant or have contracted an STD, or
- have a drug- or alcohol-related problem.

The counselor must note in the clinical record what efforts, if any, were made to involve the parents in counseling and, if none, why it was unnecessary or inappropriate to contact them.

If the therapist has knowledge or reasonable suspicion that the child is a victim of child abuse, this information must be reported to the proper authorities (Ohlschlager & Mosgofian, 1992). It may also be necessary to contact authorities or arrange for hospitalization if a child client is under sixteen and if the therapist has reasonable cause to believe that he or she is the victim of a crime and that the disclosure of this information is in the best interests of the child—or if the therapist believes that the child's emotional state is such that he or she is a danger to self, other people, or property.

CONSENT FOR TREATMENT

Since parents generally have access to their child's records, it is best to either inform the child of this status or to have the parent(s) sign a consent to treatment that releases the child to treatment without the concern of disclosure to the parent. In this regard, it is important to distinguish children younger than fourteen as clients with whom the therapist should not suggest an ability to maintain confidentiality. This is a general rule and can vary depending on the situation. However, much research supports the concept that many minors older than fourteen are capable of making well-informed treatment decisions.

For those minors fourteen and older, it is often helpful if the therapist provides a pretreatment family meeting in which the parameters of therapy and confidentiality are discussed. Then a written service agreement can be signed spelling out the limits and conditions of confidentiality. Also, the extent of family involvement should be discussed and agreed upon prior to treatment. All participating parties should sign the agreement, and it should be placed in the client's file.

If you are going to convince the older child of the therapeutic value of sharing personal information, you need to be able to assure him or her that most of this information will be kept confidential. The use of written agreements for treating children requires emphasizing to parents that the counselor will give a summary of information and progress but not details about what the child shares in the counseling appointment. If a parent should refuse to cooperate with your request for confidentiality, then it would be best to resolve this matter in consultation with the child and parent before proceeding with therapy. The parent or guardian may have a valid reason for not wanting to sign such an agreement, and it behooves the counselor to explore those reasons in an initial appointment with the parent(s) before continuing with the child.

Awkward legal and ethical dilemmas may result if the counselor refuses treatment to the child because the parent(s) will not comply with a signed release. Ultimately the parent(s) or legal guardian(s) are responsible for payment, so seeing a child without parental consent may lead to no payment. Then the counselor is left with some tough choices. If the counselor is unable to refer the minor to another professional who can treat for no cost, or if the counselor simply stops seeing the minor, it may qualify as abandonment. When the counselor is already involved in a counseling situation that develops into a payment dilemma, he or she should continue to see the minor until the situation is resolved. The Christian counselor may agree to see the minor for an agreed number of sessions either without cost or for what the minor may be able to pay.

ADOLESCENT PRACTICE ISSUES

Counseling teenagers is challenging due to their rapid development, their mistrust of authority, and their general unwillingness to be open with adults about their thoughts and feelings. Once the counselor establishes a relationship of trust with a teenager, it is essential to maintain that trust.

Teen suicide. The high suicide rate among our youth is a tragic reality. Clergy and counselors must learn how to effectively handle this important problem because of the increasing number of teens who choose this option for dealing with their pain and despair. When suicide is an issue with a teenager, a written agreement should be drafted to outline the intervention steps that will be taken and the people who will be contacted. The Christian counselor has a duty to intervene in cases where a person is suicidal or homicidal. In virtually every case this would mean that serious suicidal or homicidal intent, with a clear sense of lethality and means, requires that the helper inform parents and any intended specified victims.

Sexual behavior. A conflict between ethical and legal duties faces the Christian counselor when a minor confides that he or she is sexually involved with someone age eighteen or older. Some states stipulate that consenting minors over fourteen (or fifteen or sixteen) may be sexually involved and that the counselor is not required to report such activity. However, at the time of this writing, any voluntary sexual activity between a minor over fourteen and a minor under fourteen is considered a reportable offense for all professionals who are mandated by law to report such offenses. We advise you to check with your state attorney general's office to determine the limits of confidentiality and practice requirements. Doing so will help resolve the legal issues, but it does not resolve the ethical dilemma. It is wise to plan in advance how to treat this delicate problem in a manner that respects confidentiality and trust while meeting the legitimate concerns of the parents.

Referral practice. Making responsible referrals is a critical dimension of any counseling practice. A counselor is most apt to refer a teenager when the helper recognizes his or her own limits of competence, the need for medical or other professional help, or the teenager's need for hospitalization or a residential treatment program. It is vital for the helper to carefully attend to the reasons for making referral as well as to the reputation and practices of those to whom the referral is made. For example, it is important that any counselor who refers a teenager to a residential treatment program be very familiar with the treatment methods employed. A poorly considered referral may not only result in a disappointed family, but it could also result in legal or ethical trouble.

ACTIVE LISTENING: THE HEART OF HELPING TEENAGERS

John, thirteen, was brought to a counselor's office by his mother because he was having difficulty at school and wouldn't do his homework.

John: I don't care what they do to me. I'm not going to do another assignment.

Counselor (with great concern): Do you know you can't graduate if you don't do your homework?

John: I don't care.

Counselor (in a compassionate tone): I bet you'll care when you start looking for a job.

John: Big deal.

Counselor (desperately wanting to help): It *is* a big deal. It will affect the rest of your life.

John: I don't care.

This endless circle of conversation does not move John one inch closer to doing homework, and it does next to nothing to build a therapeutic relationship. The counselor is rational and is obviously concerned. Why isn't it working?

The missing component is the most important and fundamental skill required for a successful helping relationship: active listening. Adolescents do not readily lay out their thoughts and feelings even for a compassionate counselor. Counselors who build a therapeutic relationship with adolescents do it the old-fashioned way: "They *earrrrn* it."

An adolescent's real concerns are often closed off and opened only by continued and careful listening. "The road to the heart," wrote Voltaire, "is the ear." Look at this brief interaction again with a counselor who is hearing more than words.

John: I don't care what they do to me. I'm not going to do another assignment.

Counselor: Sounds as if you've made up your mind.

John: Yep. Those teachers are idiots, especially Mr. Wilson.

Counselor: They're not too smart, huh?

John: Well, I'm sure they're smart and everything, but they aren't very nice.

Counselor: They're kind of mean?

John: Yeah. The last time I handed in my paper, Wilson read it aloud. I didn't write that for the whole world to hear.

Like marriage, counseling is a relationship that may be for better or for worse. Artful listening determines the difference.

Active Listening Is the Heart of Counseling

Aristotle observed that while an injury to the head can make a person unconscious, a wound to the heart is invariably fatal. Active listening—listening with "the third ear," as Reik (1972) called it—is the heart of counseling. It is vital to the life of a helping relationship.

Jesus understood the importance of listening. Even as a young boy he was sitting with the teachers in the temple, "listening to them and asking them questions. Everyone…was amazed at his understanding" (Luke 2:46-47). The apostle Paul understood that listening requires diligent work. When he was before Agrippa, he said, "I beg you to listen to me patiently" (Acts 26:3). The book of James tells us to "be quick to listen, slow to speak" (James 1:19). And the book of Proverbs says, "He who answers before listening—that is his folly and his shame" (Proverbs 18:13). The word *listen* occurs more than two hundred times in the Bible.

Two major ingredients go into active listening: reflection and clarification.

Active listening requires reflection. Understanding comes through empathic reflection, through responding sensitively to the emotional rather than to the semantic meaning of a person's expression. Jesus responded on the basis of what he "heard" people feeling. After a short exchange, Nathanael declared Jesus to be the

Son of God. Jesus reflected Nathanael's meaning and said, "You believe because I told you I saw you under the fig tree" (John 1:50).

Active listening does not mean saying, "I understand." A classic cartoon shows an exasperated teenager telling her mother, "For Pete's sake, will you stop understanding me and just listen?"

Many people believe that sincerity assures understanding. But sincerity ignores the fact that we communicate in ways that severely limit our ability to get our real messages across. Between what a person intends to communicate and what others hear stands an unavoidable filter of preconception. "I'm not going to do another assignment" may mean "I was terribly embarrassed by Mr. Wilson for reading my assignment to the whole class." "I won't go" may mean "I don't want to go." Or "Do you really think so?" may mean "I disagree."

Counselors normally target three aspects of a message in their reflections: (1) the *content* of the message, (2) the *thinking* behind the message, and (3) the *feeling* behind the message. Each is equally valid and useful. Here is an example of how a single statement may be reflected at each level.

Adolescent: I couldn't believe he was accusing me for what *he* did.

Counselor (reflecting content): He blamed you.

Adolescent: Yeah. He said I was the one responsible because I was there.

Counselor (reflecting thinking): You thought he was unfair.

Adolescent: Yeah. I didn't deserve to be blamed.

Counselor (reflecting feeling): It must have made you angry.

Adolescent: I was furious. I also felt bad.

By reflecting the content of the message, counselors allow adolescents to elaborate further on what happened. By reflecting the thinking behind the message, counselors allow adolescents to understand their evaluation of what happened. And by reflecting the feeling behind the message, counselors invite adolescents to become aware of emotions resulting from what happened.

Adolescent (sitting down, looking at the floor, hunched over, and silent)…

Counselor (reflecting content): You've had a bad day.

Adolescent: My dad took away my driving privileges.

Counselor (reflecting thinking): I wonder whether you would rather be left alone.

Adolescent: No, I just wish my dad would leave me alone.

Counselor (reflecting feeling): Looks as if you don't feel so good.

Adolescent: I guess I feel that I let my dad down, but I'm mad at him.

By reflecting the content, thinking, or feeling of struggling adolescents, we are not evaluating or advising. We are saying, "I am with you and want to understand you better." Here is another example:

Adolescent: I got accepted to all three schools!

Counselor (reflecting content): You got just what you wanted.

Adolescent: Yeah, every one of them sent me a letter.

Counselor (reflecting thinking): Your hard work really paid off.

Adolescent: Yeah, I guess I didn't need to worry the way I did.

Counselor (reflecting feeling): You got just what you wanted. You must be happy.

Adolescent: I've never been so relieved. I feel great.

One caution: Making reflective comments, while very helpful, can be overdone. Eager to build rapport with an adolescent, beginning counselors sometimes

---

BOX 26.3—AN EXERCISE IN ACTIVE LISTENING

Reflecting an adolescent's feelings is one of the most helpful yet difficult listening techniques to implement. Often, important feelings are hidden behind the words of a struggling adolescent.

Following are some typical adolescent statements. Read each one separately, "listening" for feelings. Make note of the feeling you hear and write a response that reflects the feeling of each statement.

- "Every girl has a date but me."
- "I practice all the time, but it doesn't make any difference."
- "I shouldn't have slammed the door, but she shouldn't have said that."
- "I should be able to stay out past midnight if I want. Jim does."
- "Do you think I did the right thing?"
- "I'd like to punch his lights out!"
- "I don't want to talk about it anymore."
- "What's the use?"
- "What if she laughs at me? I'm not going to ask her."
- "I don't feel anything about it."

Compare your list of reflective statements with those below to see how accurately you recognize feelings. Give yourself a *2* on items where your choice matches closely, a *1* on items where your choice only partially matches, and a *0* if you missed altogether.

- "Every other girl has a date but me." *It feels as if you got left out.*

reflect everything that rolls across the kid's tongue. Continual uh-huhs and constantly nodding or parroting a client's comments interfere at best and may show superficiality and insincerity at worst. Go easy.

Active Listening Requires Clarification. How do you read the following sentence?

Love is nowhere.

Some see "Love is nowhere." Others read "Love is now here." In the same way, we, as counselors, may see an entirely different meaning from the one the client intends.

When absurd misunderstandings happened between Abbott and Costello, the famous comedy team, the whole nation chuckled. But in a counseling session, being misunderstood is no laughing matter. Misunderstanding does not result so

---

- "I practice all the time, but it doesn't make any difference." *Sounds as if you feel discouraged.*
- "I shouldn't have slammed the door, but she shouldn't have said that." *You feel kind of guilty but, at the same time, justified for what you did.*
- "I should be able to stay out past midnight if I want. Jim does." *I wonder if you feel that your parents are being overprotective.*
- "Do you think I did the right thing?" *It sounds as if you're not very sure of yourself.*
- "I'd like to punch his lights out!" *You must be really angry.*
- "I don't want to talk about it anymore." *It sounds as if you're feeling overloaded, as if it is all just too much.*
- "What's the use?" *As you say that, I get a picture of a guy who is discouraged and is about ready to give up.*
- "What if she laughs at me? I'm not going to ask her." *I get the sense that you're a little afraid and that your mind is made up.*
- "I don't feel anything about it." *I'm wondering whether you have some idea of what you should be feeling and because you don't feel that way, you register it as not feeling anything.*

Total your score. How do you rate on recognizing adolescents' feelings?

16–20: Above-average recognition of feelings

11–15: Average recognition of feelings

0–10: Below-average recognition of feelings

---

much from not hearing the words as from our not clarifying the meaning of the words. The five hundred most commonly used words in the English language carry over fourteen hundred different meanings. That's an average of nearly three meanings for each word!

In addition, some adolescents have personalized meanings for the words they use. I once heard an adolescent say he was "bailin' for a loc fiesta that's fully amped with no ancients." Translation: He was leaving for an exciting neighborhood party with no adults. Here are some more examples: *dude!* means hello; *dude* means guy; *buds* means friends; *rad* means superlative; *way rad* means extremely cool; *fresh* means cool; *weak* means uncool; *chill* means hang out; *chill* also means relax; *fly* means very stylish; *clean* means very attractive; *fundage* means cash; and *bad* means good. No wonder clarification is necessary!

Clarification serves two basic purposes: (1) to gather additional information and (2) to help explore an issue more thoroughly—to discover, for example, whether a problem is a greater concern to the adolescent or to you.

One obvious point: Clarification is necessary when you are not sure you heard correctly. Another cartoon says it beautifully: A king in the backseat of his Rolls-Royce is being carried by a group of long-haired guys with no shoes. He leans out the window and says, "I said 'radials,' not 'radicals'!"

What Active Listening Accomplishes

Active listening unearths hidden feelings. Active listening allows teenagers' hidden feelings to percolate to the top. Struggling adolescents do not often broadcast their pain. They want someone to sense their hurt without their having to admit it. The cry of fear, for example, sometimes hides behind a fuming face. Pain is sometimes muted by wordy anger. Depression may lurk behind a stiff smile.

Box 26.4—Useful Leads for the Active Listener

- "It sounds as if you're feeling…"
- "It seems as if…"
- "I get a picture of…"
- "What I hear you saying is…"
- "Could it be that…"
- "It must have been…"
- "I wonder if you're thinking…"
- "You must feel…"

To help adolescents, a counselor needs a sensitive internal seismograph to feel the tremors beneath the external calm. In effect, that is what active listening is: a way to sense the quaking of adolescence. If we have a hunch that Brian, a fourteen-year-old, is not as apathetic as he seems but is actually angry because he didn't make the team, we don't blurt out, "You are denying how angry you really are." Instead, we may probe gently, "I get the feeling you're angry and you aren't sure that's okay." A statement like this allows Brian to own his buried anger without losing face.

Active listening takes away the fear of feeling. Free of evaluation, active listening creates a safe environment. It provides a place where trembling adolescents may shed their defenses, own up to previously feared emotions, and know that their feelings are acceptable. When adolescents are guarded, it is as if they are pressing the accelerator all the way to the floor but keeping the car in neutral and a foot on the brake; they're using valuable fuel, but they're going nowhere. Your active listening gives struggling adolescents new energy and helps them begin to move in positive directions.

Active listening helps adolescents be their own counselors. Your goal is to not be needed. Too often we mistake help with throwing out a line of advice. Counseling isn't rescuing. The problem with solving people's problems is that external solutions foster unhealthful dependence. If you solve a problem for a young person who comes back with a similar problem the next week, you put out the same fire over and over. Advice-giving says, "I don't trust you to come up with your own solution." But when you listen actively, you are saying, "I believe in you." Active listening boosts the confidence of struggling adolescents and teaches them to depend on God and themselves for problem solving.

Active listening facilitates true learning. The only people who really want someone else to change them are wet babies. The goal of counseling is not to change people but to provide a relationship in which people learn to change themselves and mature.

For the most part, true learning—the kind that significantly influences behavior—is self-discovered. And active listening helps struggling adolescents discover how they can best cope with their situations. Active listening generates the principle of participation: People are motivated to act or follow through on decisions they have had a part in making. The motivation to act on advice that has been imposed is minimal at best.

WHY ADVICE CAN TURN SOUR

Too often, advice given without active listening cuts the heart out of counseling. Like a little garlic, a little advice goes a long way. The following reminders may help you keep from overdoing it.

Advice is often self-centered. When we dole out advice before we have actively listened, we may believe we are being skillfully helpful. After all, isn't it loving to relieve adolescents of suffering by helping them see the light? Actually, attempts to change adolescents by giving advice is not only naive and ineffective, but it is often also self-serving. It hurts to see adolescents struggle with psychic pain, so by doing our part—giving advice—we feel better. The driving motivation behind the practice is often the counselor's desire to feel good about him- or herself, but don't be surprised by the chaos that results from self-serving advice.

Advice may make clients feel worse. Offering advice may set young people up to feel worse because they cannot or are not ready to follow through on it. This may instill terrible pangs of guilt. The advice that Job's friends gave him in his time of affliction, for example, served only to make poor Job more miserable. The only way you can know when and whether an adolescent is ready for advice is through persistent and sensitive listening.

Advice may be threatening. Sometimes giving advice calls clients' beliefs and attitudes into question, which may reflect our own insecurity and uncertainty regarding our beliefs. It is uncomfortable for us to be uncertain of our own values on certain issues. So, we reason, if we convert adolescents to our way of thinking, our discomfort is relieved and we have reinforced the validity of our convictions. Further, we have once again proven that we are all-knowing counselors. This is much easier than making the effort to understand adolescent perspectives.

Advice may be boring. Being forced to sit through an unrewarding or even irritating monologue from the counselor causes adolescents to turn off the one-sided "conversation" and turn their minds to something else. They may feel like the bored youngster in church who said to his mom, "Pay the man and let's go home." *Advice given without active listening causes boredom.* And as Proverbs 18:13 says, advice given "before listening…is [the counselor's] folly and his shame."

Advice may be costly. Advice is effective only when it fulfills the salient needs of the listener. Too often, advice is given without considering how the client will feel about it. Those who give advice without listening enjoy the luxury of an opinion without the labor of a thought. Because a counselor is ready to give advice does not mean a person is ready to receive it. Trigger-happy advice is costly. Upon hearing advice that is not given with active listening, a teenager may say, "I don't want to talk about it anymore!" Therapy is shut down, and the counselor is at a dead end. Even good advice isn't worth that price.

The point is obvious. It is difficult to make a mistake with active listening, but advice and recommendations by themselves may clog the flow of genuine feelings. Active listening will nearly always help a person clear out the clutter.

MAKING ADVICE HELPFUL

Jung said that advice seldom hurts any of us because we so rarely take it seriously. That may be true, but there are ways to help people take good advice to heart. The key is knowing when and how to give it. As the Bible says, "Let your conversation be always full of grace, seasoned with salt, so that you may know how to answer everyone" (Colossians 4:6).

By now it should be clear that advice will usually backfire if the counselor has not earned—through active listening—the right to give it. Before offering advice, a counselor must understand what the struggling adolescent is really needing. Philosophers have always said it is more important to find someone who knows what the question is than to find someone who knows a pat answer to a question. The same holds true in counseling. Listening is not icing on the cake; it *is* the cake.

With the importance of active listening in mind, here are some specific ways to minimize the negative risks of giving advice to adolescents, *even when it is appropriate to do so.*

- Advice is heard best by a person who is calm and rational. When a person is drowning, it is not a good time to try to teach him to swim.
- Help adolescents give the advice themselves. It is sometimes helpful to say, "What would you tell someone in your predicament?"
- Advice will have more impact if it is not given routinely. Like a Mailgram, infrequent advice will stand out in importance.
- Don't hesitate to be redundant. Restating a suggestion in different ways increases the likelihood that adolescents will get the point.
- Ask clients what they hear you saying. Ask them to state in their own words what you have said.
- Suggest that clients write down what you have said. Studies have shown that note taking increases comprehension because it increases attention and personal involvement. Subsequent review of the notes maximizes the usefulness of advice.
- Pay attention to the timing of your advice. Information given first or last in a session is remembered better than that which is presented in the middle.
- If the client does not understand or accept the advice, don't push it. A counselor we know has a plaque in her office that reads, *Lord, fill my mouth with good stuff, and nudge me when I've said enough.*

CHAPTER 27

CHILD PSYCHOPHARMACOLOGY

What Counselors Need to Know About Treating Children and Adolescents

DANIEL S. SWEENEY AND ROSS J. TATUM

If a child is to keep alive his inborn sense of wonder...he needs the companionship of at least one adult who can share it, rediscovering with him the joy, excitement, and mystery of the world we live in.

—RACHEL CARSON, *The Sense of Wonder*

It is often a challenge to work with children who are experiencing significant emotional or behavioral turmoil. During the course of treatment, therapists may find it necessary to refer them for psychopharmacological evaluation and therapy. We have all heard horror stories of overmedication or of the lack of consistent medical supervision, but psychopharmacology offers wonderful success stories too.

The responsible child therapist should have at least a rudimentary knowledge of psychopharmacology and should be willing to make an appropriate psychiatric referral when necessary. Unfortunately, such knowledge and willingness is not always present. The oversight may be compounded by the helper's bias against medication or by the parents' belief that prescribing psychotropic medications amounts to an admission of parental failure or is perhaps not scriptural. While respecting the beliefs and convictions of their clients' parents, therapists should educate them about the potential value and appropriate use of medications and help them understand that psychopharmacology may be a necessary part of the overall treatment program.

This brief chapter will not undertake a detailed apologetic for the use of medications with children. However, it is our opinion that pharmacological interventions are necessary for some child clients. It is wrong to deny a child medication when it is appropriate. We also assert that it is absolutely wrong to medicate a child who does not need medication.

Furthermore, withholding medication from any client out of fear or ignorance is not only irresponsible, it is also unethical. Some children continue to suffer because many helpers are not taking advantage of modern psychiatry's increasing knowledge about the neurobiology of human beings. We therefore contend and recommend that Christian therapists working with children should recognize the benefits and limitations of medications as an adjunct treatment tool.

CHILD PSYCHOPHARMACOLOGY AND COUNSELING

Historically, psychopharmacology has not been an area of research or concern for the nonmedical child therapist. Many child therapists develop treatment programs in hopes of limiting or eliminating the need for medication rather than encouraging its use. A trend among many child therapists appears to be that medications for children are at best probably unnecessary and at worst harmful.

With the move toward managed health care and brief therapy in the mental health field, however, insurance companies and third-party payment providers are looking for the swift reduction of symptoms, which pharmacological approaches might provide. This concept may well be at odds with the goal of child therapy, which is to provide children with a safe environment in which to process intrapsychic issues in their own language (play therapy). For many child therapists, symptom reduction is a by-product, rather than a focus, of treatment. We will not attempt to address the political issues of managed health care or the appropriate focus of child mental health treatment. Our intent in this chapter is to discuss some medication considerations specific to the field of child therapy.

The need for Christian therapists to be educated about psychopharmacological issues is clear. According to the American Association of Christian Counselors *Membership Registry* (1999), the vast majority of therapists have a master's degree in some area of the mental health field. The average Christian therapist, therefore, has minimal (if any) training in psychopharmacology since the subject is not required for every accredited master's program in counseling, psychology, and marriage and family therapy (Patterson & Magulac, 1994). While most doctoral-level training programs offer pharmacology courses, many do not require them. One result of this trend is that students of psychotherapy often ignore the treatment possibilities of medications and the negative side effects that medications might have (Patterson & Magulac, 1994).

We believe that child therapists who have even a cursory knowledge of child psychopharmacology are in a better position to provide quality treatment. An understanding of a referred client's medical records and adequate knowledge to assess the necessity for a psychiatric referral are imperative in treatment planning and implementation. In order to best meet the needs of the child client, counselors must become knowledgeable about psychopharmacology and must overcome issues of power, control, and turf by being educated and aware.

PSYCHOPHARMACOLOGY WITH CHILDREN

The majority of research and experience in the field of psychopharmacology has focused on the adult population. Although the body of research is increasing, there is unfortunately a dearth of extensive empirical study on the efficacy and safety of psychotropic medication on children (Biederman, 1992; Brown & Ievers, 1999; Ellis & Singh, 1999; Gitlin, 1995). The use of psychotropics with children has not been generally addressed by the Food and Drug Administration (FDA). FDA approval, however, is not meant to direct prescribing habits, but rather to limit pharmaceutical company advertising. An additional concern is that an increasing number of nonpsychiatric physicians (including pediatricians, family doctors, and neurologists) are prescribing psychotropics for children.

Despite these and other related concerns, the use of psychotropic medications for treating children has increased dramatically beyond the common use of stimulants for attention deficit hyperactivity disorder (Wilens, Spencer, Frazier, & Biederman, 1998). These medications include antidepressants for major depression, anxiety disorders, and ADHD; lithium for bipolar disorders; neuroleptics for psychotic disorders; and some antihypertensive agents for dyscontrol (Biederman, 1992). The discovery of new pharmacological treatments and the evaluation of psychotropic uses for nonpsychiatric drugs have led to a significant increase in the pharmacologic treatment of childhood mental health issues (Gadow, 1992).

Just as nonmedical therapists would not argue the existence of physiological roots in the etiology of adult psychiatric disorders, so must they recognize this dynamic in children. Bukstein (1993) noted: "For prepubertal children, biochemical and neurophysiological correlates exist for several disorders. Research has implicated neurotransmitter dysfunction in a variety of psychopathologic behaviors and disorders" (p. 14). Whereas child therapy may address core issues of some disorders and arguably peripheral symptoms in most disorders, neurobiological contributions to childhood psychopathology must be addressed medically.

There are multiple pretreatment and treatment considerations that, although primarily the concern of the prescribing physician, the child therapist should be aware of:

- Several medications may be utilized for a variety of symptoms or diagnoses. Specific psychotropics may be effective for dissimilar disorders because of their influence on neurotransmitters and psychoendocrine events in the brain along common routes (Green, 1995).

- Developmental issues of childhood and adolescence must be considered. Children are, from a biological standpoint, immature and growing organisms, and they metabolize chemical agents differently from adults. Thus they may respond differently to psychotropic medication taken by the similarly diagnosed adult (Arnold, 1993; Biederman & Steingard, 1991; Vitiello & Jensen, 1995). Issues of absorption and disposition are primary concerns, and the prescribing physician may adjust dosage strength and frequency to achieve the maximum therapeutic effect of a medication. Blood levels may need to be closely monitored.

- Another consideration in prescribing psychotropics to children is the absolute necessity of a complete physiologic and psychiatric assessment (Kutcher, 2000). Biederman and Steingard (1991) summarized the fundamental goal of such an assessment: "Psychopharmacologic evaluation of the child should address the basic question of whether the patient has a psychiatric disorder (or disorders) that may respond to psychotropics" (p. 343). If this inquiry is answered affirmatively, a complete physical examination (sometimes including laboratory tests), psychosocial history, and baseline behavioral assessment must be conducted. The valuable contribution of the child therapist to this process will be commented upon later.

- A final concern must be the consideration of alternative or concurrent treatment approaches in psychiatric intervention with children. Green (1995) stressed that treatment with psychotropic drugs must be part of a more comprehensive treatment regimen and, as such, is rarely appropriate as the sole intervention for children. The effects of concurrent treatment interventions and environmental influences should be considered when examining the efficacy of psychopharmacology (Bukstein, 1993; Green, 1995; Wilens et al., 1998).

Pharmacologic Treatment of Childhood Disorders

Although children are brought in for psychiatric evaluation primarily to address unwanted symptoms, treatment planning generally occurs according to diagnostic category. Discussion of treatment will follow along diagnostic lines. For the sake of brevity, diagnostic definitions are not given. The table on the following page provides a summary of DSM-IV-TR (American Psychiatric Association, 2000) diagnoses and psychotropic medications that may be indicated.

Attention Deficit Hyperactivity Disorder

The category that has been most researched in the psychopharmacological treatment of children is ADHD (Spencer, Biederman, & Wilens, 2000). The most commonly prescribed medications for the ADHD diagnosis are the stimulants: Ritalin (methylphenidate), Concerta and Metadate (both are extended-release methylphenidate formulations), Dexedrine (dextroamphetamine), Adderall (mix of amphetamine salts), and Cylert (pemoline). Cylert is now used much less frequently due to concern over possible liver dysfunction. The manufacturer of Cylert now recommends biweekly blood tests.

The antidepresants Effexor (venlafaxine) and Wellbutrin (bupropion) are also used with ADHD. Tricyclic antidepressants—including Tofranil (imipramine), Pamelor (nortriptyline), and Norpramin (desipramine)—have also been used successfully. While used safely with many children, these tricyclic antidepressants are used less frequently due to cardiac events that have led to the deaths of several children. More specifically, some psychiatrists have recommended discontinuing the use of desipramine with children altogether. Catapres (clonidine) and Tenex (guanfacine) are frequently used to augment partial responses to stimulants. There is, however, some concern over the safety and efficacy of these medications with children.

Affective Disorders

Although the existence of childhood depression is no longer clinically questioned, the efficacy of the antidepressants commonly prescribed in treating this disorder has been difficult to establish. However, prescribing antidepressants for children is a common practice. The medications commonly used include Effexor, Zoloft (sertraline), Paxil (paroxetine), Prozac (fluoxetine), and Celexa (citalopram). Wellbutrin and Serzone (nefazodone) are occasionally used, and the tricyclic antidepressants are now used less frequently. Monoamine oxidase inhibitors (MAOIs) are generally not prescribed for children due to the severe dietary restrictions. Lithium is sometimes used to augment a partial response to antidepressants.

Childhood DSM-IV-TR Diagnoses and Psychotropic Medications That May be Indicated

DSM-IV Diagnosis	Medications Used
attention deficit hyperactivity disorder	stimulants, antidepressants (including Effexor, Wellbutrin, and Tricyclics), Catapres, Tenex
major depression	SSRIs, Effexor, Wellbutrin, Serzone, Remeron
mania (acute and for maintenance)	anticonvulsants, lithium, antipsychotics, benzodiazepines
mental retardation (with severe aggression or self-injurious behavior)	antipsychotics, lithium, Inderol, Trexan
pervasive developmental disorder	antipsychotics, Trexan
conduct disorder (with aggression)	antipsychotics, lithium, anticonvulsants, Inderal
anxiety disorders	
generalized anxiety disorder	antidepressants, benzodiazepines, BuSpar
obsessive-compulsive disorder	SSRIs, Clomipramine
post-traumatic stress disorder	antidepressants, benzodiazepines, BuSpar, Clonidine
separation anxiety disorder	antidepressants, benzodiazepines
panic disorder	antidepressants, benzodiazepines
schizophrenia	antipsychotics
intermittent explosive disorder	Propranolol, lithium, antipsychotics
sleep disorders	some antidepressants (Remeron, Desyrel), benzodiazepines, antihistamines
enuresis (not due to medical disorder)	DDAVP, tricyclic antidepressants
Tourette's syndrome	Haloperidol, Pimozide, Clonidine, Risperdal

Lithium and anticonvulsant medications such as Depakote (valproic acid) and Tegretol (carbamazepine) have been used for symptoms of mania. Neuroleptics (also known as antipsychotics) and benzodiazepines can be used to treat the acute agitation of mania. Long-term use of neuroleptics for the treatment of bipolar disorder is not recommended because of the risk of tardive dyskinesia, a syndrome of involuntary movements.

ANXIETY DISORDERS

Antidepressants are used most often in the treatment of anxiety problems in children. Because newer antidepressants (e.g., selective serotonin re-uptake inhibitors, Effexor) have a better safety profile, they are used more often than the tricyclic antidepressants. BuSpar (buspirone) has also been used. In addition to the antidepressants, benzodiazepines such as Xanax (alprazolam) are used with children having separation anxiety disorder. Obsessive-compulsive disorder has been shown to respond to medications that primarily affect the re-uptake of serotonin. These include Zoloft, Paxil, Prozac, Celexa, Luvox (fluvoxamine), and Anafranil (clomipramine).

Psychopharmacologic treatment of post-traumatic stress disorder (PTSD) is generally based on the treatment of comorbid anxiety or mood disorders. Antidepressants are used most often. Inderal (propranolol) and Catapres have also been used. According to clinical reports, both antidepressants and benzodiazepines may be helpful in treating children with panic disorder (Popper, 1993).

SCHIZOPHRENIA

Onset of schizophrenia in prepubertal children is rare, as is psychopharmacologic research in this population (Pomeroy & Gadow, 1998). Antipsychotics are prescribed. The newer atypical antipsychotics Risperdal (risperidone) and Zyprexa (olanzapine) are increasingly being used as an initial intervention with these children. High potency neuroleptics such as Haldol (haloperidol) and Navane (thiothixene) likely cause fewer problems with learning (but more problems with stiffness) than low-potency neuroleptics such as Mellaril (thioridazine) and Thorazine (chlorpromazine), which are more sedating (Campbell & Spencer, 1988). Clozaril (clozapine) has been used in adults showing a poor response to traditional neuroleptics and has seen some use in adolescents. It is infrequently used with children.

ENURESIS

In the authors' experience, the initial approach to enuresis should involve behavioral methods or a bed alarm. After these approaches have failed, medication may be appropriate. The antidiuretic hormone DDAVP (desmopressin) is administered intranasally or in pill form. Low doses of tricyclic antidepressants are also used. Relapse following discontinuation of medication is common.

SLEEP DISORDERS

Although sleep disorders in children are not commonly medicated, in the authors' experience these problems do respond to specific medications. Some psychiatrists use Benadryl (diphenhydramine) for brief periods for children and adolescents experiencing difficulty falling asleep. Catapres has also been used to treat the insomnia that may be associated with stimulant use. More recently, there has been increased use of Remeron (mirtazapine) and Desyrel (trazodone) for sleep difficulties. Some benzodiazepines, such as Valium (diazepam) and tricyclics, have been prescribed for night terrors and sleepwalking.

TOURETTE'S SYNDROME

Haldol and Orap (pimozide) have been used effectively to reduce tic behaviors (Gadow, 1992; Green, 1995). The tics may also respond to Catapres. Some of the newer antipsychotics, such as Risperdal, have shown some efficacy with tics and have a lower rate of tardive dyskinesia. Some psychiatrists will opt to use these new neuroleptics to avoid the potential of serious cardiovascular side effects that may be associated with clonidine.

AGGRESSION

While not a diagnostic category in itself, aggression is a common complaint encountered by therapists working with children, and it cuts across many diagnostic categories. Successful intervention takes into account comorbid symptoms such as impulsivity, depression, bipolar disorder, and psychosis. In the authors' experience, antipsychotics have been effective in reducing aggressive behavior in hyperactive and conduct-disordered children as well as children with mental retardation and autism. Because of the risks associated with these medications, they should be used long term only after other options have failed. Lithium, Inderal, and Tegretol have also been used to treat aggression. Depakote may also be of some benefit.

OTHER DISORDERS

The diagnosis of an eating disorder itself does not call for the use of pharmacotherapy. Severe anxiety, obsessive-compulsive symptoms, or psychosis that may accompany the eating disorder symptoms may be treated with appropriate medications. Likewise, severe depression may be treated with an appropriate antidepressant.

Studies with adults have noted that antidepressants can decrease the severity of binge eating (Mayer & Walsh, 1998).

In general, developmental disorders are treated according to specific indications. This is another area where the newer atypical antipsychotics are finding increased use. Neuroleptics, such as Haldol, and Trexan (naltrexone), an opiate antagonist, have been used with positive results in children with autism (Green, 1995; Kutcher, 1997). Again, children on neuroleptics must be monitored closely for the development of movement disorders. Comorbid symptoms associated with developmental disorders such as anxiety, depression, obsessive-compulsive behavior, and hyperactivity may be treated accordingly.

THERAPEUTIC AND SIDE EFFECTS OF PSYCHOTROPICS

In addition to having a basic knowledge of psychiatric medications prescribed for childhood disorders, the child therapist should be aware of the primary therapeutic effects and potential side effects of psychotropics.

ANTIDEPRESSANTS

Though there are few FDA-approved indications for the use of the newer antidepressants (SSRIs, Effexor, Serzone, Remeron, and Wellbutrin) in children, the prescribing of these medications now exceeds that of the older tricyclic antidepressants. This is primarily because of the lack of risk for severe cardiac side effects. The antidepressants may have side effects including gastrointestinal discomfort, headaches, sleep and behavioral disturbances, and weight loss or gain. Remeron is sedating and is often associated with significant weight gain. Because of these side effects, it is now occasionally used with children having the side effects of appetite and sleep difficulties due to the use of stimulants. Wellbutrin is contraindicated in persons with a history of seizures or tics, and it can cause weight loss.

Enuresis and ADHD are the only established indications for the tricyclics, although they are also prescribed for depression. Tricyclics have the possible side effects of dry mouth, constipation, blurred vision, weight change, and decreased blood pressure. Treatment requires electrocardiographic monitoring, and the monitoring of blood serum levels is recommended. Tricyclics are the most lethal of the psychotropics in an overdose.

PSYCHOSTIMULANTS

The stimulant medications commonly used with ADHD children are well researched and considered safe and effective (Barkley, DuPaul, & Costello, 1993). Common side effects include insomnia, decreased appetite, and headache. Less frequently, they may cause agitation, enuresis, and depression. Rarely, tics and psychotic symptoms may occur.

ANTIPSYCHOTICS

The neuroleptic medications are used with a variety of symptoms and disorders. These include psychosis, bipolar disorders, aggression, and tic disorders. Common side effects include dry mouth, constipation, blurred vision, sedation, stiffness, and in some cases of chronic administration, tardive dyskinesia. The newer atypical antipsychotics may lead to significant weight gain, but they are also less likely to be associated with tardive dyskinesia. Cogentin (benztropine) and Benadryl are anticholinergic medications commonly used to treat the stiffness caused by the neuroleptics.

LITHIUM

Lithium is used to treat childhood bipolar disorder, schizo-affective disorder, and aggression; it is also used to augment the treatment of depression. Common side effects include weight gain, acne, polyuria, polydipsia, gastrointestinal upset, tremor, nausea, diarrhea, and possible thyroid and renal effects with chronic administration. Treatment requires monitoring blood serum levels and thyroid and kidney tests. Electrocardiogram (EKG) monitoring has also been recommended.

ANTIANXIETY

The benzodiazepines, although used sparingly with children, have been administered effectively for sleep disorders and in overanxious and avoidant children. Possible side effects are drowsiness, disinhibition, agitation, confusion, and depression.

OTHER MEDICATIONS

Catapres, although indicated as a treatment for hypertension, has been used with some success for Tourette's symptoms, ADHD, and aggression. Possible side effects include sedation, hypotension, dry mouth, confusion, and depression. There have been recent concerns about the potential for clonidine to cause serious cardiac events. Tenex is similar to Catapres, but it is longer acting and less sedating. Inderal, a beta-adrenergic receptor blocker, has been administered for anxiety disorders, aggression, and self-abusive behaviors. The potential side effects are essentially similar to clonidine. Its use is contraindicated in the presence of diabetes or asthma. Depakote and Tegretol are anticonvulsant medications which have been used in bipolar disorder and aggression. Possible side effects include bone marrow suppression, dizziness, sedation, rashes, and nausea. It requires blood serum monitoring.

MEDICINE AND CHILD THERAPY

Child therapists who are educated in the basics of child psychopharmacology are better advocates for their clients, both in therapy and in the psychiatrist's office. The following considerations about psychopharmacological issues address this dynamic.

An initial consideration is the advantage of doing child therapy with an appropriately medicated child. The concurrence of pharmacotherapy and child therapy could provide the ideal milieu for a child. If medications can give a child an increased capacity for benefiting from therapy and are not prescribed, the potential efficacy of the therapy is diminished. Many therapists and researchers advocate concurrent psychosocial interventions as being crucial to the lasting therapeutic effects of psychoactive agents (Brown & Ievers, 1999; Campbell, Godfrey, & Magee, 1992).

The psychosocial effects on the child who is placed on medication are appropriately dealt with in the child therapy setting. Taking medications, particularly over an extended period of time, may affect the child's or adolescent's self-concept. It could begin a process of chronic self-esteem difficulties. Children who are medicated may identify themselves as having a problem and may come to see the medication as a mechanism of control.

Therapy should provide children with an opportunity to learn self-control and self-respect, to make choices, and to accept themselves (Landreth, 1991). Golden (1983) noted in his play therapy work with hospitalized children that a child can regain a sense of mastery when being medically treated through play: "The goal of the play therapist is to help the child become involved in his or her own treatment (even if only in some small way) and to help the child retain a sense of competence" (p. 226).

A related issue that might be addressed in child therapy is the perception that medications are being presented as a coercive form of behavioral control rather than as a therapeutic adjunct (Gitlin, 1995). Although this is hopefully an exceptional situation, the perceived need by parents, teachers, and therapists for an instant panacea may lead to this concern. Children in this case have not only lost a sense of power and control, but they also feel that they have been manipulated and intruded upon.

Therapy offers children opportunities to process these issues. Children can begin to make sense of and bring organization to their confusing world. They can manage an unmanageable situation through the fantasy of play therapy or another expressive intervention. They can express the grief and anger that often result from being controlled in the aforementioned manner. The attitude of both parents and children toward the use of psychotropic medications is related to both compliance and efficacy (Rappaport & Chubinsky, 2000).

With the proper authorization to release information, the child therapist is in a unique position to provide both initial input and ongoing evaluation for the pre-scribing physician. The baseline assessment necessary to appropriately initiate pharmacotherapy is often inadequate if the psychiatrist must rely solely on parent report and observation of a child in an office. The child therapist will often have

---

Box 27.1—Frequently Asked Questions About the Use of Medication

Parents of children for whom medication has been recommended often have ques-tions about the process and specific issues. Although the nonmedical therapist should defer to qualified psychiatric personnel, he or she should have a funda-mental ability to respond to these typical questions:

Question: Will my child have to take ADHD medicine forever?

Answer: Studies vary, but it has been suggested that 66% or more of ADHD patients have symptoms that continue into young adulthood.

Question: Are stimulants addictive?

Answer: Stimulants are not addictive. Stimulants have been abused, but this is usually not a problem among children.

Question: I do not want my child doped up on stimulants. Will this happen?

Answer: Rather than impairing the patient's sensorium, stimulants generally improve concentration and attention.

Question: Will stimulant medications stunt my child's growth?

Answer: It is felt that the patient's long-term height is compromised little.

Question: Does my child have to take the Ritalin and Dexedrine even on week-ends and during the summer?

Answer: If the child requires the medication in order to have a good weekend or summer, there is no reason to discontinue it. If the child's problem is mainly focusing on schoolwork and he or she can function well medica-tion free when school is out, it does not hurt to stop it.

Question: What about intermittently stopping other medications?

Answer: Because of differences in the rates of onset, metabolism, and so on, most other psychotropic medications should be taken on a regular basis.

Question: Will taking medication this early in life predispose my child to sub-stance abuse?

Answer: No. Protection against future substance abuse is a positive outcome of appropriate medication use.

greater insight into the child's basic mental status. Providing this input is not only an ethical obligation, but it is also clearly in the best interests of the child client.

Another important consideration for the therapist comes with the interpretation of the child's therapy activity. It is possible to misinterpret a child's in-session behavior if that behavior is being acted out by an unmedicated child who is in legitimate need of psychopharmacological intervention. For example, a child's agitated shifting from one activity to another may be an indication of personal anxiety due to the new experience of being in the room, getting closer to intrapsychic issues, and so forth. It may also be that the child is an undiagnosed ADHD client who would respond appropriately to stimulant medication.

An inverse situation should also be noted. It is a legitimate possibility that a child may be psychiatrically medicated for what is viewed as biologically based symptoms when, in fact, the child is responding behaviorally to an emotional trauma or inappropriate parenting. For example, children who have been severely abused physically or sexually may respond by enacting bizarre defense mechanisms to protect themselves against further adult intrusion. These bizarre behaviors may be interpreted as some level of psychosis, suggesting the need for neuroleptic medication. These behaviors may well ameliorate in the child therapy process, where the safety of boundaries and the therapeutic relationship make processing the emotional pain possible.

An example of the effects of medication on child therapy behavior is detailed in Mayes's (1991) work on play assessment of preschool hyperactive children. Using a widely published observation system for hyperactivity, she noted that, of the "hyperactive children receiving methylphenidate (Ritalin), the number of quadrant crossings decreased significantly during free play, and the number of toy changes decreased during both free and restricted play" (p. 251).

A final issue that the child therapist might consider involves the child who is uncooperative with psychiatric treatment. It is not uncommon to work with children who are noncompliant with respect to taking medications. In addition to providing children with the basic opportunity to process their possible anger, frustration, or fear in their own language, the therapist has the opportunity to utilize directive techniques if deemed appropriate. This may involve cognitive or expressive techniques such as structured doll play, artwork, or storytelling.

THE IMPORTANCE OF COLLABORATION

Child therapists have an obligation to their clients to be educated on issues of child psychopharmacology. There is also an obligation to the profession at large. Biederman (1992) noted that the long-term outlook for pediatric psychopharmacology is dependent upon research as to whether the potential risks are outweighed by the real benefits to suffering children. Child therapists must be a part of this process, which will certainly progress with or without child therapy input. Fisher (1997) asserts that

> it is important to realize that medication is just one part of the treatment plan, and it is imperative that one tend to the patient's full spectrum of needs, including his or her spiritual needs. It is also imperative that the prescribing physician collaborate closely with the child's Christian counselor. (p. 27)

This collaborative process must involve the therapist's willingness to interact and cooperate with the medical profession. In the same way that child therapists need education on psychiatric matters, the psychiatrist may need education about aspects of child therapy. As previously noted, multidisciplinary cooperation advances the best interests of both the children and our profession. One therapist noted a common frustration and a compelling view of medication: "There used to be a sense of shame when you put clients on medication. It was like an admission of failure that therapy wasn't working and that you, the therapist, had to get help" (Markowitz, 1991, p. 26).

The real shame would be to remain ignorant. Awareness, growth, and balance map the future of becoming competent advocates of our children.

CHAPTER 28

CRISIS INTERVENTION AND EMERGENCY PRACTICE

Issues and Interventions

H. NORMAN WRIGHT

---

*You are attempting to convey by your entire approach and your attitude
that the client is a capable, decent person who has been temporarily
overwhelmed by extreme stresses, and who will use your help to cope with
these stresses and get back on the track.*

—DOUGLAS PURYEAR, *Helping People in Crisis*

When he walks into your office, his appearance and response tell it all. His thought process, problem-solving skills, facial expression, and sense of confusion clearly reveal that he's someone in crisis. Many people who show up at a counselor's or pastor's office have been prompted to come because of a crisis. But in order to help them, *you* need to understand what a crisis is and how to respond.

CRISIS DEFINED

Webster's New World Dictionary defines *crisis* as a "critical time" and "a turning point in the course of anything." The term is often used for a person's internal reaction to an external hazard. A crisis usually involves a temporary loss of coping abilities, and the assumption is that the emotional dysfunction is reversible. If a person effectively copes with the threat, he then returns to prior levels of functioning.

A crisis has also been described as some event that produces a temporary state of psychological disequilibrium. This leads to a condition of emotional turmoil, and a person finds him- or herself unable to cope with a challenging or aversive situation (Aguilera, 1990; Mitchell & Everly, 1977).

The Chinese character for crisis is made up of two symbols: one is for despair and the other for opportunity. When doctors talk about a crisis, they are talking about the moment in the course of a disease when a change for the worse or better occurs. When some counselors talk about a marital crisis, they are talking about a turning point when the marriage can go in either direction: It can move toward growth and enrichment or toward further dissatisfaction and pain. When people are thrown off balance by the ensuing event and are unable to recover their equilibrium, they are experiencing a crisis.

A crisis can be the result of one or more factors (Burgess & Baldwin, 1981). It can be a problem that is overwhelming, such as the death of a child. It can be a problem that, for most people, is not serious but for a given person has special significance. It can be a problem that comes at a time of special vulnerability or when the person is unprepared. It can occur when the person's normal coping mechanisms are not functioning well or when the person does not have support from others.

Sometimes crises are caused by significant life transitions. They may be swift or gradual, and they may have a positive or devastating impact upon the person's life. All transitions, however, have the potential for being a crisis experience depending on the person involved.

Crisis is not always bad. Rather, it represents a pivotal point in a person's life. Therefore, it can bring opportunity as well as danger. As people search for methods of coping, they may choose paths of destruction, but they may also discover new and better methods than they previously had available. In order for counselors to help people at such a pivotal point, they need to understand the structure of a crisis.

COMMON ELEMENTS

Let's look briefly at the four common elements of a crisis:

1. *A hazardous event.* This is some occurrence that starts a chain reaction of events culminating in a crisis. For example, a young wife who spent seven years preparing for a career discovers she is pregnant. Or a college senior who expected to be drafted by a professional football team shatters an ankle while hiking.

2. *A vulnerable state.* For a crisis to occur, a person must be vulnerable. Even going without sleep for two nights can make a person vulnerable to a situation that he or she would usually handle with no difficulty.

3. *A precipitating factor.* To use the cliché, this is the "straw that broke the camel's back." Some people seem to hold together well during a time of extreme loss or heartache and then fall apart over a broken dish or a dropped glass. That was the "last straw," but the strong reaction and tears were really in response to the serious loss.

4. *A state of active crisis.* When a person can no longer handle the situation, the active crisis develops. There are four indications of the crisis state:

   a. *Symptoms of stress—psychological, physiological, or both.* Symptoms could include depression, headaches, anxiety, or bleeding ulcers. Some type of extreme discomfort is always present.

   b. *An attitude of panic or defeat.* The person may feel that he has tried everything and that nothing works. Therefore, he feels like a failure—defeated, overwhelmed, and helpless. He has two ways of responding at this time: The first is to become agitated and adopt unproductive behavior (pacing, drinking, taking drugs, driving fast, getting into fights); the second is to become apathetic and inert (sleeping excessively, sitting in front of the television for hours).

   c. *A focus on relief.* "Get me out of this situation!" is the concern and cry. The person wants relief from the pain of the stress. He is not in a condition to deal with the problem in a rational way. Sometimes people in crisis may appear to be in a daze, or they respond in bizarre ways. They are somewhat frantic in their efforts and will look to others for help. They may become overly dependent on others to help them out of their dilemma.

   d. *A time of lowered efficiency.* People in active crisis may continue to function normally, but instead of responding at 100%, their response may be at about 60%. The more threatened people feel by the situation, the less effective their coping resources will likely be.

A CHRISTIAN PERSPECTIVE ON CRISIS

As Christians, we have a basis for understanding crisis within the context of faith (Swihart & Richardson, 1987). From an overview of Scripture, our perspective of crisis is as follows:

- Crisis events are a part of life originating from God's specific direction, from the natural progression of creation, or from humanity's spiritual deprivation. Yet God is sovereign over all these things.
- There is a purpose for the crisis event (Proverbs 16:9). God is a God of purpose and direction, even when we in finite wisdom do not understand his mind (Proverbs 30:3-4).

- The crisis can cause a resistance to change (e.g., Pharaoh and the plagues in Exodus 7–12), or change can ultimately be accepted (see Romans 8:31).
- Spiritual resources are available for dealing with crisis.
- When we understand the crisis, we may even be able to thank God for the growth it has produced (Romans 8:28,37).

THE FOUR PHASES OF A CRISIS

There are four fairly typical and predictable phases of a crisis.

THE IMPACT PHASE

This phase is usually quite brief. People know immediately that they are facing a major event. For some individuals, it is like being hit with a two-by-four. The impact phase involves becoming aware of the crisis and being stunned. This period lasts from a few hours to a few days depending on the event and the person involved. In the case of a severe loss, tears can occur immediately or a few days later. Obviously, the more severe the crisis or loss, the greater the impact and the greater the amount of incapacitation and numbness.

It is possible for the impact phase to linger on and on, as in the case of a divorce proceeding. During this phase, the person has to decide whether to stay and fight the problem through to resolution or to run and ignore the problem. Psychologists call this the fight-or-flight pattern. During the impact state, people are usually less competent than normal, and their typical style of handling life's problems will probably emerge. If their tendency in the past has been to face problems, they will probably face the crisis. But if their tendency has been to avoid problems, they will probably run from this one.

Fighting and attempting to take charge again in the midst of crisis seems to be the healthier response. Running away only prolongs the crisis. And since each of the succeeding phases is dependent upon the adjustments made in the previous one, avoiding reality does not make for good judgment. Pain is prolonged instead of resolved.

During the impact stage, thinking capability is diminished. People become numb and disoriented. It is even possible for some to feel as though they cannot think or feel at all. It is as though their entire system shuts down. Insight is lessened and should not be expected at this time.

The factual information you give these people may not fully register during this phase and may have to be repeated later on. You may explain something to them, and they in turn will ask a question that indicates they never heard one word. Because they are numb and stunned, they may make unwise decisions. But unfortunately, important decisions may be necessary; postponing them may not be an option. This is when they need the help of other people.

Another common reaction during the impact phase is for people to actually and symbolically search for the lost object. For example, a woman whose husband dies may pore over photographs and other items that remind her of her spouse. When something is lost that means a great deal to us, we hold on to our emotional attachments for a while. It is normal to search for the lost object or a replacement, and the searching is more intense when we are not aware of what is happening to us.

Reminiscing about the loss is usually done in proportion to the value of the object or person. People need to be listened to and have their feelings accepted at this point of the crisis. Rejected feelings delay the resolution of the problem. Feelings should not be buried or denied. People in crisis may even feel strange about the feelings and thoughts they are experiencing, and negative comments from others do not help.

Feelings of guilt frequently accompany change and crisis. People feel guilty for many reasons, from having failed to having achieved. Many have difficulty handling success. They wonder if they deserve it, or they see others who do not succeed and, in their empathy for them, experience guilt over their own sense of success. Children of parents who divorce sometimes feel guilty, as though they were responsible for the destruction of the marriage. Those who witness accidents or catastrophes often experience guilt. They ask, "Why was I spared?" or "Why did my young child die and not me? He had so many more years left than I do!"

People experiencing guilt have several choices available to alleviate the guilt: They can rationalize their way out of the guilt; they can project blame onto others; they can attempt to pay penance and work off the guilt; or they can apply the forgiveness available where there has been genuine sin and violation of God's principles. God can and does remove true guilt. But there will be other feelings of guilt that have no basis. People who live by their emotions most of the time will be more guilt-prone than others during a crisis. Those who have negative patterns of thinking or self-talk will exhibit guilt more than others. Of course, people do not need to seek God's forgiveness for false guilt. What they need is help to change their perspective or self-talk. But this will take time and probably will not be accomplished during the impact phase.

The accompanying chart (box 28.1) is helpful for counseling people in crisis. Often those in crisis feel overwhelmed and wonder if their response is normal. On many occasions, I have shown people the complete chart, described the various phases, and asked them to indicate which phase they are in. After looking at the chart, they often say, "You mean my response is normal?"

By discovering the normalcy of their response, they feel relieved. Then they are able to see where they will be heading, which further alleviates anxiety. It works best, however, when they look at this chart during the withdrawal-confusion phase.

BOX 28.1—CHANGE AND CRISIS SEQUENCE*

	Phase I *Impact*	Phase II *Withdrawal, Confusion*	Phase III *Adjustment*	Phase IV *Reconstruction, Reconciliation*
Time	HOURS	DAYS	WEEKS	MONTHS
Response	fight-flight	anger-fear- guilt-rage	positive thoughts begin	hope
Thought	numbness, disorientation	ambiguity, uncertainty	problem solving	consolidation of problem solving
Direction	search for lost object	bargaining, detachment	search for new object	reattachment
Search Behavior	reminiscence	perplexed scanning	focused exploration	reality testing
Guidance Needed	acceptance of feeling	task-oriented direction	support, spiritual insight	breakthrough, reinforce hope

THE WITHDRAWAL-CONFUSION PHASE

You will note from your review of the chart that each phase becomes progressively longer. The withdrawal-confusion phase can last days and even weeks. One of the key factors in this phase is the eventual decline of emotional energy. When this occurs, there are usually feelings of depression or a sense of being worn out.

During withdrawal-confusion, the tendency to deny one's feelings is probably stronger than at any other phase. Feelings now can become ugliest. Intense anger can occur toward whatever happened, which in some cases brings on guilt

---

* Based on a similar chart by Hirschowitz (n.d.)

for having such feelings. Shame can then result, and the pain of all the various feelings can bring on the tendency and desire to suppress all emotions. Christians and non-Christians alike will refuse to let the process of grief occur. This denial leads to emotional, physical, and interpersonal difficulties.

How do people actually feel when confronted by a crisis? What goes on across their emotional spectrum when they find they are unable to adjust to life's major difficulties? The distinctive aspects of a crisis include a sense of:

- *Bewilderment:* "I've never felt this way before."
- *Danger:* "I feel so scared. Something terrible is going to happen."
- *Confusion:* "I can't think clearly. My mind doesn't seem to work."
- *Impasse:* "I'm stuck. Nothing I do seems to help."
- *Desperation:* "I've got to do something, but I don't know what to do."
- *Apathy:* "Nothing can help me. What's the use of trying."
- *Helplessness:* "I can't cope by myself. Please help me."
- *Urgency:* "I need help right now."
- *Discomfort:* "I feel so miserable and unhappy."

Knowing that these are common feelings during a crisis, you can relate to clients by making statements such as "Could it be that you feel stuck, as if nothing seems to help?" or "Perhaps you feel desperate, like you want to do *something* but you're not sure what."

If our shared feelings begin to shock and alarm our friends, we tend to repress them. But feelings must be expressed, which means people in crisis need to rely on friends, relatives, or some other type of social support system. Unfortunately, supportive friends and relatives might not be available or forthcoming. Expressions of support (meals, gifts, cards, time, and prayers) often come during the impact phase and at the beginning of the withdrawal-confusion phase. But usually in a few weeks, the support system diminishes, and that is when it may be needed most.

THE ADJUSTMENT PHASE

Notice on the chart the length of time the adjustment phase takes. It is longer than the others. Yet the emotional responses during this time are hopeful. Some depression may remain or come and go, but positive attitudes have begun. Things are looking up. People begin talking optimistically about the future, about the possibility of enjoying a new job, rebuilding a fire-destroyed home, or considering remarriage. They have just about completed their detachment from what was lost and are now looking for something new to which they can become attached.

What is occurring begins to take on new importance to these clients, who have been through the depths of the valley and are now climbing out. What they begin to attach to holds special significance for them.

Remember that people at this time are hopeful, but theirs is not a consistent sense of hope. They fluctuate and will have down times. They still need someone to be close or available. Because insight is returning, they can be objective about what has occurred and can now process new information and suggestions. They can also gain spiritual insights at this point, and their values, goals, and beliefs may have a greater depth (Ahlem, 1978).

The Reconstruction and Reconciliation Phase

During this last phase there is a sense of confidence, and plans are made out of this sense of assuredness. Doubts and self-pity are gone, because people at this point have made a logical decision not to engage in them anymore. They take the initiative for progress, and reattachments are occurring. New people, places, activities, jobs, and spiritual responses now exist. If there has been anger and blame toward others, or if relationships were broken, this is the time for reconciliation. Helpful gestures, notes, shared meals, and acts of kindness for others may be forms of reconciliation. The final resolution of a crisis is a reflection of the newness of the person. A crisis is an opportunity for a person to gain new strengths, values, and perspectives on life.

I am often asked whether it is appropriate or helpful to pray or share Scripture with a client during any or all of these phases. Sensitivity should be your guide here. If the person in crisis is angry at God for what has occurred, he or she may not be open to either prayer or Scripture. Should you decide to offer prayer or a Scripture reading, keep it brief and, of course, avoid sermonizing. Your prayer could reflect the turmoil of the individual's struggle as well as be a petition for God's comfort and guidance. Scripture that reflects life's struggles, such as the prayers of David in the Psalms, may help the person articulate what he or she is feeling. There are many passages to share that will bring a sense of comfort at this difficult time.

What to Do in a Crisis

Crisis intervention is giving emotional first aid. What you're doing is emotional damage control. In its simplest form, the goal of crisis intervention is to stop the psychological deterioration, stabilize the person's thinking and emotional processes, manage stress symptoms, and either restore him or her to a functional level or find the necessary help for continuing acute care. But remember, this is *not* therapy. It is intervention and support (Burgess & Baldwin, 1981; Mitchell & Everly, 1977).

When a crisis event is potentially or actually trauma producing, an intervention known as Critical Incident Stress Management (CISM) can be employed by a trained professional health worker. Rescue workers (firefighters, police officers, EMTs, paramedics, search-and-rescue personnel, nurses, doctors) use CISM when involved in tragedies such as plane crashes, natural disasters, or violent events (such as the recent attacks on the World Trade Center and Pentagon, the Columbine shootings, and the Oklahoma City bombing). Victims and observers of tragedies also benefit from the debriefing approach of CISM (Mitchell & Everly, 1977).

Eight basic steps are needed to help a person in crisis (adapted from Puryear, 1979). These steps are applicable to various types of crises, but you will need to be sensitive and flexible in their application.

1. *Initiate immediate intervention.* A crisis is perceived as a danger. It is threatening to the person involved, and there is a time limit on the opportunity for intervention. In the vulnerable or disturbed state, each person will respond to the problem in a different way. Some see it as a threat to their needs, their security, or their sense of control over their own lives. Others may see it as a loss. Still others see it as a challenge to grow, survive, master a situation, or achieve self-expression.

Remember that people cannot tolerate the stress of a crisis for long. In one way or another, they will resolve it within a period of six weeks. A state of equilibrium must be regained. If they must wait to see you, it shouldn't be for more than one night. And if there is a wait, at least talk with them briefly on the telephone.

The way people in crisis achieve equilibrium may or may not be healthy. They may be so overwhelmed that they become self-destructive if they do not receive immediate help. You need to act quickly because your assistance can make the crisis less severe and may help prevent people from harming themselves.

In a crisis, there are misperceptions, feelings of tension and a sense of urgency, and lowered efficiency. Therefore, many of a person's attempts to find quick relief will not be well thought out. Those efforts could even be counterproductive, worsening the problem or crisis.

The first step is to find out what happened and to let those in crisis describe it from their perspective. You may at times have to bring them back to the issue with questions such as "And then what occurred?" or "If I understand you, this is what happened."

Do not immediately ask, "How did you feel?" Instead, ask, "What thoughts went through your mind initially?" And later, when you're ready to talk about feelings, ask, "What was your reaction to all this?" rather than "How did you feel?" Some people have difficulty with the word *feelings* if they are more cognitive than emotive.

During this initial phase, sustainment techniques are used. The dual purpose is to lower anxiety, guilt, and tension and to provide emotional support. All of these are efforts to restore equilibrium. *Reassurance* is used in the beginning phase to help the person who is worried about cracking up. But remember that too much reassurance may eliminate all the anxiety when some is needed for positive change to occur. *Encouragement* helps clients overcome feelings of helplessness and hopelessness.

Procedures of *direct influence* are used to promote desired changes in clients. Used more often in crisis counseling than in other types of counseling, these procedures can include encouraging new behaviors as well as reinforcing what the person is already doing. When people are depressed, confused, or bewildered, they may need more *forceful techniques*. You might advocate a definite course of action or offer warnings of specific consequences if clients act a certain way. A suicidal person needs direct intervention (Gohan, 1978).

Some of the most severe outcomes of a crisis are suicide, homicide, running away, physical harm, or family disruption. Cutting oneself off from the acknowledged emotional ties of a family is a disaster for both the person and the family members. Therefore, one of the goals in crisis counseling is to *help avert a disastrous outcome*.

During a crisis, you have a tremendous opportunity to help and minister. The unsettled state of a crisis is also a time of change and flexibility. People in crisis are never more open to growth, never more accessible, and never less defensive. Because they are unsuccessful in their usual ways of responding and coping, they are open to trying something new. If you are going to have an effect upon the life of a person or family, it will be at this time. That is one reason crisis counseling is so important for those in ministry.

2. *Take action.* People in crisis tend to flounder, and we need to move them toward meaningful, purposeful, and goal-directed behavior. They need to know that something constructive is being done by them and for them, and they need to feel this right from the first session. This is not the time to have them fill out questionnaires, take personality tests, explore their history, or merely establish rapport. You need to be active. You will need to participate in, contribute to, and direct the first session. Listening is an important tool for gathering information.

During this time, help people understand the crisis. Usually the crisis is related to some event, but clients often are unable to bridge the two. They need to bring their feelings of despair together with the event.

As you are gathering information from the client's story and from answers to your questions, you should seek to discover the following: (1) Which issues in the person's life need to be attended to immediately, and (2) which issues can be postponed until later? Help the person make this determination, for often people in crisis are not aware of what can wait and what must be handled now. As you work more and more in crisis situations, you will discover that you seldom have to conduct a question-by-question approach to derive this information. The person will volunteer most of it. But as you discuss the situation with the person, be sure to keep all these questions and issues in mind (Slaikeu, 1984).

Be aware of the person's level of alertness and ability to communicate. Attempt to identify the cause of the crisis with prompts such as "Tell me what has happened to make you so upset" or "Can you tell me the reason you're so upset? I'd like to hear what you have to say." Those in crisis sometimes have difficulty stating clearly what they want to say. When this occurs, you will need to be patient. Any verbal or nonverbal indications of impatience, discomfort, or prodding will be detrimental.

Allow for pauses, and remain calm. Especially during the impact phase of the crisis, the mental processes do not function as they normally would. Sometimes the pain is so extreme that words will not come easily. As you listen to the person, notice if any important themes are being expressed. You can detect this either through statements being repeated or when things are said with great intensity. These are clues pointing to the person's source of distress.

On occasion you will need to redirect the conversation. In crisis situations, some issues need *immediate* action and some can wait a week or a month. Reinforce statements that are related to the crisis and avoid asking follow-up questions about unrelated topics or peripheral issues. You might say, "What you have just said sounds important to you, and in the future we can talk about it. But right now, it doesn't seem directly related to your real concern. Let's come back to that." This process of focusing helps filter out any material that is irrelevant to the crisis but that the person may not recognize as such.

If you are confused by what is said, don't hesitate to ask for clarification. When clients are able to express themselves fairly well, help them explore the available alternatives for dealing with the situation. Ask questions such as "What else might be done at this time?" Discover what type of support system the person has—spouse, parents, friends, coworkers, or fellow church members. It could be the person is new in town with no contacts or roots in the area. In such cases, you will need to help create a new support system in addition to whatever help you can personally give.

People in crisis often feel that their world is falling apart and that everything is spinning out of control. They see confusion and perhaps even chaos. Try to determine if you might be able to bring a greater sense of order to the person's environment. If you can assist in bringing a sense of calm and stability, you'll help the person. Perhaps a person needs to stay at a different location for a while, or needs some peace and quiet, or needs to be away from well-meaning people whose attempts to help only complicate matters.

Note, too, that a crisis is triggered by the person's *perception* of what has occurred. So assess what the client is telling you and compare it to the problem as you see it. At times you may feel that the person is overreacting, but remember that what triggers the reaction might not be the main problem. Some people fall apart over an insignificant occurrence that is really only a precipitating factor. They may have blocked or delayed a response to a crucial problem.

It has been suggested that you take either a facilitative or a directive role in helping the person deal with the crisis. You should take a directive role if the client (or someone else involved in the situation) is in danger, is so emotionally overwhelmed that he has no capability to function or take care of himself, is using drugs or alcohol, or has been injured.

Conversely, your role should be facilitative when the person is not a danger to others or himself and is capable of making phone calls, running errands, driving, and so on. You and the client make the plans together, but the client carries out the plan.

Whether you are taking directive or facilitative action, *listening* and *encouraging* are primary tools. Often I have people say things like "I'm cracking up," "I think I'm going crazy," "Other people don't have this much pain, do they?" or "If I had more faith, I wouldn't be responding this way." What these people are really saying is "I'm out of control. I'm afraid." They are trying to figure out what is happening to them, and such statements are their attempts to understand their predicament.

Here is your opportunity to offer realistic reassurance with statements such as "It's common to feel this way, but in reality it's doubtful that you're going crazy. Your reaction and feelings are normal considering all that you're experiencing." Or you might say, "With all you've been through, I'd be a bit concerned if you *weren't* reacting in some way." Normalizing your clients' feelings and reactions can be a source of relief for them.

When you are involved in helping a person with direct action, keep in mind the specific laws and legal procedures of your state and community. For example, do you as a minister, professional counselor, or lay counselor know your responsibility regarding privileged information or confidentiality when you counsel? What does the law state if the person talks specifically about suicidal or homicidal intent? Can someone in your county be involuntarily confined in a hospital for observation if that person appears emotionally distraught or suicidal? What if a parent tells you that he or she physically abused his or her child four years ago? What if an adolescent tells you she has been sexually abused?

Some ministers and lay counselors (and even professional counselors) take direct action too often. Before you take action, ask yourself:

- Is this something the person could do for him- or herself?
- What will this accomplish in the long run?
- How long will I need to be involved in this way?
- Are there any risks in doing this? If so, what are they?
- How could this person be helped in a different manner?

The feeling of helplessness is strong during a crisis, but you can counter it by encouraging the person to create alternatives and to take action. This will also help the person operate from a position of strength rather than weakness. One way to offer this kind of encouragement is to ask how the person has handled previous difficulties. Once again, remember to have the client do as much work as possible in order to build self-esteem.

Coach the person to consider alternatives. Some statements can be structured in this way: "Let's consider this possibility. What if you were to…" or "What might happen if you would…" Be sure to help the person anticipate any obstacles to implementing the plan. You cannot assume that the person will follow through without first considering the obstacles (Slaikeu, 1984).

3. *Avert a catastrophe.* The goal here is to restore the person to a state of balance. This is not a time to attempt personality changes. As I mentioned earlier, crisis counseling is not therapy. You must first help the person achieve some type of limited goal. There should be a bit of challenge to it, but it must also be attainable. A person who just lost a job may be able, with your help, to make a list of his or her qualifications, abilities, and job experiences. Just the simple task of completing some action can provide a sense of relief.

4. *Foster hope and positive expectations.* Since people in crisis feel hopeless, it is important to foster hope and optimism. Don't make false promises, but encourage them to solve their problems. Your belief in their capabilities will be important. This is a time when they need to "borrow" your hope and faith until their own returns. You expect the crisis to be resolved in some way at some time, and you expect them to be able to solve problems. It is your approach and interaction with them that usually conveys faith and hope rather than any blanket statements you might make.

As opposed to giving false reassurances, the problem-solving approach is a positive step. On occasion it is helpful to ask about past crises to discover how clients handled them. This helps clients realize that they have been able to work through past problems, which can instill hope for overcoming the current challenge. Also, begin to help them set goals for the future if they are in the adjustment phase of the crisis sequence.

5. *Provide support.* Sometimes a problem develops into a crisis because of the absence of an adequate social support system. Intervention in a crisis involves providing support, and initially you may be the only one offering it. Even being available to talk by phone is a means of support.

The knowledge that you are praying for the person each day and are available to pray with the person over the phone is also a source of support. Do not be surprised to receive a number of "urgent" calls during the early stages of a crisis. These need to be returned promptly. The purpose is give the client a sense of support even if it is through simple contact with you.

6. *Begin problem solving.* This has been called the backbone of crisis counseling. You and the client try to determine the main problem that led to the crisis, and then you help the person plan and implement ways to resolve it. You may discover other side issues and problems along the way, but you need to stay focused on the primary problem until it is resolved.

Think of yourself and the client as a team. Glasser (1965), author of *Reality Therapy*, uses the word *we* in his counseling: "What can *we* do?" or "How can *we* figure this out?" Involving clients in the plan accomplishes two things: It increases their chances of following through, and it helps them develop self-reliance.

During this phase, the focus is on setting goals, looking at the resources available to help solve the problem, and brainstorming alternatives. Make a list of possible alternatives. Help clients look at the probable consequences, both negative and positive, of each action. Let them give their perception of the consequences first, and then you may want to offer some other suggestions.

After you evaluate the various alternatives, help clients select a course of action. You may need to encourage and even urge them to do this. Ask for a commitment stating what they will do, how they will do it, and when they will do it. Go through the process step by step with clients and try to anticipate any roadblocks or ways they may inadvertently sabotage themselves.

Some people tend to avoid the reality of the problem and thus hope to avoid pain. Part of our task is to help them face the pain, but this must be done gradually so they are not overwhelmed. We can create an environment in which they feel safe and comfortable enough to face their situation fully.

7. *Build self-esteem.* It may sound strange to broach the subject of self-concept within the context of crisis counseling, but this seventh step is one of the most important. It involves (1) assessing and understanding the person's self-image, and

(2) discovering how the crisis is affecting that self-image and how what you do also will affect it. This is a time to protect as well as enhance the self-image.

Help your clients see how they have resolved difficulties before. When they say, "I can't handle anything; I can't even get through the day," respond with something such as "I saw you come into my office by yourself, and you have been a big help by being able to provide so much information about your difficulty." If someone says he has difficulty expressing himself, you might say, "You're concerned that you are not communicating well, but you are very clear and doing very well in telling me the problem."

8. *Instill self-reliance.* Along with helping to strengthen the person's self-image, work through the process to instill self-reliance. Remember that people in crisis are at the end of their rope. And because of this, their behavior may be regressive; they may respond at an earlier level of functioning. They want you to rescue them and heal them instantaneously. Do not respond to this need, however, for it will lower their self-esteem and may even prompt hostility toward you.

One of the most basic principles to follow in crisis counseling is this: *Do nothing for the client that he or she can do successfully.* If there is a choice between you or the client making a phone call (assuming the client is capable), have the client do it. As Puryear (1979) said,

> You are attempting to convey by your entire approach and your attitude
> that the client is a capable, decent person who has been temporarily over-
> whelmed by extreme stresses, and who will use your help to cope with these
> stresses and get back on the track. (p. 49)

When people come to us in a state of crisis, we, as counselors, have the opportunity not only to help them through the hardship, but also to minister God's grace and comfort. Christian counselors can be there at a critical juncture for those who experience a tragedy or troubling event, and we can be used by God to facilitate healing and restore hope.

CHAPTER 29

THE WORLD AT OUR DOORSTEP

Multicultural Counseling and Special Populations

KATHIE T. ERWIN, WEI-JEN HUANG, AND DIANE L. S. LIN

There are different kinds of gifts, but the same Spirit. There are different kinds of service, but the same Lord. There are different kinds of working, but the same God works all of them in all men.

—1 CORINTHIANS 12:4-6

A sea change is taking place in American demographics. The U.S. Census Bureau projects that by the year 2050, people of color will constitute a numerical majority in the United States (see Special Report, 2000). In addition, by the time baby boomers (those born between 1946 and 1964) retire, the majority of people contributing to Social Security and pension plans will be racial or ethnic minorities. Little wonder, then, that many prominent voices are raising questions about the future of cultural assimilation, of the American melting-pot experience ignited by George Washington's vision of America as a unifying experiment in liberty, freeing individuals from the tribal bondage and blood feud of Europe:

The bosom of America is open...to the oppressed and persecuted of all nations and religions—but they should not come as groups and so retain the language, habits, and principles (good or bad) which they bring with them. Rather they should settle as individuals ready for "intermixture with our people" and so become assimilated to our customs, measures, and laws; in a word, soon become *one people*. (Quoted in Guiness, 2001, p.1)

While assimilation—the "melting-pot" culture—is a growing political and ideological battleground in America, we do not intend to settle that conflict in this chapter. Herein we look at multiculturalism and special populations as a challenge in counseling. More to the point, we consider how to create the best alliance possible when working with people different from ourselves.

For more than a decade now, multiculturalism has been advocated as the "fourth force" in counseling and psychotherapy (see Sue, 1998). And while this book has argued that a paradigm shift is taking place in counseling around both empirical and spiritual axes, some have asserted that multiculturalism itself represents yet another paradigm shift in the counseling endeavor (Essandoh, 1996).

Jesus taught that one of the two greatest commandments is to "love your neighbor as yourself" (Mark 12:31). To love and serve all people is one of Christianity's highest values, as expressed in the children's Sunday-school song, "red and yellow, black and white, they are precious in his sight." Only fearful and small-minded people still argue for a monochromatic world. Our God loves variety.

The World at Our Doorstep

Over the next half-century, the challenges tied to this demographic change will likely be as significant as any wartime or economic challenge this country has ever faced (see Schlesinger, 2001). The traditional white majority and people of color will become increasingly interdependent and must learn to live together, to work together, and to help each other in order to ensure everyone's survival. We must embrace the challenge to train counselors who are capable of crossing racial and cultural barriers to serve people who are different from themselves.

Multicultural Competency

Christian counselors recognize the increasing importance of multicultural values and histories at all levels of counseling. Counseling without attention or respect to the critical differences of diversity will likely not be successful. For example, while Anglos terminate counseling after the first session at rates of 30% and below, termination rates for African, Asian, Latino, and Native Americans have been found to be 50% and higher (Sue, 1977). Therapists trained in cross-cultural counseling, however, show less premature termination with clients of different color and culture (Lopez, Lopez, & Fong, 1991). As Sue and Sue (1990) assert:

> Counselors who are willing to address cultural differences directly are those who do not perceive them as impediments. [And] counselors who view

these differences as positive attributes will most likely meet and resolve the challenges that arise in cross-cultural counseling. Such an individual is a "culturally-skilled counselor." (p. 172)

Sue (1998) advocates the development of multicultural competency for all counselors by expanding skills in:

- *Cultural-specific knowledge,* which requires building familiarity with a specific population or populations.
- *Scientific-mindedness,* which refers to the ability to form and test hypotheses, the avoidance of premature judgments or conclusions, and the awareness of personal blind spots, ethnocentricity, and the myth of sameness.
- *Dynamic sizing,* computer terminology indicating a fluctuating (cache) size, means knowing when to generalize for inclusion and when to individualize for exclusivity—as applied in a multicultural counseling context.

OVERVIEW OF WORKING WITH MINORITY POPULATIONS

Counselors must realize that all theories—even the accepted theories of multiculturalism—have their own cultural biases. For example, Bowlby's attachment theory, previously accepted as universal, is now shown to be laden with Western values and biases (Rothbaum, Weisz, Pott, Miyake, & Morelli, 2000). To be effective in counseling those culturally different from us, we must be aware of the differences in worldviews and in the underlying value assumptions between us and the clients we serve.

The challenge of discriminating between universal concepts applicable to all and client- or culture-specific variables is significantly heightened when counseling across race or culture. Trying to be culturally blind or color-blind diminishes the importance of the unique differences in the client's personality and lifestyle. Similarly, attributing too much ethnicity to a person or family who has assimilated the values of the dominant culture will also lead to mistaken perceptions and stereotypes.

In their classic volume *Ethnicity and Family Therapy*, McGoldrick, Pearce, and Giordano (1982) celebrate the distinctiveness of ethnic culture and see no danger, in clinical application, in using strong stereotypes and ethnic assumptions that are largely associated with immigrant cultures. McGoldrick herself implies that learning the English language—so crucial to political-economic assimilation and cross-cultural learning—threatens ethnic diversity and that maintaining the primary language supports preservation of the culture.

Others have cautioned that this approach overemphasizes the good of diversity and can lead to inaccurate assessment that denies the power of assimilating factors of the dominant culture. Failing to appreciate a client's assimilated behavior and values—generational status, education, socioeconomic status, religion, and language fluency—may be as serious a problem as failing to respect multiculturalism (Gelfand & Vandetti, 1995).

The differences between a parental generation emigrating from the old country and their children who are born and raised in twenty-first-century America can be significant—and a source of family and intergenerational discord. Thus we need to be humble servants just as Jesus was, always willing to learn from and serve multicultural clients.

While male-dominant and female-submissive roles are common across most ethnic boundaries, African American women are emotionally stronger and more self-reliant than other women of color. Ethnic groups are family-oriented and respect elders as well as kinship traditions. Women in all ethnic groups—except for Asian women—experience easier entry into higher education and careers than men. Socially, women of color tend to be more accepted than men of color.

In general, African Americans and Asian Americans prefer to *act*, while Latinos and Native Americans prefer to *be*. Group orientation is preferred over the rugged individualism of Western culture. Asian Americans and Latinos tend to speak softly, avoid eye contact with high-status people, and give nonverbal or indirect responses. Native Americans speak softly and slowly, interrupt less often, and are not demonstrative when encouraged. African Americans are socialized to speak with affect, to make direct and prolonged eye contact when speaking but not while listening, to interrupt and take turns speaking, to respond quickly, and to be more emotional and interpersonal in communicating.

BOX 29.1—DEFINITION OF TERMS

Culture: Behaviors, beliefs, morals, and customs transmitted over generations that characterize a people group.

Discrimination: Exclusion or oppression of any group because of their differences.

Institutional racism: A set of policies or standards that limit resources and foster dependence on the dominant society.

Racism: Devaluation, deprivation, fear of, or hatred for a group of people because of their skin color or other physical attributes that are different from one's own.

Stereotype: An artificially created standard applied to all people of a particular race of ethnicity without regard for God-given differences and potential.

AFRICAN AMERICANS

Walker (1992) addresses the problem of white people counseling people of color in a classic understatement: "Often blacks are viewed through ethnocentric glasses and evaluated by white middle-class norms" (p. 13). He then challenges the counter error of placing too much significance on ethnic factors that can easily become a counterproductive form of racial stereotyping.

Walker asserts that counselors should strive to "maintain a balanced view" (p. 13), informed by the Christian ethic that "God does not show favoritism" but accepts all those who fear him and live righteously (Acts 10:34-35). On an encouraging note, Helms (1984) finds that many African Americans enter therapy without viewing racism as their major problem and without seeing the therapist's different race as a significant deterrent to counseling.

Nonetheless, the impact of slavery and racism continues to be felt widely in the African American community. Too often, being different from the dominant racial group equals "less than" in a social as well as legal context, as evidenced in the following circumstances:

- *Racial profiling.* From surveillance in retail stores to airport security to unjustified law enforcement attention, African Americans may be followed or searched more often than others regardless of the individuals' bearing, dress, or actions.
- *Intrusive and unjustified police encounters.* "Driving while black" can be the primary reason for police to detain or search an individual. Many of these traffic stops have resulted in harassment, illegal searches, and even brutality (see Gaertner & Dovidio, 1986; Gardner, 1970; Ryan, 1971).

PSYCHOSOCIAL ISSUES FOR AFRICAN AMERICANS

Counselors working cross-culturally with African American clients or parishioners will want to keep in mind the following dynamics.

- *Powerlessness.* A consistent issue for many African Americans is powerlessness in the face of white cultural dominance. Challenging the dominant values has little to no power to effect change and is often perceived as hostile and contrary to the norms of that culture.
- *Anger and fear.* Racism and powerlessness create a pervasive climate in which many black youth feel devalued. They are often characterized as failures, are assumed to lack initiative, and are expected to rebel rather than achieve. Anger and fear are common in this powerful blend of psychosocial toxins.

- *At-risk males.* African American men face high rates of incarceration, substance abuse, and death by homicide. These statistics, however, are not destiny.
- *Intraracial discrimination.* Mainstream jobs and higher-education systems favor black women over black men and the more educated over the less educated. Discrimination may be so refined that lighter-skin minorities are preferred over those with darker skin.
- *Matriarchal system.* Under slavery, males were often sold and separated from their families. Thus women became the family leaders. From that heritage comes today's stereotype of the "angry black man" and the "strong black woman."
- *Caregiver stress.* This is particularly a concern for women who are the primary caregivers of their children and grandchildren due to the inability or unavailability of their adult children to be responsible parents.
- *Racial glass ceiling.* Unemployment remains high among the youth, and, in some fields, career progression is limited subtly, if no longer legally. Those who succeed face scrutiny if they distance themselves without reaching back to help others in the old community.
- *Isolation and marginalization.* Upper- and middle-class blacks who choose to be identifed with predominantly white neighborhoods, workplaces, or schools are often disconnected from the support system of their extended families and the black church.
- *Substance abuse.* The prevalence of drugs and alcohol as a means of escape or easy money exists in tandem with chronic unemployment or underemployment. Many black families are affected by the behaviors of a substance abuser as well as by anxiety about safety and the future of their children who could be lured into the drug culture.
- *Racial identity development.* The Cross model (Hall, Cross, & Freedle, 1972) identifies four stages through which blacks progress from identification with a white frame of reference to a positive black frame of reference. Counselors should be aware of these developmental steps:
    1. pre-encounter (idealizing and attempting to live by the values of white culture)
    2. encounter (crisis: anger or guilt causes questioning of this identity)
    3. immersion-emersion (withdraws from and becomes hostile to white culture in favor of embracing black culture)

4. internalization (global hatred and rejection of whites is replaced by tolerant, multicultural acceptance)

The process of self- and identity-development is tied to racial prejudice at many levels (see Banks, 1985; Chestang, 1972) and is most troublesome for biracial adolescents who are torn between the white and black cultures, often feeling like strangers in either world.

THERAPEUTIC APPROACHES

Effective therapy with African American clients (see Sue & Sue, 1990; Robinson, 1989) requires the non–African American counselor to observe the following guidelines:

1. Earn trust by gradually building understanding and gaining rapport. When you don't know what something means, say so and ask for clarification so that you can understand.
2. Allow clients to express concerns about having a therapist of a different race.
3. Avoid being shocked by youth who are trying to "test the therapist" with graphic details, drug language, or streetwise rap.
4. Incorporate the black church and church-based resources into all helping endeavors.
5. Consider the impact of racism on a client's defense mechanisms and coping skills.
6. Continually challenge clients to learn problem-solving skills and to accept accountability. Don't let clients excuse harmful behavior and severe disorders as acceptable responses to racism.

LATINO AMERICANS

Latinos are a diverse group who vary by history, mode of entry into the United States, race, socioeconomic status, acculturation, and ethnic identity. Generally, the one commonality is that Spanish is their spoken and written language (with the exception of Brazilians, who speak Portuguese). According to the 2000 Census, there are currently 35.3 million Latinos in the United States (12–12.6% of the population). By 2005, Latinos are expected to surpass African Americans and become the largest minority group in the United States (Special report, 2000).

PSYCHOSOCIAL ISSUES FOR LATINOS

Non-Latino therapists need to be aware of the following issues when working with Latino clients:

- *Family loyalty.* Latinos highly value family, intimacy, loyalty, and respect.
- *Machismo.* Traditional male leadership in the family is honored. In its most distorted form, it becomes oppressive and abusive toward women.
- *Marianismo.* The Virgin Mary is highly venerated, and it is an imperative for girls to remain chaste until marriage. This value also defines women's primary role as that of wife and mother.
- *Intergroup tension.* Tensions exist between Latino groups due to competition and territorial conflicts.
- *Intense ethical pressure.* Latinos place pressure on themselves to work hard and show self-discipline.

Therapeutic Approaches

Effective therapy with Latinos requires that the non-Latino therapist observe the following guidelines:

1. Never assume a Latino client's ethnicity, nationality, or affinity for either their culture or the Spanish language.
2. Make provisions for the client to express emotions in his own language by bringing in a translator or referring some clients to a therapist who speaks their language fluently.
3. Understand that a Latino client will grant respect to a doctor or professional, elevating the therapist to the level of an expert.
4. Deal with relationship issues within the context of family unity and tradition.
5. Recognize that preserving the family is all-important; thus divorce or separation may be unacceptable regardless of the nature or level of conflict in the home.
6. Utilize extended family as support system.
7. Recognize that a fatalistic view of problems and nonassertive response patterns are culturally consistent and may not be characteristics a client chooses to change.
8. Request clarification of a client's religious beliefs, which can, in Latino culture, range from Catholicism to Protestantism to various types of spiritualist cults.

Asian Americans

Asian Americans are a diverse group comprising more than twenty-nine subgroups of various nationalities and cultures, which include hundreds of regional and dialectal differences. These groups have their own immigration and social-political histories as well as conflicts or tensions with other groups due to past wars, invasions, and oppressions (e.g., the tension between Japanese and Koreans due to historical clashes in Asia).

PSYCHOSOCIAL ISSUES FOR ASIAN AMERICANS

The following issues can arise with Asian American clients:

- *Culture contrast.* Stress comes with living in contrast with the dominant culture that favors individualism. Asians traditionally favor family and heritage over the individual.
- *Reverse discrimination.* The fact that Asian Americans are often portrayed as math and science prodigies, with their successes more publicized than their failures, can cause excessively high expectations.
- *Respect for tradition.* Those who step outside the bounds of tradition can experience guilt and fear.
- *Suppressed victimizations.* Having fled war-torn countries, some men and women are haunted by scenes of rape, murder, brutality, and the conscription of youth into armies.
- *Culture assimilation.* The older generation can fear that the youth are becoming too easily assimilated into dominant Western culture.
- *Stigmas.* Acknowledging any psychological problem is viewed as insanity, a source of shame, or a lack of self-discipline. Educate clients about the various problems faced by many people and the treatment options for growth and development.
- *Family values.* Maintaining personal and family honor is a value worth any sacrifice. Unlike Westerners, Asian Americans do not put the individual ahead of family, nor do they favor personal success over the good of the whole group.

THERAPEUTIC APPROACHES

Effective therapy with Asian Americans requires that the non-Asian therapist observe the following guidelines:

1. Accept the intense family loyalty that can prohibit discussing problems with one's parents or children or within the family. These often are issues that counselors may ask about routinely in gathering a social history.
2. Proceed with restraint in asking about marriage or intergenerational relationships.
3. Be more directive than usual because of the client's respect of the therapist as an authority figure.

4. Recognize when the older generation may be trying to prevent the youth from assimilating into the dominant culture.

5. Deal with the specific problem identified by the client by setting goals and monitoring progress without meddling in areas that only you, the therapist, see as problematic.

6. Determine whether the client is a recent immigrant and connect him or her to social and church-based resources for food, housing, education, jobs, and contacts with people from the same affinity group.

7. Ask the client to share his or her religious or philosophical background. A therapist unfamiliar with polytheistic religions must be careful not to disrespect these heritages, which can take a long time for even new Christian converts to leave behind due to strong cultural connections.

Box 29.2—Cross-Cultural Treatment Strategies: A Case Study*

The following case study illustrates how counselors who have received Western training might work with culturally diverse client populations that reflect high traditionality and low acculturation.

K is a thirty-year-old PhD science student who was born and raised in South Korea and came to the United States at the age of twenty-four. He was referred to me by his Korean physician, Dr. P, who is also a friend of mine. Dr. P had called me one day out of great concern for K, who had become very depressed following his wife's tragic death while delivering their second son. Although K did not want counseling, Dr. P believed that he needed to see me as soon as possible, and he had "instructed" K to make an appointment. Knowing that this would be K's first encounter with a mental health system, I asked my secretary to show extra sensitivity when K called to set up an appointment. When nine days had passed without any word from K, I called Dr. P to let him know. He told me quite confidently that he would make sure that K came to see me...and he did.

I knew from the beginning that there was a high likelihood of K dropping out after our first session. Therefore, I was highly sensitive to the issue of shame and cultural stigma, and I looked for ways to help K feel comfortable. When I met

---

* Material for this case study was provided by Dr. Wei-Jen Huang, clinical psychologist and a medical school faculty member at Northwestern University.

him in the waiting room, I took an active stance and greeted him warmly, shaking his hand and conversing casually with him. (While I knew my actions were a violation of psychodynamic neutrality, I felt this was a situation that called for unconventional methods.)

HELPING THE CLIENT RELAX

Since I wasn't able to form an immediate connection with K by speaking Chinese—an advantage I normally have with clients—I had to quickly find common ground in order to build rapport. I sensed that K respected and appreciated Dr. P, so I started an informal conversation about Dr. P, asking K how they met, commenting on what a caring doctor Dr. P was, and so on. After some small talk, I stressed to K that our sessions would be confidential. (Reassuring clients of confidentiality is extremely important with this population.) To address K's ambivalence about counseling, I intentionally tried to give him the space he needed and told him, "I appreciate your taking the time to come. Let us work together for two sessions, and if you find this helpful, we can continue. Otherwise, I will understand if you don't want to continue. I know you have to deal with other things in your life."

My words and actions seemed to help K relax. Next, I took an active role and asked him questions about his appetite, sleep, and other physical symptoms. Clients who are less acculturated are more familiar with the medical model. Focusing initially on external symptoms or other family members' needs is more socially acceptable and can often help reduce a client's sense of shame. So, in the first session, we also talked about the behavior problems of K's three-year-old son and his worries about his one-month-old infant. I empathized with his feelings, focused on problem solving for a while, and offered him some practical help by giving him a few parenting brochures to take home. (Bibliotherapy can be a safe and useful adjunct treatment for this population.) Finally I praised him for his courage to meet with me and to face and work on his problems. I made another appointment with him and told him that I was looking forward to seeing him in our next session.

With less psychologically minded clients, I try to be very careful about "pacing and matching." It's important to understand their expectations and to meet them where they are. I often start therapy with a psychoeducational, problem-focused, symptom-relieving approach in order to engage clients in treatment. This approach helps me "buy time" to work on deeper issues later. It is also crucial to prepare clients for working on deeper issues by helping them understand the

(continued)

process of counseling. This means the therapist needs to do what Dr. Ivin Yalom (1995) termed "translating symptoms into interpersonal terms," continuously helping clients see how they can benefit from counseling.

VALIDATING AND NORMALIZING

K arrived on time for the second session, where we continued to focus on his concerns about his children, his worries about academic pressures, and other psychosomatic complaints. During the session I took a psychoeducational approach and started to teach him about the stages of grief. With less psychologically minded clients, I have found it helpful during the initial stage of therapy to empathize with their feelings by applying a multiple-choice format rather than by asking open-ended questions. Clients may feel threatened when they are asked such questions as, "So how do you feel?" They may not have a clue about how they feel or about how to respond.

Instead of making K feel uncomfortable, I helped him access and label his feelings by saying, "Other Asians in a similar situation might feel exhausted, numb, sad, or lonely, and sometimes they might not want to get up in the morning. Do you also have these feelings?" Validating and normalizing K's inner experiences helped strengthen our rapport. By the end of the second session, I gave K a "gift" (something practical to meet the client's immediate needs) by teaching him relaxation techniques to help him cope with stress.

This treatment strategy worked well with K, and he decided to continue therapy with me for a few more sessions. As the therapeutic alliance strengthened, K started to tell me more about his wife. Initially, he could talk only about external facts such as how they met and what they liked to do together as well as details about their families in Korea. Gradually, however, K was able to talk about the wonderful relationship he had had with his wife and about their dreams of building a school for poor children. He also revealed that he had been struggling with his Christian faith since his wife's death. After a while, as I mirrored, validated, and normalized K's inner experience, his inner conflict seemed to lessen.

During this period in counseling, K disclosed that he experienced bouts of sadness during the day that prevented him from concentrating on his schoolwork. He also indicated that he was having intense nightmares related to his wife's death, which woke him up during the night. I used this opportunity to share with K a few treatment metaphors. First, I reminded him of the Asian medical philosophy: It is more importance to treat the root cause than the surface symptoms. This is a philosophy with which he agreed. Then I talked about what the mental health field has learned from treating the trauma of many Vietnam War veterans: The more a person tries to bury painful feelings, the harder it is for him or her to recover. This dissociation of feelings impairs one's ability to connect emotionally with loved ones, and eventually, everyone in the family gets hurt. With this input, I tried to provide K with a rationale for verbalizing painful feelings.

This psychoeducational approach has worked well with most of my less acculturated clients, but it was not as effective with K. This was a therapeutic mistake on my part because K was not ready to work on his painful feelings. Although K complied with my request and started to share the sequence of the events surrounding his wife's death, there was not much benefit in doing so. K talked in detail about how he and his wife had joked with each other before she went into the delivery room and how she had thrown a paper clip to him, smiled, and said, "See you later." When he saw his wife again, it was in the surgery room where she withered and died before his eyes. K described this without emotion, as if it had happened to someone else. But I was overwhelmed by sadness. My intense response was probably a *projective identification* in which I carried K's pain while he covered it up. Despite our initial progress, K's treatment became stuck. K reported that his nightmares and daytime intrusive memories seemed to be getting worse. I knew we needed to go deeper into his feelings, but I also knew it would be a serious mistake to pressure him prematurely. He needed to proceed at his own pace.

Surprisingly, when I stopped pushing him and focused on supportive work, K started to get more in touch with his feelings again. Then, during the seventh session, when he asked me how to deal with his nightmares, I took a risk and tried an exercise derived from gestalt and psychodrama. To prepare him for this experiential exercise, I first gave him the allergy-shot metaphor in which I told him that coming to therapy and getting his weekly dose of grief treatment is just like taking an allergy shot. By intentionally facing his emotional pain in a safe setting, he could strengthen his mind and hopefully concentrate better on his family, schoolwork, and other responsibilities.

Verbal Letters

I then explained to K how the exercise works. With his permission, I took him through a relaxation exercise and some visualization. Then I asked him to send a

(continued)

verbal letter to his wife to tell her what her death had been like for him. He struggled initially, but when I told him to mix English with Korean (so he could access deeper feelings), it became easier. When he got stuck, I assisted by playing K's "alter-ego," and I expressed for him what I thought he might be feeling. K told me about a memorable event in which his wife and the whole family dressed in white and celebrated the hundredth-day ceremony for their first son. In my alter-ego role, I started by describing this loving family picture and expressed for him how much he missed his wife, what a wonderful dream they had had together, and how painful it was to see her leave. K broke into tears and started to talk at a much deeper emotional level.

After he had expressed much of his deep feeling, I acted as K's alter-ego one more time. I expressed for K his thanks to his wife for her friendship and companionship. On K's behalf, I praised her for being such a loving person, I blessed her, and I thanked Jesus for taking good care of her in heaven. K then took over, speaking in both English and Korean, and shared his gratitude and blessing. Then he ended the letter.

Next I asked K to do another important piece of work: to role-play his wife and to send another verbal letter from her to him. This was a very powerful and healing step for K. Through this second letter, K suddenly realized that his wife knew how much he loved her, that she wanted him to be strong, and that she is constantly praying for him and their two children. We ended this ninety-minute session by processing his intense emotional experience.

Before K left this session, I tried to take care of him by giving a *symptom prescription*. I told him that it was normal for people to feel a bit strange (more vulnerable) after an intense emotional experience. And if he felt this, it could be a sign that he was making progress in his recovery. K was obviously moved by this session, and he showed his gratitude with a firm handshake. That seventh session was a turning point in his treatment.

After that experience, K was able to grieve at a much deeper level. For the remaining sessions, we also worked on helping K build a support network, look at his future career and plans, and get his mother to come and take care of his young children. We scheduled the eleventh session two weeks after the tenth session, and the twelfth session one month after the eleventh session. By the twelfth session follow-up, K's overall functioning continued to improve, and he reported that his nightmares as well as the intrusive memories had diminished. Before we terminated our final session, I congratulated K for successfully "graduating" from our "Psychotherapy 101" class. I told him, "Now you know that counseling and psychotherapy are not for people who are crazy but for people who are mature and humble enough to want to learn and grow and who want to develop emotional intelligence, a deeper understanding of self and others, and leadership and people management skills." I told him that it might be beneficial to take "Psychotherapy 102" in the future, especially when he experiences significant changes in his life.

This coursework metaphor works quite well with most of my clients. The idea of serial "in-service" training (serial brief therapy) is developmental and can be quite empowering. After one or two good counseling experiences with the same therapist, clients may start to see the clinician as their "family doctor" and bring other family members into treatment. In my experience, this is particularly true with Asian and Latino clients. Another positive finding is that when clients come back for "Psychotherapy 102," they are much more ready to benefit from depth-oriented psychodynamic therapy.

FOLLOW-UP NOTE

Five years after the conclusion of K's therapy, I was walking toward my car in a public parking lot and heard someone call my name. I paused and looked around. It was K. He told me that both he and his family were doing well. He also told me that he had graduated from his PhD program, had gotten a good job, and had found an excellent church. For cultural reasons I did not hug him, but it was such a blessing to see his warm smile and the affection reflected in his eyes.

NATIVE AMERICANS

More than four hundred tribes that populated America before the *Mayflower* landed have been reduced to near extinction due to the federal government's misguided attempts to educate, assimilate, scatter, and isolate them on reservations. These tribes vary greatly in language, customs, family structure, and religious beliefs. But discrimination and racial slurs against Native Americans draw less attention or concern than those hurled at other minorities.

PSYCHOSOCIAL ISSUES FOR NATIVE AMERICANS

Keep the following issues in mind when working cross-culturally with Native Americans:

- *Isolation.* Segregation on reservations produced a distrust and fear of the dominant culture as well as of other minorities. Living conditions, schools, and medical care are all too often substandard, and job opportunities are few.

- *Substance abuse.* Alcoholism, drug abuse, and alcohol-related deaths are well above the national average on reservations. Children and teens are allowed to drink on social occasions and are rarely chastised for drinking, which is evidence of permissive parenting.

- *Suicide rates.* Among Native Americans, suicide rates are high, especially among adolescents.

- *Child abuse and high rates of fetal alcohol syndrome.* Both issues are related to alcoholism, which often begins in youth and persists throughout adult life.

- *Dropout rates among middle- and high-school students.* Behavioral problems, substance abuse, teen pregnancies, and lack of parental encouragement all contribute to the alarming lack of education among Native Americans, which perpetuates a cycle of poverty and welfare.

THERAPEUTIC APPROACHES

Effective therapy with Native Americans requires that the therapist observe the following guidelines:

1. Learn that honor among Native Americans is important and that it is typically gained from sharing rather than from the individual accumulation characteristic of non–Native American Western culture.

2. Characterize reluctance to compete or seek personal achievement not as low self-image but as a desire to avoid discord and to be cooperative within the family.

3. Understand that permissive parenting may be an extension of the client's belief in noninterference, and do not automatically challenge that style.

4. Realize that cultural controls prohibit the expression of strong emotions or the assertion of one's will.

5. Accept the Native American's orientation to the present, high regard for the past, and relative lack of concern about the future. Not surprisingly, Native Americans work better in the "here and now" than do Westerners.

6. Respect the wisdom of Native American elders.

7. Understand the deep-seated desire for harmony with nature in which acceptance is preferred over domination or control.

SPECIAL POPULATIONS

In the early church, people were appointed as "specialists": apostles, prophets, teachers, healers, administrators, and linguists (1 Corinthians 12:28). Likewise, among counselors, there are those who apply unique skills and interests to serve special populations such as those mentioned below.

MEDICAL AND REHABILITATION COUNSELING

Christians and secular professionals alike acknowledge the importance of the mind-body connection. When the body is compromised by injury, illness, chronic pain, or long-term disability, medical treatment alone may not be enough. Dealing with the emotional and spiritual issues of the sufferer enhances the work of the medical team. The American Psychological Association (Division 38) calls this field "health psychology" for its bio-psycho-social approach to viewing illness as a combination of biological, behavioral, and social or cultural conditioning. Health psychologists are becoming known for their work with cardiologists (Krantz, Sheps, Carney, & Natelson, 2000) and their ability to identify psychosocial risk factors for heart patients (Rozanski, Blumenthal, & Kaplan, 1999).

Psychosocial Issues of Illness and Disability

Common emotional stressors related to illness, injury, disability, or pain include the following:

- *Fear.* Lack of control, worst-case thinking, terminal illness, and severe disabilities create fears not only for the patient but even more for a family facing financial and personal sacrifices.
- *Frustration.* Enduring painful treatments, battling managed care, waiting for test results, and getting slow responses from the medical community drain limited energies and finances.
- *Stress.* Illness and recovery occur alongside the other demands of life: job, children, education. Pushing recovery into an already crowded schedule creates tension that delays healing.
- *Depression.* Feelings of helplessness and hopelessness often accompany a medical crisis. Thus depression related to a general medical condition is regarded as a problem that requires attention.
- *Anger.* Wrestling with unknowns often results in anger toward self, toward others who are healthy, and even toward God. Being stuck in that anger impedes recovery.

- *Social isolation*. The longer the incapacity, the more out of touch patients are with friends, careers, activities, and church.
- *Spiritual confusion*. The apostle Paul could view his afflictions as a way to become closer to Jesus (2 Corinthians 12:7-10), but many of us fall short of Paul's steadfastness.

Training and Work in Medical or Rehabilitative Counseling

Degrees in rehabilitative counseling, health psychology, and clinical psychology— and in most cases a professional license—are necessary for working in a hospital, medical clinic, or university. Check with prospective employers about their degree and license preferences. A person making a career transition from nutrition or nursing to medical or health psychology is highly prized for cross-field knowledge that can be applied to practice or teaching. Practitioners can also link with medical specialists, corporate wellness programs, government agencies, and academic programs.

GERIATRIC COUNSELING

Do not cast me away when I am old; do not forsake me when my strength is gone. (Psalm 71:9)

The fastest-growing population group in the United States is that of persons over age eighty-five. For some seniors, longer life is a blessing, a long-awaited opportunity to volunteer, go to the mission field, or to spend time with grandchildren. For others, long life merely increases the risk of memory impairment, disability, and depression (Older Americans, 2000).

Psychosocial Issues for Older Adults

When working with older adults, younger professionals will need to be aware of special issues many of them face:

- *Fear*. Seniors fear losing independence due to memory impairment, limited mobility, and financial loss. They are also more likely to be victims of crime and of dishonest caregivers.
- *Multiple losses*. After outliving a spouse, friends, and children, seniors know grief as a constant companion, which causes them to avoid forming new friendships rather than face more losses (APA, 1997).
- *Role loss*. When a person feels that there is no longer a meaningful role to play in the family, the workplace, or society, that person is at serious risk for depression or suicide. Some of these "role exits" (Blau, 1973) that sen-

iors encounter occur naturally (children leaving home, retirement) and others unexpectedly (job loss, illness, death).

- *Depression.* More than 20% of older adults living independently—and even more who live in institutions—have clinically significant symptoms of depression that need treatment.
- *Memory impairment.* Some decline in short-term memory is normal with age, nutritional deficiencies, grief, and certain medical conditions. A chronic interruption of memory process, permanent disorientation to person, place and time and progressive decline are signs of Alzheimer's disease or dementia (Erwin, 1997). Alzheimer's disease affects one in ten persons over sixty-five and five in ten persons over eighty-five (World Alzheimer's Congress, 2000).
- *Intergenerational adaptation.* In America today, 67% of seniors live with family members, yet only 45% remain in the family home past age eighty-five (AARP, 1998). Longer life and the costs of care add pressure to the "sandwich generation," those adults who care for their children and elderly parents in the same household.
- *Spiritual isolation.* In the final years, seniors make huge withdrawals on the "spiritual capital" invested during their lifetime. Illness and loss of mobility reduce church attendance. At that point older adults begin "values solidification" (Erwin, 1996), finding strength for today's pain in their faith experiences of years past.

Training and Work in Geriatrics
Nursing and clinical social work both have a longstanding history in geriatrics. Others working with seniors have degrees in counseling or psychology. Currently, emerging doctoral programs in gerontology are more useful for teaching and research than practice; a master's or doctoral degree in psychology with potential for licensure is more valuable. A stumbling block in the field of geriatrics is that presently only licensed clinical social workers and licensed psychologists are reimbursed for services under Medicare. As the aging population increases, there is a growing demand for counselors with various degrees to work in nursing homes, assisted-living communities, senior centers, adult day care, and community mental health programs.

SCHOOLS AND COLLEGES
Today's classroom and the dominant culture no longer support Christian ideals. Students are left on their own to learn to "stop doing wrong, [and] learn to do

right" (Isaiah 1:16-17). Yet they must do so in a society that glorifies drugs, sex, materialism, dishonesty, and selfishness.

Psychosocial Issues for Students·

Students may present one or more of the following challenges:

- *Learning disorders.* One in ten students has some type of learning problem, including ADD and dyslexia.
- *Behavioral disturbances.* Students from kindergarten through college experience performance anxiety, stress, cultural conflicts, sexual harassment, and other problems that lead to negative, peer-accepted coping skills.
- *Depression.* In the United States, 2.5% of children and 8.3% of adolescents suffer from depression, which starts earlier and recurs more frequently today than among older generations (Brimaher, Ryan, & Williamson, 1999). More than 7% of depressed adolescents later commit suicide as young adults (Weissman et al., 1999).
- *Substance abuse.* At this writing, marijuana use among teens is at the highest levels since the 1970s, yet there has been a minor decline in cocaine use among young teens (USDHHS, 1999). More than 10 million students ages twelve to twenty drink alcohol, with 6.8 million engaging in binge drinking (USDHHS, 1999). From playground to prom, students of all ages can easily obtain drugs and alcohol.
- *Violence and crime.* Nationally, 49% of all schools have problems with physical assaults, thefts, larceny, and vandalism. Fights with weapons are most common in middle school (Gottfredson Associates, 2000). More high-school students (57%) were expelled for bringing firearms to school than middle schoolers (33%) or elementary students (10%) (USDOE, 2000).
- *Peer pressure.* Desire for acceptance prompts students to take risks, defy values, and place peer acceptance ahead of safety or sanity.
- *Spiritual confusion.* Students in secular schools and colleges are exposed to peers and teachers who deny God, ridicule Christians, support evolution, and accept cults that subvert biblical truth. Young believers need the local church as a "truth meter" and support system.

Training and Work in School Counseling

Within K–12 school systems, school psychologists, school social workers, and guidance counselors provide testing and counseling. Depending on the level of work you desire, obtain a BA, MA, or doctorate in counseling, guidance, social work, or psychology. In some states, a license in school psychology can be obtained with an EdS (education specialist) degree as well as with a doctorate (EdD, PhD, PsyD).

CAREER COUNSELING

Malcolm Forbes (1919–1990) once said, "Diamonds are nothing more than chunks of coal that stuck to their jobs." How do people choose a job they can stick with for a long time? If the company suddenly downsizes or a longtime employee suddenly faces unemployment, how can that person start over at age forty, fifty, or sixty? With so much corporate turnover today and the end of the idea of having a job for life, career counseling is finally gaining the respect it deserves.

Bolles (1997), author of the frequently updated *What Color Is Your Parachute?* encourages people to look not for a job but for a mission in life because a "mission challenges us to see our [job] in relationship to our faith in God" and to "marry our religious beliefs with our work" (p. 215). The emotional and spiritual aspects of work are increasingly important to finding the right job (Luzzo, 2000).

Psychosocial Issues in Career Counseling

You will find it helpful to keep in the mind the following dynamics when working with clients in career transition:

- *Fear.* Changing or acquiring a new job is a task filled with uncertainty.
- *Performance anxiety.* Jobs are won or lost based on constant positive performance. Failure isn't rewarded. The drive for perfection leads to frustration.
- *Stress and conflict.* Coworkers can be partners or antagonists. An emotionally toxic environment can result in anger, lack of control, loss of confidence, and diminished relationships (Reinhold, 1996).
- *Sexual harassment.* Awareness and legislation have more employers working to stop this problem, but it still exists. Women are the most likely victims of offensive comments, inappropriate touching, and unwanted sexual attention.
- *Substance abuse.* Drugs and alcohol affect the workplace by causing accidents, absenteeism, crime, violence, and increased health costs. At this writing, the problem has increased 37% in five years (Institute for a Drug Free Workplace, 1995).
- *Insecurity.* Increased Internet marketing, computer graphics, and other electronic skills have pushed many longtime workers back to school or out the door, replaced by twenty-something techno-wunderkinds.

- *Spirituality and ethics.* When a salesperson's commission rides on a big sale or a friend offers insider information on a bid, personal ethics governs the course of action. For Christians, a job must never be cause to compromise. As Proverbs 13:11 teaches, "Dishonest money dwindles away." That means some jobs or companies are not places a devoted Christian can work without risking spiritual compromise.

Training and Work in Career Counseling

Career counselors need a basic knowledge of human behavior, developmental psychology, and vocational assessment as well as interview skills. BA, MA, or doctoral degrees in counseling, guidance, or psychology mean different levels of preparation. Besides colleges and universities, career counselors work in large corporations for outplacement, with government agencies, in rehabilitation programs, and with special-needs populations. Career counseling generally does not require professional licensure; however, depending on the state, some types of testing and assessment do.

SPORTS PSYCHOLOGY

Producer Roone Arledge revolutionized sports television with dramatic ways to show "the thrill of victory and the agony of defeat." From peewee leagues to the pros, sports is about the drama of human performance at its physical and mental best. Sports psychology is an emerging field in which psychological methods, behavior modification, and mental conditioning are applied to help athletes achieve their personal best in a sport.

Psychosocial Issues in Sports Psychology

Factors that come into play among athletes may include:
- *Injuries.* Pain is easier to manage than worry about reduced performance or loss of status during the healing period.
- *Drug use.* Although athletes are aware of increased drug testing and the risks associated with drug use, some feel that they can get away with selective use of both steroids and recreational drugs.
- *Depression.* If a performance falls short of the athlete's or coach's expectations, the athlete can be at risk for episodic or recurring depression. The athlete loses sleep, eats erratically, and may be lured to drugs to numb the emotional pain.
- *Body image distortion.* Sadly, eating disorders, such as bulimia and anorexia, are common among athletes who spend so much time and energy perfecting their bodies.

- *Interpersonal isolation.* Hours of daily training, traveling, and waiting to compete make many athletes feel alone in the crowd. The result is often a loss of self-esteem, recklessness, depression, or drug use.
- *Spiritual isolation.* The Christian athlete who isn't part of a team of believers may be ridiculed for depending on Jesus instead of self. Away from the home church, family, and friends who encourage the Christian lifestyle, the athlete is tempted to compromise moral standards in order to find camaraderie off the playing field.

Training and Work in Sports Psychology

As a degree program, sports psychology is relatively new, with most practitioners entering the field with degrees in exercise science or psychology. Opportunities in private practice, research, and team training are open to master's- and doctoral-level practitioners. Teaching and research jobs are mostly linked to academic settings.

OUR HERITAGE WITH MULTICULTURALISM AND SPECIAL POPULATIONS

Acts 13:1,3 tells us: "In the church at Antioch there were prophets and teachers: Barnabas, Simeon called Niger, Lucius of Cyrene, Manaen (who had been brought up with Herod the tetrarch) and Saul.... So after they had fasted and prayed, they placed their hands on [Barnabas and Saul] and sent them off."

The early church gathered men who represented different cultures and varied specialty skills to work for the common goal of evangelism. Clearly, it's time to follow this example and make connection with other counselors whose specialties, ethnicity, and fresh ideas help serve those in need. One counselor can't be all things to all clients, but you can find a Christian colleague who can help enhance your cultural and special-interest awareness.

PART VI

STRENGTHENING THE FUTURE OF CHRISTIAN COUNSELING

CHAPTER 30

RESEARCH IN CHRISTIAN COUNSELING

Proving and Promoting Our Valued Cause

IAN F. JONES

---

*Even in these post-modern times, submitting our truth claims to some
form of empirical corroboration is a good thing.*
—KEITH J. EDWARDS, 1997

Ask most counselors and they will tell you that they do not view research as
a very glamorous endeavor. Images of statistical analyses evoke fearful
reminders of tests in college over normal distribution, z-scores, t-tests, ANOVA,
regression analysis, and various other strange terms and procedures. Responses
among counselors vary when considering the necessity of conducting research, and
many reactions are negative. One response is to suggest that since the field is so
complicated, we need to leave research to the experts on statistics. Another argument is that statistical research in counseling is unnecessary since most of the conclusions could just as easily be obtained through observation and common sense.

What is research and, more important, of what use is it to Christian coun-
selors? In its most basic form, research is simply a method of acquiring knowledge.
The method involves identifying a problem and then systematically collecting
information in order to explain the causes and nature of the problem in question.
Like all areas of study, the field is subject to bias and variations in quality. Spiritual
matters, for example, are often ignored in secular counseling research (Buehler,
Hesser, & Weigert, 1973; Craigie, Liu, Larson, & Lyon, 1988; Johnson, 1993;
Larson, Pattison, Blazer, Omram, & Kaplan, 1986), although interest in religious
factors has increased in the late twentieth century and early twenty-first century

(Larson & Larson, 1994; Larson, Swyers, & McCullough, 1998; Richards & Bergin, 2000; Rose, Westefeld, & Ansley, 2001; Shafranske, 1996).

An examination of the literature reveals that Christian counselors have failed to do systematic, rigorous research and evaluation of their field. In 1983 Collins questioned the quality of the research in Christian counseling and issued a challenge for improvement. Around the same time, Royse (1985) called for more evaluative research in the field of pastoral counseling. A review of journal articles on Christian marital counseling published between 1980 and 1997 found a lack of uniquely Christian contributions to the field (Ripley & Worthington, 1998), and a review of pastoral counseling journals (1975–1984) revealed a lack of empirical research (Gartner, Larson, & Vachar-Mayberry, 1990).

Attempts to address this gap continue (Worthington, 1997). In this chapter we will look at the field of scientific research, including biblical insights into the topic, the historical development of the scientific method, the research process, and the value and limitations of research for competent Christian counseling.

A BIBLICAL PERSPECTIVE

God reveals himself through Scripture. In Genesis we discover that God is personal, that he created the heavens and the earth, and that humans bear his image. But rebellion has left every person in a state of sin and separation from the Creator (Genesis 1–3). The entire created order echoes the creative power of God, and although the echo has been distorted by sin, it is still possible to learn about God by examining what he has made (Romans 1:20-21). Such investigation permits us a general, though incomplete, revelation of God.

Put another way, natural creation is a form of sign language through which God expresses himself. The functional connection between the observation of creation and the expression of the Word of God is noted in Scripture (Psalm 19:1-7; Isaiah 55:10-11), but full comprehension is found only in the Incarnation where perfect creation and the eternal God are manifest in Christ (John 14:7-11; Colossians 1:15-17). In Jesus we find the entire alphabet (John 1:1-2; Revelation 1:8; 21:6; 22:13), the Living Word who provides the pathway of redemption from sin (John 14:6).

In contrast to the general revelation of God shown in nature, we are given a full and special revelation of God through Jesus Christ in Scripture (Hebrews 1:1-2). The Bible, illuminated by the Holy Spirit, provides the absolutely true, undistorted, and trustworthy account of the nature of creation, mankind, and the purposes of God (Romans 15:4; 16:25-26; 2 Timothy 3:15-17; Hebrews 4:12;

1 Peter 1:25; 2 Peter 1:21; 1 John 5:6-8). This foundation provides us with the necessary basis for correctly interpreting and making sense of God's general revelation in creation. The writer of Ecclesiastes, for example, set out to study and explore all wisdom in creation (Ecclesiastes 1:13), but he soon learned that accumulating a wealth of human wisdom and knowledge simply increased his grief, pain, and confusion (Ecclesiastes 1:13-18). His conclusion: Only by fearing (respecting) God and obeying his Word (commands) are we able to make sense of this world (Ecclesiastes 12:13-14).

In Scripture, we find encouragement to study God's world. From the beginning we are given authority to observe, organize, and categorize or name the creation (Genesis 1:28; 2:19-20). While we don't find a systematic, scientific methodology, we are given information and principles to guide us.

EXAMPLES OF RESEARCH PRINCIPLES FOUND IN SCRIPTURE

Knowledge and truth are observable in God's creation. A systematic study of the world around us reveals patterns and measurable relationships. The Bible tells us that there is order in both the living and the nonliving world and that creation is totally dependent on the will of God for both its origin and continued existence (Psalms 104; 135:6-12). We live in a purposeful rather than an arbitrary world. Both believers and unbelievers possess the ability to learn about creation, and even unbelievers may be recognized as wise, having a partial grasp of the truth found in the natural world (Exodus 7:11; Esther 1:13; Daniel 2:12-18). This common grace from God promotes morality and order in society and allows the development of science (Berkhof, 1939, 1941). According to Erickson (1998), "Truth arrived at apart from special revelation is still God's truth" (p. 198), but such knowledge and morality don't so much *discover* as they *uncover* both the physical and moral truth God has structured into his entire universe.

While information about God and his creation can be found in non-Christian sources, the full meaning of such knowledge cannot be understood apart from God's revelation of himself (Acts 17:22-31). We must view human knowledge from a humble perspective and recognize that, in comparison to the omniscience of God, our wisdom amounts to foolishness (1 Corinthians 3:18-21; James 4:6; Proverbs 16:5,18). Also, there are some things that lie beyond our wisdom and understanding, and they can be revealed only by the Spirit of God (1 Corinthians 2:8-11).

Close observation of the activity of creation increases godly understanding. Jesus observed the behavior of birds and the beauty of the lilies in the field and used them to illustrate God's provision in light of our propensity to worry (Matthew 6:25-34; Luke 12:22-32). Jesus' parables are filled with observations of the world around him. While he knew people's thoughts (Matthew 9:4; Luke 6:8), he did not expect others to have the complete insight he had. Instead, he encouraged people to examine the evidence and report what they saw and heard (Matthew 11:4-5; Luke 7:22). This included studying human behavior. The disciples, for example, were told to pay attention to the activities of the Pharisees and Sadducees (Matthew 16:11-12; Luke 11:37–12:12) and, in the process, to learn to avoid false teachings, reduce worry and doubt, and depend on God.

Accuracy in measurement is important. We should not be deceptive with our "weights and measures" and so mislead people or rob them (Deuteronomy 25:15; Proverbs 16:11; 20:10). In counseling research, the data gathered are often translated into activities that will have a direct impact on people's lives. Inaccurate measurements, shallow research, and misleading information can cause harm.

Motivation affects the direction and use of research. What is your purpose for doing research, and does it lie within the will of God? The census survey King David authorized (2 Samuel 24:1-10; 1 Chronicles 21:1-8) appears to have been motivated by personal pride and the quest for security and strength in numbers. The problem was not that God opposed counting the people or doing research in general (the book of Numbers is full of examples of such surveys), but rather that David's actions undermined his dependence on God for safety and protection. As a result, God punished David for his disobedience. The desire to honor God should motivate all work, including counseling research. So examine your heart and your motives before attempting to gather information.

Verification of findings is essential. We are told to "test the spirits" to see if they are from God (1 John 4:1). While this verse relates to testing human teachers who claim to be speaking for God, the general principle is that "true faith examines its object before reposing confidence in it" (Stott, 1964, p. 152). Do not accept everything you see or hear without first examining the evidence and determining whether you are being led by the Spirit of truth or the spirit of error (Alford, 1976).

The Bible rejects naive belief and superficial acceptance in favor of careful examination and assessment (Proverbs 14:15; 1 Thessalonians 5:21). We should not take anything for granted. In contrast to mystical and cultic religions, Christianity is rooted in facts existing in time and history. Any healing that Jesus did was open to examination and confirmation by others, including his critics. He insisted, for example, that the leper submit to the formal assessment and evaluation procedures of the religious authorities to corroborate his healing (Matthew 8:1-4). In terms of research, this principle means that we should examine and test all areas of counseling theory and methodology, evaluate the results in light of biblical truth, and allow others to examine our evidence.

RESEARCH WISDOM IN SCRIPTURE

The Wisdom Literature of the Bible (usually identified as the books of Proverbs, Ecclesiastes, and Job) contains numerous observations based upon personal experience as well as the study of creation. Biblical proverbs reflect God's wisdom in the context of the culture of the ancient Near East. They should not be interpreted as implying a perfect predictability; rather, they often reflect general tendencies and accumulative truths (Hilber, 1998; Welch & Powlison, 1997a). Hence, as a general principle or truth, obedience to God's Law is correlated with peace and a longer life (Proverbs 3:1-2), and foolish people die due to a lack of understanding (Proverbs 10:21). However, there are exceptions to the rule, leaving the writer of Ecclesiastes to observe that evil people may live longer lives in prosperity while good people suffer (Ecclesiastes 8:12-14).

In Proverbs we find basic assessment processes that presage the more formal scientific methods of observation and analysis. Observations from life experiences serve as examples of ways to gain wisdom. Hurley and Berry (1997) cite Proverbs 24:30-34 as an example of a study using standard research techniques. The setting for the study is a vineyard overgrown with thistles and weeds and surrounded by a broken-down stone wall. The independent variable is the vineyard owner's approach to work; the implied dependent variable is the production rate as related to the provision for survival. The data gathered include information on the condition of the field and the behavior of the owner. Analysis leads to the conclusion that a close correlation exists between a person's work attitude and quality of life and that a lack of judgment, evidenced by laziness and sleeping rather than working, will lead to poverty and scarcity. A similar conclusion can also be reached by observing the behavior of ants (Proverbs 6:6-11).

Another example of this methodology is found in a study of the relationship between sound judgment and satisfaction with life. In Proverbs 5 the actions of an immoral woman and the consequences of associating with her are described. Observation reveals that an adulterous relationship will result in a loss of self-respect, in a burdensome debt, and in disgrace. The conclusion: Remaining faithful to your wife keeps you out of trouble and increases your chances for happiness.

DEVELOPMENT OF THE SCIENTIFIC METHOD

Contemporary secular approaches have viewed science as an independent enterprise in which natural relationships of cause and effect are believed to exist within a closed system that makes the concept of God unnecessary. Logical positivism and rigid behaviorism, which have permeated much of modern scientific theory, operate on a verification principle. This principle states that if something cannot be measured, then it is not possible to know anything about it—and, in fact, the inability to measure something is a sign that it doesn't really exist. The underlying belief of modern science has been that objective truth can be discovered through rigorous empirical testing and observation, separated from value and faith orientations. Science is not an expression of a value system, according to this view, but simply a strategy for learning about life (Heppner, Kivlighan, & Wampold, 1999; Hoover & Donovan, 1995).

ORIGINS OF MODERN SCIENCE

The origins of the modern scientific method can arguably be traced back to Sir Francis Bacon (1561–1626). Bacon proposed that we cannot rely excessively or exclusively on human reason; instead, our understanding should be supplemented by science based on axioms and principles derived from nature. He stressed the use of observation and a systematic collection of information to discover the secrets of nature. In this new scientific approach, knowledge moved beyond mere contemplation, chance, and arbitrariness to experimentalism and the collection of factual information.

God was orderly in his work of creation, and observation and experimentation rather than theoretical and contemplative pursuits provided the power to transform and enlighten (Rossi, 1973). Bacon recognized that "man is but the servant and interpreter of nature; what he does and what he knows is only what he has observed of nature's order in fact or in thought; beyond this he knows nothing and can do nothing" (Bacon, 1961a, p. 8). Yet we are not infallible in our observations, he argued. Human understanding is "like a false mirror, which, receiving rays irregularly, distorts and discolors the nature of things by mingling its own nature with it" (Bacon, 1961b, p. 10).

Bacon's system of ordering and classifying is developed in his *Novum Organum,* where he sees the role of science as complementary to (or serving) religion and faith. To Bacon, science was not an autonomous enterprise; instead it was clearly rooted in a biblical worldview. He believed that as we "unrolled the volume of creation," we would recognize "the stamp of the creator himself" (Hooykaas, 1972, pp. 39-40). The ideal of science was not to rule over nature but to help us serve our neighbor.

His approach led Schaeffer (1976) to conclude that "Christianity is the mother of modern science because it insists that the God who created the universe has revealed himself in the Bible to be the kind of God he is. Consequently, there is a sufficient basis for science to study the universe" (p. 134). This unity later became separated, leading to a false dichotomy between nature and grace. Naturalistic science has rested on a belief in natural causes in a closed system that renders grace, faith, freedom, and the supernatural obsolete (Schaeffer, 1968).

IS SCIENCE OBJECTIVE OR SUBJECTIVE?

A number of critics in the secular field, most notably Popper and Kuhn, have challenged the belief in the autonomous and objective nature of scientific inquiry. Kuhn (1962) argued that scientists act on suppositions, values, and beliefs and that scientific reality is based on paradigms or explanations resting on these epistemological assumptions and the selective use of information in support of personal perceptions of reality. When evidence accumulates to the point that a view becomes untenable, then a paradigm shift occurs and the old theory is discarded for a new one.

Like Kuhn, Popper (1959) contended that scientists tend to overlook or ignore evidence that does not fit into their preferred view of reality. In other words, *their personal views shape and influence the scientific process.* One solution, according to Popper, is to have a more rigorous means of testing in which attempts are made to prove that a theory is false as opposed to the traditional approach of trying to prove that a theory is true. Yet even Popper and Kuhn fail to agree on the nature of scientific inquiry. Popper (1956, 1983), for example, believed that Kuhn was affected by "relativism, subjectivism, and elitism" (pp. xxxi–xxxii) in his claim that a scientist *must* have faith in the theory he proposes. Instead, Popper contended that scientists can assume that their theories are inadequate and that one day they will be superseded.

Christian counselors may find themselves confused by debates over the relationship between religion, values, and science; however, recognizing the relevance of faith in the practice of scientific inquiry is an important task. The inclination of some people is to go along with the status quo in the scientific community and dismiss the role of faith and values for fear of appearing ignorant, intolerant, or out of the mainstream. Competent counseling, however, requires that Christian convictions should serve as control beliefs in the practice of therapy and that Scripture should function as critic, interpreter, and guide in research (Johnson, 1997; Wolterstorff, 1984). Christian counselors can then build upon a solid biblical foundation in counseling and incorporate the benefits of scientific research into their practice.

The goal of science in counseling is to acquire facts in order to advance knowledge, which results in more effective therapeutic intervention. Christian counselors should have at least a basic knowledge of statistical analysis and the methods and procedures in scientific research. Such knowledge will enable counselors to understand research articles in journals and will provide them with additional tools of investigation. Introductory information on research and statistics is available in numerous books, including resources for people who are particularly intimidated by the subject (e.g., Kranzler & Moursand, 1995).

The Research Process

The goals of scientific research include description, explanation, testing, prediction, control, and advocacy. The most basic purpose of research is to describe the nature of a relationship in formal, often statistical, terms. Dimensions of behavior are studied to explain possible causes and consequences. Theories are tested and refined. Relationships are examined to predict the likelihood of future behavior. If behavior can be accurately described, explained, and predicted, then the possibility arises for correction of problematic behavior through prevention, intervention, and therapy.

Research may also provide visibility for an issue and give it an additional expression of support (Miller, 1986; Ragin, 1994). Such inquiry is designed to provide explanations that are

- *empirical,* based on the evidence of the senses,
- *rational,* having a logical consistency with the facts,
- *testable* or verifiable,
- *parsimonious,* seeking an explanation based upon the fewest number of assumptions,
- *general,* having broad explanatory power,
- *tentative,* acknowledging the possibility of error,
- *rigorously evaluated* for consistency with any known evidence,
- *cumulative,* building on what others have learned (Bordens & Abbot, 1999; Ellis, 1994),
- *heuristic,* useful for further practice or development and calling for future research.

Stages of Research

The rules and procedures of research provide a means of improving the accuracy of information, determining valid generalizations and theory, and allowing replication of studies. The basic stages of research include:

1. a statement of the problem and the hypotheses
2. development of a research design for collecting, analyzing, and evaluating data

3. collection of data

4. analysis of data

5. interpretation of the findings and a conclusion (see box 30.1 on the following pages for more detailed information)

The selection of a research method is usually based upon its appropriateness
for the subject matter being studied. Common designs and methods include historical studies, exploratory designs, surveys, experimental designs, developmental
designs, correlational studies, field research, and observational or case studies. All
methods have their strengths and weaknesses, and errors can occur at any point
during the research process (Isaac & Michael, 1981). Despite these concerns, research can perform a valuable function in Christian counseling.

THE VALUE OF GOOD RESEARCH

Research is a valuable tool for the Christian counselor if it is understood and used
correctly. Counselors can develop their own research projects, simple or complex,
and they can critically evaluate and learn from studies done by others. In the
process, research may serve a number of functions for the Christian counselor,
including assistance in modification, illustration, explanation, exploration, affirmation, prediction, and correction. These functions are not mutually exclusive;
they may overlap since a research study may serve multiple purposes in a single
situation.

The modification function. Scientific research can contribute information that
leads to changes in counseling theory, models, and techniques. Studies on the
effectiveness of counseling, for example, have led to modification and even transformation in the field. There are a variety of ways to define and measure effectiveness; consequently, numerous models and theories of counseling exist. Research
studies have attempted to show the efficacy of counseling (e.g., Lambert & Bergin,
1994; Pinsof & Wynne, 1995; Sanderson, 1995; Shadish, Ragsdale, Glaser, &
Montgomery, 1995; Tan, 1995). One result of this research is that the field is
beginning to move from model building to the identification of common factors
that are therapeutic regardless of the counselor's theoretical orientation (Hubble,
Duncan, & Miller, 1999). Here we see an example of the cumulative effect of
research and explanation, which leads to Kuhn's paradigm shift as new understanding emerges.

The illustration function. Scientific findings can be used to illustrate biblical
truths. One simple example of this function is found in an examination of the
research that serves to illustrate and enhance the truth of Psalm 139. In the psalm,
David marvels at the creative power of God and the incredible design of the

human body (verse 14). Studies on the complexity of the brain and its information-processing capacity reveal a vivid picture of its intricacies. This research enhances the meaning of the passage by providing additional evidence of the supernatural intelligence of God at work in the universe (Faw, 1995).

The explanation function. Research can assist in clarifying behaviors and relationships. For example, complex observational studies of conversations between males and females have led to new insights into the differences in communication styles (Tannen, 1986, 1989, 1990). On average, women speak more words daily than men do. There are also differences in the types of words they use and their intended meanings. This area of research not only explains some of the causes of gender conflict, but it also provides valuable information for more effective communication of the gospel.

The exploration function. Research studies can assist in resolving differences of opinion by systematically exploring the evidence. Even when the results of studies

---

BOX 30.1—STEPS IN THE RESEARCH PROCESS

I. Select and define the topic or problem
   A. Search for existing information
      1. Review the literature
      2. Identify biblical principles and perspectives
      3. Talk to knowledgeable people
   B. Determine the theory (and theology) related to the problem
   C. State the underlying assumptions governing interpretation of the results
   D. Clarify concepts and terms
   E. Determine the purpose of the study
   F. Select and frame the research question
      1. Decide on what will be observed
      2. Select the variables for study
   G. Describe the variables in a measurable form
   H. Form the hypotheses to be investigated
   I. Examine the value of the study: How will it contribute to the field?
II. Develop a research design
   A. Make a plan for collecting, analyzing, and evaluating data
   B. Evaluate the internal and external validity of the plan
   C. Select the participants for study

conflict, the response should not be to discard the research, but to explore the topic further. One group of researchers studied the conflict-resolution technique known as active listening and concluded, to their surprise, that it was not predictive of marital stability (Gottman, Coan, Carrere, & Swanson, 1998). Another group challenged the methodology of this research and the interpretation of the data (Stanley, Bradbury, & Markman, 2000). The debate gives us a glimpse of the disagreements that often accompany statistical research, but it also serves as a challenge to do more investigation on the subject (Lebow, 2001).

The affirmation function. Research can affirm biblical truth by confirming a biblical principle through general revelation. For example, a client was distraught over his divorce. He had not wanted it, but his wife refused to consider reconciliation. As he struggled with the issues, he discovered a book detailing a longitudinal study on the effects of divorce on children (Wallerstein, 2000). The research confirmed the troubling social effects of divorce on children and identified specific

---

    D. Set a time frame for completing the research

    E. Determine the criteria for evaluating the results

    F. Select the research method and instruments: quantitative (survey, experiment, statistical procedure) and qualitative (case study, participant observation, interview)

    G. Decide whether to use primary or secondary data

    H. Anticipate and address any ethical issues that may arise in the study

 III. Conduct the study

    A. Complete pretesting or pilot studies, if necessary

    B. Collect information or data in accordance with the research design

 IV. Analyze the data

    A. Arrange the information

    B. Apply any selected statistical procedures

    C. Evaluate and discuss data and draw inferences

    D. Determine acceptance or rejection of hypotheses

  V. Draw conclusions

    A. Summarize the findings in clear and concise language

    B. Connect the findings to theory, theology, and biblical view

    C. Discuss the significance of the results, particularly for ministry

    D. Identify related areas and issues for future research

    E. Report your findings

difficulties including such issues as loss, change, conflict, and a sense of betrayal. The client's counselor used the information to affirm biblical truths and help the client anticipate potential problems that his children might face in the future.

The prediction function. Research studies can help predict behavior and potential outcomes in relationships. A twelve-year study of 135 couples that began before they were married addressed such issues as satisfaction, adjustment, problem intensity, commitment, demographics, sexual and sensual enhancement, violence and abuse, and family development. The research also identified factors in marital growth and failure. One result was that the researchers were able to predict marital failure with a high degree of accuracy (80–91%) and, in turn, were able to provide suggestions for preventing and resolving marital problems (Stanley, Trathen, McCain, & Bryan, 1998).

The correction function. Information gathered from scientific research can lead to changes in our understanding of Scripture. This function provides an important safeguard against superimposing one's preconceived notions onto biblical passages. For example, suppose you hear that a scientific researcher has published findings that have upset church leaders. They have read his publications and believe that the researcher's conclusions have clearly contradicted a number of biblical passages regarding supernatural phenomena, including Joshua 10:12-13, Psalms 18:6-7, 19:4, 50:1, 93:1, 104:5, Ecclesiastes 1:5, and Revelation 7:1. They are skeptical of the researcher's claim to be a faithful Christian who believes the Bible.

How should Christians in the pew respond? Should they support the church leaders who are defending the Bible? Should they support the researcher who is honestly trying to communicate what he found? Should they condemn the man by criticizing his research as antibiblical and anti-Christian?

Does learning that the man's name is Galileo change your perspective? Galileo (1564–1642) concluded from his scientific observations that Copernicus was correct in theorizing that the earth revolves around the sun. In 1613 Galileo wrote a letter trying to show that the theory was consistent with Scripture, and in 1632 he published *Dialogue on the Two Great World Systems* supporting the Copernican theory over the Ptolemaic-Aristotelian theory.

The result? In 1633 Galileo was put on trial and, under formal threat of torture, forced to "abjure, curse, and detest" the "errors" in his work (Langford, 1998, p. 153). *Dialogue on the Two Great World Systems* remained in the Roman Catholic official Index of Prohibited Books until 1822. Galileo was finally acquitted 359 years later—in 1992.

Before we go any further, we need to correct some of the myths surrounding the Galileo case. First, he was never tortured and thrown into a prison. His incarceration consisted of no more than the equivalent of house arrest for a period of time. Second, although the prohibition against Copernican works was not officially removed until 1822, the Catholic Church has allowed the theory to be taught since Galileo's time. Third, although the debate has been cast in scriptural terms, the controversy is also a reflection of philosophical, scientific, theological, social, political, cultural, and personal differences.

While Galileo's predilection for argumentation and imprudent behavior and the reaction against a layman trying to tell theologians how to interpret Scripture may have played a part in Galileo's condemnation, the fact remains that the central issue revolved around the relationship between science and Scripture. In 1616, for example, Paolo Antonio Foscarini, a Carmelite friar, published a sixty-four-page book showing the compatibility of the Copernican theory with Scripture. His book was likewise condemned and placed on the Index of Prohibited Books. That same year, Galileo's theory was censured unanimously by papal authorities as "foolish and absurd in philosophy and formally heretical inasmuch as it expressly contradicts the doctrine of Holy Scripture in many passages, both in their literal meaning and according to the general interpretation of the Fathers and Doctors" (Langford, 1998, p. 89).

Social-psychological research suggests that we are all predisposed to rejecting ideas that challenge our worldview, particularly our interpretation of Scripture; therefore, we need to avoid hasty judgments. Wise counselors study scientific research carefully, even when it appears to contradict the Bible. One additional point needs to be made: Galileo was not completely correct. He was correct in his support of the Copernican theory, but some of his other scientific views were erroneous, including his theory of the tides, which he attributed to the motion of the earth around the sun rather than to the attraction of the moon.

The lesson to be learned here is that scientific research can provide a corrective influence on biblical interpretation, but we need to be both humble and cautious when applying research to this area. This perspective leads to an important principle in research for the Christian counselor: *Use scientific research to learn more about God's creation in order to counsel more effectively, but when research appears to contradict Scripture, examine your biblical interpretation just as rigorously as you evaluate the research.*

The Limitations of Research

In one of the first graduate courses I took on research and statistics, our class was given an assignment to review a textbook containing a compilation of the most current research in a social science field and critically evaluate the quality of the work. The results were illuminating. As each student reported his or her findings, it became apparent that many of the studies had weaknesses. Problems included unclear definitions, poor research design, misleading or mislabeled tables, incorrect copyediting, wrong sampling techniques, weak validity, irrelevant data, inadequate explanations, false information, bias, and other deficiencies.

One conclusion drawn from the class assignment was that all research has flaws and weaknesses. The effect of this discovery was to help us students recognize that scientific research does not provide us with unequivocal proof. We do not need to ask, "Does this scientific research have weaknesses?" We know that it does. The correct question is, "Are the problems in the research process significant enough to invalidate the conclusions?" Research is a helpful tool for discovery, but it has limitations.

Science offers a formal approach to the discovery of reality through experience, but scientific research that lacks clear guidelines can lead to false claims and unrealistic expectations. The secular field of family therapy has been criticized, for example, for promising too much and engaging in "messianic" arguments (Johnson, 2001).

Science does not have all the answers, and the information that it *does* reveal must be placed in the context of other forms of understanding truth and reality. In addition, scientific investigation is influenced by the values and moral constraints of a researcher or a society, limiting the extent and the type of research as well as the application of the results. Consequently, alternative approaches to acquiring knowledge and truth may yield better answers. A cautious approach suggested by Welch and Powlison (1997b) is to use information from research, but only with rigorous observation and with as few interpretations of the data as possible.

Humility Versus the Discoverer's Complex

Researchers can be misleading in their claims of originality and of the importance and quality of their work. Sorokin (1956) used the term *discoverer's complex* for the tendency of psychosocial researchers to claim that they are the first in history to make a particular scientific discovery, that nothing important has been discovered in their fields in the preceding centuries, and that only recently did real scientific investigation begin:

> Claiming to be particularly objective, precise, and scientific, our sociological and psychological Columbuses tirelessly repeat this delusion as a scientific truth. Accordingly, they rarely make any references to the social and psychological thinkers of the past. When they do, they hardly veil the sense of their own superiority over the unscientific old fogies. (p. 4)

Sorokin exposed this intellectual and historical amnesia by showing that many contemporary insights are actually revisions of ideas that can be traced back several centuries. Indeed, "there is nothing new under the sun" (Ecclesiastes 1:9). Sorokin also criticized social scientists for their use of obtuse jargon, sham-scientific slang, "testomania," and "quantophrenia." *Testomania* is the process of reducing personality characteristics to tests that assume scientific infallibility but are actually open to subjective interpretation and distortion. *Quantophrenia* is the replacement of true quantitative methods of psychosocial investigation with pseudomathematical imitations where the method is misused and abused in various ways.

It is not surprising, then, that scientific research is at times open to the charge of triviality. What researchers find may indeed reflect common wisdom, but even studying and documenting the obvious serves a valuable function, since the obvious sometimes turns out to be wrong (Babbie, 2001). Galileo's story is a case in point: The sun only *appears* to revolve around the earth. Job's counselors also learned that the obvious can be wrong when they made the assumption that major problems in an individual's life must always be due to that person's sin. They failed to examine the evidence, since they were already convinced that they were right. Consequently, God censured them for poor counsel and commanded them to make an offering of atonement. Then he accepted Job's intercessory prayer on their behalf (Job 42:7-8).

Mistakes occur in research for a number of reasons, including carelessness, inattention, failure to think through one's work logically, selection of an inappropriate means of assessment, and personal bias—an inflexible commitment to anticipated results that leads to a refusal to acknowledge the possibility of alternative evidence.

Mistakes can be useful for identifying pitfalls as well as directing researchers to alternative solutions. A mistake in one area can lead to a discovery in another. Mistakes, after all, are part of the learning process. Of course, we find it far easier to point out errors in the research of others than to acknowledge possible flaws in our own. Seltzer (1996), for example, has identified more than a hundred errors commonly made by researchers.

Reducing Errors in Research

Eleven suggestions can help reduce mistakes and improve the quality of your research:

1. *Do preliminary research.* Don't jump the gun and speak too early; instead, investigate first. See what research has already been done on the topic and do some preliminary testing. This will help you identify and avoid potential problems and flaws in your project.

2. *Identify your underlying theory.* Question your theoretical assumptions, and identify and examine your own prejudices. Don't let your theory limit the kinds of research questions you ask.

3. *Recognize the limitations of your research design.* Be willing to make assumptions about factors that are difficult to measure. Don't get stuck on formal definitions in a way that prevents you from proceeding with your research. Don't take responses from the people you are studying at face value, and remember that even statistical techniques are not theory-free.

4. *Avoid carelessness.* Proofread everything and carefully choose your words. Be precise and avoid errors in judgment.

5. *Check your sources.* Question and critically evaluate your sources. A "fact" may be a fiction created by someone to further an agenda.

6. *Create and maintain records.* Document the research process, keep your research notes and data, maintain files, and make backups.

7. *Avoid complacency when collecting information.* Try to identify what might go wrong with your research procedure, and plan for it. Do not assume that your original research questions and subsequent planning will be sufficient. Carefully supervise the people who assist you. Pay attention to detail throughout the entire process of your research design and implementation.

8. *Use research techniques and tools that you understand.* Before you begin, understand the concept you are studying as well as the method of analysis and the techniques you plan to use. Examine the purposes, assumptions, and limitations of the method. Check your work and don't have too much faith in your data.

9. *Use good judgment.* Study the ethical issues inherent in research, particularly the issues of confidentiality and research on human subjects, and become familiar with the ethical codes and guidelines. Protect the privacy of your subjects. Use informed consent and discuss with your prospective subjects the potential consequences of participation in the research. Do not trick or manipulate people into participating. Consider the implications of the research and anticipate the ways—whether helpful or harmful—that other people might use the results.

10. *Solicit help and collaboration.* Let your colleagues critique your work. Consultation leads to healthy examination, correction, and new ideas. Accept criticism graciously.

11. *Persevere.* Don't be discouraged. Set high standards and do your best to produce the highest quality research.

A CHALLENGE FOR THE CHRISTIAN COUNSELOR

If we as Christian counselors are to be equipped and informed advocates for our field, then we must take advantage of the resources at our disposal. Competent Christian counselors contribute to the development of the ministry of counseling at both a personal and a collective level within the community of faith. Rather than leaving the field of research to secular social scientists, Christian counselors need to be actively searching for the truths of God as revealed in his creation, and formal research methods provide the tools for examination and discovery. Basic research and evaluation techniques need to be practiced by every Christian counselor.

To be more effective as Christian counselors, we need to ask ourselves some challenging questions. How do I determine the quality of my counseling? How do I know that my clients and I agree on the meaning of particular words and phrases? How do I evaluate my skill level and measure improvement? What procedures should I use to follow up on my clients? How can I gather information that will improve my ministry? How do I evaluate the biblical efficacy of a counseling approach?

Research methods assist us in our counseling enterprise. There is a need for more formal research in Christian counseling that uses rigorous and high-quality designs as well as case-based research that confirms and graphically outlines progress and direction for clients and third-party vendors. Our findings need to be distributed to the wider counseling community, both Christian and secular, so that our research can be used not only as a means of building up the body of Christ but also as a witness and ministry to the world (Galatians 6:9-10).

We must recognize that research errors will occur, and we need to learn to distinguish good research from bad. Good scientific research will complement biblical truth. As one group of Christian researchers observed, "When and if research ever reveals findings that are inconsistent with revealed truth, we choose to follow Scripture. But one of the great blessings to us has been how wonderfully Scripture and sound marital research point in the same direction" (Stanley et al., 1998, p. 8).

In the end, we must treat scientific research as a servant, not a master; a tool, not a tyrant. Use it wisely, and always operate according to biblical revelation and under the guidance of the Spirit.

CHAPTER 31

SUPERVISION AND TRAINING

Raising Up the Next Generation of Christian Counselors

VIRGINIA TODD HOLEMAN

The best Christian counselors will be called upon to serve as supervisors and consultants—the teachers of helpers in the church.... Entrusting this call "to reliable men [and women] who will also be qualified to teach others" (2 Timothy 2:2b) will require that we invest significant resources in the training and certification of these leaders.

—OHLSCHLAGER AND MOSGOFIAN, *Law for the Christian Counselor*

Supervisors play a critical role in nurturing, training, launching, and sustaining skilled Christian counselors. Holloway (1992) states that supervision is "the critical teaching method" in the helping professions and that "professional education depends on the supervisory process to facilitate the development of the student from the novice to the autonomously functioning professional" (p. 177).

In the past thirty years, scholars and practitioners have paid serious attention to the processes and procedures that constitute counselor supervision, education, and training (Bernard & Goodyear, 1992; Borders & Leddick, 1987; Carroll, 1996; Worthington, 1987). With the increasing professionalism of counseling in general and Christian counseling in particular, and with the expansion of the lay counseling movement through programs like Stephen Ministries and Caring for People God's Way, supervisors will play an increasingly vital role in raising up the next generation of Christian counselors.

Although they are not labeled *supervisors,* we find people who are in supervisory roles described in biblical narratives. For example, Joshua developed his leadership skills under Moses. Elisha followed the footsteps of his mentor, Elijah. Jesus appointed twelve "that they might be with him and that he might send them out" (Mark 3:14) to fulfill the ministry he gave them to do (possibly the first group supervision?). Barnabus supervised Paul's early work, and Paul later supervised Timothy and Titus.

One might even think about counselor supervision, education, and training as a form of specialized discipleship. Disciples are called to be with their master, who then sends them out to do the master's work. New trainees meet with their supervisor and are then sent out to meet with their clients. Disciples embrace the ethos and values of their master. Counselors learn the ethics and standards of competent practice within their training programs and see them modeled by their supervisors. Disciples develop and grow in maturity (Ephesians 4:13; Hebrews 6:1), and so do counselors (Stoltenberg & Delworth, 1987). Disciples devote themselves to the way of the cross of Christ. Through competent training and supervision, Christian counselors learn how to bring the power and compassion of Christ to bear on their clients' dilemmas and life choices.

This chapter focuses on the formal supervisory relationship as the avenue for addressing issues related to counselor education and training. Supervision includes elements of education and training, but technically these are not synonymous terms. Counselor *education* most often refers to academic programs housed within degree-offering institutions such as colleges, universities, and seminaries, although it can also refer to programs that equip lay counselors. Supervised practica and internships are capstone courses in academic counselor education programs. Counselor *training* refers to any instruction that emphasizes the development of specific skills. For example, counselors may seek training in narrative therapy or cognitive-behavioral therapy. (A comprehensive discussion of formal counselor education and training is beyond the scope of this chapter.)

Six questions guide this chapter's exploration of supervision, education, and training. (We will be using the words *trainee, supervisee,* and *counselor* interchangeably.)

1. What is supervision?
2. What are the tasks of supervision?
3. What are models of supervision?
4. How do supervisors supervise?
5. How can supervisees maximize the benefits of supervision?
6. What are emerging issues in supervision?

What Is Supervision?

According to Bradley (1989), *supervision* is "a process in which an experienced person (supervisor) with appropriate training and experience supervises a subordinate (supervisee)" (p. 3). Holloway (1999) characterizes supervision as "an instructional method that is hand held, parsimoniously constructed in the moment, accountable in the long term, and remarkably intense as an interpersonal construction" (p. 9). Bernard and Goodyear (1992) view supervision as

> an intervention that is provided by a senior member of a profession to a junior member or members of that same profession. This relationship is evaluative, extends over time, and has the simultaneous purposes of enhancing the professional functioning of the junior members(s), monitoring the quality of professional services offered to the clients...and serving as a gatekeeper for those who are to enter the particular profession. (p. 4)

Clearly, counselor supervision is multifaceted. Supervisors teach, model, mentor, consult, and administrate (Borders & Leddick, 1987). They nurture and confront, train and evaluate. Supervisors attend to the skill development and professional socialization of trainees, and they tend to the welfare of their supervisees' clients. Because supervisor feedback is used to grade practicum students, to document professional competence for state certification or licensure, and to provide evaluation for employment and promotion decisions (Pearson, 2000), the relationship tends to be hierarchical. However, feminist (Avis, 1986; Prouty, Thomas, Johnson, & Long, 2001) and solution-oriented (Pearson, 2000; Rudes, Shilts, & Berg, 1997; Thomas, 1994) approaches challenge this assumption. Without denying the positional power of the supervisor, these newer approaches seek to empower trainees through collaboration so that they assume responsibility for their "own supervisory needs and their ongoing professional development" (Lowe, 2000, p. 512).

What characteristics are typical of good supervisors? In general, they display empathy, genuineness, warmth, flexibility, and curiosity. They are knowledgeable and experienced at both therapy and supervision. They have a sense of professional identity, approach supervision from a specified theoretical framework, show confidence in their supervisory skills, and have insight into the impact of their words and actions on supervisees (Watkins, 1997). Their feedback is concrete, direct, and closely tied to counselors' behaviors; and it is delivered in a systematic, timely, and clear fashion (Carifio & Hess, 1987; Shanfield, Matthews, & Hetherly, 1993).

Ideally, supervisors develop relationships with supervisees that are characterized by trustworthiness, respect, and care (Kaiser, 1992). They collaborate with supervisees to set clear goals, and they use a variety of supervisory methods (modeling, guided reflection, case review, and so on). Skilled supervisors promote two-way communication so that trainees can disclose case information that may be uncomfortable for them. Good supervisors maintain appropriate boundaries between themselves and trainees, facilitate skill development, and promote concise case conceptualization. Although supervisors help supervisees explore the interaction between their personal issues and counseling processes, supervisors avoid turning supervision into personal therapy.

On the other hand, ineffective supervisors are intolerant of differences between themselves and trainees. They are professionally apathetic and show little interest in the supervisee. They tend to be nonempathic, discouraging, and defensive. They fail to tailor their supervision to the supervisee's developmental level. Poor supervisors may even engage in questionable ethical behaviors. Because they lack training in supervision, they are unprepared to manage supervisory boundary issues, difficult topics within the supervisory relationship, or tense exchanges (Magnuson, Wilcoxon, & Norem, 2000; Watkins, 1997).

TASKS OF SUPERVISION

What do supervisors do? Although the counseling field lacks consensus about approaches to and practices of supervision (Rudes et al., 1997), some common processes can be identified. Worthington (1987) observes that supervisors teach process skills (how the counselor acts in session), conceptualization skills (how the counselor thinks about counseling), and personal skills (how the counselor reacts to counseling). Carroll (1996) elaborates on seven specific supervisory tasks: establishing a learning relationship, teaching, counseling, monitoring professional and ethical issues, evaluating, consulting, and administrating. Let's look briefly at these seven components:

1. *Establishing a learning relationship.* A good relationship between supervisor and supervisee is vitally important for effective supervision (Bernard & Goodyear, 1992; Bradley, 1989; Holloway, 1992; Stoltenberg & Delworth, 1987). Kaiser (1992) proposes that "the supervisory relationship is the medium through which therapy is taught" (p. 294). Supervisors bear the responsibility of clarifying the nature and scope of the supervisory relationship and establishing appropriate working boundaries. Supervisors explore issues of power, ethnicity, class, and gender that may influence the relationship between the supervisor and supervisee as well as the relationships between supervisees and their clients. Addressing these

issues is particularly important when the supervisory relationship extends over several years, as many postdegree supervisory relationships do (Pearson, 2000). Supervisors also work to foster professional autonomy in supervisees rather than to promote dependency or passivity. Therefore, collaboration is valued.

2. *Teaching.* Supervisors teach trainees how to "think like a therapist" through instructing, coaching, modeling, and experiential learning situations (Carroll, 1999). Supervisors should ascertain the congruence between their own teaching style and their supervisees' learning style, but Carroll suspects that supervisors tend to teach as they have been taught. The teaching tasks of supervision cover a broad spectrum. Supervisors may present a particular way of working with a given case, or they may help supervisees develop global conceptualization skills. As counselors become more skilled, the teaching task becomes less prominent.

3. *Counseling.* Supervision often provides a context in which supervisors help trainees examine the effect of counselors' personal issues on client care. But when does personal exploration become personal therapy? Current ethics codes differentiate between supervision and counseling (American Association of Christian Counselors, 1998; Association for Counselor Education and Supervision Interest Group, 1995) and prohibit supervisors from providing personal therapy to supervisees.

While supervisors may differ on where they draw the line (Carroll, 1996), they tend to deal with personal issues insofar as it is necessary to help supervisees grow professionally. As long as the focus of the discussion remains on client care, a boundary between personal therapy and supervision will be maintained. Supervisors should discuss the lengths and limitations of this task with supervisees before situations arise.

4. *Monitoring professional and ethical issues.* "The professional/ethical task of supervision ensures that clear boundaries are maintained within both [counseling] and supervision, that both client and supervisee are safe, that accountability is assured and that personal and organizational contexts are given reflective time" (Carroll, 1996, p. 64). This quality-control aspect of supervision is critical because supervisors carry legal liability for their supervisees' actions (Guest & Dooley, 1999; Tannenbaum & Berman, 1990). Supervisors ensure that trainees work ethically and professionally with clients. In this way, supervisors serve as gatekeepers for the profession. While all degree programs include courses on professional ethics, the implementation of these codes of conduct happens during supervision. Supervisors highlight ethical concerns for trainees and assist them in embodying ethical standards in their relationships with clients.

5. *Evaluating.* Since supervisors act as gatekeepers for the profession, evaluation is a part of their job. Supervisors should discuss evaluation with supervisees at the *beginning* of any supervisory relationship. Generally, evaluation takes two

forms: formative and summative. *Formative* evaluation provides informal and continual feedback to supervisees to help them develop clinically and professionally. *Summative* evaluation is any formal assessment used for grading, employing, and promoting decisions, or for licensure requirements.

Evaluation is facilitated when clear criteria have been established that specify which counselor competencies will be reviewed and how they will be evaluated. Often supervisors use counselor-rating scales (Bernard & Goodyear, 1992; Bradley, 1989) to minimize subjectivity and bias. The evaluating task emphasizes the supervisor's position of power. Therefore, all due process procedures should be followed to ensure that the evaluation represents the work of the supervisee fairly and accurately. Evaluation can also include an evaluation of supervisors (Bernard & Goodyear, 1992) and the supervisory process by supervisees (Williams, 1994).

6. *Consulting.* Carroll (1996) states that "consulting is about problem solving and reviewing all aspects of the [counseling] work" (p. 60). This includes the counselor-client relationship and the counselor-supervisor relationship. When the focus is on the counselor-client relationship, the supervisor examines client dynamics, intervention strategies, and transference issues. When the focus is on the counselor-supervisor relationship, the supervisor explores how the supervisory relationship mirrors dynamics present in the counseling relationship—often referred to as *isomorphic* or *parallel* process (Bernard & Goodyear, 1992; Carroll, 1996; Kaiser, 1992; Pearson, 2000; Thomas, 1994). Consulting becomes more prominent as supervisees master the basics and move from being practicum trainees to being full-time therapists. Carroll (1996) proposes that "consultative supervision then becomes the professional activity rather than training supervision" (p. 76).

7. *Administrating.* The context of supervision defines its administrative tasks. These tasks can include negotiating supervisory contracts with agencies or individuals, establishing procedures for managing supervisory notes, filing the appropriate forms with state licensure boards, and teaching supervisees how to manage their own paperwork. While administrative tasks may not be glamorous, they are nevertheless an important part of the supervisor's job. One strategy to reduce the onerous effects of administration is to recognize that accurate, timely management of paperwork can serve a clinically useful purpose. In this way, administrative tasks are framed as a means of supporting clinical work rather than detracting from it.

MODELS OF SUPERVISION

Many models have been proposed to describe supervision, including social-role models (Carroll, 1996) and psychotherapeutic models (Bradley, 1989). This section explores three models: the developmental model, the behavioral model, and the solution-informed model. Supervisors have used developmental and behavioral models since the late 1980s. The solution-informed model represents a newer supervisory approach that seeks to align supervision strategies with solution-oriented therapies.

DEVELOPMENTAL MODEL

The developmental model of supervision (Stoltenberg & Delworth, 1987) proposes that counselor development is organismic and linear. Supervision promotes maturation through four levels of counselor development (Level 1, Level 2, Level 3, and Level 3 Integrated) in three structures (awareness of self and others, motivation, autonomy) across eight domains (intervention skill competence, assessment techniques, interpersonal assessment, client conceptualization, individual differences, theoretical orientation, treatment goals and plans, ethics).

Although the developmental model supports collaborative and collegial supervision, it is implicitly hierarchical. The supervisor is responsible for facilitating maturation and competence in supervisees. Counselor development occurs through the Piagetian structures (Piaget, 1929) of assimilation and accommodation (e.g., does the counselor overassimilate or overaccommodate to the client or supervisor?) until the counselor reaches a competent level of maturation. The supervisory relationship and environment adjust to match the counselor's developmental stage (Ronnestad & Skovholt, 1993; Stoltenberg, 1981; Worthington, 1987). Researchers have found support for the developmental model (Lovell, 1999; Tryon, 1996).

Level 1 counselors are more self-focused than client-focused, are highly anxious about their performance, and are highly motivated. They overassimilate to clients (make clients fit into existing cognitive schemas), and they overaccommodate to the omniscient, omnipotent supervisor. The supervisor needs to provide a supportive and affirming environment and patiently guide the dependent Level 1 counselor through basic skill development. Supervision for Level 1 counselors is instructional, didactic, and highly focused on skill development (Ronnestad & Skovholt, 1993). Supervisors use modeling, role-playing, case presentations, and microcounseling skill development. Supervisors encourage autonomy through problem solving rather than through directives, and they maintain clear boundaries so as not to foster overdependence or enmeshment. Trainees' strengths and weaknesses are also examined.

Level 2 counselors are more client-focused than Level 1 counselors. They experience self-doubt about their competency and capability and struggle with professional autonomy and dependence. Supervisors employ facilitative, confrontative, conceptual, and prescriptive interventions with Level 2 trainees. Supervision includes challenge, affective confrontation, and clarification (Ronnestad & Skovholt, 1993). Consequently, Level 2 counselors may be resistant when their supervisor gives them suggestions or directives. This creates tension between supervisor and counselor.

Ratliff, Wampler, and Morris (2000) report that, at this level, supervisors tend to phrase directives tentatively, and supervisees act as if they may choose whether to accept or reject the directive when a lack of consensus exists between supervisors and supervisees. When this happens, it is incumbent on the supervisor to strike a balance between the trainee's autonomy to make clinical decisions and the supervisor's responsibility to ensure competent clinical practice. A flexible, less structured approach to supervision helps Level 2 trainees work through this turbulent developmental stage.

Level 3 counselors are more consistently motivated and are growing in their professional identity. At Level 3 and Level 3 Integrated stages, supervisors move into a more flexible and person-oriented stance, often acting as consultants because the trainee has mastered the basics. Supervisors need to be alert for the "pseudo Level 3" counselor who never experienced the turbulence of Level 2. Isomorphic transactions or parallel process in the supervisor-client relationship can be addressed with Level 3 counselors.

BEHAVIORAL MODEL

The behavioral model (Bradley, 1989) views counseling as the accumulation and mastery of learned skills. Supervision is an individualized lesson plan tailored to the strengths and weaknesses of the supervisee. Supervisee performance is objectively evaluated by behaviorally defining discrete counseling skills and observing the supervisee's performance and understanding of these skills. Learning how to counsel is subject to the principles of psychological learning theory.

Subsequently, the focus of the behavioral model is on skill development as defined by the supervisee's thinking, feeling, and behavior on basic through advanced levels of mastery. While the model attends to counselor behavior, it relies on the quality of the supervisory relationship for its power. A good relationship does not produce change, but a poor relationship can hinder the ease with which a supervisee gains new skills.

The methodology of this approach is clearly defined. According to Bradley (1989), the behavioral model uses a five-step process that includes:

1. establishing a facilitative relationship
2. conducting skill analysis and assessment

3. establishing supervision goals
4. constructing and implementing strategies
5. evaluating and generalizing learning

The supervisor looks for skill deficits and develops a program to facilitate improvement in those areas. Specific methods include recycling through practicum, performing specific counseling assignments, modeling and reinforcing, role-playing, conducting simulations, microteaching, providing specific feedback, and using self-management techniques. Skilled behavioral supervisors focus on specific skills rather than adopting a broadband approach. Consistent with this approach is the support of counselor autonomy. Generalization of behavioral change, transfer of learning to the clinical setting, and counselor self-direction are the final measures of counselor success.

SOLUTION-INFORMED MODEL

With the advent of solution-oriented therapies comes a reconceptualization of supervision. Supervision that is based on solution-oriented therapies is practiced as a conversation in which the supervisor and supervisee mutually shape the meaning of their experience through dialogue (Rudes et al., 1997). The supervisor's role is to facilitate a respectful discourse in order to understand supervisees' concerns. Because supervisors avoid a stance of privilege or hierarchy, collaboration is emphasized. This approach to supervision focuses on supervisees' strengths rather than on their deficits (Edwards & Chen, 1999). Supervisors believe that supervisees have the resources they need to overcome their clinical dilemmas.

Assumptions that support solution-oriented therapies also sustain solution-informed supervision (Thomas, 1994). Supervisors assume that supervisees know what is best for them. Therefore, supervisors direct the conversation to those areas of learning that are most salient for supervisees at any given point in time. Supervisors also assume that small changes are sufficient and that the supervisor's job is to identify and amplify the small changes that are already taking place within the counselor's professional life.

Because solution-informed supervision assumes that change is constant and that rapid change is possible, supervision focuses on what is possible and changeable. Multiple approaches to any given situation are explored. This model uses curiosity and respect (basic tenets of solution-oriented approaches) to "coax and author expertise from the life, experience, education, and training of a supervisee/therapist...rather than deliver or teach expertise from a hierarchically superior position" (Thomas, 1994, p. 11).

Supervisors collaborate with counselors to define the goals, directions, and options for supervision. "Supervision proceeds as a future-oriented endeavor, setting up positive expectations and building on the unique assets of the therapist" (p. 13). In this model, evaluation is a cooperative endeavor that is based on previously established goals. Thomas (1994, pp. 15-16) lists sample questions that are typical of solution-informed supervision:

- What do you do well with regard to your therapy?
- What would be most helpful for us to focus on today?
- What are you doing differently when things are better (with regard to a complaint)?
- How will you know when things have improved for you?
- What small steps could you make toward this goal?
- How did you decide to do that?

SUPERVISION STRATEGIES

Clearly, supervision is not a one-size-fits-all endeavor. Supervisors must decide what kind of supervision strategies work best with this particular counselor, under these specific circumstances, working with these kinds of clients, and in this particular setting (Bernard & Goodyear, 1992; White & Russell, 1995). This section reviews several of the major supervisory strategies used to address these issues.

THE SUPERVISION CONTRACT

At the beginning of any supervisory relationship, the supervisor and supervisee create a supervision contract. Because the supervisor will most likely evaluate the supervisee, the contract ensures that the supervisee is cognizant of "the structure of the relationship, the expectancies and goals for supervision, the criteria for evaluation, and the limits of confidentiality in supervision" (Holloway, 1999, p. 16). Hewson (1999) identifies five factors that shape supervision contracts:

1. The contract defines the nature of the supervision process. This aspect of the contract is renegotiated as the supervisee moves from novice to skilled practitioner.
2. The contract clarifies the goals of supervision. This enhances formative and summative evaluation procedures.
3. The contract serves as a measure by which each supervisory session is evaluated. It answers the question "How well have we completed the tasks we agreed to do today?"
4. Contracting creates mutuality and trust, and it guards against abuse of power.

5. The contract can be adjusted to meet specific needs. A counselor can stipulate particular learning goals for any given supervisory session.

Osborn and Davis (1996) specify six items that should be included in a supervision contract:

1. The contract should specify the supervisor's theory of supervision and delineate its purposes, goals, and objectives. Some goals focus on global concerns such as case conceptualization, whereas other goals will be case specific.
2. The contract should specify the context for supervision, including the location and frequency of supervision.
3. The contract should clarify methods of evaluation, how these means of evaluation will be used, and who will see them.
4. The contract should specify the duties and responsibilities of both the supervisor and the supervisee. Supervisors are responsible for establishing and maintaining the contract as well as for conducting their supervision in a professional and ethical manner. Supervisees are responsible for contributing to and updating the contract, specifying their goals and objectives, coming to supervision sessions prepared, and keeping the supervisor informed about what happens in therapy.
5. The contract should describe supervision procedures. Supervisors specify the methods they will use (live supervision, audiotape, case report, group supervision, and so on) and describe the degree to which supervision is collaborative (mutual feedback, presentation of options) or hierarchical (directives, modeling).
6. The contract should outline the supervisor's scope of practice. Just as counselors recognize their limits, supervisors should only supervise within the limits of their competency.

LIVE SUPERVISION

Live supervision occurs when the supervisor is present during the therapy session and is able to make immediate supervisory interventions (West, Bubenzer, & Zarski, 1989). This occurs through the use of one-way mirrors, closed-circuit television, a "bug-in-the-ear," phoning in, having the counselor take a break during the session to consult with the supervisor, or having the supervisor actually sit in on the session.

Live supervision includes (1) a presession phase where goals and strategies are discussed, (2) an in-session phase where the counselor conducts the session and the supervisor provides immediate feedback, and (3) a debriefing phase where the patterns of interaction and intrapersonal dynamics are discussed and the effectiveness of the therapist's behaviors are reviewed. Live supervision requires that the counseling context have the right equipment. Installing one-way mirrors or closed-circuit television may be more cost-effective for academic institutions or therapeutic training centers than it is for not-for-profit agencies or private practitioners.

What are the strengths and weaknesses of live supervision? One advantage is that the supervisor can intervene during the session to shape how the counselor uses counseling techniques. Because live supervision happens "in the moment," counselors can adjust their practice instantaneously and experience the shift in process. Another benefit of live supervision is that it protects client welfare because supervisors can intervene immediately if necessary. On the other hand, live supervision can encourage supervisee dependency or passivity (Liddle, 1991) and can generate tremendous anxiety for the novice counselor. It may blur the boundary between therapist and supervisor responsibilities. Also, some clients may find the interruptions disruptive. Several researchers have discovered that clients are satisfied with these procedures as long as the perceived helpfulness of the consultation exceeds its perceived intrusiveness (Locke & McCollum, 2001; Piercy, Sprenkle, & Constantine, 1986).

DELAYED REVIEW

This technique includes modes of supervision by which direct observation of the session occurs through audiotape or videotape. (Case review or verbal reports, which is a type of delayed review, will be discussed in the next section because this technique deals with *indirect* access to the session.) Supervisees present audio- or videotaped segments of their work to their supervisor after the session has concluded.

Delayed review is particularly helpful for supervisors or counselors who need more time for observation and reflection than live supervision allows. Through delayed review, supervisees improve their ability to observe intra- and interpersonal dynamics and to think like a therapist. Audiotape allows the counselor to focus on what was said and how it was said, while videotape adds the component of reviewing the nonverbal communication of both counselor and client. Delayed review requires focused attending; otherwise the supervisor and counselor can easily reach data overload (West, Bubenzer, Pinsoneault, & Holeman, 1993).

Several strategies can help maximize the benefits of delayed review:

- Counselors can select specific sections of the tape for review and come to the supervisory session prepared with particular goals in mind.
- The tapes can be set to show "the best of" and "the worst of" segments in the session.

- Previously set supervisory goals can determine the lens through which supervisors hear, watch, and evaluate the audio or video segment.
- Supervisors can model alternative ways to intervene and explore how they make clinical decisions during sessions.

Delayed review is a popular and practical supervision strategy because many states require supervisors to have direct access to counseling sessions even though many private practices and counseling centers are not equipped to conduct live supervision. Thus, delayed review offers a feasible alternative to live supervision.

VERBAL REPORTS

Verbal reports ask the supervisee to review the therapy session for the supervisor without the aid of audio- or videotape. When verbally presenting cases to supervisors, counselors learn to organize their thinking about the flow of therapy, to succinctly summarize clients' progress, and to adequately discuss client-therapist dynamics. Verbal reports also develop the counselor's case conceptualization ability (Bernard & Goodyear, 1992). According to West et al. (1993), at the beginning of a therapeutic relationship, supervisors can ask for the following:

- a clear presentation of the presenting problem
- hypotheses about the case
- identification of client strengths
- discussion of therapeutic goals and interventions

During the therapeutic relationship, supervisors can explore how earlier hypotheses have been confirmed or disconfirmed. Bernard and Goodyear (1992) suggest that supervisors can (1) inquire about the suitability of previous goals and the possibility of setting new goals, (2) discuss major themes that have emerged during the course of therapy, (3) ask what the supervisee has learned about therapy from this client, and (4) discuss future direction for counseling the client.

GROUP SUPERVISION

While all the above procedures can be used within a group context, they fall short of authentic group supervision if the focus remains on an individual counselor. Authentic group supervision "must depend on the interaction of group members and must have at its core the dynamics of group process" (Bernard & Goodyear, 1992, p. 69), including a balance of individual and group growth and development. Group supervision can be cost-effective and time-effective. Conversations are clinically rich, and the group process tends to reduce the risk of overdependence upon the supervisor and diminish hierarchical issues between supervisor and counselor.

In addition, group supervision decreases counselor isolation and provides a context for peers and supervisors to work collaboratively. Group supervisory activities (Prieto, 1996) include:

- didactic presentations—interventions are taught to the entire group
- case conceptualization
- individual development—the emphasis can be on either the counselor's relationship to the group or the counselor's relationship to clients
- group development
- organizational issues
- supervisor-supervisee issues

Supervision groups with consistent membership follow the same group development principles as all other kinds of groups. Supervisors, therefore, need to be cognizant of the general principles of group process. Hayes (1989) proposes that group supervision allows counselors to gain more accurate perceptions of self and others through consistent feedback from group members and that it gives members an opportunity to enhance their empathy and social interest. Groups offer a sense of psychological safety while at the same time providing a context in which self-defeating behaviors can be challenged.

How to Get the Most out of Supervision

While the previous sections have focused primarily on the roles and responsibilities of supervisors, this section will briefly highlight the roles and responsibilities of supervisees. How can supervisees maximize their supervisory experience?

Consider some preliminary guidelines for ascertaining the competence of one's supervisor. A counselor could ask the following questions:

- How much supervisory experience has this person had?
- How much formal or informal training in supervision has this person had?
- What is the supervisor's philosophy of supervision (e.g., hierarchical or collaborative)?
- What theoretical approach does the supervisor take to supervision?
- How does the supervisor deal with conflicts that arise between supervisor and supervisee?
- Have any ethical complaints been filed against the prospective supervisor? How were they resolved?
- How much enthusiasm does the supervisor have for the profession and for the supervisory task?

Not all counselors can choose who supervises them, but when a choice can be made, answers to these questions can help the counselor make a more informed decision.

Counselors should view supervision as a lifelong commitment, not just another hoop to jump through on the road to licensure. A strong supervisory relationship can reduce the likelihood of counselor burnout. Supervisors can remind counselors that self-care is important so that they can excel and be effective in this profession.

Counselors should be active collaborators during supervision. This includes specifying learning goals and requesting specific types of training. Through active collaboration, counselors can own the supervision hour.

Counselors should come to supervision sessions prepared. While this may be easier said than done, nothing replaces forethought prior to supervision. For example, counselors can organize their files from most critical to least critical. Audio- and videotapes should be ready to roll, and supervisees can stipulate the kind of feedback that they desire from delayed review supervision.

EMERGING ISSUES IN SUPERVISION, EDUCATION, AND TRAINING

Several issues are emerging in the twenty-first century that will affect the shape of counselor supervision, education, and training. These issues include the establishment of ethical standards for supervision, the growing influence of feminist and multicultural approaches to therapy, the role of technology in supervision, and the development of supervision for Christian counselors.

ETHICS AND SUPERVISION

According to the Association for Counselor Education and Supervision Interest Group (1995), "Supervision should be ongoing throughout a counselor's career and should not stop when a particular level of education, certification, or membership in a professional organization is attained" (p. 271). Supervision, therefore, is a lifelong commitment that counselors make to ensure the competent treatment of clients.

Both the American Association of Christian Counselors (1998) and the American Counseling Association (Association for Counselor Education and Supervision Interest Group, 1995) have written ethical guidelines for supervisors. These guidelines outline supervisory roles and describe client welfare and rights. According to these standards, supervisors should be adequately trained in teaching and supervisory methods *before* they begin to supervise. In other words, an excellent counselor does not become an excellent supervisor without additional training in supervision.

In addition, ethical as well as supervisory standards prohibit exploitative relationships between supervisor and supervisee. This prohibition includes a ban on any type of sexual relationship, a caution about dual relationships, and a warning about providing therapy within the context of supervision. Ethical standards place the burden for client welfare upon the shoulders of the supervisor and include informing clients that the supervisor is privy to counseling session content.

Borders and Leddick (1987) list ethical issues to which supervisors must attend. These include, but are not limited to, due process, evaluation, confidentiality, vicarious liability (the supervisor is liable for the supervisee's actions), and informed consent. Tannenbaum and Berman (1990) describe supervisors' ethical behaviors:

- They should provide supervision only in their areas of expertise.
- They should operate out of a clearly articulated supervisory model and formulate a sound supervisory contract with the supervisee.
- They should supervise honestly and with integrity, and they are responsible for regularly evaluating supervisee's competence.
- They must be cognizant of any financial considerations in supervision.

Feminist and Cross-Cultural Influences

Feminist and cross-cultural approaches to counseling have challenged many unexamined assumptions about power and privilege within families, therapy, and the supervisory relationship (Avis, 1986; Bernard, 1994). According to Avis (1986), feminist-informed supervision involves discussing views of gender presented by clients and counselors so that power issues are made explicit. Feminist-informed supervisors minimize competitiveness and maximize collaboration among supervisees. Without turning supervision into therapy, supervisors can help counselors explore their own perspectives on the political nature of gender (Rigazio-Digilio, Anderson, & Kunkler, 1995).

According to Prouty et al. (2001), feminist supervisors collaborate with supervisees to develop supervision contracts. Collaborative and hierarchical methods help supervisees develop therapeutic skills, increase self-confidence, and value multiple perspectives. "Supervision methods reflected the value of collaborative interaction and the minimization of hierarchy within professional relationships while simultaneously acknowledging the expertise of the supervisor and using it to teach" (p. 93). While feminist-informed therapy may not be prominent in many Christian counseling circles, its influence on the field of supervision cannot be ignored.

Multicultural awareness is expected of all counselors in today's global society. "The ability to work with a culturally diverse clientele needs to be understood as a core [counseling] competence rather than a specialization" (Coleman, 1999, p. 134). If counselors do not demonstrate this competence, then the development of multicultural competence becomes an important goal in supervision. Bernard (1994) notes that many supervisors themselves need additional training in multi-cultural counseling. Given the biblical emphasis on the global scope of Christ's message and mission, Christian counselors and supervisors ought to be setting the bar for skill mastery in cross-cultural counseling. The cultural contexts of client and counselor, counselor and supervisor, and supervisor and client interact with one another in ways that can facilitate or hinder therapy. Within supervision, counselors can integrate into effective clinical practice what they know about a given culture.

In order to enhance this integration, multiculturally informed supervisors must (1) know how cultures affect counseling relationships and processes, (2) note the degree to which supervisees attend to or ignore cultural factors, and (3) provide guidance and training on multicultural counseling as needed (Coleman, 1999). For example, counselors need to be aware of their own cultural assumptions, values, and biases. They also need to understand the worldview of culturally different clients. Finally, counselors need to develop appropriate interventions and processes for managing these differences.

TECHNOLOGY

Technological advances through the use of the Internet, LISTSERV, newsgroups, e-mail, and videoconferencing have opened new cyber opportunities for counseling in general and for counseling supervision in particular. With the ease of a keystroke, counselors in isolated corners of the globe can be linked with a supervisor or clinical consultant (Myrick & Sabella, 1995). The possibilities for peer supervision and consultation have yet to be fully explored. Of course, potential difficulties accompany this new technology (Baltimore, 2000). Unsecured sites raise issues about confidentiality. In addition, many people are concerned about protection of privacy, ease of access, and clinical and technological competence. How these cyberspace concerns are resolved will be part of the task of the next generation of Christian counselors.

Closer to home, some supervisors are using technology to augment live supervision. For example, monitors can be positioned behind clients so that a counselor can view them easily. Supervisors can type feedback to the trainee who reads it as it appears. This "bug-in-the-eye" (Klitzke & Lombardo, 1991) has several advantages.

Supervisors can reinforce appropriate behavior and provide immediate and corrective feedback (Smith, Mead, & Kinsella, 1998). Neukrug (1991) suggests that praise, specific behavioral directions, or suggested responses are communicated effectively this way. Supervisors can save these exchanges and use them later during debriefing sessions.

SUPERVISION FOR CHRISTIAN COUNSELORS

In many ways, supervision for Christian counselors is identical to supervision in other settings. The tasks, strategies, and responsibilities are basically the same. Conversely, supervision for Christian counselors is distinct in that the supervisor and supervisee can openly access the power of the Holy Spirit. Because both parties affirm the transforming power of Christ, no client situation is deemed hopeless.

Supervision can therefore directly address the spiritual issues that are present for counselor and client. Supervision can also serve as a context for the integration of theology, biblical studies, and clinical practice, especially for Christian counselors who received their training in secular settings. Theological conversations are as appropriate as clinical conversations in supervision for Christian counselors. Furthermore, supervisors can model the application of counseling techniques that are congruent with Christian counseling practice, such as therapeutic uses of prayer, Bible study, forgiveness, and clinical discussions about such topics as sin and grace.

As Christian counseling progresses into the twenty-first century, further development and description of supervision that is distinctly suited for Christian counseling is expected.

CHAPTER 32

CHRISTIAN COUNSELING PRACTICE MANAGEMENT

How to Succeed in Business by Really Trying

DWIGHT BAIN

Counseling is more than a ministry, a calling, or a profession—counseling is also a business.

—KATHIE ERWIN,

How to Start and Manage a Counseling Business

A setup for failure. That is how I would describe the training for success in business that most Christian counselors received in their formal education or graduate program. Granted, the primary purpose of graduate school is not to learn how to manage a business but how to master the interpersonal and developmental issues that affect people and help them find a better way of life. But when we do not also comprehensively instruct future counselors in the basics of day-to-day business operations, we set many of them up for failure. If counselors can't manage to stay in business, they are no longer available to provide the assistance they trained so hard to offer.

It is ironic that we spend hundreds of hours mastering the skills to help people, yet many of us graduate with little knowledge of marketing, budgeting for real expenses, income management, staffing ratios, tax liabilities, office overhead, business models for each specific patient population, and how to achieve and maintain patient satisfaction. These factors will largely determine whether you will stay in the business of counseling year after year or will not be able to pay off your student loans because of the financial failure of your practice.

This chapter addresses the major issues professional counselors need to attend to in order to find success in any type of practice setting. These issues include practice definition, corporate and office structure, fees and money management, and good business practices.

Of course, not everyone who practices counseling will offer services for a fee, but as Christian counseling continues to emerge as a respected profession, it is imperative that good business sense guide those who may expand their counseling practice or perhaps open their first counseling offices (Budman & Steenbarger, 1997; Erwin, 1993).

We, as Christian counselors, have tremendous opportunities in the twenty-first century to use the gifts God has given us to serve his people and make a living at the same time. After all, most people spend money either to get new things or to fix things that are broken, and it is with this second idea in mind that people now seek counseling (Klein, 1999). Previously, mental roadblocks such as "I don't need psychological help" or "Prayer is all I need" were prevalent; today the stigma of going to a professional therapist is largely gone. So the opportunity to reach out and serve hurting people is actually greater than it has ever been.

PRACTICE DEFINITION

The traditional model of psychotherapy is that of a practitioner working in a professional office suite with a support staff. In reality, because our field is so varied and broad, there never has been a standard business model for the practice of Christian counseling. Just as our profession promotes a wide variety of counseling models and types of counselors, there are also many models of practice definition and structure in Christian counseling.

If you grew up in the era when people worked in one office for twenty years, you are old enough to realize that this particular business model hardly exists anymore. And if you went through your professional training with the idea that you would be in the same counseling office doing the same thing for your entire professional career, you would be well advised to rethink that model.

BE RESPONSIVE TO RAPID CHANGE

Our industry is changing because our culture is changing, so let's return to our basic counseling premise: People have problems, and Christian counselors help them find answers. This sounds simple enough, except that the structure tends to change quickly and complicates how your services reach those in need.

At the beginning of the last century, most people owned and used horses as their primary transportation; it was a normal way of life for them. Many successful companies sold products and services to horse owners. Then a single technology—the automobile—changed everything. Many of those horse-oriented businesses went bankrupt because they did not adapt to societal change. However, many other horse-oriented companies downsized and restructured and redirected their marketing focus from the cities to farms and rural communities. This savvy move enabled them to stay in business for another fifty years.

As counselors, we are in the people business—not the professional medical-suite business—so it is highly likely that the manner in which people pay for services and how our industry delivers those services will drastically change in the years ahead. Are you ready?

Define Your Practice by License and Specialty

One of the best ways to define the structure of your business is to determine where you fit best in the counseling field based on your experience and educational level. To do so, answer the following questions as thoughtfully and specifically as you can:

- In what field are you trained, professionally licensed, and credentialed?
- What services do you have the experience and professional skill to provide?
- How much real experience do you have in each area in which you practice?

Once you have defined your practice by your skill and license level, you are ready to move on to the next set of questions that will help you define your counseling practice. An important strategic consideration is the development of a niche service that few others in your locale are addressing. For those who practice in small towns or rural areas, you may establish your niche service by simply advertising yourselves as Christian counselors. For the urban practitioner, however, those days are gone, since there are Christian counselors in nearly every mid-size and large city in the United States. Some experts are convinced that in order for a professional practice to survive in today's highly competitive markets, the development of a niche practice is crucial (see Connor & Davidson, 1985). In light of this, consider the following questions:

- Does your practice target a specific patient population?
- Do you need more educational training or professional certification in specific areas?

A quick review of your last twelve months of patient care will help you answer these questions. If you see, for instance, that your referrals and patient population are "all over the map," you may want to think through what you believe to be your strongest counseling skills and areas of greatest interest. On the other hand, the advantage of being a generalist is that when a specific referral population no longer exists (for example, when the hospital that sends you the most referrals is consolidated into another medical facility twenty-five miles away), you have other referral sources to draw upon. I do believe that the Lord will allow life experiences to shape our thinking, giftings, and desire to work with different populations as we grow older. For example, if early in your practice you loved working with adolescent males who have oppositional-defiant disorder, you may now have less desire to continue that specialization and may want to focus instead on the needs of the growing aging-adult population. This shift in interest and focus is part of the ongoing growth and maturation of a counselor. Consider the following questions:

- Which groups or patient populations do you see most frequently?
- Which groups or patient populations do you most enjoy working with?
- Which patient population groups are likely to change over the next twelve months?
- Could your practice benefit from limiting or adding new patient populations?

Once you have defined what you are trained and certified to do as well as what you enjoy doing, it is time to assess what has worked most effectively for you to this point. If you are a student or counselor intern, think about your experiences working with people in Sunday-school classes or youth groups or in other volunteer situations.

DEFINE YOUR PRACTICE BY PAST SUCCESSES OR FAILURES

If you have held jobs in other industries, think through which ones you really enjoyed. Discovering the best working environment and working within the strengths of your personality will help prevent emotional burnout.

In the same way, evaluate past failures. You can learn a lot about your greatest weaknesses in business by evaluating situations that didn't work out. For instance, if you dislike and tend to disregard paperwork, especially when deadlines are tight, then working with a large managed-care administration group would likely be a daily nightmare of details and deadlines.

God designed you with a caring heart and an intelligent mind. Use the cognitive side of your personality as you contemplate these issues, since you will be financially responsible to manage the details well. Consider the following questions:

- In what business setting(s) are you most comfortable (e.g., group, solo)?
- In which business setting have you been most successful?
- What business setting has the best potential to be financially rewarding?
- Based on your experiences, can you practice effectively in this setting over the long term?

Consider your personality as well as your strengths and weaknesses. By structuring a practice setting around your personality and strengths, you can experience a higher level of success. Think about working hours and schedules. If you are a morning person who loves to be around coworkers, you may be miserable if you take a job working the graveyard shift on a crisis hot line. If you are a people person from a large-city background, you may go stir-crazy working in a rural farm community. There are many wonderful assessment tools to help you determine your basic personality characteristics. The Myers-Briggs Type Indicator (MBTI) or the DISC can help you assess which practice setting is the best fit for you. Answer the following questions:

- What is your basic personality?
- Which strengths do you bring to your counseling practice?
- Which weaknesses could seriously hinder your counseling practice?
- What personality issues, if any, hinder your effectiveness as a counselor?

Consider your place in life as well as other pressing life issues. At this stage of self-evaluation, pay attention to other factors and issues in your life. For instance, if you are about to get married and want to buy a house during your first year of marriage, owning a start-up private counseling practice may not allow you to secure financing for your mortgage. Likewise, worrying about outside factors will have a bearing on your effectiveness as a therapist. Think about the age of your children or your parents, your personal financial situation, and issues such as the economy in your region of the country. If you live in an area that depends heavily on one major employer, your business structure could be seriously impacted if that company were to move, lay off staff, or close down. Consider the following questions:

- What is your personal financial condition?
- What personal health issues could impact your ability to counsel?
- What impact will the ages and health of your immediate family have on your practice?
- Are there pending issues that put serious pressure on your ability to counsel effectively?

Obviously, if you identify serious roadblocks as you answer the questions in this section, you should consider working on your own issues before attempting to help others. If your own marriage needs work, then spend time on that relationship before you counsel other couples with marital problems. If your personal finances are in terrible shape and the pressure is overwhelming you, it may be wise to work in a higher-income position prior to relying solely on income from a private counseling practice. The time and energy you spend taking care of yourself now will be rewarded later on with peace of mind and the knowledge that you are performing at your best.

CORPORATE STRUCTURE AND OFFICE ENVIRONMENT

Another major factor to consider as you define your practice is your office setting and environment. Even Bob Newhart, who played Dr. Bob Hartley in the 1970s television show, was ahead of his time: His shared office space and receptionist was an innovative practice model. You may remember that Carol, the receptionist, provided a lot of comic relief as she joked with Jerry, the orthodontist, and Mr. Carlton, one of Dr. Hartley's clients. We also assumed that she helped Dr. Hartley with his billing, scheduling, and third-party reimbursements. (No wonder they laughed so much: In the 1970s they didn't have managed care to deal with!)

Grodzki (2000) gives four rules of thumb that we should all remember as we develop our counseling practices:

1. There is no one right way to build a practice. Different strategies work for different people.
2. You must get access to the ideas and information that work best for you.
3. You must think like a businessperson, weighing costs versus benefits on everything.
4. Beyond all your degrees, titles, and licenses, you must be able to convince potential clients that you have what it takes to help them make the changes they are seeking.

TRADITIONAL MODELS OF PRACTICE

Sole practitioner. The model in which a counselor hangs out a shingle to conduct a solo business seems to be one of the most common models in metropolitan areas of the country. It may also be one of the most expensive business models from a real-cost perspective. Sometimes sole practitioners set themselves up as employees of a Subchapter S corporation, which is an IRS designation for a self-employed person working under a corporate umbrella because of greater income tax benefits and liability protection. When practicing within this model, counselors need to take great care to file taxes and state corporate records in a timely manner, since the penalties and interest can be substantial.

In a solo practice model, all expenses are the responsibility of the counselor, as are all of the paperwork and administrative duties. Many counselors working in this environment tend to overlook the issues of insurance and retirement, and paid vacations can be rare since solo counselors only generate income when they are working. It is not uncommon for Christian counselors in a private practice setting to go for years without adequate time off, which points out one of the weaknesses of this model: the high rate of burnout.

To keep overhead from eliminating profits in this practice setting, do a cost analysis of office space in your region. Discuss with your landlord the lease terms, the cost of utilities and cleaning services, and possible lower rates for a longer-term lease. Any reduction of office-space costs is vital, since you will pay these fixed costs every day whether or not you use the space to generate billable patient hours.

To further reduce costs, consider working without support staff until your practice is well established or in a setting where you can share a receptionist and major office equipment (such as a photocopier) with other businesses.

In a private practice you will also need to check on required city or county occupational licenses and on local zoning requirements, since some office settings may not be zoned for a counseling business. Also, as you consider potential office settings, don't forget to listen. That is, listen for distracting noises around you. Many offices are built with insufficient sound insulation, which means that you and your clients will be able to hear conversations or music from next door (and those next door will be able to hear your conversations!).

Group practice. This model includes all the characteristics of a solo practice, but the practitioner joins with other counselors, psychologists, or social workers to form a group. The group model is quite cost-effective since several practitioners share the overhead expenses. Each counselor may actually be working as a sole practitioner or a Subchapter S corporation while, at the same time, sharing the use and expense of support personnel, equipment, facilities, and utilities. Each counselor is responsible for his or her own practice management issues. (Some larger groups are owned and operated by a corporation where everyone works as a traditional employee, and each person receives an IRS W-2 form at the end of the calendar year.)

The key weakness of the group practice model is the tendency for everyone to become too busy to take time for one another, to listen to each other, or to gain ideas and information from one another. This lack of communication can lead to power struggles or competitiveness. An imbalance in expectations and in workload distribution, whether real or perceived, can create a lot of tension in a large group practice. Consequently, great care needs to be taken to spell out, up front and in writing, what is expected of each counselor and who is responsible for what. Attention to insurance coverage is also important, since some limited liability is carried by the entire group—even a loosely associated one—from the practice of each individual counselor.

In spite of these weaknesses, group practice is the practice model of choice right now and for the foreseeable future. Increasingly, Christian counseling is using a multidisciplinary practice model that involves many mental health professionals working together in a large group practice. According to Budman and Steenbarger (1997), the future of psychotherapy practice will be centered in "data-driven, team-based organizations" that will use their data to shape and grow dynamic practice organizations. This data will also be necessary in order to argue the additive value of psychotherapy in client's lives and to show measurable outcomes as well as clearly delineated costs (see Snyder & Ingram, 1999).

Medical or hospital setting. This model is similar to the group practice model except that in this setting the counselor works as an employee. You will often see this model in medical centers or through the chaplaincy or social service programs of many hospitals. Larger outpatient medical offices often include an on-staff counselor, especially in pediatric, geriatric, or women's health care. This is not to say that the young, the old, or women have more counseling issues than others do; rather, these medical disciplines have long recognized the value of counseling in the healing process. Medical and hospital settings are also a plus for the counselor since they provide access to physicians and often a pharmacist in the same office or building.

As an employee, the counselor receives an IRS W-2 form at the end of the year and usually significant employee benefits such as health and life insurance, retirement programs with matching funds, and paid vacations. Most counselors in this setting are salaried and have little worry regarding referrals or income.

One of the drawbacks of working in a medical or hospital setting can be the sheer volume of cases to deal with in a short period of time as well as the lack of control over many aspects of the practice—including work hours and the limited flexibility of being on call. Another weakness cited by some counselors is the definite caps on income that are set by the hospital or medical group.

Academic setting. Because many academic positions are salaried, counselors working for a school or university have the stability of predictable income. They usually have a predefined work schedule, working environment, and pay scale. This setting offers the counselor many benefits, including insurance, retirement savings programs, and paid vacations.

However, the academic model has many potential control issues. For example, it is often difficult to acquire the funding for additional products or services, and there are sometimes tremendous limitations on changing methods from the past. Also, the pay scale for counselors can be quite limited, offering little opportunity for financial advancement. Therefore it is important for counselors to hold realistic expectations of what can and cannot be accomplished within the academic setting as well as to know and enforce their personal boundaries in order to avoid burnout.

Ministry or nonprofit models. An increasing amount of professional Christian counseling is being done in nonprofit ministry. Although we typically think of a professional social worker going out to conduct a home study when working with a family on adoption, much nonprofit counseling ministry is now being done within the multidisciplinary practice center. Adoption agencies, hospice, crisis pregnancy centers, senior adult centers, church-based counseling practices, and residential treatment centers for adolescent care are common examples of settings where this type of counseling takes place.

One benefit of the nonprofit model is that it enables the counselor to avoid certain taxes on income and to qualify for foundation and donation funds. Nonprofits are usually simpler in structure and are more efficient in operation, although there is no ownership stake, and they must be governed by a board that can diffuse control. Become familiar with the board that governs a nonprofit organization, and pay special attention to how receptive board members are to change. Also, be aware that some nonprofits combine low pay with above-average time commitments required to help patient populations. Burnout levels can be high in these settings, but practitioners often believe strongly that they are working for a cause that someone needs to do something about. Long hours, low pay, and high exposure to liability issues are a normal part of this model.

Job satisfaction levels of counselors working in ministry and nonprofit settings are probably among the highest of any counseling field, since so much help is given to real people in need. In nonprofit settings where many positions are salaried, there is less concern about accounting issues such as when salaries are paid. However, in some smaller ministries timely payment of salaries and bills could present a problem. Just remember to set clear boundaries so you can enjoy the blessings of this model of counseling without experiencing the curse of living from hand to mouth.

MODERN OR NONTRADITIONAL MODELS

Church-based offices. Many Christian counselors are discovering the value of partnering with local churches and offering their services on-site at the church. This is a winning proposition for churches, which can have professional counselors immediately available to their congregations, and it benefits the counselor, who doesn't incur the usual fixed costs of private practice. Since the counselor realizes significant savings in the cost of doing business, he or she can pass along those savings to clients through a reduced-fee structure.

This model also offers a great deal of flexibility. For example, a counselor can function much as the circuit riders of the last century did, servicing several different congregations or communities in the same week without the burdensome expense of securing professional office space in each area.

It should be noted that there is a fair amount of personal marketing, accounting, and administrative responsibility in this model as well as the ongoing accountability to the governing board of the local church. But this model opens the door to some extensive marketing opportunities for innovative counselors.

One major weakness of this model is that, in the most extreme cases, the counselor could become enmeshed in church politics between different faiths or different congregations. Therefore, caution should be exercised, and roles and responsibilities should be clearly written out on paper and explained to all parties before this type of counseling relationship begins. Hasper (2001) maintains that forging a good alliance for church-based counseling requires that

- a solid pastor/counselor relationship is given priority attention,
- biblical and values compatibility between the church and counseling service is forged,
- the helping ministry is mutually promoted by the church and counseling staff and is supported by church leaders,
- a clear and detailed counseling services agreement is hammered out and agreed upon,
- affordable counseling is arranged for church parishioners.

Decisions also need to be made about how phone calls will be handled professionally, how appointments will be scheduled, and how counseling-related expenses will be processed, but the majority of other office procedures and expenses are normally handled by the church that offers the space.

Typically, church-based counselors are not salaried employees of the church, although an increasing number of churches are hiring professionally trained counselors. Most church-based counselors are independent practitioners working under the umbrella of the local church. This arrangement means that issues such as taxes, banking responsibilities, and scheduling are the therapist's responsibility. Significant professional liability issues are also present in this model. Some church liability insurers strictly limit coverage for professional counseling on church property, and others may even deny coverage.

Counselors need to be very aware of the laws of their state that govern partnerships between churches and therapists. While some states may have no guidelines, others are quite strict about how this model is structured. The IRS also has strict guidelines about working for profit in a nonprofit setting, so the wise counselor will seek professional legal and accounting guidance in order to structure this type of business properly.

Another weakness of this model is that you may experience problems with distracting noise as well as the possibility that you and your clients will be overheard by someone outside the counseling room. The space made available to you might be a Sunday-school classroom, a conference room, or a staff office. You have two options for dealing with noise: (1) eliminate or minimize any sounds with door sweeps, curtains, thicker wallpaper, tall bookshelves, or insulation in the drop ceiling, or (2) obtain a white-noise machine, which is designed to make a type of pleasant background noise that masks sounds better than background music. You may prefer a room air filter, which makes about the same sound as white noise while giving the added benefit of pulling dust and pollen out of the air.

Legal and judicial settings. As our culture has become more and more litigious, there are job opportunities for counselors at all levels of the judicial system. An increasing number of family courts are hiring counseling and mediation experts, usually professional counselors who work with family law, juvenile justice, or civil mediation cases. These family law experts and civil mediators often earn six-figure incomes. Forensic experts who specialize in divorce custody evaluations have great influence in the popular media as well as tremendous financial opportunity. Typically, mediators or forensic experts work in a professional office setting and receive a base salary, basic insurance, and office staffing, then realize additional income as their billable patient hours increase. Some highly successful experts work in a solo practice setting with control of their income and hours, while others enjoy the benefits of working with a large law firm. Either way, these counselors have to deal with the court system daily, so additional training and certification in legal matters is a must. Counselors who are not afraid of conflict or sometimes-lengthy court cases may be good matches for this growing industry and may find a niche as psycholegal experts or professional mediators.

Criminal justice and corrections. A more structured setting for counselors is the criminal justice and corrections system. Corrections is a growing multimillion dollar industry, which, for counselors, is a stable practice setting, even though it may be an indicator of the deterioration in our culture. Corrections counseling used to be poorly compensated, with limited professional requirements and no real opportunities for career advancement. That is now changing as the criminal justice and corrections system has started requiring advanced degrees and specialized training in behavioral management.

Counseling positions in this setting are classified as state or federal jobs, so while the duties are often intense and stressful, the income, hours, paid time off, and benefits are clearly structured. Senior staff positions in this field often offer significantly above-average income as well as the opportunity to guide inmates in a new direction through the use of sound Christian counseling principles.

Professional mental health corporations. A final model to consider is the professional mental health corporation. Most states have created new corporate structures that allow professional practitioners of all kinds to incorporate as professional corporations (PCs) or limited liability corporations (LLCs) and attain the special advantages that these structures offer.

A professional corporation is an excellent way to share ownership and transfer it more easily through the issuance and buying and selling of shares in the corporation. Liability is more easily managed in this structure, since the corporation can shield from risk a certain amount (though not all) of one's personal assets. While an investment of time and money is required to incorporate, corporate operations can be more centrally managed and can therefore be more efficient than other group practice models.

FEES AND MONEY MANAGEMENT

If there is a single subject that practitioners struggle with more than any other, it has to be fees. We are comfortable expressing with a virtual stranger how our faith in Jesus Christ carried us through a life crisis, but all too often we are afraid to deal with the bottom line of how professional counseling affects the pocketbook of patient and practitioner alike. Counseling takes time and costs money.

WHY CHARGE A FEE?

I will never forget the first time, back in 1984, that I received a check for thirty-five dollars for an hour of professional therapy. When the hour was up, I didn't quite know what to do! The internship I'd completed hadn't required patients to pay a fee to the intern; rather, all accounting and scheduling was done at a receptionist's station in the waiting area. I felt terrible asking for the money, but I knew that the fee had to be paid for services rendered. Admittedly, as I began paying the many expenses associated with opening a professional office, I found it a lot easier to accept payments for my counseling services.

Why is it necessary for professional Christian counselors to charge a fee? Let's go back to the basics: Life costs money. Your education cost you—or someone—thousands of dollars. You have office expenses to pay as well as personal house payments or rent, utilities, food, clothing, transportation, and myriad other expenses.

Also, people expect to pay for professional services, from the dry cleaner to the dentist, and you, too, are a professional.

If you are in a private counseling practice, all you have to "sell" is your time and expertise. If you work for a major medical counseling network, you "sell" your time to that employer, who trusts you to manage that time well. To be irresponsible with your time and finances is to be irresponsible with your counseling practice. While it may be easier to ask for fees to be paid to a major employer, the same principle holds true: Professional services require and deserve compensation.

Some Christians have the mentality that all Christian service should be free. They'll pay TicketMaster for tickets to hear Michael W. Smith, or they'll pay the admission price for a Women of Faith or Promise Keepers event, but they think that a Christian in professional counseling should not charge a fellow believer. Most Christian clients, however, understand and expect to pay a fair professional-level fee for services rendered. (I discourage any long discussion with a patient about "Why do you charge so much?" This is counterproductive in light of the emotional dynamics of counseling and often fuels the fire of a false belief that all Christian services should be offered for free.)

God's Word teaches that the laborer is worthy of his hire. The implication is clear: If you are working (providing a service), it is spiritually and ethically appropriate to be paid.

TYPICAL COUNSELING OFFICE EXPENSES
Your budget for the basics when you are starting a new business should include the following categories:
- advertising
- accounting
- banking fees
- communication services (including long distance, yellow pages, cell phones, pagers, and basic phone service)
- dry cleaning
- copier
- computer
- fax machine
- credit-card terminal
- legal fees
- office furniture
- magazines
- bottled water

- stationery
- business cards
- office supplies
- insurance (basic business, fire, health, life, and malpractice)
- travel and entertainment

A more established practice may include a budget for continuing education, retirement programs, transportation, paid vacations and sick days, and so on. If your counseling fees are inadequate to pay for the fixed costs of your business, you should carefully consider whether the counseling model you are using is out of date or if your fee structure needs to be adjusted up or down to fit the marketplace.

Interestingly, professional fees vary widely across different parts of the country. There are two ways to determine what is referred to as the UCR (usual or customary rate) for mental health counseling. One method is to politely contact several other practitioners who offer services similar to the kind you offer and ask if they would be willing to tell you their fees for various services, including group, individual, conjoint, family therapy, child therapy, professional assessment, and so on.

If other practitioners are not open to providing this information, there is another way to discover UCRs for a given region of the country. Terrie Storm (personal communication, July 19, 2001) of New Life Clinics presents an excellent method of determining how to structure your fees if you live in or near a major American city:

> To discover fees, use what is called The Resource-Based Relative Value Study (RBRVS), which was developed in 1991 for Medicare. It is a system of physician/provider compensation that is based on the amount of resources expended to produce professional health care services. Work, overhead, and malpractice units, (RVUs) are assigned to procedures as measures of their value. Geographic modifiers (GPCIs) are then employed to account for variations in costs in different regions of the U.S. The sum of these values is then multiplied by a conversion factor chosen by the carrier. Health Care Financing Administration (HCFA), as well as most insurance/benefit carriers and plans, track practice trends (including charges reported on submitted claims), geographical indices, work expense, etc. Since that time, these statistics are used in determining the Medicare fee schedule and/or other insurance plans or managed care fee schedules (often referred to as "Usual and Customary Rates") by the insurance carriers. If you are billing insurance, it is quite likely you have a provider fee profile which is being tracked individually as well as by a professional grouping. If you always

charge different rates (rates vary by patient) then you may very well be flagged for review and potential audit. They are expecting to see a pattern for your charges and that pattern is considered, along with other providers of your specialty, when determining UCRs for your geographical region. Typically, more populated metropolitan areas with higher costs of living will have higher allowable rates.[1]

Fees do vary according to practice discipline, experience, demand for service, and locale. Managed care has flattened and even reduced the upward direction of fees that had risen unabated until this past decade. The resource *Psychotherapy Finances* (Klein, 2000) has conducted a regular survey of fees charged by more than fifteen hundred clinicians from all parts of the country. The following chart reflects its most recent survey.

Discipline	Direct Fee	Managed Care Reimbursement
Psychiatry	$132/hr.	$95
Psychology	$100	$70
LCSWs	$80	$60
MFTs	$80	$60
LPCs	$79	$60

Sliding fee scales are formulated when a counseling fee is based on a percentage of the patient's annual income, and a cap is set to limit the out-of-pocket expense for the patient. While this method of payment is fair to the patient, it may make it more difficult for the practitioner to cover expenses. The therapist may then feel pressure to see a higher volume of patients. Because a sliding scale generates less income, it is best used in a setting where costs are much lower, such as in a ministry or church-based counseling practice.

Some counselors have taken to bartering their professional services in exchange for another businessperson's professional service or product. This practice is considered illegal in many states, is viewed as unethical by a growing number of professions, and could present complex tax liabilities. For these obvious reasons, the barter method of payment is not recommended.

BILLING AND COLLECTIONS

For counselors who either struggle with understanding managed care or have a difficult time managing their accounts payable, billing services are a creative way for them to solve the problem of accounting and paperwork. A billing service will take your account information and send a monthly bill to each patient who has an outstanding balance. Services typically charge from 4–15% percent of the bill collected.

Billing services are different from collection services, which are used when an account is seriously past due. (If an account is over 120 days past due, the counselor-patient relationship is already in trouble.) Collection services are last-resort formal measures that may or may not bring in the money you are owed. It is recommended that you make every effort to collect the balance due before sending a patient to collections. A good rule of thumb is to never let a patient's account balance get beyond four to five visits, or beyond five hundred dollars, before having a serious discussion about how the patient is planning to pay for the services rendered. If an account goes beyond those limits, you may never get paid. Stories of therapists being owed thousands of dollars are all too common.

It obviously behooves you to stay on top of your finances and to be able to pay your own bills in a timely fashion. While ethical issues may arise when you discontinue therapy due to financial conerns, it is not unethical or illegal per se to stop services when clients fail to pay. In fact, this is an important issue that should be addressed as a normal part of the therapeutic process. (It is important to note that counselors cannot write off the cash balance of money owed to them as a tax deduction. Tax laws won't allow for write-offs unless you are on an accrual accounting basis, which isn't likely in a private practice. A cash business counts income as it is received; an accrual business counts income as it is earned. So an accrual business eventually could write off the uncollectible debt, but a cash business never counted it and, thus, cannot write it off.)

Sometimes charging a small amount of interest or a late fee on old debt will help bring in the payments. This tactic doesn't always work, but it's still surprising that someone who lets a bill go unpaid for several months will finally pay it when interest or a late fee is going to be charged.

GOOD BUSINESS PRACTICE

The Old Testament prophet Jeremiah wrote,

> Blessed is the man who trusts in the LORD, whose confidence is in him. He
> will be like a tree planted by the water that sends out its roots by the stream.
> It does not fear when heat comes; its leaves are always green. It has no wor-
> ries in a year of drought and never fails to bear fruit. (17:7-8)

As Christian counselors, we realize that our referrals and our livelihood come from the Lord. It is wise to have as much knowledge and insight about our profession as possible, yet we always know that the blessings come from our Father. As we work to help others effectively and to make a good living in the process, we must always remember that everything we do in the practice and business of counseling must honor and glorify our Lord Jesus Christ. In that regard, I close with the following thoughts.

First, since we openly embrace the name of Jesus Christ, I believe that we are held to a higher standard of counseling practice. Excellence must be a way of life for the Christian counselor. Continuous personal growth and ongoing spiritual development are a reflection of our maturity and our faith. The gentleness of our Savior as he dealt with emotionally wounded people is our greatest model: Jesus was gentle in spirit, yet tough with direct questions and firm about personal responsibility. What's the message for us? If we are Christian in name, we must be Christian in deed. If we associate ourselves with Jesus Christ, we must do everything a notch better than those who do not.

Second, changing economies also demand that we uphold higher standards. We must be completely professional in every area of our interaction with clients. If we do not uphold higher standards, we will lose income due to a decline in client billable hours. This is a bottom-line consideration, but it is necessary if we are to raise the bar for our profession. Paying attention to the structure of your counseling business will help your financial bottom line, and ignoring the structure may leave you wide open for financial disaster.

The third factor we all have to pay attention to is client retention in proportion to the client's level of need. Many times a client will disappear from the schedule book without a trace, almost as if he or she became invisible. But these are real people with real needs. They are so much more than clients in need of care; they are God's children. He loves them and entrusts them to us for a season. When we counsel these people from a servant's heart, amazing things will happen. WWJD ("What Would Jesus Do?") is more than a buzzword for teenagers or a gimmicky concept for pop musicians to sing about. It is a way of life. Client retention is not about prolonging client care, which is totally unethical, but it is about building a level of care that removes any roadblocks to services needed.

Finally, nothing is more basic to creating a positive business image than how clients are treated. The scheduling and handling of clients' appointments, how clients are treated by office staff on their first visits, and clients' first impressions of your business operations—including the condition of the waiting room or the dust on frayed year-old magazines—are all important factors that affect the kind of image your business has. Research into why people stop using one service provider and go to another has shown that only a small percentage of clients move away; the vast majority didn't feel that they were listened to or cared for by the company's employees. Even a simple business misunderstanding can cost you a patient who may really need your services.

A positive office visit will go a long way toward building the rapport necessary for the kind of disclosure and personal insight that lead to change. If you don't present well personally (imagine a "specialist" in personal success and organization with a messy persona or a messy office), the doubt you leave in a patient's mind may very well cause him or her to seek out another level of care. This hard reality means that we, as Christian counselors, have to take fresh ownership in living out some basic elements of the human services industry, such as personal integrity and responsibility. We offer our patients insight into their own lives, but they are also watching ours!

ATTAINING THE NEXT LEVEL

I hope these reminders form the blueprint for a higher level of business success that will help you attain the next level of effectiveness in your counseling practice. As you seek to help others, with God's guidance, may you realize God's promise: "I will open rivers in desolate heights, and fountains in the midst of the valleys; I will make the wilderness a pool of water, and the dry land springs of water.... That they may see and know, and consider and understand together, that the hand of the LORD has done this, and the Holy One of Israel has created it" (Isaiah 41:18,20, NKJV).

This is an amazing time to be a Christian counselor. With a heart for helping people, a strong practice model, and continued support from organizations such as AACC, your successes will come more frequently. Be encouraged in your practice of Christian counseling. You can enjoy a satisfying and rewarding career as you touch God's people for good.

CHAPTER 33

THE MATURATION OF CHRISTIAN COUNSELING

Envisioning a Preferred Future

TIM CLINTON AND GEORGE OHLSCHLAGER

The story goes that when Walt Disney World first opened in Florida shortly after the death of Walt Disney, someone remarked to a park designer, "It is sad that Mr. Disney did not live to see this." "Oh, but he did see it," replied the designer. "That's why the park is here."

—FROM A SERMON (ATTRIBUTION UNKNOWN)

In these early years of the twenty-first century, we believe the time has come to facilitate the deliberate and systemic development of competent Christian counseling (CCC). We have labored to describe CCC to you in this book—its practice, its process, and its application across many arenas. In this chapter we will look at CCC as a macrosystem. We will consider the many challenges that are shaping and threatening it and describe where we think it should go as a larger ministry-profession.

We believe it is necessary to help CCC grow from a dynamic but disorganized movement into a more disciplined and self-directed profession. An amalgam of changes in the church, in the physical and mental health care marketplace, in the legal and regulatory environment, among the counseling and mental health professions, and in CCC itself are driving forces that will significantly transform CCC in the years ahead (Clinton & Ohlschlager, 1997).

Some of these changes are being exerted as an aggressive assault against the validity and operation of CCC. This assault is coming from both within the church (Bobgan & Bobgan, 1987; Hunt, 1987) and outside it (Ellis, 1971; Santa Rita, 1996). And even when change is presented as something other than an assault, there are still many legitimate challenges that must be addressed as Christian counseling matures in the twenty-first century. The *Psychotherapy Networker*, for example, sees the larger field of counseling being swallowed up in vertically integrated health care, with all patient decisions controlled by physicians and managed care organizations (Cummings, 2001).

So then, we posit that

1. CCC is in the stage of development best described as an "emerging profession" (Barber, 1965);
2. intentional profession and ministerial development is one necessary and honorable response to the many challenges and assaults we currently face and is essential to both the overall development and defense of this movement;
3. envisioning a systematic and structural program for directing that development is a pragmatic way to put it in front of our colleagues and friends in proposal form (Collins, 1995).

THE CHALLENGE

In light of Sweet's (1999) work *Soul Tsunami,* which paints an amazing picture of our not-too-distant future, we have been considering the challenge the twenty-first century poses to the church in general and to Christian counseling in particular. Sweet eschews prophetic labels, but if half of his cumulative forecasts come to pass, we are already living in a world so different from the one we grew up in that any comparison is like examining two completely alien planets. Those of us who are still thinking and doing ministry according to nineteenth- and twentieth-century paradigms are fossilizing at this very moment.

Sweet, a Methodist theologian and a futurist, is laboring at the Drew University seminary to define the contours of twenty-first-century church ministry. He believes we are on the cusp of a postmodern Great Awakening—a tremendous historical moment and movement of the Holy Spirit. Amazingly, however, Sweet believes that much of the modern Western church will likely miss it. He sees the church largely living in denial of the great changes now taking place around the world or, as a response to these changes, hunkering down in a fear-based bunker mentality. Sweet seems convinced that the church as we know it is a dinosaur on the edge of extinction.

The real ministers of the new millennium will be "spiritual interventionists" who understand the postmodern, post-Christian mind and are not afraid of it or of the technology that swirls around it, but who are able to move and learn and adapt to an ever-changing global-techno-enviro-relational milieu. Sweet believes that denominationalism, organizationalism, gigantism, and a host of other mostly twentieth-century "isms" are dead or soon will be.

We are struck by how this brave new world is rapidly bypassing the church as we know it. As we indicated earlier, interest in spirituality is increasing enormously. A recent poll found that 82% of Americans feel the need for greater intimacy with God, an increase of 24% in just four years (Gallup & Jones, 2000).

While commitment to church and denomination continues to slide, involvement in cults, counterfeit religions, and guru-based communities is soaring. As our knowledge of the true God wanes, alternative and cult-based religious knowledge greatly increases.

We are convinced that many Christian counselors are deeply tuned in to this new, rather alien, largely fascinating, and still-forming post-Christian paradigm. However, we must deepen our spiritual roots and improve our theological astuteness to be able to win the battle for hearts and minds in the decades ahead.

Christian counseling may well be at the forefront of this revival, a new wineskin prepared to undertake a task that the traditional church is missing. As disinterest in church and religion turns to outright hostility and persecution of Christians and as the new religion of tolerance becomes aggressively intolerant of Jesus Christ, organized religion will be targeted or co-opted and increasingly rendered powerless to effect the gospel call.

The life of Christ and the work of the church will be carried within the literal bodies of millions of believers who are networked together by a global Internet and operating in a mobile, fluid, and dynamic way. Increasingly, Christian counseling will be done outside the consulting office by creative means, and it will be done more and more in the homes and hearts of those who need our gifts.

As Dickens stated in *A Tale of Two Cities,* these truly are the best of times and the worst of times. The Human Genome Project is already revolutionizing medicine and biology to the same degree that the Manhattan Project transformed nuclear physics more than fifty years ago. Each week millions of people are logging on to the global Internet for the first time; we have barely tapped into the potential for virtual reality and distance learning from this source, including the practice of distance therapy, coaching, counselor education, and supervision—all of which are growing in importance.

These radical changes taking place on planet Earth require that we have the eyes of God to see clearly through the fog of change and the heart of God to remain at peace in the midst of the chaos these changes are creating. If we as Christian counselors are not delivering the answers to sin and brokenness, if we are not presenting Christ and his gift of love, if we are not in tune with the work of the Holy Spirit to enter and transform lives, then we are in danger of being swept along in a tide that has great power but no clear direction.

We have to ask ourselves afresh that wornout question: Are we merely Christians who counsel others with no relationship to the God who made us, or are we doing Christian counseling in a way that changes lives now and for eternity? Who we are is so much more significant than what we do in counseling. To use Sweet's language, we must ask, "In your counseling practice, are you a 'souled-out' representative of the One who saved you? If so, how may we help you become an even better representative in the days to come? If you are not souled-out yet, what will it take to help you become transformed?"

THE VISION

What is happening in the American Association of Christian Counselors (AACC) alone is sobering and is obviously something God is building—by his design and for his glory—for the church and for a desperate world. There is simply no other explanation for the phenomenal progress that has taken place.

We firmly believe that God is constructing a holy, powerful, and radiant church—a beautiful bride fit for her King—and that Christian counseling is a significant component in the construction. Above all else, we are being shaped by God to serve some of the deepest needs of his church. We must never lose sight of this divine mandate.

Remember that God is calling us to excellence and unity in Christ: "Live a life worthy of the calling you have received. Be completely humble and gentle; be patient, bearing with one another in love. Make every effort to keep the unity of the Spirit through the bond of peace" (Ephesians 4:1-3). Such godly unity will cause us to shine as lights in a world that grows ever darker as it races away from God.

We are dedicated to helping you become more compassionate soul-care providers in everything you do. We want a spirit of compassionate soul care, the spiritual heart of the *Paraklete*—the Holy Spirit himself—to be formed in you. We want Christian counselors to be a community of light, image-bearers of the living God who radiate hope and deliverance to a jaded, sated, and broken world.

We must facilitate a biblical paradigm for counseling and help shape a caring community where people are able to grow into what God intends them to be. Such dedication thrives on excellence and creativity, and it never makes excuses for sloppy counseling, substandard research, or poor teaching. Furthermore, the healing and transforming power of such a godly community offers repair and renewal in ways that are impossible in the world and maybe even in the way we have done church up to now.

We encourage you to seize this incredible moment and make the best of God's work in you and through you for others. Together we must be leaders in spiritual discernment, moral purity, insightful interventions, wise words, humble hearts, careful research, and servant natures.

The Commitment

The mission of AACC is to bring honor to Jesus Christ by the leading of the Holy Spirit and to promote excellence and unity in Christian counseling. To give this mission statement meaning, consider the metaphor of a four-legged stool.

The church and the larger community of care of which we are all a part is the seat that rests on four legs, each of which must be strong and properly attached to the seat to be of any value. Each leg represents one of the four primary groups that make up the worldwide Christian counseling community: pastors, professional clinicians, lay helpers, and students-in-training.

These four legs are fastened to the "community seat" by eight firm braces. These braces represent our commitment to the following:

- *Accessibility.* We must strive to be fully accessible to the church as a whole and to reach beyond the doors of the church to the world community.
- *Fidelity.* We must maintain an unswerving dedication to Jesus Christ, to God the Father, to the Holy Spirit, and to the revelation of this living God in the Old and New Testaments of the Bible.
- *Quality.* We must strive for excellence in all we do, aiming to produce the highest quality product, service, commitment, and ministry we can.
- *Accountability.* We must maintain the highest standards of fiscal and ministerial accountability with the church and the world at large.
- *Sensitivity.* We must listen to and strive to respect every concern about us that is voiced by the church and the world at large.
- *Creativity.* We must be dedicated to searching for and finding the most creative and clear solutions to every need or problem we face as we serve the church and world community.
- *Integrity.* We must strive always to do what is right, to do it honestly and in a timely way, and, avoiding all triumphal arrogance, to admit to and correct any problems when we fall short.

- *Advocacy.* We must be dedicated to promoting and defending Christian counseling in every legitimate way possible in the church, professions, the government, business, and the media.

THE CASE FOR INTENTIONAL TWENTY-FIRST-CENTURY DEVELOPMENT

Coming full circle with chapter 1, we believe in the intentional development of Christian counseling—in growth that is planned, rational, and actively directed as opposed to passive, unplanned, or random—because we are convinced that the transformation of competent Christian counseling will not be neutral. Intentional development of the profession will keep CCC centered in the church.

In this chapter we offer our thoughts on one path to the destination of a more mature and vibrant profession. While we invite you to join us on this path, we recognize that alternative proposals exist that could bring all of us to a similar destination.

IS THERE A CHRISTIAN COUNSELING PROFESSION?

Developmentally, we recognize that CCC is at a place similar to where psychology and social work were in the early part of the twentieth century: It is an emerging profession on the cusp of maturity and major growth. However, robust growth by itself does not necessarily ensure survival, let alone maturation into a vibrant profession. Intentional development of our profession is called for at this crucial juncture in our history.

CHRISTIAN COUNSELING PROFESSION ASSESSMENT

Barber (1965) has delineated the classic formulation of profession development in his pioneering work on the sociology of the professions. The attributes of a profession include the following:

- a distinctive definition and practice art
- a practice oriented to community service as opposed to individual self-interest
- a knowledge base that is highly developed, generalized, and systematically taught
- effective self-regulation—a high degree of professional self-control through an ethics code, recognized standards of practice, and disciplined professional association

- a system of rewards and incentives—both monetary and professional achievement honors—that motivate continued professional development at individual and corporate levels

Assessing Christian counseling across these major profession-defining variables—and comparing it to the three classical learned professions (law, medicine, and theology or ministry)—shows numerous strengths and weaknesses. Across the five variables previously noted, we make the following observations.

1. *The identity of CCC is growing more and more distinctive,* but it is still easily confused with pastoral and other forms of ministry. Some in our movement may even argue that CCC is best left as a derivative of pastoral care or professional counseling, but we argued in chapters 1 and 2 that these are the two tracks on which the Christian counseling train runs. Christian counseling is becoming better defined and understood throughout the church, but it is still not fully accepted by some segments of the church, and it is not well known in general society.

BOX 33.1—MODERN ASSAULTS ON CHRISTIAN COUNSELING

For nearly a decade now, in the conferences and publications of the American Association of Christian Counselors (AACC), we have documented the myriad challenges to and assaults on competent Christian counseling (Clinton, 1998; Clinton & Ohlschlager, 1997; Ohlschlager, 1999; Ohlschlager & Mosgofian, 1992). Following are examples of some documented cases and complaints.

- In a Midwestern state, a Christian counselor, who is also an ordained minister, passed both written and oral exams for a professional counseling license. He was known by state officials as a Christian minister and counselor who worked in a church-affiliated social services agency. When informed that he had passed his licensing exam, he also read in the letter a contingency clause that stated that the license would be issued only if he agreed to limit his employment strictly to church or church-affiliated settings. This kind of religious discrimination is patently unjust and completely illegal under the First Amendment to the U.S. Constitution, but indicative of the growing abuse of state power.
- While religion is now being recognized as a basis for multicultural and ethical respect by the mental health community, some are still compelled to attack it as "cultural baggage" (Santa Rita, 1996, p. 325). Santa Rita considered the Catholic beliefs of Filipino-Americans to be pathological

2. *A strong attribute of CCC is its dedication to Christian service:* Christ is held up as the ideal servant, and many counselors testify to their sense of calling. However, the trend toward professionalization and fee-based practice has prompted critics to question the purity of this service ideal. Also, defining distinct boundaries and specifying a clear relationship between *professional, pastoral,* and *lay helping* remains a major challenge. Giving attention to these three major divisions will help bring greater clarity of purpose to each of these important aspects of competent Christian counseling.

3. *The knowledge base of Christian counseling is likewise developing,* supported increasingly by graduate education and research, numerous professional conferences, and a growing number of journals. As McMinn (1996) points out, however, there are many holes and gaps in our models and treatment methods, we lack a solid empirical base to support their validity, and our knowledge base is not yet systematically organized and taught. We hope that this gap will close even further as new research updates and systematizes counseling knowledge and practice.

---

due to that religion's "beliefs on abortion, contraception, and homosexuality [which] contribute to a self-righteous, judgmental stance that is out of place in a pluralistic society with alternative lifestyles" (p. 326).

- Christian graduate students in California, Nebraska, and New York have complained to the AACC about blatant anti-Christian biases among graduate counseling professors and fellow students. In the name of multicultural sensitivity training, Christian students have been attacked and ridiculed—publicly and in classroom circles—for their "biases" against homosexuals and others. This has happened even when students merely indicated they were Christians. In the first semester of a program with highly competitive admissions, a student in Nebraska was told she would not graduate because her "archaic Christian beliefs" would make her a very poor counselor.

- Some church leaders still skewer Christian counseling and its leaders. It is difficult to take seriously—and there is no real dialogue with—hypercritical accusers who deem many good pioneers of our field as "psychoheretics" (Bobgan & Bobgan, 1987); who label Christian counselors as "witch doctors" and the "rot of hell" (Swaggart, 1986, p. 7); or who broadbrush and summarily dismiss our cause as "the most dangerous...form of modernism ever to have invaded the church" (Hunt, 1987, p. 130).

(continued)

4. *The size and vitality of the AACC promises an effective means of profession-wide education, identity formation, and self-regulation.* But this organization, with its twin mission of excellence of service and unity in Christian counseling, is still in its early stages of development. Such burgeoning growth in membership must be followed by disciplined service and profession development across a wide variety of concerns. Diversity in membership, in approaches to counseling, and in training and practice backgrounds is a creative hallmark of the AACC, but because of this diversity, detractors raise serious questions about the degree to which unity in Christian counseling can be attained.

5. Apart from the motivation to serve Christ and others in Christian ministry (and some would passionately argue that we need no other motivation), *Christian counseling offers few rewards and incentives to attract and motivate lifelong professional growth.* Many people are able to make a living doing CCC, but little else attracts lifelong professional dedication.

This brief observational analysis may give the impression that Christian counseling at the start of the twenty-first century is a deficient or sublevel profession.

Other criticism is more cogent. We join hands with some of our more judicious critics (Clinton, 2001, 1998; Collins, 1993; Ohlschlager & Mosgofian, 1992; Powlison, 1997; Vitz, 1977) regarding the following six concerns:

1. Has Christian counseling—and have many Christian counselors—strayed too far from Christ and the church and even rejected Christianity as the center of our identity, mission, and effort?

2. Are too many Christian counselors separate from and unaccountable to the church, to their pastors, and to counseling colleagues? Are too many counselors in danger of moral and ethical wrongdoing, arrogantly believing that they are too smart, too educated, or too complex to be understood and guided by someone else?

3. Hart (2001) has asserted that "We have borrowed uncritically from psychology and run too far ahead of our biblical roots." Do integrationists (those who accept the validity of extrabiblical sources in counseling) work too much outside the spiritual realm, helping people cope and become more confident by strengthening the self apart from God rather than helping them become more Christlike?

4. Are psychologically trained Christian counselors—including those in psychology, psychiatry, social work, counseling, and marriage and family

More constructively stated, however, CCC may be considered an *emerging profession*. Barber (1965) describes both the characteristics of an emerging profession and the challenge of those who seek to further its maturity:

> It is typical of the structure of the occupational group that is emerging as a profession that its members are not homogenous with respect to the amount of knowledge and community orientation they possess.... Probably two-thirds or more of the members are...only marginally professional. But the elite of these occupations...are clearly professional. It is the elite of an emerging profession that take the lead in pushing for the advancement of professionalism in its occupational group and in claiming public recognition of its new status....
>
> In the attempt to express and strengthen the community orientation of the group, the leaders take pains to construct and publish a code of ethics....
>
> The leaders establish or try to strengthen a professional association. In an established profession, such an association carries on the several functions

therapy—too ignorant of the Bible and church history, too timid about using the Bible and spiritual disciplines in counseling, and too uncomfortable relying on the Holy Spirit in session?

5. Are nouthetic counselors too exclusively focused on sin to be tender and helpful to clients who are broken and suffering, too engaged in biblical behavior modification to be able to help someone walk through the "dark night of soul" transformation, and too resistant to learning and becoming skilled in clinical knowledge and patterns to be widely helpful to many people?

6. After more than thirty years of development as a profession, is biblical counseling still just preaching to the choir, in danger of influencing no one outside their narrow clique and possibly stagnating in a tepid backwater while the rest of Christian counseling flows on to twenty-first-century maturity?

Is CCC strong enough to withstand these challenges and even to grow from this assault? Very much so, we are convinced. In fact, we might assert that nothing could attract so much negative attention unless it were making some significant impact on a number of levels. (The history, development, and impact of Christian counseling over the past half-century of growth are documented in chapters 1 and 2.)

of self-control, socialization and education of its members, communications with the public, and the defense of professional interest against infringement by the public or other occupational groups....

Within their own occupational ranks, the leaders establish measures and titles of more or less professional behavior, hoping, for example, to use such prestigious titles as "fellow" as an incentive for the less professional to become more so....

The leaders will, of course, seek to establish or strengthen university professional schools....

Desiring prestige and support from the general public, the leaders will engage in a program of public information about the "professional" services it provides and the "professional" standards...it maintains....

And, finally, the leaders of an emerging profession will have to engage in some conflict with elements both inside and outside their occupational group. (pp. 160-164)

CHRISTIAN COUNSELING: AN EMERGING PROFESSION

With respect to Barber's framework, we believe that Christian counseling in this new millenium is properly defined as an *emerging profession*. While those who would challenge this label might point to Barber's use of elitist language as evidence of the dangers of professionalization, we believe the benefits far outweigh its admitted costs. At the root of all good profession development—and key motivating factors in sustained activity in the face of adversity—are clear definition and visionary direction. Definition without vision is static and stagnant. Vision without clear definition of starting points and end goals eventually becomes diffuse, disorganized, and exhausting.

We must be committed to directed profession development not only because of the problems noted above but also because of the inherent benefits of professional identity. A unified profession can more clearly define practice standards, counselor ethics, and entry-level requirements; it can promote a distinctive identity to the rest of the world. American consumers are highly sophisticated and have tremendous choices, and the new marketplace is demanding even greater professional competence and certification of practice excellence. Also, advocacy of the profession's interests and views in the courts, legislatures, other professions, and society at large will be enhanced when a unified and well-supported professional voice speaks out. A single primary professional association is much better able to serve the profession's members with effectiveness and cost efficiency than can a disjointed array of several smaller organizations.

Is Christian counseling a distinctive discipline? Some will argue that there is nothing particularly distinctive about Christian counseling, that CCC is as illusory as Christian medicine or Christian accounting. It can also be argued that CCC is diffuse and imprecise, bleeding easily into its overlapping relations with pastoral ministry or psychology.

Those in the antipsychology movement might further argue that the attempt to define a distinctive discipline inherently devalues its legitimacy as a Christian ministry. Not only is a distinct and professionalized ministry corrupted beyond redemption by secular psychology, they contend, but it also stands over and against the historic gifts and ministry of the church—a ministry that has been sufficient for two thousand years without a Christian counseling arm. Many in the church are suspicious of CCC's claims and influence, while others are confused about its role.

It is one thing to assert in response—correctly, though often too easily, we believe—that CCC is here to stay. It is quite another to struggle to define the profession clearly and to discern its rightful place in the local and worldwide ministry of the church. Positively, evidence for the distinctiveness of Christian counseling is gaining strength. At present, more than ten thousand pastors are active members of the AACC, and CCC is demonstrating its acceptance by pastors and churches throughout the world. Also, the marketplace, as exemplified by the managed care demand for certified Christian counselors, is increasingly responsive to the distinctive call for CCC.

VISIONARY VIEWS

Collins outlined a comprehensive vision for Christian counseling in the winter 1995 issue of *Christian Counseling Today:*

> I have a dream for Christian counseling.... This is not a "head in the clouds" dream; it is a set of goals that are realistic, incomplete, and still forming.... Where will Christian counseling be in the year 2000 and beyond? I dream of a movement...of Christian counselors that will:
>
> - be represented by a major organization with state-of-the-art member services so that everyone senses a personal touch without being lost.
> - have established a reputation for the production and efficient distribution of the highest quality publications and other resources.
> - have a growing body of research documentation to substantiate who we are and the effectiveness of what we are doing.
> - have fully functioning regional and special-interest divisions within the organization.

- be affiliated with an international association of Christian counselors (consisting of individual country associations), characterized by clear national and international networks.
- have clear, mutually supportive, and mutually respected ties with local churches and local church leaders.
- be identified as a separate health care profession/specialty with the highest quality, nationally recognized certification procedures.
- make use of the most effective technology.
- have developed evolving, innovative, non-traditional and traditional, high-caliber training programs for pastors, professionals, lay counselors...and other(s).
- be having a recognized, Christ-honoring impact.
- have an international research-treatment-training Institute for the Development and Practice of Christian Counseling (a Christian counseling Mayo or Menninger Clinic).
- have a charitable foundation for the advancement of Christian counseling.
- have a unique, biblically-based, legally-sensitive, practical, and detailed ethics code.
- hold regular, high-quality regional, national, and international conferences.
- have an advocacy department.
- find a way to recognize excellence. (p. 8)

Collins marked out most of the factors that Barber described as essential to the fuller development of an emerging profession. (In fact, whether he did so consciously or not—and we have it on good authority that he did not—notice how Collins's statement echoes the elements of profession development previously stated by Barber.) Furthermore—and this is most exciting and hopeful for CCC— as we move farther into the twenty-first century, progress can be reported on every point of Collins's dream.

INTENTIONAL PROFESSION DEVELOPMENT IN THE TWENTY-FIRST CENTURY

Incorporating and building upon Collins's (1995) vision for our profession, and including developments actually accomplished or on the near horizon, we envision CCC maturing in the following specific ways in the days ahead.

A twenty-first-century code of ethics. The acceptance and inclusion of the final (2001) draft of the *AACC Christian Counseling Code of Ethics* into the practice of Christian counseling agencies and practices worldwide will define a standard of care for this century and serve as a sure basis for counselor defense and advocacy. This Code—already translated into six languages and adopted by Christian counselors in more than a dozen other countries—is quickly becoming a global standard of care for twenty-first-century practice and ministry.

Sure advocacy. We are convinced that Christian counseling should be at the forefront of client advocacy. In addition to developing a "patient bill of rights" and providing services to the poor and disenfranchised, Christian counselors should be advocates for those who are persecuted and suffering around the world because of their faith and for those too abused and marginalized to speak out for themselves. Aponte (1999) recognizes that Christian counselors are leading the way in delineating biblical values and giving clients the chance to consent to work within a Christian-values framework. Let's build on this and be known as leaders in client respect and advocacy.

National credentialing. The development of a nationally recognized, universally respected, and voluntary practice credential will solidly demonstrate at least minimal competence and the progressive achievement of clinical excellence, ethical practice, and fidelity to biblical principles for Christian mental health professionals of every discipline as well as for pastoral counselors, chaplains, and spiritual directors. The American Board of Christian Counselors (ABCC) has created a specialized organization, affiliated with the AACC, to accomplish this goal. Working under its own board in conjunction with AACC objectives, the ABCC and the new Code of Ethics are designed to work hand in glove in mutual ministry and become a primary credentialing, ethical standard-setting, and advocacy agency.

Program accreditation. We anticipate the rise of Christian counseling accreditation standards for graduate training programs of all kinds, including professional mental health practice training and training in pastoral counseling, the chaplaincy, and spiritual formation. We envision clinics, agencies, and practices being accredited and operating according to a standard of excellence that hopefully will be trusted throughout the church and society.

Lay helping ministry. We are on the verge of an explosion of lay helping ministries within the church that will make churches more able to serve the casualties and needy converts who come their way. Churches could be equipped to better fulfill Christ's call to evangelism and disciple making.

Spiritual and relationship formation. We realize that spiritual formation is being incorporated increasingly into Christian counseling. We also envision CCC becoming a key resource for the maturation and empowerment of discipleship in the twenty-first-century church. Christian counselors will become bio-psycho-social-spiritual interventionists and the vanguard of a uniting movement of Christians who worship God and spread his message around the world.

Biblical and theological depth. CCC is becoming more biblically grounded and theologically learned as a new wave of twenty-first-century theologians, educators, and interdisciplinary counselors join together to train and educate counselors in theology and spirituality. We believe Christian counselors will also challenge theologians to become more experiential and emotive, to apply their knowledge to real-world needs and events on an unprecedented historical scale. We hope the newly formed Geneva Institute (a division of the AACC) will be a worldwide catalyst for this kind of growth.

Cybercounseling and the use of Internet technologies. We see an explosion of service development in Christian e-care, cybercounseling, and distance learning. Practitioners of CCC will be leaders in the development of Internet, phone, and multimedia-based counseling, education, coaching, consulting, mentoring, and discipling. The reach of Christian counselors and training programs is expanding exponentially from local regions to national and global scales. The globalization of Christian counseling has already begun.

Expanding cutting-edge modes of care. Relatedly, we see Christian counselors reorienting toward doing ministry and work other than office-based psychotherapy: in-home, in-business, in-ministry, and in-church counseling and consulting; mediation and peacemaking; coaching; consulting; teaching; training and supervising lay helpers; cybercounseling; and church-based ministry of all kinds.

Interprofessional relationships. We see both increased tensions and increased collaboration with secular mental health and social service organizations across a range of issues. Tensions will increase over values conflicts, antireligious prejudice, and the explicit integration of spiritual (especially Christ-centered) practices in counseling. On the other hand, we expect increased collaboration on improving client care and client access to counseling services, improving empirical validation of treatments and outcomes, curbing abuses and unjust limitations of care by managed care and the insurance industry, and informing the public about our services and how they are to be delivered ethically.

Work with faith-based initiatives. Consistent with the national faith-based initiative, we believe that Christian counselors, the church, and mental health institutions of all kinds will collaborate more intentionally to ensure the continuity of care across the entire panoply of service modes—from outpatient to residential and day care programs to hospitalization and intensive aftercare treatment. We anticipate that Crabb's (1997, 1999, 2001) call to develop the healing power of the church and Christian community will come to fruition in miraculous and life-changing ways.

Intensive care for counselors and pastors. We see the need to facilitate the rise of a network of centers and sanctuaries to deliver intensive and high-quality care to exhausted and burned-out shepherds of the church, to pastors and counselors in need of rest, restoration, renewal, and redirection for their lives and ministries.

Distance education that emphasizes high-quality training. We envision Christian counselors demanding computer-mediated distance education that allows the learner to maintain career and family commitments. Becoming trained and gaining access to resources in new practice modalities, high-quality and responsive referral networks, law and ethics, and the business and marketing of counseling will no longer be optional. We are on the cusp of an explosion in the use of radio, television, video, the Internet, and other advanced technologies as media of service delivery.

Continuing education and focused certificate programs. A new level of continuing education and postgraduate certificate programs is being developed. These programs will train Christian counselors in specific modalities and skills. This quality training will be for licensed practitioners as well as for those desiring advanced training who have neither the desire, time, nor finances for traditional degree programs. Progressive continuing education and certificate programs, each ranging in length from six to nine to twelve months, will proliferate in schools and ministry organizations of all kinds. Topics will include Christ-centered leadership training, spiritual formation, marriage and family therapy, bio-psycho-social-spiritual assessment and intervention, clinical-medical ethics, education and supervision, psychosocial health care, mediation, coaching, and consulting.

Doctoral-level programs for training leaders in Christian counseling. We see the rise of high-quality PhD programs in Christian counseling that will stand alongside and offer alternative training to both secular and Christian psychology doctorates. These programs likely will offer core training in Christian counseling, Bible and theology, research and policy, and the bio-psycho-social-spiritual sciences. Training in alternative practice modalities such as mediation, coaching, spiritual formation, pastoral care, clinical ethics and bioethics, and policy analysis seems to be the trend.

Heightened multicultural sensitivity. CCC will increase its sensitivity and respect for multicultural differences in all aspects of its ministry and service. Due to the developing multicultural ethic in the mental health professions, CCC will increase and refine its advocacy against religious prejudice. CCC may also be on the vanguard of balancing multicultural respect with the need for some level of cultural assimilation in order to check strident and ideological multicultural extremism.

New and more refined research. A cadre of Christian counseling researchers is being trained to help advance CCC on the frontiers of empirical development. Not only are religious and faith-based variables being shown to correlate significantly with better health and well-being across a wide range of factors, but research on biblically based treatment and outcomes is just now coming into its own. Establishing a proven database for the validity of all kinds of Christian counseling applications is rapidly becoming a crucial priority in the development and defense of this work.

"Salt and light" ministry. Christian counselors of various backgrounds, working in concert with Christian counseling organizations and other ministerial partnerships, will increasingly assume leadership roles in a variety of secular arenas as "salt and light" ministry. Sadly, the attacks on the family, biblical values, and enterprising innovation continue unabated. Aggressive displays of violence, permissive sexuality, and material greed will likely grow stronger in the twenty-first century. Over the next few years we need to increase our advocacy voice in the media, in government, and in the leading mental health and managed care organizations around the country. At the same time we must partner more deliberately with like-minded ministries and organizations to increase the impact of our advocacy on a variety of cutting-edge issues.

"Glocalization." A logical and global extension of the previous trend should witness a unique twenty-first-century twist on what is now dubbed *glocalization*— "thinking globally, acting locally." Leading Christian counselors will facilitate awareness and action around issues with international consequences: missions, refugees, human rights, persecuted and tortured Christians, worldwide environmental concerns, and the development of appropriate technologies. The Internet as a global communications resource suggests that the church will increasingly break out of its institutional structure and become intensely interactive and interpersonal, a more biblical model of the effective church.

A mature interdisciplinary profession. We see Christian counseling growing into a robust adulthood during this century, maturing from an emerging profession to a full-blown interdisciplinary (ministerial and mental health) profession with room for every person who chooses to pursue this unique and challenging realm of ministry.

BUILD CAREFULLY BUT ASSUREDLY

Jesus warned against building structures that could not be finished, and he challenged us to count the cost of committing to his kingdom (Luke 14:28-30). No doubt there will be those in our movement—even some leaders—who will argue that these developments are too costly or that such development is unneeded, unwanted, or out of reach. Others will undoubtedly contend that these developments do not go far enough and that stronger medicine is needed. Legitimate cases can probably be made for either view.

Nevertheless, it is our view that the time has come for an assertive response to the various assaults on the mission of competent Christian counseling. It is time for Christian counseling to develop with intentionality and purpose, working toward goals that are both necessary and doable. We, the editors of this book, have been in unique positions that have allowed us to document some of these assaults and view them in their overlapping and interlocking perversity. Our hope, however, is always in Christ, and we regard growing to maturity in Christian counseling as a faith venture not unlike the challenge of Hebrews 11. While we do not see the exact contours of Christian counseling in the future, we are certain it will be strong and vibrant. We are confident in that hope.

Clearly, Christian counseling is an emerging but vital profession. Together, as the community of care, we are responsible for advancing our mission into the next century. But only God knows the future. So may we stay close to what he is doing and move forward together. Individually, we are weak against the various powers arrayed against us. But together, and in Christ, we are strong.

PROFILE OF A
SHEPHERD-COUNSELOR

Lessons Learned from the Good Shepherd

DIANE LANGBERG

I am the good shepherd. The good shepherd lays down his life for the
sheep.... I am the good shepherd; I know my sheep and my sheep know me.

—JOHN 10:11,14

K nowing Christ and caring for others have been inextricably woven together for me ever since I can remember. I came to Christ at the age of eleven through the teaching of my parents. It was not long afterward that I began to truly see the needs of others.

CALLED TO CARE

My father was a U.S. Air Force colonel. As I was growing up, I did not need a degree in psychology to see that most of my friends' mothers were alcoholics. They liked to come to my house after school because my mother was sober—and kind. I told my friends about Jesus and, at the age of twelve, began teaching a small group of girls from Scripture. I remember going home with one of those girls one day on the way to my house. We found her mother still in bed in a filthy nightgown. She was drunk and hanging tightly onto a bottle of something. It gave me a glimpse into the pain and horror of my friend's life, and I wanted to help.

Little did I know where the eyes to see people's hurts and the heartfelt desire to help them would take me, or how like God it is to use the broken lives I saw to bear fruit in the lives of others. Many years have passed since I was twelve, and I still have eyes that see and a heartfelt desire to help. Those two traits, plus a few degrees and some training, have given me access to many people whose lives are not unlike those of my young friends and their parents. I have witnessed a great deal of pain and horror, and, I believe, I have been called by God to tend those whose lives have been so marked.

I have nurtured women who, as little girls, were repeatedly raped by a man called Daddy. I have come alongside men who, as little boys, were repeatedly molested by a woman called Mommy. I have sat with women whose shattered, black-and-blue faces testified to a twisted form of husbanding yet who were confused as to who was responsible. I have sat with parents who had tended dying children and who desperately needed tending themselves. I have walked with those whose lives were slowly being destroyed by cancer or other diseases. Missionaries who had been raped and robbed or kidnapped and tortured have come for help and healing. Pastors, weary and broken by divisive and persecuting churches, have needed pastoring themselves.

And there has been another kind of tending, one that I never anticipated when I first began counseling others. I tend not only the women whose faces are black and blue, but also those who batter them. I care for missionaries who leave the United States to proclaim the gospel, but who have to come home because they molested those they went to help. I walk with pastors who were called to shepherd, but who ended up feeding on their sheep. I care for those whose marriages are ravaged because they cannot get their faces out of pornography. And so I find myself tending those who are damaged by others as well as those who do the damaging. Sometimes, of course, these people are one and the same.

All of us who help others are shepherds. We shepherd in various arenas. Many of us do so as pastors and therapists; some as teachers, managers, writers, and parents. I did not think of myself as a shepherd so many years ago. Now, however, I realize that this is what I am. Also, having seen the damage done by some unfit shepherds, I have realized that competent Christian counseling—shepherding—is a serious and awesome task.

UNFIT SHEPHERDS

It is far too easy to be an unfit shepherd.

One of the things I do during the course of a week is supervise several other therapists. I hear myself again and again trying to impress upon them the significance they have in the lives of their clients and the power they have to help or to harm them. Whenever you as a therapist enter the broken life of another person, you become extremely important. Many people's lives are so destroyed and barren that you are the only significant relationship they have, and so they live from one session to the next. They count the days until their next appointment with you. As you know, some people cannot even make it a week between appointments, so they call or page or write letters or request more frequent sessions.

People come wanting wisdom about their marriages or their parenting. They come confused and in need of truth. They come in bondage to sin and needing freedom. They come unable to discern right from wrong. To walk into a broken life, a life with needs of this magnitude, obviously gives the shepherd significant influence. And such potential for help also means great potential for harm.

Being an unfit shepherd begins when you abuse the power you have in the lives you've been called to care for, using that power for your own benefit instead of for the good of the client or parishioner. We find this negative model in Ezekiel 34, where the shepherds of Israel are described as feeding on their flocks. Those commissioned by God to care for his people instead used his people for their own benefit. They drank the milk of the sheep, wore their wool, and ate their flesh. In other words, they took whatever the sheep had to offer and used it for themselves.

In counseling, the most obvious example of such abuse of power is the use of a client for the therapist's own sexual gratification. Unfortunately, it is also the most common example—and the most damaging to clients. I refer not only to suicide committed by 1% of sexually abused clients, but also to the inflamed trauma, mistrust of others, destroyed marriages, and shattered lives experienced by nearly every client who has been sexually victimized by self-serving shepherds.

We can abuse our position in more subtle ways as well. For instance, it is easy to feed off others emotionally in order to help ourselves feel loved, important, or wise. We may ask questions in order to titillate our curiosity or to hear information about a third party. Anytime we orchestrate a session so as to feed some appetite or need in ourselves, we behave as unfit shepherds.

Another common abuse of power is encouraging clients to look only to us for help and healing. Certainly, the weak need our strength, the foolish need our wisdom, the despairing need our hope, the blind need our sight, and the doubters need our faith. These are good and right things to give. However, such work can also be seductive to the caregiver, for we may begin to think that we alone are able to give such things adequately. Somehow the healthy nurturing that comes from other people—such as the client's spouse, circle of friends, or church community—begins to pale in comparison to our caregiving, and we wrongly help our clients buy into the lie that we alone are what they need. There is a fine line between believing we are important to others and believing we are necessary to them. When we begin to think and teach—even by implication—that we are necessary, we take the place of the One we have been called to honor and follow.

We are never to steal the hearts of others for ourselves. Rather, as Christian counselors, we are commanded to hand our charges over to God. Our clients come to us hungry for love, truth, hope, and faith. We cannot ultimately fulfill such needs. But we can, by our lives, give them tastes of the One who is using us to draw them to himself. We are servants of the Good Shepherd. We are unfit servants if we become so inflated with our own importance that we fail to utilize the gifting of the body of Christ or fail to point our clients away from us and ultimately to the satisfaction that resides in the Good Shepherd.

Perhaps overarching all abuses, we are unfit shepherds at any point that we misrepresent the Good Shepherd. If our compassion leads us to condone sin, if our abhorrence of evil leads to harshness, if we demand justice without mercy, if our appearance of obedience cloaks hidden disobedience—we are unfit. If we abandon or fail to seek after those who have wandered away, if we rule by power rather than by love, if we leave our clients vulnerable to attack because we fail to speak truth to them—we are unfit.

In John 10, Jesus speaks of himself as the Good Shepherd, contrasting himself with those perfect examples of unfit shepherding, the Pharisees. His clear message to those unfit shepherds was "Woe...," a word used primarily as an expression of grief. Anytime you and I hurt, damage, or mislead one of the least of God's sheep, we bring great grief to the heart of our Lord.

THE FIT SHEPHERD

If it is true that those who seek us out are broken, needy, and vulnerable, and if it is true that you and I are called by God to shepherd such people, then we must learn how to shepherd fitly. Furthermore, if it is true that such a task is so serious and awesome because of its potential impact for good or evil in the lives of others, and if it is also true that shepherding selfishly and unfitly grieves the God who has called us, then we had better learn to counsel according to the Master's own heart.

Oswald Chambers wasn't inaccurate when he wrote, "The sheep are many, and the shepherds few, for the fatigue is staggering, the heights are giddy, and the sights are awful" (p. 52). Some job description—but how true it is! Given the challenge, what does it mean to be a fit shepherd? I believe the answer to that question takes us on a journey into the fellowship of Christ's sufferings—and to the Cross.

It is no coincidence that the birth of the Good Shepherd was announced to shepherds. These men were rejected, and they led isolated lives outside the camp.

Unable to observe the ritual washings, they were considered unclean. So, on the outskirts of Bethlehem, they tended flocks of sheep that were set aside for temple sacrifices. These shepherds so identified with their sheep that they entered their lives and took on their filth. They smelled like their sheep. They lived outside the camp with their sheep. They were set apart because they had stepped in the muck and mire of those they tended.

All the aspects of Jesus' good shepherding, and ours as well, are foreshadowed in this scene. Here we see the thread of sacrifice: The shepherds sacrificed in order to tend the sheep, and the sheep were intended for sacrifice. We also see the threads of tending, protecting, and being ever-watchful day and night, for that is what shepherds do. But we have another, unusual thread: the glory of God manifested in the heavens, brought down into the muck and mire.

Thirty years later the Son of God entered the scene again as John the Baptist announced, "Behold! The Lamb of God who takes away the sin of the world!" (John 1:29, NKJV). Our threads are all here. *Behold the Lamb*—the sacrifice, the unblemished One. He takes away the sin of the world. He stepped into the muck and mire of this world and was made so unclean by it that he had to go outside the camp to die.

If you and I are to learn from the Good Shepherd, we must begin here. We must first behold the Lamb. We need to seek him, to search him out. When John called his followers to behold the Lamb, he also called them to repentance. To truly behold the glory of God in the flesh is to see our own lives more clearly. So, before we can serve our clients, we must be fully aware of the fact that we are sheep ourselves, in need of the sacrificial Lamb of God and his death for our sins.

We dare not move into shepherding others if we fail to deal with our own lives. If we do not learn to behold the Lamb and repent of our sin, we will catch the soul diseases of those with whom we work. If we do not behold and repent, we will feed on the flock we have been called to feed. If we do not behold and repent, we will confuse ourselves with the Lamb and lead others to follow us rather than him. If we do not behold and repent, we will misrepresent the Good Shepherd, and others will believe lies about him, thinking we are representing him accurately.

You and I are fit to tend sheep only to the degree to which we ourselves have learned to follow the Good Shepherd. If Jesus tended us by first becoming a lamb, who are we to do otherwise? All good shepherds are, first and foremost, lambs. The shepherd who is not first a lamb will be arrogant and proud and will damage those he or she has been called to tend.

So we begin by beholding the Lamb of God, asking him to search us out and repenting of anything in our lives that displeases him. As a result, we are empowered to bring his life and influence into every relationship. If we fail to begin here, then we, like the Pharisees, may have the appearance of obedience, but in actuality we will be unfit shepherds in feeding the flock of God.

We must also begin in the same way that the announcement to the shepherds and from John the Baptist began: *Behold the Lamb!* The Lamb of God, the supreme sacrifice, is the world's only hope. Yet we tend to proclaim, "Behold a new theory!" "Behold these new methods!" "Behold our training and credentials!" "Behold this new opportunity!" "Behold our human skills!" Such things may be good and helpful, but they do not bring life. Any time we forget to declare *Behold the Lamb of God,* we lift up that which cannot bring life and healing to those we serve. Any shepherd who subordinates the life, death, and resurrection of the Good Shepherd to his or her own credentials, tools, or skills will fail.

LESSONS LEARNED FROM THE GOOD SHEPHERD

Over the years I have had the privilege of learning many lessons from our Good Shepherd, and as we conclude volume one of *Competent Christian Counseling,* I would like to share some of these lessons with you. These are not the lessons from graduate school or internship, though certainly the knowledge and training of those years are essential to our calling. Instead, the lessons of the Good Shepherd can actually infuse our knowledge, training, and experience with the life of Christ for the good of our clients and to the glory of God.

HUMILITY

The first lesson I want to share is underscored in Philippians 2:5-8: "Your attitude should be the same as that of Christ Jesus: who, being in very nature God, did not consider equality with God something to be grasped, but made himself nothing, taking the very nature of a servant.… He humbled himself and became obedient to death—even death on a cross!"

The Lamb of God identified with and served those who were cursed. I suspect that you are like me in that you prefer to be with attractive, like-minded people, those with whom you have a natural affinity. When you are in a group you want to be aligned with those who are clean, bright, healthy, and relationally adept. Jesus, on the other hand, identified with those whose personalities or abnormalities isolated them from others. He identified with the demon-possessed, the blind, the diseased, and even the dead. It is not our nature to do this. We see the afflicted and back away. We are repulsed by crime and disease and social ineptness. We have an aversion to the tormented, the odd, or the unacceptable.

I remember many years ago when I first began to see those who had been chronically sexually abused as children. I have never been abused. I enjoy what I now know is the phenomenal privilege of having a mind completely free of any memories of any kind of abuse. I never have to worry that such memories might float to the surface or be triggered by certain circumstances, for they simply do not exist. But one of the women I saw in the early years of my counseling work had been repeatedly and sadistically abused by many others. As I began to ease myself down into those memories, I found myself experiencing nightmares and crying in my sleep. I did not like the nightmares and clearly remember wrestling with whether I could go forward in my counseling work: *I don't have memories like this. Why would I want this in my head? I don't want to picture these things. I don't want them disturbing my sleep. I don't have to do this.*

Only the reminder of the Good Shepherd's humble sacrifice could help me resolve that dilemma: "Your attitude should be the same as that of Christ Jesus." A while ago another client asked me an astute question: "After all these years, does your head ever get mixed up about where your memories stop and others' memories begin?" Well, after twenty-five years in the counseling profession the answer is yes, sometimes my head gets mixed up. Sometimes I think or feel things that arise from my identification with survivors rather than from my own life experience.

It is only through the power of the Holy Spirit that you and I can humble ourselves and identify with those whose nature or experience is contrary to our own. And it is only the Holy Spirit who saves us from being overwhelmed by the secondary or vicarious trauma that has become a significant issue for many therapists. But if we are to follow the example of the Good Shepherd, we must indeed humble ourselves and wade into the muck and mire of our clients' lives in order to help and nurture them, for that is the kind of shepherding Jesus did. He so identified with the objects of his redemptive work that he became the Lamb and bore the punishment for our sin.

Choosing Lesser Things

The second powerful lesson I have learned is similar to that of humility. It has to do with choosing lesser things.

The Good Shepherd emptied himself of those things that elevated him. He demanded no recognition. He did not complain that Nazareth was too limited a sphere for his great gifts. He did not seek to dominate those under him. When the disciples started to squabble over who would be greatest in God's kingdom, Jesus got down on his hands and knees and washed their dirty feet.

Unfortunately, in recent decades, the Christian community has been infiltrated with the beliefs that bigger is better, that more means more important, and that status, money, and power are worthy of worship. Now I am not foolish enough to say that bigger is always worse or that more is always bad or that status, money, and power are inherently evil. But what I do believe with all my heart is that such things are of this earth and are transient, not worthy of our devotion.

I remember an inner struggle I experienced during the years when my two sons were quite small. Our sons were born shortly after I finished my doctorate and got my license. I had been in private practice for a short while, and it was clear that the practice was about to take off. However, I distinctly sensed God directing me to devote myself to mothering my young children. (I realize that he does not lead every young mother to do this.) I loved my work, so setting it aside to be a mom was not an easy thing to do. Also, if God had gifted me for counseling work, why would he ask me to lay down that which he had given? Nevertheless I obeyed. I kept the practice open to a minimal degree and sent most of my referrals elsewhere while I played with LEGOs and Matchbox cars.

During those precious years I learned something of what it means to set aside a good thing—something rightfully mine—for the sake of others. God had indeed called me to do some exceptional things, but he had also called me to be exceptional in the ordinary—to be holy in small places, loving with little people, unrecognized, and unapplauded.

It is a lesson I have had to learn again and again, and not just with little people but also with slow, mean, difficult, and resistant people. To follow the Good Shepherd, we must learn that greatness resides not in what we have or what we do. Rather, greatness is the freedom to set aside what we have and what we do in order to love the sheep God has entrusted to us.

RESTRAINT

Restraint is a voluntary limitation of oneself for the benefit of someone else.

The grocery store where I usually shop has a policy of hiring several employees who are intellectually limited. One particular man has been there about ten years; his job is to help people put their groceries in their cars. He is hard of hearing and lacks social skills. The first time I had him put my groceries in my car, he was slow and he threw the bags (eggs and all) into the trunk in disarray. I decided that from then on I would load the groceries myself.

On future shopping trips this man would offer help, and I would politely say, "No, thank you." One day after I declined his help, he asked, "Are you sure, ma'am?" There was almost a pleading tone to his voice, and I realized that he was being rejected by one customer after another. I felt the tug of God's Spirit. I was, of course, in a hurry. It was raining—hard. But the tug came again, so I said yes.

I stood in the rain, carefully made a couple of suggestions, and together we put my bags in the car.

When we finished, the man asked, "Did I do a good job?"

"Yes, you did a good job," I assured him.

He seemed relieved. "Lots of ladies get mad at me because I don't do so good."

I drove home weeping, asking God to teach me what that lesson was about. This man suffers. He suffers in ways I have never experienced. He is treated with anger, disregard, annoyance, and frustration. God called me that day to restrain myself—to restrain my quickness, my skill, my independence, my powers—in order to bestow dignity, value, and esteem on one who was suffering. As I pulled into my garage, I sensed God saying to me, *Is that not a picture of my incarnation? Is that not a tiny taste of what I did for you?* God of the universe, a baby. Infinite wisdom, a little boy. Creator of the worlds, a carpenter. Master of the seas, in a boat. Eternal life, dead and buried. And I didn't want to restrain myself for a retarded man!

Jesus, the Good Shepherd, says to us, "Why do you call me, 'Lord, Lord,' and do not do what I say?" (Luke 6:46). I say that I love Christ, that I am a Christian psychologist—but then I am impatient or intolerant or frustrated with a darkened, confused, or frightened person. I will not be able to wait for a trauma survivor to articulate the unspeakable unless I learn the lesson of restraint. I will be intolerant of the repeated failings of an addict unless I learn the lesson of restraint. I will throw in the towel with an Axis II personality disorder unless I learn the lesson of restraint. I will refuse to walk through the valley of the shadow of death with someone who is terminally ill unless I have learned the lesson of restraint.

The work of shepherding requires that we limit our words, because people who suffer cannot absorb a barrage of words or understand the language of high intellect. We will have to restrain the number of our syllables, the loudness of our voices, the suddenness of our movements, and the intensity of our emotions if we are to provide a safe place for the scared, the suffering, the traumatized, the silenced. Restraint allows us to connect with others, to be a blessing, and to be blessed ourselves. It also means willingly stepping down into the muck and mire of tragedy and suffering so that we may extend help and hope.

Often, when we are faced with the need to restrain some aspect of ourselves or to alter our agenda, we say, "That's just not me." I am not sure where we get the idea that we should do only that which comes naturally or easily. I have a quick mind and a quick mouth. I have a high energy level. They make jokes in the office about my going through the halls on Rollerblades. But my Shepherd is teaching me that I cannot shepherd his suffering sheep simply by doing what comes naturally. That which is immeasurable came to us in a very tiny package. If we would follow him, we too must learn the lesson of restraint in order to bring light and life to his sheep.

LOVING SERVICE

Another key lesson the Shepherd has taught me is that of service. Certainly the things we are trained to do are avenues of service: We counsel, we teach, we supervise, we write, we consult, we pastor. However, I believe that the service to which the Good Shepherd calls us goes far deeper than the skills we have been trained to utilize.

In Matthew 25 Jesus speaks of returning in all his glory and separating the people one from another as a shepherd separates the sheep from the goats. When he speaks to the sheep, he describes why he recognizes them as belonging to him: "For I was hungry and you gave me something to eat, I was thirsty and you gave me something to drink, I was a stranger and you invited me in, I needed clothes and you clothed me, I was sick and you looked after me, I was in prison and you came to visit me" (verses 35-36). Jesus is talking about acts of merciful service to particular kinds of people. I fear we often read such passages and either romanticize them or fail to really consider what our Shepherd is saying to us. Think about it with me.

What is it like to serve someone who is really hungry and thirsty? I do not mean someone who has skipped lunch. I mean someone who is starving. Hungry, thirsty people are in great need. They may be demanding. They do not care about you. They do not think clearly. They want only to have their needs met. They are desperate, clamoring, grabbing.

What is it like to serve strangers? They may make no sense to you. Their ways are foreign. They seem odd. You do not know why they do what they do. You cannot serve strangers effectively until you take the time to understand them. If you do not, it is only too easy to serve them in a manner that is frightening, inappropriate, or offensive to them.

What is it like to serve naked people? Naked people want to hide from you. They feel exposed. They do not want to be seen. To not humiliate them requires great tact and care. They do not want you close. They want you to go away. Their ambivalence is overwhelming. But you cannot cover their nakedness unless you move in close.

What is it like to serve sick people? Sick people focus on their pain. It is all they can think about, and their interest in you extends only to what you can do to help them feel better. Sick people live in small worlds. Sick people talk about what hurts. Sick people are needy and often messy. Sick people require constant care and oversight.

What is it like to serve prisoners? You cannot serve prisoners unless you go to prison. You must enter a place of locked doors and little light. You must enter a place of restricted movement. You must enter a place where you are watched and where trust is rare.

Clearly, Jesus' redemptive work demanded identification at the deepest level with the most shocking varieties of human suffering. After going through this list, Jesus makes the amazing statement that his sheep are those who do all these things for *him*: "Whatever you did for one of the least of these brothers of mine, you did for me" (verse 40). You see, the lesson I have learned about service is not that I am simply called to serve people, but rather that in serving those who suffer, I am in some mysterious way directly serving the One I follow.

At the close of each year, I try to invest some time before God asking him to show me a Scripture to truly learn to live out in the coming year. One year I was led to Colossians 1:24: "Now I rejoice in what was suffered for you, and I fill up in my flesh what is still lacking in regard to Christ's afflictions, for the sake of his body, which is the church." I believe this verse means we are called to be sensitive to the presence of the sufferings of Christ in all sufferers. Every time I encounter grief, I am encountering a grief *he* bore. Every time I encounter the sufferings of a stranger or a prisoner, I am encountering burdens *he* endured. The lesson of service means this: You and I live in solemn trust to the afflicted to mediate to them all that is to be obtained through the life and death of Christ. In so doing we serve the Lord Christ.

LEADERSHIP

When Jesus speaks of himself as the Good Shepherd, he says he "calls his own sheep by name and leads them out.... He goes on ahead of them, and his sheep follow him because they know his voice" (John 10:3-4). In order to be a fit shepherd, I must willingly go where I would take the sheep I tend.

One of my clients shared with me that a psychology professor had told her class that, if they ever decided to go into therapy, they should be very careful whom they chose as mentors. The reason? If they spent any significant amount of time in therapy, the professor explained, they would leave looking to some degree like their therapists. As the shepherd goes, so the sheep go. Only those who are faithful disciples of Jesus will be fit shepherds for the sheep.

Remember, the Good Shepherd himself became a lamb. To lead effectively we must perpetually "behold the Lamb" in our own lives. Take time to consider these questions:

- Do I really think I can lead someone out of a life of deceit if I live with ongoing, hidden sin in my own life?
- Do I really think I can lead someone away from bitterness and revenge toward his or her spouse if I harbor such feelings in my own heart?
- Do I really think I can lead someone out of captivity to an addiction if I continue be live enslaved to something in my own life?
- Do I really think I can lead someone with grace and love when I do not deal graciously and lovingly with the people in my world?

Recently, I was working with a woman who had made the commitment to learn how to love what we might call a difficult man. Her husband is fearful, selfish, and controlling. The promise of reward in this marriage is not at all great, but the wife has chosen to learn to love rather than leave. One day while we were talking about what that love might look like, she stopped me in my tracks with a question: "I just want to know one thing before we go on: Do you work to love your husband like this?"

It was a heart-searching question, one I knew was not just from her but also from God. My husband is an easy man to love; the rewards in our nearly three decades of marriage have been great. My circumstances were a piece of cake next to hers. But the challenge still stands: If I am going to teach this woman to be Christlike, to love her husband as Christ loves us, then I must be the kind of shepherd who goes before her sheep. I need to love my husband in the same way that I am calling her to learn to love her husband.

The lesson of leadership is that shepherding is not about imparting knowledge or information. Rather, shepherding is about going before someone in order to impart life. And isn't that exactly what the Good Shepherd has done for us? There is absolutely nothing Jesus asks of us that he himself has not exemplified. He who calls us to truth is Truth. He who calls us to love one another loved us unto death. He who calls us to carry the burdens of others was broken by our burdens. He who calls us to enter the muck and mire of others' lives endured our filth. He who calls us to weep with those who weep, wept over us. The Good Shepherd goes before. Those who would lead sheep are called to go before the sheep. That is true leadership.

As the Master Goes, So Goes the Servant

I have heard that a shepherd uses his pet lambs to gather lost sheep. These lambs are so fond of being near the shepherd that, when he calls out to them, they instantly follow him, bringing the lost sheep with them. Likewise, our Shepherd asks us to be so attached to him that, no matter where he places us, others will be induced to follow him because we have gone before them and have followed him ourselves. As we draw nearer to our Shepherd, we bring those lost sheep with us.

The redemptive work of Christ demanded that he identify at the deepest level with all the most shocking varieties of human suffering. As the Master was, so must his servants be. He who dealt with the enemy's occupation of the human heart has called us to do the same. As we follow him, we will learn lessons similar to those I have mentioned—and many more. Each of those lessons calls us to behold the Lamb and repent. As we are taught the lesson of restraint, we see the Lamb who is God in the flesh. As we are taught the lesson of humility, we see Eternal Glory setting aside rank and honor. As we are taught the lesson of service, we see the Sovereign Over All washing feet and touching the untouchable. As we are taught the lesson of leadership, we see Jesus going before, being and doing what he calls us to be and do.

To follow the Lamb is to enter into the fellowship of his sufferings. It means that, like him, we will get down in the filth of life in this world. The more we are willing to follow him into the dual mysteries of iniquity and suffering, the more of his beauty we will see. The threads of sacrifice that we discovered at the entrance of God into time will lead us directly to the throne of God where we will see his glory, not just in the heavens or in the flesh this time, but in its fullness.

Revelation 5:2-14 tells us that we will hear a mighty angel proclaiming in a loud voice, "Who is worthy to break the seals and open the scroll?" And the answer will be, "See, the Lion.... He is able." Then we will see a Lamb, looking as if it had been slain, standing in the center of the throne. And we will hear the voices of many angels, numbering ten thousand times ten thousand. They will encircle the throne and sing: "Worthy is the Lamb, who was slain, to receive power and wealth and wisdom and strength and honor and glory and praise!" Then you and I who have followed this Lamb will join with them, singing: "To him who sits on the throne and to the Lamb be praise and honor and glory and power, for ever and ever!"

Amen.

NOTES

CHAPTER 5

1. A great resource to begin in is Richard Foster's Renovare materials, especially *Devotional Classics* (by Foster and Smith, published by HarperSanFrancisco, 1993). Other classic works are as follows:
   - Tertullian (b. 160), *Regula Fidei* (Rule of Faith)
   - John Chrysostom (b. 345), "Dead to Sin" (a sermon)
   - Benedict of Nursia (b. 480), *The Rule*
   - John Climacus (b. 579), *The Ladder of Paradise*
   - Bernard of Clairvaux (b. 1090), *On the Love of God*
   - Francis of Assisi (b. 1182), *The Little Flowers*
   - Dante Alighieri (b. 1265), *The Divine Comedy*
   - Geoffrey Chaucer (b. 1343), *The Canterbury Tales*
   - Julian of Norwich (b. 1343), *Revelations of Divine Love*
   - Catherine of Siena (b. 1347), *The Dialogue*
   - Thomas à Kempis (b. 1380), *The Imitation of Christ*
   - Catherine of Genoa (b. 1447), *Life and Teachings*
   - Ignatius of Loyola (b. 1491), *The Spiritual Exercises of St. Ignatius*
   - John Calvin (b. 1509), *Golden Booklet of the True Christian Life*
   - Teresa of Avila (b. 1515), *The Interior Castle*
   - John of the Cross (b. 1542), *The Dark Night of the Soul*
   - Francis de Sales (b. 1567), *Introduction to the Devout Life*
   - George Herbert (b. 1593), *The Temple*
   - John Milton (b. 1608), *Paradise Lost* and *Paradise Regained*
   - Brother Lawrence (b. 1611), *The Practice of the Presence of God*
   - Jeremy Taylor (b. 1613), *The Rule and Exercise of Holy Living*
   - Isaac Pennington (b. 1617), *Letters on Spiritual Virtues*
   - George Fox (b. 1624), *The Letters of George Fox*
   - John Bunyan (b. 1628), *Grace Abounding to the Chief of Sinners*
   - François Fénelon (b. 1651), *Christian Perfection*
   - Jonathan Swift (b. 1667), *Gulliver's Travels*
   - William Law (b. 1686), *A Serious Call to a Devout and Holy Life*
   - John Wesley (b. 1703), *Christian Perfection*
   - Jonathan Edwards (b. 1703), *A Treatise Concerning Religious Affections*
   - John Woolman (b. 1720), *The Journal of John Woolman*

- Jean-Nicholas Grou (b. 1730), *How to Pray*
- John Henry, Cardinal Newman (b. 1801), *Apologia*
- Hannah Whitall Smith (b. 1832), *The Christian's Secret of a Happy Life*
- Charles Spurgeon (b. 1834), *Spiritual Revival: The Want of the Church*
- E. Stanley Jones (b. 1884), *With the Christ on the Indian Road*
- Sadhu Sundar Singh (b. 1889), *At the Feet of the Master*
- C. S. Lewis (b. 1900), *The Screwtape Letters*
- Dietrich Bonhoeffer (b. 1906), *Life Together*
- Simone Weil (b. 1909), *Waiting for God*
- Thomas Merton (b. 1915), *Contemplative Prayer*
- Aleksandr Solzhenitsyn (b. 1918), *One Day in the Life of Ivan Denisovich*
- Elizabeth O'Connor (b. 1921), *Letters to Scattered Pilgrims*
- Henri Nouwen (b. 1932), *Making All Things New: An Invitation to the Spiritual Life*

CHAPTER 6

1. The vagus nerve stimulator may be viewed at http://www.cyberonics.com.

CHAPTER 11

1. Although rooted primarily in an evangelical biblical theology, this Code is also influenced by the social justice, charismatic-Pentecostal, pietistic-holiness, liturgical, and contemplative traditions of Christian theology and church history.

2. This statement of "biblical-ethical foundations" is not a doctrinal statement, nor is it intended to substitute for one. The AACC Doctrinal Statement is a separate standard that reflects the baseline religious beliefs and biblical commitments of AACC members. However, these seven foundation statements are implicitly rooted in the AACC Doctrinal Statement. Furthermore, combined with the Scriptures, the AACC Doctrinal Statement, and the statement of "Introduction and Mission" to this Code, this section stands as the baseline ethics policy that will ground this Code, assist the search for clear meaning and common interpretation, and guide the resolution of disputed applications of ethical standards and procedural rules.

CHAPTER 18

1. The Center for Biblical Counseling may be reached at (800) 520-2268.

2. Stephen Ministries, 8016 Dale, St. Louis, MO 63117.

3. More detailed information about supervision can be found in my book *Lay Counseling: Equipping Christians for a Helping Ministry* (Tan, 1991, pp. 135-158.)

4. The *AACC Christian Counseling Code of Ethics* (2001) is available online at http://www.aacc.net.

CHAPTER 20

1. For more information on AACC's video training program, Marriage Works, contact AACC, 1639 Rustic Village Rd., Forest, VA 24551; (804) 525-9470.

2. More information on the Marriage Savers program can be found at http://www.marriagesavers.com/SixChurches.

3. A videotape demonstration is also available through the Christian Association for Psychological Studies; (830) 629-2277.

4. We heartily recommend Miller's approach for both counselors and couples. Although we draw from his method, we do not use the exact concepts that he uses.

5. The videotape demonstration is part of the course, Theories and Techniques of Counseling I (COUN 612; October 10, 1991), and is available from the Liberty University School of Lifelong Learning, P.O. Box 11803, Lynchburg, VA 24506-1803.

CHAPTER 21

1. The eight challenges are adapted from *The Second Half of Marriage* by David Arp and Claudia Arp (Grand Rapids: Zondervan, 1996). The Second Half of Marriage curriculum is also available in video form for use in group therapy, for assignments, or as a community·program. For more information, contact Marriage Alive at http://www.marriagealive.com; (888) 690-6667.

2. The marriage education program 10 Great Dates is a broad-based, low-key program for parents to help them develop marital skills through fun, positive dates. When the program is conducted through a church, childcare is provided. For more information, visit http://www.marriagealive.com.

3. Material from "Taking Stock of Your Empty-Nest Marriage" was adapted from *Fighting for Your Empty Nest Marriage* by Arp, Arp, Stanley, Markman, and Blumberg (San Francisco: Jossey-Bass, 2000).

Chapter 22

1. You can contact the Centers for Disease Control via their Web site address at http://www.cdc.gov/nchstp/dstd/dstdp.html or by calling the hot line at (800) 227-8922.

2. The Centers for Disease Control hot line can be reached at (800) 227-8922.

Chapter 32

1. From a personal e-mail communication from Terri Storm. Used by permission. To find out more about fee schedules, relative value units, geographical indices, and so forth, visit the RBRVS Web site at www.rbrvs.com.

References and Recommended Reading

Prologue

Berns, G. (2000). Spiritual recovery: Coming home to self. *Paradigm 3*(4), 12-13.

Gallup, G., & Jones, T. (2000). *The Next American Spirituality: Finding God in the Twenty-First Century.* Colorado Springs, CO: Victor/Cook Communications.

Humphrey, E. M. (2001). It's not about us: Modern spirituality begins and ends with the self; Christian spirituality, with the alpha and omega. *Christianity Today, 45*(5), 66-71.

Chapter 1

Allender, D. (1999). *The Healing Path: How the Hurts in Your Past Can Lead You to a More Abundant Life.* Colorado Springs, CO: WaterBrook.

American Counseling Association (2000). Annual Conference 2001, *Counseling Today, 43,* 39-40. Reprinted with permission.

Barna, G. (2000). *Growing True Disciples.* Ventura, CA: Issachar Resources.

Barna, G., & Hatch, M. (2001). *Boiling Point: Monitoring Cultural Shifts in the 21st Century.* Ventura, CA: Gospel Light/Regal. Used by permission.

Benner, D. (1998). *Care of Souls: Revisioning Christian Nurture and Counsel.* Grand Rapids: Baker.

Bergin, A. E. (1983). Religiosity and mental health: A critical re-evaluation and meta-analysis. *Professional Psychology: Research and Practice, 14,* 170-184.

Bergin, A. E. (1991). Values and religious issues in psychotherapy and mental health. *American Psychologist, 46,* 394-403.

Bergin, A. E., & Jensen, J. P. (1990). Religiosity of psychotherapists: A national survey. *Psychotherapy, 27,* 3-7.

Bobgan, M., & Bobgan, D. (1987). *Psychoheresy: The Psychological Seduction of Christianity.* Santa Barbara, CA: Eastgate.

Chesterton, G. K. (1997). In J. P. Moreland, *Love God with All Your Mind.* Colorado Springs, CO: NavPress.

Children's Defense Fund (1992). *Every Day in America.* Washington, DC: Children's Defense Fund.

Clinton, T. E. (1998). Getting beyond our moral shyness. *Christian Counseling Today, 6*(2), 30-32.

Clinton, T., & Ohlschlager, G. (1997). Law, ethics, and values in Christian counseling; Practice and advocacy in a brave new world. Presentation at the 1997 World Conference on Christian Counseling, Dallas, TX.

Collins, G. R. (1993). *The Biblical Basis of Christian Counseling for People Helpers.* Colorado Springs, CO: NavPress.

Collins, G. R. (1996a). *How to Be a People Helper.* Wheaton, IL: Tyndale.

Collins, G. R. (1996b). What in the world is soul care? *Christian Counseling Today, 4*(1), 9-12.

Collins, G. R. (1998). *The Soul Search: A Spiritual Journey to Authentic Ministry with God.* Nashville: Nelson.

Crabb, L. (1993). *Finding God.* Grand Rapids: Zondervan.

Crabb, L. (1997). *Connecting: Healing for Ourselves and Our Relationships. A Radical New Vision.* Nashville: Word.

Crabb, L. (2001). *Shattered Dreams: God's Unexpected Pathway to Joy.* Colorado Springs, CO: WaterBrook.

Curtis, B., & Eldridge, J. (1997). *The Sacred Romance: Drawing Closer to the Heart of God.* Nashville: Nelson.

Ellis, A. (1971). *The Case Against Religion: A Psychotherapist's View.* New York: Institute for Rational Living.

Frankl, V. (1963). *Man's Search for Meaning: An Introduction to Logotherapy.* New York: Washington Square Press.

Freud, S. (1927). *The Future of an Illusion.* Garden City, NY: Doubleday.

Gallup, G., & Jones, T. (2000). *The Next American Spirituality: Finding God in the Twenty-first Century.* Colorado Springs, CO: Victor/Cook Communications.

Gross, M. (1978). *The Psychological Society.* New York: Touchstone/Simon & Schuster.

John of the Cross (158-). *Dark Night of the Soul.* In K. Kavanaugh (Ed.) (1987), *John of the Cross: Selected Writings.* New York: Paulist Press.

Kantrowitz, B. (1994, November 28). The search for the sacred: Americans' quest for spiritual meaning. *Newsweek,* 53-58.

Kelly, E. W. (1995). *Religion and Spirituality in Counseling and Psychotherapy.* Alexandria, VA: American Counseling Association.

Langberg, D. (1999). *On the Threshold of Hope: Opening the Door to Healing for Survivors of Sexual Abuse.* Wheaton, IL: Tyndale.

Mahrer, A. (1996). Existential-humanistic psychotherapy and the religious person. In E. P. Shafranske (Ed.), *Religion and the Clinical Practice of Psychology.* Washington: American Psychological Association.

McMinn, M. (1996). *Psychology, Theology, and Spirituality in Christian Counseling*. Wheaton, IL: Tyndale.

Moon, G. (1994, Winter). Spiritual directors, Christian counselors: Where do they overlap? *Christian Counseling Today, 29-33.*

Nouwen, H. (1972). *The Wounded Healer: Ministry in Contemporary Society*. Garden City, NY: Doubleday.

Ortberg, J. (2001). *If You Want to Walk on Water, You've Got to Get Out of the Boat*. Grand Rapids: Zondervan.

Richards, P. S., & Bergin, A. E. (1997). *A Spiritual Strategy for Counseling and Psychotherapy*. Washington, DC: American Psychological Association.

Sperry, L., & Giblin, P. (1996). Marital and family therapy with religious persons. In E. P. Shafranske (Ed.), *Religion and the Clinical Practice of Psychology*. Washington: American Psychological Association.

Stafford, T. (1993, May 17). The therapeutic revolution in the church. *Christianity Today, 37,* 24-32.

Tozer, A. W. (1977). *That Incredible Christian*. Beaverlodge, Alberta: Horizon House.

Vitz, P. C. (1977). *Psychology As Religion: The Cult of Self-Worship*. Grand Rapids: Eerdmans.

Walch, A. (1999–2000, December–February). War, wealth, and water. Kids, condoms, and CDs: The world in figures. *Newsweek* (Special ed.), 64-67.

Watson. J. B. (1924, 1983). *Psychology from the Standpoint of a Behaviorist*. Dover, NH: Frances Pinter.

Willard, D. (1988). *The Spirit of the Disciplines*. San Francisco: Harper & Row.

Wilson, S. (1993). *Hurt People Hurt People*. Nashville: Nelson.

Worthington, E. L., Jr. (1986). Religious counseling: A review of published empirical research. *Journal of Counseling and Development, 64,* 421-431.

CHAPTER 2

Adams, J. (1970). *Competent to Counsel*. Grand Rapids: Zondervan.

Adams, J. (1973). *The Christian Counselor's Manual*. Grand Rapids: Baker.

Adams, J. (1979). *More than Redemption: A Theology of Christian Counseling*. Phillipsburg, NJ: Presbyterian and Reformed.

Backus, W. (1985). *Telling the Truth to Troubled People: A Manual for Christian Counselors*. Minneapolis: Bethany.

Backus, W. (2000). *What Your Counselor Never Told You: Conquer the Power of Sin in Your Life*. Minneapolis: Bethany.

Bobgan, M., & Bobgan, D. (1987). *Psychoheresy: The Psychological Seduction of Christianity*. Santa Barbara, CA: Eastgate.

Bouma-Prediger, S. (1990). The task of integration: A modest proposal. *Journal of Psychology and Theology, 18,* 21-31.

Bufford, R. (1997). Consecrated counseling: Reflection on the distinctives of Christian counseling. *Journal of Psychology and Theology, 25*(1), 111-122.

Bulkley, E. (1993). *Why Christians Can't Trust Psychology.* Eugene, OR: Harvest House.

Carlson, D. E. (1980). Relationship counseling. In G. R. Collins (Ed.), *Helping People Grow.* Ventura, CA: Regal.

Carter, J., & Mohline, R. (1976). The nature and scope of integration: A proposal. *Journal of Psychology and Theology, 4,* 3-14.

Carter, J., & Narramore, B. (1979). *The Integration of Psychology and Theology: An Introduction.* Grand Rapids: Zondervan.

Clinton, T. E. (1998). Getting beyond our moral shyness. *Christian Counseling Today, 6*(2), 30-32.

Clinton, T. E. (2001). AACC in 2001: A report from the president. *Christian Counseling Connection, 2000/2001*(4), 1-7.

Clinton, T., & Ohlschlager, G. (1997). Law, ethics, and values in Christian counseling; Practice and advocacy in a brave new world. Presentation at the 1997 World Conference on Christian Counseling, Dallas, TX.

Collins, G. R. (1977). *The Rebuilding of Psychology: An Integration of Psychology and Christianity.* Wheaton, IL: Tyndale.

Collins, G. R. (1980). *Helping People Grow: Practical Approaches to Christian Counseling.* Santa Ana, CA: Vision House.

Collins, G. R. (1988). *Christian Counseling: A Comprehensive Guide* (Rev. ed.). Dallas: Word. Used by permission.

Collins, G. R. (1993). *The Biblical Basis of Christian Counseling for People Helpers.* Colorado Springs, CO: NavPress.

Collins, G. R. (1996). What in the world is soul care? *Christian Counseling Today, 4*(1), 9-12.

Crabb, L. (1975). *Basic Principles of Biblical Counseling.* Grand Rapids: Zondervan.

Crabb, L. (1977). *Effective Biblical Counseling.* Grand Rapids: Zondervan.

Crabb, L. (1993). *Finding God.* Grand Rapids: Zondervan.

Crabb, L. (1997). *Connecting: Healing for Ourselves and Our Relationships. A Radical New Vision.* Nashville: Word. Used by permission.

Crabb, L. (2001). *Shattered Dreams: God's Unexpected Pathway to Joy.* Colorado Springs, CO: WaterBrook.

Croucher, R. (1991, Winter). Spiritual formation. *Grid.* (A publication of World Vision Australia), 1-2.

Dillon, D. (1992). *Short-Term Counseling.* Dallas: Word.

Egan, G. (1998). *The Skilled Helper: A Problem-Management Approach to Helping* (6th ed.). Pacific Grove, CA: Brooks/Cole.

Farnsworth, K. (1985). *Wholehearted Integration.* Grand Rapids: Baker.

Foster, R. (1998). *Celebration of Discipline: The Path to Spiritual Growth* (special 20th anniv. ed.). San Francisco: HarperSanFrancisco.

Hindson, E., & Eyrich, H. (1997). *Totally Sufficient: The Bible and Christian Counseling.* Eugene, OR: Harvest House.

Howard, K., Leuger, R., Maling, M., & Martinovich, Z. (1993). A phase model of psychotherapy outcomes: Causal mediation of change. *Journal of Consulting and Clinical Psychology, 61*(4), 678-685.

Hunt, D. (1987). *Beyond Seduction.* Eugene, OR: Harvest House.

Johnson, E. (1997). Christ: The lord of psychology. *Journal of Psychology and Theology, 25*(1), 11-27.

Jones, S., & Butman, R. (1991). *Modern Psychotherapies: A Comprehensive Christian Appraisal.* Downers Grove, IL: InterVarsity.

Kilpatrick, W. K. (1983). *Psychological Seduction.* Nashville: Nelson.

Kollar, C. (1997). *Solution-Focused Pastoral Counseling.* Grand Rapids: Zondervan.

Kopta, S., Howard, K., Lowry, J., & Beutler, L. (1994). Patterns of symptomatic relief in psychotherapy. *Journal of Consulting and Clinical Psychology, 62*(5), 1009-1016.

Kottler, J. A., & Brown, R. W. (2000). *Introduction to Therapeutic Counseling: Voices from the Field* (4th ed.). Belmont, CA: Wadsworth/Brooks/Cole.

Kuhn, T. (1970). *The Structure of Scientific Revolutions* (2nd ed.). Chicago: University of Chicago Press.

McMinn, M. (1996). *Psychology, Theology, and Spirituality in Christian Counseling.* Wheaton, IL: Tyndale.

McMinn, M. (1998). Exploring the role of religious experience in counseling. *Christian Counseling Today, 6*(2), 16-19.

Moon, G. (1997). *Homesick for Eden: A Soul's Journey to Joy.* Ann Arbor, MI: Vine.

Myers, D. G. (2001). A levels-of-explanation response. In E. Johnson & S. Jones (Eds.), *Psychology and Christianity: Four Views* (pp. 226-231). Downers Grove, IL: InterVarsity.

Oden, T. (1987). *Classical Pastoral Care, Vol. 3. Pastoral Counsel.* Grand Rapids: Baker.

Oliver, G., Hasz, M., & Richburg, M. (1997). *Promoting Change Through Brief Therapy in Christian Counseling*. Wheaton, IL: Tyndale.

Powlison, D. (1997). Crucial issues in biblical counseling. *Journal of Biblical Counseling* (A Selection of Readings on "Counsel the Word."), 10-22.

Powlison, D. (2001). A biblical counseling view. In E. Johnson & S. Jones, *Psychology and Christianity: Four Views*. Downers Grove, IL: InterVarsity.

Richards, P. S., & Bergin, A. E. (1997). *A Spiritual Strategy for Counseling and Psychotherapy*. Washington, DC: American Psychological Association.

Tan, S. Y., & Gregg, D. (1997). *Disciplines of the Holy Spirit: How to Connect to the Spirit's Power and Presence*. Grand Rapids: Zondervan.

Thurman, C. (1989). *The Lies We Believe*. Nashville: Nelson.

Thurman, C. (1995). *The Lies We Believe Workbook*. Nashville: Nelson.

Vernick, L. (1999). *The Truth Principle: A Life Changing Model for Spiritual Growth and Renewal*. Colorado Springs, CO: WaterBrook.

Worthington, E. L., Jr. (1994). A blueprint for interdisciplinary integration. *Journal of Psychology and Theology, 22*, 79-86.

Chapter 3

American Association of Christian Counselors (1999). The 1999 World Conference Membership Survey. Unpublished report from the 1999 AACC World Conference, Nashville, TN.

Bufford, R. (1997). Consecrated counseling: Reflection on the distinctives of Christian counseling. *Journal of Psychology and Theology, 25*(1), 111-122.

Clinton, T. (2001, Spring). 2001 president's report. *The Christian Counseling Connection*, 1-6.

Clinton, T., Hindson, E., & Ohlschlager, G. (Eds.). (2001). *The Soul Care Bible*. Nashville: Nelson. Used by permission.

Collins, G. R. (1980). *Helping People Grow: Practical Approaches to Christian Counseling*. Santa Ana, CA: Vision House.

Collins, G. R. (1988). *Christian Counseling: A Comprehensive Guide* (Rev. ed.). Dallas: Word.

Egan, G. (1998). *The Skilled Helper: A Problem-Management Approach to Helping* (6th ed.). Pacific Grove, CA: Brooks/Cole.

Ellis, A., & Greiger, R. (1977). *Handbook of Rational-Emotive Therapy, Vol. 1*. New York: Springer.

Kottler, J. A., & Brown, R. W. (2000). *Introduction to Therapeutic Counseling: Voices from the Field* (4th ed.). Belmont, CA: Wadsworth/Brooks/Cole.

McMinn, M. (1996). *Psychology, Theology, and Spirituality in Christian Counseling*. Wheaton, IL: Tyndale.

CHAPTER 4

Adams, J. E. (1970). *Competent to Counsel*. Grand Rapids: Zondervan.

Adams, J. E. (1979). *More than Redemption: A Theology of Christian Counseling*. Phillipsburg, NJ: Presbyterian and Reformed.

Allen, R. B. (1984). *The Majesty of Man: The Dignity of Being Human*. Portland, OR: Multnomah.

Anderson, N. T. (1995). *Helping Others Find Freedom in Christ*. Ventura, CA: Regal.

Barna, G. (1991). *The Barna Report: What Americans Believe*. Ventura, CA: Regal.

Barna, G. (1998). *The Second Coming of the Church*. Nashville: Word.

Benner, D. G. (1988). *Psychology and Religion*. Grand Rapids: Baker.

Benner, D. G. (1998). *Care of Souls: Revisioning Christian Nurture and Counsel*. Grand Rapids: Baker.

Bergin, A. (1991). Values and religious issues in psychotherapy and mental health. *American Psychologist, 46*(4), 394-405.

Carson, D. A. (1987). *Showing the Spirit*. Grand Rapids: Baker.

Collins, G. R. (1993). *The Biblical Basis of Christian Counseling for People Helpers*. Colorado Springs, CO: NavPress.

Covey, S. R. (1997). *The Seven Habits of Highly Effective Families*. New York: Golden Books.

Crabb, L. (1999). *The Safest Place on Earth*. Nashville: Word.

Custance, A. C. (1975). *Man in Adam and in Christ*. Grand Rapids: Zondervan.

Dillard, A. (1982). *Teaching a Stone to Talk*. New York: Harper & Row.

Egan, G. (1998). *The Skilled Helper* (6th ed.). Pacific Grove, CA: Brooks/Cole.

Erikson, M. J. (1985). *Christian Theology*. Grand Rapids: Baker.

Erikson, M. J. (1991). *The Word Became Flesh*. Grand Rapids: Baker.

Foster, R. (1988). *The Celebration of Discipline*. New York: HarperCollins.

Frankl, V. E. (1984). *Man's Search for Meaning*. New York: Simon & Schuster.

Grenz, S. J. (1994). *Theology for the Community of God*. Nashville: Broadman & Holman.

Grenz, S. J., & Olson, R. E. (1996). *Who Needs Theology?* Downers Grove, IL: InterVarsity.

Guiness, O. (1977). *In Two Minds*. Downers Grove, IL: InterVarsity.

Hart, A. D. (1992). *Me, Myself and I*. Ann Arbor, MI: Servant.

Hart, A. D. (2001). Has self-esteem lost its way? *Christian Counseling Today,* *9,*(1), 8-10.

Hindson, E., & Eyrich, H. (1997). *Totally Sufficient*. Eugene, OR: Harvest House.

Hoekema, A. A. (1986). *Created in God's Image*. Grand Rapids: Eerdmans.

Horton, M. S. (1994). *Beyond Culture Wars*. Chicago: Moody.

Landau, S. (Ed.). (1975). *The Doubleday Dictionary for Home, School and Office*. Garden City, NY: Doubleday.

Laney, J. C. (1999). *God*. Nashville: Word.

Leupold, H. C. (1952). *Exposition of Ecclesiastes*. Grand Rapids: Baker.

MacArthur, J. F., Jr., & Mack, W. A. (1994). *Introduction to Biblical Counseling*. Dallas: Word.

McMinn, M. (1996). *Psychology, Theology, and Spirituality in Christian Counseling*. Wheaton, IL: Tyndale.

Menninger, K. (1973). *Whatever Became of Sin?* New York: Hawthorne Books.

Moltmann, J. (1993). *Theology of Hope*. Minneapolis: Fortress.

Moon, G. (1997). *Homesick for Eden: A Soul's Journey to Joy*. Ann Arbor, MI: Servant.

Morris, L. (1976). *I Believe in Revelation*. Grand Rapids: Eerdmans.

Mowrer, O. H. (1960). "Sin," the lesser of two evils. *American Psychologist, 15,* 303.

Murren, D. (1991). *Churches that Heal*. West Monroe, LA: Howard.

Pache, R. (1954). *The Person and Work of the Holy Spirit*. Chicago: Moody.

Pink, A. W. (1971). *Spiritual Union and Communion*. Grand Rapids: Baker.

Powlison, D. (1997). Crucial issues in biblical counseling. *Journal of Biblical Counseling* (A selection of readings on "Counsel the Word."), 10-22.

Seamands, D. A. (1989). *Healing Grace*. Wheaton, IL: Victor.

Sire, J. (1997). *The Universe Next Door*. Downers Grove, IL: InterVarsity.

Tillich, P. (1951). *Systematic Theology, Vol. 1* (pp. 1-8). Chicago: University of Chicago Press.

Veith, G. E., Jr. (1994). *Postmodern Times*. Wheaton, IL: Crossway.

Volf, M. (2001, January). *Toward a Theology of Emotion in Christian Counseling*. Presented at the First Geneva Institute Master Series Lecture, Regent University, Virginia Beach, VA.

Von Rad, G. (1974). *Wisdom in Israel*. Nashville: Abingdon.

Weyerhaeuser, W. T. (1988). Jesus Christ. In D. G. Benner (Ed.), *Psychology and Religion*. Grand Rapids: Baker.

Willard, D. (1998). *The Divine Conspiracy*. San Francisco: HarperSanFrancisco.

Williams, D. T. (1994). *The Person and Work of the Holy Spirit*. Nashville: Broadman & Holman.

Worthington, E., Jr. (1988). Understanding the values of religious clients: A model and its application to counseling. *Journal of Counseling Psychology, 35*(2), 166-174.

Wright, S. (1991). Ecclesiastes. In F. E. Gabelein (Ed.), *The Expositors Bible Commentary*. Grand Rapids: Zondervan.

Yancey, P. (1995). *The Jesus I Never Knew*. Grand Rapids: Zondervan.

CHAPTER 5

Arterburn, S., & Felton, J. (2000). *More Jesus, Less Religion*. Colorado Springs, CO: WaterBrook.

Ball, R., & Goodyear, R. (1993). Self-reported professional practices of Christian psychotherapists. In E. Worthington Jr. (Ed.), *Psychotherapy and Religious Values*. Grand Rapids: Baker.

Benner, D. (Ed.) (1987). *Psychotherapy in Christian Perspective*. Grand Rapids: Baker.

Brown, C. (Ed.) (1971). *The New International Dictionary of New Testament Theology*. Grand Rapids: Zondervan.

Calvin, J. (1960). *The Gospel According to St. John*. Grand Rapids: Eerdmans.

Candlish, R. (1879). *A Commentary on 1 John*. Edinburgh: Banner of Truth.

Carlson, C., Bacaseta, P., & Simatona, D. (1988). A controlled evaluation of devotional meditation and progressive relaxation. *Journal of Psychology and Theology, 16*, 362-368.

Clinton, T., Hindson, E., & Ohlschlager, G. (Eds.). (2001). *The Soul Care Bible*. Nashville: Nelson.

Collins, G. (1998). *The Soul Search*. Nashville: Nelson.

Colson, C. (1989). *Against the Night*. Ann Arbor, MI: Servant.

Crabb, L. (1998). *The Safest Place on Earth*. Nashville: Word.

Crabb, L. (2001). *Shattered Dreams: God's Unexpected Pathway to Joy*. Colorado Springs, CO: WaterBrook.

Curtis, B., & Eldredge, J. (1997). *The Sacred Romance*. Nashville: Nelson.

Driskill, J. (1989). Meditation as a therapeutic technique. *Pastoral Psychology, 38*, 83-103.

Eerdman's Bible Dictionary (1987). Grand Rapids: Eerdmans.

Foster, R. (1998). *Celebration of Discipline* (20th annual ed.). San Francisco: HarperSanFrancisco.

Foster, R., & Smith, J. (1993). *Devotional Classics: A Renovare Resource for Spiritual Renewal*. San Francisco: HarperSanFrancisco.

Groeschel, B. J. (1983). *Spiritual Passages: The Psychology of Spiritual Development*. New York: Crossroad.

Haynes, L. (1998). Response to "Restoring the substance to the soul of psychology": Clincial and spiritual development applications. *Journal of Psychology and Theology, 26*(1), 44-53.

Hindson, E. (1996). *Men of the Promise*. Eugene, OR: Harvest House.

James, W. (1890). *The Principles of Psychology*. New York: Dover.

Johnson, E. (1998). Whatever happened to the human soul? A brief, Christian genealogy of a psychological term. *Journal of Psychology and Therapy, 26*(1), 16-28.

Lewis, C. S. (1969). *The Screwtape Letters*. New York: Macmillan.

McDermott, G. R. (1995). *Seeing God: Twelve Reliable Signs of True Spirituality*. Downers Grove, IL: InterVarsity.

McMinn, M. (1996). *Psychology, Theology, and Spirituality in Christian Counseling*. Wheaton, IL: Tyndale.

Moon, G. (1997). *Homesick for Eden*. Ann Arbor, MI: Servant.

Moon, G., Bailey, J., Kwasny, J., & Willis, D. (1993). Training in the use of Christian disciplines as counseling techniques within Christian graduate training programs. In E. Worthington, Jr. (Ed.), *Psychotherapy and Religious Values*. Grand Rapids: Baker.

Moore, T. (1992). *Care of the Soul*. New York: HarperCollins.

Oliver, G., Hasz, M., & Richburg, M. (1997). *Promoting Change Through Brief Therapy*. Wheaton, IL: Tyndale.

Ortberg, J. (1997). *The Life You've Always Wanted*. Grand Rapids: Zondervan.

Propst, R. (1980). The comparative efficacy of religious and nonreligious cognitive-behavioral therapy for the treatment of clinical depression in religious individuals. *Journal of Consulting and Clinical Psychology, 60*, 94-103.

Rolle, R. (1993). The fire of love. In R. Foster & J. Smith (Eds.), *Devotional Classics: A Renovare Resource for Spiritual Renewal*. San Francisco: HarperSanFrancisco. Used by permission.

Schaeffer, F. (1968). *Escape from Reason*. Chicago: Intervarsity.

"Spirit" (1987). In *Eerdman's Bible Dictionary*. Grand Rapids: Eerdmans.

"Spirit/Spiritual," (1971). In Colin Brown (Ed.), *New International Dictionary of New Testament Theology, 3*, 706-707. Grand Rapids: Zondervan.

Tan, S. Y. (1998). The spiritual disciplines and counseling, *Christian Counseling Today, 6*(2), 8-9, 20-21.

Tan, S. Y., & D. Gregg (1997). *Disciplines of the Holy Spirit.* Grand Rapids: Zondervan.

Teresa of Avila (1577). Interior castle. In R. Foster & J. Smith (1993), *Devotional Classics: A Renovare Resource for Spiritual Renewal.* San Francisco: HarperSanFrancisco.

Thomas, G. (1998). *The Glorious Pursuit: Embracing the Virtues of Christ.* Colorado Springs, CO: NavPress.

Vines, J. (1998). *Spirit Life.* Nashville: Broadman & Holman.

Watson, J. (1924). *Behaviorism.* New York: Norton.

Wesley, C. (1680). "And Can It Be?" A seventeenth-century English hymn. Public domain.

White, F. (1987). Spiritual and religious issues in therapy. In D. Benner (Ed.), *Psychotherapy in Christian Perspective.* Grand Rapids: Baker.

Whitney, D. (1991). *Spiritual Disciplines for the Christian Life.* Colorado Springs, CO: NavPress.

Willard, D. (1988). *The Spirit of the Disciplines.* San Francisco: HarperSanFrancisco.

Wilson, S. (1998). *Into Abba's Arms.* Wheaton, IL: Tyndale.

Chapter 6

Bell, R. A., Morris, R. R., & Holzer, C. E. (1976, June). The clergy as a mental health resource: Parts 1 and 2. *Journal of Pastoral Care, 103-115.*

DeBattista, C., & Schatzberg, A. F. (2000). Current psychotropic dosing and monitoring guidelines. *Primary Psychiatry, 7,* 26-64.

DeVane, C. L., & Nemeroff, C. B. (1999). Psychotropic drug interactions. *Primary Psychiatry, 6,* 39-88.

Hutto. M. (1999). The symptoms of depression in endocrine disorders. *CNS Spectrums, 4,* 51-61.

Kessler, R. C., McGonagle, K. A., & Zhao, S. (1994). Lifetime and twelve-month prevalence of DSM-III-R psychiatric disorders in the U.S.: Results from the national comorbidity survey. *General Psychiatry, 51,* 8-19.

Kleinman, A. (1980). *Patients and Healers in the Context of Culture: An Exploration of the Borderland Between Anthropology, Medicine, and Psychiatry.* Berkeley: University of California Press.

Lewis, D. A., & Oeth, K. M. (1995). Functional neuroanatomy. In H. I. Kaplan & B. J. Sadock (Eds.), *Comprehensive Textbook of Psychiatry* (pp. 4-24). Baltimore: Williams and Wilkins.

Lyles, M. R. (1992). Mental health perceptions of black pastors: Implications for psychotherapy with black patients. *Journal of Psychology and Christianity 11,* 368-377.

Lyles, M. R (1999). The patient's psychopharmacology bill of rights. *Christian Counseling Today, 7,* 75-76.

Mundy, C. (2001). The human genome project: A historical perspective. *Pharmacogenomics, 2,* 37-49.

Musselman, D. L., Evans, D. L., & Nemeroff, C. B. (1998). The relationship of depression to cardiovascular disease. *General Psychiatry, 55,* 580-592.

Nemeroff, C. B. & Schatzberg, A. F. (1999). *Recognition and Treatment of Psychiatric Disorders.* Washington, DC: American Psychiatric Press.

Penninx, B., Beekman, A., & Honig, A. (2001). Depression and cardiac mortality, *General Psychiatry, 58,* 221-227.

Regier, D. A., Narrow, N. E., Rae, D. S., Manderscheid, R. W., Locke, B. Z., & Goodwin, F. K. (1993). The de facto U.S. mental and addictive disorders service system. *General Psychiatry, 50,* 85.

Stahl, S. (2000). *Essential Psychopharmacology.* New York: Cambridge University Press.

Vogel, G. (2000). New brain cells prompt new theory of depression. *Science, 290,* 258-259.

Wong, A. H. C., Smith, M., & Boon, H. S. (1998). Herbal remedies in psychiatric practice. *General Psychiatry, 55,* 1033-1044. (Archives)

CHAPTER 7

Benner, D. (Ed.). (1987). *Psychotherapy in Christian Perspective.* Grand Rapids: Baker.

Beutler, L. E., & Clarkin, J. F. (1990). *Systematic Treatment Selection: Toward Targeted Therapeutic Interventions.* New York: Brunner/Mazel.

Blakeney, R., & Blakeney, C. (1992). Growing pains: A theory of stress and moral conflict. *Counseling and Values, 36* (3), 162-175.

Brammer, L. M., Abrego, P., & Shostrom, E. (1998). *Therapeutic Counseling and Psychotherapy* (7th ed.). Englewood Cliffs, NJ: Prentice-Hall.

Brammer, L. M., Shostrom, E. L., & Abrego, P. J. (1989). *Therapeutic Psychology: Fundamentals of Counseling and Psychotherapy* (5th ed.). Englewood Cliffs, NJ: Prentice-Hall.

Burke, J. (1989). *Contemporary Approaches to Psychotherapy and Counseling.* Pacific Grove, CA: Brooks/Cole.

Consumer Reports (1995, November). Mental health: Does therapy help? 734-739.

Corey, G. (1986). *Theory and Practice of Counseling and Psychotherapy* (3rd ed.). Pacific Grove, CA: Brooks/Cole.

Corey, G. (2000). *Theory and Practice of Counseling and Psychotherapy* (6th ed.). Pacific Grove, CA: Brooks/Cole.

Corsini, R. (Ed.). (1991). *Current Psychotherapies* (3rd ed.). Itasca, IL: F. E. Peacock.

Corsini, R., & Wedding, D. (1995). *Current Psychotherapies* (5th ed.). Itasca, IL: F. E. Peacock.

Crabb, L. (2001). *Shattered Dreams: God's Unexpected Pathway to Joy*. Colorado Springs, CO: WaterBrook.

DeJong, P., & Berg, I. (1998). *Interviewing for Solutions*. Pacific Grove, CA: Brooks/Cole.

De Shazer, S. (1991). *Putting Differences to Work*. New York: Norton.

Doherty, W. (1998). From hedgehog to fox. *Family Therapy Networker, 22*(2), 50-57.

Edwards, K. (1994, August). Evaluating object relations inpatient treatment for religiously committed patients. Paper presented at the 88th annual convention of the American Psychological Association, Los Angeles, California.

Egan, G. (1998). *The Skilled Helper: A Problem-Management Approach to Helping*. Pacific Grove, CA: Brooks/Cole.

Ellis, A. (1982a). *Rational-Emotive Therapy and Cognitive-Behavior Therapy*. New York: Springer.

Ellis, A. (1982b). Feedback—major systems. *Personnel Guidance Journal, 60*, 6-7.

Eysenck, H. (1984). The battle over psychotherapeutic effectiveness. In Hariman, J. (Ed.), *Does Psychotherapy Really Help People?* Springfield, IL: Chas. C. Thomas.

The Faith Factor Bibliography Series. (1993, 1994, 1995, 1997). Rockville, MD: National Institute for Healthcare Research.

Family Therapy Networker (2001). 24(1). (Ads referred to are scattered throughout issue.)

Fiedler, F. (1950). A comparison of therapeutic relationships in psychoanalytic, nondirective, and Adlerian therapy. *Journal of Consulting Psychology, 14*, 436-445.

Frank, J. (1961). *Persuasion and Healing*. Baltimore: Johns Hopkins University Press.

Frank, J. (1971). Therapeutic factors in psychotherapy. *American Journal of Psychotherapy, 25*, 350-361.

Garfield, S. (1994). Research on client variables in psychotherapy. In S. Garfield & A. Bergin (Eds.), *Handbook of Psychotherapy and Behavior Change* (4th ed.). New York: John Wiley & Sons.

Gartner, J. (1996). Religious commitment, mental health and prosocial behavior: A review of the empirical literature. In E. Shafrankse (Ed.), *Religion and the Practice of Psychology* (pp. 187-214). Washington, DC: American Psychological Association.

Gartner, J., Larson, D., & Allen, G. (1991). Religious commitment and mental health: A review of the empirical literature. *Journal of Psychology and Theology, 19,* 6-25.

Gibson, R., & Mitchell, M. (1995). *Introduction to Guidance and Counseling* (4th ed.). Englewood Cliffs, NJ: Prentice-Hall.

Goldfried, M. R. (Ed.). (1982). *Converging Themes in Psychotherapy*. New York: Springer.

Gross, M. (1978). *The Psychological Society*. New York: Random House.

Hampson, R., & Beavers, W. (1996). Measuring family therapy outcome in a clinical setting: Families that do better or worse in therapy. *Family Process, 35,* 347-361.

Hutchins, D. (1984). Improving the counseling relationship. *The Personnel and Guidance Journal, 62*(10), 572-575.

Hutchins, D., & Cole, C. (1992). *Helping Relationships and Strategies* (2nd ed.). Pacific Grove, CA: Brooks/Cole.

Ivey, A. (1994). *Intentional Interviewing and Counseling* (3rd ed.). Pacific Grove, CA: Brooks/Cole.

Johnson, W. B. (1993). Outcome research and religious psychotherapies: Where are we and where are we going? *Journal of Psychology and Theology, 1*(4), 297-308.

Jones, S., & Butman, R. (1991). *Modern Psychotherapies: A Comprehensive Christian Appraisal*. Downers Grove, IL: InterVarsity.

Kaminer, W. (1992). *I'm Dysfunctional, You're Dysfunctional*. Reading, MA: Addison-Wesley.

Klerman, G. (1990). The psychaitric patient's right to effective treatment: Implications of Osheroff v. Chestnut Lodge. *American Journal of Psychiatry, 147*(4), 409-18.

Koenig, H. (2000). *The Healing Connection*. Nashville, TN: Word.

Kopta, S., Howard, K., Lowry, J., & Beutler, L. (1994). Patterns of symptomatic relief in psychotherapy. *Journal of Consulting and Clinical Psychology, 62*(5), 1009-1016.

Krumboltz, J. (Ed.). (1966). *Revolution in Counseling: Implications of Behavioral Science*. Boston: Houghton Mifflin.

Kuhn, T. (1962). *The Structure of Scientific Revolutions*. Chicago: University of Chicago Press.

L'Abate, L. (1981). Classification of counseling and therapy, theorists, method process, and goals: The E-R-A model. *Personnel and Guidance Journal, 59,* 263-265.

Lambert, M. (1986). Some implications of psychotherapy outcomes research for eclectic psychotherapy. *International Journal of Eclectic Psychotherapy, 5,* 16-45.

Lambert, M., & Bergin, A. (1994). The effectiveness of psychotherapy. In A. Bergin & S. Garfield (Eds.), *Handbook of Psychotherapy and Behavior Change* (4th ed.) (pp. 143-189). New York: John Wiley & Sons.

Lambert, M., & Cattani-Thompson, K. (1996, Summer). Current findings regarding the effectiveness of counseling: Implications for practice. *Journal of Counseling and Development, 74,* 601-608.

Larson, D. B., Sawyers, J. P., & McCullough, M. E. (1998). Scientific research on spirituality and health: A consensus report. Rockville, MD: National Institute for Healthcare Research.

Lazarus, A. (1990). Multimodal applications and research: A brief overview and update. *Elementary School and Guidance Counseling, 24,* 243-247.

Lipsey, M., & Wilson, D. (1993). The efficacy of psychological, educational, and behavioral treatment: Confirmation from meta-analysis. *American Psychologist, 48*(12), 1181-1209.

Masson, J. (1988). *Against Therapy: Emotional Tyranny and the Myth of Psychological Healing.* New York: Atheneum.

McWhirter, J., & McWhirter, B. (1991). A framework for theories in counseling. In D. Capuzzi & D. R. Gross (Eds.), *Introduction to Counseling: Perspectives for the 1990s* (pp. 69-88). Boston: Allyn and Bacon.

Myers, D. (2001). A levels-of-explanation response. In E. Johnson & S. Jones (Eds.), *Psychology and Christianity: Four Views.* Downers Grove, IL: InterVarsity.

Noebel, D. (1995). *Understanding the Times* (abridged version). Colorado Springs, CO: ACSI and Summit Ministries.

Norcross, J. (1986). *Handbook of Eclectic Psychotherapy.* New York: Brunner/Mazel.

Norcross, J., & Prochaska, J. (1982). A national survey of clinical psychologists: Affiliations and orientations. *Clinical Psychologist, 35*(3), 4-6.

Ohlschlager, G., & Mosgofian, P. (1992). *Law for the Christian Counselor: A Guidebook for Clinicians and Pastors.* Dallas: Word.

Parrott, L. (1997). *Counseling and Psychotherapy*. New York: McGraw-Hill.

Powlison, D. (1997). Critical issues in biblical counseling. *Journal of Biblical Counseling* (Counsel the Word). Glenside, PA: CCEF.

Probst, L. R., Ostrom, R., Watkins, P., Dean, T., & Mashburn, D. (1992). Comparative efficacy of religious and non-religious cognitive-behavioral therapy for the treatment of clinical depression in religious individuals. *Journal of Consulting and Clinical Psychology, 60,* 94-103.

Richards, P., & Bergin, A. (1997). *A Spiritual Strategy for Counseling and Psychotherapy*. Washington DC: American Psychological Association.

Schaeffer, K. W., Nottebaum, L., Smith, P., Dech, K., & Krawczyk, J. (1999). Religiously motivated sexual orientation change: A follow-up study. *Journal of Psychology and Theology, 27*(4), 329-337.

Seligman, L. (1998). *Selecting Effective Treatments* (2nd ed.). San Francisco: Jossey-Bass.

Seligman, M. (1994). *What You Can Change and What You Can't*. New York: Knopf.

Seligman, M. (1995). The effectiveness of psychotherapy: The Consumer Report study. *American Psychologist, 50,* 965-974.

Smith, D. (1982). Trends in counseling and psychotherapy. *American Psychologist, 37,* 802-809.

Smith, M., Glass, G., & Miller, T. (1980). *The Benefit of Psychotherapy*. Baltimore, MD: Johns Hopkins University Press.

Stone, A. (1990). Law, science, and psychiatric malpractice: A response to Klerman's indictment of psychoanalytic psychiatry. *American Journal of Psychiatry, 147*(4), 419-427.

Szasz, T. (1978). *The Myth of Psychotherapy: Mental Healing As Religion, Rhetoric, and Repression*. Garden City, NY: Doubleday.

Tisdale, T., Key, T., Edwards, K., Brokaw, B., Kemperman, S., Cloud, H., Townsend, J., & Okamoto, T. (1997). Impact of treatment on God image and personal adjustment, and correlations of God image to personal adjustment and object relations development. *Journal of Psychology and Theology, 25*(2), 227-239.

Whiston, S., & Sexton, T. (1993). An overview of psychotherapy outcome research: Implications for practice. *Professional Psychology, 24,* 43-51.

Worthington, E., Jr. (1986). Religious counseling: A review of published empirical research. *Journal of Counseling and Development, 64,* 421-431.

Worthington, E., Jr., Kurusu, T., McCullough, M., & Sanders, S. (1996). Empirical research on religion and psychotherapeutic processes and outcomes: A ten year review and research prospectus. *Psychological Bulletin, 119,* 448-487.

Vitz, P. (1977). *Psychology As Religion: The Cult of Self-Worship.* Grand Rapids: Eerdmans.

Zilbergeld, B. (1983). *The Shrinking of America.* Boston: Little, Brown and Co.

CHAPTER 8

Allport, G. W. (1950). *The Individual and His Religion.* New York: Macmillian.

American Psychological Association Task Force on Psychological Intervention Guidelines (1995). *Template for Developing Guidelines: Interventions for Mental Disorders and Psychological Aspects of Physical Disorders.* Washington, DC: American Psychological Association.

Benner, D. G. (1987). *Christian Counseling and Psychotherapy.* Grand Rapids: Baker.

Bergin, A. E. & Lambert, M. J. (1978). The evaluation of therapeutic outcomes. In S. L. Garfield & A. E. Bergin (Eds.), *Handbook of Psychotherapy and Behavioral Change* (2nd ed.). New York: Wiley.

Berry, C. (1988). *When Helping You Is Hurting.* San Francisco: Harper & Row.

Boyd, J. H. (1998). A history of the concept of the soul during the 20th century. *Journal of Psychology and Theology, 26,* 66-82.

Bugental, J. F. T. (1987). *The Art of the Psychotherapist.* New York: Norton.

Cheydleur, J. R. (1999). *Called to Counsel.* Wheaton, IL: Tyndale.

Clinebell, H. J., Jr. (1966). *Basic Types of Pastoral Counseling.* Nashville: Abingdon.

Clinebell, H. J., Jr. (1984). *Basic Types of Pastoral Care and Counseling: Resources for the Ministry of Healing and Growth.* Nashville: Abingdon.

Collins, G. R. (1980). *Christian Counseling: A Comprehensive Guide.* Waco, TX: Word.

Collins, G. R. (1988). *Christian Counseling: A Comprehensive Guide* (Rev. ed.). Dallas: Word.

Combs, D., Avila, D., & Purkey, W. (1971). *Helping Relationships: Basic Concepts for the Helping Professions.* Boston: Allyn and Bacon.

Cormier, W., & Cormier, L. S. (1991). Interviewing Strategies for Helpers (3rd ed.). Pacific Grove, CA: Brooks/Cole.

Egan, G. (1998). *The Skilled Helper* (6th ed.). Pacific Grove, CA: Brooks/Cole.

Garfield, S. L. (1994). Eclecticism and integration in psychotherapy: Developments and issues. *Clinical Psychology: Science and Practice, 1,* 123-127.

Garfield, S. L. (1998). Some comments on empirically supported treatments. *Journal of Consulting and Clinical Psychology, 66,* 121-125.

Hickson, J., Housley, W., & Wages, D. (2000). Counselors' perceptions of spirituality in the therapeutic process. *Counseling and Values, Association for Spiritual, Ethical, and Religious Values in Counseling, 45,* 59.

Johnson, E. (1998). Whatever happened to the human soul? A brief, Christian genealogy of a psychological term. *Journal of Psychology and Therapy, 26*(1), 16-28.

Kennedy, E. (1977). *On Becoming a Counselor, A Basic Guide for Non-professional Counselors.* New York: Seabury.

Kottler, J. A. (1993). *On Being a Therapist* (Rev. ed.). San Francisco: Jossey-Bass.

Kottler, J. A., & Brown, R. W. (1996). *Introduction to Therapeutic Counseling* (3rd ed.). Pacific Grove, CA: Brooks/Cole.

Larson, D. B., Sawyers, J. P., & McCullough, M. E. (Eds.). (1998). *Scientific Research on Spirituality and Health: A Consensus Report.* Rockville, MD: National Institute of Healthcare Research.

McMinn, M. R. (1996). *Psychology, Theology, and Spirituality in Christian Counseling.* Wheaton, IL: Tyndale.

McMinn, M. R., & McRay, B. (1997). Spiritual discipline and the practice of integration: Possibilities and challenges for Christian psychologists. *Journal of Psychology and Theology, 25,* 102-110.

Neuhaus, E., & Astwood, W. (1980). *Practicing Psychotherapy: Basic Techniques and Practical Issues* (pp. 40-175). New York: Human Sciences Press.

Ohlschlager, G., & Mosgofian, P. (1992). *Law for the Christian Counselor: A Guidebook for Clinicians and Pastors.* Dallas: Word.

Parrott, L. (1997). *Counseling and Psychotherapy.* New York: McGraw-Hill.

Perez, J. F. (1979). *Family Counseling: Theory and Practice.* New York: Van Nostrand.

Perlman, H. H. (1979). *Relationship: The Heart of Helping People.* Chicago: University of Chicago Press.

Rogers, C. R., Gendlin, E. T., Kiesler, D. V., & Truax, C. B. (1967). *The Therapeutic Relationship and Its Impact.* Madison, WI: University of Wisconsin Press.

Rubin, T. I. (1975). *Compassion and Self-Hate.* New York: McKay.

Seligman, M. (1995). The effectiveness of psychotherapy: The Consumer Reports study. *American Psychologist, 22,* 6-78.

Small, J. (1990). *Becoming Naturally Therapeutic.* New York: Bantam.

Truax, C. B., & Mitchell, K. M. (1971). Research on certain therapist interpersonal skills in relation to process and outcome. In A. E. Bergin & S. Garfield (Eds.), *Handbook of Psychotherapy and Behavior Change*. New York: Wiley.

Vine, W. E. (1984). *An Expository Dictionary of New Testament Words*. Minneapolis: Bethany.

Welter, P. (1978). *How to Help a Friend*. Wheaton, IL: Tyndale.

White, F. J. (1987). Spiritual and religious issues in therapy. In D. G. Benner (Ed.), *Psychotherapy in Christian Perspective*. Grand Rapids: Baker.

Willard, D. (1996). Going beyond the limits: An interview with Dallas Willard. *Christian Counseling Today, 4*,1.

Willard, D. (1998). Spiritual disciplines, spiritual formation, and the restoration of the soul. *Journal of Psychology and Theology, 26,* 101-109.

Willard, D. (2000, October). *Illustrations of Spiritual Formation*. Lecture presented at For all the saints: Evangelical theology and Christian spirituality conference. Birmingham, AL.

Wilson, C. (2001, February 21). Dogs know a bad character when they see one. *USA Today,* L1.

Worthington, E. L., Jr. (1988). Understanding the values of religious clients: A model and its implication to counseling. *Journal of Counseling Psychology, 35,* 166-174.

Worthington, E. L., Jr. (Ed.). (1993). *Psychotherapy and Religious Values*. Grand Rapids: Baker.

Worthington, E. L., Jr., Kurusu, T. A., McCullough, M. E., & Sandage, S. J. (1996). Empirical research on religion and psychotherapeutic processes and outcomes: A ten-year review and research prospectus. *Psychological Bulletin, 119,* 448-487.

Chapter 9

Benner, D. G. (1987). *Christian Counseling and Psychotherapy* (pp. 17-39). Grand Rapids: Baker.

Brammer, L., & Shostrom, E. (1982). *Therapeutic Psychology: Fundamentals of Counseling and Psychotherapy* (4th ed.). Englewood Cliffs, NJ: Prentice-Hall.

Carkhuff, R. (1969). *Helping and Human Relations, Vol. 1. Selection and Training*. New York: Holt, Rinehart & Winston.

Carkhuff, R. (1987). *The Art of Helping* (6th ed.). Amherst, MA: Human Resource Development Press.

Carlson, D. (1988). *Counseling and Self-Esteem*. Waco, TX: Word.

Cormier, W., & Cormier, L. (1991). *Interviewing Strategies for Helpers: Fundamental Skills and Cognitive Behavioral Interventions* (3rd ed.). Pacific Grove, CA: Brooks/Cole.

Crabb, L. (1997). *Connecting: A Radical New Vision.* Nashville: Word.

Dayringer, R. (1998). *Heart of Pastoral Counseling: Healing Through Relationship* (Rev. ed.) (pp. 23-128). Binghamton, NY: Haworth Pastoral Press.

Egan, G. (1976). *Interpersonal Living.* Pacific Grove, CA: Brooks/Cole.

Egan, G. (1998). *The Skilled Helper* (6th ed.). Pacific Grove, CA: Brooks/Cole. Used by permission.

Gazda, G., Asbury, R., Balzer, F., Childers, W., & Walters, R. (1984). *Human Relations Development: A Manual for Educators* (3rd ed.). Boston: Allyn and Bacon.

Gendlin, E. (1979). *Focusing.* New York: Bantam.

Goleman, D. (1994). *Emotional Intelligence.* New York: Bantam.

Knapp, M. (1978). *Nonverbal Communication in Human Interaction* (2nd ed.). New York: Holt, Rinehart & Winston.

Kottler, J. (1993). *On Being a Therapist* (2nd ed.). San Francisco: Jossey-Bass.

Lambert, M., & Bergin, A. (1994). The effectiveness of psychotherapy. In A. Bergin & S. Garfield (Eds.), *Handbook of Psychotherapy and Behavior Change* (4th ed.). New York: Wiley.

Lazarus, A. (1981). *The Practice of Multimodal Therapy.* New York: Springer.

McKay, M., Davis, M., & Fanning, P. (1995). *Messages* (2nd ed.). Oakland, CA: New Harbinger.

Moustakas, C. (1986). Being in, being for, and being with. *Humanistic Psychologist, 14*(2), 100-104.

Patterson, C. H. (1985). *The Therapeutic Relationship: Foundations for an Eclectic Psychotherapy.* Pacific Grove, CA: Brooks/Cole.

Powell, J. (1969). *Why Am I Afraid to Tell You Who I Am.* Allen, TX: Tabor.

Rogers, C. (1951). *Client-Centered Therapy.* Boston: Houghton Mifflin.

Rogers, C. (1957). The necessary and sufficient conditions of therapeutic personality change. *Journal of Consulting Psychology, 21,* 95-103.

Rogers, C. (1961). *On Becoming a Person.* Boston: Houghton Mifflin.

Squires, S. (1986, June). Should you keep your therapist? *American Health.*

Strong, S. (1968). Counseling: An interpersonal influence process. *Journal of Counseling Psychology, 15,* 215-224.

Strupp, H., & Binder, J. (1984). *Psychotherapy in a New Key.* New York: Basic.

Teyber, E. (1992). *Interpersonal Process in Psychotherapy.* Pacific Grove, CA: Brooks/Cole.

Whiston, S., & Sexton, T. (1993). An overview of psychotherapy outcomes research: Implications for practice. *Professional Psychology, 24,* 43-51

Chapter 10

Adams, J. E. (1986). Potential for change. *Journal of Pastoral Practice, 8(2),* 13-14.

Bandura, A. (1982). Self-efficacy mechanism in human agency. *American Psychologist, 37,* 122-147.

Bandura, A. (1986). *Social Foundations of Thought and Action: A Social Cognitive Theory.* Englewood Cliffs, NJ: Prentice-Hall.

Bandura, A. (1989). Human agency in social cognitive theory. *American Psychologist, 44,* 1175-1184.

Cheydleur, J. R. (1999). *Called to Counsel: Counseling Skills Handbook.* Wheaton, IL: Tyndale.

Clinton, T. (1998). *Change: The Goal of Counseling.* Paper presented at the AACC regional conference in Dallas, TX.

Craigie, F., Jr. (1994). Problem-solving, discipleship, and the process of change in Christian counseling. *Journal of Psychology and Christianity, 13(3),* 205-216.

Crews, F. (2001). The secrets of Christian counseling character. Manuscript materials developed for chapter 8 in this book and for future speaking presentations.

Dayringer, R. (1998). *Heart of Pastoral Counseling: Healing Through Relationship* (Rev. ed.). Binghamton, NY: Haworth Pastoral Press.

Egan, G. (1998). *The Skilled Helper* (6th ed.). Pacific Grove, CA: Brooks/Cole.

Habermas, G. (1998). Top down thinking: Heaven and the problems on earth. *Christian Counseling Today, 6(2),* 26-28, 66-67.

Mahoney, M. (1991). *Human Change Processes: The Scientific Foundation of Psychotherapy.* New York: Basic Books.

McCollough, M., Sandage, S., & Worthington, E. (1997). *To Forgive Is Human: How to Put Your Past in the Past.* Downers Grove, IL: InterVarsity.

McMinn, M. (1996). *Psychology, Theology, and Spirituality in Christian Counseling.* Wheaton, IL: Tyndale.

Oliver, G., Hasz, M., & Richburg, M. (1997). *Promoting Change Through Brief Therapy in Christian Counseling.* Wheaton, IL: Tyndale.

Prochaska, J., DiClimente, C., & Norcross, J. (1994). *Changing for Good.* New York: Morrow.

Sandage, S. (1998). Seeking forgiveness or saving face? *Christian Counseling Today, 6(2),* 10-11, 22-24.

Seligman, M. (1994). *What You Can Change and What You Can't.* New York: Knopf.

Tan, S. Y. (1996). Religion in clinical practice. In E. Shafranske (Ed.), *Religion and the Clinical Practice of Psychology*. Washington, DC: American Psychological Association. Copyright © 1996 by the American Psychological Association. Adapted with permission.

Thurman, C. (1995). *The Lies We Believe Workbook*. Nashville: Nelson.

Trevino, J. (1996). Worldview and change in cross-cultural counseling. *Counseling Psychologist, 24*(2), 198-215.

Vernick, L. (2000). *The Truth Principle: A Life Changing Model for Spiritual Growth and Renewal*. Colorado Springs, CO: WaterBrook.

Weinrach, S. (1995). Rational emotive behavior therapy: A tough-minded therapy for a tender-minded profession. *Journal of Counseling and Development, 74*, 326-331.

CHAPTER 11

American Association of Christian Counselors (2001). *AACC Christian Counseling Code of Ethics*. Forest, VA: AACC.

American Counseling Association (1995). *Code of Ethics and Standards of Practice*. Alexandria, VA: ACA.

American Psychological Association (1995). *Ethical Principles of Psychologists and Code of Conduct* (p. 3). Washington, DC: APA.

Corey, G., Corey, M., & Callanan, P. (1998). *Issues and Ethics in the Helping Professions* (5th ed.). Pacific Grove, CA: Brooks/Cole.

Gabbard, G. (1989). *Sexual Exploitation in Professional Relationships*. Washington, DC: American Psychiatric Association.

Hart, A. (Spring, 1988). Being moral isn't always enough. *Leadership, 9*, 25.

Herlihy, B., & Corey, B. (1996). *ACA Ethical Standards Casebook* (5th ed.). Alexandria, VA: American Counseling Association.

Kottler, J. (1993). *On Being a Therapist* (Rev. ed.). San Francisco: Jossey-Bass.

Ohlschlager, G. (1999). Avoiding ethical-legal pitfalls: Embracing conformative behavior and transformative virtues. *Christian Counseling Today, 7*(3), 40-43

Ohlschlager, G., & Mosgofian, P. (1992). *Law for the Christian Counselor: A Guidebook for Clinicians and Pastors*. Dallas: Word.

Pope, K., Sonne, J., & Holroyd, J. (1993). *Sexual Feelings in Psychotherapy: Explorations for Therapists and Therapists-in-Training*. Washington, DC: American Psychological Association.

Remley, T. (1996). The relationship between law and ethics. In B. Herlihy & G. Corey (Eds.), *ACA Ethical Standards Casebook* (5th ed.). Alexandria, VA: American Counseling Association.

Trull, J., & Carter, J. (1993). *Ministerial Ethics: Being a Good Minister in a Not-So-Good World.* Nashville: Broadman & Holman.

Wind, J., Burk, R., Carmenisch, P., & McCann, D. (Eds.). (1991). *Clergy Ethics in a Changing Society.* Louisville: Westminster/John Knox.

Chapter 12

Allender, D. (1996). Emotions and the pathway to God. *Christian Counseling Today, 4*(1), 32-35.

American Association of Christian Counselors (2001). *AACC Christian Counseling Code of Ethics.* Forest, VA: AACC.

American Psychiatric Association task force report (1993). *Psychosocial Treatment Research in Psychiatry.* Washington, DC: American Psychiatric Association.

Anastasi, A. (1998). *Psychological Testing* (6th ed.). New York: Macmillan.

Cormier W., & Cormier, L. (1991). *Interviewing Strategies for Helpers* (3rd ed.). Pacific Grove, CA: Brooks/Cole.

Egan, G. (1998). *The Skilled Helper* (6th ed.). Pacific Grove, CA: Brooks/Cole. Used by permission.

Kuhn, T. (1970). *The Structure of Scientific Revolutions* (2nd ed.). Chicago: University of Chicago Press.

Lazarus, A. (1981). *The Practice of Multimodal Therapy.* New York: McGraw-Hill.

Maloney, M., & Ward, M. (1976). *Psychological Assessment: A Conceptual Approach.* New York: Oxford University Press.

McReynolds, P. (1975). Historical antecedents of personality assessment. In P. McReynolds (Ed.), *Advances in Psychological Assessment, Vol. 3.* San Francisco: Jossey-Bass.

Morrison, J. (1995). *The First Interview: Revised for DSM-IV.* New York: Guilford.

Walsh, F. (1999). *Spiritual Resources in Family Therapy* (p. 32). New York: Guilford.

Chapter 13

American Counseling Association. (1995). *Code of Ethics and Standards of Practice.* Alexandria, VA: AACC.

American Psychiatric Association. (1994). *Diagnostic and Statistical Manual of Mental Disorders* (4th ed.). Washington, DC: APA.

American Psychological Association. (1995). *Ethical Principles of Psychologists and Code of Conduct.* Washington, DC: APA.

Bergin, A. E. (1991). Values and religious issues in psychotherapy and mental health. *American Psychology, 46*(4), 393-403.

Clarkin, J. F., & Kendall, P. C. (1992). Comorbidity and treatment planning: Summary and future directions. *Journal of Consulting and Clinical Psychology, 60*(6), 904-908.

Collins, G. R. (1993). *The Biblical Basis of Christian Counseling for People Helpers.* Colorado Springs, CO: NavPress.

Corey, G., Corey, M. S., & Callanan, P. (1998). *Issues and Ethics in the Helping Professions* (5th ed.). Pacific Grove, CA: Brooks/Cole.

Fong, M. J. (1995). Assessment and DSM-IV diagnosis of personality disorder: A primer for counselors. *Journal of Counseling and Development, 73*(6), 635-639.

Hinkle, J. S. (1994). The DSM-IV: Prognosis and implications for mental health counselors. *Journal of Mental Health Counseling, 16*(2), 175-183. In L. Seligman (1996), *Diagnosis and Treatment Planning in Counseling* (2nd ed.). New York: Plenum.

Hohenshil, T. H. (1996). Editorial: Role of assessment and diagnosis in counseling. *Journal of Counseling and Development, 75*(1), 64-67.

Jones, S. L. & Butman, R. E. (1991). *Modern Psychotherapies: A Comprehensive Christian Appraisal.* Downers Grove, IL: InterVarsity.

Jongsma, A. E., & Peterson, L. M. (1995). *The Complete Psychotherapy Treatment Planner.* New York: Wiley.

Karoly, P. (1993). Goal systems: An organizing framework for clinical assessment and treatment planning. *Psychological Assessment, 5*(3), 272-280.

Morrison, J. (1995). *The First Interview: Revised for DSM-IV.* New York: Guilford.

Richards, P., & Bergin, A. E. (1997). *A Spiritual Strategy for Counseling and Psychotherapy.* Washington: American Psychological Association.

Seligman, L. (1990). *Selecting Effective Treatments.* San Francisco: Jossey-Bass.

Seligman, L. (1996). *Diagnosis and Treatment Planning in Counseling* (2nd ed.). New York: Plenum.

Stark, M. J. (1997). Treatment planning in Christian counseling: Misery or mastery. *Christian Counseling Today, 5*(4), 8-9, 44-47.

Sue, D. W., & Sue, D. (1999). *Counseling the Culturally Different: Theory and Practice.* New York: Wiley.

Tan, S. Y. (1995). Process and outcome in psychotherapy: Summary of consistent research findings for effective clinical practice. *Journal of Psychology and Christianity, 14*(3), 263-268.

Thorpe, S. A. (1987). An approach to treatment planning. *Psychotherapy, 24*(4), 729-735.

Woody, R. H. (1991). *Quality Care in Mental Health: Assuring the Best Clinical Services.* San Francisco: Jossey-Bass.

Worthington, E. L., Jr. (1986). Religious counseling: A review of published empirical research. *Journal of Counseling and Development, 61,* 421-431.

Wylie, M. S. (1995, May–June). Diagnosing for dollars? *Family Therapy Networker,* 23-33.

Chapter 14

Berg, I. K., & Miller, S. D. (1992). *Working with the Problem Drinker.* New York: Norton.

Bogard, M., & Mederos, F. (1999). Battering and couples therapy: Universal screening and selection of treatment modality. *Journal of Marital and Family Therapy, 25*(3), 291-312.

DeJong, P., & Berg, I. K. (1998). *Interviewing for Solutions.* Pacific Grove, CA: Brooks/Cole.

DeJong, P., & Hopwood, L. E. (1996). Outcome research on treatment conducted at the brief family therapy center. In S. D. Miller, M. A. Hubble, & B. L. Duncan (Eds.), *Handbook of Solution-Focused Brief Therapy* (pp. 192-193). San Francisco: Jossey-Bass.

De Shazer, S. (1988). *Clues: Investigating Solutions in Brief Therapy.* New York: Norton.

De Shazer, S. (1991). *Putting Difference to Work.* New York: Norton.

Donovan, J. M. (Ed.). (1999). *Short-Term Couple Therapy.* New York: Guilford.

Durrant, M. (1995). *Creative Strategies for School Problems.* New York: Norton.

Garfield, S. L. (1986). Research on client variables in psychotherapy. In S. L. Garfield & A. E. Bergin, *Handbook of Psychotherapy and Behavior Change: An Empirical Analysis* (3rd ed.) (pp. 213-56, 662). New York: Wiley.

Hampson, R. B., & Beavers, W. R. (1996). Measuring family therapy outcome in a clinical setting: Families that do better or do worse in therapy. *Family Process, 35,* 347-361.

Howard, K. I., Kopta, S. M., Kraus, M. S., & Orlinsky, D. E. (1986). The dose effect relationship in psychotherapy. *American Psychologist, 41,* 159-64.

Kollar, C. A. (1997). *Solution-Focused Pastoral Counseling.* Grand Rapids: Zondervan.

Koss, M. P., & Butcher, J. N. (1986). Research on brief psychotherapy. In S. L. Garfield & A. E. Bergin, *Handbook of Psychotherapy and Behavior Change: An Empirical Analysis* (3rd ed.). New York: Wiley.

Kung, W. W. (2000). The intertwined relationship between depression and marital distress: Elements of marital therapy conducive to effective treatment outcomes. *Journal of Marital and Family Therapy, 26*(1), 51-63.

Lipchik, E. (1991). Spouse abuse: Challenging the party line. *Family Therapy Networker, 15,* 59-63.

Lipchik, E., & Kublicki, A. D. (1996). Solution-focused domestic violence views. In S. D. Miller, M. A. Hubble, & B. L. Duncan (Eds.), *Handbook of Solution-Focused Brief Therapy* (pp. 65-98). San Francisco: Jossey-Bass.

Metcalf, L. (1998). *Solution-Focused Group Therapy: Ideas for Groups in Private Practice, Schools, Agencies, and Treatment Programs.* New York: Free Press.

Miller, S. D., Hubble, M. A., & Duncan, B. L. (1996). *Handbook of Solution-Focused Brief Therapy.* San Francisco: Jossey-Bass.

Murphy, J. J. (1997). *Solution-Focused Counseling in Middle and High Schools.* Alexandria, VA: American Counseling Association.

O'Hanlon, W. H. (1993). Take two people and call them in the morning: Brief solution-oriented therapy with depression. In S. Friedman (Ed.), *The New Language of Change: Constructive Collaboration in Psychotherapy.* New York: Guilford.

O'Hanlon, W. H., & Weiner-Davis, M. (1989). *In Search of Solutions: A New Direction in Psychotherapy.* New York: Norton.

Oliver, G. J., Hasz, M. & Richburg, M. (1997). *Promoting Change Through Brief Therapy in Christian Counseling.* Wheaton, IL: Tyndale.

Preston, J., Varzos, N., & Liebert, D. S. (2000). *Make Every Session Count.* Oakland, CA: New Harbinger.

Quick, E. K. (1996). *Doing What Works in Brief Therapy: A Strategic Solution Focused Approach.* San Diego: Academic.

Selekman, M. D. (1993). *Pathways to Change.* New York: Guilford.

Sells, S. (1998). *Treating the Tough Adolescent.* New York: Guilford.

Sklare, G. B. (1997). *Brief Counseling That Works: A Solution-Focused Approach for School Counselors.* Thousand Oaks, CA: Corwin.

Stanton, D., & Todd, T. (1982). *The Family Therapy of Drug Abuse and Addiction.* New York: Guilford.

Stone, H. W. (1993). *Brief Pastoral Counseling: Short-Term Approaches and Strategies.* Minneapolis: Fortress.

Stone, H. W. (2001). *Strategies for Brief Pastoral Counseling.* Minneapolis: Fortress.

Thomas, F. N., & Cockburn, J. (1998). *Competency-Based Counseling: Building on Client Strengths.* Minneapolis: Fortress.

Trute, B., Docking, B., & Hiebert-Murphy, D. (2001). Couples therapy for women survivors of child sexual abuse who are in addiction recovery: A comparative case study of the treatment process and outcome. *Journal of Marital and Family Therapy, 27*(1), 99-110.

Walter, J. L., & Peller, J. E. (1992). *Becoming Solution-Focused in Brief Therapy*. New York: Brunner/Mazel.

Walter, J. L., & Peller, J. E. (2000). *Recreating Brief Therapy: Preferences and Possibilities*. New York: Norton.

Webb, W. N., & Webb, W. H. (1999). *Solutioning: Solution-Focused Interventions for Counselors*. New York: Associated Development.

Wiersbe, W. (1993). *On Being a Servant of God* (p. 3). Nashville: Nelson.

Wright, H. N., & Oliver, G. J. (1994). *How to Change Your Spouse Without Ruining Your Marriage*. Ann Arbor, MI: Servant.

CHAPTER 15

à Kempis, T. (1981). *The Imitation of Christ*. Springdale, PA: Whitaker House.

Barker, K. (Ed.). (1995). *NIV Study Bible*. Grand Rapids: Zondervan.

Barker, P. (1996). *Psychotherapeutic Metaphors: A Guide to Theory and Practice*. New York: Brunner/Mazel.

Beck, A. T. (1976). *Cognitive Therapy and the Emotional Disorders*. New York: International Universities Press.

Beck, A. T., Rush, A. J., Shaw, B. F., & Emery, G. (1979). *Cognitive Therapy of Depression*. New York: Guilford.

Ellis, A. (1958). Rational psychotherapy. *Journal of General Psychotherapy, 58*, 35-49.

Frank, J. D., Hoehn-Saric, R., Imber, S. D., Liberman, B. L., & Stone, A. R. (1978). *Effective Ingredients of Successful Psychotherapy*. New York: Brunner/Mazel.

Freeman, A., Pretzer, J., Fleming, B., & Simon, K. M. (1991). *Clinical Applications of Cognitive Therapy*. New York: Plenum.

Gilligan, S. (2001). Getting to the core. *Family Therapy Networker, 25*(1), 22-29, 54-55.

Gordon, D. (1978). *Therapeutic Metaphors*. Cupertino, CA: Meta.

Greenberg, L. S., & Korman, L. (1993). Assimilating emotion into psychotherapy integration. *Journal of Psychotherapy Integration, 3*, 249-265.

Hill, C. E., Helms, J. E., Tichenor, V., Spiegel, S. B., O'Grady, K. E., & Perry, E. S. (1988). Effects of therapist response modes in brief psychotherapy. *Journal of Counseling Psychology, 35*, 222-233.

Johnson W. B., & Johnson, W. L. (1997). A wedding of faith and practice. *Christian Counseling Today, 5*(1), 15, 52-53.

Mahoney, M. J. (1991). *Human Change Processes: The Scientific Foundation of Psychotherapy*. New York: Basic Books.

Mahoney, M. J., Norcross, J. C., Prochaska, J. O., & Missar, C. D. (1989). Psychological development and optimal psychotherapy: Converging perspectives among clinical psychologists. *Journal of Integrative and Eclectic Psychotherapy,* 8(3), 251-261.

Nielsen, S., Johnson, W., & Ridley, C. (2000, February). Religiously sensitive rational emotive behavior therapy. *Journal of Personality and Social Psychology* [Online]. Available FTP: spider.apa.org:80/ftdocs/psp/2000/february/pro3112.html.

Ottati, V., Rhoads, S., & Graesser, A. (1999, October). The effect of metaphor on processing style in a persuasion task. *Journal of Personality and Social Psychology* [Online]. Available FTP: spider.apa.org:80/ftdocs/psp/1999/october/psp774688.html.

Peck, M. S. (1978). *The Road Less Traveled.* New York: Simon & Schuster.

Powlison, D. (1993). Critiquing modern integrationists. *Journal of Biblical Counseling, 11*(3), 24-34.

Reynolds, D. K. (1980). *The Quiet Therapies.* Honolulu: University Press of Hawaii.

Saltzberg, J. A., & Dattilio, F. M. (1996). Cognitive techniques in clinical practice. *Guidance and Counseling, 11*(2), 27, 5.

Seligman, M. (1994). *What You Can Change and What You Can't.* New York: Knopf.

Sexton, T. L., & Whiston, S. C. (1994). The status of the counseling relationship: An empirical review, theoretical implications, and research directions. *Counseling Psychologist, 22,* 6-78.

Thurman, C. (1989). *The Lies We Believe.* Nashville: Nelson.

Thurman, C. (1995). *The Lies We Believe Workbook.* Nashville: Nelson.

Thurman, C. (1999). *The Lies We Tell Ourselves.* Nashville: Nelson.

Tillich, P. (1951). *Systematic Theology, Vol. 1.* Chicago: University of Chicago Press.

Vernick, L. (2000). *The Truth Principle: A Life Changing Model for Spiritual Growth and Renewal.* Colorado Springs, CO: WaterBrook.

Vernick, L. (2001). *How to Act Right When Your Spouse Acts Wrong.* Colorado Springs, CO: WaterBrook.

Willard, D. (1998). *The Divine Conspiracy: Rediscovering Our Hidden Life in God.* San Francisco: Harper.

Wilson, S. (1995). *The Sufficiency of Christ in Counseling.* Presented at the American Association of Christian Counselors Regional Conference, Philadelphia, PA.

Zodhiates, S. (Ed.). (1991). *The Complete Word Study New Testament.* Chattanooga: AMG.

CHAPTER 16

Adler, A. (1963). *The Practice and Theory of Individual Psychology.* Patterson, NJ: Littlefield-Adams.

Anderson, C., & Stewart, S. (1983). *Mastering Resistance.* New York: Guilford.

Cavanagh, M. E. (1982). *The Counseling Experience.* Pacific Grove, CA: Brooks/Cole.

Crabb, L. (2001). *Shattered Dreams: God's Unexpected Pathway to Joy.* Colorado Springs, CO: WaterBrook.

Egan, G. (1998). *The Skilled Helper* (6th ed.). Pacific Grove, CA: Brooks/Cole.

Frankl, V. (1946, 1965). *The Doctor and the Soul* (2nd ed.) (R. Winston & C. Winston, Trans.). New York: Knopf.

Freud, S. (1900). The interpretation of dreams. In J. Strachney (Ed. and Trans.), *The Standard Edition of the Complete Psychological Works of Sigmund Freud.* (Vol. 4). London: Hogarth.

Freud, S. (1920). Beyond the pleasure principle. In J. Strachney (Ed. and Trans.), *The Standard Edition of the Complete Psychological Works of Sigmund Freud.* (Vol. 18). London: Hogarth.

Jackson, D. (1963). A suggestion for the technical handing of paranoid patients. *Psychiatry, 26,* 206-307.

Kehoe, N., & Getheil, T. (1984). Shared religious belief as resistance in psychotherapy. *American Journal of Psychotherapy, 38,* 579-585.

Lovinger, R. (1979). Therapeutic strategies with "religious" resistances. *Psychotherapy: Theory, Research, and Practice, 16,* 419-427.

Narramore, B. (1994). Dealing with religious resistances in psychotherapy. *Journal of Psychology and Theology, 22*(4), 249-258. Used by permission.

Peck, M. S. (1978). *The Road Less Traveled.* New York: Simon & Schuster.

Seligman, M. (1994). *What You Can Change and What You Can't.* New York: Knopf.

Weeks, G., & L'Abate, L. (1982). *Paradoxical Psychotherapy.* New York: Brunner/Mazel.

CHAPTER 17

Adams, J. E. (1975). *Shepherding God's Flock, Vol. 2.* Nutley, NJ: Presbyterian and Reformed.

Adams, J. E. (1979). *More than Redemption: A Theology of Christian Counseling.* Phillipsburg, NJ: Presbyterian and Reformed.

Aldrich, J. C. (1981). *Life Style Evangelism.* Portland, OR: Multnomah.

Anderson, N. T. (1995). *Helping Others Find Freedom in Christ.* Ventura, CA: Regal.

Backus, W. (1987). *Finding the Freedom of Self-Control.* Minneapolis: Bethany.

Bakke, R. (1997). *A Theology As Big As the City.* Downers Grove, IL: InterVarsity.

Barackman, F. H. (1981). *Practical Christian Theology.* Binghamton, NY: Practical Press.

Barna, G. (1998). *The Second Coming of the Church.* Nashville: Word.

Benson, H. (1975). *The Relaxation Response.* New York: Morrow.

Bradley, J., & Carty, J. (1991). *Discovering Your Natural Talents.* Colorado Springs, CO: NavPress.

Cloud, H., & Townsend, J. (1999). *Boundaries in Marriage.* Grand Rapids: Zondervan.

Clowney, E. (1976). *The Doctrine of the Church.* Philadelphia: Presbyterian and Reformed.

Cormier W., & Cormier, L. (1991). *Interviewing Strategies for Helpers* (3rd ed.). Pacific Grove, CA: Brooks/Cole.

Crabb, L. (1997). *Connecting.* Nashville: Word.

Crabb, L. (1999). *The Safest Place on Earth.* Nashville: Word.

Erikson, E. (1950). *Childhood and Society.* New York: Norton.

Foster, R. (1988). *The Celebration of Discipline.* New York: HarperCollins.

Frankl, V. (1984). *Man's Search for Meaning.* New York: Simon & Schuster.

Grenz, S. J. (1994). *Theology for the Community of God.* Nashville: Broadman & Holman.

Hart, A. D. (1989). *Unlocking the Mystery of Your Emotions.* Dallas: Word.

Hart, A. D. (1999). *The Anxiety Cure.* Nashville: Word.

Hart, A. D., Gulbranson, G. L., & Smith, J. (1992). *Mastering Pastoral Counseling.* Portland, OR: Multnomah.

Horton, M. S. (1994). *Beyond Culture Wars.* Chicago: Moody.

Jeremias, J. (1971). *New Testament Theology.* London: SCM.

MacArthur, J. F., Jr., & Mack, W. A. (1994). *Introduction to Biblical Counseling.* Dallas: Word.

Miller, W. R. (1985). *Practical Psychology for Pastors.* Englewood Cliffs, NJ: Prentice-Hall.

Moltmann, J. (1993). *Theology of Hope.* Minneapolis: Fortress.

Murren, D. (1999). *Churches that Heal.* West Monroe, LA: Howard.

Stoop, D., & Masteller, J. (1996). *Forgiving Our Parents/Forgiving Ourselves.* Ann Arbor, MI: Servant.

Sweet, L. (1999). *Soul Tsunami.* Grand Rapids: Zondervan.

Thurman, C. (1995). *The Lies We Believe.* Nashville: Nelson.

Wagner, E. G., & Martin, C. S. (1998). *Your Pastor's Heart.* Chicago: Moody.

Warren, R. (1995). *The Purpose Driven Church.* Grand Rapids: Zondervan.

Willard, D. (1998). *The Divine Conspiracy.* San Francisco: HarperSanFrancisco.

Wilson, E., Wilson, S., Friesen, P., Paulson, V. L., & Paulson, N. (1997). *Restoring the Fallen.* Downers Grove, IL: InterVarsity.

Wilson, S. D. (1990). *Released from Shame.* Downers Grove, IL: InterVarsity.

CHAPTER 18

Adams, J. E. (1970). *Competent to Counsel.* Grand Rapids: Baker.

Adams, J. E. (1973). *The Christian Counselor's Manual.* Grand Rapids: Baker.

Adams, J. E. (1981). *Ready to Restore: The Layman's Guide to Christian Counseling.* Grand Rapids: Baker.

Backus, W. (1985). *Telling the Truth to Troubled People.* Minneapolis: Bethany.

Backus, W. (1987). A counseling center staffed by trained Christian lay persons. *Journal of Psychology and Christianity, 6*(2), 39-44.

Backus, W., & Chapian, M. (1980). *Telling Yourself the Truth.* Minneapolis: Bethany.

Becker, W. W. (1987). The paraprofessional counselor in the church: Legal and ethical considerations. *Journal of Psychology and Christianity, 6*(2), 78-82.

Berman, J. S., & Norton, N. C. (1985). Does professional training make a therapist more effective? *Psychological Bulletin, 98,* 401-406.

Beutler, L. E., & Kendall, P. C. (1995). Introduction to the special section: The case for training in the provision of psychological therapy. *Journal of Consulting and Clinical Psychology, 63,* 179-181.

Bickman, L. (1999). Practice makes perfect and other myths about mental health services. *American Psychologist, 54,* 965-978.

Boan, D. M., & Owens, T. (1985). Peer ratings of lay counselor skill as related to client satisfaction. *Journal of Psychology and Christianity, 4*(1), 79-81.

Bright, J. I., Baker, K. D., & Neimeyer, R. A. (1999). Professional and paraprofessional group treatments for depression: A comparison of cognitive-behavioral and mutual support interventions. *Journal of Consulting and Clinical Psychology, 67,* 491-501.

Bufford, R. K., & Buckler, R. E. (1987). Counseling in the church: A proposed strategy for ministering to mental health needs in the church. *Journal of Psychology and Christianity, 6*(2), 21-29.

Burlingame, G. M., Fuhriman, A., Paul, S., & Ogles, B. M. (1989). Implementing a time-limited therapy program: Differential effects of training and experience. *Psychotherapy, 26,* 303-313.

Cheydleur, J. R. (1999). *Called to Counsel.* Wheaton, IL: Tyndale.

Christensen, A., & Jacobson, N. S. (1994). Who (or what) can do psychotherapy: The status and challenge of nonprofessional therapies. *Psychological Science, 5,* 8-14.

Collins, G. R. (1976a). *How to Be a People Helper.* Santa Ana, CA: Vision House.

Collins, G. R. (1976b). *People Helper Growthbook.* Santa Ana, CA: Vision House.

Collins, G. R. (1980). Lay counseling within the local church. *Leadership, 7*(4), 78-86.

Crabb, L. (1977). *Effective Biblical Counseling.* Grand Rapids: Zondervan.

Crabb, L. (1996). Struggling without a shepherd. *Christian Counseling Today, 4*(1), 14-15.

Crabb, L. (1997). *Connecting.* Nashville: Word.

Crabb, L. (1999). *The Safest Place on Earth.* Nashville: Word.

Crabb, L. J., & Allender, D. (1984). *Encouragement: The Key to Caring.* Grand Rapids: Zondervan.

Durlak, J. (1979). Comparative effectiveness of paraprofessional and professional helpers. *Psychological Bulletin, 86,* 80-92.

Durlak, J. (1981). Comparative effectiveness of paraprofessional and professional helpers: A reply to Nietzel and Fisher. *Psychological Bulletin, 89,* 566-569.

Harris, J. (1985). Non-professionals as effective helpers for pastoral counselors. *Journal of Pastoral Care, 39,* 165-172.

Hattie, J. A., Sharpley, C. F., & Rogers, H. J. (1984). Comparative effectiveness of professional and paraprofessional helpers. *Psychological Bulletin, 95,* 534-541.

Haugk, K. C. (1984). *Christian Caregiving—A Way of Life.* Minneapolis: Augsburg.

Kendall, P. C., Reber, M., McLeer, S., Epps, J., & Ronan, K. R. (1990). Cognitive-behavioral treatment of conduct-disordered children. *Cognitive Therapy and Research, 14,* 279-297.

Lambert, M. J., & Bergin, A. E. (1994). The effectiveness of psychotherapy. In A. E. Bergin & S. L. Garfield (Eds.), *Handbook of Psychotherapy and Behavior Change* (4th ed) (pp. 143-189). New York: Wiley.

McManus, E. (2001). *An Unstoppable Force.* Loveland, CO: Group Publishing.

Miller, G. A. (1969). Psychology as a means of promoting human welfare. *American Psychologist, 24,* 1063-1075.

Nietzel, N. T., & Fisher, S. G. (1981). Effectiveness of professional and paraprofessional helpers: A comment on Durlak. *Psychological Bulletin, 89,* 555-565.

Ohlschlager, G., & Mosgofian, P. (1992). *Law for the Christian Counselor: A Guidebook for Clinicians and Pastors.* Dallas: Word.

Partridge, T. J. (1983). Ten considerations in establishing a Christian counseling center. *Christian Counselor's Journal, 4*(4), 31-33.

Scanish, J. D., & McMinn, M. R. (1996). The competent lay Christian counselor. *Journal of Psychology and Christianity, 15,* 29-37.

Shadish, W. R., Montgomery, L. M., Wilson, P., Wilson, M. R., Bright, I., & Okwumabua, T. (1993). Effects of family and marital psychotherapies: A meta-analysis. *Journal of Consulting and Clinical Psychology, 61,* 992-1002.

Solomon, C. R. (1975). *Handbook to Happiness.* Wheaton, IL: Tyndale.

Solomon, C. R. (1977). *Counseling with the Mind of Christ.* Old Tappan, NJ: Revell.

Stein, D. M., & Lambert, M. J. (1995). Graduate training in psychotherapy: Are therapy outcomes enhanced? *Journal of Consulting and Clinical Psychology, 63,* 182-196.

Steinbron, M. J. (1987). *Can the Pastor Do It Alone? A Model for Preparing Lay People for Lay Pastoring.* Ventura, CA: Regal.

Steinbron, M. J. (1997). *The Lay Driven Church.* Ventura, CA: Regal.

Strupp, H. H., & Hadley, S. W. (1979). Specific versus nonspecific factors in psychotherapy: A controlled study of outcome (Archive ed.). *General Psychiatry, 36,* 1125-1136.

Sweeten, G., Ping, D., & Clippard, A. (1993). *Listening for Heaven's Sake.* Cincinnati, OH: Teleios.

Tan, S. Y. (1991). *Lay Counseling: Equipping Christians for a Helping Ministry.* Grand Rapids: Zondervan.

Tan, S. Y. (1993). Lay Christian counseling. In R. J. Wicks & R. D. Parsons (Eds.), *Clinical Handbook of Pastoral Counseling, Vol. 2* (pp. 27-50). Mahwah, NJ: Paulist.

Tan, S. Y. (1994). Lay counseling: A Christian approach. *Journal of Psychology and Christianity, 13,* 264-269.

Tan, S. Y. (1995). Starting a lay counseling ministry. *Christian Counseling Today, 3*(1), 56-57.

Tan, S. Y. (1997a). Lay counselor training. In R. K. Sanders (Ed.), *Christian Counseling Ethics* (pp. 235-245). Downers Grove, IL: InterVarsity.

Tan, S. Y. (1997b). The role of the psychologist in paraprofessional helping. *Professional Psychology: Research and Practice, 28,* 368-372.

Tan, S. Y. (1999a). Holy Spirit, role in counseling. In D. G. Benner & P. C. Hill (Eds.), *Baker Encyclopedia of Psychology and Counseling* (2nd ed.) (pp. 568-569). Grand Rapids: Baker.

Tan, S. Y. (1999b). Lay counseling. In D. G. Benner & P. C. Hill (Eds.), *Baker Encyclopedia of Psychology and Counseling* (2nd ed.) (pp. 672-674). Grand Rapids: Baker.

Tan, S. Y. (1999c). Lay counseling: The state of the art. *Christian Counseling Today, 7*(2), 32-34.

Toh, Y. M., & Tan, S. Y. (1997). The effectiveness of church-based lay counselors: A controlled outcome study. *Journal of Psychology and Christianity, 16,* 260-267.

Toh, Y. M., Tan, S. Y., Osburn, C. D., & Faber, D. E. (1994). The evaluation of a church-based lay counseling program: Some preliminary data. *Journal of Psychology and Christianity, 13,* 270-275.

Voss, S. L. (1996). The church as an agent in rural mental health. *Journal of Psychology and Theology, 24,* 114-123.

Walters, R. P. (1987). A survey of client satisfaction in a lay counseling program. *Journal of Psychology and Christianity, 6*(2), 62-69.

Worthington, E. L., Jr., Kurusu, T. A., McCullough, M. E., & Sandage, S. J. (1996). Empirical research on religion and psychotherapeutic processes and outcomes: A ten-year review and research prospectus. *Psychological Bulletin, 119,* 448-487.

CHAPTER 19

American Association of Christian Counselors (2000). *AACC Christian Counseling Code of Ethics.* Forest, VA: AACC.

Bales, R. F., & Strodbeck, F. L. (1951). Phases in group problem solving. *Journal of Abnormal and Social Psychology, 46,* 485-495.

Brown, N. W. (1998). *Psycho-educational Groups.* Philadelphia: Acceleration Development Press.

Coleman, L. E. (1989). *Serendipity Youth Ministry Encyclopedia.* Littleton, CO: Serendipity House.

Conyne, R. K. (1999). *Failures in Group Work: How Can We Learn from Our Mistakes.* Thousand Oaks, CA: Sage.

Corey, G., Corey, M., Callanan, P., & Russell, J. M. (1992). *Group Techniques* (3rd ed.). Pacific Grove, CA: Brooks/Cole.

Corey, M. S., & Corey, G. (1997). *Groups: Process and Practice* (5th ed.). Pacific Grove, CA: Brooks/Cole.

Corey, M. S., & Corey, G. (2001). *Groups: Process and Practice* (6th ed.). Pacific Grove, CA: Brooks/Cole.

Crabb, L. (1999). *The Safest Place on Earth*. Nashville: Word.

Crabb, L. J., & Allender, D. B. (1984). *Encouragement: The Key to Caring*. Grand Rapids: Zondervan.

Dibbert, M. T., & Wichern, F. B. (1985). *Growth Groups: A Key to Christian Fellowship and Spiritual Maturity in the Church*. Grand Rapids: Zondervan.

Donahue, B. (1996). *The Willow Creek Guide to Leading Life-Changing Small Groups*. Grand Rapids: Zondervan.

Earley, J. (1999). *Interactive Group Therapy*. Ann Arbor, MI: Brunner/Mazel.

Fuhriman, A., & Burlingame, G. M. (Eds.). (1994). Group psychotherapy: Research and practice. *Handbook of Group Psychotherapy: An Empirical and Clinical Synthesis*. New York: Wiley.

Galloway, D. (1995). *The Small Group Book*. Grand Rapids: Revell.

George, C. F. (1997). *Nine Keys to Effective Small Group Leadership*. Mansfield, PA: Kingdom Publishing.

Gladding, S. T. (1995). *Group Work: A Counseling Specialty* (2nd ed.). Englewood Cliffs, NJ: Prentice-Hall.

Glanz, E. C., & Hayes, R. W. (1967). *Groups in Guidance* (2nd ed.). Boston: Allyn and Bacon.

Herlihy, B., & Corey, G. (1996). *Ethical Standard Casebook*. Alexandria, VA: American Counseling Association.

Icenogle, G. W. (1994). *A Biblical, Theological, and Integrative Foundation for Small Group Ministry*. Unpublished doctoral dissertation, Fuller Theological Seminary. Pasadena, CA.

Jacobs, E. E., Harvill, R., & Masson, R. L. (2000). *Group Counseling: Strategies and Skills* (4th ed.). Pacific Grove, CA: Brooks/Cole.

Jones, J. (1993). *Life Support—Leader's Handbook: Your Church's Lifeline to Hurting People*. Nashville: Lifeway.

Krech, D., & Crutchfield, R. S. (1959). *Elements of Psychology*. New York: Knopf.

Lifton, W. M. (1972). *Groups: Facilitating Individual Growth and Societal Change*. New York: Wiley.

Loeser, L. (1957, January). Groups: What are they? *International Journal of Group Psychotherapy, 8*(1), 5-19.

Mahler, C. C. (1969). *Group Counseling in the Schools*. Boston: Houghton Mifflin.

McBride, N. F. (1995). *How to Build a Small Group Ministry.* Colorado Springs, CO: NavPress.

Olsen, C. M. (1973). *The Base Church: Creating Community Through Multiple Forms.* Atlanta, GA: Forum House Publishers.

Price, R., Springle, P., & Kloba, J. (1991). *Rapha's Handbook for Group Leaders.* Houston: Rapha.

Rapin, L., & Keel, L. (1998, September). Association for specialists in group work: best practical guidelines. *Journal for Specialists in Group Work, 23*(3), 237-244.

Riva, M. T., & Smith, R. D. (1997). Looking into the future of group research. Where do we go from here? *Journal for Specialists in Group Work, 22*(4), 266-276.

Smith, M., Glass, G., & Miller, T. (1980). *The Benefits of Psychology.* Baltimore: Johns Hopkins University Press.

Spitz, H. I. (1996). *Group Psychotherapy and Managed Mental Health Care: A Clinical Guide for Providers.* New York: Brunner.

Toseland, R. W., & Siporin, M. (1986). When to recommend group treatment: A review of the clerical and research literature. *International Journal of Group Psychotherapy, 36*(2), 171-20.

Tuckman, B. W. (1965). Developmental sequences in small groups. *Psychological Bulletin, 63,* 384-399.

Wheeler, I. (1989). Self-help groups. In G. M. Gazda (Ed.), *Group Counseling* (4th ed.). Boston: Allyn and Bacon.

Wuthnow, R. S. (1994). *Sharing the Journey: Support Groups and America's New Quest for Community.* New York: Free Press.

Yalom, I. D. (1995). *Theory and Practice of Group Psychotherapy* (4th ed.). New York: Basic Books.

Zimpfer, D. G. (1970). Lecture notes, PSY 543. Group counseling at the University of Rochester.

CHAPTER 20

Beck, A. T. (1988). *Love Is Never Enough.* New York: Harper & Row.

Benner, D. (1992). *Strategic Pastoral Counseling: A Short-Term Structural Model.* Grand Rapids: Baker.

Bowen, M. (1994). *Family Therapy in Clinical Practice.* New York: J. Aronson.

Burchard, G., Yarhouse, M., Worthington, E. L., Jr., Berry, J. W., & Canter, D. E. (2001, March). A pilot study of two marriage-enrichment interventions versus a retested control. Poster presented at the meeting of the Christian Association for Psychological Studies, Richmond, VA.

Butler, M. H., & Wampler, K. S. (1999). A meta-analytic update of research on the Couple Communication Program. *American Journal of Family Therapy, 27,* 223-238.

Clinton, T. (1999). *Before a Bad Goodbye: How to Turn Your Marriage Around.* Nashville: Word.

Clinton, T., & Clinton, J. (2000). *The Marriage You've Always Wanted: How to Grow a Stronger, More Intimate Relationship.* Nashville: Word.

Combs, C. W., Bufford, R. K., Campbell, C. D., & Halter, L. L. (2000). Effects of cognitive-behavioral marriage enrichment: A controlled study. *Marriage and Family: A Christian Journal, 3,* 99-111.

De Shazer, S. (1988). *Clues: Investigating Solutions in Brief Therapy.* New York: Norton.

Doherty, W. J., Lester, M. E., & Leigh, G. K. (1986). Marriage encounter weekends: Couples who win and couples who lose. *Journal of Marriage and Family Therapy, 12,* 49-61.

Fisher, R., & Ury, W. (1981). *Getting to Yes: Negotiating Agreements Without Giving In.* Boston: Houghton Mifflin.

Friessen, D. D., & Friessen, R. M. (1989). *Counseling and Marriage.* Dallas: Word.

Giblin, P., Sprenkle, D. H., & Sheehan, R. (1985). Enrichment outcome research: A meta-analysis of premarital, marital, & family interventions. *Journal of Marital and Family Therapy, 11,* 257-271.

Gottman, J. M. (1994). *What Predicts Divorce? The Relationship Between Marital Processes and Marital Outcomes.* Hillsdale, NJ: Lawrence Erlbaum Associates.

Gottman, J. M., Coan, J., Carrere, S., & Swanson, C. (1998). Predicting marital happiness and stability from newlywed interactions. *Journal of Marriage and the Family, 60,* 5-22.

Gottman, J. M., Notarius, C., Gonso, J., & Markman, H. (1975). *A Couple's Guide to Communication.* Champaign, IL: Research Press.

Greenberg, L. S., & Johnson, S. M. (1988). *Emotionally Focused Therapy for Couples.* New York: Guilford.

Guerin, P. J., Jr., Fay, L. F., Burden, S. L., & Kautto, J. G. (1987). *The Evolution and Treatment of Marital Conflict: A Four-Stage Approach.* New York: Basic Books.

Guerney, B. (1977). *Relationship Enhancement.* San Francisco: Jossey-Bass.

Gurin, G., Veroff, J., & Feld, S. (1960). *Americans' View of Mental Health.* New York: Basic Books.

Hahlweg, K., & Klaan, N. (1997). The effectiveness of marital counseling in Germany: A contribution to health services research. *Journal of Family Psychology, 11,* 410-421.

Hahlweg, K., Markman, H. J., Thurmaier, F., Engl, J., & Eckert, V. (1998). Prevention of marital distress: Results of a German prospective longitudinal study. *Journal of Family Psychology, 12,* 543-556.

Hammonds, T. M., & Worthington, E. L., Jr. (1985). The effect of facilitator utterances on participant responses in a brief ACME-type marriage enrichment group. *American Journal of Family Therapy, 13,* 59-69.

Harley, W. F., Jr. (1994). *His Needs, Her Needs: Building an Affair-Proof Marriage.* Grand Rapids: Revell.

Harley, W. F., Jr. (1997). *Love Busters: Overcoming Habits that Destroy Romantic Love.* Grand Rapids: Revell.

Hasz, M., Oliver, G. J., & Carmack, J. (2000). What to do in sessions two and beyond in solution-based brief therapy: A case study. *Marriage and Family: A Christian Journal, 3,* 363-372.

Hight, T. L. (2000). *A Meta-Analysis of Marital-Enrichment Interventions.* Unpublished doctoral dissertation, Virginia Commonwealth University, Richmond.

Jacobson, N. S., & Addis, M. E. (1993). Research on couples and couple therapy: What do we know? Where are we going? *Journal of Consulting and Clinical Psychology, 61,* 85-93.

Jacobson, N. S., & Christensen, A. (1996). *Integrative Couple Therapy: Promoting Acceptance and Change.* New York: Norton.

Marcel, G. (1962). *Homo Viator: An Introduction to the Metaphysics of Hope.* New York: Harper & Row.

Markman, H. J., Renick, M. J., Floyd, F. J., Stanley, S. M., & Clements, M. (1993). Preventing marital distress through communication and conflict management training: A 4- and 5-year follow-up. *Journal of Consulting and Clinical Psychology, 61,* 70-77.

McCullough, M. E., & Worthington, E. L., Jr. (1995). Promoting forgiveness: The comparison of two brief psychoeducational interventions with a waiting-list control. *Counseling and Values, 40,* 55-68.

McCullough, M. E., Worthington, E. L., Jr., & Rachal, K. C. (1997). Interpersonal forgiveness in close relationships. *Journal of Personality and Social Psychology, 75,* 321-326.

McManus, M. J. (1993). *Marriage Savers.* Grand Rapids: Zondervan.

Miller, S., Wachman, D., Nunnally, E., & Miller, P. (1988). *Connecting: With Self and Others.* Denver: Interpersonal Communications Program.

Miller, W. R., & Jackson, K. A. (1995). *Practical Psychology for Pastors.* Englewood Cliffs, NJ: Prentice-Hall.

Norval, L. S., Combs, C. W., Wiinamak, M., Bufford, R. K., & Halter, L. L. (1996). Effects of cognitive-behavioral marriage enrichment on marital adjustment of church couples. *Journal of Psychology and Theology, 24,* 47-53.

Oliver, G. J., Hasz, M., & Richburg, M. (1997). *Promoting Change Through Brief Therapy in Christian Counseling.* Wheaton, IL: Tyndale.

Oliver, G. J., & Miller, S. (1996). Couple communication. In E. L. Worthington, Jr. (Ed.), *Christian Marital Counseling: 8 Approaches to Helping Couples* (pp. 87-108). Grand Rapids: Baker.

Oliver, G. J., & Wright, H. N. (1997). One approach to helping couples change. *Marriage and Family: A Christian Journal, 1,* 17-27.

Parrott, L., III, & Parrott, L. (1995). *Saving Your Marriage Before It Starts.* Grand Rapids: Zondervan.

Parrott, L., III, & Parrott, L. (2001). *When Bad Things Happen to Good Marriages: How to Stay Together When Life Pulls You Apart.* Grand Rapids: Zondervan.

Ripley, J. S., Borden, C., Barlow, L., Hawxhurst, K., Kemper, S., Smith, C., Valdez, S., Babcock, J., & Page, M. (2000, November). Distance Couples Assessment and Feedback with Christian Married Couples: A Pilot Study. Paper presented at Christian Association for Psychological Studies, East Region Conference, Waymart, PA.

Ripley, J. S., Parrott, L., III, Worthington, E. L., Jr., & Parrott, L. (2000). Program evaluation of the SYMBIS pre-marital course. *Marriage and Family: A Christian Journal, 3,* 13-26.

Ripley, J. S., Parrott, L., III, Worthington, E. L., Jr., Parrott, L., & Smith, C. (2001). An initial empirical examination of the Parrotts' marriage mentoring: Outcomes in confidence, knowledge and training the program coordinators. *Marriage and Family: A Christian Journal, 4,* 77-94.

Ripley, J. S., & Worthington, E. L., Jr. (1998). What the journals reveal about Christian marital counseling: An inadequate (but emerging) scientific base. *Marriage and Family: A Christian Journal, 1,* 375-396.

Ripley, J. S., & Worthington, E. L., Jr. (2001). Married Christians' preferences for and expectations of Christian and non-Christian marital therapists and interventions. *American Journal of Family Therapy, 29,* 39-58.

Snyder, C. R. (1994). *The Psychology of Hope: You Can Get There from Here.* New York: Free Press.

Stanley, S. M., Bradbury, T. N., & Markman, H. J. (2000). Structural flaws in the bridge from basic research on marriage to interventions for couples. *Journal of Marriage and the Family, 62,* 256-264.

Stanley, S. M., Markman, H. J., Prado, L. M., Olmos-Gallo, P. A., Tonelli, L., St. Peters, M., Leber, B. D., Bobulinski, M., Cordova, A., & Whitton, S. W. (2001). Community based premarital prevention: Clergy and lay leaders on the front lines. *Family Relations, 50,* 67-76.

Stanley, S. M., & Trathen, D. (1994). Christian PREP: An empirically based model for marital and premarital intervention. *Journal of Psychology and Christianity, 13,* 158-165.

Stanley, S. M., Trathen, D., McCain, S., & Bryan, M. (1998). *A Lasting Promise: A Christian Guide to Fighting for Your Marriage.* San Francisco: Jossey-Bass.

Thomas, G. (2000). *Sacred Marriage.* Grand Rapids: Zondervan.

Trathen, D. W. (1995). A comparison of effectiveness of two Christian premarital counseling programs (skills and information-based) utilized by evangelical Protestant churches. (Doctoral dissertation, University of Denver, 1995). *Dissertation Abstracts International 56*(06-A), 2277.

Wimberly, E. P. (1997). *Counseling African-American Marriages and Families: Counseling and Pastoral Theology.* Louisville, KY: Westminster/John Knox.

Worthington, E. L., Jr. (1989). *Marriage Counseling: A Christian Approach to Counseling Couples.* Downers Grove, IL: InterVarsity.

Worthington, E. L., Jr. (1990). Marriage counseling: A Christian approach for counseling couples. *Counseling and Values, 35,* 3-15.

Worthington, E. L., Jr. (1991). Marriage counseling with Christian couples. In G. R. Collins (Ed.), *Case Studies in Christian Counseling* (pp. 87-108). Dallas: Word.

Worthington, E. L., Jr. (1993). *Hope for Troubled Marriages: Overcoming Common Problems and Major Difficulties.* Downers Grove, IL: InterVarsity.

Worthington, E. L., Jr. (1994). *I Care About Your Marriage.* Chicago: Moody.

Worthington, E. L., Jr. (1995). Religious education and marital issues. In H. Atkinson (Ed.), *Handbook of Young Adult Religious Education* (pp. 291-313). Birmingham, AL: Religious Education Press.

Worthington, E. L., Jr. (1996). Speculations about new directions in helping marriages and families that arise from pressures of managed mental health care. *Journal of Psychology and Christianity, 15,* 197-212.

Worthington, E. L., Jr. (1998). The pyramid model of forgiveness: Some inter-disciplinary speculations about unforgiveness and the promotion of forgive-ness. In Worthington, E. L., Jr. (Ed.), *Dimensions of Forgiveness: Psychological Research and Theological Perspectives* (pp. 107-137). Philadelphia: Templeton Foundation Press.

Worthington, E. L., Jr. (1999). Hope-focused marriage counseling. *Enrichment: A Journal for Pentecostal Ministry, 5*(2), 54-58.

Worthington, E. L., Jr., Buston, B. G., & Hammonds, T. M. (1989). A compo-nent analysis of marriage enrichment: Information and treatment modality. *Journal of Counseling and Development, 67,* 555-560.

Worthington, E. L., Jr., Hight, T. L., Ripley, J. S., Perrone, K. M., Kurusu, T. A., & Jones, D. R. (1997). Strategic hope-focused relationship-enrichment counseling with individual couples. *Journal of Counseling Psychology, 44,* 381-389.

Worthington, E. L., Jr., Kurusu, T. A., Collins, W. B., Berry, J. W., Ripley, J. S., & Baier, S. N. (2000). Forgiving usually takes time: A lesson learned by studying interventions to promote forgiveness. *Journal of Psychology and Theology, 28,* 3-20.

Worthington, E. L., Jr., McCullough, M. E., Shortz, J. L., Mindes, E. J., Sandage, S. J., & Chartrand, J. M. (1995). Can marital assessment and feedback improve marriages? Assessment as a brief marital enrichment procedure. *Journal of Counseling Psychology, 42,* 466-475.

Worthington, E. L., Jr., & McMurry, D. (1994). *Marriage Conflicts.* Grand Rapids: Baker.

Worthington, E. L., Jr., Shortz, J. L., & McCullough, M. E. (1993). A call for emphasis on scholarship on Christian marriage and marriage counseling. *Journal of Psychology and Christianity, 12,* 13-23.

Wright, H. N. (1981). *Marital Counseling: A Biblical, Behavioral, Cognitive Approach.* New York: Harper & Row.

Wright, H. N. (1992). *The Premarital Counseling Handbook* (2nd rev. ed.). Chicago: Moody.

Wright, H. N. (1995). *Finding Your Perfect Mate.* Eugene, OR: Harvest House.

Wright, H. N. (1997). *So You're Getting Married.* Ventura, CA: Regal.

Wright, H. N. (1999a). *After You Say I Do.* Eugene, OR: Harvest House.

Wright, H. N. (1999b). *Before You Remarry.* Eugene, OR: Harvest House.

Wright, H. N. (2000). *Communication: Key to Your Marriage.* Ventura, CA: Regal.

CHAPTER 21

Arp, D., & Arp, C. (1993). *52 Dates for You and Your Mate.* Nashville: Nelson.

Arp, D., & Arp, C. (1996). *The Second Half of Marriage: Facing the Eight Challenges of the Empty-Nest Years.* Grand Rapids: Zondervan. Used by permission.

Arp, D., & Arp, C. (1997a). *10 Great Dates to Energize Your Marriage.* Grand Rapids: Zondervan.

Arp, D., & Arp, C. (1997b). *10 Great Dates Video Curriculum Kit.* Grand Rapids: Zondervan. Contains ten video date launches, leader's guide, and participant's book.

Arp, D., & Arp, C. (2000). *The Second Half of Marriage Video Curriculum Kit.* Grand Rapids: Zondervan. Contains nine video sessions, leader's guide, and participant's guide.

Arp, D., Arp, C., Stanley, S. M., Markman, H. J., & Blumberg, S. L. (2000). *Fighting for Your Empty Nest Marriage: Reinventing Your Relationship When the Kids Leave Home.* San Francisco: Jossey-Bass. Used by permission.

Collins, G., & Clinton, T. (1992). *Baby Boomer Blues.* Dallas: Word.

Gallup, G., & Jones, T. (2000). *The Next American Spirituality: Finding God in the Twenty-First Century.* Colorado Springs, CO: Cook.

Gottman, J. (1994). *Why Marriages Succeed or Fail.* New York: Simon & Schuster.

National Center for Health Statistics (1991). Census report 1981–1991 by National Center for Health Statistics in Hyattsville, Maryland. Washington, DC: Centers for Disease Control; U.S. Department of Health and Human Services.

Olson, David, PhD, University of Minnesota, PREPARE/ENRICH, has recently developed an inventory for long-term marriages, which should prove to be very helpful for counselors and clergy—especially those who already utilize PREPARE/ENRICH. For information about PREPARE/ENRICH, write to PREPARE/ENRICH, P.O. Box 190, Minneapolis, MN 55440-0190.

Sheehy, G. (1995). *New Passages.* New York: Random House.

Stanley, S. (1998). *The Heart of Commitment: Compelling Research That Reveals the Secrets of a Lifelong, Intimate Marriage.* Nashville: Nelson.

Stanley, S., Trathen, D., McCain, S., & Bryan, M. (1998). *A Lasting Promise.* San Francisco: Jossey-Bass.

Waldrop, J. (1991, January). The baby boomer turns 45. *American Demographics, 22-27.*

Wallerstein, J., & Blakeslee, S. (1995). *The Good Marriage.* Boston: Houghton Mifflin.

Chapter 22

Basson, R. (2000). The female sexual response: A different model. *Journal of Sex and Marital Therapy, 26,* 51-65.

Centers for Disease Control and Prevention (1998). *HIV/AIDS Surveillance Report,* 1998. 10(2). Atlanta: CDC.

Cutrer, W., & Glahn, S. (1998). *Sexual Intimacy in Marriage.* Grand Rapids: Kregel.

Gray, J. (1992). *Men Are from Mars, Women Are from Venus: A Practical Guide for Improving Communication and Getting What You Want in Your Relationships.* New York: HarperCollins.

Hart, A. D. (Speaker). (1998). *The Mystery of Female Sexuality.* (An audio CounselTape). Lynchburg, VA: American Association of Christian Counselors.

Hart, A. D., Weber, C. H., & Taylor, D. (1998). *Secrets of Eve: Understanding the Mystery of Female Sexuality.* Nashville: Word.

Kaplan, H. S. (1974). *The New Sex Therapy.* New York: Brunner/Mazel.

Kaplan, H. S. (1995). *The Sexual Desire Disorders: Dysfunctional Regulation of Sexual Motivation.* New York: Brunner/Mazel.

Laumann, E. O., Paik, A., & Rosen, R. C. (1999). Sexual dysfunction in the United States: Prevalence and predictors. *Journal of American Medical Association, 281*(6), 537-544.

Leiblum, S. R., & Rosen, R. C. (2000). *Principles and Practice of Sex Therapy* (3rd ed.). New York: Guilford.

LoPiccolo, J. (1985). Diagnosis and treatment of male sexual dysfunction. *Journal of Sex and Marital Therapy, 11,* 215-232.

LoPiccolo, J. (1993). *Becoming Orgasmic.* Chapel Hill, NC: Sinclair Institute.

LoPiccolo, J., & LoPiccolo, L. (Eds.). (1978). *Handbook of Sex Therapy.* New York: Plenum.

McCluskey, C. (2001). *Coaching Couples into Passionate Intimacy* [Videotape]. Edgar Springs, MO: Coaching for Christian Living.

Masters, W. H., & Johnson, V. E. (1966). *Human Sexual Response.* Boston: Little, Brown.

Masters, W. H., & Johnson, V. E. (1970). *Human Sexual Inadequacy.* New York: Little, Brown.

Penner, C. L., & Penner, J. J. (1981). *The Gift of Sex: A Guide to Sexual Fulfillment.* Waco, TX: Word.

Penner, C. L., & Penner, J. J. (1993). *Restoring the Pleasure.* Dallas: Word.

Penner, C. L., & Penner, J. J. (1994a). *52 Ways to Have Fun, Fantastic Sex.* Nashville: Nelson.

Penner, C. L., & Penner, J. J. (1994b). *Getting Your Sex Life off to a Great Start: A Guide for Engaged and Newlywed Couples.* Dallas: Word.

Penner, C. L., & Penner, J. J. (1997). *Men and Sex: Discovering Greater Love, Passion and Intimacy with Your Wife.* Nashville: Nelson.

Penner, J. J., & Penner, C. L. (1990). *Counseling for Sexual Disorders.* Dallas: Word.

Rosenau, D. (1994). *A Celebration of Sex.* Nashville: Nelson.

Schnarch, D. (1991). *Constructing the Sexual Crucible: An Integration of Sexual and Marital Therapy.* New York: Norton.

Schnarch, D. (1995). A family systems approach to sex therapy and intimacy. In R. H. Mikesell, D. Lusterman, & S. McDaniel (Eds.), *Integrating Family Therapy: Handbook of Family Psychology and Systems Therapy.* Washington, DC: APA Press.

Vine, W. E. (1996). *Vine's Complete Expository of Old and New Testament Words: With Topical Index.* M. F. Unger, & W. White, Jr. (Eds.). Nashville: Nelson.

Walen, S. R., & Roth, D. (1987). A cognitive approach. In J. H. Greet & W. T. O'Donohue (Eds.), *Theories of Human Sexuality.* New York: Plenum.

Worthington, E. L., Jr. (1989). *Marriage Counseling: A Christian Approach to Counseling Couples.* Downer's Grove, IL: InterVarsity.

Zilbergeld, B. (1999). *The New Male Sexuality* (Rev. ed.). New York: Doubleday Dell.

CHAPTER 23

Ackerman, N. (1966). *Treating the Troubled Family.* New York: Basic Books.

Barna, G., & Hatch, M. (2001). *Boiling Point: Monitoring Cultural Shifts in the 21st Century.* Ventura, CA: Regal.

Bateson, G. (1972). *Steps to an Ecology of the Mind.* New York: Dutton.

Bedrosian, R. C., & Bozicas, G. D. (1994). *Treating Family of Origin Problems: A Cognitive Approach.* New York: Guilford.

Borzormenyi-Nagy, I., & Spark, G. N. (1973). *Invisible Loyalties: Reciprocity in Intergeneration Family Therapy.* New York: Harper & Row.

Bowen, M. (1978). *Family Therapy in Clinical Practice.* New York: Aronson.

Carter, B., & McGoldrick, M. (1980). *The Family Life Cycle: A Framework for Family Therapy.* New York: Gardner.

De Shazer, S. (1980). *Keys to Solution in Brief Therapy.* New York: Norton.

Fisch, R., Weakland, J., & Segal, L. (1980). *The Tactics of Change: Doing Therapy Briefly.* San Francisco: Jossey-Bass.

Framo, J. L. (1982). *Explorations in Marital and Family Therapy: Selected Papers of James L. Framo.* New York: Springer.

Freedman, E. H. (1985). *Generation to Generation: Family Process in Church and Synagogue.* New York: Guilford.

Goldenberg, I., & Goldenberg, H. (1985). *Family Therapy: An Overview* (2nd ed.). Pacific Grove, CA: Brooks/Cole.

Grunlan, S. (1984). *Marriage and Family: A Christian Perspective.* Grand Rapids: Zondervan.

Guerin, P. J., Jr. (Ed.) (1976). *Family Therapy: Theory and Practice.* New York: Gardner.

Haley, J. (1973). *Uncommon Therapy: The Psychiatric Techniques of Milton H. Erickson, M.D.* New York: Norton.

Haley, J. (1981). *Reflections on Therapy and Other Essays.* Chevy Chase, MD: The Family Therapy Institute of Washington, D.C.

Haley, J. (1984). *Ordeal Therapy: Unusual Ways to Change Behavior.* San Francisco: Jossey-Bass.

Haley, J., & Hoffman, L. (1967). *Techniques of Family Therapy.* New York: Basic Books.

Hoffman, L. (1981). *Foundations of Family Therapy.* New York: Basic Books.

Imber-Black, E. (1988). *Families and Larger Systems: A Family Therapist's Guide Through the Labyrinth.* New York: Guilford.

Kantor, D., & Lehr, W. (1975). *Inside the Family.* San Francisco: Jossey-Bass.

Kerr, M. E., & Bowen, M. (1988). *Family Evaluation: An Approach Based on Bowen Theory.* New York: Norton.

Madanes, C. (1981). *Strategic Family Therapy.* San Francisco: Jossey-Bass.

Madanes, C. (1984). *Behind the One-Way Mirror: Advances in the Practice of Strategic Therapy.* San Francisco: Jossey-Bass.

McGoldrick, M., & Gerson, R. (1985). *Genograms in Family Assessment.* New York: Norton.

McGoldrick, M., Pearce, J. K., & Giordano, J. (1982). *Ethnicity and Family Therapy.* New York: Guilford.

Minuchin, S. (1974). *Families and Family Therapy,* Cambridge, MA: Harvard University Press.

Minuchin, S. (1984). *Family Kaleidoscope.* Cambridge, MA: Harvard University Press.

Minuchin, S., and Fishman, H. C. (1981). *Family Therapy Techniques.* Cambridge, MA: Harvard University Press.

Napier, A. Y., & Whitaker, C. A. (1978.). *The Family Crucible*. New York: Harper & Row.

Papp, P. (1977). *Family Therapy: Full-Length Case Studies*. New York: Gardner.

Pittman, F. (1987). *Turning Points: Treating Families in Transitions and Crisis*. New York: Norton.

Satir, V. M. (1964). *Conjoint Family Therapy*. Palo Alto, CA: Science and Behavior Books.

Satir, V. M. (1972). *Peoplemaking*. Palo Alto, CA: Science and Behavior Books.

Scharff, D. E., & Scharff, J. S. (1991). *Object Relations Family Therapy*. Northvale, NJ: Aronson.

Selvini-Palazzoli, M., Cirillo, S., Selvini, M., & Sorrentino, A. M. (1989). *Family Games: General Models of Psychotic Processes in the Family*. New York: Norton.

Slipp, S. (1988). *The Technique and Practice of Object Relations Family Therapy*. Northvale, NJ: Aronson.

Stoop, D. A., & Masteller, J. (1991). *Forgiving Our Parents, Forgiving Ourselves*. Ann Arbor, MI: Servant.

von Bertalanffy, L. (1968). *General Systems Theory: Foundations, Development, Applications*. New York: Braziller.

Walsh, F. (1999). *Spiritual Resources in Family Therapy*. New York: Guilford.

Watzlawick, P. (1978). *The Language of Change*. New York: Basic Books.

Watzlawick, P., Beavin, J. H., & Jackson, D. D. (1967). *Pragmatics of Human Communication*. New York: Norton.

Watzlawick, P., Weakland, J. H., & Fisch, R. (1974). *Change: Principles of Problem Formation and Problem Resolution*. New York: Norton.

Whitaker, C. A., & Bumberry, W. M. (1988). *Dancing with the Family: A Symbolic-Experiential Approach*. New York: Brunner/Mazel.

Chapter 24

Ackerman, N. W. (1970). Child participation in family therapy. *Family Process, 9*, 403-410.

Alsdurf, J., & Alsdurf, P. (1998). *Battered into Submission: The Tragedy of Wife Abuse in the Christian Home*. Eugene, OR: Wipf and Stock.

American Psychiatric Association (2000). *Diagnostic and Statistical Manual of Mental Disorders* (4th ed.). Washington, DC: APA.

Angelou, M. (1970). *I Know Why the Caged Bird Sings*. New York: Bantam.

Barna Research Online (1999). Christians are more likely to experience divorce than are non-Christians. Barna Research Ltd. Retrieved February 16, 2001, from Barna database on http://www.barna.org/.

Bennett, W. (1993). *The Index of Leading Cultural Indicators, Vol. 1.* Washington, DC: Empower America, Heritage Foundation, and Free Congress Foundation.

Birmaher, B., Ryan, N., Williamson, D., Brent, D., & Kaufman, J. (1996a). Childhood and adolescent depression: A review of the past 10 years, pt. 2. *Journal of the American Academy of Child and Adolescent Psychiatry, 35,* 1575-1583.

Birmaher, B., Ryan, N., Williamson, D., Brent, D., & Kaufman, J. (1996b). Childhood and adolescent depression: A review of the past 10 years, pt. 1. *Journal of the American Academy of Child and Adolescent Psychiatry, 35,* 1427-1439.

Center for Mental Health Services. (2001). Comprehensive community mental health services for children program. Washington, DC: Center for Mental Health Services. Retrieved March 29, 2001, from CMHS database on http://www.mentalhealth.org/publications.

Chasin, R. (1989). Interviewing families with children: Guidelines and suggestions. *Journal of Psychotherapy and the Family, 5*(3/4), 15-30.

Culbertson, J. (1993). Clinical child psychology in the 1990s: Broadening our scope. *Journal of Clinical Child Psychology, 22*(1), 116-122.

Ellison, C., Bartkowski, J., & Anderson, K. (1999). Are there religious variations in domestic violence? *Journal of Family Issues, 20*(1), 87-114.

Federman, J. (Ed.). (1998). *National Television Violence Study, Vol. 3.* Thousand Oaks, CA: Sage.

Field, A., Cheung, L., Wolf, A., Herzog, D., Gortmaker, S., & Colditz, G. (1999). Exposure to the mass media and weight concerns among girls. *Pediatrics, 103*(3), 660.

Flisher, A., Kramer, R., Hoven, C., King, R., Bird, H., Davies, M., Gould, M., Greenwald, S., Lahey, B., Regier, D., Schwab-Stone, M., & Shaffer, D. (2000). Risk behavior in a community sample of children and adolescents. *Journal of the Academy of Child and Adolescent Psychiatry, 39*(7), 881-887.

Gil, E. (1994). *Play in Family Therapy.* New York: Guilford.

Hofstra, M., Van Der Ende, J., & Verhulst, J. (2000). Continuity and change of psychopathology from childhood into adulthood: A 14-year follow-up study. *Journal of the Academy of Child and Adolescent Psychiatry, 39*(7), 850-858.

Illback, R. (1994). Poverty and the crisis in children's services: The need for services integration. *Journal of Clinical Child Psychology, 23*(4), 413-424.

Korner, S., & Brown, G. (1990). Exclusion of children from family psychotherapy: Family therapists' beliefs and practices. *Journal of Family Psychology, 3,* 420-430.

La Greca, A., & Hughes, J. (1999). United we stand, divided we fall: The education and training needs of clinical child psychologists. *Journal of Clinical Child Psychology, 28*(4), 435-448.

Landreth, G. (1991). *Play Therapy: The Art of the Relationship*. Philadelphia: Taylor and Francis.

Landreth, G., & Sweeney, D. (1997). Child-centered play therapy. In K. O'Connor & L. Braverman (Eds.), *Play Therapy: Theory and Practice*. New York: Wiley.

Lavigne, J., Gibbons, R., Christoffel, K., Arend, R., Rosenbaum, D., Binns, H., Dawson, N., Sobel, H., & Isaacs, C. (1996). Prevalence rates and correlates of psychiatric disorders among preschool children. *Journal of the Academy of Child and Adolescent Psychiatry, 35*(2), 204-214.

Martin, G. (1992). *Critical Problems in Children and Youth*. Dallas: Word.

Martin, G. (1995). *Help! My Child Isn't Learning*. Colorado Springs, CO: Focus on the Family.

Martin, G. (1998). *The Attention Deficit Child*. Colorado Springs, CO: Chariot Victor.

National Clearinghouse for Alcohol and Drug Information. (2001). Children of alcoholics: Important facts. Washington, DC: SAMHSA. Retrieved February 16, 2001, from SAMHSA database on http://www.health.org/nongovpubs/coafacts.

National Institute of Mental Health. (1998). *Genetics and Mental Disorders: Report of the National Institute of Mental Health's Genetics Workshop* (NIH Publication No. 98-4268). Rockville, MD: NIMH.

National Institute of Mental Health. (2001). Brief notes on the mental health of children and adolescents. Bethesda, MD: NIMH. Retrieved March 23, 2001, from NIMH database on http://www.nimh.nih.gov/publicat/childnotes.cfm.

Roberts, D., Foehr, U., Rideout, V., & Brodie, M. (1999). *Kids and Media at the New Millennium: A Comprehensive National Analysis of Children's Media Use*. Menlo Park, CA: Kaiser Family Foundation Report.

Roberts, M. (1994). Models for service delivery in children's mental health: Common characteristics. *Journal of Clinical Child Psychology, 23*(2), 212-219.

Sweeney, D. (1997). *Counseling Children Through the World of Play*. Wheaton, IL: Tyndale.

Sweeney, D. (2001). Legal and ethical issues in play therapy. In G. Landreth (Ed.), *Innovations in Play Therapy: Issues, Process and Special Populations* (pp. 51-63). Philadelphia: Brunner-Routledge.

Sweeney, D., Homeyer, L., & Pavlishina, O. (2000). Filial therapy: Healing children through relationship parenting. *Marriage and Family: A Christian Journal, 3*(3), 239-254.

Tuma, J. (1989). Mental health services for children: The state of the art. *American Psychologist, 44,* 188-199.

U.S. Department of Health and Human Services. (1999). *Mental Health: A Report of the Surgeon General.* Washington, DC: U.S. Government Printing Office.

U.S. Department of Health and Human Services. (2000). *Child Maltreatment 1998: Reports from the States to the National Child Abuse and Neglect Date System.* Washington, DC: U.S. Government Printing Office.

Wickramaratne, P., & Weissman, M. (1998). Onset of psychopathology in offspring by developmental phase and parental depression. *Journal of the American Academy of Child and Adolescent Psychiatry, 37,* 933-942.

CHAPTER 25

American Psychiatric Association. (2000). *Diagnostic and Statistical Manual of Mental Disorders* (4th ed.). Washington, DC: APA.

Association for Play Therapy. (1999). What the research shows about play therapy. Association for Play Therapy. Retrieved March 28, 2001, from the Association for Play Therapy database on http://www.iapt.org/research.html/.

Children's Defense Fund. (2000). *Every Day in America.* Washington, DC: CDF. Retrieved March 24, 2001, from the Children's Defense Fund database on http://www.chidrensdefensefund.org.

Gordon, R., & Wraith, R. (1993). Responses of children and adolescents to disaster. In J. Wilson & B. Raphael (Eds.), *International Handbook of Traumatic Stress Syndromes* (pp. 561-567). New York: Plenum.

James, B. (1989). *Treating Traumatized Children.* Lexington, MA: Lexington Books.

Landreth, G. (1991). *Play Therapy: The Art of the Relationship.* Philadelphia: Taylor and Francis.

Landreth, G., Homeyer, L., Glover, G., & Sweeney, D. (1996). *Play Therapy Interventions with Children's Problems.* Northvale, NJ: Jason Aronson.

Martin, G. (1992). *Critical Problems in Children and Youth.* Dallas: Word.

Moustakas, C. (1974). *Portraits of Loneliness and Love.* New York: Prentice-Hall.

Neale, R. (1969). *In Praise of Play: Toward a Psychology of Religion.* New York: Harper & Row.

Piers, M., & Landau, G. (1980). *The Gift of Play.* New York: Walker and Co.

Schaefer, C. (1994). Play therapy for psychic trauma in children. In K. O'Connor & C. Schaefer (Eds.), *Handbook of Play Therapy, Vol. 2.* New York: Wiley.

Shengold, L. (1989). *Soul Murder: The Effects of Childhood Abuse and Deprivation.* New Haven, CT: Yale University Press.

Sweeney, D. (1997). *Counseling Children Through the World of Play.* Wheaton, IL: Tyndale.

Sweeney, D., & Homeyer, L. (1999). *Handbook of Group Play Therapy: How to Do It, How It Works, Whom It's Best For.* San Francisco: Jossey-Bass.

Terr, L. (1990). *Too Scared to Cry: Psychic Trauma in Childhood.* New York: Harper & Row.

U.S. Department of Health and Human Services. (2000). *Child Maltreatment 1998: Reports from the States to the National Child Abuse and Neglect Data System.* Washington, DC: U.S. Government Printing Office.

van der Kolk, B. (1996). The body keeps score: Approaches to the psychobiology of posttraumatic stress disorder. In B. Van der Kolk, A. McFarlane, & L. Weisaeth (Eds.), *Traumatic Stress: The Effects of Overwhelming Experience on Mind, Body, and Society.* New York: Guilford.

Chapter 26

Arkoff, A. (1980). *Psychology and Personal Growth* (2nd ed.). Boston: Allyn and Bacon.

Arnett, J. J. (1999). Adolescent storm and stress, reconsidered. *American Psychologist, 54,* 317-326.

Brenner, D. (1982). *The Effective Psychotherapist: Conclusions from Practice and Research.* Elmsford, NY: Pergamon.

Collins, G. R. (1988). *Christian Counseling: A Comprehensive Guide* (Rev. ed.). Waco, TX: Word.

Erikson, E. H. (1965). *The Challenge of Youth.* New York: Anchor.

Erikson, E. H. (1968). *Identity: Youth and Crisis.* New York: Norton.

Glasser, W. (1972). *The Identity Society.* New York: Harper & Row.

Kohlberg, L. (1969). *Stages in the Development of Moral Thought and Action.* New York: Holt.

McDowell, J., & Day, D. (1987). *Why Wait? What You Need to Know About the Teen Sexuality Crisis.* San Bernardino, CA: Here's Life.

Mitchell, J. (1975). Moral growth during adolescence. *Adolescence, 10,* 221-26.

Ohlschlager, G., & Mosgofian, P. (1992). *Law for the Christian Counselor: A Guidebook for Clinicians and Pastors.* Dallas: Word.

Olson, G. (1984). *Counseling Teenagers: The Complete Christian Guide to Understanding and Helping Adolescents*. Loveland, CO: Group Books.

Parrott, L. (1997). *Counseling and Psychotherapy* (p. 24). New York: McGraw-Hill.

Piaget, J. (1969). The intellectual development of the adolescent. In G. Caplan & S. Lebovici (Eds.), *Adolescence: Psychosocial Perspectives* (pp. 22-26). New York: Basic Books.

Reik, T. (1972). *Listening with the Third Ear*. New York: Harper & Row.

Rogers, C., Gendlin, G. T., Kiesler, D. V., & Traux, C. B. (1967). *The Therapeutic Relationship and Its Impact*. Madison, WI: University of Wisconsin Press.

Smith, G., & Fogg, C. P. (1974). Teenage drug use: A search for causes and consequences, *Personality and Social Psychology* [Bulletin 1], 426-429.

Chapter 27

American Association of Christian Counselors. (1999). *Membership Registry*. Forest, VA: AACC.

American Psychiatric Association. (2000). *Diagnostic and Statistical Manual of Mental Disorders* (4th ed.) Washington, DC: APA.

Arnold, L. (1993). A comparative overview of treatment research methodology: Adult vs. child and adolescent, psychopharmacological vs. psychosocial treatments. *Psychopharmacology Bulletin, 29*(1), 5-17.

Barkley, R., DuPaul, G., & Costello, A. (1993). Stimulants. In J. Werry & M. Aman (Eds.), *Practitioner's Guide to Psychoactive Drugs for Children and Adolescents* (pp. 205-237). New York: Plenum.

Biederman, J. (1992). New developments in pediatric psychopharmacology. *Journal of the Academy of Child and Adolescent Psychiatry, 31*(1), 14-15.

Biederman, J., & Steingard, R. (1991). Pediatric psychopharmacology. In A. Gelengerg, E. Bassuk, & S. Schoonover (Eds.), *The Practitioner's Guide to Psychoactive Drugs* (3rd ed.) (pp. 341-381). New York: Plenum.

Brown, R., & Ievers, C. (1999). Psychotherapy and pharmacotherapy treatment outcome research in pediatric populations. *Journal of Clinical Psychology in Medical Settings, 6*(1), 63-88.

Bukstein, O. (1993). Overview of pharmacological treatment. In V. Van Hasselt & M. Hersen (Eds.), *Handbook of Behavior Therapy and Pharmacotherapy for Children* (pp. 13-27). Boston: Allyn and Bacon.

Campbell, M., Godfrey, K., & Magee, H. (1992). Pharmacotherapy. In C. Walker & M. Roberts (Eds.), *Handbook of Clinical Child Psychology* (pp. 873-902). New York: Wiley.

Campbell, M., & Spencer, E. (1988). Psychopharmacology in child and adolescent psychiatry: A review of the past five years. *Journal of the American Academy of Child and Adolescent Psychiatry, 27,* 269-279.

Carson, R. (1965). *The Sense of Wonder.* New York: Harper & Row.

Ellis, C., & Singh, N. (1999). Pharmacological approaches. In S. Russ & T. Ollendick (Eds.), *Handbook of Psychotherapies with Children and Families* (pp. 199-216). New York: Kluwer Academic/Plenum.

Fisher, J. G. (1997). A primer on the use of psychotropic medications in prepubertal children. *Christian Counseling Today, 5*(2), 24-27.

Gadow, K. (1992). Pediatric psychopharmacotherapy: A review of recent research. *Journal of Child Psychology and Psychiatry and Allied Disciplines, 33*(1), 153-195.

Gitlin, M. (1995). *The Psychotherapist's Guide to Psychopharmacology* (2nd ed.). New York: Free Press.

Golden, D. (1983). Play therapy for hospitalized children. In C. Schaefer & K. O'Connor (Eds.), *Handbook of Play Therapy* (pp. 213-233). New York: Wiley.

Green, W. (1995). *Child and Adolescent Clinical Psychopharmacology* (2nd ed.). Baltimore, MD: Williams and Wilkins.

Kutcher, S. (1997). *Child and Adolescent Psychopharmacology.* Philadelphia: Saunders.

Kutcher, S. (2000). Practical clinical issues regarding child and adolescent psychopharmacology. *Child and Adolescent Psychiatric Clinics of North America, 9*(1), 245-260.

Landreth, G. (1991). *Play Therapy: The Art of the Relationship.* Muncie, IN: Accelerated Development.

Markowitz, L. (1991, May-June). Better therapy through chemistry. *Family Therapy Networker,* 22-31.

Mayer, L., & Walsh, T. (1998). Eating disorders. In T. Walsh (Ed.), *Child Psychopharmacology.* Washington, DC: American Psychiatric Press.

Mayes, S. (1991). Play assessment of preschool hyperactivity. In C. Schaefer, K. Gitlin, & A. Sandgrund (Eds.), *Play Diagnosis and Assessment* (pp. 249-271). New York: Wiley.

Patterson, J., & Magulac, M. (1994). The family therapist's guide to psychopharmacology: A graduate level course. *Journal of Marital and Family Therapy, 2*(2), 151-173.

Pomeroy, J., & Gadow, K. (1998). An overview of psychopharmacotherapy for children and adolescents. In R. Morris & T. Kratochwill (Eds.), *The Practice of Child Therapy* (pp. 419-470). Boston: Allyn and Bacon.

Popper, C. (1993). Psychopharmacologic treatment of anxiety disorders in adolescents and children. *Journal of Clinical Psychiatry, 50*(Supplement), 52-63.

Rappaport, N., & Chubinsky, P. (2000). The meaning of psychotropic medications for children, adolescents, and their families. *Journal of the American Academy of Child and Adolescent Psychiatry, 39*(9), 1198-1200.

Spencer, T., Biederman, J., & Wilens, T. (2000). Pharmacotherapy of attention deficit hyperactivity disorder. *Child and Adolescent Psychiatric Clinics of North America, 9*(1), 77-97.

Vitiello, B., & Jensen, P. (1995). Developmental perspectives in pediatric psychopharmacology. *Psychopharmacology Bulletin, 31*(1), 75-81.

Wilens, T., Spencer, T., Frazier, J., & Biederman, J. (1998). Child and adolescent psychopharmacology. In T. Ollendick & M. Hersen (Eds.), *Handbook of Child Psychopathology* (3rd ed.) (pp. 603-636). New York: Plenum.

Chapter 28

Aguilera, D. (1990). *Crisis Intervention* (6th ed.). St. Louis, MO: Mosby.

Ahlem, L. (1978). Phases of crisis. *Living with Stress* (pp. 31-64, adapted). Ventura, CA: Regal.

Brown, S. L. (1991). *Counseling Victims of Violence.* American Association for Counseling and Development, (703) 823-9800, order number 72108.

Burgess, A., & Baldwin, B. (1981). *Crisis Intervention: Theory and Practice.* Englewood Cliffs, NJ: Prentice-Hall.

Glasser, W. (1965). *Reality Therapy.* New York: Harper & Row.

Gohan, N. (1978). Crisis intervention as a mode of brief treatment. In R. W. Roberts & R. H. Nee (Eds.), *Theories of Social Casework* (pp. 98, 99). Chicago: University of Chicago Press. (Adapted.)

Hirschowitz, R. (n.d.). Addendum, in the *Levinson Letter* (adapted chart on 4). Cambridge: Levinson Institute.

Mitchell, J. T., & Everly, G. S., Jr. (1977). *Critical Incident Stress Debriefing.* Ellicott City, MD: Chevron Publishing Co.

Puryear, D. (1979). *Helping People in Crisis.* San Francisco: Jossey-Bass. (Eight steps, adapted).

Slaikeu, K. A. (1984). *Crisis Intervention: A Handbook for Practice and Research.* Boston: Allyn and Bacon.

Swihart, J. J., & Richardson, G. C. (1987). *Counseling in Times of Crisis.* Waco, TX: Word.

Wright, H. N. (1999). *Crisis Counseling: What to Do and Say During the First 72 Hours.* Ventura, CA: Regal.

Wright, H. N. (2001). *Recovering from the Losses of Life.* Grand Rapids: Baker.

Chapter 29

American Association of Retired Persons (1998). *Profile of Older Americans.* Washington, DC: AARP.

American Psychological Association (1997). *What Practitioners Should Know About Working with Older Adults.* Washington, DC: APA.

Banks, J. (1985). Racial prejudice and the black self-concept. In J. Banks & J. Gambs (Eds.), *Black Self-Concept.* New York: McGraw-Hill.

Birhamer, B., Ryan, N. D., & Williamson, D. E. (1999). Childhood and adolescent depression: A review of the past 10 years, pt. 1. *Journal of the American Academy of Child and Adolescent Psychiatry, 35*(11), 1427-1429.

Blau, Z. S. (1973). *Old Age in a Changing Society.* New York: New Viewpoints.

Bolles, R. N. (1997). *What Color Is Your Parachute?* Berkeley, CA: Ten Speed Press.

Chestang, L. (1972). *Character Development in a Hostile Environment.* Chicago: University of Chicago Press.

Erwin, K. T. (1996). *Group Techniques for Aging Adults.* Washington, DC: Taylor and Francis.

Erwin, K. T. (1997). *Lifeline to Care with Dignity.* St. Petersburg, FL: Caremore Publications.

Essandoh, P. (1996). Multicultural counseling as the "fourth force": A call to arms. *Counseling Psychologist, 24*(1), 126-137.

Gaertner, S., & Dovidio, J. (1986). The aversive form of racism. In J. Dovidio & S. Gaertner (Eds.), *Prejudice, Discrimination, and Racism.* Orlando, FL: Academic Press.

Gardner, L. (1970). Psychotherapy under varying conditions of race. In R. Pugh (Ed.), *Psychology and the Black Experience.* Pacific Grove, CA: Brooks/Cole.

Gelfand, D., & Vandetti, D. (1995). The emergent nature of ethnicity: Dilemmas in assessment. In F. Turner (Ed.), *Differential Diagnosis and Treatment in Social Work* (4th ed.). New York: Free Press.

Guiness, O. (2001). *The Great Experiment: Faith and Freedom in America.* Colorado Springs, CO: NavPress.

Hall, E., Cross, W., & Freedle, R. (1972). Stages in the development of black awareness: An exploratory investigation. In R. L. Jones (Ed.), *Black Psychology.* New York: Harper & Row.

Helms, J. (1984). Toward a theoretical explanation of the effects of race in counseling: A black and white model. *Counseling Psychologist, 12,* 153-165.

Institute for a Drug Free Workplace. (1995). What American employees think about drug abuse. Survey by Gallup Polls. www.drugfreeworkplace.org.

Krantz, D., Sheps, D. S., Carney, R. M., & Natelson, B. H. (2000). Effects of mental stress in patients with coronary artery disease. *Journal of the American Medical Association, 283*(14).

Lopez, R., Lopez, A., & Fong, K. (1991). Mexican Americans' initial preference for counselors: The role of ethnic factors. *Journal of Counseling Psychology, 38,* 487-496.

Luzzo, D. A. (2000). *Career Counseling of College Students: An Empirical Guide to Strategies That Work.* Washington, DC: APA.

McGoldrick, M. (1982). Ethnicity and family therapy: An overview. In M. McGoldrick, M., Pearce, J., & Giordano, J. (Eds.). (1982). *Ethnicity and Family Therapy.* New York: Guilford.

National study of delinquency prevention in schools (2000). Gottfredson Associates. (Available at www.gottfredson.com/national.htm.)

Older Americans 2000: Key indicators of well-being (2000). Federal Interagency Forum on Aging-Related Statistics.

Reinhold, B. B (1996). *Toxic Work.* New York: Penguin.

Robinson, J. (1989). Clinical treatment of black families: Issues and strategies. *Social Work, 34*(4), 323-329.

Rothbaum, F., Weisz, J., Pott, M., Miyake, K., & Morelli, G. (2000). Attachment and culture: Security in the United States and Japan. *American Psychologist, 55*(10), 1093-1104.

Rozanski, A., Blumenthal, J., & Kaplan, J. (1999). Impact of psychological factors on the pathogenesis of cardiovascular disease and implications for therapy. *Circulation, 99*(16), 2192-2217.

Ryan, W. (1971). *Blaming the Victim.* New York: Pantheon.

Schlesinger, A. M., Jr. (2001). The disuniting of America. In O. Guiness, *The Great Experiment: Faith and Freedom in America.* Colorado Springs, CO: NavPress.

Special report: Redefining race in America. (2000, September 18). *Newsweek,* 38-64.

Sue, D. W. (1977). Counseling the culturally different: A conceptual analysis. *Personnel and Guidance Journal, 55,* 422-425.

Sue, D. W. (1998). Multicultural counseling: Models, methods, and actions. *Counseling Psychologist, 24*(2), 279-284.

Sue, D. W., & Sue, D. (1990). *Counseling the Culturally Different: Theory and Practice* (2nd ed.) New York: Wiley.

U.S. Department of Education (2000). *Gun-Free Schools Act Report: 1998-2000.* www.ed.gov/offices/OESE/SDFS/GFSA.

U.S. Department of Health and Human Services (1999). *National Household Survey on Drug Abuse (NHSDA).* Washington, DC: HHS.

Walker, C. (1992). *Biblical Counseling with African-Americans.* Grand Rapids: Zondervan.

Weissman, M. M., Wolk, S., Goldstein, R. B., Moreau, D., Adams, P., Greenwald, S., Klier, C. M., Ryan, N. D., Dahl, R. E., & Wickramaratne, P., (1999). Depressed adolescents grown up. *Journal of the American Medical Association, 281,* 1901-1913.

World Alzheimer's Congress (2000). *Fact Sheet: Alzheimer's Disease Statistics.* Alzheimer's Association USA. www.alzheimer2000.org/news/alzstats.htm.

Yalom, I. (1995). *Theory and Practice of Group Psychotherapy* (4th ed.). Boston: Allyn and Bacon.

CHAPTER 30

Alford, H. (1976). *Alford's Greek Testament: An Exegetical and Critical Commentary, Vol. 4, Pt. 2. James–Revelation.* Grand Rapids, MI: Guardian Press.

Babbie, E. (2001). *The Practice of Social Research* (9th ed.). Belmont, CA: Wadsworth/Thomson Learning.

Bacon, F. (1961a). Selections from *The Great Instauration.* In W. Kaufman (Ed.), *Philosophic Classics: Bacon to Kant* (pp. 3-9). Englewood Cliffs, NJ: Prentice-Hall.

Bacon, F. (1961b). Selections from *Novum Organum.* In W. Kaufman (Ed.), *Philosophic Classics: Bacon to Kant* (pp. 9-25). Englewood Cliffs, NJ: Prentice-Hall.

Berkhof, L. (1939, 1941). *Systematic Theology* (4th ed.). Grand Rapids: Eerdmans.

Bordens, K. S., & Abbot, B. B. (1999). *Research Design and Methods: A Process Approach.* Mountain View, CA: Mayfield.

Buehler, C., Hesser, G., & Weigert, A. (1973). A study of articles on religion in major sociology journals. *Journal for the Scientific Study of Religion, 11,* 165-170.

Collins, G. R. (1983). Moving through the jungle: A decade of integration. *Journal of Psychology and Theology, 11,* 2-7.

Craigie, F. C., Liu, I. Y., Larson, D. B., & Lyon, J. S. (1988). A systematic analysis of religious variables in the Journal of Family Practice 1976-1986. *Journal of Family Practice, 27,* 509-513.

Edwards, K. (1997). Research on religious issues: Is this intergration? *Journal of Psychology and Theology, 25*(2), 186-187.

Ellis, L. (1994). *Research Methods in the Social Sciences.* Madison, WI: Brown and Benchmark.

Erickson, M. J. (1998). *Christian Theology* (2nd ed.). Grand Rapids: Baker.

Faw, H. W. (1995). *Psychology in Christian Perspective: An Analysis of Key Issues.* Grand Rapids: Baker.

Gartner, J., Larson, D. B., & Vachar-Mayberry, C. D. (1990). A systematic review of the quantity and quality of empirical research published in four pastoral counseling journals: 1975-1984. *Journal of Pastoral Care, 44*(2), 115-129.

Gottman, J. M., Coan, J., Carrere, S., & Swanson, C. (1998). Predicting marital happiness and stability from newlywed interactions. *Journal of Marriage and the Family, 60,* 5-22.

Heppner, P. P., Kivlighan, D. M., Jr., & Wampold, B. E. (1999). *Research Design in Counseling* (2nd ed.). Pacific Grove, CA: Brooks/Cole.

Hilber, J. W. (1998). Old Testament wisdom and the integration debate in Christian counseling. *Bibliotheca Sacra, 155,* 411-422.

Hoover, K., & Donovan, T. (1995). *The Elements of Social Scientific Thinking* (6th ed.). New York: St. Martin's Press.

Hooykaas, R. (1972). *Religion and the Rise of Modern Science.* Grand Rapids: Eerdmans.

Hubble, M. A., Duncan, B. L., & Miller, S. D. (Eds.). (1999). *The Heart and Soul of Change: What Works in Therapy.* Washington, DC: American Psychological Association.

Hurley, J. B., & Berry, J. T. (1997). The relation of scripture and psychology in counseling from a pro-integration position. *Journal of Psychology and Christianity, 16,* 323-345.

Isaac, S., & Michael, W. B. (1981). *Handbook in Research and Evaluation: A Collection of Principles, Methods, and Strategies Useful in the Planning, Design, and Evaluation of Studies in Education and the Behavioral Sciences* (2nd ed.). San Diego, CA: EdITS Publishers.

Johnson, E. L. (1997). Christ, the Lord of psychology. *Journal of Psychology and Theology, 25,* 11-27.

Johnson, S. (2001). Family therapy saves the planet: Messianic tendencies in the family systems literature. *Journal of Marital and Family Therapy, 27*(1), 3-11.

Johnson, W. B. (1993). Outcome research and religious psychotherapies: Where are we and where are we going? *Journal of Psychology and Theology, 21,* 297-308.

Kranzler, G., & Moursand, J. (1995). *Statistics for the Terrified.* Englewood Cliffs, NJ: Prentice-Hall.

Kuhn, T. S. (1962). *The Structure of Scientific Revolutions.* Chicago: University of Chicago Press.

Lambert, M. J., & Bergin, A. E. (1994). The effectiveness of psychotherapy. In A. E. Bergin & L. L. Garfield (Eds.), *Handbook of Psychotherapy and Behavior Change* (4th ed.) (pp. 143-189). New York: Wiley.

Langford, J. J. (1998). *Galileo, Science and the Church.* South Bend, IN: St. Augustine's Press.

Larson, D. B., & Larson, S. S. (1994). *The Forgotten Factor in Physical and Mental Health: What Does the Research Show?* Rockville, MD: National Institute for Healthcare Research.

Larson, D. B., Pattison, E. M., Blazer, D. G., Omran, A. R., & Kaplan, B. H. (1986). Systematic analysis of research on religious variables in four major psychiatric journals, 1978–1982. *American Journal of Psychiatry, 143,* 329-334.

Larson, D. B., Swyers, J. P., & McCullough, M. E. (Eds.). (1998). *Scientific Research on Spirituality and Health: A Consensus Report.* Rockville, MD: National Institute for Healthcare Research.

Lebow, J. (2001). What "really" makes couples happy? *Family Therapy Networker, 25*(1), 59-62.

Miller, B. C. (1986). *Family Research Methods.* Newbury Park, CA: Sage.

Pinsof, W. M., & Wynne, L. C. (1995). The efficacy of marital and family therapy: An empirical overview, conclusions, and recommendations. *Journal of Marital and Family Therapy, 21,* 585-613.

Popper, K. R. (1956, 1983). *Realism and the Aim of Science.* Totowa, NJ: Rowman and Littlefield.

Popper, K. R. (1959). *The Logic of Scientific Discovery.* New York: Basic Books.

Ragin, C. C. (1994). *Constructing Social Research: The Unity and Diversity of Method.* Thousand Oaks, CA: Pine Forge Press.

Richards, P. S., & Bergin, A. E. (Eds.). (2000). *Handbook of Psychotherapy and Religious Diversity.* Washington, DC: American Psychological Association.

Ripley, J. S., & Worthington, E. L., Jr. (1998). What the journals reveal about Christian marital counseling: An inadequate (but emerging) scientific base. *Marriage and Family: A Christian Journal, 1,* 375-396.

Rose, E. M., Westefeld, J. S., & Ansley, T. N. (2001). Spiritual issues in counseling: Clients' beliefs and preferences. *Journal of Counseling Psychology, 48*(1), 61-71.

Rossi, P. (1973). Baconianism. In P. P. Weiner (Ed.), *Dictionary of the History of Ideas: Studies of Selected Pivotal Ideas, Vol. 1* (pp. 172-179). New York: Scribner.

Royse, D. (1985). Client satisfaction with the helping process: A review for the pastoral counselor. *Journal of Pastoral Care, 39*(1), 3-11.

Sanderson, W. C. (1995). Which therapies are proven effective? *APA Monitor, 26*(3), 4.

Schaeffer, F. A. (1968). *Escape from Reason.* Downers Grove, IL: InterVarsity.

Schaeffer, F. A. (1976). *How Should We Then Live? The Rise and Decline of Western Thought and Culture.* Old Tappan, NJ: Revell.

Seltzer, R. A. (1996). *Mistakes That Social Scientists Make: Errors and Redemption in the Research Process.* New York: St. Martin's Press.

Shadish, W. R., Ragsdale, K., Glaser, R. R., & Montgomery, L. M. (1995). The efficacy and effectiveness of marital and family therapy: A perspective from meta-analysis. *Journal of Marital and Family Therapy, 21,* 345-360.

Shafranske, E. P. (Ed.). (1996). *Religion and the Clinical Practice of Psychology.* Washington, DC: American Psychological Association.

Sorokin P. A. (1956). *Fads and Foibles in Modern Sociology and Related Sciences.* Chicago: Regnery.

Stanley, S., Bradbury, T., & Markman, H. (2000). Structural flaws in the bridge from basic research on marriage to intervention for couples. *Journal of Marriage and the Family, 62*(1), 256-264.

Stanley, S., Trathen, D., McCain, S., & Bryan, M. (1998). *A Lasting Promise: A Christian Guide to Fighting for Your Marriage.* San Francisco: Jossey-Bass.

Stott, J. R. W. (1964). *The Epistles of John: An Introduction and Commentary.* Grand Rapids, MI: Eerdmans.

Tan, S. Y. (1995). The effectiveness of psychotherapy: Implications of outcome research findings for clinical practice. *Journal of Psychology and Christianity, 14,* 66-72.

Tannen, D. (1986). *That's Not What I Meant! How Conversational Style Makes or Breaks Your Relations with Others.* New York: Morrow.

Tannen, D. (1989). *Talking Voices: Repetition, Dialogue, and Imagery in Conversational Discourse.* Cambridge: Cambridge University Press.

Tannen, D. (1990). *You Just Don't Understand: Women and Men in Conversation.* New York: Ballantine.

Wallerstein, J. S. (2000). *The Unexpected Legacy of Divorce: A 25-Year Landmark Study.* New York: Hyperion.

Welch, E., & Powlison, D. (1997a). Every common bush afire with God: The Scripture's constitutive role for counseling. *Journal of Psychology and Christianity, 16,* 303-322.

Welch, E., & Powlison, D. (1997b). Response to Hurley and Berry. *Journal of Psychology and Christianity, 16,* 346-349.

Wolterstorff, N. (1984). Integration of faith and science—The very idea. *Journal of Psychology and Christianity, 3*(2), 12-19.

Worthington, E. L., Jr. (1997). From the editor. *Marriage and Family: A Christian Journal, 1,* 5.

Chapter 31

American Association of Christian Counselors. (1998). *AACC Christian Counseling Code of Ethics.* Forest, VA: AACC.

Association for Counselor Education and Supervision Interest Group. (1995). Ethical guidelines for counseling supervisors. *Counselor Education and Supervision, 34,* 270-276.

Avis, J. (1986). *Training and Supervision in Feminist-Informed Family Therapy: A Delphi Study.* Unpublished doctoral dissertation, Purdue University, West Lafayette, IN.

Baltimore, M. L. (2000). Ethical considerations in the use of technology for marriage and family counselors. *Family Journal: Counseling and Therapy for Couples and Families, 8*(4), 390-393.

Bernard, J. M. (1994). Multicultural supervision: A reaction to Leong and Wagner, Cook, Priest, and Fukuyama. *Counselor Education and Supervision, 34,* 159-171.

Bernard, J. M., & Goodyear, R. (1992). *Fundamentals of Clinical Supervision.* Boston: Allyn and Bacon.

Borders, L. D., & Leddick, G. R. (1987). *Handbook of Counseling Supervision.* Alexandria, VA: Association of Counselor Educators and Supervisors.

Bradley, L. J. (1989). *Counselor Supervision: Principles, Process, and Practice* (2nd ed.). Muncie, IN: Accelerated Development.

Carifio, M. S., & Hess, A. K. (1987). Who is the ideal supervisor? *Professional Psychology: Research and Practice, 18*(3), 244-250.

Carroll, M. (1996). *Counselling Supervision: Theory, Skills, and Practice.* New York: Cassell.

Carroll, M. (1999). Training in the tasks of supervision. In E. Holloway & M. Carroll (Eds.), *Training Counselling Supervisors: Strategies, Methods, and Techniques* (pp. 44-66). Thousand Oaks, CA: Sage.

Coleman, H. L. K. (1999). Training for multi-cultural supervision. In E. Holloway & M. Carroll (Eds.), *Training Counselling Supervisors: Strategies, Methods, and Techniques* (pp. 130-161). Thousand Oaks, CA: Sage.

Edwards, J. K., & Chen, M. W. (1999). Strength-based supervision: Frameworks, current practice, and future directions. *Family Journal: Counseling and Therapy for Couples and Families, 7*(4), 349-357.

Guest, C. L., Jr., & Dooley, K. (1999). Supervisor malpractice: Liability to the supervisee in clinical supervision. *Counselor Education and Supervision, 38*(4), 269-279.

Hayes, R. (1989). Group supervision. In L. Bradley (Ed.), *Counselor Supervision: Principles, Process, and Practice* (pp. 399-422). Muncie, IN: Accelerated Development.

Hewson, J. (1999). Training supervisors to contract in supervision. In E. Holloway & M. Carroll (Eds.), *Training Counseling Supervisors: Strategies, Methods, and Techniques* (pp. 67-91). Thousand Oaks, CA: Sage.

Holloway, E. L. (1992). Supervision: A way of learning and teaching. In S. D. Brown & R. W. Lent (Eds.), *Handbook of Counseling Psychology* (2nd ed.) (pp. 177-214). New York: Wiley.

Holloway, E. L. (1999). A framework for supervision training. In E. Holloway & M. Carroll (Eds.), *Training Counseling Supervisors: Strategies, Methods, and Techniques* (pp. 8-43). Thousand Oaks, CA: Sage.

Kaiser, T. L. (1992). The supervisory relationship: An identification of the primary elements in the relationship and an application of two theories of ethical relationships. *Journal of Marital and Family Therapy, 18*(3), 283-296.

Klitzke, M. J., & Lombardo, T. W. (1991). A "bug-in-the-eye" can be better than a "bug-in-the-ear": A teleprompter technique for on-line therapy skills training. *Behavior Modification, 15,* 113-117.

Liddle, H. A. (1991). Training and supervision in family therapy: A comprehensive and critical analysis. In A. S. Gurman & D. P. Kniskern (Eds.), *Handbook of Family Therapy, Vol. 2* (pp. 638-697). New York: Brunner/Mazel.

Locke, L. D., & McCollum, E. E. (2001). Clients' views of live supervision and satisfaction with therapy. *Journal of Marital and Family Therapy, 27*(1), 129-133.

Lovell, C. (1999). Supervisee cognitive complexity and the Integrated Developmental Model. *Clinical Supervision, 18*(1), 191-201.

Lowe, R. (2000). Supervising self-supervision: Constructive inquiry and embedded narrative in case consultation. *Journal of Marital and Family Therapy, 26*(4), 511-521.

Magnuson, S., Wilcoxon, S. A., & Norem, K. (2000). A profile of lousy supervision: Experienced counselors' perspectives. *Counselor Education and Supervision, 39*(3), 189-202.

Myrick, R. D., & Sabella, R. A. (1995). Cyberspace: New place for counselor supervision. *Elementary School Guidance and Counseling, 30*(1), 35-44.

Neukrug, E. S. (1991). Computer-assisted live supervision in counselor skill training. *Counselor Education and Supervision, 31*(2), 132-138.

Ohlschlager, G., & Mosgofian, P. (1992). *Law for the Christian Counselor: A Guidebook for Clinicians and Pastors.* Dallas: Word.

Osborn, C. J., & Davis, T. E. (1996). The supervision contract: Making it perfectly clear. *Clinical Supervision, 14*(2), 121-134.

Pearson, Q. M. (2000). Opportunities and challenges in the supervisory relationship: Implication for counselor supervision. *Journal of Mental Health Counseling, 22*(4), 283-295.

Piaget, J. (1929). *The Child's Conception of the World.* Orlando, FL: Harcourt Brace Jovanovich.

Piercy, F. P., Sprenkle, D. H., & Constantine, J. A. (1986). Family members' perceptions of live observation/supervision: An exploratory study. *Contemporary Family Therapy, 8*(3), 171-187.

Prieto, L. R. (1996). Group supervision: Still widely practiced but poorly understood. *Counselor Education and Supervision, 35*(4), 295-307.

Prouty, A. M., Thomas, V., Johnson, S., & Long, J. K. (2001). Methods of feminist family therapy supervision. *Journal of Marital and Family Therapy, 27*(1), 85-98.

Ratliff, D. A., Wampler, K. S., & Morris, G. H. (2000). Lack of consensus in supervision. *Journal of Marital and Family Therapy, 26*(3), 373-384.

Rigazio-Digilio, S. A., Anderson, S. A., & Kunkler, K. A. (1995). Gender-aware supervision in marriage and family counseling and therapy: How far have we actually come? *Counselor Education and Supervision, 34*(4), 344-355.

Ronnestad, M., & Skovholt, T. (1993). Supervision of beginning and advanced graduate students of counseling and psychotherapy. *Journal of Counseling and Development, 71*, 396-405.

Rudes, J., Shilts, L., & Berg, I. K. (1997). Focused supervision seen through recursive frame analysis. *Journal of Marital and Family Therapy, 23*(2), 203-215.

Shanfield, S., Matthews, K., & Hetherly, V. (1993). What do excellent psychotherapy supervisors do? *American Journal of Psychiatry, 150*, 1081-1084.

Smith, R. C., Mead, D. E., & Kinsella, J. A. (1998). Direct supervision: Adding computer-assisted feedback and data capture to live supervision. *Journal of Marital and Family Therapy, 24*(1), 113-125.

Stoltenberg, C. D. (1981). Approaching supervision from a develomental perspective: The counselor complexity model. *Journal of Counseling Psychology, 28*, 59-65.

Stoltenberg, C. D., & Delworth, U. (1987). *Supervising Counselors and Therapists: A Developmental Approach.* San Francisco, CA: Jossey-Bass.

Tannenbaum, R. L., & Berman, M. A. (1990). Ethical and legal issues in psychotherapy supervision. *Psychotherapy in Private Practice, 8*(1), 65-77.

Thomas, F. N. (1994). Solution-oriented supervision: The coaxing of expertise. *Family Journal: Counseling and Therapy for Couples and Families, 2*(1), 11-18.

Tryon, G. S. (1996). Supervisee development during the practicum year. *Counselor Education and Supervision, 35*(4), 287-294.

Watkins, C. E. (1997). The ineffective psychotherapy supervisor: Some reflections about bad behaviors, poor process, and offensive outcomes. *Clinical Supervisor, 16*(1), 163-180.

West, J., Bubenzer, D., Pinsoneault, T., & Holeman, V. (1993). Three supervision modalities for training marital and family counselors. *Counselor Education and Supervision, 33*(2), 127-139.

West, J., Bubenzer, D., & Zarski, J. (1989). Live supervision in family therapy. An interview with Barbara Okun and Fred Piercy. *Counselor Education and Supervision, 29,* 25-34.

White, M. B., & Russell, C. S. (1995). The essential elements of supervisory systems: A modified Delphi study. *Journal of Marital and Family Therapy, 21*(1), 33-53.

Williams, L. (1994). A tool for training supervisors: Using the Supervision Feedback Form (SSF). *Journal of Marital and Family Therapy, 20*(3), 311-316.

Worthington, E. L., Jr. (1987). Changes in supervision as counselors and supervisors gain experience: A review. *Professional Psychology: Research and Practice, 18,* 189-208.

Chapter 32

Budman, S., & Steenbarger, B. (1997). *The Essential Guide to Group Practice in Mental Health: Clinical, Legal, and Financial Fundamentals.* New York: Guilford.

Connor R., & Davidson, J. (1985). *Marketing Your Consulting and Professional Services.* New York: Wiley.

Erwin, K. (1993). *How to Start and Manage a Counseling Business.* Dallas: Word.

Grodzki, L. (2000). *Building Your Ideal Private Practice: A Guide for Therapists and Other Healing Professionals.* New York: Norton.

Hasper, R. (2001, Winter). Win-win-win referrals: How to forge a good pastor-therapist relationship. *Leadership Journal* (1), 45.

Klein, H. (1999, December). A recipe for enchanted marketing. *Psychotherapy Finances,* 12/99, 1 [Online]. Available FTP: www.psyfin.com.

Klein, H. (2000, October). Fee, practice, and managed care survey. *Psychotherapy Finances,* 10/00, 1 [Online]. Available FTP: www.psyfin.com.

Snyder, C., & Ingram, R. (1999). *Handbook of Psychological Change: Psychotherapy Processes and Practices for the 21st Century.* New York: Wiley.

CHAPTER 33

American Association of Christian Counselors (2001). *AACC Christian Counseling Code of Ethics.* Forest, VA: AACC.

Aponte, H. (1999). The stresses of poverty and the comfort of spirituality. In F. Walsh (Ed.), *Spiritual Resources in Family Therapy.* New York: Guilford.

Barber (1965). The sociology of the professions. In K. S. Lynn (Ed.), *The Professions in America.* Boston: Houghton Mifflin. Used by permission.

Bobgan, M., & Bobgan, D. (1987). *Psychoheresy: The Psychological Seduction of Christianity.* Santa Barbara, CA: Eastgate.

Clinton, T. (1998). Getting beyond our moral shyness. *Christian Counseling Today,* 6(2), 30-32.

Clinton, T. (2001, Winter). AACC 2001 Report. *Christian Counseling Connection, 2000/2001*(4), 1-6.

Clinton, T., & Ohlschlager, G. (1997). Law, ethics, and values in Christian counseling: Practice and advocacy in a brave new world. Presentation at the 1997 World Conference on Christian Counseling, Dallas, TX.

Collins, G. R. (1993). *The Biblical Basis of Christian Counseling for People Helpers.* Colorado Springs, CO: NavPress.

Collins, G. R. (1995, Winter). A vision for Christian counseling. *Christian Counseling Today,* 3(1), 8

Crabb, L. (1997). *Connecting: Healing for Ourselves and Our Relationships. A Radical New Vision.* Nashville: Word.

Crabb, L. (1999). *The Safest Place on Earth.* Nashville: Word.

Crabb, L. (2001). *Shattered Dreams: God's Unexpected Pathway to Joy.* Colorado Springs, CO: WaterBrook.

Cummings, N. (2001). Is managed care on its way out? *Psychotherapy Networker,* 25(4), 34.

Ellis, A. (1971). *The Case Against Religion: A Psychotherapist's View.* New York: Institute for Rational Living.

Gallup, G., & Jones, T. (2000). *The Next American Spirituality: Finding God in the Twenty-first Century.* Colorado Springs, CO: Victor.

Hart, A. (2001). Toward an integrated psychology and theology of emotions. Presentation at the 1st annual Geneva Institute Master's Series. Virginia Beach, VA.

Hunt, D. (1987). *Beyond Seduction.* Eugene, OR: Harvest House.

McMinn, M. (1996). *Psychology, Theology, and Spirituality in Christian Counseling.* Wheaton, IL: AACC-Tyndale.

Ohlschlager, G. (1999). Avoiding ethical-legal pitfalls: Embracing conformative behavior and transformative virtues. *Christian Counseling Today, 7*(3), 40-43

Ohlschlager, G., & Mosgofian, P. (1992). *Law for the Christian Counselor: A Guidebook for Clinicians and Pastors.* Dallas: Word.

Powlison, D. (1997). Critical issues in biblical counseling. In D. Powlison (Ed.), *Counseling the Word: A Selection of Readings from the Journal of Biblical Counseling.* Glenside, PA: Christian Counseling and Education Foundation.

Santa Rita, E. (1996). Filipino families. In M. McGoldrick, J. Pearce, & J. Giordano (Eds.), *Ethnicity and Family Therapy.* New York: Guilford.

Swaggart, J. (1986, November). Christian psychology? *The Evangelist,* 7.

Sweet, L. (1999). *Soul Tsunami: Sink or Swim in the New Millennium Culture.* Grand Rapids: Zondervan.

Vitz, P. C. (1977). *Psychology As Religion: The Cult of Self-Worship.* Grand Rapids: Eerdmans.

Epilogue

Chambers, O. (1960). *Studies in the Sermon on the Mount.* Hants., U. K.: Publications Association.

EXECUTIVE EDITORS AND CONTRIBUTORS

EXECUTIVE EDITORS

TIM CLINTON (EdD, LPC, LMFT) is president of the forty-thousand-member American Association of Christian Counselors (AACC), the largest and most diverse Christian counseling association in the world. He is professor of counseling and pastoral care and executive director of the Center for Counseling and Family Studies at Liberty University, where he helps deliver residence- and distance-learning MA and PhD degrees in professional counseling and pastoral care.

Licensed in Virginia as both a professional counselor (LPC) and a marriage and family therapist (LMFT), Tim is president of and maintains a part-time counseling practice with Light Counseling, Inc., in Lynchburg, Virginia, and is currently a distinguished visiting professor in the School of Psychology and Counseling at Regent University (2002).

Licensed and ordained as a pastor, Tim conceived and directed the development of the lay helping, marriage, and women's ministry programs of the AACC's Center for Biblical Counseling. He holds certification from the National Board of Certified Counselors, recently served on the Virginia Board of Health Professions, and continues to serve on the Board of Counseling, regulating professional counselors, marriage and family therapists, and substance abuse providers. He hosts *Live the Life,* a national call-in radio program on Christian counseling and living, and is a featured guest expert on the nationally syndicated *Al Denson* television show.

Tim has written many articles on Christian counseling, counselor education and development, and marriage and family life. He coauthored *Baby Boomer Blues* in the W Publishing Group's Contemporary Christian Counselor series and is the author of *Before a Bad Goodbye: How to Turn Your Marriage Around.* He and his wife, Julie, also coauthored *The Marriage You Always Wanted.*

Tim is executive editor of *The Soul Care Bible,* a joint project of the AACC and Thomas Nelson Publishers. He is also a contributing editor for *The National Liberty Journal* and *Christian Counseling Today* magazine and serves as a columnist for *Parent Life* and *Shine* magazines.

Tim is a Liberty University graduate with BS and MA degrees in pastoral ministries and counseling. He earned EdS and EdD degrees in counselor education from the College of William and Mary in Virginia.

Tim and his wife, Julie, have been married twenty-one years and have two children, Megan and Zachary. They live in Forest, Virginia.

GEORGE OHLSCHLAGER (JD, LCSW) is executive director of the American Board of Christian Counselors, the national Christian counselor credentialing, ethics management, and advocacy agency of the AACC. He is director of policy and professional affairs for the AACC and helps supervise AACC's Division for Mental Health Professionals. He is program director of the Geneva Institute, AACC's think tank and ministry innovator that delivers education, research, policy, and action programs advancing Christian counseling worldwide. He is also founding editor and primary writer of *AACC eNews & cNotes,* a monthly electronic newsletter exclusively for AACC members. George chairs the Law and Ethics Committee of the AACC and drafted the AACC Christian Counseling Code of Ethics.

After twenty-five years of professional Christian counseling, mediation, supervision, and agency development and administration as a licensed clinical social worker (LCSW), George now maintains a worldwide consulting, coaching, training, and clinical-ethical development practice with and through AACC. He teaches part-time in the doctor of ministry program in pastoral counseling at Western Seminary in Portland, Oregon, is a faculty member in AACC's Center for Biblical Counseling, and will teach and assist in development at the Center for Counseling and Family Studies at Liberty University.

George has authored and coauthored more than one hundred articles, chapters, notes, reviews, and columns on Christian counseling practice, law and ethics, marriage and family therapy and ministry, and interdisciplinary mental health practice and policy. He is coauthor of *Law for the Christian Counselor* and *Sexual Misconduct in Counseling and Ministry,* both published by the W Publishing Group, and the *Liability Management Notebook for Pastoral Counselors* by Rapha Resources. He is also a writer and consulting editor for *The Soul Care Bible* and is co-columnist for "Inside Law & Ethics" in *The Christian Counseling Connection* as well as for the "Editor's Afterword" in *AACC eNews & cNotes.*

A psychology and religious studies graduate of Humboldt State University in California, George holds an MA in counseling psychology and biblical-theological studies from Trinity International University (Trinity Evangelical Divinity School). He earned MSW and JD degrees from a dual-degree, interdisciplinary studies program in social work and law at the University of Iowa.

George and his wife, Lorraine, have been married twenty-eight years and have three children, Noelle, Justin, and Rea. They live in Lynchburg, Virginia.

CONTRIBUTORS

DAVID ARP (MSSW) and CLAUDIA ARP (BS) are educators, popular speakers, columnists, and award-winning authors. They are cofounders and codirectors of Marriage Alive International.

DWIGHT BAIN (MA), popular speaker, seminar leader, counselor, and mediator, is founder and director of the Orlando Counseling Center.

JOHN CARMACK (PhD), an LPC-, LMFT-, and AAMFT-approved supervisor, is assistant professor and chair of the Graduate Counseling Department at John Brown University.

FREDA CREWS (DMin) is a licensed professional counselor, author, speaker, popular host of the television program *Time for Hope*, and member of the AACC executive board.

KATHIE T. ERWIN (PhD, EdD) is director of the Discovery Program at Community Christian School in Largo, Florida.

RON HAWKINS (DMin, EdD), pastor and professional counselor, is dean of the College of Arts and Sciences at Liberty University and a member of the executive board of the AACC.

EDWARD HINDSON (ThD, DMin, DPhil), award-winning Bible editor and popular speaker, is dean of the Institute for Biblical Studies and professor and assistant to the chancellor at Liberty University. He also serves as director of ministerial relations for the AACC.

VIRGINIA TODD HOLEMAN (PhD) is a professor of counseling and associate dean of the School of Theology at Asbury Theological Seminary in Wilmore, Kentucky.

JAN HOOK (EdD) serves as director of the Marital Restoration Ministry at Willow Creek Community Church in South Barrington, Illinois, and is in private clinical practice.

WEI-JEN HUANG (PhD) is a staff psychologist and outreach director with the Counseling and Psychological Services Center at Northwestern University.

IAN F. JONES (PhD, PhD) is professor of counseling and director of the Baptist Marriage and Family Counseling Center at Southwestern Baptist Theological Seminary in Fort Worth, Texas.

JOSEPH A. KLOBA (EdD) is associate provost, professor of psychology, and director of the graduate counseling psychology program at Palm Beach Atlantic College in West Palm Beach, Florida.

DIANE LANGBERG (PhD), author and popular speaker, maintains a private practice in clinical psychology and is director of Diane Langberg and Associates near Philadelphia.

DIANE L. S. LIN (PhD) is a staff psychologist with the Counseling and Psychological Services Center at Northwestern University.

MICHAEL R. LYLES (MD) is a board-certified psychiatrist and founding partner of Lyles and Crawford Clinical Consulting. He is a member of the AACC executive board.

GRANT L. MARTIN (PhD) is in private clinical practice and serves as adjunct professor in the clinical family psychology doctoral program at Seattle Pacific University.

GARY W. MOON (PhD) is vice president of the Psychological Studies Institute in Atlanta and director of research and development for LifeSpring Resources.

GARY J. OLIVER (ThM, PhD) is executive director of the Center for Marriage and Family Studies and professor of psychology and practical theology at John Brown University. He serves as director of the Geneva Institute, is a member of the AACC executive board, and serves as editor of *Marriage & Family: A Christian Journal.*

LES PARROTT (PhD), popular speaker and best-selling author, is professor of psychology and codirector of the Center for Relationship Development at Seattle Pacific University.

LESLIE PARROTT (EdD) maintains a private practice in marriage and family therapy and is codirector of the Center for Relationship Development at Seattle Pacific University.

JENNIFER S. RIPLEY (PhD) is assistant professor in the School of Psychology and Counseling at Regent University in Virginia Beach.

DOUGLAS E. ROSENAU (EdD), speaker and best-selling author, maintains a private counseling and sex therapy practice. He is codirector of Sexual Wholeness and adjunct professor at the Psychological Studies Institute and Reformed Theological Seminary.

MIRIAM STARK PARENT (PhD) is associate professor of pastoral counseling and counseling psychology in the graduate and divinity schools of Trinity International University.

DAVID STOOP (PhD) is founder and director of the Center for Family Therapy in Newport Beach, California, and adjunct professor in the Fuller Seminary Graduate School of Psychology.

DANIEL S. SWEENEY (PhD), author, educator, and counselor, is an associate professor and clinical director in the graduate department of counseling at George Fox University in Portland, Oregon.

MICHAEL SYTSMA (PhD, LPC) is president of Building Intimate Marriages and cofounder of Sexual Wholeness.

SIANG-YANG TAN (PhD), author and popular speaker, is senior pastor of First Evangelical Church in Glendale and Arcadia, California, and professor of psychology in the Fuller Seminary Graduate School of Psychology.

ROSS J. TATUM (MD) is a board-certified child and adolescent psychiatrist in private practice. He speaks and writes on child and parenting issues.

DEBRA L. TAYLOR (MA, LMFT) is a certified sex therapist and is in private practice in marriage, family, and sex therapy.

CHRIS THURMAN (PhD), popular speaker and best-selling author, maintains a private counseling practice in Austin, Texas.

LESLIE VERNICK (MSW, LCSW), popular speaker, author, and seminar leader, maintains a private counseling practice in Orefield, Pennsylvania.

EVERETT L. WORTHINGTON JR. (PhD) is professor of psychology at Virginia Commonwealth University and executive director of the Campaign for Forgiveness Research (www.forgiving.org).

H. NORMAN WRIGHT (MA, MEd), best-selling author, counselor, teacher, and speaker, is founder and director of Christian Marriage Enrichment, pastor of enrichment at Rolling Hills Covenant Church, dean of Marriage Works, and a member of the AACC executive board.

Subject Index

To learn more about WaterBrook Press and view
our catalog of products, log on to our Web site:
www.waterbrookpress.com

WATERBROOK
PRESS